MAJOR PSYCHIATRIC DISORDERS
OVERVIEWS AND SELECTED READINGS

MAJOR PSYCHIATRIC DISORDERS
OVERVIEWS AND SELECTED READINGS

Edited by

FREDERICK G. GUGGENHEIM, M.D.
Associate Professor of Psychiatry
Chief, Psychiatric Consultation Liaison Division
Department of Psychiatry
Southwestern Medical School
University of Texas Health Science Center at Dallas, Dallas, Texas

and

CAROL NADELSON, M.D.
Professor and Vice Chairman, Department of Psychiatry
Associate Psychiatrist in Chief, Director, Training and Education
Tufts University School of Medicine
New England Medical Center Hospital, Boston, Massachusetts

ELSEVIER
New York • Amsterdam • Oxford

Elsevier Science Publishing Co., Inc.
52 Vanderbilt Avenue, New York, New York 10017

Sole distributors outside the United States and Canada:

Elsevier Science Publishers B.V.
P.O. Box 211, 1000 AE Amsterdam, The Netherlands

Library of Congress Cataloging in Publication Data

Main entry under title:

Major psychiatric disorders.

    Includes bibliographies and index.
    1. Psychology, Pathological—Addresses, essays,
    lectures. I. Guggenheim, Frederick G. II. Nadelson, Carol C.
RC454.M256   616.89   82-1453
ISBN 0-444-00663-X   AACR2

Current printing (last digit)
10 9 8 7 6 5 4 3

Manufactured in the United States of America

This book is dedicated to our children:

Hannah Carol Guggenheim
Jennifer Nicole Guggenheim
Jennifer Ann Nadelson
Robert Erik Nadelson

The authors gratefully acknowledge the help
of the following people who contributed to our preparation of the manuscript:
Robert Spitzer, M.D.,
and the many people who contributed to DSM-III,
George Arana, M.D., Donna Giles, Ph.D., Janet Gornick, B.A.,
Margorie Gibson Guggenheim, M.A., Susan Okie, M.D.,
members of the Harvard Medical School classes of 1976–1980,
and our colleagues at Harvard Medical School,
Southwestern Medical School, and Tufts Medical School.

CONTENTS

LIST OF CONTRIBUTORS

HAGOP S. AKISKAL, M.D.
Professor of Psychiatry and Associate Professor of Pharmacology; Director, Mood Clinic and Affective Disorders Program, University of Tennessee College of Medicine, Memphis, Tennessee

GEORGE ARANA, M.D.
Instructor in Psychiatry, Harvard Medical School, Boston, Massachusetts

DAVID BEAR, M.D.
Assistant Professor of Psychiatry, Harvard Medical School; Neuropsychiatric Consultant, Behavioral Neurology Unit, Beth Israel Hospital, Boston, Massachusetts

JAMES D. BELLUZZI, Ph.D.
Associate Adjunct Professor, Department of Pharmacology, University of California at Irvine, Irvine, California

GRETE L. BIBRING, M.D. (deceased)
Clinical Professor of Psychiatry, Emeritus, Harvard Medical School; Chief of Psychiatry, Emeritus, Beth Israel Hospital, Boston, Massachusetts

RICHARD L. BYYNY, M.D.
Professor and Vice Chairman of Medicine; Head of the Division of Internal Medicine, University of Colorado Medical Center, Denver, Colorado

GABRIELLE A. CARLSON, M.D.
Assistant Professor of Psychiatry, University of California, Los Angeles, School of Medicine, Division of Mental Retardation and Child Psychiatry; Ward Chief, Children's Unit, University of California, Los Angeles—Neuropsychiatric Institute, Los Angeles, California

JOHN CLANCY, M.D., F.R.C.P.(C)
Professor of Psychiatry, Director of Outpatient and Consultation Services, University of Iowa Hospitals, Iowa City, Iowa

C. ROBERT CLONINGER, M.D.
Professor of Psychiatry and Genetics, Department of Psychiatry and Genetics, Washington University School of Medicine and The Jewish Hospital of St. Louis, St. Louis, Missouri

RICHARD A. DeVAUL, M.D.
Associate Professor of Psychiatry and Behavioral Sciences, University of Texas Medical School, Houston, Texas

H. WARREN DUNHAM, Ph.D.
Professor of Psychiatry (Medical Sociology), Department of Psychiatry and Behavioral Science, Health Service Center, State University of New York at Stony Brook, New York

GEORGE L. ENGEL, M.D.
Professor of Psychiatry and Professor of Medicine, University of Rochester School of Medicine, Rochester, New York

LOUIS A. FAILLACE, M.D.
Professor and Chairman, Department of Psychiatry and Behavioral Sciences, University of Texas Medical School at Houston, Houston, Texas

CARL J. GETTO, M.D.
Assistant Professor of Psychiatry, University of Wisconsin, Madison, Wisconsin

FREDERICK K. GOODWIN, M.D.
Chief, Clinical Psychobiology Branch, National Institutes of Mental Health, Bethesda, Maryland

FREDERICK G. GUGGENHEIM, M.D.
Associate Professor of Psychiatry, Chief, Psychiatric Consultation Liaison Division, Department of Psychiatry, Southwestern Medical School, University of Texas Health Science Center at Dallas, Dallas, Texas

JOHN G. GUNDERSON, M.D.
Director of Psychotherapy, McLean Hospital, Boston,
Massachusetts; Associate Professor of Psychiatry,
Harvard Medical School, Boston, Massachusetts

THOMAS P. HACKETT, M.D.
Eben S. Draper Professor of Psychiatry, Harvard
Medical School, Boston, Massachusetts; Chief of
Psychiatry, Massachusetts General Hospital, Boston,
Massachusetts

RALPH J. KAHANA, M.D.
Associate Clinical Professor of Psychiatry, Harvard
Medical School; President of the Boston
Psychoanalytic Society and Institute, Boston,
Massachusetts

GERALD L. KLERMAN, M.D.
Professor of Psychiatry, Harvard Medical School;
Director of Research, The Stanley Cobb Psychiatry
Research Laboratories, Massachusetts General
Hospital, Boston, Massachusetts

ERICH LINDEMANN, M.D. (deceased)
Department of Diseases of the Nervous System,
Harvard Medical School, and the Department of
Psychiatry, Massachusetts General Hospital, Boston,
Massachusetts

JOHN M. LUCE, M.D.
Assistant Professor of Medicine, University of
California, San Francisco General Hospital, San
Francisco, California

BRENDAN A. MAHER, Ph.D.
Professor of the Psychology of Personality, Harvard
University, Cambridge, Massachusetts

E. JAMES McCRANIE, M.D.
Professor of Psychiatry, Department of Psychiatry,
Medical College of Georgia, Augusta, Georgia

WILLIAM T. McKINNEY, M.D.
Professor of Psychiatry, University of Wisconsin
Medical School, Madison, Wisconsin

CAROL NADELSON, M.D.
Professor and Vice Chairman, Department of
Psychiatry; Associate Psychiatrist in Chief; Director,
Training and Education, Tufts University School of
Medicine, New England Medical Center Hospital,
Boston, Massachusetts

THEODORE NADELSON, M.D.
Chief of Psychiatry, Boston Veterans Administration
Medical Center; Clinical Professor, Department of
Psychiatry, Tufts University School of Medicine,
Boston, Massachusetts

JOHN C. NEMIAH, M.D.
Psychiatrist-in-Chief, Beth Israel Hospital, Boston,
Massachusetts; Professor of Psychiatry, Harvard
Medical School, Boston, Massachusetts

MALKAH T. NOTMAN, M.D.
Clinical Professor of Psychiatry, Tufts University
Medical School, Boston, Massachusetts

RUSSELL NOYES, M.D.
Professor of Psychiatry, University of Iowa, College of
Medicine, Iowa City, Iowa

FERRIS N. PITTS, Jr., M.D.
Professor of Psychiatry and Behavioral Science,
University of Southern California School of Medicine,
Los Angeles, California

WILLIAM POLLIN, M.D.
Director of the National Institute on Drug Abuse,
Bethesda, Maryland

LEON SALZMAN, M.D.
Professor of Clinical Psychiatry, Georgetown
University Medical School, Washington, D.C.

ARTHUR H. SCHMALE, Jr., M.D.
Professor of Psychiatry and Associate Professor of
Medicine; Acting Director, Medical Psychiatric
Liaison Group, University of Rochester Medical
Center, Rochester, New York

RICHARD I. SHADER, M.D.
Professor and Chairman, Department of Psychiatry,
New England Medical Center, Boston, Massachusetts

EDWARD R. SHAPIRO, M.D.
Assistant Clinical Professor of Psychiatry, Harvard
Medical School, Boston, Massachusetts; Associate
Psychiatrist, McLean Hospital, Belmont,
Massachusetts; Director and Founder, Adolescent and
Family Treatment and Study Center, McLean Hospital,
Belmont, Massachusetts

MARGARET T. SINGER, Ph.D.
Professor, Department of Psychiatry, University of
California, San Francisco, School of Medicine;
Professor, Department of Psychiatry, University of
California at Berkeley, Berkeley, California

SOLOMON H. SNYDER, M.D.
Director, Department of Neuroscience, Distinguished
Service Professor of Neuroscience, Pharmacology and
Psychiatry, The Johns Hopkins University School of
Medicine, Baltimore, Maryland

LARRY STEIN, Ph.D.
Professor and Chair, Department of Pharmacology,
University of California at Irvine, Irvine, California

GEORGE TALLAND, Ph.D. (*deceased*)
Assistant Professor of Psychology, Department of
Psychiatry, Harvard Medical School; Psychologist,
Massachusetts General Hospital, Boston,
Massachusetts

TROY L. THOMPSON, II, M.D.
Assistant Professor of Psychiatry and Medicine;
Program Director, General Internal Medicine
Residency, University of Colorado School of Medicine,
Denver, Colorado

TERRY A. TRAVIS, M.D.
Professor, Department of Psychiatry, Southern Illinois
University School of Medicine, Springfield, Illinois

GEORGE E. VAILLANT, M.D.
Professor of Psychiatry, Harvard Medical School at
Massachusetts Mental Health Center; Director of
Training, Massachusetts Mental Health Center, Boston,
Massachusetts

AVERY D. WEISMAN, M.D.
Senior Psychiatrist, Massachusetts General Hospital,
Boston, Massachusetts; Professor of Psychiatry,
Harvard Medical School, Boston, Massachusetts

MYRNA M. WEISSMAN, Ph.D.
Professor, Departments of Psychiatry and
Epidemiology, Yale University School of Medicine;
Director, Depression Research Unit, Connecticut
Mental Health Center, New Haven, Connecticut

CHARLES E. WELLS, M.D.
Professor of Psychiatry and Neurology; Vice-
Chairman, Department of Psychiatry, Vanderbilt
University School of Medicine, Nashville, Tennessee

C. DAVID WISE, Ph.D.
Grants Associate, Department of Health and Human
Services, National Institutes of Health, Bethesda,
Maryland

INTRODUCTION

The human condition has been described, categorized, and satirized throughout the ages. But how difficult at times it is to distinguish those innately human characteristics common to all of us from those that are troublesome, pathological, and even indicative of mild or early mental illness.

Cartoonists, novelists, and playwrights often present poignant views of how we appear in health and sometimes in disease. For example, does winter's stroller in Figure 1 delineate contentment, denial, or a manic episode with feelings of euphoria and unreality?

Does Mr. Wilmer in Figure 2 represent a sardonic, embittered speaker or a man afflicted with a dysthymic disorder manifested by irritability and undue pessimism?

Is the woman in Figure 3 sentimental or is she dealing with a prolonged, unsolved grief reaction?

Does the woman who is the subject of the comment in Figure 4 have a flair for the dramatic (a marvelous gift), or does she have a dysfunctional personality disorder that will interfere with some aspect of living, loving, or working?

Does the middle-aged man in Figure 5 have an overly critical wife, or is he showing subtle signs of an early organic brain disorder? The answer is, of course, that without more facts, we just don't know.

We hope to provide the reader with the conceptual framework needed to assess the predicaments of cartoon characters and real people and to know what clues to look for, what questions to ask.

This book is not a comprehensive manual for diagnosis. We have left out some important disorders and our discussion of the six disorders that we have included is not encyclopedic. We have written not a textbook to be consulted occasionally, but rather a series of overviews and an anthology of

FIGURE 1. Does winter's stroller delineate contentment, denial, or a manic episode with feelings of euphoria and unreality? *Drawing by C. Barsotti;* © *1979 The New Yorker Magazine, Inc.*

"Last week, the management of this station wished our listeners a happy New Year. Here now is Mr. Clyde Wilmer with an opposing view."

FIGURE 2. Does Mr. Wilmer represent a sardonic, embittered speaker, or a man afflicted with a dysthymic disorder manifested by irritability and undue pessimism? *Drawing by Dana Fradon;* © *1979 The New Yorker Magazine, Inc.*

FIGURE 3. Is the woman sentimental or is she dealing with a prolonged, unresolved grief reaction? *Drawing by Modell;* © *1979 The New Yorker Magazine, Inc.*

"Everyone simply adores her, but he's the interesting one."

well-written and concise papers to be read, often a section at a time—given the appropriate clinical stimulus (or course assignment).

The book focuses on six groups of psychiatric conditions commonly encountered in general medical hospitals, psychiatric inpatient services, medical/surgical wards, and outpatient clinics: schizophrenic disorders; affective disorders; personality disorders; anxiety disorders and somatoform disorders (together comprising most of what used to be called the neuroses); and organic brain disorders (including delirium and dementia). The aim of the book is to describe clinically these six major disorders. In a preliminary way, the book also addresses the questions of *why* some people develop certain mental disorders. To illustrate current scientific thinking on the origins of mental illness, we have surveyed a vast array of articles from the psychiatric literature of the past several decades and have selected those articles that we feel are the clearest and most illustrative.

In organizing and writing this material we have relied heavily on the new *Diagnostic and Statisti-*

FIGURE 4. Does the woman, who is the subject of the comment, have a flair for the dramatic (a marvelous gift), or does she have a dysfunctional personality disorder that will interfere with some aspect of living, loving, or working? *Drawing by Saxon;* © *1979 The New Yorker Magazine, Inc.*

cal Manual of Mental Disorders (Third Edition) of the American Psychiatric Association (*DSM-III*), so that our terminology, in a field very much in flux, should be quite current. To help the reader apply this, we have included a *DSM-III* Quick Check that can be removed from the back of this book.

In this volume we have not covered alcohol and substance abuse, anorexia nervosa and other eating disorders, psychosexual disorders, dissociative disorders, conduct disorders, mental retardation, and disturbances of childhood. We have also left out of our collection articles dealing specifically with treatment. These might well be the subject for subsequent volumes.

We originally prepared this material for use by

"This is not, after all, the Middle Ages. This is 1978."   *"1979."*

FIGURE 5. Does the middle-aged man have an overly critical wife, or is he showing subtle signs of an early organic brain disorder? *Drawing by Mulligan;* © 1979 *The New Yorker Magazine, Inc.*

medical students of diverse backgrounds and experiences, as well as beginning residents in psychiatry, primary care, and family practice. For more than six years we have student-tested these articles and have discarded many that lacked readability (clarity, compactness, interest), were too complex, or contained too few relevant ideas for the amount of time taken to read them. Because many of our students were unfamiliar with technical vocabulary, we wrote a series of explanatory overview sections, one for each disorder, to spell out the key concepts used in the articles to follow. These overviews contain material on description and etiology and a brief section on treatment. In our overviews, we have tried to define important new terms in the text itself. Other terms are italicized when they first appear and are defined in the Glossary at the back of the book. At the end of each section we have listed Suggested Readings, organized according to a biopsychosocial format, for students' or teachers' further use. For ease of availability, we have, when possible, cited journal articles rather than book chapters. Many of the articles in the Suggested Readings are classics and others are current.

Our goal has been to allow the reader to develop a basic understanding of these six psychiatric disorders biologically and psychodynamically, so that heuristic hypotheses can be generated, and perhaps even tested. An understanding of some disorders implies knowledge of biochemical events in the brain (e.g., pre- and post-synaptic uptake) and knowledge of psychodynamic formulations (coping strategies and ego defense mechanisms). Twenty years ago, debates raged in the academic community about whether severe psychiatric illness was caused by nature or nurture. Now we recognize that many of the psychoses and some other disorders evolve because of the interplay of underlying biologic vulnerability (diathesis) and precipitating or predisposing psycho-social stresses. Basic to the selection of the articles reprinted in the book is our conviction that for some conditions psychodynamic considerations are paramount, while for other conditions bio-chemical factors play a predominant role, with personality factors often shaping the form and course that an illness follows.

Finally, a word about our own psychiatric ori-entation seems appropriate. In an era of divergent schools of thought, our own clinical experience and that of our medical students have helped us to become eclectic in our approach, looking at the biopsychosocial model as it applies to mental ill-ness. As psychotherapists, we find our patients have been helped with a variety of techniques, including psychodynamic psychotherapy, psy-choanalysis, behavior therapy, drug therapy, and milieu support—depending on the patient, the disorder, and the available resources.

Frederick G. Guggenheim
Dallas, Texas

Carol C. Nadelson
Boston, Massachusetts

1982

SUGGESTED READINGS

General

Mental disease classification: Significance for primary physicians. Guze S. Hospital Practice 15:77–81, 1980.

DSM-III: The major achievements and an overview. Spitzer RL, Williams JBW, Skodol AE. American Journal of Psychiatry 137:151–164, 1980

The clinical application of the biopsychosocial model. Engel GL. American Journal of Psychiatry 137:535–544, 1980.

Hidden conceptual models in clinical psychiatry. Lazare A. New England Journal of Medicine 288:345–351, 1973

Comprehensive Textbook of Psychiatry/III. Freedman AM, Kaplan HI, Sadock BJ. Baltimore, The Williams & Wilkins Co., 1980.

Quick Reference to Diagnostic Criteria from DSM-III. Washington, D.C., American Psychiatric Association, 1980.

Biological Factors

Brain peptides as neurotransmitters. Synder S. Science 209:976–983, 1980.

Psychological Factors

An Elementary Textbook of Psychoanalysis. Brenner C. Garden City, New York, International Universities Press, Inc., 1955.

Elements of Psychopathology: The Mechanisms of Defense. White RB, Gilliland RM. New York, Grune & Stratton, 1975.

PART

I

SCHIZOPHRENIC DISORDERS

OVERVIEW

Schizophrenia is a severe, persistent, or recurrent condition in which hallucinations and delusions disrupt clear logical thinking, leading to impoverished interpersonal relationships and a diminished capacity for effective work. Called *dementia* praecox in the past century, we now know that it does not necessarily lead to diminished memory or awareness and that its onset is not confined to adolescence.

The term "schizophrenia" was coined by the Swiss psychiatrist Eugen Bleuler in 1911 to describe a group of disorders, presumably of diverse and unknown organic origin, sharing in common certain basically similar clinical manifestations. Bleuler chose his term to connote the splitting or fragmentation of the mind's functions, producing a disconnectedness in the linking of ideas, the expression of feelings appropriate to thoughts and behavior, and the ability to assess reality. Bleuler enumerated what have been called the "4 A's," defects in mental functioning manifest in: (1) *Association*, loose association of thoughts; (2) *Affect*, lack of connection between emotional feelings and events; (3) *Autism*, withdrawal of interest in the outside world and in its place preoccupation with an internal fantasy life; and (4) *Ambivalence*, intense contradictory feelings about similar situations or people. He called these fundamental, or primary, symptoms.

Further, he delineated secondary, or accessory, symptoms. These include (1) *delusions*, false beliefs which cannot be corrected by reason (e.g., believing that someone is about to attack when there is no evidence for this); (2) *hallucinations*, perceptions, especially auditory, not based on real stimuli from the external world (e.g., hearing voices that are not there); (3) *illusions*, perceptions that cause misinterpretation of actual events; and

(4) *catatonia*, marked motor abnormalities, either inhibition or excitement. These experiences and perceptions occurring during the psychotic process may indeed be based on prior feelings and experiences that become elaborated to emerge in a distorted and bizarre form. For example, during the patient's childhood, the father may have been rejecting or attacking. Years later, in a psychotic episode, a distorted father figure may reemerge into importance, seen lurking in shadows, gazing through windows, menacing with a knife, and threatening mayhem.

Bleuler recognized that the person with schizophrenia does not have any gross defect in memory; orientation to date, person, or place; or perception such as may be seen in patients with neurological abnormalities caused by known toxins, infections, metabolic disturbances, and the like.

Another system used in diagnosing schizophrenia complemented the Bleulerian criteria and centered around an impairment of *ego* functioning. Thus, patients were sometimes diagnosed as having schizophrenia if they demonstrated defects in reality perception and *reality testing*, logical and abstract thought processes, capacity for relationships, impulse control, ability to regulate activity, and the maintenance of defense mechanisms (see Part III: Personality Disorders, for further discussion of ego functions and defense mechanisms). But diagnostic schemas involving the use of Bleulerian symptoms and ego deficits are rather imprecise and can invite misuse. The criteria are subjective and so broad in nature that they are potentially overinclusive.

The next major advance in diagnostic conceptualization was marked by Kurt Schneider's description of "first rank" and "second rank" symptoms. His first rank symptoms derived from his long clinical experience with mental patients without detectable brain disease who were chronically psychotic. His criteria, therefore, were not related to any theoretical position but rather reflected his observations of clinical course and prognosis. "First rank" symptoms included thought broadcasting (thoughts are experienced as escaping from the patient's head into the external world); experiences of alienation (thoughts, feelings, and volition derive from an external force and are not internally generated); experiences of influence (body sensations, feelings, impulses, and thoughts are felt to be imposed by an external agency, thus the patient is controlled and must submit); complete auditory hallucinations (clearly audible voices are experienced as coming from the outside that are prolonged, commenting on the patient's actions, and even arguing); and delusional perceptions (events that have special private meaning to the patient). Schneider believed that when any one of these is present, and there is no other organic cause, then the clinical diagnosis of schizophrenia can be made.

A further advance in the objectification of the diagnostic criteria for schizophrenia was made by Robins and Guze. They delineated criteria that distinguished schizophrenics with a poor prognosis from those mental patients who were nonschizophrenics and had a good prognosis.

Indicative of a good prognosis	Indicative of a poor prognosis
1. Good premorbid adjustment	1. Poor premorbid adjustment (schizoid/paranoid personality)
2. Clear-cut precipitating factors	2. No obvious precipitating factors
3. Sudden onset (less than six months)	3. Insidious onset (greater than six months)
4. Absence of a family history of schizophrenia	4. Family history of schizophrenia
5. Family history of affective disorders	5. Absence of a family history of affective disorders
6. Prominent affective symptoms	6. Blunted affect
7. Dreamlike or altered state of consciousness on admission	7. Clear sensorium
8. "Paranoid" symptoms (delusional mood and notions)	

Their clinical investigations substantially influenced further diagnostic criteria recently adapted by the American Psychiatric Association (*DSM-III*).

DSM-III CRITERIA

To develop an even more specific diagnostic criteria for clinical care and research, the American Psychiatric Association was engaged from 1975 to 1980 in a nationwide, multicenter project to evolve a set of reliable and valid criteria for diagnosis. This was codified in a new *Diagnostic and Statistical Manual*, referred to as *DSM-III*, that sets forth an objective set of symptoms and signs based on specific information about the patient's observable behavior and inner experiences.

DSM-III takes into account the fact that many psychiatric disorders can produce emotional turmoil and even hallucinations and delusions for varying periods of time. Examples include ingestion of drugs (e.g., "angel dust") or alcohol, alcohol withdrawal, *reactive* or stress-induced psychoses, and temporal lobe epilepsy. Thus, for schizophrenia, the single most stringent diagnostic criterion involves the history of onset and course. Importantly, some psychotic episodes of shorter duration phenomenologically resemble schizophrenic disorder (*schizophreniform* reactions) but have a more benign course. This fact becomes reflected in an important criterion for schizophrenia: the psychiatric disorder must have been continuous for at least six months and have occurred before age 45.

During the often tumultuous active phase of the disorder, one of these six symptoms must be present:

1. Bizarre delusions (content is patently absurd and there is no possible real basis) such as delusions of being controlled, thought broadcasting, thought insertion, or thought withdrawal
2. Somatic, grandiose, religious, nihilistic, or other delusions without persecutory or jealous content
3. Delusions with persecutory or jealous content, if accompanied by hallucinations of any type
4. Auditory hallucinations in which either a voice keeps up a running commentary on the individual's behaviors or thoughts as they occur, or two or more voices converse with each other
5. Auditory hallucinations on several occasions, the content of which has no apparent relation to depression or elation and is not limited to one or two words.

6. Incoherence, marked loosening of associations, marked illogicality, or marked poverty of content of speech, if associated with at least one of the following:
   a. blunted, flat, or inappropriate affect
   b. delusions or hallucinations
   c. catatonic or other grossly disorganized behavior.

The time period need not be occupied solely by active phase symptoms; during some of that period the patient may have manifested signs of social impairment, bizarre behavior, or unusual thinking, which is characteristic of the onset (*prodromal*) phase or the resolution (residual) phase of the schizophrenic episode.

During the prodromal and residual phases, there must be evidence of impairment and deterioration of function in areas such as work or role functioning, social relationships and self-care. There may be eccentric behavior, for example, talking to oneself in public or shouting to strangers on street corners, poor personal hygiene or grooming, or blunted or inappropriate affect. Finally, there may be evidence of distorted thinking, such as speech that is vague, overelaborate, or constantly digressive, ideas and beliefs that are bizarre or magical, or experiences of a hallucinatory or peculiar nature.

In addition to these inclusion criteria (duration, signs, and symptoms), some important exclusion criteria assist in making the diagnosis of schizophrenia: There must be no evidence of affective disorder, organic brain disorder, or mental retardation.

COURSE

Acute episodes of schizophrenia may appear immediately following well-defined precipitating stressful events. Recoveries may be complete or there may be recurrences with other stresses. In contrast to the acute reactive form, there is another form of schizophrenia with clinically similar signs that begins insidiously and does not declare itself completely for a number of months or years. This chronic process type of schizophrenia (or nuclear schizophrenia) runs a downhill course with eventual personality disintegration, inability to carry out normal social functioning, and, in some cases, even disruption of language function. Intermediate forms between acute and chronic types of schizophrenia are also found. In such situations, a recurrent pattern of acute *psychosis* may be followed by return to a baseline that is close to the previous, impaired level of functioning. In such cases deterioration is not marked.

Generally, it is estimated that one-third of those with schizophrenia recover completely, one-third improve somewhat, and in one-third the disease follows a deteriorating downhill course.

CLINICAL FORMS

Schizophrenia can appear in a variety of ways. Some patients develop *catatonia* with bizarre motor behavior. They may appear stuporous though covertly attentive. Or they may be highly agitated or even randomly destructive and negativistic. They may present with hebephrenia, the disorganized type of schizophrenia. These people show disordered social behavior with odd dress, jumbled speech, inappropriate laughing, and an inability to be cognizant of the feelings of others. The paranoid type shows suspiciousness and persecution. At times there may also be grandiosity, jealousy, imagined poverty, or morbid physical illness. The residual, or simple, type of schizophrenia does not present with current hallucinations or delusions, but there is blunted or inappropriate affect, loosening of associations, and a sense of social and personal apathy.

Another type of schizophrenia that shares characteristics with other disorders is the *schizoaffective* type. In this type there is marked affective symptomatology, e.g., depression or elation, and there are also secondary schizophrenic symptoms, for example, delusions and hallucinations.

Not all people with hallucinations and delusions have schizophrenia. Other mental disorders that must be differentiated from schizophrenia include brief psychotic reactions, acute psychotic episodes in affective disorders (see Part II), somatoform disorders (see Part V), and personality disorders (see Part III). Finally, psychoses with physical causes such as drug or metabolic disorders (see Section IV) such as amphetamine psychosis often mimic paranoid schizophrenia.

EPIDEMIOLOGY

Although there are reported differences in incidence and prevalence of schizophrenia throughout the world, many of these probably result from differences in diagnostic criteria utilized and populations sampled. The world wide prevalence (or occurrence of cases at this time) of chronic schizophrenic appears to be approximately one percent of the population. Because of its early onset, protracted course, and social disability, it is one of the most important psychiatric illnesses. Currently, one-quarter of all hospital beds in the United States are occupied by patients whose illness has been diagnosed as schizophrenia. The prevalence of acute schizophrenic disorders is not so well known, but available evidence suggests that it is more common than chronic schizophrenia.

Schizophrenia is found in all cultures. A number of studies have indicated that it is more prevalent among people from lower socioeconomic backgrounds. This may be partially explained by the fact that the disease itself produces some "downward drift" in the individual's socioeconomic status because of the resultant social disability. Another possible explanation relates to being labeled: that is, more affluent, educated people may be able to use their money and power to avoid some of the serious consequences of their symptoms or behavior.

ETIOLOGY

There is much speculation about the cause of schizophrenic illness but no definitive or specific etiology has been clearly delineated. Some authors consider the structure and function of the family to be responsible. Specifically, they cite *double-binding* "schizophrenogenic" mothers, befuddling communication, and marital *schisms* as having paramount importance in the genesis of schizophrenia.

Other researchers have relegated the role of nurturing to a rather minor position and have given a central position to genetic and prenatally or natally induced constitutional factors, particularly in response to stress. For example, a set of aversive interpersonal events in a susceptible individual could overload a neural circuit, producing an exaggerated biochemical/neurophysiological response. Defective neural integration could in turn produce aberrant behaviors, further adversely affecting the individual's relationships in the community, creating more interpersonal stress.

Research on the children of schizophrenics indicates that some of these psychosis-prone subjects have detectable neurophysiological instability, demonstrated on certain types of testing even prior to the onset of psychosis. Although no clearcut and consistent neurological deficit has been found, subtle and fluctuating neurological signs do appear in schizophrenia, including one-sided tremors, *diplopia, anisocoria*, temperature dyscontrol, localized weakness, plus inequality of knee jerks and other deep tendon reflexes. Investigators have elucidated cognitive slippage, psychomotor dyscontrol, and body image and other special aberrations. Researchers, using a new radiologic technique on chronic schizophrenics, have discovered with computerized axial tomography (CAT scans) that some have dilated cerebral *ventricles*. Of course, it is always difficult to know whether such phenomena are the cause or the effect of the disease.

Although exact etiologic mechanisms are unclear, one fact has emerged in the past decade that must be accounted for in theories of schizophrenia. There is now substantial evidence for a hereditary component in chronic schizophrenia spectrum illness. Heston and Kety have shown the one-quarter to one-half of those who have a genetic propensity for the chronic form of illness develop some form of it.

At a biochemical level, a mechanism has been proposed to account for clinical findings in schizophrenia: the relative excess of *dopamine* (a metabolic precursor of the neurohormone norepinephrine) at certain midbrain centers. Other endogenous biochemical compounds that have also been suspected of playing a role in schizophrenia include such endogenous substances as beta-endorphins and hallucinogens such as dimethoxy phenylethylamine (DMPEA). These substances may be produced in genetically predisposed people during stressful conditions.

In summary, schizophrenia can be seen as a manifestation of an interaction of a number of components: genetic characteristics, constitutional predispositions, brain *neurotransmitters*, and some sort of disadvantageous environment, much as in the case of tuberculosis or carcinoma. Apparently each factor is necessary and no one alone is sufficient to produce the full-blown clinical picture of a schizophrenic disorder.

Several factors have complicated research in schizophrenia. First, schizophrenia is a protean disorder that probably represents a heterogenity of etiologies; but our clinical observation, technology, and level of understanding have not yet enabled us to differentiate heuristically useful discrete subgroups. This inability relates to a second factor: the current basis for the diagnosis of schizophrenia rests on discernible behavior rather than on pathognomonic physical signs or laboratory tests. Finally, objective clinical findings in this disorder can be substantially changed by a cardinal feature of the disorder, emotional upset. Of course, this is the case for other neurological diseases, such as *Parkinson's disease*, but in comparison with Parkinson's disease, schizophrenia has a more polymorphic set of symptoms and may possibly have more causes. Research over the next decade may well demonstrate that there are a group of chronic and acute schizophrenia disorders with differing genetic transmission and biochemical mechanisms, each responding to somewhat different psychosocial and biochemical treatment. But as is the case with catatonia, one cannot currently deduce etiologic factors from phenomenology alone.

TREATMENT

Most patients with schizophrenia require psychiatric hospitalization at some point in the course of the illness. Treatment generally includes phenothiazines or other similar medication, brief hospitalization with utilization of milieu and other therapeutic approaches, and attempts to reduce ongoing personal and family conflicts. Thus, traditional comprehensive treatment programs include somatic therapy and a number of approaches that attempt to be supportive and nonregressive while promoting adaptation to stress and rehabilitation.

Somatic Therapy

Phenothiazine medication and other drugs of slightly different structural configurations such as butyrophenones, thioxanthenes, dihydroindolones, and tricyclic dibenzoxazepines are all *neuroleptics* (antipsychotic agents referred to at times as major tranquilizers). These medications decrease or eliminate hallucinations and delusions and facilitate reintegration of thought processes and associations. Additional target symptoms (symptoms that can be objectively measured), which include disordered sleep and appetite, may be considerably improved and mood may return to normal. These drugs, however, probably do not affect the personality changes associated with chronic schizophrenia. Larger doses of medication are usually required during acute exacerbations, and they may be reduced or, in certain instances, discontinued when symptoms abate.

Many patients will omit medication if not carefully supervised, because there are, at least for some, unpleasant side effects such as lethargy, stiff muscles, impotence, and skin sensitivity to sunlight. *Extrapyramidal* symptoms include *Parkinson's syndrome*, which produces tremors, slowing of muscular activity, muscular aches, restless legs, and occasionally acute *torticollis* (wry neck).

These side effects can usually be controlled by antiparkinsonism drugs such as benztropine, (Cogentin) trihexyphenidyl, (Artane) or biperiden (Akineton).

About 5% of patients receiving antipsychotic medications develop permanent involuntary writhing movements, especially of the mouth, cheeks, or tongue (*tardive dyskinesia*), after prolonged periods of exposure, especially if they have been receiving high doses and/or are elderly. This recently noted complication of treatment has led many physicians to advocate "drug holidays" for all but the most disturbed patients with schizophrenia.

Electroconvulsive therapy (ECT) sometimes is administered when the patient has marked psychomotor excitement, stupor, or depressive symptoms. Because this treatment is rarely indicated in schizophrenia except in these specific situations, it is discussed in Part II: Affective Disorders, where it has a broader applicability.

Other physical treatments have been proposed; these include *megavitamin therapy*. The scientific proof of its efficacy does not match the claims made by proponents. While it is possible that a small subgroup of patients with schizophrenia may achieve some benefit from this treatment or even from dietary restrictions of gluten, it is likely that the enthusiasm of proponents and uncertainty about diagnosis account for the good results reported.

Psychotherapy

During the acute phase of a schizophrenic disorder, the patient is often flooded with thoughts, besieged by *primitive* (uncensored) impulses, and confused by conflicting or alien ideas. Plunged precipitously into an estranged, uncharted new world, the patient is usually in pain and often frightened. Hence, psychotherapy is oriented toward empathic understanding and structured practical support. Interpretations of unconscious motives and aggressive confrontations about past behaviors have no role in this phase. Rather, the therapist can be most helpful to his or her patient by providing an active, genuine interest, gathering routine historical data, and "staying and being"—yet avoiding overwhelming the patient.

The incredible sensitivity of the psychotic schizophrenic patient to the subtle nuances of interpersonal relationships makes it essential for therapists to consider even such elementary details as: whether the patient is comforted or frightened by the therapist's walking side-by-side with the patient on the way to a psychotherapy session; or whether the patient needs to sit close to the door to facilitate hasty departure during a family meeting.

Later, after the tumultuous acute phase of the patient's illness has passed, the therapist will want to focus on difficulties the patient has experienced with interpersonal relationships and life events. Then it may be useful to examine the patient's role in the problems that may have evolved in a relationship and how the patient can ameliorate matters.

An ongoing relationship with a therapist can be an important source of support. Patients often need encouragement to continue their neuroleptic medication because of irksome side effects, and they should be monitored to prevent development of serious long-term toxic effects such as *tardive dyskinesia*. In times of crisis, the therapist can be an anchor by giving practical advice and by temporarily increasing dosage of antipsychotic medication, thus staving off the necessity of rehospitalization.

Institutional Therapy

Hospitalization in a *therapeutic community* may at times be necessary. Accompanying *milieu therapy* are rehabilitative efforts such as close contact with other patients and staff as well as vocational rehabilitation. The transition to the home and the community can be effected through halfway houses and aftercare centers.

THE SHATTERED LANGUAGE
OF SCHIZOPHRENIA

BRENDAN A. MAHER

Somewhere in a hospital ward a patient writes:

> The subterfuge and the mistaken planned substitutions for that demanded American action can produce nothing but the general results of negative contention and the impractical results of careless applications, the natural results of misplacement, of mistaken purpose and unrighteous position, the impractical serviceabilities of unnecessary contradictions. For answers to this dilemma, consult Webster.

The document is never sent to anyone; it is addressed to no one; and perhaps intended for no reader. Another patient, miles away, writes:

> I am of I-Building in B..State Hospital. With my nostrils clogged and Winter here, I chanced to be reading the magazine that Mentholatum advertised from. Kindly send it to me at the hospital. Send it to me Joseph Nemo in care of Joseph Nemo and me who answers by the name of Joseph Nemo and will care for it myself. Thanks everlasting and Merry New Year to Mentholatum Company for my nose for my nose for my nose for my nose for my nose.

EDITORS' COMMENTS:
ALTHOUGH THIS IS NOT A FORMAL ACADEMIC PAPER, IT PROVIDES A GOOD CLINICAL SENSE OF THE BAFFLEMENT OF SCHIZOPHRENIC LANGUAGE. SEVERELY DISABLED PEOPLE WITH SCHIZOPHRENIA OFTEN HAVE PATTERNS OF SPEECH AND WRITING THAT ARE NOTICEABLY ODD. BRENDAN MAHER'S PAPER PRESENTS SEVERAL HYPOTHESES THAT ACCOUNT FOR THIS.

Reprinted from Psychology Today Magazine 1:378–381. Copyright © 1968, Ziff-Davis Publishing Company.

A British patient writes:

> I hope to be home soon, very soon. I fancy chocolate éclairs, chocolate eclairs, Doenuts. I want some doenuts, I do want some golden syrup, a tin of golden syrup or treacle, jam . . . See the Committee about me coming home for Easter my twenty-fourth birthday. I hope all is well at home, how is Father getting on. Never mind there is hope, heaven will come, time heals all wounds, Rise again Glorious Greece and come to Hindoo Heavens, the Indian Heavens, The Dear old times will come back. We shall see Heaven and Glory yet, come everlasting life. I want a new writing pad of note paper. . . .*

Yet another writes:

> Now to eat if one cannot the other can—and if we cant the girseau Q. C. Washpots prize-bloom capacities—turning out—replaced by the head patterns my own capacities—I was not very kind to them. Q. C. Washpots under-patterned against—bred to pattern. Animal sequestration capacities and animal sequestired capacities under leash—and animal secretions. . . .*

Experienced clinicians, when called upon to diagnose the writers of language like this, agree closely with each other (80 per cent of the time or more). The diagnosis: schizophrenia. Nearly every textbook on psychopathology presents similar examples, and nobody seems to have much difficulty in finding appropriate samples. It would seem obvious that there must be a well-established and explicit definition of what characteristics lan-

---

*These quotations are taken from *The Neurology of Psychotic Speech* by McDonald Critchley.

guage must possess to be called schizophrenic. But when we ask clinicians to tell us exactly what specific features of an individual language sample led them to decide that the writer was schizophrenic, it turns out that they aren't exactly sure. Instead of explicit description, the expert comment is likely to be: "It has that schizophrenic flavor" or "It is the confusion of thought that convinces me."

Impressionistic descriptions abound. The language is described as circumlocutious, repetitive, incoherent, suffering from an interpenetration of ideas, excessively concrete, regressed, and the like. Doubtless, all of these descriptions have merit as clinical characterizations of the language. Unfortunately, they are quite imprecise, and they give us no adequate basis for developing theoretical accounts of the origin of schizophrenic language. This is, of course, hardly surprising. Quantitative studies of language have been notoriously laborious to undertake. However, two recent developments in behavioral sciences have combined to change the situation quite significantly. The first of these is the development of language-analysis programs for computer use, and the second is the increasing sophistication of psycholinguistics as a framework for the study of applied problems in the psychology of language.

Before turning to look at the consequences of these developments, we should glance at the kinds of hypotheses that have already been advanced to account for schizophrenic language. The first of these might be termed the Cipher Hypothesis. In its simplest form this says that the patient is trying to communicate something to a listener (actual or potential) but is afraid to say what he means in plain language. He is somewhat in the same straits as the normal individual faced with the problem of conveying, let us say, some very bad news to a listener. Rather than come right out and tell someone directly that a family member is dying, the informant may become circumlocutious and perhaps so oblique that his message simply does not make sense at all.

In the case of the schizophrenic patient, however, it is assumed that the motives which drive him to disguise his message may be largely unconscious—that he could not put the message into plain language if he tried. Where the normal person is trying to spare the feelings of the listener by his distortions and evasions, the patient purportedly is sparing his own feelings by the use of similar techniques. This analogy can be stretched a little further. Just as the normal speaker is caught in a dilemma—the necessity to convey the message and the pressure to avoid conveying it too roughly—so the patient is caught in a conflict between the necessity of expressing himself on important personal topics and the imperative need to avoid being aware of his own real meanings. Thus, so the Cipher Hypothesis maintains, it is possible in principle to decipher the patient's message—provided one can crack the code. This hypothesis assumes, of course, that there really is a message.

Obviously, the Cipher Hypothesis owes its genesis to psychoanalytic theory. In essence, it is identical with Freud's interpretation of the relationship between manifest and latent dream content. Unfortunately, from a research point of view, this hypothesis suffers from the weakness of being very hard to disprove. No two patients are assumed to have the same code, and so the translation of schizophrenic language into a normal communication requires a detailed analysis of the case history of the individual writer. As the code that is discovered for any one case cannot be validated against any other case, the hypothesis rests its claim to acceptance upon its intrinsic plausibility vis-à-vis the facts of the life history of the patient. But plausible interpretations of a patient's language may reflect the creative (or empathetic) imagination of the clinician, rather than a valid discovery of an underlying process governing the patient's utterances.

One more or less necessary deduction from the Cipher Hypothesis is that language should become most disorganized when the topic under discussion is one of personal significance, and less disorganized when the topic is neutral. To date, no adequate test of this deduction has been reported. In the absence of this or other independent tests of the Cipher Hypothesis, it must be regarded for the time being as, at best, an interesting speculation.

A second explanation has been that the patient's communications are confusing and garbled precisely because he wishes to avoid communicating with other people. This hypothesis, which we shall call the Avoidance Hypothesis, interprets the disordered language as a response that is maintained and strengthened by its effectiveness in keeping other people away. Presumably, the normal listener becomes frustrated or bored with such a speaker and simply goes away, leaving the schizophrenic in the solitude he seeks. This theory rests, in turn, upon the assumption that the patient finds personal interactions threatening. We might expect that casual interactions—such as chatting about the weather—are relatively unthreatening and do not provoke avoidant disorder in language. The language disturbance should become more evident when the threat of personal involvement arises.

At this level, the Avoidance Hypothesis cannot be distinguished from the Cipher Hypothesis. The main difference between the two is that the Avoidance Hypothesis is concerned with a dimension of incomprehensibility and does not imply that the incomprehensible can be unscrambled. Both of these hypotheses have their attractions.

"For answers to this dilemma, consult Webster," wrote the first patient we have quoted. Is he just playing a word game with an imaginary reader or is there a meaning to his message? We might remark on the similarity of the prefix in many of the words he uses: *subterfuge, substitution; unrighteous, unnecessary; mistaken, misplacement, contention, contradiction*. His message might, indeed, sound like a random sampling from a dictionary.

Or did the dictionarylike nature of the "message" only occur to the patient himself toward the end—and hence the closing remark? In any event, the sample seems to fit plausibly into the notion that some kind of enciphering was going on between the patient's basic "message" and the language that he wrote.

Our fourth sample of schizophrenic language, on the other hand, seems to be absolutely incomprehensible. Fragments of phrases, neologisms ("girseau") and repetitions—*sequestration* and *sequestired*—combine into a jumble that seems to defy understanding. It is hard to believe that there might be a message in disguise here, or even that the language was uttered with any wish to communicate.

Although both hypotheses can be made to seem plausible, they are intrinsically unsatisfying to the psychopathologist. They do not deal with the most fascinating problem of schizophrenic language: why does a particular patient utter the particular words that he does, rather than some other jumbled-up sequence?

Some beginnings of an answer to this question have begun to emerge. Years ago, Eugen Bleuler commented on the presence of interfering associations in schizophrenic language. He suggested that the difficulty for the patient was that ideas associated with the content of his message somehow intruded into the message and thus distorted it. A patient of his, whom he had seen walking around the hospital grounds with her father and son, was asked who her visitors were. "The father, son and Holy Ghost," she replied. These words have a strong mutual association as a single phrase and although the last item, "Holy Ghost," was probably not meant as part of her message, it intruded because of its strong associative links with other units in the message.

Bleuler also noticed the difficulty that patients seemed to have in understanding a pun, despite their tendency to talk in punning fashion. A patient asked about her relationships with people at home says, "I have many ties with my home! My father wears them around his collar." The pun on the word *tie* was unintentional, hence humorless.

Against the background of this general hypothesis of interfering associations, my students and I began investigations of schizophrenic language some years ago in Harvard's Laboratory of Social Relations. Our first concern was with the original question of definition. What must language contain to be labeled schizophrenic? Our work began with a plea to over 200 hospitals for examples of patients' writings—whether the patients were schizophrenic or not. Colleaguial response was rather overwhelming, and we amassed a very large number of letters, documents, diaries and simple messages written in almost every state of the Union. (Many of these were inappropriate to our purposes. A carton load of documents in Spanish from a Texas hospital, some brief obscenities scribbled on matchcovers and dropped daily onto the desk of a colleague in a St. Louis hospital and other similar items were eliminated, of course.)

From this mass, we selected a set of documents that were legible, long enough to include several consecutive sentences—and written in English. These texts were then read by a panel of clinicians. Each text was judged independently, and then was classified as schizophrenic language or normal language. (We obtained typical interjudge agreements of around 80 per cent.) At this juncture we did not know whether the writers of the letters had been diagnosed as schizophrenic or not. Our concern was with the characteristics of the language—and with the clinicians' reactions to it.

Our two sets of texts then were submitted for computer analysis with the aid of the General Inquirer program. This program codes and categorizes language in terms of content, and also provides a summary of grammatical features of the language. Out of this analysis, we developed some empirical rules (or a guide on how to write a document that a clinician will judge schizophrenic). Two of the most reliable rules were:

1. Write about politics, religion or science. Letters dealing with global social issues of this kind are highly likely to be regarded as schizophrenic by clinicians.
2. Write more objects than subjects in sentences. Typical sentences consist of enumerations of classes of objects in a form illustrated in our second and third examples above: "send it to me, Joseph Nemo, in care of Joseph Nemo and me who answers by the name of Joseph Nemo"; or "I fancy chocolate eclairs, chocolate eclairs, doenuts." Or in chains of associations at the end of a sentence. When, for example, a woman patient writes: "I like coffee, cream, cows, Elizabeth Taylor," the association links between each word and the one following seem obvious.

This kind of associative chaining already had been described clinically by Bleuler; hence it was hardly surprising that the computer should find it to be a reliable discriminator in our document samples. What began to interest us, however, was the fact that these associations interfere most readily at the end of a sentence. Why not chains of subjects or chains of verbs, and why not at the beginning or middle of a sentence? Furthermore, why is this kind of interference found clearly in some schizophrenic patients and yet never occurs at all in others?

For some time it has become increasingly apparent that, in schizophrenia, attention is greatly disrupted. It is hard for a patient to remain focused on any one stimulus for any length of time. He is unable to "tune out" or ignore other surrounding stimuli. These distract him; they enter consciousness at full strength and not in an attenuated fashion as they do with the normal person. Reports by the patients themselves make the point dramatically:

"Things are coming in too fast. I lose my grip of it and get lost. I am attending to everything at once and as a result I do not really attend to anything."†

"Everything seems to grip my attention, although I am not particularly interested in anything. I am speaking to you just now but I can hear noises going on next door and in the corridor. I find it difficult to concentrate on what I am saying to you."†

"I cannot seem to think or even put any plans together. I cannot see the picture. I get the book out and read the story but the activities and the story all just do not jar me into action."†

Experimental tasks that require close attention, tasks that call for fast reactions to sudden stimuli, or any continuous monitoring of a changing stimulus field are almost invariably done poorly by schizophrenics. Sorting tasks, where the subject must organize objects or words into conceptual groups, are progressively more difficult for the schizophrenic if irrelevant or puzzling factors appear in the material.

We may regard the focusing of attention as a process whereby we effectively inhibit attention to everything but certain relevant stimuli in the environment. As attention lapses, we find ourselves being aware of various irrelevant stimuli—the inhibitory mechanism has failed temporarily.

It is possible that an analogous set of events takes place when we produce a complex sequence of language. Attention may be greater or lesser at some points in a language sequence than at others. The end of a sentence—the period point—may be particularly vulnerable to momentary attentional lapses: one thought has been successfully completed, but the next one may not yet have been formed into utterable shape. Within a single sentence itself, there may be other points of comparative vulnerability, though not perhaps as marked as at the sentence ending.

Uttering a sentence without disruption is an extremely skilled performance, but one that most of us acquire so early in life that we are unaware of its remarkable complexity. (However, we become more aware of how difficult it is to "make sense" when we are extremely tired, or ripped out of sleep by the telephone, or distraught, or drunk.)

Single words have strong associational bonds with other words—as the classic technique of word association indicates. We know that the word "black" will elicit the response "white" almost instantaneously from the majority of people. The associational bond between black and white is clearly very strong. Strong as it is, it will not be allowed to dominate consciousness when one is uttering a sentence such as "I am thinking about buying a black car." Our successful sentences come from the successful, sequential inhibition of all interfering associations that individual words in the sentence might generate. Just as successful visual attention involves tuning out irrelevant visual material, so successful utterance may involve tuning out irrelevant verbal static.

By the same token, disordered attention should lead to an increasing likelihood that this kind of interference will not be inhibited, but will actually

---

†These quotations are taken from McGhie & Chapman's *Disorders of Attention in Schizophrenia*.

intrude into language utterance. Its most probable point of intrusion is wherever attention is normally lowest.

"Portmanteau" words or puns provide unusually good occasions for disruptive intrusions. Consider, for example, the word "stock." This word has several possible meanings, each of them with its own set of associations. Financial associations might be *Wall Street, bonds, dividend,* etc. Agricultural associations might include *cattle, barn* and *farm;* theatrical associations might be *summer, company,* and the like. Webster's Third International Dictionary gives 42 different definitions of the word *stock,* many of them archaic or unusual, but many of them common. If one set of meanings intrudes into a sentence that is clearly built around another set of meanings, the effect is a pun, and an accompanying digression or cross-current in surface content. The sentences—"I have many ties with my home. My father wears them around his collar,"—seem to skip, like a stone on a lake, from *ties* (bonds) to *home* to *father* to *ties* (neckties). On the surface, this is a witty statement, but the speaker had no idea of what was really going on inside or underneath the form of words. The statement was therefore unwitting and hence unwitty.

Loren Chapman and his associates, in work at Southern Illinois University, demonstrated that schizophrenics as a group are more open to interference from the most common meaning of a punning word. When we use a word like *stock* as a stimulus for word association, we discover that most normal respondents give financial associations first, and may find it difficult to respond when asked to "give associations to another meaning." Associations to the other meaning are weaker or less prepotent and only emerge under special instructional sets. Chapman's work suggests that if the plan of a sentence calls for the use of a weaker meaning, the schizophrenic runs some risk that associational intrusions will interfere and actually produce a punning effect.

On the other hand, if the plan of a sentence involves the stronger meaning, then there may be no intrusion of associations. And if associations do intrude, these intrusions will appear relevant to the sentence and will not strike the listener as strange. Which meanings will be strong or weak will depend to some extent upon the culture from which the patient comes. (Personal experience may of course produce uniquely strong or weak associations in individual cases.) However, Chapman was able to predict correctly the direction of errors for schizophrenic patients as a group on the basis of estimates of strength obtained from normal respondents. Thus, some patients may have personal idiosyncrasies, but the associations that interrupt the schizophrenic are generally the same as those that are strong for the population at large.

A parallel investigation I conducted at the University of Copenhagen included a study of the language of Danish schizophrenics. I observed the same general effect: patients were liable to interference from strong meanings of double-meaning words. English is a language, of course, that is unusually rich in puns, homonyms, cognates and indeed a whole lexicon of verbal trickery. But it seems plausible to suppose that in any language in which double-meaning words are to be found, this kind of schizophrenic disturbance may be found.

From these observations we can begin to piece together a picture of what happens when schizophrenic intrusions occur in a sentence that started out more or less normally. Where a punning word occurs at a vulnerable point, the sequence becomes disrupted and rapidly disintegrates into associative chaining until it terminates (see Figure 1).

FIGURE 1. A look at a schizophrenic utterance. Where a punning word occurs at a vulnerable point, the sequence becomes disrupted and disintegrates into associative chaining until it terminates. The emotional significance of what the schizophrenic plans to say may have little or no bearing on when an intrusion occurs or what it seems to mean.

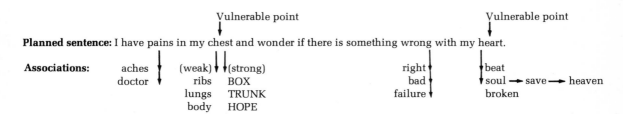

Planned sentence: I have pains in my chest and wonder if there is something wrong with my heart.

Utterance: "Doctor, I have pains in my chest and hope and wonder if my box is broken and heart is beaten for my soul and salvation and heaven, Amen."

We may look at schizophrenic utterances as the end result of a combination of two factors: the vulnerability of sentence structure to attentional lapses, and the inability of patients to inhibit associational intrusions, particularly at these lapse points. From this point of view, the problem of language is directly related to the other attentional difficulties which the schizophrenic has; he is handicapped in making language work clearly, just as he is at any other task that requires sustained attention. The emotional significance of what the schizophrenic plans to say may have little or no bearing on when an intrusion occurs, or what it seems to mean. Any sentence with vulnerable points in its syntactic or semantic structure may result in confusion, whether the topic is of great psychological importance or has to do with a patient's harmless liking for chocolate eclairs and doughnuts.

Serious and sustained difficulties in the maintenance of attention suggest a biological defect. Peter Venables at the University of London has suggested swimming or unfocusable attention in schizophrenia may be connected with low thresholds of physiological arousal—stimuli can be very weak and yet trigger strong physiological reactions. This low arousal threshold is found mostly in acute, rather than chronic, schizophrenia.

Evidence from studies of a variety of attentional tasks supports this interpretation. Additional and intriguing evidence was obtained by one of my students, Dr. Joy Rice at the University of Wisconsin. Using electrochemical (galvanic) changes in the skin as a measure, she found that schizophrenic patients who were most responsive to noise stimulation were also the patients who showed the most difficulty in dealing with the meaning of punning sentences. The magnitude of galvanic skin response to external stimulation is presumably greatest in patients with low initial arousal levels (and hence the most receptivity to external stimulation). Rice's data may therefore support the notion that verbal associational interference is part and parcel of a total syndrome of which biological control of attention is a crucial central focus.

Recent research into the effects of LSD has shown that it is people with low initial arousal systems who have the "good trips"; the most cursory glance at literary biography will reveal an extraordinary number of poets and writers who were "sensitive," "neurasthenic," and so on. Which leads me to a sort of Parthian speculation.

Look again at the four samples quoted in the beginning of this article. What you see there, I think, is the literary imagination gone mad, if I may use so unclinical a term here. The first sample, had it come from the pen of someone whose brain we trusted, might almost be a crude parody of ponderous political tracts or socio-economo-political gobbledygook of one sort or another. In the second, the fragment, "With my nostrils clogged and Winter here," is really not bad, and one wouldn't be terribly surprised to find it occurring in, say, the *Cantos* of Ezra Pound. In the third quotation, there are unmistakable echoes from the New Testament, Lord Byron, and Ralph Waldo Emerson, or rather echoes from an entire chamber of the literary heritage. The kind of wordplay indulged in throughout the fourth quote is not essentially different technically from that employed by the later James Joyce, or by the John Lennon of *In his own write*.

What is lacking from these samples, so far as we can tell, is context and control and the critical, or pattern-imposing, intelligence. It would seem, therefore, that the mental substrata in which certain kinds of poetry are born probably are associative in a more or less schizophrenic way. (In the case of poets like Dylan Thomas or Hart Crane, of course, these substrata had to be blasted open by liquor.) The intelligence that shapes, cuts, edits, revises and erases is fed by many conscious sources, most of them cultural; but the wellsprings seem to be, as poets have been telling us for centuries, sort of divine and sort of mad.

BIOCHEMICAL FACTORS
IN SCHIZOPHRENIA

SOLOMON H. SNYDER

Many false trails have been followed over the years in attempts to associate schizophrenia with biochemical anomalies. Recently it has been found that there is a close correlation between the efficacy of certain neuroleptic agents in the management of the disease and their ability to block CNS receptor sites activated by dopamine. It is suggested that this may be a clue to one of many genetic bases of schizophrenia.

Almost since schizophrenia was first defined in the mid-nineteenth century, psychiatrists and others have speculated on possible biochemical factors in the disease. The severe and generalized nature of its symptoms suggested the operations of some toxic process, a view that was strengthened by the discovery, around the turn of the twentieth century, that the severe neuropsychiatric disorder general paresis has an organic cause: syphilitic infection of the brain.

Perhaps the first systematic work on the biochemistry of schizophrenia involved attempts to isolate abnormal substances in the blood or urine of patients. Thus, for example, a group at Tulane University reported the discovery in the serum of schizophrenics of a protein they called taraxein that was supposedly not present in nor-

mal individuals and that could cause hallucinations when injected into normal volunteers. Subsequent attempts to duplicate these findings, however, were unsuccessful: the blood proteins of schizophrenics turned out to be identical with those of normal individuals, apart from changes that could be most easily accounted for by chronic illness and institutionalization. Moreover, the hallucinatory reactions ascribed to taraxein could equally well be produced by a placebo if the latter were given in a similar experimental situation where such effects were suggested to the subjects.

Another apparently false lead turned up a few years later, with the discovery of a chromatographic abnormality in the urine of schizophrenics, called, from its staining properties, the pink spot. Some researchers tentatively identified the compound giving rise to the spot as 3,4-dimethoxyphenylamine, a substance related both to the neurotransmitter dopamine and the hallucinogenic drug mescaline. Further work, however, showed that the pink spot was in fact composed of many compounds, its major components being metabolites of the drugs that the patients were taking.

The failure of these attempts to demonstrate biochemical abnormalities in schizophrenics strengthened the view of some psychiatrists—notably, those of the psychodynamic or psychoanalytic school—that the disease was entirely functional in its etiology. More recently, however, the whole question has been reopened with the demonstration that the disease possesses a strong hereditary component. Whether, and to what extent, patterns of behavior or tendencies to behave in a particular way can be transmitted genetically in man or other animals is still a matter of debate. What is not in dispute is that the mechanism of

EDITORS' COMMENTS:

THE AUTHOR REVIEWS SOME OF THE BIOLOGICAL THEORIES ASSOCIATED WITH THE ETIOLOGY OF SCHIZOPHRENIA. A DOPAMINERGIC HYPOTHESIS IS DEVELOPED FROM THE OBSERVATION THAT CERTAIN OF THE PHENOTHIAZINES ARE MUCH MORE EFFECTIVE IN TREATING SCHIZOPHRENIA THAN OTHERS.

Reprinted from Hospital Practice 12:133–140, 1977. Figures by Albert Miller and Nancy Lou Gahan. Reproduced with permission.

Tyrosine

3-hydroxytyrosine (dopa)

Dopamine

Norepinephrine

Homovanillic Acid

Diagrams show structural similarity of precursors and a breakdown product, homovanillic acid, to dopamine and norepinephrine, the two principal catecholamines found in the brain. In studies of biochemical factors that may underlie schizophrenia, much emphasis has been given to dopamine because of strong correlations between the clinical effectiveness of many neuroleptic drugs with their ability to block receptor sites in the brain that are activated by dopamine.

transmission must be chemical: the passing from parent to offspring of certain compounds (nucleic-acid sequences) that control the biosynthesis of other compounds (proteins). Inherited abnormalities of either physiology or behavior, in short, imply abnormalities somewhere in the body's protein complement.

In the case of behavioral abnormalities, the obvious place to look for aberrant biochemistry is the CNS. Abnormal metabolites produced elsewhere in the body can, indeed, sometimes affect the brain, but many such substances are ruled out of consideration by the blood-brain barrier, which tends to protect the brain from physiologic perturbations elsewhere in the organism. Unfortunately, even limiting our search to the CNS does not help much, since that system—like most others—contains many thousands of different chemical species, many still unidentified or of unknown or little-known function. One must therefore approach the problem indirectly and by inference.

Attempts to seek clues to abnormalities of the brain by examining the urine are not likely to be productive, since much experimental work has shown that most brain chemicals have little access to the urine. One potentially profitable line of approach is through investigation of the effects of drugs, notably those that exert selective effects on schizophrenic behavior. If a drug can indeed relieve the symptoms of schizophrenia—and only those symptoms—then there is at least a fair chance that by learning how the drug works we can secure clues to the biochemical lesion involved in the disease.

As is well known, a number of drugs do selectively relieve symptoms of schizophrenia. These so-called neuroleptic agents are of different molecular structures but fall mainly into two chemical families: the phenothiazines and the butyrophenones. When Jean Delay and Pierre Deniker introduced chlorpromazine, the first of the phenothiazines, into clinical practice in 1952, they expected merely that it would sedate hyperactive patients. They found, however, that it could also activate withdrawn schizophrenics and, accordingly, suggested that it was acting selectively on the fundamental schizophrenic abnormality, whatever that was.

For many years, American physicians treated this conclusion with considerable skepticism. Eventually, however, the two French clinicians' conclusions were confirmed by a number of well-controlled, multi-hospital studies in the Veterans Administration and elsewhere. When the neuroleptics were compared with many other agents that affect mental functioning (notably, sedatives and antianxiety drugs), they proved to be the only compounds that could produce significant overall improvement in schizophrenic behavior and thought. Sedatives could reduce hyperactivity or violent behavior but had no effect on the disordered thinking associated with them—and made withdrawn schizophrenics even more withdrawn. The antianxiety agents such as diazepam (Valium) and chlordiazepoxide (Librium), by contrast, proved to be considerably more effective than the neuroleptics in relieving anxiety but exerted no clear beneficial effect on schizophrenia. This latter finding, incidentally, seriously weakened the theory, suggested by some psychologists, that the immediate cause of schizophrenia is an overwhelming "pan-anxiety."

Ascertaining the mode of action of neuroleptic drugs, however, has been difficult, since these substances, like many other drugs, are highly reactive and can influence large numbers of biochemical processes not merely in the brain but elsewhere in the body. They can, for example, alter energy metabolism and protein turnover, as well as brain levels of a number of compounds that serve as neurotransmitters. How, then, does one determine which of these effects accounts for the drugs' therapeutic actions in patients with schizophrenia and which are simply irrelevant?

One way of tackling this problem is to evaluate a large number of chemically related drugs. The phenothiazines, for example, include numerous agents of similar structure that have been tested in patients; some have proved highly effective in relieving schizophrenic symptoms, some totally ineffective, with many falling into the middle ground between the two extremes. If, then, a given chemical action of these drugs is exerted most potently by the most clinically efficacious compounds and is least marked in the ineffective ones, one can feel reasonably confident that the action in question is related to the drugs' therapeutic effect. Conversely, if a given chemical action is shared by drugs of widely varying clinical potency, it seems unlikely that it will have much relevance to the biochemistry of schizophrenia.

The second principle enables us to exclude a large number of chemical effects. For example, promethazine is closely related in structure to chlorpromazine but is devoid of antischizophrenic activity (it is an effective antihistamine). Yet most of chlorpromazine's biochemical effects are elicited just as potently by promethazine and, therefore, cannot represent chlorpromazine's therapeutic mode of action.

This technique of elimination has over the years revealed only one biochemical action that consistently correlates closely with the clinical effects of large numbers of neuroleptics: the apparent ability of some neuroleptics to blockade receptor sites in the brain that are activated by the neurotransmitter dopamine. To evaluate these findings, however, we must first consider what dopamine is and what, so far as we know, it does.

Dopamine is one of the body's three principal catecholamines (catechol referring to a benzene ring with two attached hydroxyl groups and amine referring to the presence of an amino [$-NH_2$] group in the molecule), the other two being norepinephrine and epinephrine. Only dopamine and norepinephrine are found in the brain to any great extent, epinephrine exerting its activity mainly on the peripheral nervous system.

The ultimate (dietary) progenitor of dopamine in the body is the amino acid tyrosine, which is transformed successively into dihydroxyphenylalanine (dopa) and then into dopamine itself. In most parts of the brain, dopamine is then further transformed into norepinephrine by the action of the enzyme dopamine hydroxylase. In some areas, however, the enzyme is missing, meaning

Although dopamine is transformed to norepinephrine in most parts of the brain, in others the converting enzyme is missing and dopamine itself serves as neurotransmitter. The dopaminergic pathways thought most likely to be involved in schizophrenia are suggested in the drawing; they are components of, or linked functionally to, the limbic system, which is known to play a significant regulatory role in emotional behavior.

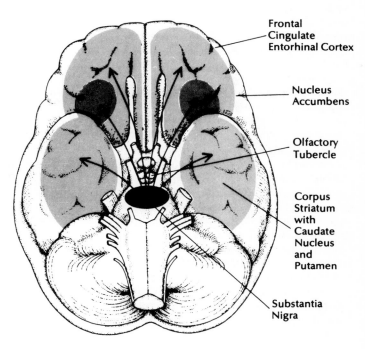

Frontal
Cingulate
Entorhinal Cortex

Nucleus
Accumbens

Olfactory
Tubercle

Corpus
Striatum
with
Caudate
Nucleus
and
Putamen

Substantia
Nigra

that dopamine rather than norepinephrine must serve as the neurotransmitter. The best known of these areas involves neurons in the substantia nigra with axonal terminals in the corpus striatum, which includes the caudate nucleus and putamen; the neurons act by releasing dopamine at the terminals. The neurons are selectively destroyed (by unknown causes) in patients with idiopathic Parkinson's disease. As is well known, parkinsonian symptoms can be dramatically alleviated by administering the dopamine precursor, L-dopa, indicating that dopamine depletion is causally related to the disease. Significantly, the neuroleptic drugs themselves can produce extrapyramidal, parkinsonianlike symptoms, but presumably by blocking the dopamine receptors rather than by engendering the depletion of dopamine.

Other dopaminergic pathways are probably more important in schizophrenia. We know, for example, that pathways with neurons close to the substantia nigra project to the nucleus accumbens and the olfactory tubercle; both of these are components of the limbic system of the brain, which, significantly, regulates emotional behavior. Other, more recently described, dopaminergic pathways run from the same area to parts of the frontal, cingulate, and entorhinal cortex, which, though anatomically part of the brain's cortical associative centers, have been functionally linked to the limbic system. It is reasonable, therefore, that abnormalities in these dopaminergic pathways would induce emotional abnormalities that neuroleptic drugs, by further changing the pathways' functioning, would alleviate or abolish. But how does one demonstrate that neuroleptics do in fact act on the dopaminergic system? Specifically, can it be shown that they bind to dopamine receptor sites on the target neurons?

The earliest findings in this area were obtained by the Swedish pharmacologist Arvid Carlsson. From a number of animal experiments with neuroleptic drugs, he had concluded that the behavioral changes observed seemed most consistent with a depletion of dopamine. However, when he measured brain levels of dopamine breakdown products (e.g., homovanillic acid), he found that the neuroleptic drugs actually increased these levels, implying an increase rather than a decrease in dopamine. To reconcile this finding with the animal behavioral data, Carlsson hypothesized that the rise was a secondary effect, resulting from biochemical feedback. That is, the drugs blocked dopamine receptors, which in turn stimulated the dopamine-releasing cells to fire more frequently, thereby producing the observed excess of the neurohumor.

Many subsequent experiments, both pharmacologic and neurophysiologic, have demonstrated conclusively that the neuroleptics do indeed accelerate the firing of dopamine-releasing neurons. Demonstrating that they also block the receptor sites, however, has proved much more difficult, and for a long time much of the evidence was indirect.

There was, for example, the matter of the extrapyramidal (parkinsonian) side effects frequently seen with neuroleptics, which it has become increasingly clear must be due to interference with some dopaminergic pathway. And since the drugs were clearly not blocking dopamine production or release (as occurs in Parkinson's disease itself), the obvious alternative was that they were interfering with its reception. In this connection it has been observed that schizophrenic patients treated with neuroleptics who do not develop extrapyramidal side effects tend to have much higher levels of dopamine breakdown products in the spinal fluid than those who show such effects. This suggests that the feedback effect that Carlsson postulated does indeed liberate excess dopamine, which in turn prevents the appearance of parkinsonian symptoms.

One might then wonder, however, how it is that the patients respond at all to the drugs. That is, if the excess dopamine liberated is sufficient to prevent the extrapyramidal symptoms, why is it not also sufficient to cancel any therapeutic effect of the drugs elsewhere in the brain? Delay and Deniker, in fact, postulated just such a relationship; they believed that unless the patient showed a neurologic (extrapyramidal) response to the drug, he would derive no therapeutic benefit. Subsequently, however, it has become clear that this relationship between therapeutic benefit and side effects need not obtain—that the neurologic and emotional effects of the drugs do not correlate perfectly. The reason has to do with various other pharmacologic properties of the drugs that we do not have space to detail here. One might note, however, that an overcompensation to neuroleptics, by release of excess dopamine, may explain why some schizophrenics fail to respond to the drugs.

Another line of evidence on the mode of action of the neuroleptics came from studies of other, quite different, drugs. If the neuroleptics control schizophrenia by blocking dopamine receptors, thereby functionally reducing dopamine levels at

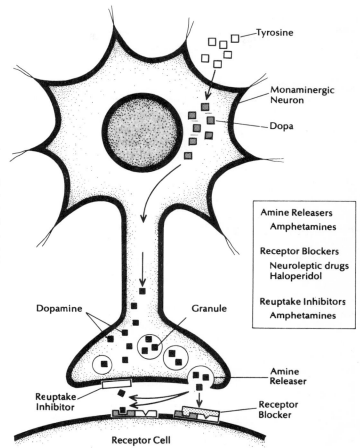

Support for concept that neuroleptic drugs ameliorate schizophrenia by blocking receptors for dopamine, thus reducing its functional level at certain brain sites, comes also from the finding of an exacerbating effect on the disease by drugs, e.g., the amphetamines, that stimulate dopamine release or prevent its reuptake by the nerve terminal.

certain sites in the brain, one would expect that drugs that increased dopamine levels at these sites would exacerbate the disease.

As it happens, the amphetamines exert their clinical actions by increasing the amount of both norepinephrine and dopamine in the synaptic cleft. It has been found that even in very low doses these stimulants can dramatically exacerbate the symptoms of schizophrenic patients. Yet they do not exert such effects on patients with other emotional disorders (e.g., mania, depression) nor on normal individuals at low doses. Experiments using different amphetamine analogues, with differential effects on the dopamine and norepinephrine systems, indicate that the exacerbation is more likely to be mediated through the former rather than the latter. One would expect, too, that L-dopa, which is used routinely in parkinsonian patients to raise dopamine levels, would also worsen schizophrenic symptoms, and in fact several clinical studies have shown that it does.

It is important to note, by the way, that neither the amphetamines nor L-dopa in any way superimpose a different psychosis on the schizophrenic; rather, they exacerbate the patient's own constellation of symptoms: a hebephrenic patient becomes more hebephrenic, a catatonic more catatonic, and so on.

If amphetamines and L-dopa can exacerbate the symptoms of schizophrenics by engendering an excess of dopamine, one might expect that in large enough doses they could induce psychotic symptoms even in nonschizophrenic individuals. So far as the amphetamines, at least, are concerned, this is the case. Amphetamine addicts—especially the "speed freaks" who take the drug intravenously—often administer themselves doses of up to 500 mg, or 50 times the normal therapeutic dose. Such individuals will almost invariably, at one time or another, develop acute paranoid psychosis that can be clinically indistinguishable from acute paranoid schizophrenia. There are, in-

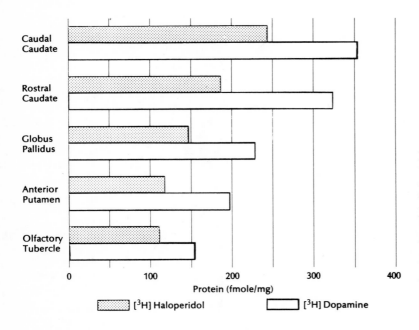

[³H] Haloperidol   [³H] Dopamine

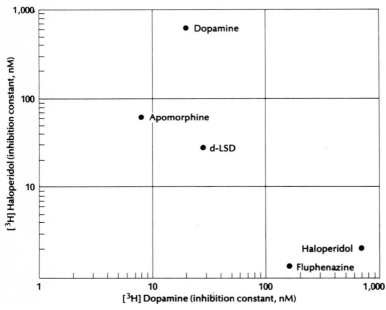

Evidence that the dopamine receptor exists in two states (i.e., with selective affinity, respectively, for agonist and antagonist compounds of a given type) was obtained in binding experiments. As seen in graph above, testing sections of calf brain with labeled dopamine and a labeled antagonist, haloperidol, showed that the same brain areas bind both substances and do so in similar proportions (in other parts of the brain neither is bound). At the same time, testing the ability of agonist and antagonist to inhibit binding of each other indicated that they do not bind to the same sites within the given locus. Graph below shows that dopamine inhibits dopamine binding much more than haloperidol binding, and vice versa. Apomorphine, an agonist, has similar effects to dopamine's; fluphenazine, an antagonist, has effects similar to haloperidol's. The mixed agonist-antagonist, d-LSD, inhibits binding of both dopamine and haloperidol.

deed, numerous reports of individuals admitted to psychiatric hospitals with a diagnosis of schizophrenia that had to be revised when the history of drug abuse became known. Cocaine, which is believed to facilitate the actions of the catecholamines, can produce a very similar type of psychosis—an observation summed up by a famous jazz musician as, "If you aren't crazy before you take it, you're crazy afterward."

The use of amphetamine or cocaine psychosis as a model for schizophrenia has been attacked on the ground that such individuals do not display all the abnormalities of thought and action typical of schizophrenia. Moreover, amphetamine psychosis is invariably paranoid in form, whereas paranoid schizophrenia is merely one type of the disease. Such objections do not seem to me necessarily fatal. For one thing, one can see the pathology of amphetamine psychosis as similar to that of schizophrenia without regarding them as identical. For another, the fact that amphetamine is acting in a nonschizophrenic who "knows" that the episode is likely to be transient should in itself make for major differences. The schizophrenic, by contrast, has been experiencing a more or less abnormal mental state for months or (usually) years, with little or no hope of major relief.

Nonetheless, all these lines of indirect evidence, while certainly persuasive, fall considerably short of hard proof that schizophrenia is linked to some disorder in the brain's dopaminergic pathways. For this reason, I and my associates Ian Creese and David Burt have attempted to obtain more direct evidence by studying the binding of neuroleptic drugs to dopamine-binding sites in brain tissue.

As is well known, many hormones, neurotransmitters, and other physiologically active substances produce their effects by binding to specific sites on the exterior (plasma) membranes of their target cells, by which process they activate other processes in the cell interior by means of a "second messenger" substance such as cyclic AMP. Often the action of these substances can be antagonized by other compounds which, by themselves binding to the same membrane sites, block the action of the active, or agonist, substance. Such systems are often visualized in terms of a "lock-and-key" model: the binding site is the lock, the agonist compound the key, while the antagonist is an "incorrectly cut" key that cannot turn the lock, but by filling the keyhole can prevent insertion of the correct key.

Identification of neurotransmitter receptors is a very young science, dating only from about 1970, when several groups succeeded in isotopically labeling a particular type of acetylcholine receptor in certain invertebrates. Further progress in the area was hampered by the fact that both neurotransmitters and their antagonists are rather loosely bound to the receptor sites, meaning that it is hard to distinguish specific binding there from nonspecific adsorption. Only recently has this problem been overcome—by using low concentrations of binding substance with high levels of radioactivity plus rapid but vigorous washing of the tissues to remove the nonspecifically bound molecules.

A number of experiments using this technique have indicated that for many brain receptor sites, at least, the lock-and-key model is an oversimplification. Rather, it appears that the receptor site exists in two states, one with selective affinity for

agonist compounds of a given type, the other with similar affinity for the appropriate antagonists. The evidence supporting this view is too complex to detail here, but it includes, for example, the observation that the physiologic potency of antagonists of a particular class often does not correlate well with their capacity to displace an agonist from the binding site (as would be the case in the simple lock-and-key model), though it correlates very well with their capacity to displace other antagonists. The two-state model also explains how compounds with no structural similarity to the agonist can still act as antagonists, and how other compounds can exert both types of effect— antagonist and agonist—simultaneously.

It appears that the two states can in many cases be converted into one another, though in most cases we do not know how or why conversion occurs. With the opiate receptor, however, it has been shown that it binds opiates (agonists) much more effectively in the absence of sodium ion, while opiate antagonists are bound selectively when the ion is present. Exactly how this two-state model should be visualized at the molecular level is still uncertain and will probably remain so until someone succeeds in actually determining the structure of a receptor site. It may involve a stereochemical change in the receptor, as is the case with, for example, the visual pigments in their response to light. Alternatively, it may involve two adjacent molecules or adjacent sites on the same molecule. One of these might selectively bind agonists, the other antagonists, and the molecules could be so arranged that the occupation of either site (or molecule) desensitizes the other to the action of "its" compound. Additional models are also possible, but in the present state of knowledge there seems little point in speculating about them.

A good deal of evidence obtained in our laboratory indicates that the dopamine receptors operate according to the two-state model. To begin with, labeling experiments show clearly that both dopamine and its antagonists bind to the same portions of the brain and, moreover, that the amount of binding in different areas is in the same proportion. For example, when sections of calf brain are tested with labeled dopamine and a labeled antagonist, haloperidol (an antischizophrenic drug), the greatest amount of binding for both drugs is in the caudal caudate region. The next highest amount is in the rostral caudate, with 76% (of the maximum caudal caudate level) for haloperidol and 90% for dopamine. Levels are lower in the globus pallidus, anterior putamen, and olfactory tubercle, which for both drugs show about 60%,

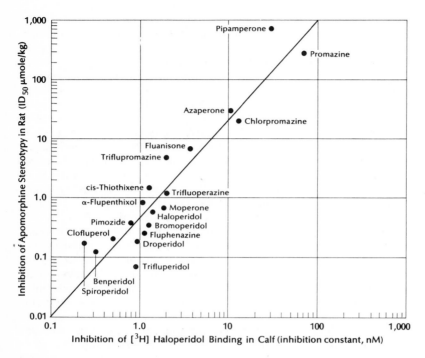

Binding studies have provided a method of ranking antischizophrenic drugs according to potency. Graph above shows a correlation coefficient of .94 between affinity for haloperidol binding sites and pharmacologic effectiveness in animals. Correlation with potency in schizophrenia is almost as high, .84 (graph below).

50%, and 40% to 45% of the maximum, respectively.

A second point is that the binding in question does not involve presynaptic dopamine receptors, though these are known to exist. This can be demonstrated by injecting the compound 6-hydroxy-

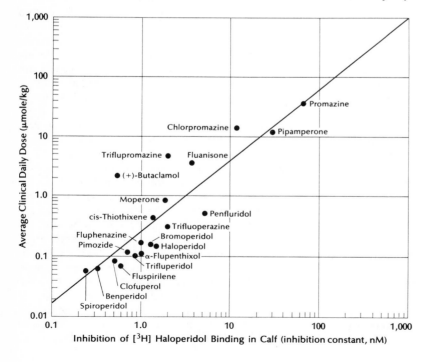

dopamine into the substantia nigra of the rat brain, thereby destroying nearly all the dopamine-releasing presynaptic nerve terminals. Such treatment does not reduce binding of either dopamine or haloperidol.

Thus, it seems clear that both drugs bind in the same locus (postsynaptic receptors) in the same parts of the brain and in the same proportions. Yet when we test their ability to inhibit binding of each other, and of other agonists and antagonists, it seems equally clear that they are not binding to the same sites. Thus, dopamine inhibits dopamine binding 30 times more effectively than it does haloperidol binding, while haloperidol inhibits haloperidol binding far more effectively than it does dopamine binding. (The difference in the latter situation is on the order of 300 to 1.) Apomorphine, an agonist (i.e., its physiologic effects resemble those of dopamine), inhibits dopamine binding more than it does haloperidol binding. Fluphenazine, an antagonist, inhibits haloperidol binding more effectively than dopamine binding. Finally, d-LSD, which physiologically shows both agonistic and antagonistic effects in relation to dopamine, inhibits binding of both compounds.

On the basis of these findings, we have ranked a whole series of antischizophrenic drugs by their ability to inhibit haloperidol binding, by their ability to antagonize the action of apomorphine and amphetamine in animals, by the average clinical dose, and by their ability to inhibit dopamine binding. The in vivo animal potency of the drugs correlates almost perfectly with their haloperidol-binding inhibition, with correlation coefficients averaging .94, and the correlation is almost as good for the clinical potency (.84). Ranked against dopamine-binding inhibition, however, the correlation is only moderately good (.58). (The nature of correlation coefficients makes this figure much "worse" than .94, considerably more so than the raw numerical difference would suggest.)

These findings, we believe, provide strong evidence that the brain's dopaminergic pathways are involved in the therapeutic effects of neuroleptics in schizophrenia, and also that the dopamine postsynaptic receptor indeed exists in the two-state form. The haloperidol-binding inhibition test, moreover, provides a quick and cheap method for screening new antischizophrenic drugs, requiring only a few micrograms of the drug and a few milligrams of brain tissue; up to 100 drugs can be screened in a morning. Thus, the two most clinically potent antischizophrenic drugs, spiroperidol and benperidol, rank first and second in haloperidol-binding inhibition but 16th and 21st (out of 25) in dopamine-binding inhibition, while (+)-butaclamol, the top drug for inhibiting dopamine binding, ranks only 15th in clinical potency.

However, more efficient drug screening, though certainly a beneficial side effect of our experiments, was not the main goal of these studies, which was rather to elucidate the biochemistry of schizophrenia. As indicated above, the studies are

Dopamine-binding inhibition correlates less well than haloperidol-binding inhibition with clinical potency (r = .58). As shown in preceding graph, the two most potent antischizophrenic drugs, spiroperidol and benperidol, ranked first and second in haloperidol-binding inhibition but are 16th and 21st here. Similarly, (+)-butaclamol, first here in dopamine-binding inhibition, was only 15th in clinical potency.

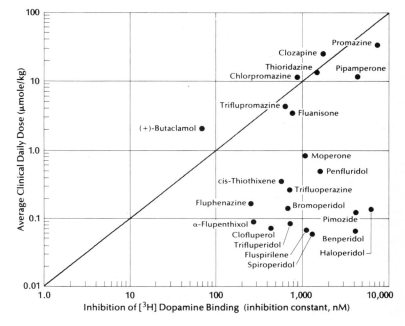

consistent with the dopamine theory of schizophrenia but have by no means demonstrated that the brain defect in that disease involves dopamine itself. This somewhat paradoxical conclusion may perhaps be clarified by an electrical analogy: the fact that a dangerous short circuit can be abolished by tripping the appropriate circuit breaker does not mean that the short is in the breaker—it may be anywhere in the circuit. Equally, the fact that schizophrenic symptoms can be ameliorated, by "breaking" the dopaminergic pathways of the brain (by administering dopamine antagonists) need not imply that the symptoms' primary cause is some defect in release or reception of that substance.

One should emphasize that the dopamine mediation of the therapeutic actions of neuroleptics does not necessarily mean that dopamine synapses are disturbed in schizophrenia. Possible schizophrenic abnormalities might involve systems several steps distant, but which can be modulated by changes in dopamine transmission.

If dopamine systems are in fact abnormal in such schizophrenia, there are several candidate sites for the abnormality. The transmitter is synthesized in specialized dopamine-releasing neurons (as well as other neurons where it serves as a substrate for norepinephrine). When these neurons fire, dopamine is released into the synaptic cleft, where it can bind to the receptors of the target neurons. Being only loosely bound, however, it becomes detached rather easily and is then swept up from the synaptic cleft by an uptake system in the releasing neurons, whence it can be released once more. Whatever is not scavenged this way is broken down by the enzyme monoamine oxidase, which is widespread in the CNS, notably in the glia.

Possible schizophrenic abnormalities in the dopamine system, then, would include the manufacture and/or release of excess dopamine, a too-avid binding of it to the receptors, and a failure of the uptake system and/or the monoamine oxidase system, either of which would presumably lead to excess dopamine in and around the synaptic cleft. It is by blocking the uptake system and directly releasing dopamine that amphetamine produces many of its pharmacologic effects (including the exacerbation of schizophrenia); the antidepressant drugs known as monoamine oxidase inhibitors can also aggravate the disease by slowing dopamine breakdown.

Most of these possibilities, however, have been ruled out as potential mechanisms for schizophrenia, at least on a gross scale. Studies of dopamine and breakdown products such as homovanillic acid in the spinal fluid of schizophrenics indicate that their dopamine production and release are normal. Measurements of receptor binding in the brains of schizophrenics indicate nothing unusual there either. Whether the uptake system is also normal remains to be determined. In principle, it should be possible to measure this (e.g., by measuring dopamine binding to receptor sites on the secreting cells), but so far no one has managed to do it.

Even if it should turn out that dopamine uptake is abnormal in schizophrenics, there is little reason to think that this would amount to the biochemical defect in schizophrenia. Studies of the genetics of the disease indicate that it is almost certainly the product not of one genetic defect but of several (see L. L. Heston, "Schizophrenia: Genetic Factors," Hospital Practice, June 1977), which are in turn heavily influenced by environmental factors. About all we can say at present is that these defects involve substances that interact at some level with the dopaminergic pathways of the brain. As we learn more about the architecture and function of those pathways and the ways in which they are activated, we should be able to throw more light on schizophrenic biochemistry.

SELECTED READING

Bunney BS, Aghajanian GK: Evidence for drug actions on both pre- and postsynaptic catecholamine receptors in the CNS. Pre- and Postsynaptic Receptors, Usdin E, Bunney WE Jr, (Eds). Marcel Dekker Inc., New York, 1975, pp. 89–122

Carlsson A, Lindqvist J: Effect of chlorpromazine and haloperidol on formation of 3-methoxytyramine and normetanephrine in mouse brain. Acta Pharmacol Toxicol 20:140, 1963

Creese I, Burt DR, Snyder SH: Dopamine receptor binding predicts clinical and pharmacological potencies of antischizophrenic drugs. Science 192:481, 1976

Deniker P: Introduction of neuroleptic chemotherapy into psychiatry. Discoveries in Biological Psychiatry (Ayd FJ Jr, Blackwell B (Eds). Lippincott Company, Philadelphia, 1970, pp. 155–164

Kebabian JW, Petzold GL, Greengard P: Dopamine-sensitive adenylate cyclase in caudate nucleus of rat brain and its similarity to the "dopamine receptor." Proc Natl Acad Sci USA 69:2145, 1972

Snyder SH, Banerjee SP, Yamamura HI, Greenberg D: Drugs, neurotransmitters and schizophrenia. Science 184:1243, 1974

THE PATHOGENESIS OF SCHIZOPHRENIA

WILLIAM POLLIN

A series of studies in schizophrenia, using several varieties of the twin study method, are reviewed and five major conclusions or hypotheses drawn. A modified twin study design—the co-twin comparison method—is described, with which these conclusions and hypotheses can be tested; and two additional major issues— specificity to schizophrenia, and the antecedent-consequent question—dealt with. A stress model of schizophrenia pathogenesis is presented, which attempts to integrate genetic, biochemical, and experiential variables.

A series of studies by this research group in recent years has investigated the pathogenesis of schizophrenia.[1-10] This report summarizes five major related conclusions or hypotheses which have emerged from these studies. These conclusions clarify, and suggest the relationships between, pathogenic factors that operate at different, increasing levels of organization: the genetic and biochemical, the organ level and physiological processes, the level of the total person and his entire life experience, and, finally, factors at the level of class and social organization. They also lead to a number of new, testable questions, and a new study design, which will also be described.

The five conclusions and hypotheses are: (1) There exists a genetic predisposition to schizophrenia which may, however, be nonspecific for this particular psychosis. (2) The genetic predisposition does not take the form of a single, major dominant gene. (3) The genetic predisposition may be expressed, in part, as an abnormality in one or both of two interrelated systems of biogenic amines, the catecholamines and the indolamines. Both quantitative and qualitative abnormalities may be involved. These biochemical abnormalities may contribute to a predisposition to a neurophysiological state of hyperarousal. (4) Additional major pathogenic determinants are, however, nongenetic, and derive from historical and familial experiences, and nongenetic constitutional factors that reflect intrauterine experience. (5) Conceptual integration of the role of genetic and biochemical determinants, on the one hand, and experiential determinants, on the other, by the use of the weak ego boundary construct, cannot be empirically validated. An alternative formulation, based on the concept of life-history stress, is consistent with a wide range of data, from the biochemical to the sociological, once the different mechanisms by which stress operates are teased apart.

A new study design—the co-twin comparison method—will be described. It offers possibilities of testing definitively a number of these conclusions, exploring their specificity to schizophrenia, and determining whether the resultant findings are antecedent and causal, or secondary and consequent to the presence of the illness.

These conclusions emerge from a series of studies employing or contributing to a basic research tactic: the use of discordant life-histories within the same family, by comparison of same-sexed siblings, or identical twins, discordant for schizophrenia. With few exceptions, the data referred to in this paper have been previously pre-

EDITORS' COMMENTS:

THIS DENSE ARTICLE PROVIDES A PERSPECTIVE FROM PSYCHOANALYSTS, NEUROLOGISTS, BIOLOGICAL PSYCHIATRISTS, PSYCHOLOGISTS, AND PSYCHO-PHYSIOLOGISTS, ATTEMPTING TO DISENTANGLE NATURE/NURTURE ISSUES IN THE GENESIS OF SCHIZOPHRENIA.

Reprinted, with author revisions, from Archives of General Psychiatry 27:29–37, 1972. Copyright 1972, American Medical Association.

sented and/or published; these previous sources, in which subject populations, methodology, and results were described in detail, are cited, where relevant. The previous reports also detail the operational definition of schizophrenia employed in these studies.

GENETIC PREDISPOSITION TO SCHIZOPHRENIA

Until 1963, the evidence for a predominant genetic role in the pathogenesis of schizophrenia was compelling. The major source of such evidence was the consistency of twin study data obtained in different countries and different decades. Between 1928 and 1938, eight studies by six authors reported that 60% to 86% of monozygotic (MZ) pairs

in which schizophrenia appeared became concordant for the illness (age corrected, wide concept of schizophrenia; see Table 1).[10] The dizygotic (DZ) concordance rate in the same series of studies varied between 0% and 22%. It was widely accepted that the only significant difference between monozygotic and dizygotic twin pairs was the degree of genetic similarity, the MZ pairs being genetically identical and the DZ pairs, on average, no more genetically alike than same-sexed siblings. Therefore, the consistent, substantial difference between MZ and DZ concordance rates (M = × 5) was widely accepted as an approximate measure of the degree of genetic contribution to the illness.

In the 1960s, two diverse sets of observations raised serious questions concerning this conclu-

TABLE 1. Concordance Rates of Schizophrenia in Twins

Investigator		No. MZ pairs	% MZ concordance	No. DZ pairs	& DZ concordance	MZ/DZ ratio	Sampling*	Diagnosis†
Luxenberger	1928	17	60–76‡	33	0		R, C	A
	1930	21	67	37	...	...	...	...
	1934	27	33	...	...	...	...	...
Rosanoff	1934	41	61	101	10	$\frac{61}{10} = 6.1$	R	H
Essen Möller	1941	11	55–64	27	15	$\frac{64}{15} = 4.3$	C	A
Kallmann	1946	174	69–86§	517	10–15	$\frac{86}{15} = 5.7$	R, C	A
Slater	1953	41	68–76§	115	11–14§	$\frac{76}{14} = 5.4$	R, C	A
Inouye	1961	55	36–60‡	17	22	$\frac{60}{22} = 2.7$	R	A
Tienari	1963	16	6‖	21	5	$\frac{6}{5} = 1.2$	B	A
Harvald & Hauge	1965	9	44	62	10	$\frac{44}{10} = 4.4$	B	H
Gottesman & Shields	1966	24	42–65§	33	9–17§	$\frac{65}{17} = 3.8$	C	H
Kringlen	1967	55	25–38‡	172	4–10‡	$\frac{38}{10} = 3.8$	B	A
Pollin et al	1969	80	14–16§	146	4–4§	$\frac{15.5}{4.4} = 3.5$	B	H

*R, Resident hospital population; C, consecutive hospital admissions; and B, birth registry.

†A, Diagnosis by author and H, diagnosis by hospital.

‡"Wide" concept of schizophrenia used.

§Aged corrected.

‖The 1967 follow-up report on the 1963 series: Tienari P: Schizophrenia in monozygotic male twins, conference on Transmission of Schizophrenia, San Juan, PR, June 1967.

sion. Scandinavian investigators (Tienari,[11] Kringlen,[12] and Harvald and Hauge[13]) using the superior Scandinavian birth and mental hospital records, undertook twin studies which analyzed national cohorts of twins born during a given decade, rather than pairs identified on the basis of mental hospitalization. These methodologically advanced studies, stimulated in part by Rosenthal's valuable critique of the earlier twin studies,[14] sharply reduced the difference between MZ and DZ concordance rates. The initial findings for MZ pair concordance now ranged between 6% and 44%, and the difference between MZ and DZ pairs averaged only × 3.3 rather than × 5.

At approximately the same time a new question was raised concerning the core assumption of the classical twin method; that differences between MZ and DZ concordance rates could be attributed almost entirely to differences in degree of genetic similarity. After reviewing a series of psychoanalytic and psychological studies of twins, Kety[15] and Jackson[16] emphasized the degree to which MZ twins shared their life space in a uniquely intimate way, and in consequence, probably shared considerably more psychological, as well as genetic, determinants than did DZ pairs.

The two points taken together—a substantially lowered MZ/DZ concordance ratio, and persuasive reasoning that a significant part of this sharply reduced MZ/DZ preponderance of concordance could be attributed to psychological rather than

genetic factors, left uncertain the extent, if any, of the role of genetic pathogenic factors.

We undertook an analysis of the distribution of psychopathology in the National Academy of Science pool of 15,909 veteran twin pairs,[17] as part of our search for a replication sample, described below. The design made it possible to deal with the problem raised by Kety and Jackson therefore to again use MZ/DZ comparisons as meaningful indicators of the role of genetic factors. The initial analysis of computer-stored data, based on armed forces, Veterans Administration, and questionnaire diagnoses, showed that 11 of 80 MZ pairs were concordant and six of 146 DZ pairs were concordant, yielding an uncorrected pairwise concordance rate of 13.8% for MZ pairs and 4.1% for DZ pairs. Though these absolute concordance rates were somewhat low (in part due to the fact that the veteran sample was one selected for health) the MZ pair concordance rate was 3.3 times greater than the DZ rate. When the same ratio was calculated for other psychiatric diagnoses in the same sample, it was found to be significantly greater for schizophrenia than for neurosis. We then reanalyzed all previously reported twin studies in the literature which made possible the computation of similar MZ/DZ concordance ratios for schizophrenia and for neurosis.[10] As shown on Fig 1, a highly consis-

FIGURE 1. MZ/DZ concordance ratios in twin studies of neurosis and schizophrenia.

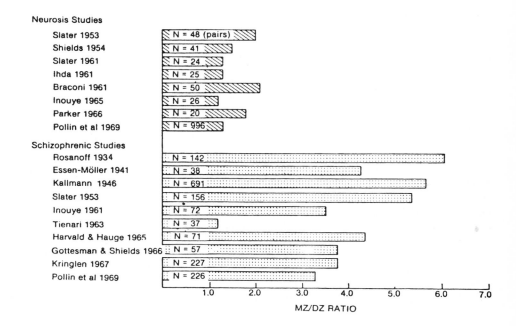

tent difference appeared, with very little overlap; the MZ/DZ concordance ratio varied between 1 and 2 in all nine studies of neurosis, but was over three in all but one of ten studies of schizophrenia (range: 1.2 to 6.1). This comparison of the MZ/DZ ratio for two different diagnostic entities could be interpreted, we felt, to mean that there was a significant genetic component in the causation of schizophrenia, substantially greater than for neurosis. In comparing two diagnostic categories, the relative contribution of greater psychic similarity, in MZ as compared to DZ pairs is controlled ie, matched, in both disease entities. Therefore, this data concerning relative concordance rates can be used as a measure of genetic contribution to pathogenesis.

An alternative explanation for the higher MZ/DZ ratio in schizophrenia than in neurosis would be that environmental congruities are more important in schizophrenia than in neurosis. However, the only serious theoretical construct which has been advanced that would support such an alternative interpretation—the weak ego boundary hypothesis—is not supported by available twin study data, as detailed below.

EXTENT AND NATURE OF THE GENETIC PREDISPOSITION

The above data, taken in conjunction with the adoption studies of Heston[18] and Kety, Rosenthal, Wender et al,[19,20] led us to conclude that there clearly exists a genetic factor that plays a significant predisposing role in the pathogenesis of schizophrenia. However, since 50% to 75% of all MZ pairs in which one member of the twin pair becomes schizophrenic, do not become concordant, we further conclude that nongenetic factors must also play a substantial pathogenic role. We infer that for most, if not all, cases of schizophrenia, neither genetic nor environmental factors is sufficient, and that most often both are necessary, though we know of no direct evidence to support this conclusion.

The nature, as well as the extent, of the mechanism which constitutes the genetic predisposition has significant consequences in shaping one's model of the pathogenic process. One major hypothesis has been that there exists a single dominant gene which expresses itself in some instances as clinical schizophrenia, and as schizoid symptoms or character structure when the full disease does not appear. In a major recent review Heston[21] marshalled the evidence for this point of view. Our extensive evaluation of the nonschizo-

TABLE 2. Schizoid Features

	Mean Schizoid Ratings		Clinical "Schizoid" Mentions
	Slater-Heston*	DSM II†	
Co-twins, 15 MZ pairs discordant for schizophrenia (N = 15)	6.6	0.5	2 (1 of 3 interviewers)
4 "normal control" pairs (N = 8)	7.5	0.6	1 (1 of 3 interviewers)

*Maximum possible score, 183.
†Maximum possible score, 24.

phrenic co-twins, in our series of 15 pairs of MZ pairs discordant for schizophrenia made it possible to test this hypothesis empirically.[22] The protocol entailed some 25 hours of intensive psychiatric interviewing by three or more highly experienced psychiatrists, and included similar inpatient evaluation of four "NC" ("normal controls")[1] pairs of twins, and their families. Three tests of the Heston hypothesis were undertaken. The first was based on Heston's own set of schizoid descripters, derived by him from Slater's list of 61 such descripters. This, and the eight descripters which comprise the DSM II (*Diagnostic and Statistical Manual,* American Psychiatric Association's second edition) definition of "schizoid," were used to rate the extensive clinical material on a three-point scale (0, not present; 1, present; and 2, strongly present). Finally, the extensive formulations were searched for any mention of the use of the word "schizoid" in describing the twins, without requiring that it be part of the final diagnosis. As shown in Table 2, by all three of these measures, the nonschizophrenic co-twins in the discordant pairs, as a group, ranked low with respect to schizoid features and did not differ from the ratings shown by the normal control pairs. The frequency of the use of the word "schizoid" in diagnostic formulations is of the same order of magnitude as that reported in two other twin series which permit similar evaluation. Thus, though there is a greater likelihood of diagnosable psychopathology of various types in the co-twins of monozygotic discordant pairs than would be expected in an unselected population, this psychopathology is not schizoid in nature, as called for by the single dominant gene hypothesis.

MECHANISM OF THE GENETIC PREDISPOSITION

Genetic factors express themselves in biochemical phenomena. Our investigation of biochemical findings and patterns in the discordant twin series,[9] suggests that a biochemical process, which results in a type of "functional hyperactivity" at some level of catecholamine metabolism, and presumed central nervous system function, is genetically determined and plays a significant role in the predisposition to schizophrenia. The evidence for this tentative conclusion is as follows. Urinary excretion values for seven catecholamines (dopamine, norepinephrine, epinephrine, normetanephrine, metanephrine, vanillylmandelic acid [VMA], and 3-methoxy-4-hydroxy-phenylglycol [MHPG]) and for 17-hydroxysteroids were obtained on index schizophrenic twins, their nonschizophrenic co-twins, and two series of controls: four normal control twin pairs and four concordant-for-schizophrenia control pairs. All subjects were studied in Bethesda, Md, during a two to three week inpatient admission research protocol, on similar wards, similar protocols, and presented with similar diets, though precise dietary control was not attempted. A highly significant intraclass correlation coefficient for the catecholamines, independent of the presence or absence of schizophrenia in the discordant pairs, strongly suggests, though it does not definitively establish, a high degree of genetic control for these substances (Table 3). Most catecholamines and their metabolites in this series (with the significant

exception of MHPG), were found to be approximately equally elevated in index schizophrenic twins and their nonschizophrenic co-twin controls, independent of the presence or absence of psychosis (Fig 2 and 3). Such elevations suggest a relationship to the genetic predisposition. The fact that 17-OH steroids, determined at the same time, are elevated in the index schizophrenic twins and not in their genetically identical co-twin controls, strongly suggests that the catecholamine elevation in the discordant pairs cannot be solely or predominantly attributed to secondary phenomena such as agitation and tension. In effect, the catecholamines parallel the schizophrenic genotype; and 17-OH steroids, the schizophrenic phenotype, in this series of twins.

These data need be accepted cautiously at this point for a number of reasons: (a) urinary excretion levels are far removed from possible CNS processes, particularly with regard to these complex, as yet only partially understood systems, in which these elevated levels could be due variously to changes in rates of synthesis, neuronal storage, release, uptake, postsynaptic sensitivity, or feedback mechanisms. (b) Elevations such as those reported here are not consistently reported in the literature, though for theoretical reasons described elsewhere, the use of co-twin controls may make more available an obscure though significant relationship. (c) The elevations are group means and do not hold for all patients and are not consistently true of the concordant controls in the series. (d) The pattern is not true for the one metabolite—MHPG—which is currently viewed as most di-

TABLE 3. Catecholamines and 17-OH Steroids: Intraclass Correlations

	All Pairs (N = 18*)		Discordants (N = 11†)		Concordants (N = 3)		Normals (N = 4)	
	r	P	r	P	r	P	r	P
Dopamine	.716	<.001	.769	<.01	.665	NS	.493	NS
Norepinephrine	.788	<.001	.787	<.001	−.816	NS	.913	<.01
Epinephrine	.401	<.05	.323	NS	−.015	NS	.450	NS
Normetanephrine	.648	<.001	.617	<.05	.550	NS	.909	<.01
Metanephrine	.767	<.001	.795	<.001	.403	NS	.890	<.01
VMA	.565	<.01	.475	NS	.731	NS	.106	NS
MHPG	.351	NS	.384	NS	—	—	.004	NS
17-OH steroids	−.062	NS	−.347	NS	—	—	.910	<.01
Urine volume	.214	NS	.485	.05	.117	NS	—	—

*N = 16 for MHPG, 10 for 17-OH.
†N = 10 for MHPG, 6 for 17-OH.

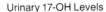

Urinary 17-OH Levels

Urinary Epinephrine Levels

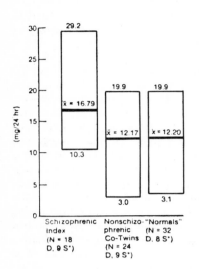

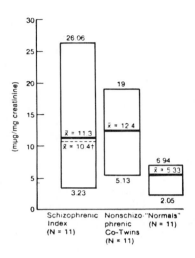

FIGURE 2. Urinary 17-OH and urinary epinephrine levels. *D indicates number of determinations and S, number of subjects. † indicates cc pair group means.

rectly reflecting CNS catecholamine metabolism. If these cautions are kept in mind, it is then appropriate, however, to consider the other side of the coin, and to evaluate the positive and ancillary evidence from other sources. There is a considerable body of evidence which seems consistent with the conclusion that the use of chemical agents which increase or mobilize functionally effective CNS catecholamines cause an exacerbation of psychosis; conversely, that chemical agents which are effective in attenuating or terminating psychotic symptoms share the capacity to decrease functionally effective central nervous system catecholamines. L-dopa, the precursor of dopamine, norepinephrine, and epinephrine, has been reported to reactivate or exacerbate psychosis in schizophrenic, depressive, and manic patients. It is notable that in these reports, the symptom picture of the exacerbation is a reappearance of the prior dominant psychotic picture, ie, either depressed, manic, or schizophrenic, as was previously the case.[23] In this extensive review of L-dopa effects Murphy concluded that "activation or hyperarousal mediated by catecholamines may constitute a common factor in the triggering of the varied psychologic reaction patterns in specifi-

Urinary Dopamine Levels

Urinary Norepinephrine Levels

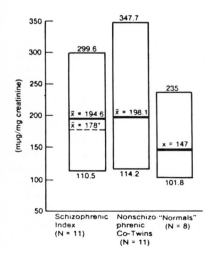

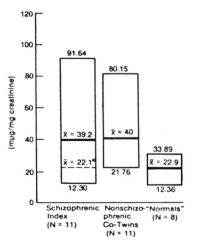

FIGURE 3. Urinary dopamine and urinary norepinephrine levels. * indicates concordant pair group means.

cally susceptible individuals." He reaches a conclusion similar to that we recently proposed[9]: that such activation is an important central phenomenon in the development of a variety of psychotic states. Other drugs which show similar ability to worsen or reactivate psychosis, including monoamine oxidase (MAO) inhibitors, tricyclic antidepressants, amphetamines, and steroids, may share the same common final denominator: functional hyperactivity of strategic catecholamine systems. Conversely, it is notable that all but one of the potent antipsychotic medications, representing several different classes of drugs which have become available during the past two decades, are capable of causing parkinsonism-like symptoms in a majority of patients to whom they are given. A deficiency of dopamine is believed to be the chemical lesion in parkinsonism. Thus, it appears that antipsychotic activity goes along with, if it is not directly related to, processes which cause a decrease in functionally effective CNS dopamine, and presumably, therefore, catecholamines in general.

From the clinical and psychodynamic point of view, it should be noted that this oversimplified formulation relating chronic hypercatecholamine mobilization to predilection to psychosis is consistent with the clinical descriptions of the preschizophrenic individual (which usually includes fearfulness, hypersensitivity, and problems in focal attention), and to current psychodynamic formulations of psychosis, which picture the intrusion of libidinal and instinctual processes into, and then as overwhelming, ego structures.

It is suggested that a genetically determined, "high functional hyperactivity" of certain strategic catecholamine-mediated CNS systems related to a predisposition to schizophrenia, on the basis of a prepsychotic, chronic state, or a greater susceptibility to an acute onset, of hyperarousal. In addition to this hypothesized quantitative abnormality, there is also evidence to indicate that a concomitant qualitative abnormality in catecholamine or indolamine metabolism relates to the actual appearance of psychotic symptoms, possibly helping to determine the specific nature of the psychotic episode that the predisposition is likely to lead to. It has long been noted that there are interesting structural similarities between the dimethylated derivatives of a number of catecholamines and indolamines, on the one hand, and demonstrated psychotogenic substances, on the other. The hypothesis that abnormalities in transmethylation processes create an abnormal psychotogenic metabolite, first proposed in 1952

by Harley Mason, was initially tested by administration of very large doses of methionine to schizophrenic patients ten years ago, by Pollin, Cardon, and Kety.[24] We reported significant exacerbations in four of nine schizophrenics. A current review by Cohen and Pollin analyses ten subsequent replication studies, which have all been positive, and finds that 58% of 107 schizophrenic patients studied in these studies show an exacerbation of a functional psychosis and that 56% of these showed such an exacerbation of functional psychosis in the absence of organic signs (disorientation, delirium, visual hallucinations, and/or confusion).[25] There is some evidence to suggest that the presence of a MAO inhibitor, given along with methionine in most of these studies, is responsible for a significant part of the organic symptomatology prominent in a number of these reports. (Antun et al[26] in a careful study, reported relatively few organic symptoms in a study employing methionine without a MAO inhibitor.)

These hypotheses concerning the role of possible quantitative and/or qualitative abnormalities of biogenic amines in the pathogenesis of schizophrenia continue to elicit considerable interest, and significant new directions of inquiry (eg, Stein's recent observations concerning a possible abnormal dopamine metabolite in schizophrenia[27]; and Horn and Snyder's report of conformational similarities in the molecules of chlorpromazine and dopamine that correlate with the antischizophrenic activity of phenothiazines).[28] It should be emphasized, however, that the evidence to date is far from conclusive, and definitive confirmation or refutation still remains to be accomplished.

EXPERIENTIAL FACTORS INVOLVED IN PATHOGENESIS

As noted above, 50% to 75% of identical twin pairs in which one twin is schizophrenic, do not become concordant for schizophrenia. We interpret this to mean, therefore, that a significant portion of the pathogenic determinants are nongenetic and, therefore, experiential. The bulk of our data and effort have gone into attempting to study and formulate these nongenetic experiential factors, as observed in our discordant twin series. Analysis and integration of this data is more difficult than that of biochemical data. To date, we have found a rather consistent interrelated pattern of intrauterine, nongenetic constitutional factors, family characteristics and relationships, and life-history events which relate to the development of schizophrenia.[2,29]

Group 1. The nongenetic constitutional factors include: (a) evidence for a less-favored intrauterine development, based on relative biological deficiency at birth, as manifested by lower birth weight (11 of 15 pairs); less adequate early psychophysiologic regulations; and relatively disordered feeding and sleep behavior. Of the four of 15 index schizophrenic twins not showing this pattern at birth, two were quickly propelled into it by severe childhood illness (severe cyanosis due to heating gas accident at month two; severe Rocky Mountain spotted fever at year 3½). (b) The preponderance of neurological soft signs demonstrated currently by the index schizophrenic twins may be secondary to the presence of schizophrenia; or may have existed pre-illness.[8] The latter would be consistent with the preponderant number of episodes of cyanosis in this group, and possibly be related to the decreased capacity for focal attention that appears to be a common denominator of many early developmental problems shown by the group of schizophrenics-to-be, in comparison to their co-twin controls.

Group 2. A second major group of findings has to do with differences in family perceptions and relationships.[7] (a) The constitutionally disadvantaged twin was viewed as the more vulnerable and weaker one, in a particularly rigid, unyielding, and unchanging manner, by the families in question. (b) This rigidity seemingly resulted from a type of projective identification in one or both parents. Resonating to cues in one of the twins, often quite minor ones, he would attribute to that one twin denied or conflicted aspects of his own personality by which he felt especially threatened. (c) The relationship of parent and vulnerable twin tended to be characterized by significantly greater intensity, exclusiveness, ambivalence, uncertainty, and unresolved conflicts, thus constituting a very different model for identification than that received by the co-twin. Consistent pre-illness life course and personality differences between the schizophrenic index and the nonschizophrenic co-twins constitute a third major group of observations. These included, in the schizophrenic-to-be, the following: increased fearfulness and dependence; submissiveness; decreased competence, differentiation, relatedness, emotional openness and sharing; depreciated self-image; decreased satisfaction; and increased frustration as he moved from one developmental stage to another.

CONCEPTUAL INTEGRATION

Our first effort to integrate the genetic, biologic, and psychological variables developed in the discordant twin series was via the concept of weak ego boundaries.[30] Bellak had reported that this was the most widely used concept in psychodynamic studies of schizophrenia during the past several decades.[31] In brief, it suggested that diminished clarity concerning one's sense of self, and the limits of one's subjective experience of self, reflected a significant impairment in major ego functions, and predisposed toward schizophrenia. Monozygotic twins, because of certain unique life experiences, such as being frequently misidentified one for the other by parents and parent surrogates, had been typically described as primary examples of individuals with weak ego boundaries. It therefore followed, if the concept was valid

TABLE 4. Incidence of Schizophrenia in MZ Twins Compared to DZ Twins

	MZ incidence	DZ incidence
Luxenberger*	$\frac{1}{228.6} = 0.44\%$†	$\frac{1}{117.8} = 0.85\%$†
Essen-Möller*	$\frac{1}{542.4} = 0.18\%$	$\frac{1}{61.2} = 1.63\%$
Harvald & Hauge‡	$\frac{13}{1,528} = 0.85\%$	$\frac{68}{5,134} = 1.32\%$
Kringlen‡	$\frac{69}{13,158} = 0.52\%$	$\frac{186}{36,842} = 0.50\%$
Allen & Pollin‡	$\frac{91}{9,428} = 0.97\%$†	$\frac{152}{12,484} = 1.22\%$†

*From Rosenthal (1960) where incidence is based on the ratio of schizophrenic twins to schizophrenic nontwins within a hospital-clinic population. For example, in Luxenberger, there are 228.6 times more nontwin schizophrenics than MZ twin schizophrenics.

†When incidence is computed as limits, depending on whether cases of unknown zygosity are classified as all MZ or all DZ, the rates are: Luxenberger—MZ: 0.44%–0.82%; DZ: 0.84%–1.23%. Pollin and Allen—MZ: 0.65%–1.51%; DZ: 0.85%–1.53%. Forty-four percent of the veteran sample is MZ (14,000 individuals) and 56% DZ (17,818) (Jablon et al. 1967).

MZ incidence is:

$$\frac{91}{14,000} = 0.65\% \text{ to } \frac{(91 + 121)}{14,000} = 1.51\%;$$

DZ incidence is:

$$\frac{152}{17,818} = 0.85\% \text{ to } \frac{(152 + 121)}{17,818} = 1.53\%.$$

‡Incidence is based on the total twin population studies, eg, a large, population-based twin registry.

and relevant to schizophrenia, that there should be a higher incidence of schizophrenia in monozygotic than in dizygotic twins, who are much less alike and hardly ever misidentified one for the other. As shown in Table 4, in the NAS twin series and then in re-analysis of two Scandinavian twin series, our observations confirmed Rosenthal's earlier conclusion,[32] based on indirect computation indicating that no such hypothesized increased incidence of schizophrenia in MZ twins exists. Thus, we were unable to empirically validate this tempting formulation.

An alternative stress model does appear to satisfactorily integrate a wide variety of observations that range from the biochemical, at one end of the spectrum, to the sociological, at the other. This formulation goes as follows: (1) hyperactivity of catecholamine-mediated CNS systems leads to a state of hyperarousal which predisposes to psychosis, or can cause exacerbation in already psychotic individuals. The similarity in the clinical state, which results from massive methionine administration, suggests that a methylated catecholamine derivative may be involved in this process; (2) some part of this hyperactivity is genetically predetermined and predisposing; (3) experiential factors substantially influence this process by several quite different mechanisms. These include the following: (a) increased life-stress can induce substantial sustained increases in levels of major enzymes that regulate the rate of amine metabolism. Axelrod et al[33] have reported threefold and fourfold increases in the level of tyrosine-hydroxalase, the rate-limiting enzyme in catecholamine synthesis, resulting from living situations which caused, in an experimental group of mice, substantial increase in dominance-submission confrontations, and increased social stimulation. Similar changes in humans as a result of more stressful life histories would presumably be reflected in the fact that two individuals, in the face of equal external stress, would produce very different amounts of bioactive amines, both in the CNS and peripherally. (b) Stress is a bridge phenomenon, involving the integration of psychodynamic and biologic phenomena, and influenced by sociologic factors, as well. Thus, phenomena occurring at several different levels of organization—biochemical phenomena at subcellular levels, neurophysiological at cellular and organ levels, psychological phenomena at the total person level, and social phenomena at the group level—are involved.

Before enzyme systems are stimulated to manufacture increased quantities of catecholamines—and in some instances, perhaps, abnormal psychotogenic metabolites—these systems must receive a triggering signal. How often and how intensely this signal is delivered depends on psychological rather than cellular responsivity. It is a whole person experience. The individual reared in a family of circus trapeze artists, finding himself perched at the very edge of a rock overlooking the Grand Canyon, will probably have little stress response and will, instead, be very aware of the view. Another individual, standing on the same rock, reared by two parents with a height phobia, will likely have little time for the view and be, instead, bathed in a cold sweat.

One of the most strikingly discordant pairs in our series was found in the M family. The index twin had done poorly in school, had few friends, had rarely left home or the family, where she was overprotected, had relatively few interests, and a paucity of social and academic achievements and competence. The co-twin, on the other hand, was very popular, academically successful, involved in numerous extracurricular activities, actively pursued a variety of religious activities and hobbies, and had a much more differentiated and complete experience of the world, and ways to deal with it and the people in it. The first major psychotic break for the index occurred shortly before graduation from high school and was clearly related to the stress of having to choose some type of postschool, new life-course for herself, outside of the family. The family, though in many ways overprotective in a quite rigid fashion, insistently assumed that one, of course, went out of the family and did something new and independent upon graduation from high school, educationally or vocationally. Thus, the same challenge presented to these two genetically identical individuals constituted an entirely different magnitude of external stressor event. For the co-twin, it was not a significantly new or totally different step she was now called upon to take compared to previous experience. For the index, however, it was a step of a much greater order of magnitude of change, and a totally new degree of threatening expectation—a level of demand she had not previously encountered.

This case demonstrated the manner in which both family characteristics and prior life-history experiences interact to determine the extent to which any given life-experience will be stressful for any given individual. The families in this series, as has so often been reported in the literature, tended to be rigid households, in which contradictory expectations were frequently presented to the offspring, with the index-to-be, because of his family role, more caught up in these contradictory demands than was the control. For example, an intense need for achievement was often signaled; and simultaneously a parallel signal given, stating that the type of aggressive initiative such success required constituted a great danger, and was unacceptable. Characteristically, family rigidity and communication blocks led to a decreased opportunity to freely discuss and reconcile such apparently incompatible goals and standards, and the index-to-be experienced increasing high chronic stress in adolescence and young adulthood, determined in part by his living a type of chronic double-blind life.

Kohn has carefully analyzed the relationship between lower social class and a higher incidence of schizophrenia.[34] He defined several ways in which positioning at different levels in the social matrix can contribute to the development of schizophrenia. In persons who are both genetically predisposed and subjected to stress, he believes, lower-class parents transmit an orientational system too limited and too rigid for dealing effectively with complexity, change, and more specifically, with stress.

Thus, we have pictured a sequence which involves an external event, the potential stressor—its resultant psychological meaning and signal, which is based on previous experience, role within the family and within the social structure—the resultant biochemical and physiologic response on the organ and cellular level, its extent determined in part by genetically controlled enzyme activity, and in part by changes in enzyme levels induced by previous experience.

In summary, experiential factors are seen as operating in four distinct ways. (1) They form the dictionary with which an individual translates the meaning and significance of any given current experience; and the yardstick by which he automatically measures the amount of threat, ie, stress, it constitutes for him. (2) Their residue determines the quantity and style of defenses and coping abilities with which the individual will attempt to deal with a stressful current life-situation. The determinants include such varied processes as the clarity of intrafamilial communication,[35] the nature and extent of intrafamilial alliances and identifications,[7] and the pattern of perceptions and coping mechanisms associated with one's location in the social class matrix.[34] (3) Prior experience determines, in part, the extent of biochemical response to stress by influencing the level of enzymes available, through enzyme induction.[33] (4)

It seems likely that certain events, possibly concentrated in the intrauterine period, are relevant because of a direct slight effect on CNS structure, ie, neonatal anoxia causing minimal brain changes that later appear as subtle decrease in the capacity to maintain focal attention.

In this paper it is suggested that changes in biogenic amine metabolism are especially relevant to the pathogenesis of schizophrenia. Whether or not these indeed prove to be the relevant biochemical processes, the above schema is believed to be independently valid.

REPLICATION, SPECIFICITY, AND THE ANTECEDENT-CONSEQUENT QUESTION

Methodological advances and a more complete picture of amine metabolism make it possible to now test some parts of this formulation in a more precise manner than was heretofore possible. Instead of merely looking at urinary excretion levels, a number of enzymes in the catecholamine cycle can now be measured in serum or platelets (dopamine-β-oxidase, catechol-O-methyl transferase [COMT], MAO). Of especially great interest is nonspecific N-methyl transferase. This enzyme, which can catalyze the formation of a potent psychotomimetic (dimethyltryptamine), was originally identified by Axelrod in rabbit lung, and has recently been described in human brain by Morgan and Mandell.[36] Wyatt and Axelrod (personal communication) believe a technique for measuring it in platelets may soon be available. Contradictory reports concerning the presence or absence of DMT and similar possible psychotomimetic compounds in schizophrenic urine may be resolvable by mass spectography. Thus, we wish to ask the following questions: (a) can we replicate and establish the finding of a genetically controlled increased excretion of catecholamines by schizophrenic patients and their co-twins, compared to other psychotics, severe neurotics, and normals? (b) Do schizophrenic patients show higher levels of enzymes involved in amine metabolism on the basis of prior life experience and resultant enzyme induction than do their co-twins? Do they, therefore, show higher levels of catecholamine production than their co-twins, in the face of an experimental stress? (c) Can we identify any abnormal psychotomimetic metabolite—such as DMT—in schizophrenic subjects, under baseline or dietary challenge conditions? (d) Can we replicate and clarify the experiential variables which account for the discordance in discordant MZ twin pairs, and which we assume would point to more gener-

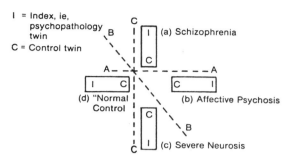

FIGURE 4. Co-twin comparison research design.

ally applicable nonorganic pathogenic determinants?

The co-twin comparison design offers promise of providing a technique for attempting to answer these questions. In particular, it can deal with the issues of antecedent-consequent phenomena, and of specificity to schizophrenia.

The bulk of research into schizophrenia and other psychoses is not able to deal satisfactorily with the major question as to whether findings are antecedent or consequent to the psychosis being studied. The design proposed in recent years that deals most satisfactorily with this issue is the prospective study of high-risk populations. The co-twin comparison method—comparing cohorts of MZ twins discordant for three different, well-defined psychopathologies, and a fourth group of matched controls, with comparative emphasis on the nonpathology co-twins—is an alternate design that can deal with these questions.

Optimally, one would attempt to assemble four matched cohorts of MZ pairs (15/cohort), drawn perhaps from the NAS veteran twin pool, and additional available state twin registries. (a) The key cohort would be composed of 15 MZ pairs discordant for schizophrenia. Matched on demographic variables would be cohorts of (b) 15 pairs discordant for affective psychosis, (c) 15 pairs discordant for nonpsychotic severe neurotic psychopathology, and (d) 15 normal control pairs with no diagnosed or treatable psychopathology. The design is diagrammed in Fig 4.

Within each cohort, intrapair comparisons between index and nonpsychopathology co-twin controls could be undertaken, along previously studied lines, and could be expected to yield significant results. However, the unique power of this design involves the comparison of the four subgroups of control subjects. Variables genetically related to the pathogenesis of schizophrenia should manifest themselves not only in the index schizophrenic, but also in the nonschizophrenic

co-twin control in cohort (a: discordant for schizophrenia). If this factor is specific for schizophrenia, it would be found in the control subjects of cohort (a) (and thus clearly not be secondary to the presence of the illness) but not appear in the control subjects of the other three cohorts. Factors which may possibly be related to psychosis in general would be found in the co-twin controls in cohorts (a) and (b). Factors relevant to any type of severe psychopathology independent of the distinction between psychosis and neurosis would be found in the co-twin controls of cohorts (a), (b), and (c).

The implementation of this design would be a difficult task. However, its central notion—a focus on the comparative evaluation of the nonpathology co-twins in a series of MZ pairs discordant for a given condition—would seem to offer substantial promise of helping to tease apart genetic and nongenetic determinants of various phenomena.

The work summarized in this paper has resulted from the joint efforts of the staff of the Section on Twin and Sibling Studies, and numerous collaborating investigations. Acknowledgment is due, in particular, to the senior investigators who have maintained ongoing involvement in the work, most notably, Dr. James Stabenau, and additionally Drs. Loren Mosher, Martin Allen, and Joe Tupin.

Dr. I. Kopin, of the National Institute of Mental Health, did the catecholamine determinations and Dr. M. Lipsett the steroid determinations.

Figures 1, 2, and 3 and Tables 1, 3, and 4 are reprinted with permission of the *American Journal of Psychiatry*.

REFERENCES

1. Pollin W, Stabenau J, Mosher L, et al: Life history differences in identical twins discordant for schizophrenia. Amer J Orthopsychiat 36:492–509, 1966.

2. Pollin W, Stabenau JR: Biological, psychological and historical differences in a series of monozygotic twins discordant for schizophrenia. J Psychiat Res 6(suppl 1):317–332, 1968.

3. Stabenau JR, Pollin W: Early characteristics of monozygotic twins discordant for schizophrenia. Arch Gen Psychiat 17:723–734, 1967.

4. Stabenau JR, Pollin W: Comparative life history differences for families of schizophrenics, delinquents and "normals." Amer J Psychiat 124:1526–1534, 1968.

5. Stabenau JR, Pollin W: The pathogenesis of schizophrenia: II. Contributions from the NIMH study of 16 pairs of monozygotic twins discordant for schizophrenia, in Sankar DV (ed): Schizophrenia—Current Concepts and Research. Hicksville, NY, PJD Publications, 1969, pp 336–351.

6. Mosher LR: Etiological implications of studies of identical twins discordant for schizophrenia. Read

before the British Schizophrenia Association Meeting, London, 1971.

7. Mosher L, Pollin W, Stabenau JR: Families with identical twins discordant for schizophrenia: Some relationships between identification, thinking styles, psychopathology and dominance-submissiveness. Brit J Psychiat 118:29–42, 1971.

8. Mosher L, Pollin W, Stabenau JR: Identical twins discordant for schizophrenia: Neurological findings. Arch Gen Psychiat 24:422–430, 1971.

9. Pollin W: A possible genetic factor related to psychosis. Amer J Psychiat 128:311–317, 1971.

10. Pollin W, Allen MG, Hoffer A, et al: Psychopathology in 15,909 pairs of veteran twins: Evidence for a genetic factor in the pathogenesis of schizophrenia and its relative absence in psychoneurosis. Amer J. Psychiat 126:597–611, 1969.

11. Tienari P: Schizophrenia in monozygotic male twins, in Rosenthal D, Kety SS (eds): The Transmission of Schizophrenia, NY, Pergamon Press, 1968, pp 27–36.

12. Kringlen E: Heredity and Environment in the Functional Psychoses, an Epidemiological-Clinical Twin Study. Oslo, Norway, Universitsforlaget, 1967.

13. Harvald B, Hauge M: Heredity factors elucidated by twin studies, in Neel J (ed): Genetics and the Epidemiology of Chronic Disease: PHS1163. Government Printing Office, Department of Health, Education and Welfare, 1965.

14. Rosenthal D: Some factors associated with concordance and discordance with respect to schizophrenia in monozygotic twins. J Nerv Ment Dis 129:1–10, 1959.

15. Kety SS: Biochemical theories of schizophrenia. Science 129:1528, 1590, 1959.

16. Jackson DD: A critique of the literature on the genetics of schizophrenia, in Jackson DD (ed): The Etiology of Schizophrenia. New York, Basic Books Inc Publishers, 1959, pp 37–90.

17. Hoffer A, Pollin W: Schizophrenia in the NAS-NRC panel of 15,909 veteran twin pairs. Arch Gen Psychiat 23:469–477, 1970.

18. Heston LL, Denney D: Interactions between early life experience and biological factors in schizophrenia, in Rosenthal D, Kety SS (eds): The Transmission of Schizophrenia. New York, Pergamon Press, 1968, pp 363–376.

19. Kety SS, Rosenthal D, Wender PH, et al: The types and prevalence of mental illness in the biological and adoptive families of adopted schizophrenics, in Rosenthal D, Kety SS (eds): The Transmission of Schizophrenia. New York, Pergamon Press, 1968, pp 345–362.

20. Rosenthal D, Wender PH, Kety SS, et al: Schizophrenics' offspring reared in adoptive homes, in Rosenthal D, Kety SS (eds): The Transmission of Schizophrenia. New York, Pergamon Press, 1968, pp 377–391.

21. Heston LL: The genetics of schizophrenia and schizoid disease. Science 167:249, 1970.

22. Mosher L, Stabenau J, Pollin W: Schizoidness in the nonschizophrenic identical co-twins of schizophrenics. Read at a symposium "Transmission of Schizophrenia," Fifth World Congress of Psychiatry, International Congress and Convention Association, Mexico City, 1971.

23. Murphy DL: L-Dopa, behavioral activation and psychopathology. Research Proceedings, Association for Research in Nervous and Mental Disease, 1971.

24. Pollin W, Cardon P, Kety S: Effects of amino acids feedings in schizophrenic patients treated with iproniazid. Science 133:104–105, 1961.

25. Cohen SM, Pollin W, et al: Methionine administration to schizophrenic patients: A review.

26. Antun F, Burnett G, Cooper A, et al: The effects of L-methionine (without MAOI) in schizophrenia. J Psychiat Res 8:63–71, 1971.

27. Stein L: Neurochemistry of reward and punishment: Some implications for the etiology of schizophrenia. J Psychiat Res 8:345–361, 1971.

28. Horn AS, Snyder SH: Chlorpromazine and dopamine: Conformational similarities that correlate with the antischizophrenic activity of phenothiazine drugs. Proc Nat Acad Sci 68:2325–2328, 1971.

29. Stabenau JR, Pollin W: Experiential differences for schizophrenics as compared with their nonschizophrenic siblings: Twin and family studies, in Roff M, Ricks DF (eds): Life History Research in Psychopathology. Minneapolis, University of Minnesota Press, 1970, pp 94–126.

30. Allen M, Pollin W: Schizophrenia in twins and the diffuse ego boundary hypothesis. Amer J Psychiat 127:437–443, 1970.

31. Bellak L, Loeb L: The Schizophrenia Syndrome. New York, Grune & Stratton Inc, 1969.

32. Rosenthal D: Confusion of identity and the frequency of schizophrenia in twins. Arch Gen Psychiat 3:297–304, 1960.

33. Axelrod J, Mueller RA, Henry JP, et al: Changes in enzyme involved in the biosynthesis and metabolism of Nor-Adrenaline and Adrenaline after psychosocial stimulation. Nature 225:1059–1060, 1970.

34. Kohn ML: Class, family, and schizophrenia: A reformulation. Social Forces.

35. Singer MT, Wynne LC: Family transactions and schizophrenia, in The Origins of Schizophrenia, Proceedings of the First Rochester International Conference. Amsterdam, Excerpta Medica, International Congress Series No. 151, 1967, pp 147–178.

36. Morgan M, Mandell AJ: Indole(ethyl)amine N-methyl-transferase in the brain. Science 165:492, 1969.

SCHIZOPHRENIA:
THE IMPACT OF SOCIOCULTURAL FACTORS

H. WARREN DUNHAM

Since genetic factors cannot wholly explain why some people develop schizophrenia, environmental factors continue to be probed in depth. The author's findings of far higher incidence rates in neighborhoods of low economic level than in high-income neighborhoods lead him to conclude, not that "social isolation" in poor areas causes residents to become schizophrenic, but rather that schizophrenia tends to make or keep people poor.

Any attempt to assess the etiologic role of sociocultural factors in schizophrenia is immediately thrown into question because of the mounting evidence for a strong genetic component. Shields, Heston, and Gottesman in a recent review of some of the evidence point out that studies of monozygotic twins, assumed to be genetically identical, show a concordance percentage for schizophrenics ranging from 38 to 69. However, the fact that normality in the co-twin ranged from 5% to 43% suggested clearly that the genetic components are necessary but not sufficient to explain the phenotype. Thus, the search for the impact of the en-

vironment in the molding of a schizophrenic is a continuous and timely effort.

However, when it comes to the actual nature of these inferred sociocultural factors, we are almost totally in the dark. Some have sought them in various types of interpersonal relationships within the patient's family, but have thus far amassed very little hard evidence to support their theories. Others, including myself, have investigated the possible role of social, economic, and cultural factors—with equal lack of success. Yet these latter studies, inconclusive though they have been, are not without significance for several reasons. First, they provide an opportunity for noting some basic epidemiologic facts about schizophrenia. Second, they warn us against the danger of too quickly drawing etiologic conclusions from epidemiologic data. Finally, they serve to remind us that in science negative findings can in their own way be as useful as positive ones. Even though they may not provide immediate answers to our questions, they may at least tell us where and where not to look for answers.

Epidemiologic observations relative to disease go back at least to Hippocrates, who noted (among many other pioneering observations) that gout seldom affects either premenopausal women or eunuchs. Significantly, this ancient observation has still not led to any firm etiologic conclusions. It clearly implies that sex hormones must play some role in the disease, but no one has yet demonstrated conclusively what that role is.

Epidemiologic studies of schizophrenia, of course, date from much later, since the disease was not even defined with any precision until the latter part of the nineteenth century. (As most clinicians are aware, even present definitions are not as precise as they would like.) Some 40 years ago, Ø.

EDITORS' COMMENTS:

THIS MEDICAL SOCIOLOGIST QUESTIONS THE MYTH THAT POVERTY CAUSES SCHIZOPHRENIA. HE POINTS OUT THAT WHATEVER THE ENVIRONMENTAL INFLUENCES MAY BE THAT TURN LATENT SCHIZOPHRENICS INTO CLINICALLY ILL ONES, THEY ARE NOT SO SIMPLE AND OBVIOUS AS MEMBERSHIP IN A PARTICULAR CULTURE, SUBCULTURE, OR SOCIAL CLASS. THE SOCIALIZATION EXPERIENCE OF THE PERSON, RATHER THAN THE SOCIETAL STRUCTURE ITSELF, APPEARS TO INCREASE AN INDIVIDUAL'S SUSCEPTIBILITY TO SCHIZOPHRENIA.

Reprinted from Hospital Practice 12:61–68, 1977. Figures by Albert Miller and A. Tomko. Reproduced with permission.

Ødegaard reported that mental illness (notably, schizophrenia) was more common among Norwegians who had migrated to the U.S. than among those who had remained at home; he concluded that this was due to selective migration, with those most prone to the disease also most likely to migrate. Other investigators, however, pointed out that his findings were equally consistent with other conclusions, for example, that the migrants had been subject to greater environmental stresses. Forty years later, we still do not know which explanation, if either, is correct.

My own initial epidemiologic study of schizophrenia, in collaboration with Robert Faris, was published in 1939. Before considering its findings and the conclusions we drew from them, however, I must say a word about the general methodology of such studies.

Censuses of disease in a given community are designed to obtain either the prevalence or the incidence of the disease, or both. Prevalence refers to the number suffering from the disease at the time of the survey. This may refer either to point prevalence on a given day (which for obvious reasons is seldom measured) or period prevalence, which counts the number of sufferers during a given time period, ranging from a week to several months. Incidence, by contrast, measures the number of new cases of a given disease appearing for a given time interval (usually a year). In general, prevalence studies of schizophrenia have identified cases for follow-up by a house-to-house survey or a birth register cohort (drawing a random sample from the birth register 50 years before the date of the study), while incidence studies have been based on first admissions to hospitals and other psychiatric facilities.

It will be evident that in the case of chronic conditions, such as schizophrenia, incidence will be substantially lower than prevalence, since the latter will measure not merely new cases during the census period but old cases (those who developed the disease in an earlier year but are still sick at the census period).

A further complication arises with schizophrenia, namely, that European studies measure prevalence by counting anyone who has suffered from the disease at any time, while most American studies limit their figures to those actually sick during the survey period. This may perhaps reflect a difference in outlook among psychiatrists in the two regions, with the Europeans assuming that schizophrenia is almost certain to recur sooner or later, while the Americans take a more optimistic view. One should also note that for schizophrenia, and many other diseases, some investigators have attempted to estimate the lifetime risk of contracting the condition—which will evidently be greater than either the prevalence or the incidence, since at any given time there is a certain proportion of the population that has not developed the disease but will do so eventually (as is true also with cancer).

Given these differences in methodology, not to speak of differences in diagnostic criteria, it is hardly surprising that estimates of both the incidence and the prevalence of schizophrenia vary considerably from one study to another. More surprising, perhaps, is that the reported figures still fall within a relatively narrow compass, varying by less than a factor of 10 worldwide, and considerably less than that if only U.S. studies are considered. Thus, European censuses have yielded prevalence figures ranging from 1.9 to 9.6/1,000

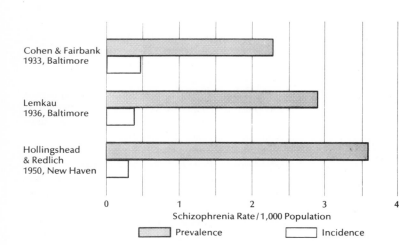

Cohen & Fairbank
1933, Baltimore

Lemkau
1936, Baltimore

Hollingshead
& Redlich
1950, New Haven

Schizophrenia Rate / 1,000 Population

Prevalence   Incidence

As graph shows, different epidemiologic studies yield different values for incidence and prevalence of schizophrenia, depending on methods and diagnostic criteria. Note, however, that as with many other chronic conditions, incidence (rate of new cases per year) is always lower than prevalence (total patient load at a given time).

people; American studies from 1.0 to 3.6. (The few Asian surveys have yielded figures ranging from 2.1 to 3.8.) Incidence rates found in the U.S. range from 0.10 to 0.47/1,000/year. Lifetime risk of the disease is probably on the order of 10/1,000, but with a considerable margin for error either way.

From all these considerations, it will be evident that comparing the prevalence or incidence of schizophrenia among different nations or cultures is difficult, if not impossible, on the basis of existing data. Equally important, in assessing any given study of the disease, one must be quite clear on what is being measured, and how.

Our Chicago study was carried out during the early 1930s and was based on first-admission figures from state and private hospitals during a 13-year period (1922–1934). During that time, the average yearly population of Chicago, ages 15 to 64, was about 2.42 million, and the total first admissions for schizophrenia were 10,575, for an average incidence of 0.34/1,000/year. First admissions were divided between public and private institutions in a ratio of 5.67 to 1. Significantly, however, the total case load of schizophrenics (which would have reflected prevalence rather than incidence) was overwhelmingly (98%) in public rather than private hospitals. This reflected the fact that almost no family could afford the costs of prolonged private hospitalization, so that schizophrenics inevitably accumulated in public institutions.

A number of people criticized these incidence figures on the ground that they did not include cases that developed during the survey period but were not hospitalized. While this was of course true, I do not myself consider it as having much weight. My reason for saying this is the conviction that virtually all schizophrenics in an urban setting are hospitalized sooner or later, at least temporarily, those who are not will in all likelihood fall into the diagnostically ambiguous category of "schizoid." Thus, while our study undoubtedly omitted a number of cases that had developed during or prior to 1934 (the end of our study period) but were not hospitalized until later, it equally must have included cases that had developed before 1922 but were hospitalized during the study period. The only assumption under which this "displacement" of cases in time might have biased our overall incidence figure was that of a marked change in incidence between the beginning and end of the study; of this we found no evidence.

In any case, the possibility of missed (undiagnosed) cases had little if any bearing on our central finding: a marked difference in incidence rates among neighborhoods of different economic levels. Specifically, incidence in the high-income areas of the city averaged 0.21/1,000, while in the poorest neighborhoods it was 0.64, or three times as high. (I might note parenthetically that subsequent studies have obtained very similar figures, with ratios between rich and poor neighborhoods pretty uniformly on the order of one to three.) That the difference was real was confirmed by the contrasting figure on incidence of manic-depressive psychosis, which showed no significant difference related to economic level.

To explain this socioeconomic difference in incidence, we theorized that the impoverished parts of the city, with high incidence rates, were also areas that tended to be high in "social isolation." Such neighborhoods would include the residents of cheap rooming houses, hobos, and economically depressed ethnic groups among whom interpersonal communication was (presumably) limited. Individuals prone to schizophrenia might thereby be "encouraged" to develop the symptoms that led to hospitalization. To oversimply somewhat, we hypothesized that poor people were more isolated and therefore were at a greater risk of developing schizophrenia.

The alert reader will at this point probably have noted something that we, alas, were too young and enthusiastic to see at the time: our findings, while consistent with the notion that poor people tend to become schizophrenic, were no less consistent with the almost diametrically opposite notion that schizophrenic people tend to become poor. One should recall, however, that in 1939, at the tail end of the Great Depression, with "one third of a nation ill-clothed, ill-house, ill-fed," many people in the social sciences (and out of them, for that matter) were intensely—and rightly—concerned about the destructive effects of poverty on families and individuals. Given the evident and easily demonstrated impact of economic deprivation on nutrition and the incidence of organic disease, they—and we—were ready to see a comparable impact on the incidence of the functional psychoses.

Despite its shaky logic, our conclusion was in tune with the Zeitgeist, and as such it won a wide acceptance. Indeed, the hypothetical correlation between high schizophrenia rates and social isolation is still quoted by sociologists who have not critically examined the evidence.

As the years rolled by, I grew increasingly troubled about the gaps in our reasoning. It was easy enough to conjecture that people in poverty areas were socially isolated and perhaps prone, as a result, to become schizophrenic, but quite another thing to demonstrate that such people were in fact

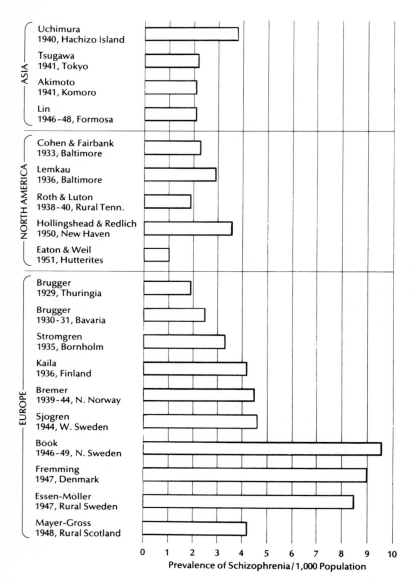

Although prevalence rates of schizophrenia vary in different studies, they fall within a fairly narrow range. The higher rates found by some European investigators are believed to reflect different assumptions about the probable future course of the disease.

socially isolated to a greater degree than residents of more prosperous areas. In fact some 15 years after the completion of our study, Clausen and Kohn designed a study that provided some evidence to answer the question. They collected data on isolation during the adolescent years for three case samples—schizophrenics, manic-depressives, and normals used as controls. For the groups under study, they found little evidence that schizophrenics or manic-depressives were isolated in their adolescent years, and that social isolation was a predisposing factor in either disease.

There remained the possibility that poverty, though it may not engender any notable degree of

social isolation, may yet help to beget schizophrenia by some other mechanism—say, by increasing the psychic stress on the vulnerable individual. In an attempt to resolve this and other questions that had arisen in my mind concerning the Chicago study, I undertook during the late 1950s to examine the question de novo, in a different city and with a more sophisticated methodology.

The city was Detroit (I was at that time at Wayne State University). After considerable preliminary investigation, my associates and I selected two subcommunities for intensive study: Cass, an inner-city neighborhood just north of downtown Detroit; and Conner-Burbank, a semisuburban area

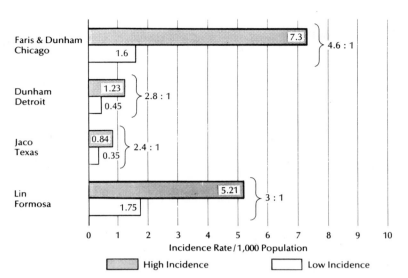

Ratio of schizophrenia incidence between high-incidence (low-income) and low-incidence (high-income) neighborhoods in a community ranges between 2.4:1 and 4.6:1.

in the city's northeast corner. The Cass population was predominantly native-born white (mostly of southern origin), but with a rapidly growing nonwhite (mainly black) population—5.5% in 1950, 37.4% in 1960; at the time of our study (1959) the nonwhite proportion was around 35%. As of 1950, more than 30% of the population in Cass was considered "mobile"—i.e., had lived in the area for less than a year. Conner-Burbank was also predominantly native-born white, but with a substantial

and growing foreign-born element; the nonwhite population was virtually nil.

Contrast in incidence rates for schizophrenia is shown by two Detroit neighborhoods. Cass, a racially mixed inner-city community, had almost twice as many cases (46, shown by dots) as Conner-Burbank, a white semisuburban area (24). Yet in the late 1950s when the communities were studied, the population of Cass was much less: 57,100 vs 76,564 for Conner-Burbank.

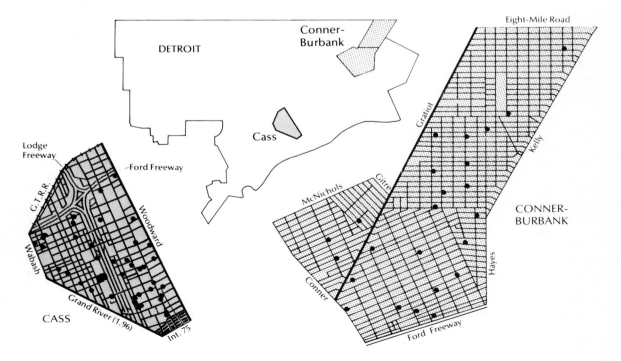

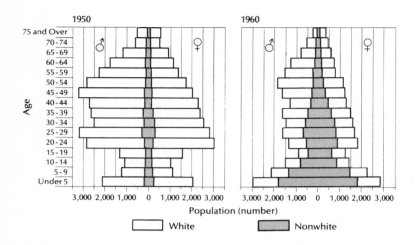

1950   1960

Rapidity of change in Cass area is shown by population "pyramids" a decade apart (1950 and 1960). Marked increase of nonwhite (mostly black) population is more than off-set by decline in white residents, with overall population drop. However, rapid change per se seems to have little relationship to incidence of schizophrenia.

Perhaps the most striking demographic differences between the communities concerned social class and income. In Cass, only 19% of the population fell into the three highest classes (proprietors, professionals, clerical and skilled workers), with 36% in the lowest class (unskilled and manual laborers); nearly 80% of the families had incomes below $6,000 a year, with a median for the whole community of $2,693. In Conner-Burbank, by contrast, over 30% of the population fell into the three highest classes, with but 15% in the lowest. Only 36% of the families had incomes under $6,000, with the median a reasonably comfortable (by 1960 standards) $7,048, or more than double the figure for Cass.

Our preliminary survey (which included a tabulation of first admissions for schizophrenia to state hospitals from 1956 to 1958) had indicated that the two communities differed considerably in their incidence of schizophrenia. They were, in fact, reasonably typical of high-incidence and low-incidence communities in Detroit, with Conner-Burbank about average for the low-incidence group and Cass below average for the high-incidence neighborhoods. We now set out to establish "true" incidence figures for the two communities by comprehensive case finding.

For this purpose we checked over the records of 176 psychiatric facilities in southeastern Michigan. These included 13 federal, state, and city-county hospitals, 11 private sanatoriums, eight private general hospitals with psychiatric services, 10 outpatient clinics, three diagnostic centers, and 131 private psychiatrists. Among the last, we received cooperation from 82% of psychiatrists in private practice in the Detroit metropolitan area. Altogether, our field workers screened some 500,000 psychiatric records. This com-

prehensive screening, which concentrated on the years 1956 to 1958 but also covered 1959 and 1960 and (less accurately) the years before 1956, turned up 3,086 cases of mental illness. Of these, 490 had been diagnosed at one time or another as schizophrenic, 549 as severely ill but nonschizophrenic (primarily cyclothymic, involutional, psychoneurotic, and schizoid cases), while the remainder (2,047), termed "additional," included most of the psychopathies, some addictions, and undiagnosed cases.

We then went over these lists intensively to eliminate duplications (persons who had been seen by more than one facility) and to ascertain as precisely as possible the year of first admission. By this process we winnowed out 454 individuals who had been seen by a psychiatric facility for the first time in 1958. Of these, 70 were schizophrenics, 111 were nonschizophrenics, and the remainder fell into the "additional" category. These people, we believe, represented essentially the entire patient population in question: a comprehensive count of cases of mental illness coming to medical attention during the year.

We were now in a position to calculate incidence rates for the two communities as well as for various subgroups within them. For this purpose, we based our rate computations on the population 15 years of age and over, since our survey did not tap childhood schizophrenia. On this basis, we found an incidence of 1.24/1,000 for Cass as against only 0.45/1,000 for Conner-Burbank. This difference was of the same order of magnitude as that found in earlier comparisons of impoverished and prosperous communities. We then tried to isolate demographic factors that might explain the differences.

One possibility was that the excess cases in

Cass might be accounted for by selective immigration, and the figures provided some support for this. In fact, when we eliminated the schizophrenics who had been living in Cass for less than five years, the incidence rates of the two communities were practically identical. But we then had to take into account the fact that a much larger percentage of the total population in Cass had been living there for less than five years (65% as compared with a little over 30% in Conner-Burbank). This meant of course that a larger proportion of the Cass schizophrenics could be expected to have been in residence for a period shorter than five years. And indeed when we divided the populations into subgroups according to length of residence (i.e., under or over five years) and compared incidence in each, we found that the differences between the two communities reappeared.

We then tried analyzing the two communities in various other ways: by previous residence (inner city, outer city, outside Detroit), by birthplace (in a large city or elsewhere), and by living arrangements (alone or with others); but in no case did any meaningful differences become manifest.

A useful clue emerged, however, when we analyzed the populations by social class, based on occupation and educational level (or for some cases, such as housewives or adolescents, by the social class of the husband or father). Some earlier studies had indicated an inverse relationship between schizophrenia and class—the higher the class, the lower the incidence of the disease. With one exception, we found no such relationship. For the four upper classes, there were no significant differences in incidence. Indeed, for both communities the incidence in Class IV (next to lowest) was lower than for any other, though since these figures were based on three and six cases respectively, they should be interpreted with caution.

The big exception was the lowest class, Class V, where incidence rates for both communities were markedly above those for any of the other four classes. Indeed, when we considered Classes I to IV only, the rates for the two communities were identical. The difference between them was in Class V where the rate in Cass was twice as high as the rate in Conner-Burbank. In Cass, the ratio between Class V and the Classes I to IV was approximately eight to one, while the ratio in Conner-Burbank was four to one.

From these and other findings we were able to draw a number of tentative conclusions. First, mere residence in a deteriorated, relatively unstable inner-city community had no influence on the incidence of schizophrenia, with the possible exception of Class V individuals in such a community. Second, class position, based on occupation and education, equally had no relationship to incidence, with the clear exception of Class V.

One obvious question emerged from this. If Class V individuals showed an abnormally high incidence of schizophrenia, was the relationship one of cause or effect? That is, had their class position helped to engender the disease, or was the disease, perhaps, the cause of their class position? In an attempt to answer this, we reclassified our patients according to their fathers' class positions, at which point the predominance of Class V vanished. For Cass, the incidence rates according to this scheme ranged from a low of 0.65 for Class III to a high of 1.47 for Class II; for Conner-Burbank, from 0.43 for Class IV to 0.87 for Class I. In both communities, the incidence for individuals with Class V fathers was about the middle of the range, and none of the class differences was statistically significant. Putting it another way, of the total of 62 patients whom we were able to classify according to these schemes, 40 (or nearly two thirds) were themselves in Class V, but only 19 (fewer than a third) had fathers in Class V, which was not much greater than the proportion of Class V individuals in the total population.

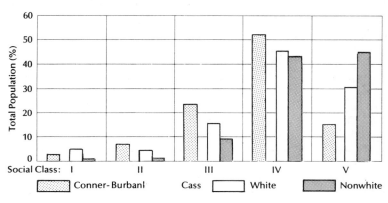

Chief difference between the neighborhoods was in class structure. In Cass, largest percentage of population, especially the nonwhite group, was in lowest classes (IV and V). In Conner-Burbank (all white) bulk of population was in Classes III and IV. Income distribution between the two areas showed similar differences; Cass was much poorer.

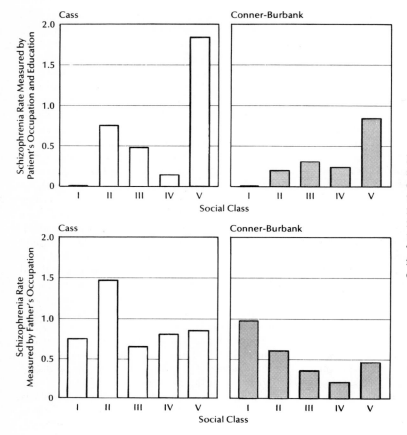

In both communities, only Class V showed significantly higher incidence of schizophrenia. However, when patient was grouped by his father's class rather than his own, Class V predominance disappeared, indicating that the high Class V incidence reflects "fallout" or downward movement from higher classes, probably because of the disease.

The conclusion seemed clear: the "excess" of schizophrenics in Class V was apparently composed of people who had dropped into Class V from higher classes or who, born into Class V families, had failed to move into a higher class (as not a few lower-class individuals normally do) or both. And by far the most likely explanation for this movement downward—or failure to move upward—was the disease itself. Clearly the chance that a schizophrenic or incipient schizophrenic will reach a given level of education or employment must be significantly poorer than that of a normal person of the same background, whether that background be of a middle-class family in a middle-class community (Conner-Burbank) or of a lower-class family in an inner-city community (Cass).

One further question remained to be elucidated. As noted above, while the rates for Classes I to IV were essentially identical in the two communities, the rate for Class V was higher in Cass than in Conner-Burbank. The only obvious difference in Class V between the two communities was that in Conner-Burbank its members were ex-

clusively white, while in Cass they were more than a third black (37%). In fact, when we reclassified our cases by race, we found that while rates for Class V whites were almost identical in the two communities (about 1.0/1,000), the incidence for Class V blacks (in Cass only, of course) was nearly three times that figure (2.78/1,000).

What is one to make of this difference? In the first place, one would expect, other things being equal, that Class V blacks would, if anything, have a lower incidence than Class V whites. This would follow on the basis of our earlier reasoning. That is, to the extent that the preponderance of schizophrenics in Class V is due to "fallout" from higher classes (i.e., individuals from higher-class families whose class position has dropped due to their disease), fewer blacks would have undergone this process, since there were fewer of them in the higher classes to begin with. Our other conclusion—that Class V preponderance could be due in part to diminished social mobility in schizophrenics of Class V origin as compared with normal individuals—would also be expected to affect blacks differentially. Social mobility among blacks is, of course, considerably less than among whites (this was even more true in the 1950s), meaning that fewer normal blacks would have been able to move out of Class V.

On the face of it, then, the Class V black-white difference in Cass, lying in the opposite direction to the expected difference, could point to some differential etiologic factor(s) in the two groups. Conceivably blacks—or at any rate these blacks— taken as a group could be viewed as having a higher hereditary predisposition to schizophrenia (though I know of no evidence that this was or is the case). Other possibilities are that the experience of being black imposes additional stresses on the personality, which, given an inherited predisposition, makes the emergence of schizophrenia more likely. Or some hidden factor in the structure of the poor black family (or some black families) might have a similar effect. Still other potential influences might be a higher incidence of such putative predisposing factors as chronic unemployment, alcoholism, and the like.

A number of points need to be made about all these hypotheses. First, we do not at this point have sufficient data to test any of them. Second, many of them are difficult, if not impossible, to state in a testable form. The importance of this can be seen from our earlier study in Chicago, in which socioeconomic differences in the incidence of schizophrenia were put down to "social isolation." Granted that some aspects of "the black experience" in America are unpleasant and stressful, how does one define them with sufficient precision to measure them, and thereby, perhaps, to show how they relate to schizophrenia?

But perhaps the most important aspect of our racial findings is that they reflect only a small number of cases (nine whites and 22 blacks) and, as such, have only a borderline statistical significance. Thus, before attempting to determine the reason(s) for racial differences in the incidence of schizophrenia, it would perhaps be wiser to make certain that such differences in fact exist (other studies in this area have concluded both that they do and that they do not). And this, I believe, would require a case-finding study as comprehensive as ours, but on a considerably larger scale.

Having described our Detroit study and the conclusions (mostly negative!) that can be drawn from it, I should like to summarize briefly the existing evidence on sociocultural factors in schizophrenia.

To begin with, schizophrenia is found in every culture in the world. So far as we can tell, its incidence does not differ greatly from one culture to another, though differences in diagnostic criteria naturally make this conclusion rather tentative. There seems little doubt that cultures differ substantially in their incidence of mental disease in the broad sense, but such differences seem to involve largely or entirely the "milder," nonpsychotic, mental illnesses (e.g., psychoneurosis, alcoholism).

This conclusion is particularly interesting in the light of the nineteenth century theory that mental disease did not exist in primitive societies. So far as the psychoses are concerned, at least, this theory is untrue. Rather, it probably grew out of the eighteenth century vision of the "noble savage" and may be considered another example of how psychologic theories are shaped by the Zeitgeist.

Second, historical studies (notably, one by H. Goldhamer and A. W. Marshall of the Rand Corporation) indicate that in the United States the incidence of psychosis in the central age groups has not increased over the last hundred years. In a study of seven states, done with H. Medow, I was able to confirm this finding for the period 1910 to 1950. Thus if, as is often said, the "stresses of modern life" are producing more mental illness, this generalization does not apply to the psychoses.

It is worth noting, however, that though the form of psychoses does not seem to vary much between cultures or historical periods, the content certainly does. Putting it another way, the fact that a person has delusions or hallucinations does not depend on the culture, but the substance of the delusions does; in 1840, a paranoid might have thought he was Napoleon, while in 1940 he more likely would have thought he was Hitler.

Third, and along the same lines, rapid social change as such does not appear to engender mental disease (for example, by increasing anxiety), though certain kinds of change may do so. Thus, a comprehensive survey of epidemiologic evidence by H. B. M. Murphy of McGill University found that where non-Western peoples are shifting toward Western cultural patterns (urban, industrialized, market economy, etc.), the rate of mental disease goes up—but it still does not (or has not) become as high as it is among peoples already enjoying (if that is the word) Western culture. In other words, it is the nature of the change, not change itself, that is decisive. Again, the increases do not seem to involve the psychoses. Thus, for example, two studies in Taiwan by T. Y. Lin, made 15 years apart, indicated that while psychoneuroses had increased by 100%, psychoses had not increased at all.

Finally, while the incidence of psychosis differs within cultures or communities (especially in being concentrated in the lowest class), these differentials provide no foundation for inferences about etiology. Social class does not appear to be an etiologic factor in schizophrenia; rather, schizophrenia appears to be an etiologic factor in social class.

Turning from the etiologic to the clinical aspects of schizophrenia, the role of environment is somewhat—but only somewhat—clearer. Where the disease already exists, it appears that certain types of situations can make the patient more or less likely to undergo an acute psychotic episode. This involves what Ernest M. Gruenberg has diagnosed as the "social breakdown syndrome," resulting from social demands placed on mental patients (especially those suffering from schizophrenia, mental retardation, and certain organic syndromes) that they, because of their disease, cannot meet. One may contrast, for example, the schizophrenic performing some relatively simple mechanical job with one forced by the nature of his job to deal with people (e.g., as a sales person); the latter will be more likely to undergo a psychotic breakdown.

If certain kinds of situations can make a schizophrenic more sick, it would seem not unreasonable to suppose that such situations, or others, can turn a latent schizophrenic into a clinically ill one. It seems likely, however, that whatever these environmental influences may be (and as indicated at the beginning of this article, we know they must exist), they are nothing so simple and obvious as membership in a particular culture, subculture, or social class. More probably they involve the combined, perhaps cumulative, operation of a number of specific social situations and incidents in the life history of the individual schizophrenic.

As such, they will have to be uncovered and their effects explained on the basis of the socialization experience of the person rather than on the basis of a societal structure.

SELECTED READING

Clausen JA, Kohn M: Social isolation and schizophrenia. Am Sociol Rev 20:265, June 1955

Dohrenwend BP, Dohrenwend BS: Social and cultural influences on psychopathology. Annu Rev Psychol 25:417, 1974

Dunham HW: Community and Schizophrenia. Wayne State University Press, Detroit 1965

Faris REL, Dunham HW: Mental Disorders in Urban Areas. University of Chicago Press, Chicago, 1939

Goldhamer H, Marshall AW: Psychosis and Civilization: Two Studies in the Frequency of Mental Disease. The Free Press, Glencoe, Ill., 1953

Gruenberg EM et al: Social breakdown syndrome: environmental and host factors associated with chronicity. Am J Public Health 62:91, 1972

Hollingshead A, Redlich F: Social Class and Mental Illness. John Wiley & Sons, Inc., New York, 1958

Leighton DC, Harding JS, Macklin DB, Leighton AH: The Character of Danger. Basic Books, Inc., New York, 1963

Linton R: Culture and Mental Disorders, Devereux G, Ed. Charles C Thomas Publisher, Springfield, Ill., 1956

Murphy HBM: Social change and mental health. Causes of Mental Disorder: A Review of Epidemiological Knowledge, 1959. Milbank Memorial Fund, New York, 1961, pp 280–329

Ødegaard Ø: Emigration and mental health. Mental Hygiene 20:546, 1936

Shields J, Heston L, Gottesman II: Schizophrenia and the schizoid: the problem for genetic analysis. Genetic Research in Psychiatry, Fieve R, Rosenthal D, Brill H, Eds. The Johns Hopkins University Press, Baltimore, 1975 (table IV, pp 167–197)

SUGGESTED READINGS

General

Schneiderian first-rank symptoms and clinical prognostic features in schizophrenia. Taylor M. Archives of General Psychiatry 26:64–67, 1972.

The diagnosis of schizophrenia: A review of recent developments. Haier RJ. Schizophrenia Bulletin 6:417–428, 1980.

Early characteristics of monozygotic twins discordant for schizophrenia. Stabenau JR, Pollin W. Archives of General Psychiatry 17:723–743, 1967.

Catatonic schizophrenia: Epidemiology and clinical course. Guggenheim FG, Babigian HM. Journal of Nervous and Mental Diseases 158:140–154, 1974.

Biological Factors

Schizophrenia: Genetic factors. Heston L. Hospital Practice 12:43–49, 1977.

Mental illness in the biological and adoptive families of adopted individuals who have become schizophrenic: A preliminary report based on psychiatric interviews. Kety SS, Rosenthal D, Wender PH, Schulsinger, F, Jacobsen B. In Genetic Research in Psychiatry (edited by Fieve R, Rosenthal D, Brill H). Baltimore, Johns Hopkins Press, 1975, pp 147–165.

Schizophrenia. Baldessarini R. New England Journal of Medicine 297:988–995, 1977.

Relevance of dopamine autoreceptors for psychiatry: Preclinical and clinical studies. Meltzer HY. Schizophrenia Bulletin 6:456–475, 1980.

An un-dopamine hypothesis of schizophrenia. Alpert, M, Friedhoff AJ. Schizophrenia Bulletin 6:387–390, 1980.

Biochemistry and the Schizophrenias: Old Concepts and New Hypotheses. Berger PA. Journal of Nervous and Mental Disease 169:90–99, 1981.

The Schizophrenia Syndrome: Examples of Biological Tools for Subclassification. Wyatt RJ, Potkin SG, Kleinman JE, Weinberger DR, Luchins DL, Geste DV Journal of Nervous and Mental Disease 169:100–112, 1981.

An Anatomy of schizophrenia? Stevens J. Archives of General Psychiatry 29:177–189, 1973.

Cerebral ventricular size and neuropsychological impairment in young chronic schizophrenics. Golden CJ, Moses JA, Zelazowski R, et al. Archives of General Psychiatry 37:619–623, 1980.

Gross pathology of the cerebellum in patients diagnosed and treated as functional psychiatric disorders. Heath RG, Franklin DE, Shraberg D. Journal of Nervous and Mental Disease 167:585–592, 1979.

Psychoendocrine Aspects of Acute Schizophrenic Reactions. Sachar EJ, Mason JW, Kolmer MS, Artiss KL. Psychosomatic Medicine 30:510–537, 1963.

Psychological Factors

Psychological deficit in schizophrenia. Shaskow D. Behavioral Science 8:275, 1963.

Children at Risk for Schizophrenia. MacCrimmon DJ, Cleghorn JM, Asarnow RF, Steffy RA. Archives of General Psychiatry 37:671–674, 1980.

Psychogenic theories of schizophrenia. Chodoff R, Carpenter W. In Schizophrenia, Biological and Psychological Perspectives (edited by G. Usein). New York, Brunner/Mazel, 1975, pp 56–79.

An overview of schizophrenia from a predominantly psychological approach. Arieti S. American Journal of Psychiatry 131:241–249, 1974.

Is disordered thinking unique to schizophrenia? Harrow M, Quinlan D. Archives of General Psychiatry 34:15–21, 1977.

Schizophrenia: Language and thought. Maher B. In Principles of Psychopathology (edited by Maher B). New York, McGraw-Hill, 1966, Chapter 15.

Nonsense and sense in schizophrenic language. Forrest DV. Schizophrenia Bulletin 2:286–301, 1976.

Sociocultural and Familial Factors

Toward a Theory of Schizophrenia. Bateson G, Jackson DD, Haley J, Weakland JH. Behavioral Science 1:251–264, 1956.

Intrafamilial environment of the schizophrenic relationships. Lidz T. American Medical Association Archives of Neurology and Psychiatry 79:305–316, 1958.

Family studies of schizophrenia: An update and commentary. Liem JH. Schizophrenia Bulletin 6:429–455, 1980.

On the nature and sources of the psychiatrist's experience with the family of the schizophrenic. Schaffer L, Wynn LC, Day J, Ryckoff IM, Halpenn A. Psychiatry 24:32–45, 1961.

Can mother/infant interaction produce vulnerability to schizophrenia? Brodie EB. Journal of Nervous and Mental Disease 169:72–81, 1981.

Current concepts about schizophrenics and family relationships. Wynne LC. Journal of Nervous and Mental Disease 169:82–89, 1981.

Social Support and Schizophrenia. Beels CC. Schizophrenia Bulletin 7:58–72, 1981.

Recent stressful life events and episodes of schizophrenia. Dohrenwend B, Egri G. Schizophrenia Bulletin 7:12–23, 1981.

PART

II

AFFECTIVE DISORDERS

OVERVIEW

After a loss we often experience sadness; after a victory we experience elation. These are transient moods in response to life events. These moods alert us, and those around us. They are a signal. When they are observable, we call them *affective* states. But moods can go awry and seemingly change out of proportion to the situation; and they can linger on far longer than seems appropriate. Moods can be a symptom of medical illness. For example, a sad feeling can sometimes be a harbinger of viral hepatitis, coming on briefly "out of the blue" before jaundice develops. A depressed mood can follow in the wake of a heart attack, clearing as the individual resumes normal activities. Similarly, an elated state can be a symptom of *encephalitis*, or can be a toxic effect of an antimalarial drug such as quinacrine.

If moods can be signals and symptoms, they can also be part of a syndrome, i.e., a complex of signs, symptoms, and laboratory findings that comprise a disease or a cluster of similar diseases. Merely being sad for a week doesn't meet the criteria for depressive disease. The beginning clinician may think it difficult to determine whether a mood is a signal, a symptom, or a tip-off to a psychiatric syndrome, but careful observation and history taking help to differentiate and diagnose appropriately.

Moods can vary, from mild to extreme. Except in the most severe cases, the depth of the depression per se is usually not diagnostic of depressive disease. A mild depression manifests itself by one's loss of interest in the usual affairs of life. Spontaneity disappears; everything requires an extra effort yet provides less gratification than previously. Fatigue may be excessive; and realistic worries and ordinary bodily discomforts become prominent, while positive memories, hopes, and plans appear difficult to remember. A person with mild depression generally can work, can attend to obligations and responsibilities, and often appears "normal" to acquaintances. To the patient and to his or her intimate friends, however, something has changed.

In depressive disorders of moderate extent, the individual feels frankly despondent and may feel physically ill most of the time. Psychological symptoms include poor concentration, indecisiveness, slowed thinking, apprehension, fatigue, boredom, and even suicidal ideation. Not all moderate depressions have the same symptoms, either from episode to episode or from person to person.

In severe depression, the individual is unable to function at work or school and cannot do simple tasks around the home. Most individuals with severe disturbance of mood have depressive disease, a major episodic affective disorder. Formerly the term "melancholia" was used for the state of a person with a mood of marked despondency. Sometimes the depth of the depression is so great that the patient becomes psychotic. When this happens, the content of the delusion is usually congruent with mood. The patient may hear accusatory voices describing bad behavior, highlighting guilt and worthlessness and producing an unbearable feeling of foreboding doom. For example, an accountant may become convinced he is about to be arrested for making an arithmetic error on an income tax form filed 15 years ago. Delusional themes usually concern (1) personal inadequacy and guilt, (2) disease or rotting organs (nihilistic delusions), (3) poverty, (4) deserved punishment or unbearable persecution, and (5) jealousy.

TYPES OF AFFECTIVE DISORDERS

A variety of terms have been used to describe pathological depressions and elations, including manic–depressive disease, primary affective reaction, melancholia, *endogenous* depression, psychotic depression, bipolar and unipolar affective disturbance, and dysphoric or dysthymic conditions. The *DSM-III* classification is useful in that it divides affective disorders into two broad forms: (1) major affective disorders and (2) other affective disorders, including cyclothymic disorder (having some of the same characteristics of major affective disorder but not of sufficient severity or duration to meet the diagnostic criteria) and *dysthymic disorder*. The term "atypical affective disorder" refers to a third residual category reserved for those affective disorders not meeting criteria for major or other affective disorders (see below).

Major Affective Disorders

Major affective disorders are characterized by three features: (1) episodic nature; (2) at least one episode enduring for more than one week; and (3) associated somatic symptoms.

Episodes of major affective disorder generally have a clear beginning and usually a distinct ending. The patient can often pinpoint the season, month, and sometimes even the day when the definite and distinctly different feeling state was noted. The episode itself may be one of depression or of mania. Occasionally episodes have rapid alterations or cycling of moods, and at times there may even be elements of depression and mania concurrently. These episodes may or may not be accompanied at the onset by a psychosocial stressor (a psychological or social stress). Between episodes, the individual is "as good as new," in marked contrast to the patient with schizophrenia, who will almost always have some residual impairment in personality or coping ability.

These affective episodes can last weeks to many years; most last six weeks to two years. Although "minor episodes" are not uncommon early in the course of affective disorder, it is not valid to make the diagnosis of a major affective disorder with depression on the basis of an episode of less than two weeks' duration, or mania based on an episode of less than one week's duration.

During an episode of severe depression or melancholia, the individual will experience certain specific somatic signs and symptoms that, along with laboratory findings, aid in appropriate diagnosis. Among the signs seen, there will be weight loss (at times approaching 7 pounds per month); psychomotor retardation (slowed bodily movement); prolonged response latency (pauses during response to questions); decreased rate of salivation; slowed bowel transit time; and disordered sleep (usually early morning awakening with a feeling of dread, but in some cases hypersomnia (an irresistible urge to sleep much longer than usual); and a decreased ability to concentrate or think abstractly.

Symptoms in melancholia include decreased appetite for food and even *anorexia*; decreased interest in usual activities and decreased libido (loss of interest in sex); loss of energy; fatigue; feelings of worthlessness, self-reproach, and inappropriate guilt; recurrent thoughts of death or suicidal ideation. Other *vegetative* or somatic symptoms include headaches, constricting feeling about the head, muscular tension, abdominal discomfort, facial or low back pain, palpitations (sensation of irregular heart beat), hot flashes, coldness of the extremities, dry mouth, and constipation. A symptom often noted when the patient has a severe depression with somatic symptoms is *diurnal* mood fluctuations—here, a sadness that is particularly prominent in the early morning.

A new and rather specific laboratory finding in melancholia relates to the dexamethasone suppression test (DST). For reasons that have not been clearly defined yet, during an episode of melancholia, there is an insensitivity of the hypothalamic–pituitary axis to agents that would ordinarily suppress it, such as dexamethasone. During an episode of melancholia the patient's adrenal cortex will continue to produce *cortisol*, "oblivious" of efforts to suppress it. This feedback inflexibility or dyscontrol clears up after the patient's severe depression has completely lifted. The DST seems to be rather specific, in the absense of certain medical conditions (including pregnancy, *Cushing's disease*, severe weight loss, and *anorexia nervosa*) and certain medications (including high-dose estrogens, *steroids*, and high doses of diazepam (Valium).

When an individual experiences a manic episode, the clinical characteristics often are a mirror image of depression. The mood is elated, not sad. There is a sense of optimism, not futility. There is evidence of greatly increased tempo in thinking, speaking, and moving (psychomotor acceleration). Accompanying the euphoria is an increased level of physical activity plus an expansiveness of planning. Thoughts dart from one idea to the next (flight of ideas). There is also an increased push or pressure of speech. The individual is inordinately aware of his or her environment, highly distractible yet relatively insensitive to interpersonal consequences. Approach to others is positive, and often accompanied by a contagious sense of humor. As the disorder becomes more severe, critical good judgment and common sense are lost and the individual may be feverishly overextended in business deals and engage in atypical or changed sexual behaviors. When events tend to be displeasing, the manic may display a marked degree of irritability and may even be briefly violent.

During a manic episode, *vegetative symptoms* include a sleep disorder, with the individual requiring three or less hours of sleep per night, an increase in sexual libido, and appetite for food (although some manics are in such a hurry to accomplish plans they defer eating and actually lose weight).

Multiple episodes of either mania or depression are referred to as recurrent manic disorder or recurrent depressive disorder. Major affective disorders that produce one or many discrete episodes of depression are called unipolar depressions. When a patient has both discrete major manic and depressive episodes, the condition is diagnosed as bipolar mood disorder, or Bipolar I, once referred to as manic–depressive disease. When depression is the major mood, and the *hypomanias* are mild and never associated with hospitalization, the diagnosis is Bipolar II. With advancing age, depressive episodes are more frequent, more severe, and longer lasting than are manic episodes.

The episode may vary from extremely severe, with psychotic thinking, vegetative symptoms, hopelessness–helplessness, and suicidal ideation, or it may be very mild and diagnosed only in retrospect. A mild episode may resemble a period of unexplained depression that many people transiently experience, accompanied by difficulty in initiating new projects and making decisions and reduced sexual drive.

When depression accompanies other psychiatric disease, the depression is referred to as a secondary phenomenon. For example, depression may occur in schizophrenia, but there a thought disorder predominates; in hysteria, there may be depression, but somatic symptoms may be more striking; and in anxiety disorders, the anxious overconcern begins first and generally anxiety symptoms dominate the clinical picture.

Dysthymic Disorders

A common form of affective disorder is chronic minor depressive disorder, now referred to as dysthymic disorder. In the past this condition was also called depressive neurosis or sometimes characterological depression. Such depressions are usually mild or moderate in extent and usually last for years.

In taking a history on people with chronic depression, one can sometimes trace a dysphoric (unpleasant) mood accompanying a negative sense of self all the way back to childhood. With some of the most persistent and long-lasting depressions, often a history of early deprivation in relationships and affection can be elicited. Vegetative symptoms other than a sleep disorder are infrequent. These individuals often complain of low energy level or chronic fatigue. There may be other complaints also, including loss of interest or pleasure, recurrent thoughts of death, pessimistic attitude, or brooding about past or current unpleasant events. People whose depressive stance seems to be part of their character (characterological depression) see this way of feeling as their lot in life. They rarely go to a physician because of depression per se. In summary, they have always believed that they are powerless to help themselves and that others can do little to benefit them, except briefly in a crisis.

Another type of chronic minor depression begins in the adult years. Here the patient may state that he or she has not always felt this way and depression may be seen as a sign of disease, or dis-ease, requiring the intervention of a physician or other mental health professional.

Many people have occasional moods of sadness for a few days. But in order to merit a psychiatric diagnosis of a dysthymic disorder, the depressed feeling must be present most of the time for at least two years and must impede functioning to some extent. The individual may experience periods of bouncing back to being "one's good old self" for a few days or a few months, but there is a pervasive sense of depressed mood and loss of interest and pleasure. Additionally, the individual will have some of the following: feelings of inadequacy, a pessimistic attitude about the future; decreased attentiveness to work, school, or home; reduced effectiveness; social withdrawal; feeling slowed down; decreased interest in sex, brooding about the past, tearfulness; and recurrent thoughts about death and suicide. Symptoms may vary from hour to hour and day to day, depending on the circumstances of the moment and the vulnerability of the individual.

Many times neither the beginning nor the ending of a period of demoralization, dejection, or depression is particularly clear cut, unless it begins with a dramatic event such as a death, divorce, or some other psychosocial stressor. Some dysthymic disorders do not seem to be initiated by a specific occurrence while others appear in response to an upsetting event, the individual experiencing a considerable degree of distress for six weeks, with lesser degrees of depression continuing for one or two years. If a depression lasts for less than two years, it would not be diagnosed as a dysthymic disorder; rather, it would be called an adjustment disorder with depressive features. A depression that accompanies a physical illness may last as long as that physical illness is symptomatic or it may persist after the physical disease has remitted. An important differential diagnostic point is that vegetative signs and symptoms other than a sleep disorder are rare in a dysthymic disorder.

EPIDEMIOLOGY

Prevalence studies of major affective disorders have not been carried out as extensively as those of schizophrenia, but recent evidence indicates that, over a lifetime, 22% of all women and 10% of all men will have at least one diagnosable episode of depression. Both unipolar and bipolar disorders are seen twice as often in women as in men and more frequently in upper than in lower socioeconomic classes. Only a quarter of people with depression seek medical advice. Chronic minor depressions are two to three times more prevalent than episodic severe depressions.

ETIOLOGY

Affective disorders appear to be caused by one or several factors, such as: biochemical imbalance secondary to inherited genetic tendencies; a toxic effect from a drug prescribed for a medical disorder; and/or psychodynamically important factors such as loss of supports, especially at vulnerable times.

From the perspective of individual *psychodynamics*, Freud described and attempted to differentiate mourning from *melancholia* (deep depression). He noted that anger could be turned against the self (*retroflection* of the aggressive instincts of the id) following the loss of a significant person, particularly when that person was regarded with mixed feelings (the ambivalently held object). Later, Edward Bibring observed that depression occurred most often when there was loss of a sought-after goal or a significant person. He saw depression as an emotional expression of helplessness and powerlessness of the ego.

Specific types of losses have been noted to produce clinically recognizable syndromes. Lindemann, in his description of responses to the catastrophic Coconut Grove fire in Boston in 1942, described a normal but profound type of depression: the response to sudden bereavement. Abnormal *unresolved grief reactions* also have been studied by Parkes. He interviewed a sample of bereaved widows and noted that the deepest depres-

sions were often found in widows who had the strongest attachment to, or dependency on, the deceased.

From a behavioral point of view, depression is a maladaptive response elicited by a loss of positive reinforcement or by an uncontrollable aversive (painful) stimulus. Both psychoanalysts and behaviorists generally agree that in the severest depressions, certain signs and symptoms cannot be accounted for on purely psychological grounds.

Evidence has accumulated over the past two decades to suggest a biochemical basis for the major affective disorders. This does not preclude psychological factors, since it is not clear in which order changes occur—does the mood cause the biochemical change or does the biochemical change make the individual especially vulnerable to developing a depression as the result of even a trivial loss?

Certain *neurohormones* (substances elaborated in the brain to assist in regulation of thought, feeling, and movements) seem to be temporarily decreased in some types of depression. Norepinephrine (representing the *catecholamines*) and *serotonin* (representing the indoleamines) may be considerably affected in depression. However, the understanding of relevant metabolic products and their chemical detection in body fluids has proved to be exceedingly complicated. Hence, even experts in the field have yet to pull together all the diverse biochemical findings in depression into one unified, comprehensive theoretical model to explain the phenomenon.

TREATMENT

Management of the affective disorders varies considerably, depending upon (1) severity and type, (2) associated health problems, and (3) physician's treatment plan.

Always to be kept in mind when dealing with a patient with affective disease is the possibility of suicide, a leading cause of death among teenagers and young adults. The best deterent is awareness of its possibility, especially in someone with a history of suicide attempts, where there is a feeling of hopelessness, where there are vague comments such as, "You'll be better off without me," or where there is sudden tidying up of affairs such as making out a will. Most successful suicide attempts occur in those with some type of depressive disorder.

For those episodic affective disorders of a presumed biological basis, somatic treatments are indicated. Additionally, psychotherapy or hospitalization may be an important adjunct in selected instances. For those intermittent or chronic dysthymic disorders of presumed psychogenic origin, psychotherapy or some form of psychosocial intervention is usual. Additionally, drugs may be useful in certain patients in whom vegetative signs are prominent. Patients with intermittent or chronic mild hypomanias rarely seek or accept medical intervention that might interfere with their euphoria.

Somatic Therapy

Although many types of somatic treatments are used in moderate to severe affective disorders, five classes of drugs are of particular importance for alleviation of symptoms. For depression, the tricyclics are the most widely used agents. Examples of tricyclics are imipramine (Tofranil, Presamine, Imarate), amitriptyline (Elavil, Endep) protryptyline (Vivactil), nortriptyline (Aventyl, Pamelar), desipramine (Pertofrane, Norpramin), and doxepin (Sinequan). Recently approved by the Federal Drug Administration, are amoxapine (Asendin) and trimipramine (Surmontil) plus the tetracyclic, maprotiline (Ludiomil). These agents take from one to three weeks to become effective in altering depressed mood, the sense of hopelessness, and guilt feelings. Disturbed sleep pattern and decreased interest often improve in just a few days, however.

A major drawback of tricyclic antidepressants is side effects, which usually occur when serum drug levels are in the therapeutic range. Dry mouth and other *anticholinergic* effects including constipation, increased *intraocular pressure*, delayed bladder emptying, *orthostatic hypotension*, and increased heart rate are more prominent with certain tricyclics and may pose problems for some patients, especially the elderly and the medically infirm. Another drawback is the delayed onset of action of both the tricyclics and the monoamine oxidase inhibitors (vide infra). Also, the tricyclics induce manic symptoms in some predisposed people with bipolar disease. Tricyclics may be effective because they block neuronal reuptake of norepinephrine and serotonin, increasing available neurohormonal levels, presumably at the interface between the presynaptic and the postsynaptic neurons. The gap between these neurons is referred to as the *synaptic cleft*, with the tricyclics blocking the reuptake of neurohormones such as norepinephrine by the presynaptic neuron. (By contrast, neuroleptics are thought to block reuptake at the postsynaptic neuron.)

Those depressions with severe agitation may also be treated with a second class of drugs, the antipsychotic neuroleptics. These agents are also useful in dampening the frenzied activity often seen in severe mania. Here such drugs as chlorpromazine (Thorazine), thioridazine (Mellaril), trifluoperazine (Stelazine), fluphenazine (Prolixin), and haloperidol (Haldol) are particularly useful when symptoms of irritability and hostility prevail.

A third type of agent effective in some depressions is the monoamine oxidase inhibitors (MAOIs). These agents, including phenelzine (Nardil) and tranylcypramine (Parnate), work not at the neuronal membrane level but rather within the cell, inhibiting the oxidation of monoamines (including the catechol norepinephrine and the indole serotonin). The effect of an MAOI is to augment the supply of norepinephrine by decreasing its degradation. But because metabolic breakdown of other amines is also inhibited, certain ordinarily benign foodstuffs containing the amino acid tyramine as well as medications with high concentrations of adrenalin-like properties become potentially toxic. Thus pressor responses (increased blood pressure and pulse rate) may occur in response to ingestion of even small amounts of aged cheese and certain wines as well as cold tablets and other drugs. The MAOIs are reportedly better for treating depressions characterized more by hypochondriacal concerns than by neurovegetative symptoms. In these atypical depressions, dysphoria (unpleasant affect) is present though not prominent.

A fourth type of agent used for depressions is represented by psychomotor stimulants such as methylphenidate (Ritalin) and dextroamphetamine. However, these drugs are no longer so widely used, partly because of the better reliability of tricyclic antidepressants and partly because of the dangers of drug dependence and drug-induced paranoid psychoses. Apparently the psychostimulant agents activate the release of stored norepinephrine and inhibit the presynaptic reuptake of neurotransmitter from the *synaptic cleft*. Reportedly, stimulants do transiently help the patient who is feeling a lack of confidence, hopelessness, and fatigue. A prompt response often predicts a good response to the tricyclic amitriptyline.

A fifth type of pharmacological agent used in depression is lithium carbonate, (Eskalith, Lithonate), which may have some mild antidepressant properties for certain patients. Lithium also has acute antimanic properties that usually decrease psychomotor acceleration within a week. But more importantly, for many bipolar patients, lithium is a highly successful prophylactic agent against further episodes of both depression and mania, dramatically decreasing the frequency and/or intensity of episodes, and decreases hospitalization.

Another effective form of somatic treatment is electroconvulsive therapy (ECT). Here, electrodes are placed on the scalp and a carefully controlled pulse of electricity is passed through one or both cerebral hemispheres, producing a *grand mal seizure* with contralateral muscular contractions and a brief loss of consciousness. At present, the procedure is done with an anesthesiologist in attendance to maintain a clear airway and to medicate the patient with a rapid action muscle relaxant and an anesthetic agent to reduce the thrashing activity during the seizure. There is no residual damage to mental functioning or personality structure with a small number of treatments (4–20). The risk to the patient is only that of general anesthesia. Prolonged and excessive ECT or improper ventilation immediately after a seizure can, however, result in brain damage. Ten to 30 years ago, improperly used ECT did give this procedure a bad image among the public.

In certain instances of severe suicidal impulsivity or refractoriness to drug treatment, ECT may be the treatment of choice, for it can be quickly effective. The troublesome but transient memory loss associated with bilateral treatments has been decreased by the use of unilateral treatment. A successful course of ECT will generally include four to eight treatments given over two to three weeks. The proposed mechanism of action centers on the ability of ECT to increase available neurotransmitter at the synaptic cleft, increasing its synthesis, storage, and/or release.

Psychotherapy

When depressive affect is due to bereavement, then sympathy, support, and companionship are helpful. Family, friends, and/or the primary care physician can share the grief, review the relationship and doubts about what could have been done, and help the patient face a new reality—all important therapeutic tasks. However, persistent depressive affect that interferes with functioning requires more skillful intervention, with psychiatric referral.

When a psychogenic depression is less dramatic, roots of the depression can often be traced to loss of love or loss of an important goal. Difficulty in appropriately expressing anger and failure to maintain self-esteem often accompany the depression. The task of a therapist is to enable the patient to delineate the problem, to encourage ventilation of feelings, to facilitate the understanding of how this response is connected to past events, and to encourage development of alternate coping strategies upon the patient's entering into hurtful situations. Thus, psychotherapy for the depressed patient can be supportive and it can lead to insight that frees the patient to make satisfying and productive life choices.

Institutional Therapy

Occasionally, depressed persons become suicidal. Indeed, one of six people with recurrent major depressive episodes dies of suicide. Self-destructive behavior may require vigorous and vigilant intervention as a lifesaving measure. Estimation of degree of potential lethality depends upon: the clinician's sense of the patient's intentionality; the degree of the patient's impulse control; the extent and nature of current psychosocial supports; whether or not a plan has actually been formulated; and the patient's past history. Legal commitment to a psychiatric facility for care may be necessary for the days of a suicidal crisis until effective treatment procedures have reduced the patient's push toward death. Also, some depressed and some manic patients require hospitalization because for a period of several weeks, they lack the ability or the judgment to care for themselves in the community. Ninety-five percent of patients with major affective disorders recover promptly and resume the life they were leading before the disruptive affective episode.

SYMPTOMATOLOGY AND MANAGEMENT OF ACUTE GRIEF

ERICH LINDEMANN

INTRODUCTION

At first glance, acute grief would not seem to be a medical or psychiatric disorder in the strict sense of the word but rather a normal reaction to a distressing situation. However, the understanding of reactions to traumatic experiences whether or not they represent clear-cut neuroses has become of ever-increasing importance to the psychiatrist. Bereavement or the sudden cessation of social interaction seems to be of special interest because it is often cited among the alleged psychogenic factors in psychosomatic disorders. The enormous increase in grief reactions due to war casualties, furthermore, demands an evaluation of their probable effect on the mental and physical health of our population.

The points to be made in this paper are as follows:

1. Acute grief is a definite syndrome with psychological and somatic symptomatology.
2. This syndrome may appear immediately after a crisis; it may be delayed; it may be exaggerated or apparently absent.

EDITORS' COMMENTS:

THIS CLASSIC PAPER WAS WRITTEN AFTER THE AUTHOR PARTICIPATED IN CARE OF FAMILIES AND VICTIMS OF A MAJOR FIRE THAT KILLED OR MAIMED HUNDREDS. ALTHOUGH THE USE OF PSYCHOACTIVE AGENTS IN THE TREATMENT OF AGITATION AND DEPRESSION HAS CHANGED DRAMATICALLY OVER THE PAST 35 YEARS, THE AUTHOR'S OBSERVATIONS ARE PARTICULARLY LUCID.

Reprinted from the American Journal of Psychiatry 101:141–148, 1944. Copyright 1944, the American Psychiatric Association.

3. In place of the typical syndrome there may appear distorted pictures, each of which represents one special aspect of the grief syndrome.
4. By appropriate techniques these distorted pictures can be successfully transformed into a normal grief reaction with resolution.

Our observations comprise 101 patients. Included are (1) psychoneurotic patients who lost a relative during the course of treatment, (2) relatives of patients who died in the hospital, (3) bereaved disaster victims (Cocoanut Grove Fire) and their close relatives, (4) relatives of members of the armed forces.

The investigation consisted of a series of psychiatric interviews. Both the timing and the content of the discussions were recorded. These records were subsequently analysed in terms of the symptoms reported and of the changes in mental status observed progressively through a series of interviews. The psychiatrist avoided all suggestions and interpretations until the picture of symptomatology and spontaneous reaction tendencies of the patients had become clear from the records. The somatic complaints offered important leads for objective study. Careful laboratory work on spirograms, g.-i. functions, and metabolic studies are in progress and will be reported separately. At present we wish to present only our psychological observations.

SYMPTOMATOLOGY OF NORMAL GRIEF

The picture shown by persons in acute grief is remarkably uniform. Common to all is the following syndrome: sensations of somatic distress occurring in waves lasting from twenty minutes to an hour at a time, a feeling of tightness in the throat, choking with shortness of breath, need for sighing, and an empty feeling in the abdomen, lack of muscular power, and an intense subjective distress described as tension or mental pain. The patient soon learns that these waves of discomfort can be precipitated by visits, by mentioning the deceased, and by receiving sympathy. There is a tendency to avoid the syndrome at any cost, to refuse visits lest they should precipitate the reaction, and to keep deliberately from thought all references to the deceased.

The striking features are (1) the marked tendency to sighing respiration; this respiratory disturbance was most conspicuous when the patient was made to discuss his grief. (2) The complaint about lack of strength and exhaustion is universal and is described as follows: "It is almost impossible to climb up a stairway." "Everything I lift seems so heavy." "The slightest effort makes me feel exhausted." "I can't walk to the corner without feeling exhausted." (3) Digestive symptoms are described as follows: "The food tastes like sand." "I have no appetite at all." "I stuff the food down because I have to eat." "My saliva won't flow." "My abdomen feels hollow." "Everything seems slowed up in my stomach."

The sensorium is generally somewhat altered. There is commonly a slight sense of unreality, a feeling of increased emotional distance from other people (sometimes they appear shadowy or small), and there is intense preoccupation with the image of the deceased. A patient who lost his daughter in the Cocoanut Grove disaster visualized his girl in the telephone booth calling for him and was much troubled by the loudness with which his name was called by her and was so vividly preoccupied with the scene that he became oblivious of his surroundings. A young navy pilot lost a close friend; he remained a vivid part of his imagery, not in terms of a religious survival but in terms of an imaginary companion. He ate with him and talked over problems with him, for instance, discussing with him his plan of joining the Air Corps. Up to the time of the study, six months later, he denied the fact that the boy was no longer with him. Some patients are much concerned about this aspect of their grief reaction because they feel it indicates approaching insanity.

Another strong preoccupation is with feelings of guilt. The bereaved searches the time before the death for evidence of failure to do right by the lost one. He accuses himself of negligence and exaggerates minor omissions. After the first disaster the central topic of discussion for a young married woman was the fact that her husband died after he left her following a quarrel, and of a young man whose wife died that he fainted too soon to save her.

In addition, there is often disconcerting loss of warmth in relationship to other people, a tendency to respond with irritability and anger, a wish not to be bothered by others at a time when friends and relatives make a special effort to keep up friendly relationships.

These feelings of hostility, surprising and quite inexplicable to the patients, disturbed them and again were often taken as signs of approaching insanity. Great efforts are made to handle them, and the result is often a formalized, stiff manner of social interaction.

The activity throughout the day of the severely bereaved person shows remarkable changes. There is no retardation of action and speech; quite to the contrary, there is a push of speech, especially when talking about the deceased. There is restlessness, inability to sit still, moving about in an aimless fashion, continually searching for something to do. There is, however, at the same time, a painful lack of capacity to initiate and maintain organized patterns of activity. What is done is done with lack of zest, as though one were going through the motions. The bereaved clings to the daily routine of prescribed activities; but these activities do not proceed in the automatic, self-sustaining fashion which characterizes normal work but have to be carried on with effort, as though each fragment of the activity became a special task. The bereaved is surprised to find how large a part of his customary activity was done in some meaningful relationships to the deceased and has now lost its significance. Especially the habits of social interaction—meeting friends, making conversation, sharing enterprises with others—seem to have been lost. This loss leads to a strong dependence on anyone who will stimulate the bereaved to activity and serve as the initiating agent.

These five points—(1) somatic distress, (2) preoccupation with the image of the deceased, (3) guilt, (4) hostile reactions, and (5) loss of patterns of conduct—seem to be pathognomonic for grief. There may be added a sixth characteristic, shown by patients who border on pathological reactions, which is not so conspicuous as the others but nevertheless often striking enough to color the whole picture. This is the appearance of traits of the deceased in the behavior of the bereaved, especially symptoms shown during the last illness, or behavior which may have been shown at the time of the tragedy. A bereaved person is observed or finds himself walking in the manner of his deceased father. He looks in the mirror and believes that his face appears just like that of the deceased. He may show a change of interests in the direction of the former activities of the deceased and may start enterprises entirely different from his former pursuits. A wife who lost her husband, an insurance agent, found herself writing to many insurance companies offering her services with somewhat exaggerated schemes. It seemed a regular observation in these patients that the painful preoccupation with the image of the deceased described above was transformed into preoccupation with symptoms or personality traits of the lost person, but now displaced to their own bodies and activities by identification.

COURSE OF NORMAL GRIEF REACTIONS

The duration of a grief reaction seems to depend upon the success with which a person does the grief work, namely; emancipation from the bondage to the deceased, readjustment to the environment in which the deceased is missing, and the formation of new relationships. One of the big obstacles to this work seems to be the fact that many patients try to avoid the intense distress connected with the grief experience and to avoid the expression of emotion necessary for it. The men victims after the Cocoanut Grove fire appeared in the early psychiatric interviews to be in a state of tension with tightened facial musculature, unable to relax for fear they might "break down." It required considerable persuasion to yield to the grief process before they were willing to accept the discomfort of bereavement. One assumed a hostile attitude toward the psychiatrist, refusing to allow any references to the deceased and rather rudely asking him to leave. This attitude remained throughout his stay on the ward, and the prognosis for his condition is not good in the light of other observations. Hostility of this sort was encountered on only occasional visits with the other patients. They became willing to accept the grief process and to embark on a program of dealing in memory with the deceased person. As soon as this became possible there seemed to be a rapid relief of tension and the subsequent interviews were rather animated conversations in which the deceased was idealized and in which misgivings about the future adjustment were worked through.

Examples of the psychiatrist's role in assisting patients in their readjustment after bereavement are contained in the following case histories. The first shows a very successful readjustment.

A woman, aged 40, lost her husband in the fire. She had a history of good adjustment previously. One child, ten years old. When she heard about her husband's death she was extremely depressed, cried bitterly, did not want to live, and for three days showed a state of utter dejection.

When seen by the psychiatrist, she was glad to have assistance and described her painful preoccupation with memories of her husband and her fear that she might lose her mind. She had a vivid visual image of his presence, picturing him as going to work in the morning and herself as wondering whether he would return in the evening, whether she could stand his not returning, then, describing to herself how he does return, plays with the dog, receives his child, and gradually tried to accept the fact that he is not there any more. It was only after ten days that she succeeded in accepting his loss and then only after having described in detail the remarkable qualities of her husband, the tragedy of his having to stop his activities at the pinnacle of his success, and his deep devotion to her.

In the subsequent interviews she explained with some distress that she had become very much attached to the examiner and that she waited for the hour of his coming. This reaction she considered disloyal to her husband but at the same time she could accept the fact that it was a hopeful sign of her ability to fill the gap he had left in her life. She then showed a marked drive for activity, making plans for supporting herself and her little girl, mapping out the preliminary steps for resuming her old profession as secretary, and making efforts to secure help from the occupational therapy department in reviewing her knowledge of French.

Her convalescence, both emotional and somatic, progressed smoothly, and she made a good adjustment immediately on her return home.

A man of 52, successful in business, lost his wife, with whom he had lived in happy marriage. The information given him about his wife's death confirmed his suspicions of several days. He responded with a severe grief reaction, with which he was unable to cope. He did not want to see visitors, was ashamed of breaking down, and asked to be permitted to stay in the hospital on the psychiatric service, when his physical condition would have permitted his discharge, because he wanted further assistance. Any mention of his wife produced a severe wave of depressive reaction, but with psychiatric assistance he gradually became willing to go through this painful process, and after three days on the psychiatric service he seemed well enough to go home.

He showed a high rate of verbal activity, was restless, needed to be occupied continually, and felt that the experience had whipped him into a state of restless overactivity.

As soon as he returned home he took an active part in his business, assuming a post in which he had a great many telephone calls. He also took over the role of amateur psychiatrist to another bereaved person, spending time with him and comforting him for his loss. In his eagerness to start anew, he developed a plan to sell all his former holdings, including his house, his furniture, and giving away anything which could remind him of his wife. Only after considerable discussion was he able to see that this would mean avoiding immediate grief at the price of an act of poor judgment. Again he had to be encouraged to deal with his grief reactions in a more direct manner. He has made a good adjustment.

With eight to ten interviews in which the psychiatrist shares the grief work, and with a period of from four to six weeks, it was ordinarily possible to settle an uncomplicated and undistorted grief reaction. This was the case in all but one of the 13 Cocoanut Grove fire victims.

MORBID GRIEF REACTIONS

Morbid grief reactions represent distortions of normal grief. The conditions mentioned here were transformed into "normal reactions" and then found their resolution.

a. Delay of Reaction. The most striking and most frequent reaction of this sort is delay or postponement. If the bereavement occurs at a time when the patient is confronted with important tasks and when there is necessity for maintaining the morale of others, he may show little or no reaction for weeks or even much longer. A brief delay is described in the following example.

A girl of 17 lost both parents and her boy friend in the fire and was herself burned severely, with marked involvement of the lungs. Throughout her stay in the hospital her attitude was that of cheerful acceptance without any sign of adequate distress. When she was discharged at the end of three weeks she appeared cheerful, talked rapidly, with a considerable flow of ideas, seemed eager to return home and to assume the role of parent for her two younger siblings. Except for slight feelings of "lonesomeness" she complained of no distress.

This period of griefless acceptance continued for the next two months, even when the household was dispersed and her younger siblings were placed in other homes. Not until the end of the tenth week did she begin to show a true state of grief with marked feelings of depression, intestinal emptiness, tightness in her throat, frequent crying, and vivid preoccupation with her deceased parents.

That this delay may involve years became obvious first by the fact that patients in acute bereavement about a recent death may soon upon exploration be found preoccupied with grief about a person who died many years ago. In this manner a woman of 38, whose mother had died recently and who had responded to the mother's death with a surprisingly severe reaction, was found to be but mildly concerned with her mother's death but deeply engrossed with unhappy and perplexing fantasies concerning the death of her brother, who died twenty years ago under dramatic circumstances from metastasizing carcinoma after amputation of his arm had been postponed too long. The discovery that a former unresolved grief reaction may be precipitated in the course of the discussion of another recent event was soon demonstrated in psychiatric interviews by patients who showed all the traits of a true grief reaction when the topic of a former loss arose.

The precipitating factor for the delayed reaction may be a deliberate recall of circumstances surrounding the death or may be a spontaneous occurrence in the patient's life. A peculiar form of this is the circumstance that a patient develops the grief reaction at the time when he himself is as old as the person who died. For instance, a railroad worker, aged 42, appeared in the psychiatric clinic with a picture which was undoubtedly a grief reaction for which he had no explanation. It turned out that when he was 22, his mother, then 42, had committed suicide.

b. Distorted Reactions. The delayed reactions may occur after an interval which was not marked by any abnormal behavior or distress, but in which there developed an alteration in the patient's conduct perhaps not conspicuous or serious enough to lead him to a psychiatrist. These alterations may be considered as the surface manifestations of an unresolved grief reaction, which may respond to fairly simple and quick psychiatric management if recognized. They may be classified as follows: (1) overactivity without a sense of loss, rather with a sense of wellbeing and zest, the activities being of an expansive and adventurous nature and bearing semblance to the activities formerly carried out by the deceased, as described above; (2) the acquisition of symptoms belonging to the last illness of the deceased. This type of patient appears in medical clinics and is often labelled hypochondriasis or hysteria. To what extent actual alterations of physiological functions occur under these circumstances will have to be a field of further careful inquiry. I owe to Dr. Chester Jones a report about a patient whose electrocardiogram showed a definite change during a period of three weeks, which started two weeks after the time her father died of heart disease.

While this sort of symptom formation "by identification" may still be considered as conversion symptoms such as we know from hysteria, there is another type of disorder doubtlessly presenting (3) a recognized *medical disease*, namely, a group of psychosomatic conditions, predominantly ulcerative colitis, rheumatoid arthritis, and asthma. Extensive studies in ulcerative colitis have produced evidence that 33 out of 41 patients with ulcerative colitis developed their disease in close time relationship to the loss of an important person. Indeed, it was this observation which first gave the impetus for the present detailed study of grief. Two of the patients developed bloody diarrhea at funerals. In the others it developed within a few weeks after the loss. The course of the ulcerative colitis was strikingly benefited when this grief reaction was resolved by psychiatric technique.

At the level of social adjustment there often occurs a conspicuous (4) alteration in relationship to friends and relatives. The patient feels irritable, does not want to be bothered, avoids former social activities, and is afraid he might antagonize his friends by his lack of interest and his critical attitudes. Progressive social isolation follows, and the patient needs considerable encouragement in re-establishing his social relationships.

While overflowing hostility appears to be spread out over all relationships, it may also occur as (5) furious hostility against specific persons; the doctor or the surgeon are accused bitterly for neglect of duty and the patient may assume that foul play has led to the death. It is characteristic that while patients talk a good deal about their suspicions and their bitter feelings, they are not likely to take any action against the accused, as a truly paranoid person might do.

(6) Many bereaved persons struggled with much effort against these feelings of hostility, which to them seem absurd, representing a vicious change in their characters and to be hidden as much as possible. Some patients succeed in hiding their hostility but become wooden and formal, with affectivity and conduct resembling *schizophrenic pictures*. A typical report is this, "I go through all the motions of living. I look after my children. I do my errands. I go to social functions, but it is like being in a play; it doesn't really concern me. I can't have any warm feelings. If I were to have any feelings at all I would be angry with everybody." This patient's reaction to therapy was characterized by growing hostility against the therapist, and it required considerable skill to make her continue interviews in spite of the disconcerting hostility which she had been fighting so much. The absence of emotional display in this patient's face and actions was quite striking. Her face had a mask-like appearance, her movements were formal, stilted, robot-like, without the fine play of emotional expression.

(7) Closely related to this picture is a lasting loss of patterns of social interaction. The patient cannot initiate any activity, is full of eagerness to be active—restless, can't sleep—but throughout the day he will not start any activity unless "primed" by somebody else. He will be grateful at sharing activities with others but will not be able to make up his mind to do anything alone. The picture is one of lack of decision and initiative. Organized activities along social lines occur only if a friend takes the patient along and shares the activity with him. Nothing seems to promise reward; only the ordinary activities of the day are carried on, and these in a routine manner, falling apart into small steps, each of which has to be carried out with much effort and without zest.

(8) There is, in addition, a picture in which a patient is active but in which most of his activities attain a coloring which is detrimental to his own social and economic existence. Such patients with uncalled for generosity, give away their belongings, are easily lured into foolish economic dealings, lose their friends and professional standing by a series of "stupid acts," and find themselves finally without family, friends, social status or money. This protracted self-punitive behavior seems to take place without any awareness of excessive feelings of guilt. It is a particularly distressing grief picture because it is likely to hurt other members of the family and drag down friends and business associates.

(9) This leads finally to the picture in which the grief reaction takes the form of a straight agitated depression with tension, agitation, insomnia, feelings of worthlessness, bitter self-accusation, and obvious need for punishment. Such patients may be dangerously suicidal.

A young man aged 32 had received only minor burns and left the hospital apparently well on the road to recovery just before the psychiatric survey of the disaster victims took place. On the fifth day he had learned that his wife had died. He seemed somewhat relieved of his worry about her fate; impressed the surgeon as being unusually well-controlled during the following short period of his stay in the hospital.

On January 1st he was returned to the hospital by his family. Shortly after his return home he had become restless, did not want to stay at home, had taken a trip to relatives trying to find rest, had not succeeded, and had returned home in a state of marked agitation, appearing preoccupied, frightened, and unable to concentrate on any organized activity. The mental status presented a somewhat unusual picture. He was restless, could not sit still or participate in any activity on the ward. He would try to read, drop it after a few minutes, or try to play pingpong, give it up after a short time. He would try to start conversations, break them off abruptly, and then fall into repeated murmured utterances: "Nobody can help

me. When is it going to happen? I am doomed, am I not?"
With great effort it was possible to establish enough rapport to carry on interviews. He complained about his
feeling of extreme tension, inability to breathe, generalized weakness and exhaustion, and his frantic fear
that something terrible was going to happen. "I'm destined to live in insanity or I must die. I know that it is
God's will. I have this awful feeling of guilt." With intense morbid guilt feelings, he reviewed incessantly the
events of the fire. His wife had stayed behind. When he
tried to pull her out, he had fainted and was shoved out
by the crowd. She was burned while he was saved. "I
should have saved her or I should have died too." He
complained about being filled with an incredible violence and did not know what to do about it. The rapport
established with him lasted for only brief periods of time.
He then would fall back into his state of intense agitation
and muttering. He slept poorly even with large sedation.
In the course of four days he became somewhat more
composed, had longer periods of contact with the psychiatrist, and seemed to feel that he was being understood and might be able to cope with his morbid feelings
of guilt and violent impulses. On the sixth day of his
hospital stay, however, after skillfully distracting the attention of his special nurse, he jumped through a closed
window to a violent death.

If the patient is not conspicuously suicidal, it
may nevertheless be true that he has a strong desire
for painful experiences, and such patients are
likely to desire shock treatment of some sort,
which they picture as a cruel experience, such as
electrocution might be.

A 28-year-old woman, whose 20 months-old son was accidentally smothered developed a state of severe agitated
depression with self-accusation, inability to enjoy anything, hopelessness about the future, overflow of hostility against the husband and his parents, also with excessive hostility against the psychiatrist. She insisted upon
electric-shock treatment and was finally referred to
another physician who treated her. She responded to the
shock treatments very well and felt relieved of her sense
of guilt.

It is remarkable that agitated depressions of this
sort represent only a small fraction of the pictures
of grief in our series.

PROGNOSTIC EVALUATION

Our observations indicate that to a certain extent
the type and severity of the grief reaction can be
predicted. Patients with obsessive personality
make-up and with a history of former depressions
are likely to develop an agitated depression. Severe reactions seem to occur in mothers who have
lost young children. The intensity of interaction
with the deceased before his death seems to be

significant. It is important to realize that such interaction does not have to be of the affectionate
type; on the contrary, the death of a person who
invited much hostility, especially hostility which
could not well be expressed because of his status
and claim to loyalty, may be followed by a severe
grief reaction in which hostile impulses are the
most conspicuous feature. Not infrequently the
person who passed away represented a key person
in a social system, his death being followed by
disintegration of this social system and by a profound alteration of the living and social conditions
for the bereaved. In such cases readjustment presents a severe task quite apart from the reaction to
the loss incurred. All these factors seem to be more
important than a tendency to react with neurotic
symptoms in previous life. In this way the most
conspicuous forms of morbid identification were
found in persons who had no former history of a
tendency to psychoneurotic reactions.

MANAGEMENT

Proper psychiatric management of grief reactions
may prevent prolonged and serious alterations in
the patient's social adjustment, as well as potential
medical disease. The essential task facing the psychiatrist is that of sharing the patient's grief work,
namely, his efforts at extricating himself from the
bondage to the deceased and at finding new patterns of rewarding interaction. It is of the greatest
importance to notice that not only over-reaction
but under-reaction of the bereaved must be given
attention, because delayed responses may occur at
unpredictable moments and the dangerous distortions of the grief reaction, not conspicuous at first,
be quite destructive later and these may be prevented.

Religious agencies have led in dealing with the
bereaved. They have provided comfort by giving
the backing of dogma to the patient's wish for continued interaction with the deceased, have developed rituals which maintain the patient's interaction with others, and have counteracted the
morbid guilt feelings of the patient by Divine
Grace and by promising an opportunity for "making up" to the deceased at the time of a later reunion. While these measures have helped countless mourners, comfort alone does not provide
adequate assistance in the patient's grief work. He
has to accept the pain of the bereavement. He has to
review his relationships with the deceased, and
has to become acquainted with the alterations in
his own modes of emotional reaction. His fear of
insanity, his fear of accepting the surprising
changes in his feelings, especially the overflow of

hostility, have to be worked through. He will have to express his sorrow and sense of loss. He will have to find an acceptable formulation of his future relationship to the deceased. He will have to verbalize his feelings of guilt, and he will have to find persons around him whom he can use as "primers" for the acquisition of new patterns of conduct. All this can be done in eight to ten interviews.

Special techniques are needed if hostility is the most marked feature of the grief reaction. The hostility may be directed against the psychiatrist, and the patient will have such guilt over his hostility that he will avoid further interviews. The help of a social worker or a minister, or if these are not available, a member of the family, to urge the patient to continue coming to see the psychiatrist may be indispensable. If the tension and the depressive features are too great, a combination of benzedrine sulphate, 5–10 mgm. b.i.d., and sodium amytal, 3 gr. before retiring, may be useful in first reducing emotional distress to a tolerable degree. Severe agitated depressive reactions may defy all efforts of psychotherapy and may respond well to shock treatment.

Since it is obvious that not all bereaved persons, especially those suffering because of war casualties, can have the benefit of expert psychiatric help, much of this knowledge will have to be passed on to auxiliary workers. Social workers and ministers will have to be on the look-out for the more ominous pictures, referring these to the psychiatrist while assisting the more normal reactions themselves.

ANTICIPATORY GRIEF REACTIONS

While our studies were at first limited to reactions to actual death, it must be understood that grief reactions are just one form of separation reactions. Separation by death is characterized by its irreversibility and finality. Separation may, of course, occur for other reasons. We were at first surprised to find genuine grief reactions in patients who had not experienced a bereavement but who had experienced separation, for instance with the departure of a member of the family into the armed forces. Separation in this case is not due to death but is under the threat of death. A common picture hitherto not appreciated is a syndrome which we have designated anticipatory grief. The patient is so concerned with her adjustment after the potential death of father or son that she goes through all the phases of grief—depression, heightened preoccupation with the departed, a review of all the forms of death which might befall him, and anticipation of the modes of readjustment which

might be necessitated by it. While this reaction may well form a safeguard against the impact of a sudden death notice, it can turn out to be of a disadvantage at the occasion of reunion. Several instances of this sort came to our attention when a soldier just returned from the battlefront complained that his wife did not love him anymore and demanded immediate divorce. In such situations apparently the grief work had been done so effectively that the patient has emancipated herself and the readjustment must now be directed towards new interaction. It is important to know this because many family disasters of this sort may be avoided through prophylactic measures.

BIBLIOGRAPHY

Many of the observations are, of course, not entirely new. Delayed reactions were described by Helene Deutsch(1). Shock treatment in agitated depressions due to bereavement has recently been advocated by Myerson(2). Morbid identification has been stressed at many points in the psychoanalytic literature and recently by H. A. Murray(3). The relation of mourning and depressive psychoses has been discussed by Freud(4), Melanie Klein(5), and Abraham(6). Bereavement reactions in war time were discussed by Wilson(7). The reactions after the Cocoanut Grove fire were described in some detail in a chapter of the monograph on this civilian disaster(8). The effect of wartime separations was reported by Rosenbaum(9). The incidence of grief reactions among the psychogenic factors in asthma and rheumatoid arthritis has been mentioned by Cobb, et al.(10, 11).

1. Deutsch, Helene. Absence of grief. Psychoanalyt. Quart., **6**:12, 1937.
2. Myerson, Abraham. The use of shock therapy in prolonged grief reactions. New England J. Med., **230**:9, Mar. 2, 1944.
3. Murray, H. A. Visual manifestations of personality. Jr. Abn. & Social Psychol., **32**:161–184, 1937.
4. Freud, Sigmund. Mourning and melancholia. Collected Papers IV, 288–317; 152–170.
5. Klein, Melanie. Mourning and its relation to manic-depressive states. Internat. J. Psychoan., **21**:125–153, 1940.
6. Abraham, C. Notes on the psycho-analytical investigation and treatment of the libido, viewed in the light of mental disorder. Selected Papers.
7. Wilson, A. T. M. Reactive emotional disorders. Practitioner, **146**:254–258.
8. Cobb, S., & Lindemann, E. Neuropsychiatric observations after the Cocoanut Grove fire. Ann. Surg., June 1943.
9. Rosenbaum, Milton. Emotional aspects of wartime separations. Family, **24**:337–341, 1944.
10. Cobb, S., Bauer, W., and Whitney. I. Environmental factors in rheumatoid arthritis. J. A. M. A., **113**:668–670, 1939.
11. McDermott, N., and Cobb, S. Psychogenic factors in asthma. Psychosom. Med., **1**:204–341, 1939.
12. Lindemann, Erich. Psychiatric factors in the treatment of ulcerative colitis. In press.

OVERVIEW OF DEPRESSION: INTEGRATION OF TEN CONCEPTUAL MODELS INTO A COMPREHENSIVE CLINICAL FRAME

HAGOP S. AKISKAL AND WILLIAM T. MCKINNEY, Jr.

Disciplinary fragmentation and nosological and semantic controversies have obscured the impressive advances made in the area of depressive disorders during the past decade. This article is an attempt to translate data derived from psychodynamic, sociobehavioral, and neurobiologic research into a clinically meaningful framework.

We review ten models of depression with special emphasis on newer models supported by empirical and experimental studies, and present a new model, which incorporates and synthesizes findings from different schools. Depressive illness is conceptualized as the feedback interaction of three sets of variables at chemical, experiential, and behavioral levels with the diencephalon serving as the field of action.

The progress made in the general area of affective disorders during the past decade is probably unmatched by that in any other area of psychiatric research. The progress has been especially visible in neurobiology. Yet, equally impressive advances have been made in the psychology, epidemiology, and sociology of depression. The rapid turnover of knowledge in part reflects changes in study method and perspective. Psychiatry is becoming a behavioral science.[1] There has been a decisive shift from anecdotal observations to carefully designed cross-sectional and longitudinal studies employing sophisticated methodology. Moreover, experimental manipulation of variables, at times carried to the level of animal models,[2,3] has permitted behavioral scientists to supplement naturalistic observations on human depressions.

Unfortunately, the impact of such advances is not always visible in psychiatric education,[4-7] nor does it seem reflected in the official international and American Psychiatric Association (APA) nomenclature on affective disorders.[8,9]

This report represents an attempt to translate recent research into a form that can be put into clinical use.

MODELS OF DEPRESSION

According to Havens, "the present-day fragmentation and disputatiousness not only confuse practice but also obscure the extraordinary advances that have been made" by modern psychiatry.[10] Psychiatry today is subdivided into multiple factions of "pseudopsychiatry,"[4] whose advocates seldom communicate. Nosological and semantic dissonance prevails. Depressive disorders, as well as other disorders of behavior, are conceptualized along specialized frames of reference that largely depend on the training and indoctrination of the clinician or researcher.

Ten models of depression, reflecting five dominant schools of thought, are summarized in Table 1. For those in the psychoanalytic tradition, depression represents the introjection of hostility resulting from the loss of an ambivalently loved object,[11,12] or a reaction to separation from a significant object of attachment.[13-15] More recent ego psychological approaches focus on helplessness, lowered self-esteem,[16] and negative cognitive

Reprinted, with author revisions, from Archives of General Psychiatry 32:285–305, 1975. Copyright 1975, American Medical Association.

TABLE 1. Ten Models of Depression

School	Model	Mechanism
Psychoanalytical	Aggression-turned-inward [11,12]	Conversion of aggression instinct into depressive affect
	Object loss [13–15]	Separation: disruption of an attachment bond
	Loss of self-esteem [16]	Helplessness in attaining goals of ego-ideal
	Negative cognitive set [17]	Hopelessness
Behavioral	Learned helplessness [18]	Uncontrollable aversive stimulation
	Loss of reinforcement [19–21]	Rewards of "sick role" substitute for lost sources of reinforcement
Sociological	Sociological [22]	Loss of role status
Existential	Existential [23]	Loss of meaning of existence
Biological	Biogenic amine [24–27]	Impaired monoaminergic neurotransmission
	Neurophysiological [28–30]	Hyperarousal secondary to intraneuronal sodium accumulation
		Cholinergic dominance
		Reversible functional derangement of diencephalic mechanisms of reinforcement

set.[17] For the behaviorist, depression is a set of maladaptive behavioral responses—elicited by uncontrollable aversive stimuli or by loss of reinforcement—that are additionally maintained by the rewards of the "sick-role."[18–21] The sociologist regards depression as the outcome of a social structure that deprives individuals with certain roles, eg, middle-class middle-aged housewives, from control over their destiny.[22] For the existentialist, depression supervenes when the individual discovers that his world has lost its meaning and purpose.[23] Finally, the biological psychiatrist conceptualizes depression as the behavioral output of a genetically vulnerable central nervous system (CNS) depleted from biogenic amines[24–27] and characterized by hyperarousal.[28] More recent hypotheses emphasize cholinergic dominance[29] or reversible deficits in the diencephalic mechanisms of reinforcement.[30] Each theoretical framework has generated its own therapeutic modalities that, unfortunately, tend to be competitive rather than complementary. They range from psychoanalysis to behavior therapy, from socio-political activism to pharmacotherapy, and electric convulsive therapy (ECT).

Attempts at reconciling these diverse theoretical positions have been sporadic and incomplete. Wilkins[31] and Liberman and Raskin,[32] for instance, reformulated the psychoanalytical models in behavioral terminology. Bart[22] synthesized the psychoanalytical and existential models into a sociological theory of depression. Mallerstein[33] reviewed the psychoanalytical models in the light of ethological and biological advances. Whybrow

and Mendels[28] related psychophysiological and biochemical abnormalities to a neurophysiological dysfunction. In a comprehensive review of the biology of affective disorders, Goodwin and Bunney[34] suggested a model that embraces the interface between stress and biogenic amines. More recently, Whybrow and Parlatore[35] presented a general systems' scheme that provided an elegant synthesis of the psychobiologic literature on affective disorders, integrating the biochemistry, endocrinology, and neurophysiology of depression.

We have elsewhere presented a unified hypothesis that integrates the various conceptual models of depression.[30] The depressive syndrome is conceived as the psychobiological final common pathway of various processes that result in a reversible, functional derangement of the diencephalic mechanisms of reinforcement. In our model, depression is simultaneously conceptualized at several levels, rather than having any one-to-one relationship with a single event—whether defined in chemical, psychodynamic, or behavioral language. In this report, we shall elaborate on the clinical implications of our model in an attempt to provide a cohesive conceptual framework for the phenomena of depression. In other words, depression will serve as a paradigm to illustrate the heuristic value of such an integrative model for psychiatric theory and practice.

In the first third of this report, we shall consider semantic, nosological, and diagnostic issues and present a nosological scheme which takes into consideration recent advances in genetics and neuropharmacology. In the middle part, we shall review the empirical evidence for the ten conceptual models of depression and attempt a stepwise integration as we proceed to the last section, which will provide the final neurobehavioral synthesis. Philosophical, methodological, and clinical issues will be addressed throughout the presentation.

UNHAPPINESS, DEPRESSION, AND MELANCHOLIA

A major source of confusion in the area of depression stems from the fact that psychiatrists use the term depression with different meanings. As Lipowski[36] remarks, an unfortunate dichotomy, psychodynamic vs descriptive psychopathology, so prevalent among US psychiatrists, further confuses issues. The tendency to favor "understanding" depression over objective description of observable signs and symptoms hinders clinical research. During the past five to six years, however, there has been a healthy revival of interest in psychiatric nosology with emphasis on clusterings of clinical signs and symptoms viewed in longitudinal context. In this country the "St. Louis" school[7] has pioneered in this approach. The impact of such trends on research in the area of depression, reviewed by Klerman and Barret,[38,39] has resulted in nosological clarifications based on detailed clinical descriptions.

Primary and Secondary Depression

One major effort in this direction is the Robins-Guze classification[40] of depressive phenomena into primary and secondary subgroups (summarized in Table 2). This classification provides a clear nosological framework within which one can place many of the current research efforts in the area of affective disorders. Feelings of sadness, inadequacy, and hopelessness that occur during the course of preexisting nonaffective psychiatric disorders, such as hysteria or anxiety disorders, constitute "secondary depression." Depressive symptomatology can also be secondary to or associated with medical illnesses, such as viral infections, rheumatoid arthritis, hypothyroidism, multiple sclerosis, and chronic heart conditions. The designation "primary depression," on the other hand, refers to a combination of signs and symptoms that involve varying degrees of psychomotor and vegetative dysfunction, dysphoria, hopelessness, worthlessness, guilt, and suicidal preoccupations, occurring de novo as a primary disorder of mood, ie, unrelated to a nonaffective psychiatric disorder. It is to the credit of Robin's group that

TABLE 2. The "St. Louis" Classificatory Scheme of Depressive Disorders

---

Primary Depression

Definition
  An affective illness:
    With no preexisting major psychiatric syndromes such as:
      Process schizophrenia
      Hysteria; panic, phobic, and obsessive-compulsive disorders
      Sociopathy; chronic alcoholism; drug dependency
      Homosexuality or other sexual deviation
      Mental retardation and organic brain syndrome
    Also excluded are affective reactions superimposed on life-threatening or incapacitating medical/surgical illnesses
  Length of illness: at least one month
  Signs and symptoms:
    Dysphoric mood (depressed, blue, despondent, hopeless, discouraged, fearful, worried, irritable)
    Anorexia and/or unintentional weight loss; rarely hyperphagia
    Insomnia or hypersomnia
    Loss of energy with easy fatigability
    Psychomotor retardation or agitation
    Anhedonia (including diminished libido) and/or decreased interest in usual activities
    Lowered self-esteem and self-reproach
    Poor concentration, slow thinking, or mixed-up thoughts
    Recurrent thoughts of death or suicide
  Subtypes
    Unipolar: single or recurrent episodes of depression with no history of mania or hypomania
    Bipolar (true manic-depressive illness): single or recurrent episodes of depression with history of mania or hypomania

---

Secondary Depression

Signs and symptoms as under primary depression
Superimposed on:
  Either a preexisting nonaffective psychiatric illness
  Or paralleling the course of a life-threatening or incapacitating medical/surgical illness

---

they have published operationally defined criteria for the diagnosis of the major psychiatric disorders,[41] in which reasonable interrater agreement can be achieved. Recent biochemical work, such as differential rates of urinary 3-methoxy-4-hydroxyphenylethylene glycol (MHPG) excretion in the two conditions, has been reported in further substantiation of the primary-secondary dichotomy.[42] The major virtue of this classification lies in the fact that diagnosis is made independent from etiological considerations such as precipitating stress, thereby bypassing the familiar controversies generated by the endogenous-reactive and psychotic-neurotic dichotomies.

But where does unhappiness, so-called normal depression end and depressive illness begin? Some psychiatrists do not distinguish between depression and misfortune: the depressed individual is merely seen as the unfortunate victim of adverse life situations. For others, depression represents a masochistic life style, which serves the purpose of obtaining interpersonal favors. Many clinicians, on the other hand, classify a sustained state of depression as an illness, the phenotypic expression of an underlying genetic diathesis. Such opposing viewpoints are largely due to artificial semantic controversies, such as organic vs functional, heredity vs environment, and medical vs psychosocial models that continue to obfuscate psychiatric thinking.[4, 7, 43, 44]

The distinction between "melancholia" and "depression" as introduced by Whybrow and Parlatore,[35] constitutes an important conceptual clarification of such issues. These authors reserve the term "depression" as a synonym for sadness. In this sense, depression is a ubiquitous, universal emotional response to everyday adaptation to stress, frustration, and loss. Such states of normal mood are ordinarily self-limited and, therefore, do not warrant syndromal status. They suggest the term "melancholia" for sustained states of deep dejection that are most commonly seen in the syndrome of primary depression. Melancholia (black bile)—with its biochemical connotations—is an appropriate designation here because, once attained, it becomes biologically autonomous and, as Prange[45] remarks, it assumes the dimensions of illness—namely, disruption of psychomotor and vegetative functions, morbidity, mortality, and response to pharmacological therapies. Melancholia represents the "biological" phase in the course of a depressive disorder. To continue labeling such melancholic states as "depression" with the implication that they represent accentuation of normal unhappiness is clinically disastrous. The individual so afflicted is in profound despair, suffers from serious somatic dysregulation, and is simply too sick to benefit from psychotherapeutic modalities alone; biological intervention is necessary if one expects the patient to survive and respond to interpersonal feedback.

Consequently, the distinction between normal sadness, depressive symptoms, and melancholia is important from clinical and research standpoints. For instance, tricyclic antidepressants alone are generally contraindicated for symptoms of depression (eg, schizophrenics with secondary depression may get worse[46]) but constitute an effective therapeutic modality in melancholia. Also, tricyclic antidepressants are not indicated for normal unhappiness, and the differentiation of unhappiness from melancholia requires systematic, careful, and detailed history and mental status, where well-designed depression rating scales,[47-49] can be of great practical utility. Thus, the researchers' task is to define why most individuals undergo transient and minor fluctuations in response to everyday stresses, while 5% of men and 10% of women[37(p7)] make one or several descents into the abyss of despair.

THE ENDOGENOUS-REACTIVE DICHOTOMY

Having classified depressive phenomena into primary and secondary, how does one go about subdividing the syndrome of primary depression?

The official system of classification developed by the APA in the second edition of its manual (*DSM-II*)[9]—which was essentially adapted from the eighth edition of the International Classification of Diseases (*ICD-8*)[8]—heavily relied on "precipitating stress" as the criterion for taxonomy.

As Mendelson remarks, it is misleading to profess that a consensus exists about the clinical boundaries of "neurotic" and "psychotic" depressions.[50] Do these labels designate the severity of the illness? Is "neurotic" synonymous with "reactive" or "psychogenic"; if so, how does one operationally define these concepts? Or does it refer to "neurotic" symptomatology, such as anxiety, obsessions, and inordinate fatigue superimposed on a primary disturbance of mood? Or does "neurotic" refer to a characterological propensity to overreact with depressive symptoms when confronted with minor frustrations?

While cautiously avoiding terms, such as "endogenous" and "reactive," both the international and the APA diagnostic manuals basically adhered to the endogenous-reactive dichotomy. Thus, psychotic depressive reaction and neurotic depression were said to be "attributable to some experience."[9(p38)] Involutional melancholia and manic-depressive illness, on the other hand, "do not seem to be related directly to a precipitating life experience."[9(p35)] But, when presented with an individual patient, how will the clinician assess the etiological relevance of poorly-defined, universal, and everyday occurrences, such as stressful psychosocial events, in the pathogenesis of the depressive illness?

Although *DSM-III* has largely avoided such dichotomies, the dualistic approach to depressive phenomena is deeply ingrained in current clinical practice. For instance, psychiatrists who subscribe to psychosocial schools and, therefore, search for stressful life events or intrapsychic conflicts preceding the onset of the depressive mood, may show a distinct preference for the diagnosis of adjustment disorder with mixed emotional features rather than melancholic and bipolar disorders. It has been stated that the decline in the diagnosis of manic-depressive illness in the United States is accounted to a large degree by a proportional overdiagnosis of the schizophrenias. To the extent psychosocial schools have numerically dominated US psychiatry, the decline in manic-depressive diagnoses may have in part resulted from a preference for the diagnosis of "psychodynamically understandable" depressions, such as "neurotic depression." In a recently completed 3- to 4-year follow-up study[51] of "neurotic depression," we discovered that 22% of patients, so labeled, satisfied the criteria of recurrent (unipolar) depressions, while another 14% were suffering from manic-depressive illness, bipolar type II, ie, a course of illness characterized by depressive attacks and periods of hypomania, rather than clearly defined manic episodes. The more accurate diagnosis was missed because personality labels, such as "histrionic," "narcissistic," "emotionally unstable," and "passive-aggressive" were advanced in "explaining" the unstable mood and the "acting out" behavior of these "orally fixated neurotics." In the bipolar group, transient hypomanic symptomatology was in many instances interpreted as "flight into health" or attributed to the "activating" side effect of tricyclic medication; this fact alone should have provided a clue to the correct diagnosis, in view of reports of induction of hypomania by tricyclics and sympathomimetics in bipolar depressives.[52,53] It is of interest in this regard that in a longitudinal follow-up study by Small et al,[54] "passive-aggressive personality" occupied a position midway between alcoholism and affective illness. Welner and coworkers[55] have verified the pitfalls involved in utilizing loosely defined "character diagnoses" in that some 75% of patients, so-labeled, were shown to suffer from a major psychiatric disorder, such as unipolar and bipolar affective illness, hysteria, schizophrenia, and anxiety disorders. Thus, diagnostic concepts based on psychodynamic theorizing have added nothing but confusion as far as the nosology of depressive disorders is concerned.

In summary, the ideal approach to the diagnosis of depressive disorders should distinguish descriptive or observational criteria from inferred psychological processes based on one theory or another.

Studies designed to assess the etiological and nosological significance of psychosocial stress in primary depressive illness have generated three viewpoints:

1. The association between stress and primary depressive illness is coincidental.[56-58] Stress may precipitate hospitalization, rather than the depressive episode.

2. Primary depressive illness produces stress.[59] Individuals predisposed to affective illness display abnormal reactivity to normative stresses; hence, the so-called precipitating stressful events actually represent the prodromal manifestations of the illness. For instance, a man who ascribes his depression to having lost his job may have in reality lost his job as a result of his depressive illness.

3. Stress does play a role in precipitating the depressive illness,[60-63] usually in individuals who are genetically or developmentally predisposed to such illness.

It is interesting, however, that much of current research employing sophisticated statistical computations has verified the findings of Sir Aubrey Lewis[60] published some 40 years ago. A study by Leff et al,[61] for instance, failed to find any significant differences in the frequency and kinds of stresses that preceded "reactive" and "endogenous" depressions. Instead of limiting the search for stressful events to the initial phase of hospitalization (when "reactive" and "endogenous" labels had been applied), these investigators obtained careful history for psychosocial antecedents during the recovery phase of the illness. The rationale for such retrospective anamnesis was that many patients in the acute phase of their illness were too sick to fully appraise the psychosocial context within which their illness manifested itself and, therefore, would not have verbalized stressful events. Paykel et al[62] have reported similar findings. Finally, a study by Thomson and Hendrie[63] extended earlier findings by Kendell and Gourlay[64] in that they failed to verify three major predictions derived from the hypothesis that psychosocial stress provides a sufficient criterion for subdividing depressive disorders into reactive and endogenous groups. In other words, these investigators could not demonstrate: (1) a bimodal distribution of stress scores in a depressed population; (2) an inverse relationship between stress and positive family history of depressive illness; and (3) greater stress scores in patients labeled "reactive depression." The taxonomic criteria of depressive disorders, then, should preferably be free from any consideration of precipitating stress.

The endogenous-reactive subdivision of depressive illness is the expression of a dualistic and reductionistic philosophy for which the mind-body dichotomy is central. It hinges on the belief that certain events in the universe are "psychological," ie determined by psychological causes, while others are "physical" and enjoy relative freedom from psychic influences. Many authorities, notably Graham[43] and Lipowski,[65] have pointed out the clinical impasses that have resulted from such semantic misconceptions. Suffice it to mention in this context that depressive phenomena are neither inherently psychological (reactive) nor organic (endogenous). Like other emotional states, they should be defined at psychological (verbal-cognitive-experiential), somatic (physiological-biochemical), and psychomotor (motor-behavioral) levels. As the final common pathway of various processes that impinge on the functioning of the organism, melancholia can be described in many frames of reference, both psychological and biological, and at multiple levels of sophistication.[4,44] One of the major challenges for modern psychiatry is to build conceptual bridges between these various frames of reference.

In Great Britain the terms "reactive" and "endogenous" are used in a broader sense to refer to certain clinical features and not necessarily to the presence or absence of precipitating stress.[59] Indeed, there is considerable evidence that the endogenous-reactive dichotomy subdivides depressive disorders into prognostically and therapeutically meaningful classes.[66-68] Those who fall into the endogenous group, for instance, show good response to somatic therapies and generally have favorable outcome. However, because of the reasons given in the preceding paragraph, it is best to avoid these designations. The melancholic phase of primary depression largely overlaps with the endogenous clinical picture, while secondary depression probably includes many of the cases that are now officially labeled "dysthymic" and "neurotic." Alternatively, a certain percentage of what is subsumed under the rubric of "dysthymic disorder" represents cases of primary affective illness that have not attained melancholic proportions.[50]

TOWARD A GENETIC TAXONOMY OF DEPRESSIVE PHENOMENA

If psychosocial stress, psychodynamic criteria, and "neurotic" and "psychotic" labels fall short in providing satisfactory criteria for classifying affective illness, then how does one go about classifying the heterogeneous population of depressed individuals?

The first major advance in the nosology of primary affective illness came from family studies, such as those conducted by Leonhard,[69] Angst,[70] Perris,[71] and Winokur's group.[72] It was observed that families with mania had high familial loading for affective illness in two consecutive generations, while families without mania had low genetic loading for depression with a lower incidence of two-generation positive history. This suggested that the former condition, labeled bipolar affective illness, was a dominant trait; while the latter, unipolar affective illness, could not be so characterized. Current genetic studies suggest that bipolar illness can be transmitted as either X-linked dominant[72-74] or autosomal dominant.[75] There is less uniformity of opinion on unipolar illness, though some studies favor polygenic inheritance.[76,77] The importance of the bipolar-unipolar dichotomy lies in the fact that epidemiological,[78,79] clinical,[80,81] biochemical,[82-84] neurophysiological,[85,86] and pharmacological[52,53-87,88] studies have substantiated its validity and utility. Some of these differences are summarized in Table 3.

The exact mode of genetic transmission in primary affective illness will not be elucidated until further meaningful subdivision of the heterogeneous group of the bipolar and unipolar depressions is achieved. For instance, recent studies by Taylor and Abrams[89,90] suggest that bipolar illness might comprise two species of illness, early onset bipolar illness with typical bipolar course and late onset bipolar illness characterized by predominance of manic attacks. Fieve[91] proposes subdividing bipolar and unipolar depressions into six groups on the basis of positive or negative family history of depression and mania. This approach is promising inasmuch as bipolar illness with positive family history for mania—as compared with bipolar affective illness with negative family history for affective illness—has been shown to run a severe course with higher rates of suicide and to predict good response to lithium carbonate.[92,93] Much current research, such as that of Paykel et al,[94,95] Winokur et al,[96] Overall et al,[97] and Roth et al[98] is directed at additional attempts to subclassify unipolar depression on the basis of phenomenological, epidemiological, and pharmacological criteria. Such efforts would hopefully subdivide unipolar depressions into subgroupings that would aid the clinician in his approach to the largest group of depressed patients. Winokur et al,[96] for instance, have presented data that favor the classification of unipolar depressions into two groups: (1) pure depressive disease, where the proband is a middle-aged man with positive family history of depression in first degree relatives of both sexes; and (2) depression spectrum disease, where the proband is a young women with depression in female and alcoholism and sociopathy in male first-degree relatives. It would appear that under some yet undefined circumstances the unipolar depressive genotype may manifest itself in nondepressive phenotypes.

PHARMACOGENETICS AS A DIAGNOSTIC TOOL

Robins and Guze[99] have described five phases for the validation of psychiatric diagnoses. In addi-

tion to careful clinical descriptions and delimitation from contiguous syndromes (utilizing laboratory data when applicable), these investigators have emphasized the importance of family history and prognosis. Fieve and his group at the New York Psychiatric Institute seem to deemphasize the clinical picture in favor of family history and pharmacological response.[91–93] Schizophreniform symptomatology has been described in patients who are responsive to lithium carbonate and have a longitudinal course consistent with affective illness.[100–102] Ollerenshaw contends that if one utilizes pharmacological and prognostic criteria, "much of what is currently classed as acute schizophrenia is really manic-depressive psychosis."[102(p528)] Mendelewicz et al[93] have demonstrated positive family history for bipolar affective illness to be a reliable predictor of lithium

TABLE 3. Differential Characteristics of Bipolar, Unipolar, and Secondary Depressions

	Clinical Features 80,81	Family History 69–72,96*	Follow-up 78,79	Biochemistry 82–84†	Neuro-physiology 85,86	Pharmacology 53,87,88,107
Bipolar	Retarded in psycho-motor activity; postpartum episodes	+ Mania + Depression + Suicide + Alcoholism + 2-generation affective illness	>3 episodes per lifetime; episode lasts 3–6 mo	Subnormal steroid output; low platelet MAO activity	"Augmenter" on evoked potentials	Lithium carbonate-responsive; may switch to hypomania with tricyclics
Unipolar	Agitated (sometimes retarded) in psycho-motor activity	− Mania + Depression, sociopathy & alcoholism in early onset (<40 yr) + Depression in late onset (>40 yr)	Fewer episodes per lifetime; episode lasts 6–9 mo	Above normal steroid output; normal platelet MAO activity	"Reducer" on evoked potentials	Less likely to respond to lithium carbonate; tricyclic responsive
"Atypical depressions" and "Hysteroid dysphorias"	Depressive features super-imposed on nonaffective psychiatric symptom-atology	Variable	Usually intermittent or chronic	(No data available)	(No data available)	May respond to MAO inhibitor

*Positive history is indicated by plus sign, negative history by minus sign.

*For new developments since this review was written, see Mendels J and Amsterdam JD (eds): *The Psychobiology of Affective Disorders*, S. Karger, Basel, 1980.

carbonate-responsiveness. Pare and others[103] have described tricyclic-responsive families and mono-amine oxidase (MAO) inhibitor responsive families. The MAO inhibitor-responsive[104,105] group includes patients classified by other investigators as "atypical depressions"[105] and "hysteroid dysphorias,"[106] and would largely belong in the secondary depression category. A recent controlled study by Robinson et al[107] supported earlier claims by British psychiatrists, notably Sargant,[105] that the MAO inhibitors are superior to the tricyclics in this subgroup of depressed patients.

Table 3 lists clinically relevant research contributions that support the classification of affective disorders into bipolar, unipolar, and secondary categories. The classification is more refined than current official nosological schemes inasmuch as it takes into consideration differences in family history, prognosis, biochemistry, neurophysiology, and response to pharmacotherapy.

The clinical implications of such a perspective are far reaching. At a pragmatic level, the precipitation of hypomanic symptoms during the course of tricyclic therapy in a depressed patient would lend support for a bipolar diagnosis and would perhaps suggest the wisdom of adding lithium carbonate to the therapeutic regimen. Also, most cases of schizoaffective disorder appear to be variants of bipolar affective illness inasmuch as the family history and prognosis overlap with that of manic-depressive illness.[102,108] Therefore, one would expect schizoaffective illness to be lithium carbonate-responsive. Prien et al[109] found lithium carbonate effective in "mildly active" schizoaffectives and ineffective in "severe" cases. The *DSM-II* criteria for schizoaffective illness, however, were ill-defined, and it quite likely that Prien et al were dealing with a diagnostically heterogeneous population.

Lithium carbonate therapy has generated many intriguing questions. The entire concept of manic-depressive illness needs careful reevaluation. For instance, individuals with "emotionally unstable character disorder" have been reported to stabilize with lithium carbonate.[110] It is not unusual for the clinician to be faced with the problem of assigning a diagnosis for patients with "schizophreniform" clinical features and who, on therapeutic trial with lithium carbonate, respond as well as manic-depressives do. Johnson and co-workers and Shopsin and Gershon[111,112] have reported lithium carbonate to be neurotoxic in schizophrenic patients; confusional states, delirium, and accentuation of psychotic symptoms occur as common side effects. Based on findings

such as these, one should preferably separate lithium carbonate-responsive psychoses from the group of the schizophrenias. Whether or not one subscribes to the hypothesis that lithium carbonate is disease-specific for bipolar affective illness, there is little rationale for classifying lithium carbonate-responsive psychotic conditions, even when they have "schizophreniform" features, with the schizophrenias. Indeed, the recent trend in the research literature is to subsume these psychoses under manic-depressive illness.[91,100-102] Thus, pharmacological criteria may ultimately prove to be quite important and sensitive discriminators, as much so as standard clinical criteria, in the classification of psychotic disorders. The idea that genetic factors determine such differential responses to pharmacotherapy may revolutionize psychiatric practice.

DEPRESSIVE ILLNESS AS A PSYCHOBIOLOGICAL FINAL COMMON PATHWAY

Although genetic and pharmacological factors are becoming increasingly important in differentiating among the heterogeneous group of depressive disorders, the defining characteristics of the depressive syndrome are still largely phenomenological and provide the common denominator for the different subgroups of depressive disorders. Depressive illness, as a final common pathway, is the culmination of various processes that conceivably converge in those areas of the diencephalon that modulate arousal, mood, motivation, and psychomotor function. The specific form that the syndrome will take in a given individual depends on the interaction of several factors.

1. **Genetic Vulnerability:** the importance of which has been conclusively demonstrated in bipolar illness and recurrent unipolar depressions.[69-77]

2. **Developmental Events:** eg, early object loss, which may sensitize the organism to the pathoplastic influence of certain kinds of psychosocial events in adult life.

3. **Psychosocial Events:** events in adult life that overwhelm the coping mechanisms of the organism.

4. **Physiological Stressors**[59]**:** stressors such as reserpine, viral infections, childbirth, and hypothyroidism, which impinge on diencephalic function.

5. **Personality Traits:** traits that determine or modify the reactivity of the organism to stress, including the stress of being depressed. The hys-

terical individual, for instance, may exploit depressive symptomatology in order to obtain interpersonal favors; hence, the dramatic, attention-seeking suicidal gestures. The obsessive-compulsive, on the other hand, will be too threatened by impending decompensation and will consequently experience additional turmoil, hopelessness, and lowering self-esteem.

The interaction of such diverse factors is expected to result in a variety of biochemical alterations in the CNS. One can conceive that several biochemical species of depression exist, as originally proposed by Schildkraut.[24] No wonder then that catecholamines,[24,25] indoleamines,[26,27] false neurotransmitters,[113] and sodium metabolism[26,28] have all been incriminated in the biochemical etiology of these disorders. A diencephalic final common pathway (to be elaborated in the final section of this article) may provide a neurophysiological system where different biochemical events converge and account for the common features shared by the heterogeneous group of depressive disorders.

The ten models of depression are attempts, from different disciplinary perspectives, to delineate the mechanisms by which this psychobiological final common pathway is reached.

FROM RETROFLEXED ANGER TO LOWERED SELF-ESTEEM

The Abraham-Freud Formulation

The Abraham-Freud model[11,12] views depression as the inward turning of the aggressive instinct that, for some reason, is not directed at the appropriate object. The retroflexion of hostility is triggered by the loss of an ambivalently loved object. Formulated in the days of id psychology, the model disregarded the consequences of object loss on the ego, and instead focused on the retroflexion of thanatotic energy. The model is phrased in metapsychological terms and does not lend itself easily to empirical verification. Even though this is the most widely quoted psychological conceptualization of depression, there is little systematic evidence to substantiate it.

Epidemiological data have demonstrated an inverse relationship between suicide and homicide.[114,115] To the extent these two events measure "anger-in" and "anger-out," respectively, such data are grossly compatible with the "aggression-turned-inward" model. In a clinical study, depressed patients were found to have less

outwardly expressed anger as compared with normal volunteers.[116] However, redirection of hostility at outside objects has not been correlated with clinical improvement[117]; it may actually have disastrous consequences.[50] It has been suggested that the direction of hostility at intimate objects rather than at casual acquaintances is consistent with the ambivalence, which according to psychoanalytic investigators, plays a key role in the pathogenesis of depression.[118] On the other hand, several investigators have identified a subgroup of "hostile depressives," characterized by the concomitant presence of depression and outwardly expressed anger.[94,97,119] A study by Weissman and coworkers[120] on the relationship between hostility, suicide, and depression concluded that the coexistence of hostility and depression in the same patient favors the view that aggression and depression are separate affects and sheds considerable doubt on the universality of the aggression-turned-inward model as an explanatory hypothesis for depression.

Mallerstein[33] notes that the Abraham-Freud formulation views depression as a derivative of dammed-up aggression, much as dammed-up libido was considered to be the origin of anxiety in Freud's early writings. This style of conceptualizing affects as derivatives of instincts is characteristic of the days of id psychology, when the "hydraulic model" of the mind was fashionable. While the "sexual frustration" hypothesis of anxiety has been abandoned, the same style of conceptualizing depression has survived.

Bibring's Model

Ego-psychological reformulations of the original psychoanalytical model have paid greater attention to object loss and its consequences on the ego. Bibring's model,[16] the first major conceptual break with the id-psychological approach to depression, views depression as an ego state, an affect independent from the vicissitudes of the aggressive drive. Much recent empirical work has supported this position. Helplessness is the focal point in Bibring's model. Depression supervenes when the ego is cognizant of its goal and simultaneously aware of its helplessness to attain it. The ego suffers a narcissistic injury and collapse in self-esteem. Depression, in other words, appears when one cannot live up to one's ego ideals—the wish to be worthy and to be loved, the striving to be secure, strong and superior, the aspiration to be good, kind, loving, and humane. In this model, hostility is an inconstant, secondary phenomenon unleashed by object losses or objects that prevent the attainment of cherished aspirations.

Existential and Sociological Ramifications

To define depression as an ego phenomenon, according to Becker,[23] is to define it as a social phenomenon. The ego, unlike the id, is rooted in social reality, and the ego ideal is composed of socially learned symbols and motives. A breakdown of self-esteem may involve, in addition to object losses, man's symbolic possessions, such as power, status, roles, identity, values, and purpose for existence. Depression may easily befall the overintegrated, the conventional, the individual with upward social mobility, and women who strongly identify with the role prescribed to them by their culture.[22] Thus one can see the broad existential, sociological, and political implications of Bibring's concept of depression.

COGNITIVE AND BEHAVIORAL MODELS

Beck's Model

Beck's model[17] of depression carries the ego-psychological approach to its fullest implications. An altered style of cognition, characterized by negative expectations, is said to be the basis of depressive mood states. According to this viewpoint, hopelessness and helplessness represent the central features of human depression and reflect a peculiar "cognitive triad" of negative conception of the self, negative interpretations of one's experiences, and a negative view of the future. The depressed individual finds the world presenting insuperable obstacles to carrying out his goals, views himself helpless to surmount these obstacles, and has given up any hope of exercising future control over his destiny.

This cognitive approach to depression is interesting from several perspectives. It represents a radical departure from psychodynamic theories of affective disorders in that it emphasizes the role that disturbances in thinking play in determining emotional states.[121] It succinctly identifies the central feature of depression inasmuch as empirical studies have demonstrated hopelessness to be the best correlate of the depth of melancholia and suicide.[122] It provides the rationale for a unique psychotherapeutic approach to depression. The focus is on altering the negative cognitive set with the expectation that the remaining symptoms and behaviors characteristic of depression will be eliminated. This method of psychotherapy, which

bears some resemblance to Ellis' rational-emotive-therapy,[123] could conceivably fortify the individual against future attacks. Whereas it would be impossible to create animal analogues for metapsychological models, such as retroflexed anger and lowered self-esteem, Beck's model lends itself to experimental verification at the animal level.

Learned Helplessness: An Animal Model of Depression

Seligman and his co-workers[124-127] at the University of Pennsylvania, while testing a particular learning theory that involved administering inescapable electric shock to dogs, accidentally discovered a phenomenon they have termed "learned helplessness." This interesting behavioral condition provides many parallels to human depressions.[18] The experimental paradigm consists of two phases. During the first phase, the animal undergoes repeated noxious stimulation and at the same time it is prevented from engaging in any activities that would bring relief from such stimulation. For instance, a dog is subjected to electrical shock while strapped in a pavlovian harness so that no response on its part can terminate the shock. During the second phase, the animal is unharnessed when exposed to the noxious stimulus, thereby providing it with the opportunity of evading the noxious stimulus. Normally, an unharnessed dog that has not previously experienced inescapable shock would immediately jump the barrier that separates the electrified grid from the nonelectrified section of the shuttlebox. The remarkable finding in the studies of Seligman et al is that exposure to multiple sessions of inescapable aversive stimuli (phase I) impairs the animal's adaptive responding in future situations where an escape from aversive stimuli is readily available (phase II). While in the shuttlebox, the dog seems to "give up" inasmuch as it passively accepts the highly traumatic shock experience. Learned helplessness can be lysed by forcibly dragging the animal to the nonelectrified section of the shuttlebox, ie, by compelling the animal to respond in such a way as to obtain reinforcement through its own actions.

It can be hypothesized that when one is confronted with aversive stimuli, adaptive behavior depends on the expectation that one's own responses would provide relief from such stimulation.[18] Learned helplessness, on the other hand, describes a behavioral state characterized by the nonemission of adaptive behaviors, because one recognizes no relationship between one's responses and relief from aversive events. The similarities between learned helplessness and depression as described by Beck are striking, including the therapeutic prescriptions. Furthermore, learned helplessness is not only a stimulus-specific behavioral state, but may well represent a personality trait, the expectation that one's efforts are generally futile. Seligman[18] suggests that the depression-prone individual has a life-long history characterized by relative failure in exercising control over the reinforcers in his environment and that depression supervenes whenever the individual perceives himself losing all control over such reinforcers and is paralyzed by helplessness, passivity, and inability to assert himself. This lack of aggression (which Freud assumed to have been retroflexed from the frustrating love object), seen in many depressives, may well be a symptom derived from pervasive feelings of helplessness and powerlessness. Notice that Seligman's behavioral model encompasses the cognitive, sociological, and existential models of depression.

Clinical Behavioral Approaches

A review of the clinical literature on behavioral approaches to depression discloses a paucity of well-controlled studies. A more serious methodological flaw is the failure to distinguish between unhappiness ("depression") and clinical depression ("melancholia.") Some investigators utilize a classical conditioning paradigm,[19,128] while others emphasize operant conditioning.[32,129] In many of these writings, however, the distinction between the two is blurred.

Wolpe[128] postulates that chronic frustration in one's personal or professional life results in chronic anxiety with the outcome that the individual cannot achieve anxiety-reduction with his usual behavioral repertoire. A maladaptive depressive syndrome develops characterized by passivity and hopelessness, very much like Seligman's dogs. Both Wolpe[128] and Lazarus[20] believe that systematic desensitization of such anxiety, or assertive training to countercondition it—especially if the anxiety results from failure in controlling interpersonal relationships—are useful in treating mild depressions. In another therapeutic strategy prescribed by Lazarus,[20] the patient is instructed to actively fantasize that he is in the future and has overcome the noxious event. Thus, the patient is provided with some freedom from his depressive inertia to engage in some formerly enjoyable activity. In effect, the patient's negative cognitive set is altered so that he becomes susceptible to substitute reinforcement.

Lewinsohn et al[21,130-132] seem to be in agreement with Seligman[18] when they postulate a low rate of response-contingent positive reinforcement to be the historical antecedent of depressive behaviors. For instance, the retired exadministrator who receives his retirement check is not receiving response-contingent reinforcement and is, therefore, at high risk for depressive illness. Two sets of variables should be considered here. The environment may repeatedly fail in providing reinforcement, placing the individual on a prolonged extinction schedule. Or, more importantly, the individual may fail to emit the appropriate responses to potentially reinforcing stimuli. At the therapeutic end, positive reinforcement is provided for emitting active behaviors that substitute for the lost source of reinforcement, coupled with selective inattention to depressive behaviors, leading to their extinction.

Some clinicians have focused on the rewards of the "sick role" in maintaining depressive behaviors.[32,129,133] It is true that some depressed patients manipulate their interpersonal environment for attention and sympathy. Such operant conditioning is expected to maintain the depressive symptomatology or favor its future recurrence when interpersonal rewards are desired. This subgroup of depressed patients received a classical description by Lazare and Klerman.[119] They observed that the histrionic behavior and aggressive manipulation of the environment, so characteristic of this subgroup of female depressives, made them appear less depressed in comparison with other depressed patients. This characterological propensity to exploit the sick role for obtaining interpersonal favors is appropriately labeled "hysteroid dysphoria" by Klein and Davis.[106] They also remark that the manipulative behavior seen in this subgroup of patients has unfortunately led some clinicians into elevating coercive manipulation to etiological status in all depressive disorders. It should be abundantly clear from the foregoing presentation of the behavioral literature that the major defining feature of melancholia lies in the patient's inability to derive gratification or reinforcement from the environment, ie, anhedonia. The exploitation of the sick role is, at best, a meager and sometimes a desperate attempt to substitute for more basic kinds of reinforcement and represents the special coloring that certain personality structures, such as the hysterical, impart to the more typical depressive symptomatology.

In summary, then, there is clinical evidence that a variety of behavioral techniques can ameliorate the course of depressive states. One major advantage of the behavioral formulations of depression over psychodynamic formulations is that the former can be effectively operationalized for experimental verification as well as for psychotherapeutic purposes. But both Wolpe[128] and Lazarus[20] remark that the behavioral approaches are effective in mild depressions of "neurotic" proportion and that more severe depressions usually require antidepressants or ECT. It would appear that no matter what interpersonal factors mobilize depressive behaviors, once the latter reach the melancholic phase, they become biologically autonomous and become relatively refractory to psychotherapeutic intervention. Also, the inability of the depressive to derive gratification (reinforcement) from the environment suggests some kind of disorder in the biological substrates of reinforcement.[30] It is of interest, in this regard, that chronic aversive stimulation beyond the coping ability of an animal does lead to serious biological dysfunction. For instance, rats exposed to inescapable aversive stimuli—unlike rats exposed to aversive stimuli that they can terminate by bar pressing—suffer anorexia, weight loss, and central norepinephrine depletion.[134]

SEPARATION AND DEPRESSION

In id psychology, the focus is on the hostility unleashed by object loss. The behavioral schools emphasize the helplessness derived from loss of control over reinforcement. Experimental psychologists, notably the Harlows,[135,136] have demonstrated the vital role of attachment behavior as a primary reinforcer. There is abundant evidence that the disruption of a significant attachment bond may well represent the most traumatic kind of withdrawal of reinforcement in primate species, including man. Therefore, it is not surprising that theorists of depression have paid great attention to the possible depressionogenic effects of separation events that disrupt interpersonal attachment bonds. The reader is referred to Ainsworth's extensive review of the subject,[137] to Bowlby's two volumes on attachment and loss,[138,139] and to the work of the Robertsons.[140]

In psychoanalytical language, object loss generally refers to traumatic separation from significant objects of attachment. Since the meaning of a loss is a matter of subjective interpretation, it is frequently stated that, in fantasy, trivial losses or separations may actually function as real ones. In the present section, where we shall consider the empirical literature on object loss and depression, object loss and separation will be used interchangeably in the former sense.

That separation from a loved object, especially from an ambivalently loved one, could have depressionogenic consequences was first emphasized by Freud in "Mourning and melancholia."[12] Since then, many papers and monographs have dealt with the proposed relationship between object loss and depression. In this section, we shall selectively focus on overall trends, controversies, and methodological issues in the separation literature that are of direct relevance to clinical psychiatry, and briefly consider the separation studies in nonhuman primates that have provided one kind of animal model for human depression.

The hypotheses that propose a causal relationship between object loss and depression have considered two interrelated issues: (1) separation in adult life as a proximate precipitating stress for depression; and (2) bereavement during childhood, or other kinds of early object losses, as predisposing factors for the occurrence of adult depressions. Many of the studies designed to test these hypotheses have suffered from serious methodological flaws. Psychoanalytical data have largely been of an anecdotal nature; while both psychoanalytical and epidemiological studies have, in general, shared the disadvantage of being retrospective.

Separation as a Precipitating Stress

In spite of the foregoing limitations in methodology, many studies have concluded that a depressed population, however defined, has an increased frequency of separation or "exit type" events[62] surrounding the onset of depression, and that separation events are among the most common stressful events associated with depressive illness.[61-63] However, other studies have failed to demonstrate such an association between separation and depression.[56-58] Even if one assumes the statistical relationship between recent separation and depression to be reliable, the causal relationship is open to different interpretations. Separation may precipitate the depressive episode, but it is equally possible that a depressed individual may engage in behaviors that would have the net effect of alienating those close to him, thereby leading to what would be experienced as object loss.[56,59] Studies in which data are obtained from relatives in part circumvent this problem, thus controlling for the experiential distortions of the clinically depressed individual.

A different approach to the study of separation and depression involves a prospective follow-up of a nonpsychiatric population that has suffered a recent object loss to examine whether or not it represents a high risk group for depressive illness. Clayton et al[141] followed up 109 recently bereaved individuals with systematic interviews and found that, within one month from bereavement, 35% had developed symptoms similar to those seen in patients with primary depressive illness. It is of interest, however, that the depression of widowhood was a self-limited condition that, on the average, lasted two to three months and did not persist unless the widowed individual had no substitute objects of association or attachment in the form of close family ties and friends. It would appear that the depressionogenic potential of separation depends, to some extent, on the nonavailability of substitute forms of interpersonal reinforcement.

Another approach to this problem is a study by Parkes[142,143] whose patient population consisted of 3,245 psychiatric inpatients with the entire gamut of psychiatric diagnoses. He found that patients who had the onset of symptoms within six months of the death of a parent, spouse, sibling, or a child were at high risk for affective illness only. But apparently separation is not specific for depression. Schmale,[144,145] for instance, reported a high incidence of separation events preceding the onset of medical illnesses.

The separation data thus far reviewed, then, warrant the following tentative conclusions: (1) separation events figure prominently among the possible precipitating stresses of depressive illness; (2) they are probably not specific for depressive illness; (3) separation is not a sufficient cause of depression, because many individuals who have apparently suffered it do not develop a depressive illness; (4) nor is separation a necessary antecedent of depression, since many depressed individuals have not experienced it; and (5) finally, separation may result from the depressive illness.

Childhood Bereavement and Adult Depression

The role of object loss during childhood as a sensitizing or predisposing event for the development of depression in adult life is a complex topic but one of great clinical significance.[146] Although

Freud[12] noted the relationship between object loss and depression, he did not specifically relate adult depression to childhood bereavement. Abraham[147] believed that children who had suffered certain kinds of trauma or losses were subject to "primal parathymia," which made them vulnerable to melancholia later in life.

Rene Spitz[13] in 1945 reported a deprivational reaction in human infants separated from their mothers in the second half of the first year of life. The condition was characterized by apprehension, crying, withdrawal, psychomotor slowing, dejection, stupor, insomnia, anorexia, weight loss, and gross retardation in growth and development. It has been questioned whether the essential ingredient of the syndrome, known as "anaclitic depression," is separation or the adverse effects of institutionalization in an orphanage. A similar reaction to separation from the mother was described in somewhat older children by Robertson and Bowlby.[14,15] The syndrome was triphasic; a "protest" stage during which the child appeared restless and tearful, apparently in search for the mother; a "despair" stage with apathetic withdrawal; and a final "detachment" phase seen only in some children and characterized by rejection of the mother on reunion. Recent work by the Robertsons,[140] however, casts doubt on the universality of these responses and suggests that appropriate substitute mothering during the separation period can greatly attenuate the behavioral responses described.

The relationship of early deprivation, such as those described by Spitz and Bowlby, and other "subclinical" forms of anaclitic depression, to adult depression has been the subject of numerous studies. Gregory,[148-150] Bowlby,[138,139] and Granville-Grossman[151] have dealt with the systematic and unsystematic errors that have characterized many of the investigations in this area. One of the most widely quoted studies—and in many ways representative of their retrospective study method—is that of Brown[152] who reported on 216 patients with depressive disorders as compared with two groups of controls derived from medical inpatients and the British orphanhood census. He found an increased incidence of 41% of childhood bereavement—loss of a parent by death—before the age of 15 years in the depressive patients in comparison to the figures of 16% and 12%, respectively, for the control groups. He noted that the loss of the mother was significant in each of the five-year periods of childhood (0 to 4, 5 to 9, and 10 to 14), whereas the loss of the father was more significant in later childhood (5 to 9 and 10 to 14).

Other authors have attempted to relate different forms of childhood bereavement to adult depression and other kinds of adult psychiatric disorders.[153-166] The results of such investigative efforts have often been conflicting and difficult to compare because of differences in methodology. Reliable trends are difficult to detect. Heinicke[167] recently surveyed the literature in this area. Some authorities suggest that the loss of the father from ages 10 to 14 years is the critical predisposing variable for adult depression; the age period 0 to 4 years being considered the critical age period for sociopathy. From a research standpoint, the causal connection between early object loss and adult depression can be considered unproved. Indeed, some researchers indicate a lack of association between the two,[168,169] while others have even speculated about the possible beneficial or "immunizing" effects of having successfully coped with a loss early during development."[170] Unfortunately, meticulous research strategy[171] has been the exception in this area, in contrast to its wide use in psychobiological research on depression.

Separation in Primates

The importance of separation as a stressful event capable of inducing dramatic behavioral changes has also been investigated in nonhuman primates. The elegance of such models lies in the fact that one can control for other variables, so that separation can be studied as an independent variable. In general, by separating a rhesus infant from its mother, one can replicate a biphasic protest-despair reaction very similar to that described by Robertson and Bowlby.[172-179] Of course, this can be done at certain ages only, ie, after the infant-mother bond has had sufficient time to develop but before the infant has emancipated itself from the mother. Many other variables influence the nature of the separation response and the investigation of these factors may offer valuable clues to our understanding of the basic mechanisms underlying reactions to separation.[180-183] One such factor is the nature of the preseparation mother-infant relationship; the more an infant has been off the mother, the less clinging it does on reunion.[180] Another variable is whether or not the infant has visual access to the mother during the separation period, visual contact apparently contributing to the intensity of the despair phase. Finally, the ready availability of substitute mothering, eg, in Bonnett macaques who freely share their infants among themselves, substantially attenuates the infant's response to separation.[177]

Separation of peers from one another can also produce behavioral reactions similar to infant-mother separation. Here again, the age at separation is critical. For example, peer-peer separation under 1 year of age induces the typical biphasic protest-despair reaction as described above[182]; whereas juvenile-aged rhesus monkeys (3 to 4 years old) exhibit a uniphasic protest or hyperactive reaction only, which persists throughout the period of separation.[183,184]

The behavior of rhesus infants that have undergone traumatic separation, whether from mother or peers, bears striking resemblance to that described for human infants experiencing anaclitic depression. Such similarity in the two syndromes, the fact that monkeys establish strong social interactional bonds, and the proximity of humans to monkeys on an evolutionary scale provide the justification for cross-species generalizations. The monkey model of object loss depression may offer important clues to unresolved clinical problems. For instance, the occurrence, on separation from peers, of a "despair-like" phase in monkeys 3 to 4 years old with a history of traumatic separation during infancy, suggests that the experience of traumatic events during early life may predispose to adult psychopathology.[185]

THE "PHARMACOLOGICAL BRIDGE"

Models of depression thus far reviewed conceptualize depressive disorders in intrapsychic, interpersonal, and behavioral terms. The central theme in these formulations is a peculiar alteration in one's self-perceptions, whereby one gives up hope in controlling environmental reinforcers. Such negative self-cognitions have, as their behavioral counterpart, an impaired motivation in obtaining consummatory reward from interpersonal feedback. Whatever the nature of the stressful events that culminate in such states of despair, depression is accompanied by a temporary disruption in one's interpersonal, vocational, and ideologic bonds. In other words, the depressed individual suffers a diminution in his relatedness to other humans, human institutions, and the world at large. The disruption of such bonds may precede the depression and thus play a precipitant role in the causation of the depressive state, or it may result from the illness, thereby additionally maintaining the maladaptive nonrelatedness. We have already presented data strongly suggesting that the dissolution of interpersonal attachment bonds in nonhuman primates results in significant loss of reinforcement and induces a behavioral state that may be associated with helplessness and break-down of motivated behavior. Thus, primate models of separation provide a common denominator for the various conceptual frames of depression. With the expansion of our knowledge concerning the neuroanatomical and neurochemical substrates of reinforcement during the past decade, concepts derived from primatology may also help in establishing conceptual bridges with biological models of depression.

The Biological Substrates of Reinforcement

Evidence from work with animals suggests that lesions that interfere with the anatomical or chemical integrity of the reinforcement system in the diencephalon impair the ability of the organism to respond to environmental reinforcers.[186] Therefore, whatever the nature of the interpersonally defined events that mobilize depressive behaviors, their field of action would involve the diencephalic centers of reinforcement. Since the pioneering studies of Olds and Milner,[187] the literature in this area has grown rapidly. A symposium edited by Heath[188] and recent reviews by Stein,[189] Crow,[190] and Wise et al[191] have attempted to relate such work to psychiatric disorders. Much evidence from pharmacological research in animals suggests that both classes of biogenic amines—the catecholamines and the indoleamines—and acetylcholine play significant roles in modulating the function of the medial forebrain bundle (MFB) and the periventricular system (PVS), the neuroanatomical substrates of "reward" and "punishment," respectively. Pharmacological agents, such as the amphetamines, which are clinically known to increase drive, motivation, and psychomotor activity when injected through permanently implanted electrodes along the paths of the MFB, increase rewarding self-stimulation. Antidepressant drugs, eg, the tricyclics, potentiate the action of amphetamines. Administration of reserpine or alpha-methyl-para-tyrosine (AMPT), which are known to precipitate a "depression-like" syndrome in monkeys[192] with decreased initiative and psychomotor activity, diminish the action of amphetamines. In Stein's words, the MFB functions as "a behavior-facilitating or 'go' mechanism that initiates facilitatory feedback and increases the probability that the behavior will run off to completion."[193(p348)] The MFB is antagonized by the PVS, a system that generally exercises inhibitory control on on-going behavior. Stimulation along the reward pathways resembles the action of primary reinforcers in that neutral stimuli, pre-sented with such stimulation, acquire secondary reinforcing properties. Therefore, disturbances in the functional level of biogenic amines, however achieved, would disrupt the ability of the organism to respond to reinforcement and to experience pleasure and consummatory reward with resultant impairment in psychomotor functions and biological drives.

Biogenic Amines and Affective Disorders

Biological hypotheses concerning the biochemical correlates of affective disorders, enunciated in the mid 60s, were based on pharmacological inference.[24-27] A group of drugs that elevates the central level of catecholamines and indoleamines in animals was found effective in alleviating clinical depressions in man, while another class of drugs, known to decrease these neurotransmitters, precipitated depressive illness in certain individuals. It was hypothesized that these same neurotransmitters were involved in naturally occurring human depressions. The line of reasoning that links behavior to brain chemistry has been appropriately labeled the "pharmacological bridge" by Schildkraut.[194] The extensive literature on the possible role of biogenic amines in the pathogenesis of depressive illness has been summarized in several scholarly reviews.[34,35,194-196] We shall try to relate the research efforts in this area to clinical and philosophical issues generated by such research.

Much of the theorizing has dealt with two major classes of neurotransmitters, the catecholamines (norepinephrine and dopamine) and the indoleamines (largely serotonin). Their metabolism is presented in Fig 1. The pharmacological evidence that implicated biogenic amines in depression failed to favor one class over the other. For instance, reserpine, which precipitates depression in 15% to 20% of hypertensive subjects, depletes the brain of dopamine and norepinephrine, as well as serotonin.[197]

Two major research strategies have been employed to test the catecholamine (specifically the norepinephrine) vs the indoleamine (specifically the serotonin) hypothesis. One approach, the precursor loading technique, consists of selective administration of the precursor amino acids of the respective classes of biogenic amines and observation of the therapeutic response. The more direct approach consists of measuring the metabolites of these amines in the brains (postmortem) and body fluids of depressed individuals.

A recent study by Coppen et al[198] employing

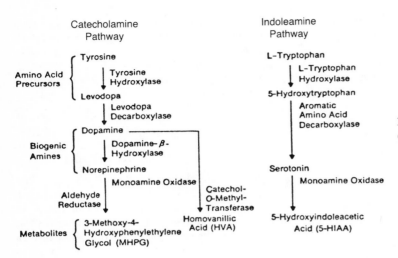

FIGURE 1. Catecholamine and indoleamine metabolic pathways.

the precursor loading strategy found the serotonin precursor L-tryptophan, with or without attempted potentiation with a MAO inhibitor, to be an effective antidepressant.[199] Despite several negative reports, accounts of which can be found in the review papers,[34,35,194-196] the amino acid is already marketed in England as an antidepressant. Prange et al[200] found L-tryptophan to be effective in mania as well, providing indirect support to the notion of a shared indoleaminergic deficiency in mania and depression. The catecholamine precursor levodopa, on the other hand, has been consistently disappointing in therapeutic trials in depression except for a small subgroup of retarded depressives.[201,202] In studies conducted at the National Institute of Mental Health (NIMH), bipolar depressives given levodopa did switch to hypomania without any significant decrease in depression.[53] As previously noted, such a switch has been observed with tricyclic antidepressants and other sympathomimetic drugs as well.[52] The clinical literature on levodopa treatment of Parkinson disease suggests that depression, hypomania, and delirium could all result from levodopa administration.[203] Such observations, according to Bunney et al[204] raise serious doubts about the role of catecholamines in depression but implicate them in the switch process from depression to mania. One major methodological problem with the precursor loading strategy is the distinct possibility that many neurochemical systems are simultaneously affected in the brain. Levodopa, for instance, in addition to raising brain catecholamine levels, lowers brain serotonin concentration.[205]

Measurement of biogenic amine metabolites in the tissues and body fluids of depressed individuals presents even more formidable methodological problems. Two studies[206,207] have reported subnormal levels of indoleamine metabolites and normal levels of norepinephrine metabolites in the hindbrain of depressive suicides, thereby strengthening the indoleamine hypothesis. But how reliably do postmortem neurochemical findings reflect antemortem conditions? Also, the presuicide clinical state is uncertain, since suicide may result from a variety of disorders. Studies[208-211] reporting a lowered level of the serotonin metabolite 5-hydroxyindoleacetic acid (5-HIAA) in the lumbar cerebrospinal fluid (CSF) of depressed patients, manic patients, and recovered depressed patients have been criticized on the ground that peripheral (gastrointestinal) sources may contribute to the CSF levels of this acid. Van Praag,[84] however, employing the probenecid technique—which selectively permits the CSF accumulation of central 5-HIAA—has found support for the idea that serotonin turnover is decreased in a selected subgroup of depressives. Thus indoleaminergic deficiency seems to characterize both manic and depressive states and, at least in depression, persists with clinical recovery, suggesting a common biological denominator for the two conditions. This viewpoint is additionally strengthened by the previously noted effectiveness of the serotonin precursor L-tryptophan in the two affective states. Somewhat inconsistent with this viewpoint is a report by Ashcroft et al who demonstrated subnormal 5-HIAA levels in unipolar depressives but not in bipolar depressives.[212]

Another controversy involves 3-methoxy-4-hydroxyphenylethylene glycol (MHPG). 50 to 80% of this metabolite of norepinephrine measured in the urine is believed to reflect central norepinephrine catabolism.[213,214] Maas and

TABLE 4. Biogenic Amine Hypotheses of Affective Illness Compared

Hypothesis	Predisposition	Melancholia	Mania
Catecholamine	(Unspecified)	Decrease in catecholamines	Increase in catecholamines
Indoleamine	(Unspecified)	Decrease in indoleamines	(Unspecified)
Biogenic amine permissive hypothesis	Indoleaminergic deficiency; normal level of catecholamines	Indoleaminergic deficiency; decrease in catecholamines	Indoleaminergic deficiency; increase in catecholamines
Two Disease Theory	(Unspecified)	Low indoleamines *or* low catecholamines	(Unspecified)

others[215,216] have reported low levels of the urinary level of this acid in depression, returning to normal with successful treatment with tricyclic antidepressants. Goode et al[217] have presented data to suggest that urinary levels of MHPG are independent from exercise and psychomotor activity in general. On the other hand, Post and co-workers[218,219] at NIMH have reported a correlation between MHPG and psychomotor activity. For instance, CSF levels of MHPG tended to rise to normal levels in depressed patients in "simulated mania" (induced hyperactivity). Could it be that alterations in catecholamine metabolism represent epiphenomena of depression? Consistent with this viewpoint is the lowered level of homovanillic acid (HVA), the dopamine metabolite, in the CSF of retarded depressives.[84]

In a heuristic effort to bypass these controversies, Maas[220] hypothesized the existence of two chemical species of clinical depression: a low norepinephrine and a low serotonin, depression. The permissive amine hypothesis of affective disorders developed by Prange and coworkers is another attempt to account for the current data on biogenic amines and depression (see Table 4). It states that central serotonergic deficiency may represent the vulnerability to affective illness, lowered catecholamines correlate with depression and increased catecholamines with mania. Thus, depression and mania are hypothesized to be on a continuum rather than being polar opposites, mania representing a more severe deviation from normal mood. The continuum model, originally proposed by Court,[221] is based on clinical and biological dysfunction shared by both depression and mania, with mania having the more severe dysfunction. Manics, for example, have more pronounced arousal, insomnia, anorexia, and increase in residual sodium.[28] Also the manic phase of bipolar illness is usually preceded by a short period of mild depression; similarly, recovery from mania is followed by mild depression. Finally, the coexistence of manic and depressive symptoms in rare episodes of mixed manic-depressive illness can be explained by a continuum model.

The Leap from Chemistry to Behavior

Biochemical statements that propose a causal relationship between a chemical event in the brain and a set of observable behaviors or subjective experiences present serious philosophical problems. The notion of a direct one-to-one relationship between a specific chemical event in the brain and a behavioral syndrome has been discarded in most areas of neurobiology. Smythies[222] has succinctly expressed this point:

> . . . One can be certain that all reductionist attempts to explain 'mind' in terms of brain chemistry (only), or reinforcement schedules (only), or computer logic (only), or any combinations of these, will fail. The facts of conscious experience are irreducible and must enter in their own right as basic irreducible elements, into any comprehensive account of mind.

Unfortunately, one often gains the impression that in psychiatry such reductionistic thinking lingers on. In the area of depression and affective disorders in particular, our theories concerning their physiochemical bases are in need of revision. This is not to say that the original hypotheses concerning biogenic amines and depressive disorders have not been useful. From a heuristic standpoint they have. However, with the recent influx of data from many sources, both clinical and experimental, they require modification before a kind of premature closure hinders additional advances in our scientific understanding of these disorders. We have been concerned with the creation of new conceptual schemes that incorporate recent findings, provide more sophisticated ways of integrating seemingly diverse sets of data, and stimulate new lines of inquiry. In a previous report,[30] we reviewed chemically induced "depressive" syndromes in monkeys with pharmacological agents that permit selective depletion of one class of neurotransmitters rather than another, and concluded that no one-to-one relationship could be postulated to exist between one specific class of neurotransmitters and depressive behaviors. For instance, we noted that AMPT, a selective inhibitor of catecholamine metabolism, induced a "depressive" syndrome in monkeys[192]; yet, a more permanent destruction of the central catecholaminergic system with 6-hydroxydopamine (6-OHDA), resulted only in a reversible behavioral deficit.[223] Since the publication of our work, a provocative study by Mendels and Frazer[224] appeared, emphasizing the difficulties one encounters in building "pharmacological bridges" with the biogenic amines. After a careful review of the clinical and experimental literature on parachlorphenylalanine (PCPA), the selective inhibitor of serotonin synthesis, AMPT and reserpine, these investigators concluded that depletion of brain norepinephrine, dopamine, or serotonin was not sufficient to account for the clinical phenomena of depression. They suggested that, along with the chemical changes, one should consider the genetic and constitutional background, the cognitive state of the organism (following the theory of emotions by Schacter and Singer,[225]) and the differential ability of the individual to cope with the altered physiological and psychomotor state.

Bridges are supposed to handle two-way traffic. Whereas in the psychiatric literature the focus has largely been on behavioral alterations occurring secondary to changes in biogenic amines, there is another line of research that indicates that the reverse may also be true. That is, one can selectively manipulate social variables and induce major changes in brain amines.[226–235]

Barchas and Freedman,[226] for instance, swam rats to exhaustion and found that brain serotonin levels were increased 15% and norepinephrine levels decreased 20%. The alterations in the central levels of the two amines followed different time courses; the increase in serotonin was seen immediately after the exercise was over, returning to normal levels within two hours; norepinephrine levels, on the other hand, did not return to normal for six hours. Bliss et al,[232,233] based on work in cats, have contended that "heightened emotion-

ality," whether aversive or pleasurable, results in lowering of brain norepinephrine levels. That is, self-stimulation in the so-called punishment (PVS) and reward (MFB) areas does not produce differential norepinephrine changes, even though opposite affects are evoked with stimulation in these areas. Welch and Welch[234,235] found that neurochemical reaction to stress is influenced by rearing conditions. The stress of being restrained resulted in increases in brain norepinephrine, dopamine, and serotonin levels with the increase being most pronounced in mice that had been reared in isolation as compared to group-reared mice. Most recently, separation of infant rhesus monkeys from their mothers has been found to result in an increase of the major enzymes involved in catecholamine synthesis in the adrenals and a significant increase in hypothalamic levels of serotonin, with no appreciable changes in central norepinephrine and dopamine.[236]

Clearly, the data from all these studies are difficult to reconcile at this point. Nor have we attempted to cover all the studies in this area. Nevertheless, there is sufficient empirical support developing from psychochemical work in animals to suggest that a variety of stresses, including separation, can induce changes in biogenic amines and that any comprehensive theory of depression must take into account this line of work. Theorists of depression have assumed that some underlying defect in biogenic amine metabolism was primary. We propose that such a defect, if indeed it does exist, can also be secondary to developmental and interpersonal events. Such secondary biochemical alterations, in their turn, could maintain depressive behaviors via their effects on the neurophysiological mechanisms of reinforcement.

AROUSAL AND DEPRESSION

Recent studies of patients with affective disorders, including those with severe psychomotor retardation, indicate that central hyperarousal is a prominent characteristic of both depressive and manic states. Neurophysiological studies of affective disorders were reviewed by Whybrow and Mendels.[28] They reported that the most consistently reported abnormalities include lowered thresholds of arousal, disruption of rapid eye movement (REM) sleep patterns, and disappearance of delta sleep, the deepest stage of non-REM sleep. They presented a cogent argument, largely based on data from Coppen, Shaw and coworkers[237–240] that such states of central arousal could in part result from intraneuronal sodium accumulation with consequent lowering of the resting membrane potential. Redistribution of sodium into the intracellular compartment is a well-documented pharmacological effect of alcohol in clinical and experimental populations.[241,242] Moreover, depressive symptomatology and suicidal behavior are frequently associated with alcoholic binges in these same populations.[243,244] Contrary to popular myths, alcohol, when consumed over a period of days, causes autonomic and central arousal, manifested behaviorally in autonomic hyperactivity, psychomotor agitation, and insomnia.[245,246] Many of these behavioral effects of alcohol are conceivably mediated through sodium retention in the brain. Intraneuronal sodium leakage—in states of alcoholic inebriation and, should it occur, in melancholic states—would lower the resting membrane potential and thus contribute to neuronal hyperexcitability. Psychic turmoil, agitation and disruption of vegetative functions, and an impending sense of decompensation could, in part, represent the psychological-behavioral correlates of a hyperaroused CNS. Depressed patients who drink to excess with the hope of "drowning their sorrow in alcohol" may indeed aggravate their depressive state.[246]

Although the arousal seen in affective disorders may have its basis in disordered electrolyte metabolism,[247-249] it could also result from disturbances in biogenic amines. Jouvet's work,[250] for instance, implicates serotonin in the regulation of arousal and sleep; thus, inhibition of serotonin synthesis with PCPA, the inhibitor of tryptophan hydroxylase, produces insomnia, arousal, and psychomotor activation. However, the literature that relates biogenic amines to sleep is in rapid flux and the interactional patterns of central neurohumoral substances in the regulation of sleep await additional clarification.[251] Disturbances in biogenic amines could also secondarily result from intraneuronal sodium accumulation, since the transport of monoamine neurotransmitters across the presynaptic membrane is partially determined by the distribution of electrolytes between the intraneuronal and extraneuronal compartments.[249,252,253] Disordered biogenic amine function, in turn, may disturb the diencephalic mechanisms of reinforcement with the resultant impairment in mood, psychomotor activity, appetite, sleep, and libido. The relationship among biogenic amines, sleep, and depression was recently reviewed by Hauri.[251] One of the most exciting developments in this area is the finding that REM deprivation, either via tricyclics and MAO inhibitors or mechanically (eg, through forced awakening as performed by Vogel et al[254]), has been correlated with significant relief from depression.

AN INTEGRATIVE MODEL OF DEPRESSION

It would be an oversimplification, however, to conceive the syndrome of depression as the outcome of a single set of physiochemical variables. Depression cannot be equated with the depletion of one or another class of neurotransmitters or disordered electrolyte metabolism. It appears that a potentially reversible neurophysiological state of hyperarousal—which may in part be based on disordered biogenic amine function or intraneuronal sodium accumulation, or both—should co-occur with the experience of frustrating environmental events that signal intense turmoil, impending decompensation, and hopelessness. The net result is nonrelatedness and anhedonia, while the concomitant failure in vegetative and psychomotor functions is experienced as additional evidence for such negative self-perceptions. Depression, then, represents the feedback interactions of three sets of variables at chemical, experiential, and behavioral levels—with the diencephalon serving as the field of action. These ideas are schematically presented in Fig 2. The MFB and the PVS, which represent the anatomical substrates of reinforcement, establish feedback connections with other systems in the brain. Functional impairments in one system, then, could result in functional shifts in one or more of these systems. For illustrative purposes, and at the expense of oversimplification, it would be instructive to consider the following three systems that are intimately related to the "reinforcement" (MFB-PVS) system: the "stress" (hypothalamopituitary) system; the "arousal" (reticular activating) system; and the "psychomotor" (pyramidal-extrapyramidal) system. All four systems, with their feedback connections, are diagrammed in Fig 3.

Melancholic and manic behaviors, according to our scheme, result from a failure in the homeostatic mechanisms that maintain these systems in negative feedback[255]—when physiochemical alterations in these systems produce increasing levels of positive feedback in the reinforcement system. Stress or frustration beyond the coping ability of the individual—together with their psychic (anxiety, hopelessness) and neuroendocrine (increased cortisol,[256]) correlates—are expected to produce heightened arousal and could

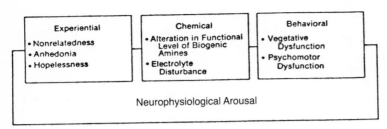

FIGURE 2. Definition of depression at experiential, chemical, behavioral, and neurophysiological levels.

disrupt the functional integrity of the reinforcement system. The resultant decline in vegetative and psychomotor functions and the perception of oneself as losing control in an impending state of decompensation serve as novel sources of stress with additional increments in arousal and additional decrements in coping mechanisms. Thus a vicious cycle of more arousal, more hopelessness, and more evidence of purposeless psychomotor activity. In a system's scheme like this, the controversy whether altered catecholamine metabolism is a cause or effect of depression can be easily resolved. Lowering of norepinephrine in the reinforcement system would contribute to functional impairment whether it is primary or secondary. In other words, norepinephrine depletion can be an effect that, in its own right, can then serve as a cause in the pathogenetic chain of events. Besides, it is not necessary to postulate norepinephrine depletion for all types of depressive illness. The final common pathway of derangement in the homeostatic mechanisms, that normally maintain the reinforcement system in optimal balance, may result from a variety of causes. Janowsky et al,[29] for instance, hypothesized that melancholia involves a functional shift in the noradrenergic-cholinergic balance toward the cholinergic side. Stated in neurophysiological terms, depression may result from predominance of the PVS (cholinergic), without any primary change in the MFB (noradrenergic).

FIGURE 3. Diagrammatic illustration of neurophysiological systems in melancholia.

The diencephalic final common pathway of melancholia can be reached via numerous routes. Whybrow and Parlatore[35] suggested that melancholia is the most readily available final common pathway when, confronted with stress beyond one's coping ability, the homeostatic mechanisms are set in the direction of positive feedback. Unipolar depressions of nonrecurrent type probably occur in the absence of major genetic vulnerability; recurrent unipolar and bipolar depressions, on the other hand, apparently require specific genetic permission to enter the final common path of decompensation. The diencephalic disturbance in affective illness is of such a nature that, in the majority of instances, it permits full restitution to the predecompensation level. (In the schizophrenias, on the other hand, the genetic permission is such that other systems are involved and positive feedback, once set, generally assumes an irreversible course. Stein and Wise[193,257] hypothesized schizophrenic disorders to result from an irreversible functional destruction of the MFB.)

To recapitulate, melancholia can be conceptualized as the final common pathway of various interlocking processes at chemical, experiential, and behavioral levels that, in the language of neurophysiology, translate into a functional impairment of the diencephalic centers of reinforcement (see Fig 4).

1. Genetic Factors. These may provide metabolic loopholes that permit profound changes in biogenic amines or intraneuronal sodium, or both, before homeostatic mechanisms could restore them to normative levels. Of all possible levels

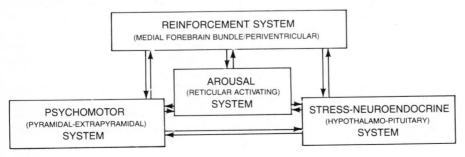

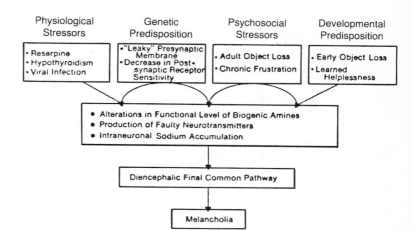

FIGURE 4. Melancholia as final common pathway.

of dysfunction, three deserve special mention: (1) A mutation in the control gene(s) that monitors the availability of rate-limiting enzymes in the biosynthetic pathways of biogenic amines. Heretofore no evidence has been presented for dysfunction at this level. For instance, in depressed patients, the enzyme tryptophan hydroxylase metabolizes the entire tryptophan load, up to 9 gm/day, administered in such patients.[258,259] (2) A genetic defect that interferes with the transport of electrolytes or biogenic amines, or both, across the presynaptic membrane is another plausible locus of dysfunction. This may either involve deficiency in the membrane sodium ion/potassium ion (Na^+/ K^+) dependent adenosine triphosphatase (ATPase)—as proposed by Singh[260] and Bunney et

FIGURE 5. Schematic presentation of three plausible hypothetical loci of genetic dysfunction in depressive illness.

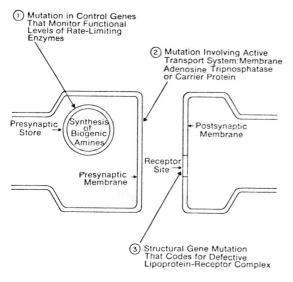

al[204]—or the carrier protein. Mendels and Frazer[261] have demonstrated that the erythrocyte membrane in bipolar depressives permits higher rates of intraerythrocyte lithium ion accumulation than in control subjects, suggesting that there may be a generalized membrane dysfunction in this disorder. More recently, Naylor et al[262] and Hokin-Nyverson et al[263] reported that the erythrocyte Na^+/K^+ ATPase activity was significantly lowered in female inpatients with depressive illness. (3) A structural gene mutation that codes for a defective lipoprotein-receptor complex on the postsynaptic membrane is another attractive possibility. The sensitivity of this receptor to monoamine neurotransmitters is dependent on thyroid hormone. The work of Prange et al[264,265] who demonstrated enhancement of tricyclic antidepressant action by thyroid hormone is consistent with this kind of dysfunction. Figure 5 summarizes, in schematic form, these three hypothetical loci of dysfunction.

2. Developmental Events. These may sensitize certain individuals to the depressionogenic effects of frustration and separation in adult life. Negative cognitive schemata, early object loss, and lifelong failure in controlling environmental reinforcers may weaken the homeostatic mechanisms of the diencephalon. The end result is an exquisite vulnerability to adult disappointment and rapid development of positive feedback loops.

3. Physiological Stressors. Stressors such as reserpine, viral infections, or hypothyroidism may, theoretically, bypass genetic and developmental mechanisms in that direct physiochemical changes can be induced. It appears, however, that at least in the case of reserpine-precipitated depressions, genetic predisposition is required.[197] The experience of somatic and psychomotor debilitation, which frequently accompanies such stresses, may itself be depressionogenic.

4. *Psychosocially Defined Acute or Chronic Stress.* This in adult life has to be considered in relation to genetic and developmental factors. In the absence of developmental events that predispose to helplessness and easy despair, one would generally expect human adults to continue to cope and to experience anxiety. Severe, debilitating cardiac, rheumatological, and other chronic diseases, however, could in some instances serve as sufficient causes for depression. Seligman remarks that depression of helpless proportions supervenes only when one loses the ability to experience adaptive anxiety.[3] Of course, paralyzing anxiety may result from one's perception of oneself in a helpless state of melancholia.

Such a diencephalic final common pathway accounts for the shared clinical features seen in the heterogeneous group of depressive disorders—especially when they attain the melancholic phase—while the phenomenologic heterogeneity (unipolar, bipolar, and secondary) is explainable by differences in the pathogenetic factors and the multilevel interaction possible among these factors. Recently, Klein[266] argued that the final common pathway that we have identified as the diencephalic field of action in depressive disorders represents the underlying biologic dysfunction in what he termed "endogenomorphic" depressions (which correspond to mild or severe episodes of genetically determined primary depression), and that "chronic hysteroid dysphorias" (one of the subtypes of secondary depression) and "acute dysphorias" (acute normal unhappiness) represent disturbances in reinforcement mechanisms that are qualitatively different from the former, ie, unrelated to the "reward" centers of the diencephalon. The studies of Poschell[186] and other experimental work[187-191] conducted largely in infrahuman animals suggest that environmental reinforcers cannot bypass the reward centers, since their effect is annuled on chemical or anatomical lesioning in the reward system. Therefore, it is our position that the depressive's anhedonia—whether mild, transient, or reactive (as seen in normal unhappiness, hysteroid dysphorias, and mild attacks of primary depression) or severe, pervasive, and sustained (most commonly observed in primary affective illness of melancholic proportions)—represents dysfunction in the same biological substrates variously achieved. Thus, our unified model attempts integration of the various conceptual models of de-

pression, while permitting phenomenologic heterogeneity.

According to Senay,[267] who translated depressive phenomena into the language of general systems theory,[255] depression is perhaps the only psychopathological phenomenon that is not limited to humans. As a reduction or elimination of the tendency of any open system to seek relationship with the world, it represents a behavioral state for which there is universal vulnerability. It thus explains the occurrence of depressive behaviors in dogs, monkeys, and humans; in children, adults, and the elderly; and in the hysteric, the obsessive-compulsive, and the alcoholic. Although milder forms of "depression" may befall almost anybody, the more severe melancholic depressions, as defined in this report, seem to involve genetic and interpersonal-developmental events that impart a special fragility to the diencephalic mechanisms of reinforcement or to the feedback loops, or both, that maintain them in homeostasis with contiguous neurophysiological systems.

ADDENDUM BY AUTHORS AT PROOF STAGE

Two biological diagnostic markers in support for limbic-diencephalic dysfunction in melancholia have emerged since this review was published in 1975. These are the REM Latency Test (Kupfer et al., *American Journal of Psychiatry* 135:69, 1978) and the Dexamethasone Suppression Test (Carroll et al., *Archives of General Psychiatry* 38:15, 1981).

This investigation was supported in part by the Tennessee Department of Mental Health, Alcohol and Drug Abuse Section (H.S.A.); by National Institute of Mental Health grants MH-47353, MH-21892 and MH-18070; and by the Wisconsin Psychiatric Research Institute. (W.T.M.).

REFERENCES

1. Hamburg D (ed): Psychiatry as a Behavioral Science. Englewood Cliffs, NJ, Prentice-Hall Inc, 1970.
2. McKinney WT Jr, Bunney WE Jr: Animal model of depression: I. Review of evidence: Implications for research. Arch Gen Psychiatry 21:240–248, 1969.
3. Seligman M: Fall into helplessness. Psychol Today 7:43–48, 1973.
4. Akiskal HS, McKinney WT Jr: Psychiatry and pseudopsychiatry. Arch Gen Psychiatry 28:367–373, 1973.
5. Arthur R: Social psychiatry: An overview. Am J Psychiatry 130:841–849, 1973.
6. Freedman D, Gordon R: Psychiatry under siege: Attacks from without. Ann Psychiatry 3:10–34, 1973.
7. Whybrow P: The use and the abuse of the "medical model" as a conceptual frame in psychiatry. Psychiatr Med 3:333–342, 1972.

8. Eighth Revision International Classification of Diseases Adapted for Use in the United States, Public Health Service publication 1693. Washington, DC, US Government Printing Office, 1968.

9. American Psychiatric Association: DSM-II: Diagnostic and Statistical Manual, ed 2, 1968.

10. Havens L: Approaches to the Mind. Boston, Little Brown & Co, 1973, p vii.

11. Abraham K: Notes on the psychoanalytic investigation and treatment of manic-depressive insanity and allied conditions (1911), in Selected Papers on Psychoanalysis. New York, Basic Books, 1960, pp 137–156.

12. Freud S: Mourning and melancholia (1917), in Collected Papers. London, Hogarth Press, 1950, vol 4, pp 152–172.

13. Spitz R: Anaclitic depression: An inquiry into the genesis of psychiatric conditions in early childhood. Psychoanal Study Child 2:313–342, 1942.

14. Robertson J, Bowlby J: Responses of young children to separation from their mothers. Courrier Centre Inter Enfance 2:131–142, 1952.

15. Bowlby J: Grief and mourning in infancy and early childhood. Psychoanal Study Child 15:9–52, 1960.

16. Bibring E: The mechanism of depression, in Greenacre P (ed): Affective Disorders. New York, International Universities Press, 1965, pp 13–48.

17. Beck A: Depression: Clinical, Experimental and Theoretical Aspects. New York, Harper & Row Publishers Inc, 1967.

18. Seligman M: Learned helplessness and depression, in Friedman R, Katz M (eds): The Psychology of Depression: Contemporary Theory and Research. Washington, DC, US Government Printing House, to be published.

19. Ferster C: Classification of behavior pathology, in Krasner L, Ullman L (eds): Research in Behavior Modification. New York, Holt Rinehart & Winston Inc, 1965, pp 6–26.

20. Lazarus A: Learning theory and the treatment of depression. Behav Res Ther 6:83–89, 1968.

21. Lewinsohn P: A behavioral approach to depression, in Friedman R, Katz M (eds): The Psychology of Depression: Contemporary Theory and Research. Washington, DC, US Government Printing House, to be published.

22. Bart P: Depression: A sociological theory, in Roman P, Trice H (eds): Explorations in Psychiatric Sociology. Philadelphia, FA Davis Co, 1974, to be published.

23. Becker E: The Revolution in Psychiatry. London, Free Press of Glencoe, Collier-MacMillian Ltd, 1964, pp 108–135.

24. Schildkraut J: Catecholamine hypothesis of affective disorders. Am J Psychiatry 122:509–522, 1965.

25. Bunney WE Jr, Davis M: Norepinephrine in depressive reactions. Arch Gen Psychiatry 13:483–494, 1965.

26. Coppen A: The biochemistry of affective disorders. Br J Psychiatry 113:1237–1264, 1967.

27. Lapin I, Oxenkrug G: Intensification of the central serotonergic process as a possible determinant of thymoleptic effect. Lancet 1:132–136, 1969.

28. Whybrow P, Mendels J: Toward a biology of depression: Some suggestions from neurophysiology. Am J Psychiatry 125:45–54, 1969.

29. Janowsky D, El-Yousef K, Davis M, et al: A cholinergic-adrenergic hypothesis of mania and depression. Lancet 2:632–635, 1972.

30. Akiskal HS, McKinney WT Jr: Depressive disorders: Toward a unified hypothesis. Science 182:20–29, 1973.

31. Wilkins W: Psychoanalytic and behavioristic approaches toward depression: A synthesis? Am J Psychiatry 128:358–359, 1971.

32. Liberman R, Raskin D: Depression: A behavioral formulation. Arch Gen Psychiatry 24:515–523, 1971.

33. Mallerstein J: Depression as a pivotal affect. Am J Psychother 22:202–217, 1968.

34. Goodwin F, Bunney WE Jr: A psychobiological approach to affective illness. Psychiatric Ann 3:19–53, 1973.

35. Whybrow P, Parlatore A: Melancholia, a model in madness: A discussion of recent psychobiologic research into depressive illness. Psychiatr Med 4:351–378, 1973.

36. Lipowski B: Psychopathology as a science: Its scope and tasks. Compr Psychiatry 7:175–181, 1966.

37. Woodruff R, Goodwin D, Guze S: Psychiatric Diagnosis. New York, Oxford University Press, 1974.

38. Klerman G: Clinical research in depression. Arch Gen Psychiatry 24:305–319, 1971.

39. Klerman G, Barrett J: The affective disorders: Clinical and epidemiological aspects, in Gershon S, Shopsin B (eds): Lithium, its Role in Psychiatric Research and Treatment. New York, Plenum Press, 1973, pp 201–236.

40. Robins E, Guze S: Establishment of diagnostic validity in psychiatric illness: Its application to schizophrenia. Am J Psychiatry 126:983–987, 1970.

41. Feighner J, Robins E, Guze S, et al: Diagnostic criteria for use in psychiatric research. Arch Gen Psychiatry 26:57–63, 1972.

42. Deleon-Jones F, Maas J, Dekirmenjian H, et al: MHPG excretion in primary and secondary depression. Read before the 126th annual meeting of the American Psychiatric Association, Honolulu, 1973.

43. Graham D: Psychophysiology and medicine. Psychophysiology 8:121–311, 1971.

44. Lazare A: Hidden conceptual models in clinical psychiatry. N Engl J Med 288:345–351, 1973.

45. Prange A: The use of drugs in depression: Its theoretical and practical basis. Psychiatr Ann 3:55–75, 1973.

46. Simpson G, Mohammed A, Angus J, et al: Role of antidepressants and neuroleptics in the treatment of depression. Arch Gen Psychiatry 27:337–345, 1972.

47. Hamilton M: A rating scale for depression. J Neurol Neurosurg Psychiatry 23:56–62, 1960.

48. Beck A, Ward C, Mendelson M, et al: An inventory for measuring depression. Arch Gen Psychiatry 4:561–571, 1961.

49. Zung W: From art to science: The diagnosis and treatment of depression. Arch Gen Psychiatry 29:328–337, 1973.

50. Mendelson M: Neurotic depressive reaction, in Freedman A, Kaplan HI (eds): Comprehensive Textbook of Psychiatry. Baltimore, Williams & Wilkins Co, 1967, pp 928–936.

51. Akiskal HS, Bitar AH, Puzanhan VR, et al: The nosological status of neurotic depression: a prospective 3–4 year examination in the light of the primary-secondary and the unipolar-bipolar dichotomies. Arch Gen Psychiatry 35:756, 1978.

52. Bunney WE Jr, Murphy D, Goodwin F: The switch process from depression to mania: Relationship to drugs which alter brain amines. Lancet 2:1022–1027, 1970.

53. Murphy D, Brodie K, Goodwin F, et al: Regular induction of hypomania by l-dopa in "bipolar" manic-depressive patients. Nature 229:135–136, 1971.

54. Small I, Small J, Alig V, et al: Passive-aggressive personality disorder: A search for a syndrome. Am J Psychiatry 126:973–983, 1970.

55. Welner A, Liss J, Robins E: Personality disorder: II. Follow-up study. Br J Psychiatry 124:359–366, 1974.

56. Hudgens R, Morrison J, Barchha R: Life events and onset of primary affective disorders. Arch Gen Psychiatry 16:134–145, 1967.

57. Morrison J, Hudgens R, Barchha R: Life events and psychiatric illness. Br J Psychiatry 114:423–432, 1968.

58. Cadoret R, Winokur G, Dorzab J, et al: Depressive disease: Life events and onset of illness. Arch Gen Psychiatry 26:133–136, 1972.

59. Slater E, Roth M: Mayer Gross' Clinical Psychiatry, ed 3. Baltimore, Williams & Wilkins Co, 1969, pp 77–81, 188–236.

60. Lewis A: Melancholia: A clinical survey of depressive states. J Mental Science 80:277–378, 1934.

61. Leff M, Roatch J, Bunney WE Jr: Environmental factors preceding the onset of severe depressions. Psychiatry 33:293–311, 1970.

62. Paykel E, Myers J, Dienelt M, et al: Life events and depression. Arch Gen Psychiatry 21:753–760, 1970.

63. Thomson K, Hendrie H: Environmental stress in primary depressive illness. Arch Gen Psychiatry 26:130–132, 1972.

64. Kendell R, Gourlay J: The clinical distinction between psychotic and neurotic depressions. Br J Psychiatry 117:257–266, 1970.

65. Lipowski J: New perspectives in psychosomatic medicine. Can Psychiatr Assoc J 15:515–525, 1970.

66. Astrup C, Fossum A, Holmboe R: A follow-up study of 270 patients with acute affective psychoses. Acta Psychiatr Neurol Scand 34 (suppl 135):11–65, 1959.

67. Kay D, Garside R, Roy J, et al: "Endogenous" and "neurotic" syndromes of depression: A five- to seven-year follow-up of 104 cases. Br J Psychiatry 115:389–399, 1969.

68. Paykel E, Klerman G, Prusoff B: Prognosis of depression and the endogenous-neurotic distinction. Psychol Med 4:57–64, 1974.

69. Leonard K: Über monopolare und bipolare endogene Psychosen. Der Nervenarzt 39:104–106, 1968.

70. Angst J: Zur Atiologie und Nosologie Endogener Depressiver Psychosen. Berlin, Springer Verlag, 1966.

71. Perris C: A study of bipolar (manic-depressive) and unipolar recurrent depressive psychoses. Acta Psychiatr Scand 42 (suppl 194):7–189, 1966.

72. Winokur G, Clayton P, Reich T: Manic-Depressive Illness. St. Louis, CV Mosby Co, 1969.

73. Reich T, Clayton P, Winokur G: Family history studies: V. The genetics of mania. Am J Psychiatry 125:1358–1369, 1969.

74. Mendlewicz J, Fleiss J, Fieve R: Evidence for X-linkage in the transmission of manic-depressive illness. JAMA 222:1624–1627, 1972.

75. Green R, Goetzl U, Whybrow P, et al: X-linked transmission of manic-depressive illness. JAMA 223:1289, 1973.

76. Gershon E, Dunner D, Goodwin F: Toward a biology of affective disorders: Genetic contributions. Arch Gen Psychiatry 25:1–15, 1971.

77. Baker M, Dorzab J, Winokur G, et al: Depressive disease: Evidence favoring polygenic inheritance based on an analysis of ancestral cases. Arch Gen Psychiatry 27:320–327, 1972.

78. Perris C: The course of depressive psychoses. Acta Psychiatry Scand 44:238–248, 1968.

79. Winokur G: The natural history of the affective disorders (manias and depressions). Semin Psychiatry 2:451–463, 1970.

80. Beigel A, Murphy D: Unipolar and bipolar affective illness: Differences in clinical characteristics accompanying depression. Arch Gen Psychiatry 24:215–220, 1971.

81. Reich T, Winokur G: Postpartum psychoses in patients with manic-depressive disease. J Nerv Ment Dis 151:60–68, 1970.

82. Dunner D, Goodwin F, Gershon E, et al: Excretion of 17-OHCS in unipolar and bipolar depressed patients. Arch Gen Psychiatry 26:360–363, 1972.

83. Murphy D, Weiss R: Reduced monoamine oxidase activity in blood platelets from bipolar depressed patients. Am J Psychiatry 128:1351–1357, 1972.

84. van Praag H, Korf J, Schut D: Cerebral monoamines and depression: An investigation with the probenecid technique. Arch Gen Psychiatry 28:827–831, 1973.

85. Buchsbaum M, Goodwin FK, Murphy MD, et al: Average evoked response in affective disorders. Am J Psychiatry 128:19–25, 1971.

86. Borge F, Buchsbaum M, Goodwin F, et al: Neuropsychological correlates of affective disorders. Arch Gen Psychiatry 24:501–504, 1971.

87. Goodwin F, Murphy D, Dunner D, et al: Lithium response in unipolar versus bipolar depression. Am J Psychiatry 129:44–47, 1972.

88. Noyes R, Dempsey M, Blum A, et al: Lithium treatment of depression. Compr Psychiatry 15:187–193, 1974.

89. Taylor M, Abrams R: Manic states: A genetic study of early and late onset affective disorders. Arch Gen Psychiatry 28:656–658, 1973.

90. Abrams R, Taylor M: Unipolar mania: A preliminary report. Arch Gen Psychiatry 30:441–443, 1974.

91. Fieve R: Overview of therapeutic and prophylactic trials with lithium in psychiatric patients, in Gershon S, Shopsin B (eds): Lithium, its Role in Psychiatric Research and Treatment. New York, Plenum Press, 1973, pp 317–349.

92. Mendelewicz J, Fieve R, Rainer D, et al: Manic-depressive illness: A comparative study of patients with and without a family history. Br J Psychiatry 120:523–530, 1972.

93. Mendelewicz J, Fieve R, Stallone F: Relationship between the effectiveness of lithium therapy and family history. Am J Psychiatry 130:1011–1013, 1973.

94. Paykel E: Classification of depressed patients: A cluster analysis derived grouping. Br J Psychiatry 118:275–288, 1971.

95. Paykel E, Prusoff B, Klerman G, et al: Clinical response to amitriptyline among depressed women. J Nerv Ment Dis 156:149–165, 1973.

96. Winokur G, Cadoret R, Dorzab J, et al: Depressive disease: A genetic study. Arch Gen Psychiatry 24:135–144, 1971.

97. Overall J, Hollister C, Johnson M, et al: Nosology of depression and differential response to drugs. JAMA 195:946–948, 1966.

98. Roth R, Gurney C, Garside R, et al: Studies in the classification of affective disorders: The relationship between anxiety states and depressive illnesses. Br J Psychiatry 121:147–166, 1972.

99. Robins E, Guze S: Establishment of diagnostic validity in psychiatric illness: Its application to schizophrenia. Am J Psychiatry 126:983–987, 1970.

100. Carlson G, Goodwin F: The stages of mania. Arch Gen Psychiatry 28:221–288, 1973.

101. Taylor M, Gaztanaga P, Abrams R: Manic-depressive illness and acute schizophrenia: A clinical, family history and treatment-response study. Am J Psychiatry 131:678–682, 1974.

102. Ollerenshaw D: Classification of functional psychoses. Br J Psychiatry 122:517–530, 1973.

103. Pare C, Rees L, Sainsbury M: Differentiation of two genetically specific types of depression by response to antidepressant drugs. Lancet 2:1340–1343, 1962.

104. West D, Dally P: Effects of iproniazid in depressive syndromes. Br Med J 1:1491–1494, 1959.

105. Sargant W: Drugs in the treatment of depression. Br Med J 1:225–227, 1961.

106. Klein D, Davis J: Diagnosis and Drug Treatment of Psychiatric Disorders. Baltimore, Williams & Wilkins Co, 1969, pp 180–185.

107. Robinson D, Nies A, Ravaris L, et al: The monoamine oxidase inhibitor, phenelzine, in the treatment of depressive-anxiety states: A controlled clinical trial. Arch Gen Psychiatry 29:407–413, 1973.

108. Clayton P, Rodin L, Winokur G: Family history studies: III. Schizoaffective disorder: Clinical and genetic factors, including a one to two year follow-up. Compr Psychiatry 9:31–49, 1968.

109. Prien R, Caffey EM Jr, Klett J: A comparison of lithium carbonate and chlorpromazine in the treatment of excited schizoaffectives. Arch Gen Psychiatry 27:182–189, 1972.

110. Rifkin A, Quitkin F, Carrillo C, et al: Lithium carbonate in emotionally unstable character disorder. Arch Gen Psychiatry 27:519–523, 1972.

111. Johnson G, Gershon S, Hekimian L: Controlled evaluation of lithium and chlorpromazine in the treatment of manic states: An interim report. Compr Psychiatry 9:563–573, 1968.

112. Shopsin B, Gershon S: Pharmacology—toxicology of the lithium ion, in Gershon S, Shopsin B (eds): Lithium, its Role in Psychiatric Research and Treatment. New York, Plenum Press, 1973, pp 107–146.

113. Murphy D: Amine precursors, amines and false neurotransmitters in depressed patients. Am J Psychiatry 129:41–48, 1972.

114. Kendell R: Relationship between aggression and depression: Epidemiological implications of a hypothesis. Arch Gen Psychiatry 22:308–318, 1970.

115. Henry A, Short J: Suicide and Homicide. New York, Free Press of Glencoe Inc, 1954.

116. Friedman A: Hostility factors and clinical improvement in depressed patients. Arch Gen Psychiatry 23:524–537, 1970.

117. Klerman G, Gershon E: Imipramine effects upon hostility in depression. J Nerv Ment Dis 150:127–132, 1970.

118. Weissman M, Klerman G, Paykel E: Clinical evaluation of hostility in depression. Am J Psychiatry 128:261–266, 1971.

119. Lazare A, Klerman G: Hysteria and depression: The frequency and significance of hysterical personality features in hospitalized depressed women. Am J Psychiatry 124:48–56, 1968.

120. Weissman M, Fox K, Klerman G: Hostility and depression associated with suicide attempts. Am J Psychiatry 130:450–455, 1973.

121. Beck A: Cognition, affect, and psychopathology. Arch Gen Psychiatry 24:495–500, 1971.

122. Minkoff K, Bergman E, Beck A, et al: Hopelessness, depression, and attempted suicide. Am J Psychiatry 130:455–460, 1973.

123. Ellis A: Rational psychotherapy. J Gen Psychol 59:35–49, 1958.

124. Seligman M, Maier S: Failure to escape traumatic shock. J Exp Psychol 74:1–9, 1967.

125. Overmier J, Seligman M: Effects of inescapable shock upon subsequent escape and avoidance responding. J Comp Physiol Psychol 63:28–33, 1967.

126. Seligman M, Maier S, Geer J: The alleviation of learned helplessness in the dog. J Abnorm Soc Psychol 73:256–262, 1968.

127. Seligman M, Groves D: Non-transient learned helplessness. Psychonom Sci 19:191–192, 1970.

128. Wolpe J: Neurotic depression: Experimental analog, clinical syndromes and treatment. Am J Psychother 25:362–368, 1971.

129. Ullman L, Krasner L: A Psychological Approach to Abnormal Behavior. Englewood Cliffs, NJ, Prentice-Hall, 1969, p 414.

130. Lewinsohn P, Weinstein M, Alper T: A behavioral approach to the group treatment of depressed persons: A methodological contribution. J Clin Psychol 26:525–532, 1970.

131. Lewinsohn P, Shaw D: Feedback about interpersonal behavior as an agent of behavior change: A case study in the treatment of depression. Psychother Psychosom 17:82–88, 1969.

132. Lewinsohn P, Shaffer M: Use of home observations as an integral part of the treatment of depression. J Consult Clin Psychol 37:87–94, 1971.

133. Bonime W: The psychodynamics of neurotic depression, in Arieti S (ed): American Handbook of Psychiatry, ed 1. New York, Basic Books, 1966, vol 3, pp 239–255.

134. Weiss M, Stone E, Harrel N: Coping behavior and brain norepinephrine level in rats. J. Comp Physiol Psychol 72:153–160, 1970.

135. Harlow M, Harlow H: Affection in primates. Discovery 27:11–17, 1966.

136. Harlow H, Harlow M: Learning to love. Am Sci 54:244–272, 1966.

137. Ainsworth M: Object relations, dependency and attachment. Child Dev 40:969–1025, 1969.

138. Bowlby J: Attachment, New York, Basic Books Inc, 1969.

139. Bowlby J: Separation: Anxiety and Anger. New York, Basic Books Inc, 1973.

140. Robertson J, Robertson J: Young children in brief separation: A fresh look. Psychoanal Study Child 26:264–315, 1971.

141. Clayton P, Halikas J, Maurice W: The depression of widowhood. Br J Psychiatry 120:71–77, 1972.

142. Parkes C: Bereavement and mental illness: A clinical study of the grief of bereaved psychiatric patients. Br J Med Psychol 38:1–12, 1965.

143. Parkes C: Recent bereavement as a cause of mental illness. Br J Psychiatry 110:198–204, 1964.

144. Schmale A: Importance of life setting for disease onset. Mod Treat 6:643–655, 1969.

145. Schmale A: Relationship of separation and depression to disease. Psychosom Med 20:259–277, 1958.

146. Bowlby J: Childhood mourning and its implication for psychiatry. Am J Psychiatry 118:481–498, 1961.

147. Abraham K: A short study of the development of the libido viewed in the light of mental disorders (1924), in On Character and Libido Development. New York, WW Norton & Co Inc, 1966, pp 67–150.

148. Gregory I: Studies of parental deprivation in psychiatric patients. Am J Psychiatry 115:432–442, 1958.

149. Gregory I: Retrospective data concerning childhood loss of a parent: I. Arch Gen Psychiatry 15:354–361, 1966.

150. Gregory I: Retrospective data concerning childhood loss of a parent: II. Arch Gen Psychiatry 15:362–367, 1966.

151. Granville-Grossman K: The early environment in affective disorder, in Coppen A, Walk A (eds): Recent Developments in Affective Disorders. London, Headley Brothers Ltd, 1968, pp 65–79.

152. Brown F: Depression and childhood bereavement. J Ment Sci 107:754–777, 1961.

153. Birtchnell J: Some psychiatric sequelae of childhood bereavement. Br J Psychiatry 116:346–347, 1970.

154. Birtchnell J: Psychiatric sequelae of childhood bereavement. Br J Psychiatry 116:572–573, 1970.

155. Birtchnell J: Early parent death and mental illness. Br J Psychiatry 116:281–288, 1970.

156. Caplan M, Douglas V: Incidence of parental loss in children with depressed mood. J Child Psychol Psychiatry 10:225–232, 1969.

157. Hill O: The association of childhood bereavement with suicidal attempt in depressive illness. Br J Psychiatry 115:301–304, 1969.

158. Abrahams M, Whitlock F: Childhood experience and depression. Br J Psychiatry 115:883–888, 1969.

159. Moran P: Maternal age and parental loss. Br J Psychiatry 114:207–214, 1968.

160. Munro A: Parental deprivation in depressive patients. Br J Psychiatry 112:443–457, 1966.

161. Dennehy C: Childhood bereavement and psychiatric illness. Br J Psychiatry 212:1049–1069, 1966.

162. Brown F: Childhood bereavement and subsequent psychiatric disorder. Br J Psychiatry 112:1035–1041, 1966.

163. Brill N, Liston E: Parental loss in adults with emotional disorders. Arch Gen Psychiatry 14:307–314, 1966.

164. Greer S: The relationship between parental loss and attempted suicide: A control study. Br J Psychiatry 110:698–705, 1964.

165. Archibald H, Bell D, Miller C, et al: Bereavement in childhood and adult psychiatric disturbance. Psychosom Med 24:343–351, 1962.

166. Barry H, Lindemann E: Critical ages for maternal bereavement in psychoneuroses. Psychosom Med 22:166–179, 1960.

167. Heinicke C: Parental deprivation in early childhood, in Scott J, Senay E (eds): Separation and Depression: Clinical and Research Aspects. Washington, DC, American Association for the Advancement of Science, 1973, pp 141–160.

168. Pitts F, Meyer J, Brooks M, et al: Adult psychiatric illness assessed for parent loss. Am J Psychiatry 121 (Childhood suppl 12):I–X, 1965.

169. Hellman I: Sudden separation and its effect followed over 20 years: Psychoanal Study Child 17:159–174, 1962.

170. Goertzel V, Goertzel M: Cradles of Eminence. Boston, Little Brown & Co, 1962, pp 149–152, 214–216, 272.

171. Beck A, Sethi B, Tuthill R: Childhood bereavement and adult depression. Arch Gen Psychiatry 9:295–302, 1963.

172. Seay B, Hansen E, Harlow H: Mother-infant separation in monkeys. J Child Psychol Psychiatry 3:123–132, 1962.

173. Seay B, Harlow H: Maternal separation in the

rhesus monkey. J Nerv Mental Dis 140:434–441, 1965.

174. Hinde R, Spencer-Booth Y: Effects of brief separation from mother on rhesus monkeys. Science 173:111–119, 1971.

175. Hinde R, Spencer-Booth Y, Bruce M: Effects of six-day maternal deprivation on rhesus monkey infants. Nature 210:1021–1023, 1966.

176. McKinney WT Jr, Suomi S, Harlow H: Depression in primates. Am J Psychiatry 127:1313–1320, 1971.

177. Rosenblum L, Kaufman I: Variations in infant development and response to maternal loss in monkeys. Am J Orthopsychiatry 83:418–426, 1968.

178. Kaufman I, Rosenblum L: Depression in infant monkeys separated from their mothers. Science 155:1030–1031, 1967.

179. Jensen G, Toleman C: Mother-infant relationship in the monkey, macaca nemestrina: The effect of brief separation and mother-infant specificity. J Comp Physiol Psychol 55:131–136, 1962.

180. Hinde R, Spencer-Booth Y: Individual differences in the responses of rhesus monkeys to a period of separation from their mothers. J Child Psychol Psychiatry 11:159–176, 1970.

181. Hinde R, Davies L: Removing infant rhesus from mother for 13 days compared with removing mother from infant. J Child Psychol Psychiatry 13:227–237, 1972.

182. Suomi S, Domek C, Harlow H: Effects of repetitive infant-infant separation of young monkeys. J Abnorm Psychology 76:161–172, 1970.

183. McKinney WT Jr, Suomi S, Harlow H: Repetitive peer separations of juvenile-age rhesus monkeys. Arch Gen Psychiatry 27:200–203, 1972.

184. Bowden D, McKinney WT Jr: Behavioral effects of peer separation, isolation, and reunion on adolescent male rhesus monkeys. Develop Psychobiology 5:353–362, 1972.

185. Young L, Suomi S, Harlow H, et al: Early stress and later response to separation in rhesus monkeys. Am J Psychiatry 130:400–405, 1973.

186. Poschell BPH: Do biological reinforcers act via the self-stimulation areas of the brain? Physiol Behav 3:53–60, 1968.

187. Olds J, Milner P: Positive reinforcement produced by electrical stimulation of septal area and other regions of rat brain. J Comp Physiol Psychol 47:419–427, 1954.

188. Heath R (ed): The Role of Pleasure in Behavior. New York, Paul B Hoeber Inc, 1964.

189. Stein L: Chemistry of reward and punishment, in Efron D (ed): Psychopharmacology: A Review of Progress 1957–1967. Washington, DC, US Government Printing Office, 1968, pp 105–123.

190. Crow T: Catecholamine-containing neurones and electrical self-stimulation: II. A theoretical interpretation and some psychiatric implications. Psychol Med 3:66–73, 1973.

191. Wise C, Berger B, Stein L: Evidence of alpha-noradrenergic reward receptors and serotonergic punishment receptors in the rat brain. Biol Psychiatry 6:3–21, 1973.

192. Redmond D, Maas, J, Kling A, et al: Changes in primate social behavior after treatment with alpha-methyl-para-tyrosine. Psychosom Med 33:97–113, 1971.

193. Stein L: Neurochemistry of reward and punishment: Some implications for the etiology of schizophrenia. J Psychiatr Res 8:345–361, 1971.

194. Schildkraut J: Neuropsychopharmacology and the Affective Disorders. Boston, Little Brown and Co, 1970.

195. Coppen A: Indoleamines and affective disorders. J Psychiatr Res 9:163–171, 1972.

196. Bunney WE Jr, Gershon E, Murphy D, et al: Psychobiological and pharmacological studies of manic-depressive illness. J Psychiatr Res 9:207–226, 1972.

197. Goodwin F, Bunney WE Jr: Depression following reserpine: A reevaluation. Semin Psychiatry 3:435–448, 1971.

198. Coppen A, Whybrow P, Noguera R, et al: The comparative antidepressant value of L-tryptophan and imipramine with and without attempted potentiation by liothyronine. Arch Gen Psychiatry 26:234–241, 1972.

199. Coppen A, Shaw D, Farrell J: Potentiation of the antidepressant effect of a monoamine-oxidase inhibitor by tryptophan. Lancet 1:79–81, 1963.

200. Prange A, Wilson I, Lynn CW, et al: L-Tryptophan in mania: Contribution to a permissive hypothesis of affective disorders. Arch Gen Psychiatry 30:56–62, 1974.

201. Klerman G, Schildkraut J, Hassenbush J: Clinical experience with dihydroxyphenylalanine (dopa) in depression. J Psychiatr Res 1:289–297, 1963.

202. Goodwin F, Brodie H, Murphy D, et al: L-Dopa, catecholamines and behavior: A clinical and biochemical study in depressed patients. Biol Psychiatry 2:341–366, 1970.

203. Goodwin F: Behavioral effects of 1-dopa in man. Semin Psychiatry 3:477–492, 1971.

204. Bunney WE Jr, Goodwin F, Murphy D: The "switch process" in manic-depressive illness: III. Theoretical implications. Arch Gen Psychiatry 27:312–317, 1972.

205. Goodwin F, Dunner D, Gershon E: Effect of 1-dopa, treatment on brain serotonin metabolism in depressed patients. Life Sci 10:751–759, 1971.

206. Shaw D, Camps F, Eccleston E: 5-Hydroxytryptamine in the hindbrain of depressive suicides. Br J Psychiatry 113:1407–1411, 1967.

207. Bourne H, Bunney WE Jr, Colburn R, et al: Noradrenaline, 5-hydroxytryptamine, and 5-hydroxyindoleacetic acid in hindbrains of suicidal patients. Lancet 2:805–808, 1968.

208. Ashcroft G, Crawford T, Eccleston E, et al: 5-Hydroxyindole compounds in the cerebrospinal fluid of patients with psychiatric or neurological diseases. Lancet 2:1049–1052, 1966.

209. Dencker S, Malm U, Roos B, et al: Acid monoamine metabolites of cerebrospinal fluid in mental depression and mania. J Neurochem 13:1545–1548, 1966.

210. Mendels J, Frazer A, Fitzgerald R, et al: Biogenic amine metabolites in the cerebrospinal fluid of depressed and manic patients. Science 175:1380–1382, 1972.

211. Coppen A, Prange A, Whybrow P, et al: Abnormalities of indoleamines in affective disorders. Arch Gen Psychiatry 26:474–478, 1972.

212. Ashcroft G, Blackburn I, Eccleston D, et al: Changes on recovery in the concentration of L-tryptophan and the biogenic amine metabolites in the cerebrospinal fluid of patients with affective illness. Psychol Med 3:319–325, 1973.

213. Maas J, Landis D: In vivo studies of metabolism of norepinephrine in central nervous system. J Pharmacol Exp Ther 163:147–162, 1968.

214. Schanberg S, Schildkraut J, Breese G, et al: Metabolism of normetanephrine-H in rat brain: Identification of conjugated 3-methoxy-4-hydroxyphenylglycol as major metabolite. Biochem Pharmacol 17:247–254, 1968.

215. Maas J, Fawcett J, Dekirmenjian H: Catecholamine metabolism, depressive illness, and drug response. Arch Gen Psychiatry 26:252–262, 1972.

216. Fawcett J, Maas J, Dekirmenjian H: Depression and MHPG excretion: Response to dextroamphetamine and tricyclic antidepressants. Arch Gen Psychiatry 26:246–251, 1972.

217. Goode D, Dekirmenjian H, Meltzer H, et al: Relation of exercise to MHPG excretion in normal subjects. Arch Gen Psychiatry 29:391–396, 1973.

218. Post R, Kotin J, Goodwin F, et al: Psychomotor activity and cerebrospinal fluid amine metabolites in affective illness. Am J Psychiatry 130:67–72, 1973.

219. Post R, Goodwin F, Gordon E: Amine metabolites in the human cerebrospinal fluid: Effects of cord transection and spinal fluid block. Science 179:897–898, 1973.

220. Maas JW: Biogenic amines and depression. Arch Gen Psychiatry 32:1357–1361, 1975.

221. Court J: Manic-depressive psychosis: An alternative conceptual model. Br J Psychiatry 114:1523–1530, 1968.

222. Smythies J: Psychiatry and neurosciences. Psychol Med 3:267–269, 1973.

223. Breese G, Prange A, Howard J, et al: 3-Methoxy-4-hydroxyphenylglycol excretion and behavioral changes in rat and monkey after central sympathectomy with 6-hydroxydopamine. Nature New Biol 240:286–288, 1972.

224. Mendels J, Frazer A: Brain biogenic amine depletion and mood. Arch Gen Psychiatry 30:447–451, 1974.

225. Schacter S, Singer J: Cognitive, social and physiological determinants of emotional state. Psychol Rev 69:379–399, 1962.

226. Barchas J, Freedman D: Brain amines: Response to physiological stress. Biochem Pharmacol 12:1232–1235, 1963.

227. Ordy J, Samorajski T, Schroeder D: Concurrent changes in hypothalamic and cardiac catecholamine levels after anesthetics, tranquilizers and stress in a subhuman primate. J Pharm Exp Ther 152:445–457, 1966.

228. Maynert E, Roberto L: Stress-induced release of brain norepinephrine and its inhibition by drugs. J Pharm Exp Ther 143:90–95, 1964.

229. Paulson E, Hess S: The rate of synthesis of catecholamines following depletion in guinea pig brain and heart. J Neurochem 10:453–459, 1963.

230. Theirry A, Javou F, Glowinski J, et al: Effects of stress on the metabolism of noradrenaline, dopamine and serotonin in the CNS of the rat: I. Modification of norepinephrine turnover. J Pharm Exp Ther 163:163–171, 1968.

231. Hineshey R, Norton J, Aprison M: Serotonin, norepinephrine and 3,4-dihydroxyphenyl-ethylamine in rat brain parts following electroconvulsive shock. J Psychiatr Res 6:143–152, 1968.

232. Bliss E, Wilson V, Zwanziger J: Changes in brain norepinephrine in self-stimulating and "aversive" animals. J Psychiatr Res 4:59–63, 1966.

233. Bliss E, Zwanziger J: Brain amines and emotional stress. J Psychiatr Res. 4:189–198, 1966.

234. Welch A, Welch B: Failure of natural stimuli to accelerate brain catecholamine depletion after biosynthetic inhibition with alpha-methyl-para-tyrosine. Brain Res 9:402–405, 1968.

235. Welch B, Welch A: Differential activation by restraint stress of a mechanism to conserve brain catecholamines and serotonin in mice differing in excitability. Nature 218:575–577, 1968.

236. Young L, McKinney WT Jr, Lewis J, et al: Induction of adrenal catecholamine synthesizing enzymes following mother-infant separation. Nature New Biol 246:94–96, 1973.

237. Coppen A, Shaw D: Mineral metabolism in melancholia. Br Med J 2:1439–1444, 1963.

238. Coppen A, Shaw D, Mallerson A, et al: Mineral metabolism in mania. Br Med J 1:71–75, 1966.

239. Shaw D, Frizel D, Camps F, et al: Brain electrolytes in depressive and alcoholic suicides. Br J Psychiatry 115:69–79, 1969.

240. Shaw D, Camps F, Robinson A, et al: Electrolyte content of the brain in alcoholism. Br J Psychiatry 116:185–193, 1970.

241. Beard J, Knott D: Fluid and electrolyte balance during acute withdrawal in chronic alcoholic patients. JAMA 204:135–139, 1968.

242. Ogata M, Mendelson J, Mello N: Electrolytes and osmolality in alcoholics during experimentally induced intoxication. Psychosom Med 30:463–468, 1968.

243. Butterworth A: Depression associated with alcohol withdrawal. Q J Stud Alcohol 32:343–348, 1971.

244. Mayfield D, Montgomery D: Alcoholism, alcohol intoxication and suicide attempts. Arch Gen Psychiatry 27:349–353. 1972.

245. Knott D, Beard J: Diagnosis and therapy of acute withdrawal from alcohol. Curr Psychiatr Ther 10:145–153, 1970.

246. Akiskal HS, Beard J, Fink R, et al: Diuretic-antidepressant combination in alcoholic depressives: Preliminary findings. Dis Nerv Syst 35:207–211, 1974.

247. Baer L, Platman S, Fieve R: The role of electrolytes in affective disorders. Arch Gen Psychiatry 22:108–113, 1970.

248. Shaw D: Mineral metabolism, mania and melancholia. Br Med J 2:262–267, 1966.

249. Maas J: Adrenocortical steroid hormones, electrolytes and the disposition of the catecholamines with particular reference to depressive states. J Psychiatr Res 9:227–241, 1972.

250. Jouvet M: Biogenic amines and the states of sleep. Science 163:32–41, 1969.

251. Hauri P: Sleep in depression. Psychiatr Ann 4:45–62, 1974.

252. Bogdanski D, Tissari A, Brodie B: The effects of inorganic ions on uptake, storage and metabolism of biogenic amines in nerve endings, in Efron D (ed): Psychopharmacology: A Review of Progress 1957–1967. Washington, DC, US Government Printing Office, 1968, pp 17–26.

253. White T, Paton D: Effect of external N+ and K+ on the initial rates of noradrenaline uptake by synaptosomes prepared from rat brain. Biochem Biophys Acta 266:116–127, 1972.

254. Vogel G, Thompson F, Thurmond A, et al: The effect of REM deprivation on depression. Psychosomatics 14:104–107, 1973.

255. von Bertalanffy L: General System Theory. New York, George Braziller, 1968.

256. Sachar E, Kanter S, Buie D, et al: Psychoendocrinology of ego disintegration. Am J Psychiatry 126:1067–1072, 1970.

257. Stein L, Wise C: Possible etiology of schizophrenia: Progressive damage to the noradrenergic reward system by 6-hydroxy-dopamine. Science 171:1032–1036, 1971.

258. Frazer A, Pandey G, Mendels J: Metabolism of tryptophan in depressive disease, Arch Gen Psychiatry 29:528–535, 1973.

259. Ashcroft G, Crawford T, Cundall R, et al: 5-Hydroxytryptamine metabolism in affective illness: The effect of tryptophan administration. Psychol Med 3:326–332, 1973.

260. Singh M: A unifying hypothesis on the biochemical basis of affective disorders. Psychiatr Q 44:706–724, 1970.

261. Mendels J, Frazer A: Intracellular lithium concentration and clinical response: Towards a membrane theory of depression. J Psychiatr Res 10:9–18, 1973.

262. Naylor G, Dick D, Dick E, et al: Erythrocyte membrane cation carrier in depressive illness. Psychol Med 3:502–508, 1973.

263. Hokin-Nyverson M, Spiegel D, Lewis W: Deficiency of erythrocyte sodium pump activity in bipolar manic depressive psychosis. Life Sci, to be published.

264. Prange A, Wilson I, Rabon A, et al: Enhancement of imipramine antidepressant activity by thyroid hormone. Am J Psychiatry 126:457–468, 1969.

265. Prange A, Wilson I, Knox A, et al: Thyroid-imipramine clinical and chemical interaction: Evidence for a receptor deficit in depression. J Psychiatr Res 9:187–205, 1972.

266. Klein D: Endogenomorphic depression: A conceptual and terminological revision. Arch Gen Psychiatry 31:447–454, 1974.

267. Senay E: General systems theory and depression, in Scott J, Senay E (eds): Separation and Depression: Clinical and Research Aspects. Washington, DC, American Association for the Advancement of Science, 1973, pp 237–246.

SEX DIFFERENCES
AND THE EPIDEMIOLOGY OF DEPRESSION

MYRNA M. WEISSMAN AND GERALD L. KLERMAN

This article reviews the evidence for differing rates of depression between the sexes in the United States and elsewhere during the last 40 years, and then critically analyzes the various explanations offered. These explanations include the possibility that the trends are spurious because of artifacts produced by methods of reporting symptoms, or that they are real because of biological susceptibility (possibly genetic or female endocrine), psychosocial factors such as social discrimination, or female-learned helplessness.

A frequent observation in epidemiologic studies of depression is that women preponderate. Observations of a sex difference in the frequency of any disease attracts attention and stimulates explanations. Depression has recently gained the attention of biologists, sociologists, feminists, and the educated public. Is it a "true" finding that women are more prone to depression? Or are the observations the result of confounding factors in case reporting or the organization of the health care system? If the finding is "real," what processes, biological or psychosocial, can best explain the differences?

The topic is timely for a number of reasons. All aspects of women's roles are currently under scrutiny. Demographic changes in the past century have increased longevity for women more than for men. However, while these changes have resulted in a larger population of women in the sixth to eighth decades, the aging of the female population in itself cannot account for the predominance of women in epidemiologic studies. For one thing, the preponderance of women is not just in absolute numbers of depressed patients but, more significantly, in rates per population group adjusted for age. At every age group, rates of depression are higher for women. If anything, there is evidence for a shift in the peak age of onset of depression. Whereas pre-World War II textbooks characterized the onset of depression as rising after the fourth decade of life, recent reports emphasize depressions in young adults, again with a predominance of females.

A number of explanations for the female preponderance have been offered. One set of explanations questions whether the findings are "real" and hypothesizes that they are more likely an artifact accounted for by women's perceptions of stress-coping responses, their willingness to express affective symptoms, and the high frequency with which they seek medical help. Alternately, the finding is considered a real phenomenon and attributed to female biological susceptibility or to social causes. In this article, we first review the evidence for differing rates of depression between the sexes and then critically analyze the various explanations offered.

METHODOLOGICAL ISSUES

In any discussion of epidemiological issues, it is customary to express cautions about the meth-

EDITORS' COMMENTS:

MANY MORE WOMEN THAN MEN ARE DEPRESSED IN WESTERN SOCIETY. THE AUTHORS EXPLORE VARIOUS EXPLANATIONS TO ACCOUNT FOR THE PREPONDERANCE OF DEPRESSION IN WOMEN AND THEY CONCLUDE THAT IT IS HIGHLY UNLIKELY THAT ANY ONE OF THESE WILL BE THE SOLE FACTOR ACCOUNTING FOR THE PHENOMENON.

Reprinted from: Archives of General Psychiatry 34:98–111, 1977. Copyright 1977, American Medical Association.

odologic problems in gathering data and the consequent difficulties in comparing findings across studies. A detailed discussion of these issues can be found in several recent reviews.[1-4]

One major source of discrepancy is that of case definition. There are at least three meanings to the term depression—a mood, a symptom, a syndrome.

Although the boundaries between mood, symptom, and syndrome are not always clear, in this article we will be interested in the depressive syndrome of primary affective disorders.[5,6] We will not be focusing on normal mood states or demoralization as reported, for example, in the studies on happiness,[7] or on secondary depressions associated with medical or psychiatric disorders.

Some of the variations in rates can be explained by variations in methodology, particularly case definition. The problems in methodological difficulties notwithstanding, it is striking that the findings show amazing consistency—the preponderance of females among depressives.

EVIDENCE THAT WOMEN PREPONDERATE AMONG DEPRESSIVES

The available evidence for the preponderance of females among depressives comes from four sources: (1) clinical observations of patients coming for treatment; (2) surveys of persons not under treatment; (3) studies of suicide and suicide attempters; (4) studies of grief and bereavement. These sources, from which a number of trends have emerged, are reviewed in Tables 1 through 3. The data are arranged by place and time of reporting.[8-76]

Most Diagnosed Depressives are Women

Rates of treated depressions are underestimates, subject to the availability of treatment facilities, the individual's willingness to seek and ability to afford care, and other factors related to utilization of health care. Therefore, such rates do not represent true estimates of the prevalence of the disorder.

Table 1 summarizes reported findings of the sex ratios for treated depressives for the United States and elsewhere, between 1936 and 1973. Looking first at the United States, a 2:1 sex ratio is fairly consistent over the time period. When a specific diagnosis is given, the ratios are lower for manic depressives (1.2:1) and higher for neurotic depres-

sives. Countries other than the United States report similar preponderances of females, with the exception of a number of developing countries such as India, Iraq, New Guinea, and Rhodesia. Interesting exceptions to the sex ratios among highly industrialized countries are Finland in 1965, and Norway in 1969, where reports describe nearly equal sex ratios.

Do More Women Get Depressed?

Since rates of treated cases do not represent true prevalence, epidemiologic analysis requires data from community surveys. Such surveys usually involve a random sample drawn from a total community, and therefore provide information on many persons who have the disorder but have not received treatment.

Table 2 summarizes data from community surveys in the United States and elsewhere. In clinical studies of diagnosed cases, the sex ratios show minor variations, but in the community surveys there are no variations, with the exception of bereaved widows (which will be discussed separately). Women preponderate in all countries and over all time periods.

Suicide and Suicide Attempters

Since Stengel's work,[77] it is conventional to distinguish between persons who die from suicide (completers) and those who make attempts (suicide attempters). Suicide attempters tend to be young females while completers are older males. Rates of suicide attempts are an indirect index of depression since many suicide attempters are depressed.

The sex ratios reported for suicide attempters in recent years are especially interesting because of the rise in rates among youthful adults (mostly under 30 years of age), a consistent trend reported internationally. All countries report an increase in suicide attempts over the last decade, which persists even after correcting for population growth or changes in reporting. Reviewing the figures (Table 3) from Australia, Great Britain, the United States, Israel, and India, the sex ratio in suicide attempts is about 2:1. The only exception is India, where the sex ratios are reversed. This reversal is consistent with the ratios of treated cases of depression but not with data from community surveys, suggesting that this may be due to a national pattern of help-seeking. In Poland the sex ratios are nearly equal for suicide attempts, but this is consistent with the

TABLE 1. Sex Ratios in Depression: Treated Cases

Place and time	Sex ratios (female/male)	Reference
UNITED STATES		
Baltimore	2:1 (psychoneurosis, including depression and manic-depressive)	8
Boston, 1945, 1955, 1965	Marked increase in young females with diagnosis of depressive reaction)	9
Pittsfield, Mass, 1946–1968	2.4:1 (patients treated with electroconvulsive therapy)	10
New York State, 1949	1.7:1	11
Massachusetts, 1957–1958	2.5:1 (all depressives)	12
Ohio, 1958–1961	First admissions: 1.9:1 (white) 2.7:1 (nonwhite)	13
Madison, Wis, 1958–1969	Increase in depression for women over decade (patients referred for psychological testing)	14
Monroe County, New York, 1960	2.1:1 (affective psychosis)	15
United States, 1961	Outpatient admissions: 1.4:1 (psychotic depression) 1.2:1 (manic depression) 1.8:1 (involutional psychosis) 1.6:1 (depressive reactions)	16
Monroe County, New York, 1961–1962	1.6:1 (prevalence) 1.3:1 (incidence)	17
New Haven, Conn, 1966	3:1 (all depressions)	18
United States, 1970	Admissions to all psychiatric facilities: 2.1:1 (all depressive disorders)	19
OUTSIDE UNITED STATES		
Amsterdam, 1916–1940	2.3:1 (Ashkenazim Jews) 2.4:1 (Gentiles)	20
Gaustad, Norway, 1926–1955	Lifetime risk of first admission: 1.37:1 (1926–1935) 1.36:1 (1946–1950) 1.33:1 (1951–1955)	21
Buckinghamshire, England, 1931–1947	1.8:1 (1931–1933) 1.9:1 (1945–1947)	11
Basel, Switzerland, 1945–1957	1.5:1 (approximately)	22
1965–1971	First admissions of manic-depressives; involutional melancholia and affective psychosis	N. Sartorius, written communication 1974 (World Health Organization data)

	1965	1967	1969	1971
Canada	1.8:1	1.7:1	1.8:1	1.7:1
Czechoslovakia	2.1:1	...	...	2.1:1

(continued)

TABLE 1 (*continued*)

Place and time	Sex ratios (female/male)				Reference
	1965	1967	1969	1971	
Denmark	2.4:1	1.9:1	1.8:1	1.8:1	
Finland*	1:1	1.3:1	...	...	
France	...	...	1.7:1	1.6:1	
Norway	1.2:1	1.2:1	0.9:1	1.5:1	
Poland*	1.4:1	1.4:1	1.4:1	...	
Sweden†	1.8:1	1.8:1	...	...	
Switzerland*	1.6:1	1.3:1	1.4:1	...	
England and Wales	1.9:1	1.9:1	1.8:1	...	
New Zealand	1.5:1	2.2:1	1.8:1	...	

Place and time		Reference
London, 1947–1949	2.1	11
Scania, Sweden, 1947, 1957	1.8:1 (Lifetime prevalence of severe depression)	23
England and Wales, 1952, 1960	1.6:1 (1952) 1.7:1 (1960)	11
Aarhus County, Denmark, 1958	2:1 (endogenous depression) 4:1 (psychogenic depression) 3:1 (depressive neurosis)	24
Salford, England, 1959–1963	1.9:1 (depressive psychosis)	25
Dakar, Guinea, 1960–1961	0.5:1	26
Madras and Madurai, India, 1961–1963	0.2:1	27
Tokyo and Taiwan, 1963–1964	Women have more depressive symptoms	28
Madurai, India, 1964–1966	0.56:1 (endogenous depression)	29
Bulaways, Rhodesia, 1965–1967	1.1:1 (N = 76)	30
Baghdad, Iraq, 1966–1967	1.1:1	31
Honduras, 1967	1.6:1 (admissions) 6.7:1 (outpatients)	32
New Delhi, 1968	0.55:1	33
Jerusalem, 1969–1972	2.1:1 (affective disorders)	34
Papua, New Guinea, 1970–1973	0.4:1 (based on a few cases)	35
Denmark, 1973	1.9:1 (first admissions for manic depression)	36
Bangkok, Thailand (time not indicated)	1.3:1 (Far East Orientals) 0.8:1 (Occidentals)	37

*Manic depressives only.
†Discharges only.

TABLE 2. Sex Differences in Depression: Community Surveys

Place and time	Sex ratios (female/male)	Reference
UNITED STATES		
Brooklyn and Queens, NY, 1960	Women were more depressed	38
Baltimore, 1968	1.6:1 (Includes wives of blue collar workers only)	39
Northern Florida, 1968	1.8:1	40
Carroll County, Maryland, 1968	Women were more nervous, helpless, anxious	41
New Haven, Conn, 1969	2:1 (suicidal feelings)	42
St. Louis, 1968–1969	No significant sex differences in depression in bereaved spouse	43
New York City, 20-year period	More referrals for minor depression in female employees in one company	44
OUTSIDE UNITED STATES		
Iceland, 1910–1957	1.6:1 (all depressions)	24
Samso, Denmark, 1960	3.5:1 (all depressions)	45
Ghiraz, Iran, 1964	3.6:1 (N = 23)	46,47
Luchnow, India, 1969–1971	2:1	B. B. Sethi, MD written communication, March 1974
Herfordshire, England, 1949–1954	2.4:1	48
Agra, India, (time not indicated)	1.6:1 (manic depression)	49
Aarhus County, Denmark, 1960–1964	1.6:1 (manic depression) 3.8:1 (psychogenic depression) 2.9:1 (neurotic depression)	50

data from first admissions (Table 1); no survey data could be found.

The Depression of Bereavement: Is it Normal?

The data on the bereaved spouse from community surveys deserve special mention since the sex ratios found in studies of bereavement are different from those found in clinical depression. The naturally occurring depression accompanying bereavement, usually called grief, has been universally noted in almost all societies, and unlike depression is considered normal and adaptive.[78–81]

The fact that there are few differences between men and women in frequency or types of depressive symptoms in the first year following bereavement lends support to the view that regards grief as qualitatively different from clinical depression. Longer-term studies are required to determine possible delayed consequences of bereavement per se, or whether absent, delayed, or atypical grief predisposes to psychosomatic, medical, or psychiatric illness. Such studies may show male-female differences, but the current evidence is that there are no differences between the sexes in the frequency of depressive symptoms following bereavements.

TABLE 3. Sex Ratios in Suicide Attempts

Place and time	Sex ratio (female/male)	Reference	Place and time	Sex Ratio (female/male)	Reference
UNITED STATES			AUSTRALIA (*cont.*)		
New York, 1960	3.1	51	Victoria, 1963	1.3:1	62
Window Rock, Ariz, 1968	2.1	52	Melbourne, 1963–1968	2.4:1	63
St. Louis, 1968–1969	2.1	53	Brisbane, 1965–1966	2.5:1	64
Providence, RI, 1968	3.1	54	Southern Tasmania, 1968–1969	2.5:1	65
New Haven, Conn, 1970	2.1	55	Melbourne, 1970	2.2:1	66
			GREAT BRITAIN		
ISRAEL			Glasgow, Scotland, 1960–1962	1.3:1	67
Israel, 1962–1963	1.5:1	56	Sheffield, England, 1960–1961	1.7:1	68
Jerusalem, 1967–1969	2.1:1	34	Edinburgh, 1962, 1967	2.1 (1962) 1.6 (1967)	69
INDIA			Leicester, England, 1961	2.4:1	70
New Delhi, 1967–1969	0.8:1	57	London, 1963	2.1:1	71
Madurai, 1964	0.8:1	58	Bristol, England, 1964–1965	2:1	72
POLAND			Shropshire, Montgomeryshire, England, 1965–1966	2.3:1	73
Krakow, 1960–1969	1.5:1 (1960) 0.6:1 (1962) 1.0:1 (1966) 1.2:1 (1967) 0.8:1 (1969)	59			
Poznania, 1970	1.1:1	59	Brighton, England, 1967	2:1	74
			Newcastle-upon-Tyne, England, 1962–1964, 1966–1969	2.5:1	75
AUSTRALIA					
Western Australia, 1961	2.1	60			
Northeast Tasmania, 1961–1963	1.7:1	61	Glasgow, Scotland, 1970	1.4:1	76

Summary of Evidence for Female Preponderance

To summarize, the evidence from international comparisons of diagnosed and treated depressed patients and from community surveys that include both treated and untreated "cases" is consistent. Women preponderate in the rates of depression.

IS THE PREPONDERANCE OF FEMALE DEPRESSIVES AN ARTIFACT OF SEX DIFFERENCES IN REPORTING STRESS AND DISTRESS?

The "artifact" hypothesis proposes that women perceive, acknowledge, report, and seek help for stress and symptoms differently than men and that these factors account for the sex ratio findings. Put another way, the "artifact" hypothesis would hold that response set and labeling processes serve to overestimate the number of female depressives.

Are Women Under More Stress?

Before the sex differences in rates of depression can be regarded as an artifact, the possibility must be considered that women are under more stressful life events and therefore are at greater risk for depression. There is an extensive research literature concerning the relationship between stress and general illness.

Many clinicians have observed stressful events occurring before the onset of clinical depression and, therefore, concluded that these events serve as precipitating events. In spite of this clinical conviction relating stress to depression, until recently there had been relatively little systematic research testing of these hypotheses. Holmes and Rahe[82] provided great impetus to these studies by developing a simple quantitative scale for assessing life events that have been used in epidemiologic and clinical studies. The results support the hypothesized relationship between stressful life events and the onset and severity of numerous medical illnesses and psychiatric disorders, particularly depression. No consistent sex differences in stress reports have appeared.[83]

Uhlenhuth and Paykel and colleagues have conducted elegant studies to examine the relationship between actual or perceived stress, using newer life events scales and the report of symptoms among patients in both psychiatric settings and normal populations in community studies.[84,85] They found a direct relationship between stress and symptom intensity, but did not find that women reported more stressful life events. At the same levels of stress, women reported symptom intensities about 25% higher than men. This study was repeated in a probability sample of all households in Oakland, Calif. with similar results.[86]

One possible criticism of these studies is that most stress scales emphasize discrete life events and acute changes in life conditions. They are relatively insensitive to certain chronic conditions, such as poverty, the impact of large family size, or health problems, that might differentially impact to a greater extent on women than men. However, pending empirical research, the available evidence is that women do not experience or report more stressful events.

Do Women Weigh Events as More Stressful?

While women may not report more stressful life events, they may evaluate events as more stressful. To study the weighing given to stress, Paykel et al[87] asked patients and their relatives to judge the degree to which various life events were upsetting; they found no sex differences. Men and women do not appear to evaluate the standard lists of life events as having different impacts on their lives.

Women Report More Symptoms, Especially Affective Distress

One hypothesis proposed to account for the excess of symptoms among women is that women respond to stress with affective distress because they feel freer to acknowledge symptoms.[88] Clancy and Gove[89] examined the possible role of social disapproval in affecting the reporting of symptoms, and they found no significant sex difference. Women did not report more desire for social approval and did not judge having psychiatric symptoms as less undesirable. They concluded that sex differences in symptom reporting appear to reflect actual differences and are not an artifact of response bias. Women experienced more symptoms.

Women Go to Doctors More Often

Women cope with problems by visiting doctors and, by every measure of utilization of the general health care system, women preponderate. They have increased rates of use of outpatient facilities, of visiting physicians, of prescriptions, and of psychotropic drug use.[90,91] Hinkle et al,[44] in a 25-year study of over 200 telephone company employees in New York City, found that women had more visits to the doctor and were away from work for health reasons more frequently, but these differences were accounted for almost entirely by minor illnesses. On the other hand, life-endangering illness occurred among men. Analysis of the risk of death based on expected case fatality rates led to an estimate that, over a 20-year period, men experienced a greater risk of death from illness than did women, in a ratio of about 4:3. On the basis of this evidence, Hinkle inferred that men and women probably experience a similar variety of minor illnesses, but men do not seek medical attention.

There is a consistency in the findings for help seeking. Women come for help for minor complaints, and mortalities show that men die sooner.

For depression, women seek treatment more often and men have a higher suicide rate.[1] In our society the public assumption of the sick role is interpreted by men as a sign of weakness. Moreover, the health care system is organized in ways that make it difficult for most men to come for treatment, ie, office hours usually conflict with hours of employment.

Help-seeking patterns alone cannot account for the preponderance of depressed women in community surveys. The majority of persons judged depressed in community surveys have not been treated in psychiatric clinics. Therefore, they have not been included in any official treatment rates. Consequently, health care-seeking behavior cannot account for the female preponderance.

Men Use More Alcohol

While depression is more common in women, alcohol use and abuse are considerably more common in men.[92] It has been hypothesized that depression and alcoholism are different but equivalent disorders. Women get depressed. Men are reluctant to admit being depressed or to seek treatment and mitigate this by drinking. Thus, men self-prescribe alcohol as a psychopharmacological treatment for depression.

Winokur and Clayton[93] noted that environmental factors may render it difficult for women to drink excessively. In families that discourage drinking by women, the same "illness" might manifest itself as depression rather than alcoholism. This hypothesis holds that alcoholism and depression are different manifestations of the same familial-genetic disorder.

While alcohol in moderate to high amounts is a central nervous system pharmacologic depressant,[94,95] in small amounts it is a psychic relaxant. Moreover, the social context of the consumption can provide support. The working-class man seeks the local pub, while middle- and upper-class men seek the country clubs or cocktail lounges; all settings provide a group atmosphere for psychopharmacological self-treatment. The psychosocial supports provided by these group situations should not be overlooked as powerful reinforcers for participation, synergistically reinforcing the pharmacological actions of alcohol itself on mood and self-esteem.

Many treated alcoholics have symptoms of depression. Tyndel,[96] in a study of 1,000 alcoholic patients, found serious depressive symptoms either at interview or in the past history of approximately 35% of alcoholics. Studies of outpatients coming for treatment of alcoholism in New Haven, Conn, found that over 50% had depressive disorders of sufficient magnitude to require antidepressant treatment. These results are consistent with earlier reports by Winokur.[97] However, studies of frequency of depression among alcoholics coming for treatment are not suitable for assessing the true incidence of depression among alcoholics, since people with two serious conditions (in this case, alcoholism and depression) have a greater probability of coming for treatment.[98]

As further evidence for an association between alcoholism and depression, excessive alcohol use has been reported in patients with bipolar illness.[99] Female depressed patients who have an early onset of depression have an increased rate of alcoholism in their first-degree relatives.[100] Suicide and suicide attempts frequently occur in the context of alcohol abuse. Depression is associated with alcohol postwithdrawal states,[101] and antidepressants and other psychotropic drugs have suggested therapeutic value in the treatment of detoxified alcoholics.[95,102-104]

These studies have not successfully sorted out causes from consequences. Two processes certainly operate. Alcohol is used by men to mitigate their symptoms of depression. For others, chronic alcohol abuse and the consequent social impairment can lead to depression. Whether cause (primary) or effect (secondary), the hypothesis that a substantial portion of depressed men appear under the diagnostic rubric of alcoholism cannot be ruled out.

Males Preponderate in Law Enforcement and Correctional Systems

In most industrial nations, women preponderate in the health care system and men in the law enforcement system and correctional institutions. It is hypothesized, therefore, that depressed men may show up in the courts rather than in the clinics, eg, a depressed man may get drunk, get into a fight, and end up in court. This hypothesis has been supported by Mazer's studies in Martha's Vineyard.[90]

If these hypotheses are verified, epidemiological studies of rates of depression must include more extensive case reporting from correctional institutions. Where this has been done in studies ascertaining rates of suicide attempts, a higher number of male attempters than is usually reported has been found.[53,105]

Summary of Evidence for Female Preponderance

Women do not have more stressful life events and do not judge life events as more stressful. While women acknowledge having symptoms and affective distress more frequently, this does not seem to be because they feel less stigma or because they wish to win approval. Women and men have different help-seeking patterns. However, increased female utilization of health care would not account for the preponderance of depressed women in community surveys, since most survey "cases" are not in psychiatric treatment either at the time of the interview or in the past.

There is no question that more males than females have alcohol abuse problems, so that some unknown proportion of depressed men appear in the alcoholism rates and are not identified as depressed. It could be debatable, however, as to whether or not these men are really depressed. Accurate diagnostic assessments are required to determine the morbid risk of depression and the time sequence of onset in relationship to alcoholism. Similar considerations apply to the possibility that the depressed men are to be found in the law enforcement system. Pending future research to test this possibility, it remains an interesting, but unproved, hypothesis. When all these possibilities are considered, our conclusion is that the female preponderance is not an artifact.

THE FEMALE PREPONDERANCE IS REAL

We must regard the sex differences as real findings and examine the possible explanations. These include hypotheses involving biological susceptibility and others involving social discrimination and its psychological consequences. Among the biological hypotheses, possible genetic transmission and female endocrine physiological processes have been investigated.

Is There a Genetic Transmission for Depression?

The possibility of a genetic factor in the etiology of depression has regularly attracted attention. There are mainly four sources of evidence for the genetic hypothesis: family aggregation studies that compare illness rates within and between generations of a particular family on the basis of the fact that members of the same family share the same genes to varying degrees; studies of twins comparing illness rates in monozygotic twins with those of dizygotic twins; cross-rearing studies; and linkage studies in which known genetic markers are used to follow other traits through several generations or in siblings. The majority of genetic studies in depression are concerned with evidence from the first two types of studies.

The available evidence summarized by several investigators[4,106,107] shows an increased morbid risk of affective disorder in the first-degree relatives of diagnosed depressives as compared with the general population, and a higher concordance rate for affective disorders in monozygotic than dizygotic twins. Taking all the studies, there is reasonable evidence for a genetic factor operating in depressive illness.

A greater frequency of a disorder in one sex is a genetically interesting phenomenon. One possible explanation is X-linkage, that is, the location of the relevant locus on the X chromosome. For an X-linked locus, if the trait is dominant, females (with two X chromosomes) will be affected more commonly. A rare X-linked recessive trait will seldom appear in the parents of children of an affected male but will always be found in both the father and all sons of an affected female. A rare X-linked dominant trait will usually appear in the mother and all of the daughters of an affected male and will occur in at least one parent and at least half of the children of an affected female. The exact frequencies with which first-degree relatives are affected is also a function of the allele frequency in the population and of the mating pattern. Based on assumptions of random mating and an X-linked dominant trait, Slater and Cowie[107] calculated that for every affected male sibling of an affected female there would be three affected female siblings.

The examination of possible X-linkage in depression has been accelerated by the identification of at least two groups of affective disorders: unipolar, which includes persons only with a major depressive illness, usually of a recurring nature (although the definition varies); and bipolar, which includes persons with episodes of both mania and depression.[108–112] The results of family studies investigating X-linkage are conflicting. Perris[113] has reported data consistent with X-linked transmission for unipolar but not for bipolar depression. However, Helzer and Winokur[114] and Reich et al[115] found data suggesting X-linkage for bipolar but not for unipolar depression. The inconsistency of studies has continued into recent work as well. Gershon et al[116] have found no evidence for X-linkage of bipolar affective disorder in a study in Jerusalem; Goetzl et al[117] had similar results in a study conducted in New Hampshire.

Another possible explanation of the different incidences in the two sexes is a differential interaction of genotype and environment depending on sex. Kidd and colleagues, in published[118] and unpublished studies, have shown that a sex effect can be treated as a differential threshold, with the less commonly affected sex having a higher threshold. The underlying liability is determined by a combination of genetic and environmental factors. They have considered two types of inheritance: a polygenic model and a single major autosomal locus. While they have not applied these models to data on depression, they have shown that many of the commonly observed aspects of the sex effect could be explained by these models. The results of Uhlenhuth and Paykel[84,85] suggest that at the same level of stress females have more symptoms than males, which is consistent with the concept of females having a lower threshold.

At this stage the findings are in need of further examination. The samples studied are small and family data on depressives who may not fit either the unipolar or bipolar classification are not available. Currently, the evidence from genetic studies is insufficient to draw conclusions about the mode of transmission or to explain the sex differences.

CAN FEMALE ENDOCRINE PHYSIOLOGY CAUSE DEPRESSION?

Interest in the possible relationships between female sex hormones and affective states derives from observations that clinical depression tends to occur in association with events in the reproductive cycle. Included are the menstrual cycle, use of contraceptive drugs, the postpartum period, and the menopause. Four questions are raised for each event: (1) are depressive symptoms more likely to be associated with these events; (2) do they occur with sufficient frequency to account for the excess of depressed women; (3) is there a specific clinical syndrome associated with the event; and (4) is any specific female hormone implicated as mediating the depression?

Premenstrual Tension

Mood changes associated with hormonal fluctuation during the normal menstrual cycle have received much attention.[119–123] The syndrome, called premenstrual tension, includes irritability, depression, bloated feelings, and headaches during the four to five days before the onset of the menses. If a substantial number of women undergo such changes on a regular monthly basis, this could account for some of the excess of female depressives. Moreover, it would suggest that some aspect of female hormonal balance plays a role in pathogenesis of depression.

The frequency of premenstrual tension as a real phenomenon has received systematic study, and a few careful clinical studies are available. Sommer,[121] in a critical review, has identified the major methodologic problem inherent in these studies, including variations in the cycle phase and response bias, and notes that studies asking the subject to report behavior changes associated with the menses are positive, whereas studies using actual objective performance measures generally fail to demonstrate menstrual cycle-related changes. Morton et al noted premenstrual tension in 80% of a volunteer sample of women prisoners, 5% of whom reported severe symptoms.[123] Lamb et al found such symptoms in 73% of a sample of student nurses.[123] McCance, on the other hand, in a study of 167 women who gave daily information about mood, found great discrepancies between what they claimed were their symptoms related to menstruation and what was actually reported on the forms.[123]

Numerous etiological hypotheses, both physiological and psychological, have been offered to explain premenstrual tension. These hypotheses have been reviewed by Tonks,[123] with no definitive conclusions, and no one sex hormone can be implicated.

Oral Contraceptive Use

The use of oral contraceptives, which provide exogenous gonadal steroids, is believed to be associated with increased depression. This hypothesis is supported by findings from case reports, uncontrolled studies, and overall side effect incidence rates. Adequately controlled studies are lacking because of the problems inherent in their design. For example, ideal control groups are difficult to establish because contraceptives cannot easily be randomly assigned or compared to placebos. Moreover, the suggestability attendant to use of all medication requires placebo controls to differentiate the psychological from the pharmacologic effects of oral contraceptives.

Weissman and Slaby[124] have reviewed the evidence and conclude that there is insufficient data to justify the conclusion that oral contraceptives cause depressive symptoms on a pharmacologic basis. There is evidence that women with a prior psychiatric history and those with an expectation of adverse side effects tend to develop more depressive symptoms while taking oral contraceptives. One well-controlled study[124] showed that mild psychiatric disturbances may develop during the first four weeks of use with high estrogen preparations. These symptoms, however, gradually disappear.

While these studies do not exclude the hypothesized physiological basis to psychiatric symptoms associated with oral contraceptive use, such an association is probably of low incidence. For example, Adams et al[125] and Winston[126] have suggested that a small number of women taking steroid hormones may become depressed because of the inhibition of the synthesis of biogenic amines in the central nervous system. This is the result of a functional pyridoxine deficiency caused by the estrogens in the oral contraceptive and may be alleviated or prevented by supplementary vitamin B_6 administration. Both studies agree that this occurs in a small number of women.

Evidence based on experiences with oral contraceptive use, like that from premenstrual tension, is not conclusive. In summary, the amount of female depression that could be attributed to the possible psychopharmacologic effects of oral contraceptives is small.

Postpartum Depression

In the postpartum period, significant hormonal changes occur and depressive mood changes have been described. Transient emotional disturbances in the first weeks following delivery, the "new baby blues," occur with such frequency as to be considered normal and resolve without treatment.[127] However, there is overwhelming evidence that the longer postpartum period (up to six months) carries an excess risk for more serious psychiatric disorders.[128-132] The most comprehensive studies on the risk of mental illness in the prepartum and postpartum periods were reported by Paffenberger and McCabe[133] and by Pugh et al.[134] Paffenberger and McCabe studied the medical records of all women in Cincinnati during a two-year period, aged 15 through 44, who were inpatients on any psychiatric service. They found that age-adjusted rates of mental illness were low for married women in general, but they were higher for women in the postpartum period and lowest for pregnant women. The peak rates of mental illness occurred in the first months following delivery. Moreover, about half of the women who suffered a postpartum illness had a recurrence in one third of their subsequent pregnancies.

Paffenberger and McCabe's results were very similar to those of Pugh et al, who studied all females, aged 15 to 44, who were first admissions to Massachusetts mental hospitals during 1950. Pugh and colleagues also found an excess of psychosis, especially the manic-depressive type, during the first three months postpartum. While all authors agree that endocrine changes are involved in the postpartum psychiatric illness, in a previous era many acute psychotic states, including delirium, may have been related to infections, fevers, dehydration, and hemorrhage following childbirth. However, with better medical care, these are rare occurrences in industrialized countries. Currently, the severe psychiatric reactions of postpartum are almost all of a depressive nature. It must be concluded that women are at greater risk for psychiatric disorders, particularly depression, in the postpartum period although, if any specific endocrine abnormality is involved, the mechanism is not understood.

Menopause

The menopausal period is presumed to produce an increased risk of depression, and depressions occurring in this period are supposed to have a distinct clinical entity. It is believed that women who are normally symptom-free experience depressive changes during this period. Moreover, the depression occurring in the menopause is described as a separate entity, and involutional melancholia appears in the official American Psychiatric Association diagnostic classification.

In regard to the supposedly characteristic clinical picture, Rosenthal reviewed 30 years of studies and concluded that involutional melancholia never existed as a separate entity. The early clinical studies were poorly controlled and contained small samples, and the recent studies find few patients with the characteristic symptom pattern. If such an entity existed in the past, its relative absence now may have to do with the availability of better case finding and effective treatments, so that depressed patients are seen earlier, before the full-blown "involutional" syndrome emerges.[135]

In regard to the possible increased risk of depression around the menopause, Winokur[136] found that there was no greater risk for depression during the menopause than during other times of the life span. Similar findings have been noted by others[1,24,25,43,137] McKinley and Jeffreys[138] conducted a community survey of over 600 women in the premenopausal and menopausal age range to ascertain the prevalence of depressive symptoms. They found that hot flashes occurred more frequently in women whose menstrual flow showed evidence of change or cessation, but few of the women sought treatment for this symptom. There was no direct relationship between depression and menopausal status. Moreover, the majority of respondents did not experience any difficulties at menopause and only 10% expressed regret at the cessation of menses. These conclusions have also been reported by Neugarten,[139] although this may vary in rural cultures, and by Hallstrom.[140]

The most definitive epidemiologic study of mental disorder in the climacteric was recently completed in Sweden.[140] Between 1968 and 1970, more than 800 women, aged 38 to 60, were surveyed to determine possible changes in mental health status during the climacteric. No significant differences were observed in the incidence rates for mental illness, depressive states, or psychiatric morbidity in the different age strata as a function of menopause. Moreover, there was no evidence that characteristic personality or emotional changes took place.

The psychologic impact of the menopause has also been implicated along with the hypothesized hormonal changes. Deykin et al,[141] Bart,[142] and others have pointed out that the period coinciding with the menopause may be associated with other life events such as departure of children from the home. These psychosocial changes may have more of an impact on women than the cessation of the menses itself.

In summary, there is no evidence that women are at greater risk for depression during the menopausal period or that depressions occurring in this period have a distinct clinical pattern.

Summary of the Endocrine Evidence

The pattern of the relationship of endocrine to clinical states is inconsistent. There is good evidence that premenstrual tension and use of oral contraceptives have an effect to increase rates, but these effects are probably of small magnitude. There is excellent evidence that the postpartum period does induce an increase in depression. Contrary to widely held views, there is good evidence that the menopause has no effect to increase rates of depression.

There is little evidence to relate these mood changes and clinical states to altered endocrine balance or specific hormones. However, it must be emphasized that no study could be located that correlated clinical state with female endocrines, utilizing modern endocrinological methods or sensitive quantitative hormonal assays. Here is an area for fruitful collaboration between endocrinol-ogy and psychiatry. While some portion of the sex differences in depression, probably during the childrearing years, may be explained endocrinologically, this factor is not sufficient to account for the large differences.

PSYCHOSOCIAL EXPLANATIONS

Sociologists, psychologists, feminists, and others concerned with women have become increasingly occupied with explaining why more women become depressed. The conventional wisdom is that the long-standing disadvantaged social status of women has psychological consequences that are depressing, and the persistence of social status discrimination is proposed to explain the long-term trends of female preponderance in depression. In addition to this hypothesis based on social status differences, there are explanations offered based on psychoanalytic theories of female personality and historical changes associated with rapid social stress.

Psychological Disadvantages of Women's Social Status

Various hypotheses have been proposed specifying the pathways whereby women's disadvantaged status might contribute to clinical depression. Our review of these hypotheses indicates two main proposed pathways. One emphasizes the low social status, legal, and economic discrimination of women; the other emphasizes women's internalization of role expectations, which results in a state of learned helplessness.

The first pathway, which we call the social status hypothesis, is widely accepted in the recent discussions on social discrimination against women. Many women find their situation depressing because the real social discriminations make it difficult for them to achieve mastery by direct action and self-assertation, further contributing to their psychological distress. Applied to depression, it is hypothesized that these inequities lead to legal and economic helplessness, dependency on others, chronically low self-esteem, low aspirations, and, ultimately, clinical depression.

The second pathway, which we call the learned helplessness hypothesis, proposes that socially conditioned, stereotypical images produce in women a cognitive set against assertion, which is reinforced by societal expectations. In this hypothesis, the classic "femininity" values are redefined as a variant of "learned helplessness," characteristic of depression.[143] Young girls learn to be helpless during their socialization and thus develop a limited response repertoire when under stress. These self-images and expectations are internalized in childhood, so that the young girl comes to believe that the stereotype of femininity is expected, valued, and normative.[144-154]

Marriage and Depression

In the few attempts to test this hypothesis that the high rates of depression are related to the disadvantages of the woman's social status, particular attention has been given to differential rates of mental illness among married and unmarried women. If this hypothesis is correct, marriage should be of greater disadvantage to the woman than to the man, since married women are likely to embody the traditional stereotyped role and should, therefore, have higher rates of depression. Gove, in particular, has focused his research on examining whether rates of mental illness among married women compare to those of other women and married men. Gove and his associates found that the higher overall rates of many mental illnesses for females are largely accounted for by higher rates for married women. In each marital status category, single, divorced, and widowed women have lower rates of mental illness than men. He concludes that being married has a protective effect for males but a detrimental effect for females.[155,156] Similar conclusions were reached by Radloff[157] from data from a community survey of depressive symptoms conducted in Kansas City, Mo, and Washington County, Maryland; by Porter in a study of depressive illness in Surrey, England, general practice;[158] by a National Health Survey of psychological distress;[158] and by Manheimer et al in a California survey of factors related to psychotropic drug use.[158]

Gove and others attribute the disadvantages of the married female to several factors: role restriction (most men occupy two roles, as household head and worker, and therefore have two sources of gratification whereas women have only one); housekeeping being frustrating and of low prestige; the unstructured role of housewife, allowing time for brooding; and even if the married woman works, her position is usually less favorable than a working man's.

Additional, but indirect, support for the hypothesized disadvantage of the female role comes from experimental research on boredom in humans. Ramsey[159] presented evidence for the negative effect of boredom, which characterized the lives of many married women. In one experiment, human subjects were exposed to a uniformly uninteresting environment; reaction time, sensory acuity, power of abstract reasoning, verbal ability, space visualization, and internal motivation to move, to daydream, or to think all decreased.

Boredom and role restriction may not be the major or only risk factors in marriage; other intervening factors such as family size and financial resources must also be taken into account. An elegant study of the interaction of some of these factors was recently reported by Brown et al.[160] Using data collected from a community survey in London, they examined the relationship between psychosocial stress and subsequent affective disorders and found that working-class married women with young children living at home had the highest rates of depression. Subject to equivalent levels of stress, working-class women were five times more likely to become depressed than middle-class women. Four factors were found to contribute to this class difference: loss of a mother in childhood; three or more children under age 14 living at home; absence of an intimate and confiding relationship with husband or boyfriend; lack of full- or part-time employment outside of home. The first three factors were more frequent among working-class women. Confidants other than spouse or boyfriend did not have a protective effect. Rather, the general levels of satisfaction and intimacy in the relationship with the husband or boyfriend and the amount of emotional support he gave the woman in her role was the important factor in preventing against depression in the face of life stress. Employment outside the home, it was suggested, provided a protective effect by alleviating boredom, increasing self-esteem, improving economic circumstances, and increasing social contacts.

The association of poor interpersonal relations within the marriage and clinical depression is further supported by studies of depressed women during psychiatric treatment. The New Haven group found that marital discord was the most common event in the previous six months reported by depressed patients compared to normals.[161] Weissman and Paykel[162] found that acutely depressed women as compared to matched normal controls reported considerably more problems in marital intimacy, especially ability to communicate with the spouse. Moreover, these marital problems often were enduring and did not completely subside with symptomatic remission of the acute depression. Furthermore, the data that unmarried women have lower rates of mental illness than unmarried men, but that married women have higher rates than married men, are cited as evidence that the excess of symptoms noted currently are not entirely due to biological factors intrinsic to being female, but are contributed to by the conflicts generated by the traditional female role.

Psychoanalytic Explanations

Among mental health clinicians, a widely held explanation for the high rates of depression among women locates the cause in female intrapsychic conflicts. It is of interest that two parallel psychoanalytic theories related to this issue were developed in the early decades of this century but were not linked together until recently with the emergence of the feminist critique. These two theories are (1) the psychoanalytic theory of female psychological development and (2) the psychodynamic theory of the psychogenesis of depression.

As regards the psychoanalytic theory of the psychology of women, Freud and others proposed that the personality of adult women, normal and neurotic, is characterized by narcissism, masochism, low self-esteem, dependency, and inhibited hostility as a consequence of the young girl's special resolution of her Oedipal complex. As is widely known, this theory has been extensively criticized, recently by Kate Millet[163] but earlier by Clara Thompson and Karen Horney.

In parallel with the theory of femininity, the classic psychodynamic theory of depression emphasized that individuals prone to depression were characterized by difficulties in close relationships, excess dependency, early childhood deprivation, excessive guilt, and tendency to turn hostility against themselves. The immediate precipitant for the overt clinical depression was hypothesized to be a loss, either actual or symbolic.

Interestingly, these two theories developed in parallel with each other for almost 50 years. Few psychoanalysts attempted to deal with the epidemiologic fact that women preponderate among depressives by linking the predisposition to depression among women to their presumed characteristic psychic conflicts related to childhood experiences of penis envy, narcissism, low self-esteem, dependency, etc.

Although these two theories in one form or another have been widely accepted among clinicians, empirical evidence in their support has been meager.[164]

The Mental Health System's Contribution

The predominance of these psychodynamic views among clinicians has contributed to criticism of the mental health system by feminists. It is claimed that women find difficulty in freeing themselves from the feminine stereotype because it has been consistently reinforced in public by "experts" on child development and psychology.

Keller,[149] Kirsh,[165] and others state that psychotherapeutic treatment too often reinforces the negative self-image of women and perpetuates the problems of women who suffer symptoms from their life situation. Psychotherapy, it is claimed, promotes dependency by reinforcing stereotypical roles.

The most pertinent work supporting the existence of sex role stereotype among mental health professionals is that of Broverman et al,[153] who asked mental health clinicians what behaviors they considered healthy in men, women, and adults with sex unspecified. These researchers found a powerful negative assessment of women. The standard for a healthy adult was the same for a healthy man, but not for a healthy woman. Healthy women were seen as differing from healthy men in that the healthy women were supposed to be submissive, dependent, subjective, emotional, and easily hurt. Thus, a double standard of mental health was found that parallels the sex role stereotypes in our society. Moreover, both sexes incorporated the better or worse aspects of the stereotypical role in their image of themselves and women tended to have a more negative self-concept than men.[153]

Feminist critics have been intense in their assertions that psychiatry is a male-oriented profession that has perpetuated male-dominated theories. Attempts have been made to encourage women to seek female therapists and to join groups for consciousness-raising. Before these assertions can be accepted, the results of some recent studies on the attitudes and views of female mental health practitioners need to be appraised.[166] In response to various case histories, male psychotherapists actually judged protocols of female patients less stringently than did female counselors. Male mental health professionals were not necessarily bound by their ideology to discriminate against women.

Historical Change, Rising Expectations, and Changing Rates of Depression

Any attempt to understand the female preponderance in depression must explain both the long-term and the short-term trends. Conventional explanations have assumed that the female preponderance in depression has been a long-term trend. Most of the studies do support this and the data that exist from the 19th century indicate a female preponderance of depression. These enduring trends can be interpreted as supporting either the biological or the social status theories.

On the other hand, recent evidence suggests short-term trends. There has been an increase in the rates of depression,[167] especially among young women, manifested by rising suicide attempt rates among young women[59] and by high attendance by women at psychiatric outpatient clinics.[168] This has prompted speculation about the possible role of recent historical changes, especially the presumed pathogenic pressures of modern life.

Rising expectations, increased life events, separations, and loss of attachment bonds are all risk factors of depression that have been suggested as mechanisms by which social change can be psychic stressors.[169] These stressors are proposed to have a greater impact on women because of their more vulnerable social position.

Rate increases in depression have been reported to have occurred during earlier periods of rapid social change. Schwab[170] has pointed to possible historical parallels to the current era in late Elizabethan and early 17th-century England, when depression was described to have reached epidemic proportions. Similarly, Rosen,[171] citing the example of late 18th-century England, quotes Edgar Shepherd (1773) who, attributing the rise in mental illness to the "wear and tear of a civilization," speculated on the reasons for the differential prevalences of mental disorder between the sexes.

Rising expectations, access to new opportunities, and efforts to redress the social inequalities of women have been suggested as further explanation for the recent increase in depression among women. Depressions may occur not when things are at their worse, but when there is a possibility of improvement, and a discrepancy between one's rising aspirations and the likelihood of fulfilling these wishes. The women's movement, governmental legislation, and efforts to improve educational and employment opportunities for women have created higher expectations. Social and economic achievement often have not kept pace with the promises, especially in a decreasing job market and where long-standing discriminatory practices perpetuate unequal opportunities.

These new role expectations may also create intrapsychic personal conflicts, particularly for those women involved in traditional family tasks but who also desire employment and recognition outside the family. While the women's movement has mainly involved middle- and upper-class and educated women, it has had an impact on women from other social classes where opportunities for work outside the home, management of money, dominance in the marriage, etc, may be crucial. Even for the educated and economically comfortable women, ambivalence and conflict continue about careers not conventionally seen as feminine.[172,173] The documented increase in suicides and suicide attempts among women suggests that social changes may be exacting psychological costs for many young women. In this regard, Gove and Tudor[152] note that communities that are extremely close-knit, stable, traditionally family-oriented, and culturally isolated have lower rates of mental illness in general, with the women having even lower rates than the men. Although support can be adduced for the hypothesis that participation in the women's movement is associated with psychological distress, it is unlikely that this is the major factor for the excess of depression among women. The differing rates substantially predate the women's movement. The shortterm changes may be disruptive, but in the long term a new equilibrium may be reached and the high female rates may begin to decrease. Such a reduction in rate of depression would be indirect confirmation of the hypothesis that the female excess of depression is due to psychological disadvantages of the female role. As behaviors become more similar between the sexes, females may begin to employ modes of coping with stress that are similar to men. There are some indications that this may be occurring in that the female rates of alcoholism, suicide, and crime (predominantly male behaviors) have begun to rise. Alternatively, the sex ratios for depression could become equal because of an increase in depression among men due to the stress produced by the change in the roles of women and by the uncertainty of the male role. In this regard, it would be interesting to determine the rates of depression among educated and emancipated women. Similarly, are the rates of depression equalized between the sexes in cultural subgroups whose sex role allocations are less rigid or nonconventional?

Summary of the Psychosocial Explanations

The most convincing evidence that social role plays an important role in the vulnerability of women to depression is the data that suggest that marriage has a protective effect for males but a detrimental effect for women. This supports the view that elements of the traditional female role may contribute to depression. Further understanding of social stress and its interactions with components of the female vulnerability in the traditional role is a promising area of research. This research would need to take into account intervening variables such as women's employment and the quality of the marriage. Any comprehensive theory, including biological ones proposed to account for the preponderance of depression among women, must explain both long-term rates and recent changes in rates.

CONCLUSIONS

The male-female differences in rates of depression are real. The evidence in support of these differential rates is best established in Western industrialized societies. Further studies in non-Western countries, particularly in Africa and Asia, are necessary before any conclusions can be drawn as to the universality of this differential rate.

There is little doubt, however, that the sex differences found in depression are a promising lead that requires considerably broader-based inquiry in epidemiology. It is highly unlikely that any one of the explanations already described will be the sole factor accounting for the phenomena, or that all types of depressions will be associated with the same risk factors. As was shown, the explanations cross such a wide variety of disciplines that rarely are all interactions entertained by any one group of investigators. There has been an unfortunate tendency for fragmentation, so that the investigators in genetics, social psychology, or endocrinology are not specifically aware of attempts by their scientific colleagues to deal with similar phenomena. The purpose of this review has been to assess different positions and, hopefully, to guide future research. The salient areas include (1) broad community-based epidemiologic studies that use consistent and operationalized diagnostic criteria and ovecome the problem of reporting and response set; (2) further research on the genetics of depression, including the nonbipolar and less severe forms of the disorder, and examination of the rates of depression in first-degree relatives of depressed patients to see if they fit frequencies and patterns consistent with a particular mode of inheritance; (3) endocrine studies on the relationship between hormones and mood; (4) cross-cultural epidemiologic studies, using consistent and similar diagnostic criteria, that examine the suggestion that depression may be less frequent in females in nonindustrialized countries; (5) longitudinal studies of the help-seeking pattern and rates of depression of women who do not assume the traditional female roles, especially in countries where women have achieved increased emancipa-

tion; and (6) close surveillance of changes in rates by sex and marital status.

In summary, we have reviewed the evidence critically and believe that the sex differences in depression in Western society are, in fact, real and not an artifact of reporting or health care behavior.

This research was supported in part by Public Health Service grant 1 RO1 MH25712 from the Center for Epidemiologic Studies, National Institute of Mental Health, Rockville, Md.

Kenneth Kidd, PhD, assisted in the preparation of the section on genetics. Ben Locke, MPH, reviewed this manuscript.

REFERENCES

1. Silverman C: The Epidemiology of Depression. Baltimore, Johns Hopkins Press, 1968.
2. Winokur GW, Clayton PJ, Reich T: Manic Depressive Illness. St. Louis, CV Mosby Co, 1969.
3. Kramer M: Cross-national study of diagnosis of the mental disorders: Origin of the problem. Am J Psychiatry 125(suppl 10):1–11, 1969.
4. Klerman GL, Barrett JE: The affective disorders: Clinical and epidemiological aspects, in Gershon S, Shopsin B (eds): Lithium: Its Role in Psychiatric Research and Treatment. New York, Plenum Press Inc, 1973.
5. Weissman MM, Pincus C, Prusoff B: Symptom patterns in depressed patients and depressed normals. J Nerv Ment Dis 160:15–23, 1975.
6. Katz MM: The classification of depression: Normal, clinical and ethnocultural, in Fieve RR (ed): Depression in the 70s. The Hague, Excerpta Medica, 1971.
7. Bradburn N, Caplowitz A: Reports on Happiness: A Pilot Study on Four Small Towns, Chicago, Aldine Publishing Co, 1965.
8. Cooper M, Lemkau P, Tietze C: Complaint of nervousness and the psychoneuroses: An epidemiological viewpoint. Am J Orthopsychiatry 12:214–223, 1942.
9. Rosenthal SH: Changes in a population of hospitalized patients with affective disorders, 1945–1965. Am J Psychiatry 123:671–681, 1966.
10. Tarnower SM, Humphries M: Depression: A recurring, genetic illness more common in females. Dis Nerv Syst 30:601–604, 1969.
11. Lehmann HE: The epidemiology of depressive disorders, in Fieve RR (ed): Depression in the 70s. The Hague, Excerpta Medica, 1971.
12. Weschler H: Community growth, depressive disorders, and suicide. Am J Sociol 67:9–16, 1961.
13. Duvall HJ, Kramer M, Locke BZ: Psychoneuroses among first admissions to psychiatric facilities in Ohio, 1958–1961. Community Ment Health J 2:237–243, 1966.
14. Rice DG, Kepecs JG: Patient sex differences and MMPI changes—1958 to 1969. Arch Gen Psychiatry 23:185–192, 1970.

15. Gardner EA, Bahn AK, Miles HC, et al: All psychiatric experience in a community. Arch Gen Psychiatry 9:365–378, 1963.

16. Rosen BF, Bahn AK, Kramer M: Demographic and diagnostic characteristics of psychiatric clinic outpatients in the U.S.A., 1961. Am J Orthopsychiatry 34:455–468, 1964.

17. Pedersen AM, Barry DJ, Babigian HM: Epidemiological considerations of psychotic depression. Arch Gen Psychiatry 27:193–197, 1972.

18. Paykel ES, Dienelt MN: Suicide attempts following acute depression. J Nerv Ment Dis 153:234–243, 1971.

19. Cannon M, Redick R: Differential Utilization of Psychiatric Facilities by Men and Women: U.S. 1970, Statistical Note 81. Surveys and Reports Section, US Dept of Health, Education, and Welfare, June 1973.

20. Grewel F: Psychiatric differences in Ashkenazim and Sephardim. Psychiatr Neurol Neurochir 70:339–347, 1967.

21. Odegaard O: The epidemiology of depressive psychoses. Acta Psychiatr Scand 162:33–38, 1961.

22. Kielholz P: Drug treatment of depressive states. Can Psychiatr Assoc J 4:S129–137, 1959.

23. Essen-Moller E, Hagnell O: The frequency and risk of depression within a rural population in Scania. Acta Psychiatr Scand 162(suppl):28–32, 1961.

24. Juel-Nielson N, Bille M, Flygenring J, et al: Frequency of depressive states within geographically delimited population groups. Acta Psychiatr Scand 162:69–80, 1961.

25. Adelstein AM, Downham DY, Stein Z, et al: The epidemiology of mental illness in an English city: Inceptions recognized by Salford Psychiatric Services, Soc Psychiatry 3:455–468, 1964.

26. Collomb H, Zwingelstein J: Depressive states in an African community, in Lamba J (ed): First Pan-African Psychiatric Conference Report. Abeokuta, Nigeria, 1961.

27. Venkoba Rao A: Depression in Southern India. International Congress Series 150, The Hague, Excerpta Medica, 1966, pp 1882–1885.

28. Rin H, Schooler C, Caudill W: Symptomatology and hospitalization: Culture, social structure and psychopathology in Taiwan and Japan. J Nerv Ment Dis 157:296–312, 1973.

29. Venkoba Rao A: A study of depression as prevalent in South India. Transcult Psychiatr Res 7:166–168, 1970.

30. Buchan T: Depression in African patients. S Afr Med J 43:1055–1058, 1969.

31. Bazzoui W: Affective disorders in Iraq. Br J Psychiatry 117:195–203, 1970.

32. Hudgens R, deCastro MI, deZuniga EA: Psychiatric illness in a developing country: A clinical study. Am J Psychiatry 60:1788–1805, 1970.

33. Teja J, Aggarwal AK, Narang RL: Depression across cultures. Br J Psychiatry 119:253–260, 1971.

34. Gershon ES, Liebowitz JH: Sociocultural and demographic correlates of affective disorders in Jerusalem. J Psychiatr Res 12:37–50, 1975.

35. Torrey EF: Is schizophrenia universal? An open question. Schizophrenia Bull 7:53–59, 1973.

36. Dupont A, Videbech T, Weeke A: A cumulative national psychiatric register: Its structure and application. Acta Psychiatr Scand 50:161–173, 1974.

37. Tongyonk J: Depression in Thailand in the perspective of comparative-transcultural psychiatry. J Psychiatr Assoc Thailand 16:337–354, 1971.

38. Benfari RC, Beiser M, Leighton AH, et al: Some dimensions of psychoneurotic behavior in an urban sample. J Nerv Ment Dis 155:77–90, 1972.

39. Siessi I, Crocetti G, Spiro H: Loneliness and dissatisfaction in a blue-collar population. Arch Gen Psychiatry 30:261–265, 1974.

40. Schwab JJ, McGinnis NH, Warheit GJ: Social psychiatric impairment: Racial comparisons. Am J Psychiatry 130:183–187, 1973.

41. Hogarty GE, Katz MM: Norms of adjustment and social behavior. Arch Gen Psychiatry 25:470–480, 1971.

42. Paykel ES, Myers JK, Lindenthal JJ, et al: Suicidal feelings in the general population: A prevalence study. Br J Psychiatry 124:1–10, 1974.

43. Clayton PJ, Halikas JA, Maurice W: The depression of widowhood. Br J Psychiatry 120:71–77, 1972.

44. Hinkle LE, Redmont R, Plummer N, et al: II. An explanation of the relation between symptoms, disability, and serious illness in two homogeneous groups of men and women. J Public Health 50:1327–1336, 1960.

45. Sorenson A, Stromgren E: Frequency of depressive states within geographically delimited population groups. Acta Psychiatr Scand 37:32–68, 1961.

46. Bash KW, Bash-Liechti J: Studies on the epidemiology of neuropsychiatric disorders among the rural population of the province of Khuzestran, Iran. Soc Psychiatry 4:137–143, 1969.

47. Bash KW, Bash-Liechti J: Studies on the epidemiology of neuropsychiatric disorders among the population of the city of Shiraz, Iran. Soc Psychiatry 9:163–171, 1974.

48. Martin FF, Brotherston JHF, Chave SPW: Br J Prev Soc Med 11:196–202, 1957.

49. Dube KC, Kumar N: An epidemiologic study of manic-depressive psychosis. Acta Psychiatr Scand 49:691–697, 1973.

50. Weeke AB, Videbeck T, Dupont A, et al: The incidence of depressive syndromes in a Danish County. Acta Psychiatr Scand 51:28–41, 1975.

51. Hirsh J, Zauder HL, Drolette BM: Suicide attempts with ingestants. Arch Environ Health 3:94–98, 1961.

52. Miller SI, Schoenfeld LS: Suicide attempts patterns among the Navajo Indians. Int J Soc Psychiatry 17:180–193, 1971.

53. Clendenin WW, Murphy GE: Wrist cutting: New epidemiological findings. Arch Gen Psychiatry 25:465–469, 1971.

54. Ianzito BM: Attempted suicide by drug ingestion. Dis Nerv Syst 31:453–458, 1970.

55. Weissman MM, Paykel ES, French N, et al: Suicide attempts in an urban community, 1955 and 1970. Soc Psychiatry 8:82–91, 1973.

56. Modan B, Nissenkorn I, Lewkowski SR: Comparative epidemiologic aspects of suicide and attempted suicide in Israel. Am J Epidemiol 91:393–399, 1970.

57. Venkoba Rao A: Attempted suicide (an analysis of 114 medical admissions into the Erskine Hospital, Madurai). Indian J Psychiatry 7:253–264, 1965.

58. Venkoba Rao A: Suicide attempters in Madurai. J Indian Med Assoc 57:278–284, 1971.

59. Weissman MM: The epidemiology of suicide attempts. Arch Gen Psychiatry 30:737–746, 1974.

60. James IP, Derham SP, Scott-Orr DN: Attempted suicide: A study of 100 patients referred to a general hospital. Med J Aust 1:375–380, 1963.

61. Gold N: Attempted suicide with chlorpromazine. Med J Aust 1:492–493, 1966.

62. Krupinski J, Stoller A, Polke P: Attempted suicides admitted to the mental health department, Victoria, Australia: A sociodemographic study. Int J Soc Psychiatry 13:5–13, 1966.

63. Hetzel BS: The epidemiology of suicidal behavior in Australia. Aust NZ J Psychiatry 5:156–166, 1971.

64. Edwards JE, Whitlock FA: Suicide and attempted suicide in Brisbane: I. Med J Aust 1:932–938, 1968.

65. Freeman JW, Ryan CA, Beattie RR: Epidemiology of drug overdosage in Southern Tasmania. Med J Aust 57:1168–1172, 1970.

66. Oliver RG, Kaminski, Z, Tudor K, et al: The epidemiology of attempted suicide as seen in the casualty department, Alfred Hospital, Melbourne. Med J Aust 1:833–839, 1971.

67. Sclare AB, Hamilton CM: Attempted suicide in Glasgow. Br J Psychiatry 109:609–615, 1963.

68. Parkin D, Stengel E: Incidence of suicidal attempts in an urban community. Br Med J 2:133–138, 1965.

69. Aitken RCB, Buglass D, Kreitman N: The changing pattern of attempted suicide in Edinburgh, 1962–1967. Br J Prev Soc Med 23:111–115, 1969.

70. Ellis GG, Comish KA, Hewer, RL: Attempted suicide in Leicester. Practitioner 196:557–561, 1966.

71. Bridges PK, Koller KM: Attempted suicide: A comparative study. Compr Psychiatry 7:240–247, 1966.

72. Roberts J, Hooper D: The natural history of attempted suicide in Bristol. Br J Med Psychol 42:303–312, 1969.

73. Hershon HI: Attempted suicide in a largely rural area during an eight year period. Br J Psychiatry 114:279–284, 1968.

74. Jacobson S, Tribe P: Deliberate self-injury (attempted suicide) in patients admitted to hospital in Mid-Sussex. Br J Psychiatry 121:379–386, 1972.

75. Smith JS, Davison K: Changes in the pattern of admissions for attempted suicide in Newcastle-upon-Tyne during the 1960s. Br Med J 4:412–415, 1971.

76. Patel AR, Roy M, Wilson GM: Self-poisoning and alcohol. Lancet 2:1099–1102, 1972.

77. Stengel E: Suicide and Attempted Suicide. Middlesex, England, Penguin Books, 1964.

78. Clayton PJ, Halikas JA, Maurice WL: The bereavement of the widowed. Dis Nerv Syst 32:597–604, 1971.

79. Klerman G, Izen J: The effects of grief and bereavement on physical health and general well being, in Reicksman F (ed): Advances in Psychosomatic Medicine: Epidemiologic Studies in Psychosomatic Medicine. Basel, Switzerland, S Karger, 1977.

80. Lindemann E: The symptomatology and management of acute grief. Am J Psychiatry 101:141–148, 1944.

81. Engel G: Is grief a disease? Psychosom Med 23:18–22, 1961.

82. Holmes TH, Rahe RH: The social readjustment rating scale. J Psychosom Res 11:213–218, 1967.

83. Horowitz M: New directions in epidemiology. Science 188:850–851, 1975.

84. Uhlenhuth EH, Paykel ES: Symptom intensity and life events. Arch Gen Psychiatry 28:473–477, 1973.

85. Uhlenhuth EH, Paykel ES: Symptom configuration and life events. Arch Gen Psychiatry 28:744–748, 1973.

86. Uhlenhuth EH, Lipman RS, Balter MB, et al: Symptom intensity and life stress in the city. Arch Gen Psychiatry 31:759–764, 1974.

87. Paykel ES, Prusoff BA, Uhlenhuth EH: Scaling of life events. Arch Gen Psychiatry 25:340–347, 1971.

88. Blumenthal MD: Measuring depressive symptomatology in a general population. Arch Gen Psychiatry 32:971–978, 1975.

89. Clancy K, Gove W: Sex differences in mental illness: An analysis of response bias in self reports. Am J Sociol 80:205–216, 1974.

90. Mazer M: People in predicament: A study in psychiatric and psychosocial epidemiology. Soc Psychiatry 9:85–90, 1974.

91. Parry HJ, Balter MB, Mellinger GD, et al: National patterns of psychotherapeutic drug use. Arch Gen Psychiatry 28:769–783, 1973.

92. Gomberg ES: Women and alcoholism, in Franks V, Burtle V (eds): Women in Therapy. New York, Brunner/Mazel Inc, 1974.

93. Winokur G, Clayton P: Family history studies: II. Sex differences and alcoholism in primary affective illness. Br J Psychiatry 113:973–979, 1967.

94. Mayfield DG, Coleman LL: Alcohol use and affective disorder. Dis Nerv Syst 29:467–474, 1968.

95. Mayfield DG: Psychopharmacology of alcohol: I. Affective change with intoxication, drinking, behavior and affective state. J Nerv Ment Dis 146:314–321, 1968.

96. Tyndel M: Psychiatric study of 1,000 alcoholic patients. Can Psychiatr Assoc J 19:21–24, 1974.

97. Winokur G: Family history studies. VIII. "Secondary depression is alive and well, and . . ." Dis Nerv Syst 33:94–99, 1972.

98. Lilienfeld A, Pedersen E, Dowd JE: Cancer Epidemiology: Methods of Study. Baltimore, Johns Hopkins Press, 1967.

99. Reich LH, Davies RK, Himmelhoch JM: Excessive alcohol use in manic-depressive illness. Am J Psychiatry 131:83–86, 1974.

100. Winokur G, Clayton P: Family history studies: IV. Comparison of male and female alcoholics. Q J Stud Alcohol 29:885–891, 1968.

101. Butterworth AT: Depression associated with alcohol withdrawal: Imipramine therapy compared with placebo. Q J Stud Alcohol 32:343–348, 1971.

102. Overall JE, Brown D, Williams JD, et al: Drug treatment of anxiety and depression in detoxified alcoholic patients. Arch Gen Psychiatry 29:218–221, 1973.

103. Rosenberg C: Drug maintenance in the outpatient treatment of chronic alcoholism. Arch Gen Psychiatry 30:373–377, 1974.

104. Wren JC, Kline NS, Cooper TB, et al: Evaluation of lithium therapy in chronic alcoholism. Clin Med 81:33–36, 1974.

105. Whitehead PC, Johnson FG, Ferrence R: Measuring the incidence of self-injury: Some methodological and design considerations. Am J Orthopsychiatry 43:142–148, 1973.

106. Gershon ES, Dunner DL, Goodwin FK: Toward a biology of affective disorders. Arch Gen Psychiatry 25:1–15, 1971.

107. Slater E, Cowie V: The Genetics of Mental Disorders, Oxford Monographs on Medical Genetics, London, Oxford University Press, 1971.

108. Leonhard K: Aufteilung der Endogenen Psychosen. Berlin, Akademieverlag, 1957.

109. Leonhard K, Korff I, Schulz H: Die temperamente in den familien der monopolaren und bipolaren phasischen psychosen. Psychiatr Neurol 143:416–434, 1962.

110. Winokur G, Clayton P: Family history studies: I. Two types of affective disorders separated according to genetic and clinical factors, in Wartis IJ (ed): Recent Advances in Biological Psychiatry. New York, Plenum Press Inc, 1967.

111. Perris C: A study of bipolar (manic-depressive) and unipolar recurrent depressive psychoses. Acta Psychiatr Scand 42(suppl 194):1–89, 1966.

112. Goodwin FK, Ebert MH: Lithium in mania: Clinical trials and controlled studies, in Gershon S, Shopsin B (eds): Lithium: Its Role in Psychiatric Research and Treatment. New York, Plenum Press Inc, 1973.

113. Perris C: Abnormality on paternal and maternal sides: Observations in bipolar (manic-depressive) and unipolar depressive psychoses. Br J Psychiatry 118:207–210, 1971.

114. Helzer JE, Winokur G: A family interview study of male manic depressives. Arch Gen Psychiatry 31:73–77, 1974.

115. Reich T, Clayton P, Winokur G: Family history studies: V. The genetics of mania. Am J Psychiatry 125:1358–1369, 1969.

116. Gershon ES, Bunney WE, Leckman JF, et al: The inheritance of affective disorders: A review of data and of hypotheses. Behav Genet. 6:227, 1976.

117. Goetzl U, Green R, Whybrow P, et al: X linkage revisited. Arch Gen Psychiatry 31:665–672, 1974.

118. Kidd KK, Reich T, Kessler S: A genetic analysis of stuttering suggesting a single major locus, abstracted. Genetics 74:s137, 1973.

119. Neu C, DiMascio A: Variations in the menstrual cycle. Medical Aspects of Human Sexuality. February 1974, pp 164–180.

120. Shader RI, Ohly JI: Premenstrual tension, femininity, and sexual drive. Medical Aspects of Human Sexuality. April 1970, pp 42–49.

121. Sommer T: The effect of menstruation on cognitive and perceptual-motor behavior: A review. Psychosom Med 35:515–534, 1973.

122. Bardwick JM: The sex hormones, the central nervous system and affect variability in humans, in Frank V, Burtle V (eds): Women in Therapy. New York, Brunner/Mazel Inc, 1974.

123. Tonks C: Premenstrual tension. Br J Hosp Med 7:383–387, 1968.

124. Weissman MM, Slaby AE: Oral contraceptives and psychiatric disturbance: Evidence from research. Br J Psychiatry 123:513–518, 1973.

125. Adams PW, Rose DP, Folkard J, et al: Effect of pyridoxine hydrochloride (vitamin B_6) upon depression associated with oral contraception. Lancet 1:897–904, 1973.

126. Winston F: Oral contraceptives, pyridoxine, and depression. Am J Psychiatry 130:1217–1221, 1973.

127. Yalom ID, Lunde TT, Moos RH, et al: Postpartum blues syndrome. Arch Gen Psychiatry 18:16–27, 1968.

128. Thuwe I: Genetic factors in puerperal psychosis. Br J Psychiatry 125:378–385, 1974.

129. Brown WA, Shereshefsky P: Seven women: A prospective study of postpartum psychiatric disorders. Psychiatry 35:139–159, 1972.

130. Butts HF: Postpartum psychiatric problems. J Natl Med Assoc 61:136–139, 1969.

131. Gordon R, Gordon K: Social factors in the prediction and treatment of emotional disorders of pregnancy. Am J Obstet Gynecol 77:1074–1083, 1959.

132. Asch SS, Rubin LJ: Postpartum reactions: Some unrecognized variations. Am J Psychiatry 131:870–874, 1974.

133. Paffenberger RS, McCabe LJ: The effect of obstetric and perinatal events on risk of mental illness in women of childbearing age. Am J Public Health 56:400–407, 1966.

134. Pugh TF, Jerath BK, Schmidt WM, et al: Rates of mental disease related to childbearing. N Engl J Med 268:1224–1228, 1963.

135. Rosenthal SH: The involutional depressive syndrome. Am J Psychiatry 124(suppl):21–35, 1968.

136. Winokur G: Depression in the menopause. Am J Psychiatry 130:92–93, 1973.

137. Juel-Nielsen N, Stromgren E: A five-year survey of a psychiatric service in a geographically delimited rural population given easy access to this service. Compr Psychiatry 6:139–165, 1965.

138. McKinley SM, Jeffreys M: The menopausal syndrome. Br J Prev Soc Med 28:108–115, 1974.

139. Neugarten B: Middle Age and Aging. University of Chicago Press, 1968.

140. Hallstrom T: Mental Disorder and Sexuality in the Climacteric. Goteberg, Sweden, Orstadius Biktryckeri AB, 1973.

141. Deykin EY, Jacobson S, Klerman GL, et al: The empty nest: Psychosocial aspects of conflict be-

tween depressed women and their grown children. Am J Psychiatry 122:1422–1426, 1966.

142. Bart P: Mother Portnoy's complaints. Trans-Action, November–December 1970, pp 69–74.

143. Seligman ME: Depression and learned helplessness, in Friedman RJ, Katz MM (eds): The Psychology of Depression: Contemporary Theory and Research. Washington, DC, VH Winston & Sons, 1974.

144. Cole JD, Pennington BF, Buckley HH: Effects of situational stress and sex roles on the attribution of psychological disorder. J Consult Clin Psychol. to be published.

145. Menaker E: The therapy of women in the light of psychoanalytic theory and the emergence of a new view, in Franks V, Burtle V (eds): Women in Therapy. New York, Brunner/Mazel Inc, 1974.

146. Beck AT, Greenberg RL: Cognitive therapy with depressed women, in Franks V, Burtle V (eds): Women in Therapy. New York, Brunner/Mazel Inc, 1974.

147. Maccoby EE, Jacklin CN: Psychology of Sex Differences. Palo Alto, Calif, Stanford University Press, 1975.

148. Friedman RC, Richart RM, Vande Wiele RL (eds): Sex Differences in Behavior, New York, John Wiley & Sons, 1975.

149. Keller S: The female role: Constants and change, in Franks V, Burtle V (eds): Women in Therapy, New York, Brunner/Mazel Inc, 1974.

150. Bart P: Unalienating abortion, demystifying depression, and restoring rape victims. Read before the American Psychiatric Association, Anaheim, Calif, May 7, 1975.

151. Chesler P: Women and Madness. New York, Doubleday & Co Inc, 1972.

152. Gove WR, Tudor JF: Adult sex roles and mental illness. Am J Sociol 78:812–835, 1973.

153. Broverman IK, Broverman DM, Clarkson FE, et al: Sex-role stereotypes and clinical judgments of mental health. J Consult Clin Psychol 34:1–7, 1970.

154. Gove WR, Lester BJ: Social position and self-evaluation: A reanalysis of the Yancy, Rigsby, and McCarthy data. Am J Sociol 79:1308–1314, 1974.

155. Gove WR: The relationship between sex roles, marital status, and mental illness. Soc Forces 51:34–44, 1972.

156. Gove WR: Sex, marital status, and mortality. Am J Sociol 79:45–67, 1973.

157. Radloff L: Sex differences in depression: The effects of occupation and marital status. Sex Roles 1:249–269, 1975.

158. Bachrach L: Marital Status and Mental Disorder: An Analytical Review, publication (ADM) 75-217. US Dept of Health, Education, and Welfare, 1975.

159. Ramsey ER: Boredom: The most prevalent American disease. Harpers 249:12–22, November 1974.

160. Brown G, Bhrolchain M, Harris T: Social class and psychiatric disturbance among women in an urban population. Sociology 9:225–254, 1975.

161. Paykel ES, Myers JK, Dienelt MN, et al: Life events and depression: A controlled study. Arch Gen Psychiatry 21:753–760, 1969.

162. Weissman MM, Paykel ES: The Depressed Woman: A Study of Social Relationships. University of Chicago Press, 1974.

163. Millet K: Sexual Politics. New York, Doubleday & Co Inc, 1970.

164. Chodoff P: The depressive personality: A critical review. Arch Gen Psychiatry 27:666–673, 1972.

165. Kirsh B: Consciousness-raising groups as therapy for women, in Franks V, Burtle V (eds): Women in Therapy. New York, Brunner/Mazel Inc, 1974.

166. Schwartz JM, Abramovitz SI: Value-related effects on psychiatric judgment. Arch Gen Psychiatry 32:1525–1529, 1975.

167. Secunda S, Katz M, Friedman R, et al: The Depressive Disorders. US Dept of Health, Education, and Welfare, 1973.

168. Zonana H, Henisz J, Levine M: Psychiatric emergency service a decade later. Psychiatry Med 4:273–290, 1973.

169. Klerman GL: Depression and adaptation, in Friedman R, Katz M (eds): The Psychology of Depression: Contemporary Theory and Research. Washington, DC, VH Winston & Sons, 1974.

170. Schwab J: Coming in the 70's—An epidemic of depression. Attitude 1:2–6, 1970.

171. Rosen G: Social stress and mental disease from the 18th century to the present: Some origins of social psychiatry. Milbank Mem Fund Q 37:5–32, 1959.

172. Horner M: Towards an understanding of achievement related conflicts in women. J Soc Issues 28:157–175, 1972.

173. Weissman MM, Pincus C, Radding R, et al: The educated housewife: Mild depression and the search for work. Am J Orthopsychiatry 43:565–573, 1973.

ASSESSMENT OF SUICIDE RISK

RICHARD I. SHADER

As with other human behaviors, suicide (attempted or completed) can reflect several motivational determinants, personal and interpersonal as well as cultural. Self-immolation is a well-known *religious* (or nationalistic or political) phenomenon. At the same time, death can be seen as a *release* from despair, pain, old age, or a sense of a barren future, or as a means of *rebirth*. It can be experienced as *revenge* (e.g., "you'll be sorry when I'm dead") or as *reunification* with a lost loved one. Suicide also can be a *response* to the disordered thinking of a psychotic decompensation (e.g., hearing a voice directing one to die) or to the disordered thinking of a toxic state (e.g., stepping out of a window and falling to one's death in a response to a belief that one can walk on air or fly).

Just as vital signs are a fundamental part of a physical examination, in a psychiatric examination an assessment of suicidal risk is fundamental. It should *not* be restricted solely to those appearing depressed. Since suicidal impulses may wax and wane and may be more or less evident, continuing reassessment may be required for some patients. Inquiry about suicidal concerns and impulses can be conducted in a systematic manner,

progressing from more general to more specific questions, such as: "How depressed do you feel?" "Do you ever want to die?" "What was going on in your life when you were thinking about killing yourself?" "Did you have a plan?" Clinical experience does not support the fear that asking patients about suicide will put the idea into their minds. Observation of the patient for facial, postural, and other nonverbal clues also is an important part of suicide risk assessment. It may be important with some patients to question family members or other informants about their sense of the patient's suicide potential.

Since the assessment of an individual patient's potential for suicide is a complex and difficult task, attention must be paid to what is said (and *not* said), what has happened (or *not* happened), who is available to the patient (with particular attention to those who feel no one is available or who have just lost or been separated from their last or only caring relationship), and what has been done (or *not* done). The mélange of suicidal variants—attempts, manipulative gestures, thoughts, preoccupations and obsessive ruminations, and the act per se—must be sorted out. Examples are the hurt and angry young child who says "You'll be sorry when I die myself"; the young woman who tries to hold onto her lover by ingesting a nonlethal dose of aspirin; the smoker who says "I wonder why I'm paying someone to kill me"; the recently widowed, 60-year-old man who wants to die; or the middle-aged man who shoots himself when he learns that he has an inoperable carcinoma.

It is important to learn how the patient feels about the future. Does he have evidence of an orientation toward the future? Does he entertain realizable goals and realistic expectations, or is he setting himself up for disappointment and loss?

EDITORS' COMMENTS:

SUICIDE IS A MAJOR CONCERN FOR THE DEPRESSED PATIENT. THE ASSESSMENT OF THE SUICIDAL PATIENT, BASED ON ALL THE AVAILABLE DATA THAT ONE HAS FOLLOWING AN INTERVIEW, THUS BECOMES VERY IMPORTANT.

Reprinted from Manual of Psychiatric Therapeutics, Boston, Little, Brown and Company, pp. 305–310, 1975. Copyright 1975, Little Brown and Company.

Assessment must be a continuing process, and one must remain alert to newly appearing stresses in the patient's life and to changes in the patient's available interpersonal and material resources.

No single sign or set of signs is a reliable indicator of a patient's suicide potential. Attention must be paid to the patient's appearance, mood, and thought content and to the overall significance of biographic elements (e.g., the fact that a patient is known to have put his affairs in order* may suggest a plan for suicide). It is likely that the recognized incidence of suicide (20,000 to 25,000 suicides annually reported in the United States) is an underestimate, ignoring the suicidal implications of numerous automobile accidents, home fires, and such. At least transient suicidal thoughts are reported in some surveys to occur in about 15 percent of the general population. The following section details specific factors that may serve to increase the clinician's index of suspicion.

I. **Biographic Factors Relevant to Suicide Risk Assessment**

   A. **History of previous attempts**
      1. A pattern of repeated threats of attempts is common. Depending on samples and methods of study, from 20 to 60 percent of suicides have tried before. Known attempts are about ten times more frequent than successful suicides.
      2. Those who have attempted suicide before are more likely to succeed than nonattempters.
      3. Second attempts commonly come within three months after the first attempt.

   B. **Occupational status**
      1. The unemployed and the unskilled have higher suicide rates than those who are skilled and employed.
      2. By profession, higher suicide rates occur in policemen, musicians, dentists, insurance agents, physicians (especially psychiatrists, ophthamologists, and anesthesiologists), and lawyers.
      3. A sense of failure in fulfilling one's occupational role (e.g., in job or as wife-mother) is a common factor in suicides.

   C. **Marital status**   Single (never married) persons are at greater risk for suicide, followed in rank order by persons widowed, separated and divorced, married without children, and married with children. Those who live "all alone in the world," or who feel alone (with no one who cares or no one to care about), and those who have recently lost a loved one or failed in a love relationship (particularly within the preceding six months to a year) always must be considered serious suicide risks.

   D. **Sex**
      1. **Men successfully** *commit* suicide more frequently than women, perhaps three times as often. Perhaps at highest risk for suicide is the middle-aged male with a recent life crisis (e.g., a health problem, such as myocardial infarction, carcinoma, or kidney disease; a major financial setback; a significant loss of a loved one) who makes use of alcohol and tends to deny depression.
      2. Women *attempt* suicide more often (two or three times) than men.

   E. **Age**
      1. Suicides may occur in the young, but they are uncommon prior to adolescense.
      2. The frequency of suicide increases with age for men until the seventh decade; a decline begins in the 75 to 85 age range.
      3. In women the peak frequency for suicide is between 55 and 65 years of age.

   F. **Family history**   Successful and attempted suicides are more common among those with a family history of attempts or suicides.

   G. **Emotional factors**
      1. Depression (grief, hypochondriasis, insomnia, guilt, gloominess, despair about the future) is a major factor in suicides.
      2. Psychosis—particularly with associated terror, suspiciousness, persecutory delusions, hallucinations urging suicide or reasons for dying. Psychotic depressives and young catatonics are especially high risk groups.
      3. Acute and chronic alcoholism and other forms of drug-dependency.
      4. For women of childbearing age, postpartum months and the premenstrual week are high risk times.

   H. **Health factors**
      1. Patients who have undergone recent surgery are at special risk.
      2. Patients with intractable pain.

---

*Examples are writing of or changes in last will and testament; buying a burial plot; or making a plan for the disposition of one's remains or effects.

3. Chronic or protracted diseases.
4. Terminal illnesses.

I. **Help-seeking** Although many suicides have sought medical or psychiatric care within the year preceding an attempt, help-seeking is not a reliable factor, as illustrated by a study of suicides among college students in which none had sought help nor had they appeared depressed to those who knew them.

J. **Race** Within the United States, recorded suicide rates are higher for whites than for nonwhites.

K. **Geographic location** Rates are higher in urban as compared to rural settings.

II. Treatment

Unfortunately, assessment of suicide risk and treatment planning may be influenced by clinicians' varied reactions to suicidal patients. Some, for example, imply or openly state that they cannot take responsibility for someone else's life. This attitude often confuses feelings of helplessness, anger, and disappointment-rejection with civil liberties and philosophical positions about individuals' rights. It is important to realize that in all states suicide has legal implications, and commitment laws may allow the hospitalization of those who are considered a danger to themselves. Some clinicians banter with suicide attempters, trying to mimimize or undercut the seriousness of the attempt. Some clinicians restrict banter to those who have made repeated attempts. This therapeutic style often assumes a manipulative aspect to the attempt. There are, by contrast, clinicians who hospitalize suicide attempters and then are reluctant to discharge them, feeling uncertain about judging patients' freedom from suicidal impulses.

Although it is beyond the scope of this chapter to offer guidelines for treatment of individual patients, consideration of aspects of one approach to treatment may be helpful. The author approaches most suicidal patients with a bias based on clinical experience—*the majority of suicidal patients change their minds.* When patients have suicidal thoughts or behavior associated with endogenous depressive syndromes, effective treatment of the depression usually is sufficient. Similarly, in suicidal behavior secondary to the hallucinations or delusions of a psychotic state, adequate treatment of the psychosis should be effective. Borderline

patients with intense dysphoria also may respond to therapeutic strategies. The recently widowed may be helped to grieve and may find support and companionship from association with others who are successfully handling widowhood.

With each patient, however, the aim is to come to understand and have the patient understand why he wants to die and what might help to make life more worthwhile. Some key elements in working with suicidal patients are: listening to the patient, being open to hearing their often ambivalently expressed cries for help and their deep despair or loneliness; understanding and managing one's own countertransference reactions, such as helplessness, anger, or rejection; *taking seriously all threats of suicide;* providing a safe, nonrejecting environment—this may range from helping the patient to reveal his feelings and impulses to family and friends so that they will be more open and, if necessary, spend increased time with the patient, to hospitalization with continuous observation; the patient's person and his immediate environment may require attention to minimize destructive opportunities—safety screens for hospital windows must not be overlooked; use of appropriate interpersonal and somatic therapies; an awareness that improvement in the patient's mood may reflect a decision to try again—continued support and involvement during this phase are essential; taking the crucial risk of reducing suicide precautions and permitting the patient more freedom—the timing of this shift must include consideration of the amount of improvement in the patient's suicidal thoughts, depressed mood, or withdrawal, evidence of an orientation toward the future, and a sense that the patient is engaged with staff in some form of therapeutic alliance; involvement of family members and friends, when appropriate, so that the patient does not return to the same circumstances that contributed to the patient's decision to die; working out with the patient a plan for aftercare and followup—such planning should take into consideration that some patients feel less suicidal when a therapist temporarily fills some void, and that this can lead to a reemergence of suicidal impulses when treatment termination or interruption is discussed—therapeutic planning must face this possibility, and the therapist must be aware of the quality of other relationships available to the patient; the absence of other available object relationships must be considered, and part of treatment planning should include helping the patient to develop them—group therapy may be beneficial; involvement of community resource persons (e.g., teacher, family, physician, clergyman) may be beneficial to some patients.

A second bias has emerged from the author's clinical experience—*patients who continue to want to die will usually find a way.* We can delay death and provide an opportunity for the patient to improve from a particular episode of depression, demoralization, grief, or psychosis. Some patients, however, find life so empty or painful that a second chance to them means a second chance to die, not a second chance to find something to live for or to work out their disappointment in themselves. A word of caution is in order—the clinician must not let his own feeling that he would not want to live under a particular set of conditions dictate his care of the patient. For example, this can be especially difficult when working with a patient with inoperable and painful metastatic carcinoma.

Suicidal patients should be viewed as medical emergencies, and program planning must recognize the need for 24-hour services.

REFERENCES

Dublin, L. I. Suicide. New York: Ronald, 1963.

Durkheim, E. Le Suicide. Glencoe, Ill.: Free Press, 1950.

Farberow, N. L., and Schneidman, E. S. The Cry for Help. New York: McGraw-Hill, 1961.

Schneidman, E. S., and Farberow, N. L. Clues to Suicide. New York: McGraw-Hill, 1957.

THE STAGES OF MANIA:
A LONGITUDINAL ANALYSIS OF THE MANIC EPISODE

GABRIELLE A. CARLSON AND FREDERICK K. GOODWIN

The progression of symptoms during an acute manic episode was studied retrospectively in 20 bipolar manic-depressive patients whose diagnosis was reconfirmed at follow-up. Three stages were delineated, the most severe of which was manifested by bizarre behavior, hallucinations, paranoia, and extreme dysphoria. Despite symptoms that might have otherwise prompted a diagnosis of schizophrenia, patients appeared clearly manic both earlier in the course and later as the episode was resolving.

The level of functioning was ascertained at follow-up and compared statistically with the level of psychotic disorganization during the acute manic episode; no relationship was found. The advantages of using a longitudinal view of a psychotic episode as a diagnostic tool is discussed.

In the course of longitudinal studies of manic-depressive illness during the past seven years we have frequently observed periods during the patient's manic episode when his symptoms appeared to be indistinguishable from those of acute schizophrenia. Because of the recent availability of lithium carbonate for the acute and prophylactic treatment of mania,[1,2] the task of recognizing his illness and differentiating it from schizophrenia has assumed renewed importance.

We have attempted to investigate systematically the course of the manic episode in 20 patients who by strict diagnostic criteria were considered on admission to have manic-depressive illness, who had a complete manic episode at some time during hospitalization, and in whom the diagnosis of manic-depressive illness was confirmed on follow-up. The data reviewed suggest that the occurrence of "schizophrenic-like" symptoms during the manic episode in some patients does not differentiate them diagnostically or prognostically from manic patients without such symptoms.

METHODS

Prior to admission to either of two metabolic research units at the National Institute of Mental Health (NIMH), patients were screened for primary affective disorder by at least one psychiatrist and a psychiatric social worker. Patients were referred by private psychiatrists or mental health clinics, generally from the Washington, DC, area. The referral sources were aware of our group's interest in affective illness and of the free inpatient treatment available at NIMH. More specifically, referrals were stimulated by the availability of lithium carbonate through our program.

Twenty consecutively admitted patients were selected for this study on the basis of having participated in an ongoing follow-up reexamination of manic-depressive patients and having had at least one complete manic episode during hospitalization. A complete manic episode is one in which patients proceed from a depressed or normal mood state, thru mania, and returning to a depressed or normal state while hospitalized, so that the entire course was observed. The manic episodes under study averaged four weeks in duration. The total length of hospitalization (averaging four months) was longer than is usual for affective

Reprinted from Archives of General Psychiatry 28:221–228, 1973. Copyright 1973, American Medical Association.

illness—a consequence of the fact that the research protocols involved long periods off medication. In addition, some patients were kept in the hospital through more than one manic or depressive episode.

The diagnosis of bipolar affective disorder was based on a history of relatively good premorbid adjustment, a history of previous episodes of mania and depression, no history of personality deterioration, and symptoms compatible with the diagnosis of mania or depression at the time of admission.[3] Though not required for the diagnosis, patients frequently had a family history of affective disorder. Special care was taken to exclude patients whose histories were suggestive of schizophrenia, particularly patients with any of Schneider's first-rank symptoms of schizophrenia (experiences of alienation, thought insertion, thought withdrawal, thought broadcasting, persistent feelings of influence, complete auditory hallucinations, and delusional perceptions).[4]

Hospital Study

The manic episode was first identified by using global mania ratings for each patient; these global ratings were obtained twice daily by consensus of the nursing research team. This method of evaluation, originally designed to measure depression,[5] has been revised to include a global mania item.[6] The episode was analyzed if the mania rating averaged at least 4 over three consecutive days (equivalent to a moderate degree of mania, ie, hypomania).

Additional corroboration of the manic nature of the episode was obtained from the psychiatrists' and nurses' written descriptions of the patient's affect, psychomotor activity, and cognitive state. Using these daily written observations, we recorded the sequence of symptoms from the beginning to the end of the episode, specifically following longitudinal changes in affect, behavior, and cognition. Both the nurses who originally recorded the observations and we who reviewed the clinical data were blind to all research or therapeutic medications given to these patients.

Follow-Up Study

Follow-up data described in detail elsewhere (Carlson GA et al, unpublished data) were obtained independently through two-hour systematic interviews with the patient and most significant family member available (spouse, sibling, or parent) without prior knowledge of the patient's course during hospitalization. A 200-item questionnaire was used which focused on job status, changes in family and social relationships, mental status, further hospitalization, and the status of psychiatric treatment. The degree of return to premorbid level of function was assessed by scoring each patient's job status, social function, and interpersonal relationships at the time of interview as compared to those parameters before the first episode of manic-depressive illness. The scoring method was the following:

Areas of Functioning Rated at Follow-up

Job Status
    4—Return to the same or better job with same responsibilities
    3—Return to full-time work but in position of lesser status
    2—Employed irregularly or works around the home
    1—Sustained unemployment

Interpersonal and Family Relationships
    4—Patient and family satisfied
    3—Family less satisfied but tolerant
    2—Family dissatisfied but together
    1—Family disruption due to illness

Social Function
    4—Normal social function
    3—Some social withdrawal
    2—Moderate social withdrawal
    1—Complete social withdrawal

Mental Status
    4—Completely normal
    3—Very mild affective symptoms
    2—Obvious affective symptoms
    1—Symptoms requiring constant care

These points were totaled and the patients were ranked from best to worst functioning. These rankings and the rankings of the severity of the acute manic episode (as measured by the extent of progression towards psychotic disorganization) were compared using Spearman's rank order correlation technique.

RESULTS

Patients had an average age of onset of first episode at 28 years with a mean of 4.4 manic episodes and 2.2 depressive episodes over an average of 12.3 years. These demographic data are summarized below:

	Demographic Data	
Sex	Men, 10	Women, 10
Age of onset	Average 28 (range 17 to 57)	
No. of episodes	Average 6.6 (range 1 to 20)	
	1 to 3 episodes	8 patients
	4 to 6 episodes	4 patients
	7 episodes or more	8 patients (including 2 patients with frequent, severe, alternating manic and depressive episodes)
Frequency of episodes	Mania—4.4 per patient	
	Depression—2.2 per patient	
Duration of illness	Average 12.3 years (range 3 to 31 years)	

Family history of affective disorder (either parent, sibling or both treated for or incapacitated by a depressive episode, manic episode, or both): 15 patients (75%).

Depression immediately prior to index mania: 6 patients (30%)

These demographic data are similar to those derived from other studies of manic-depressive patients,[3] suggesting that our patients are not atypical with respect to relapse frequency, duration of illness, and so forth.

The patient's longitudinal course was divided into three stages based mainly on the predominant mood: in stage 1 euphoria predominated, in stage 2 anger and irritability prevailed, while stage 3 was dominated by severe panic.

In all 20 patients the initial phase of the manic episode was characterized by increased psychomotor activity which included increased initiation and rate of speech and increased physical activity. The accompanying mood was labile but euphoria predominated, although irritability became obvious when the patient's many demands were not instantly satisfied.

The cognitive state during the initial stage was characterized by expansiveness, grandiosity, and overconfidence. Thoughts were coherent though sometimes tangential. Also frequently observed during this stage were increased sexuality or sexual preoccupations, increased interest in religion, increased and inappropriate spending of money, increased smoking, telephone use, and letter writing. Some of the patients were aware of the mood change on some level and described the feeling of

"going high," having racing thoughts, and feeling like they were in an airplane. At this stage patients were not out of control.

The second or intermediate stage was also observed in all patients. During this period the pressure of speech and psychomotor activity increased still further. Mood, although euphoric at times, was now more prominently characterized by increasing dysphoria and depression. The irritability observed initially had progressed to open hostility and anger, and the accompanying behavior was frequently explosive and assaultive. Racing thoughts progressed to a definite flight of ideas with increasing disorganization of the cognitive state. Preoccupations that were present earlier became more intense with earlier paranoid and grandiose trends now apparent as frank delusions.

The final stage was seen in 14 of 20 patients (70%) and was characterized by a desperate, panic stricken, hopeless state experienced as clearly dysphoric, accompanied by frenzied and frequently even more bizarre psychomotor activity. Thought processes that earlier had been only difficult to follow now became incoherent and a definite loosening of associations was often described. Delusions were bizarre and idiosyncratic; hallucinations were present in six patients; disorientation to time and place was observed in six patients during this stage; and three patients also had ideas of reference. The diagnosis of schizophrenia, at least as described by Bleuler,[7] was most often entertained at this state. (Schizophrenia, according to Bleuler, was "characterized by a specific type of thinking, feelings and relation to the external world," and included many nonspecific symptoms and a variable prognosis. We, however, are using the narrower concept of K. Schneider,[4] and none of his first-rank symptoms were observed in these patients at any time during their hospitalization.) Quotes from patients in each of the three stages appear in Table 1.

The clinical material on which the staging was based is illustrated in Fig 1 to 3 which present individual patient data showing the progressive changes in the nurses' ratings of mania, psychosis, and dysphoria (an average of the ratings for depression and anxiety) along with clinical vignettes and quotes. This material emphasizes the following points: (1) the mania ratings rise first, followed closely by the psychosis ratings; (2) the dysphoria rating is always fairly high, but as mania and psychosis increase so does dysphoria; (3) stage III, the most intense stage, is represented on the graph as a concatenation of the peaks of mania, psy-

TABLE 1. Excerpts from Daily Nursing Notes, Including Patient Verbalizations

Stage I	Stage II	Stage III
"Now I feel like talking" and does so, increasing intrusiveness and irritability, flight of ideas, restless; "I'm not feeling so depressed."	Hypersexual, bizarre (wearing 3 dresses at a time), screaming, angry, delusion; in control but frightened that other patients are against her; grandiose, incessant talking.	Very frightened, talking and crying constantly, pacing. "I'll never get out." "I have cat eyes. He crawls around inside me and he can't stand the light." Profane, hypersexual, uncooperative. "Oh please let me die. I can't take it anymore." "National Institute of Hell."
"I'm going higher than a Georgia Pine. I'm going to fly tonight. I could kill you."	Pacing, manipulative, religious; says he can't trust people; crude, hypersexual, assaultive; wants to be King Kong; grimaced and postured as if anguished; felt "life on the unit is designed to test my tolerance."	Much pacing, grimacing, and bodily shaking; slaps self on arms; afraid of dying. "They're going to cut out my heart." Afraid of being given TNT; thought there was special meaning when his doctor pointed a finger at him; running up and down hall making animalistic noises.
Hyperactive, pressure of speech, sarcastic, playful; "I'm having a ball." Talks of spending $3,000,000.	Took bath in nightgown, yelling, crying, laughing, throwing food, threatening, combative.	Throwing things, exposing herself, trying to escape, parading around in flimsy pajamas crying, "even God has given up" and later, "I'm dying. The radioactivity has made my hair straight." Voided on the seclusion room floor.
"I'm excited but I don't think I'm worried about anything." Later, "You'd rather have me on top of the table than under it wouldn't you?"	Talking about big plans for Christmas party; very loud, profane, almost assaultive, slightly paranoid, very inappropriate telephone use (calling people to solicit money.)	
Some labile, good frame of mind, very busy.	Hypersexual, hyperverbal, hyperactive, suspicious; very angry, assaultive, obscene; banging urinal on door; wanting to use phone to buy stocks.	

chosis, and dysphoria not observed in stage II patients.

While the sequence of symptom progression was remarkably consistent, the rate of acceleration was variable. Some patients progressed to stage III in hours, others took several days. All of the stage III patients, even the six most psychotic, passed through earlier stages where their symptoms were typically manic. In their deceleration phase they again passed through stages in which they appeared more typically manic. Delusions and hallucinations disappeared as mood returned to normal. Although treatment with antimanic agents hastened the return to a normal mood state, the disappearance of symptoms followed the same course in both spontaneously remitting and treated patients.

Hyperactivity, extreme verbosity, pressure of speech, grandiosity, manipulativeness, and irritability, ie, the manic symptoms most frequently reported in other studies,[3,8] were found in all patients. Table 2 shows the prevalance of symptoms. Examples of some of the delusions, ideas of reference, and bizarre behaviors are illustrated in the patients' quotes in Table 1. Examples of the hallucinations were "hearing the theme from Rawhide," "hearing the hallelujah chorus from the Messiah," "seeing a box open with beautiful flowers emerge," "seeing a kaleidoscope of colors running together," and "talking to my dead daughter."

No significant relationship between the severity of the acute manic episode and the level of function to which the patients returned during the follow-up period were shown by Spearman's rank order correlations technique.

Follow-up data per se are discussed in detail elsewhere. However no patient at the time of discharge or follow-up showed signs of persistent delusions or hallucinations. All patients showed insight, recognizing themselves as having been ill and requiring help for their illness. Four patients who showed an abnormal mental status at the time of follow-up had a mental status compatible with affective disorder, not schizophrenia. Those patients who exhibited symptoms of stage III mania had no greater frequency of relapse or abnormal

mental status at the time of follow-up than did stage II manic patients.

COMMENT

We have presented longitudinal clinical data on the sequence of symptoms occurring during the manic episodes of 20 patients admitted with the diagnosis of manic-depressive illness based on the criteria of Winokur et al.[3] None of Schneider's[4] first-rank symptoms of schizophrenia was revealed by history or observed on admission. Six of the patients, however, at the peak of their manic episodes became grossly psychotic with disorganized thoughts, extremely labile affect, delusions, hallucinations, and brief ideas of reference.

FIGURE 1. Relationship between stages of a manic episode and daily behavior ratings (patient 69).

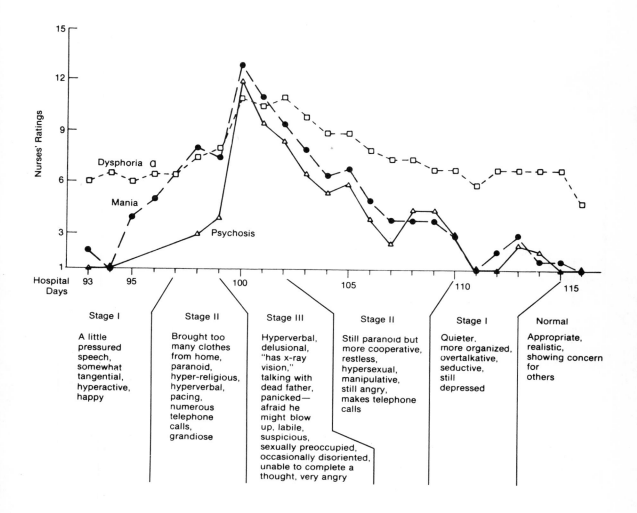

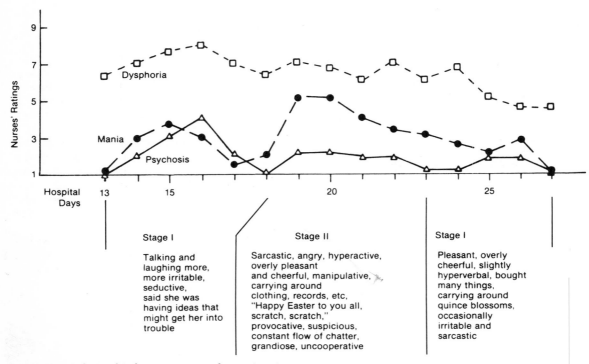

FIGURE 2. Relationship between stages of a manic episode and daily behavior ratings (patient 15).

FIGURE 3. Relationship between stages of a manic episode and daily behavior ratings (patient 72).

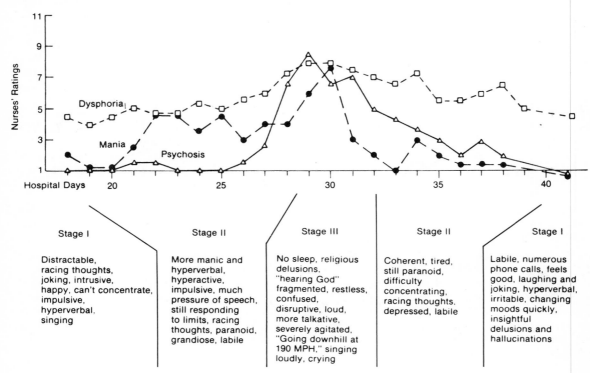

TABLE 2. Classical and "Atypical" Symptoms in 20 Manic Patients

Symptoms	Patients Manifesting Symptoms, %
Hyperactivity	100
Extreme verbosity	100
Pressure of speech	100
Grandiosity	100
Manipulativeness	100
Irritability	100
Euphoria	90
Mood lability	90
Hypersexuality	80
Flight of ideas	75
Delusions	75
Sexual	(25)
Persecutory	(65)
Passivity	(20)
Religious	(15)
Assaultiveness or threatening behavior	75
Distractibility	70
Loosened associations	70
Fear of dying	70
Intrusiveness	60
Somatic complaints	55
Some depression	55
Religiosity	50
Telephone abuse	45
Regressive behavior (urinating or defecating inappropriately; exposing self)	45
Symbolization or gesturing	40
Hallucinations (auditory and visual)	40
Confused	35
Ideas of reference	20

Because of these symptoms the diagnosis of schizophrenia was sometimes entertained.

Reference to schizophrenia-like psychotic symptoms occurring during manic episodes can be found in some of the older literature.[9-11] The current view as reflected in recent textbooks of psychiatry is that mania is a syndrome in which euphoria predominates and behavior and preoccupations are really secondary to the prevailing mood. For example, Arieti,[12] Noyes and Kolb,[13] and Freedman and Kaplan[14] have briefly paraphrased Kraepelin's description of "delirious"

mania[10] but it is presented as a variant of the normal clinical picture in mania, given little emphasis, and may consequently be rarely recognized. Redlich and Freedman,[15] and Slater and Roth[16] emphasize that delusions are part of the grandiosity seen in mania. Only Henderson and Gillespie[17] describe in some detail the bizarre and frenetic picture possible in severe mania, but they add that it is rarely seen.

Before somatic treatments were available, psychiatrists had the opportunity to observe the natural history of the manic episode and their clinical descriptions and reports of the incidents of psychotic symptoms are of interest. Kraepelin's[9] description of three types of mania are perhaps the most thorough: acute mania, delusional mania, and delirious mania. His descriptions of these latter two types bear clear similarities to the clinical picture described here. Thus in delusional mania, paranoid delusions and hallucinations prevail, while in delirious mania hallucinations are numerous and the mood changes from euphoria to "anxious, despairing thoughts of death," psychomotor activity is "senseless" and "raving," patients "pass their motions under them, smear everything, make impulsive attempts at suicide, take off their clothes," and articulations are incoherent. Kraepelin, however, does not provide a longitudinal picture of the episodes he describes under the three "types" and it is not clear whether the acute "delusional" and the "delirious" descriptions apply to separate populations or to different phases in the same patients as we have described here.

Some studies which have attempted to relate the presence of psychotic symptoms in mania to the clinical condition at follow-up are summarized in Table 3.

Rennie, in his follow-up from the predrug era,[10] has described some psychotic symptoms in his manic-depressive patients. Although he does not say what percentage of those having hallucinations or delusions were manic or depressed, he does give some examples of hallucinations, eg, "see something white," "saw and heard God and the angels," "saw trees glitter like gold," "saw dead father," "heard voices say, they've got me now," "heard God's voice," etc (hallucinations similar to those verbalized by our patients). He also described bizarre behavior which included grimacing, smearing, "fear with screaming of being killed," posturing, spitting, wetting, soiling, refusing medication, hoarding, and mannerisms. He concluded that the depth of psychosis had no relation to the clinical status at follow-up since

TABLE 3. Psychotic Symptoms in Manic Patients, Review of the Literature

Follow-up studies	% Patients								
	Persecutory Delusions	Passivity Delusions	No Delusions	Ideas of Reference	Incoherence	Symbolism	Hallucinations	No Hallucinations	Confusion
NIMH (1972) 20 patients with complete manic episodes	65	15	25	20	70	40	40	60	35
Astrup (1959)[18] 96 manic-depressives No. of manics not specified									
77 recovered	9	8	27	4	9	5	55	45	...
13 chronic schizophrenic	38	23	10	15	23	38	62	38	...
Winokur (1969)[3] 100 manic episodes in 61 patients	19	22	52	...	...	28	30	70	8
Clayton & Winokur (1965)[8] 31 patients	...	48	16	84	...	...	...	...	58
Rennie (1942)[10] 208 patients (66 manics)	24		52	...	...	...	22	...	...
Lundquist (1945)[11] 95 recovered manics	...	...	...	...	...	...	13	...	23

76% of those recovered had been "seriously psychotic."

Lundquist,[11] in 1945, discussed the symptoms of confusion and hallucinations occurring during the acute phase of the first manic episode in relation to the outcome of manic-depressive illness. He found that the duration of untreated manic episodes was shorter in patients with confusion, while the duration of the episode did not seem to be related to the presence of hallucinations.

Astrup et al,[18] while not clarifying which of their patients had mania or depression as their predominant mood at admission, felt that the presence of ideas of reference, paranoia, passivity, or symbolism during the acute episode was a poor prognostic sign because more patients with those symptoms in their study had a chronic schizophrenic course. Again, the presence of hallucinations did not necessarily correlate with outcome.

Langfeldt,[19] on the other hand, found that some patients diagnosed as schizophrenic because of Astrup's "poor prognostic" symptoms on their first admission, go on to have manic-depressive course. The clinical descriptions of both these populations sound very similar and one can only conclude that the presence of Astrup's "poor prognosis" symptoms is in no way pathognomonic or even diagnostic of schizophrenia.

Winokur et al,[3] studying a population of manic patients very similar to ours, recorded the prevalence of symptoms in 100 directly observed manic episodes. In this study, and in an earlier one of 31 manics,[8] they note that delusions (persecutory, passivity, sexual, religious, and depressive), hallucinations, posturing, and symbolism may occur in mania even though these features are often considered symptoms of schizophrenia. Finally, Lipkin et al[20] reported three patients with paranoid delusions, bizarre behavior, and excitement who were first diagnosed as schizophrenia or paranoid state, but who later responded to lithium carbonate. In the brief case histories presented, the authors record but do not emphasize the occurrence of typical "manic" symptoms preceding the onset of a disorganized, agitated, paranoid psychotic state.

There are several possible explanations for our findings of a higher incidence of psychotic symptoms during mania than is generally emphasized in the literature. Our study, in contrast to others, included only patients hospitalized with a complete manic episode rather than patients who had already been manic for some time before hospitalization. The inclusion of patients admitted to the research unit when the episode was already beginning to subside would have increased the proportion of "nonpsychotic" to "psychotic" patients.

Furthermore, because of our interest in studying the natural phenomenonology of mania, drug treatment was not instituted in the earlier phases as it would be in most other settings. Thus, the full clinical picture is more likely to unfold. This suggests one reason that the observations of Kraepelin,[9] Lundquist,[11] and Rennie[10] from the predrug era are in reasonable agreement with our data. Finally, Mendlewicz et al[21] have reported that in manic patients with a positive family history of affective disorder (ie, similar to our patients), almost half had previously been misdiagnosed as schizophrenic. They speculate that this is the result of a higher incidence of psychotic symptoms during mania and therefore the tendency to misdiagnose schizophrenia in patients with more psychotic manias.

The course of the illness and response to medication in these patients has been no different from those parameters in groups of manic patients reported in the literature.[1] All 20 patients eventually received lithium carbonate in a double-blind fashion and showed an antimanic response; 40% of the most disturbed were treated simultaneously with phenothiazines for the acute episode. Despite continuation of the phenothiazines, manic episodes recurred when lithium carbonate was replaced by a placebo. Moreover, ultimate withdrawal of phenothiazines with lithium carbonate maintenance was accomplished without return of symptoms. In addition, a prophylactic benefit of lithium carbonate was observed in all the stage III patients and in all but one of the stage II patients, a success rate comparable to that reported in the literature.[1,22]

Do the data presented here suggest that these cases should be classified as "schizo-affective" psychosis? The meaning of this question awaits further clarification of what constitutes this diagnostic category. Clayton et al[23] have presented evidence that the "schizo-affective" psychoses can be reasonably considered variants of manic-depressive illness. Our data are compatible with such a view, and we realize that others may choose to diagnose the patients discussed as schizo-affective.

We have, however, presented clinical and therapeutic reasons as well as historical precedents to support the conclusion that they are manic. Whether or not these patients ultimately will become chronic schizophrenics also cannot be assessed. The average duration of illness thus far is only 14 years. In Astrup's "atypical" cases, chronic schizophrenia became obvious anywhere from one to 52 years after onset of initial psychiatric symptoms.[18] It seems that a conclusive diagnosis cannot be made because of the evidently long age of risk for the late-developing schizophrenias.

Although to our knowledge no one has systematically examined the sequence, progression, and significance of symptoms over the course of the entire manic episode itself, there are several reports examining the onset and early phases of the episode. Bunney et al[24] describe three phases occurring in the first ten days following the switch into mania. They note the progression of behavior from euphoria, irritability, and hyperactivity to more psychotic behavior. Their emphasis is on the "switch process" itself, however, and the more psychotic symptoms were not highlighted since they usually occur later in the course of the illness.

Both Cohen[13] and Henderson and Gillespie[17] have noted that delirious mania may follow earlier stages of mania or begin acutely. We found even in those cases with a fairly abrupt onset of severe mania, the earlier stages were present even though transient. To recapitulate then, although the sequence of symptom appearance is rather consistent, the rate of progression of mania varies considerably in different individuals.

This study has demonstrated that cross-sectional observations are not always reliable in making a diagnosis, and that the presence during mania of symptoms sometimes thought of as schizophrenic (eg, hallucinations, paranoid delusions, and ideas of reference) should not necessarily rule out the diagnosis of affective disorder. Finally, even when such symptoms are present they apparently do not distinguish that population of patients from those without psychotic symptoms in terms of subsequent functioning.

The ability to distinguish mania from schizophrenia during the acute psychotic episode has both practical and theoretical importance. The therapeutic modalities for both the treatment and prophylaxis of mania now includes lithium carbonate, a medication probably contraindicated in schizophrenia.[25] Furthermore, the lack of clarity concerning proper diagnostic boundaries has often clouded the interpretation of the psychobiological data in affective illness. The use of longitudinal sequential analysis of changing symptom patterns, rather than simple cross-sectional enumeration of symptoms, should result in increased diagnostic clarity.

The nursing staff of 4-West contributed valuable behavioral observations and ratings; Martin Matzen and Eloise Orr provided technical assistance.

REFERENCES

1. Schou M: Special review: Lithium in psychiatric therapy and prophylaxis. J Psychiatr Res 6:67–95, 1968.
2. Goodwin FK, Ebert M: Lithium in mania, in Gershon S, Shopsin B (eds): Lithium: Its Role in Psychiatric Research and Treatment. New York, Plenum Press Inc, to be published.
3. Winokur GW, Clayton PJ, Reich T: Manic-depressive Illness. St. Louis, CV Mosby Co Publishers, 1969.
4. Schneider K: Clinical Psychopathology. New York, Grune & Stratton Inc, 1959.

5. Bunney WE Jr, Hamburg DA: Methods for reliable longitudinal observation of behavior. Arch Gen Psychiatry 9:280–294, 1963.

6. Kotin J, Goodwin FK: Depression during mania: Clinical observations and theoretical implications. Am J Psychiatry 129:679–686, 1972.

7. Bleuler E: Dementia Praecox of the Group of Schizophrenias. New York, International University Press Inc, 1911.

8. Clayton P, Pitts FN Jr, Winokur G: Affective disorder: IV. Mania. Compr Psychiatry 6:313–322, 1965.

9. Kraepelin E: Manic-Depressive Insanity and Paranoia. Edinburgh, ES Livingston Publishers, 1921.

10. Rennie TAC: Prognosis in manic-depressive psychosis. Am J Psychiatry 98:801–814, 1942.

11. Lundquist G: Prognosis and course in manic-depressive psychosis. Acta Psychiatr Neurol Scand, suppl 35, 1945.

12. Arieti S (ed): American Handbook of Psychiatry. New York, Basic Books Inc Publishers, 1965.

13. Noyes AP, Kolb LC: Modern Clinical Psychiatry, ed 7. Philadelphia, Saunders Co, 1968.

14. Freedman AM, Kaplan HI (eds): Comprehensive Textbook of Psychiatry. Baltimore, Williams & Wilkins Co, 1967.

15. Redlich FC, Freedman DX: The Theory and Practice of Psychiatry. New York, Basic Books Inc Publishers, 1966.

16. Slater E, Roth M: Mayer-Gross Clinical Psychiatry, ed 3. London, Williams & Wilkins Co, 1969.

17. Batchelor RC: Henderson and Gillespie's Textbook of Psychiatry for Students and Practitioners, ed 10. New York, Oxford University Press Inc, 1969.

18. Astrup C, Fossum A, Holmboe R: A follow-up study of 270 patients with acute affective psychoses. Acta Psychiatr Neurol Scand 34(suppl 135), 1959.

19. Langfeldt G: The Schizophreniform States. Copenhagen, Munksgaard, 1939.

20. Lipkin KM, Dyrud J, Meyer GG: The many faces of mania. Arch Gen Psychiatry 22:262–267, 1970.

21. Mendlewicz J, et al: Manic-depressive illness: A comparative study of patients with and without a family history. Br J Psychiatry 120:523–530, 1972.

22. Gershon S: Lithium in mania. Clin Pharmacol Ther 11:168–187, 1970.

23. Clayton PJ, Rodin L, Winokur G: Family history studies: III. Schizoaffective disorder, clinical and genetic factors including a one to two year follow-up. Compr Psychiatry 9:31–49, 1968.

24. Bunney WE Jr, et al: The "switch process" in manic-depressive illness. Arch Gen Psychiatry 27:295–302, 1972.

25. Shopsin B, Kim SS, Gershon S: A controlled study of lithium vs chlorpromazine in acute schizophrenics. Br J Psychiatry 119:435–440, 1971.

SUGGESTED READINGS

General

Characterological depressions: Clinical and sleep EEG findings separating "subaffective dysthymias" from "character spectrum disorders." Akiskal HS, Rosenthal TL, Haykal RF, Lemmi H, Rosenthal RH, Scott-Strauss A. Archives of General Psychiatry 37:777–783, 1980.

Conditions predisposing to suicide: A review. Miles CP. Journal of Nervous and Mental Disease 164:231–246, 1977.

Current Trends in Suicidal Behavior in the United States. Frederick CJ. American Journal of Psychotherapy 32:172–200, 1978.

The Presuicidal syndrome. Ringel F. Suicide and Life-Threatening Behavior 6:131–149, 1976.

Suicide in the Subway: Psychodynamic Considerations. Guggenheim FG, Weisman A. Life-Threatening Behavior 4:43–53, 1974.

The psychodynamics of suicide. Hendin H. Journal of Nervous and Mental Disease 136:236–244, 1963.

Cognitive therapy of depression and suicide. Rush AJ, Beck AT. American Journal of Psychotherapy 32:201–219, 1978.

Hopelessness and suicidal behavior. Beck AT et al. Journal of the American Medical Association 234:1146–1149, 1975.

The Myth of involutional Melancholia. Weissman MM Journal of the American Medical Association 242:742–744, 1979.

The bereavement of the widowed. Clayton PJ, Halakas JA, Maurice WL. Diseases of the Nervous System 32:597–604, 1971.

Depression in Bereavement and Divorce. Briscoe CW, Smith JV. Archives of General Psychiatry 32:439–445, 1975.

Interpersonal maneuvers of manic patients. Janowsky DS, El-Yousef K, Davis JM. American Journal of Psychiatry 131:250–255, 1974.

Biological Factors

Genetics of the affective disorders. Gershon ES. Hospital Practice, 117–122, 1979.

Biochemistry of the affective disorders. Maas JW. Hospital Practice 14:113–120, 1979.

Depression in the Elderly. II. Possible Drug Etiologies; Differential Diagnostic Criteria. Salzman, C, Shader, R. I. Journal of American Geriatrics Society 26:303–308, 1978.

Drug-induced depression. Editorial. Lancet pp 1333–1334, 1977.

Hypothalamic-pituitary-adrenal axis activity in depressive illness: Its relationship to classification. Schlesser MA, Winokur G, Sherman BM. Archives of General Psychiatry 37:737–743, 1980.

Endocrine changes in depressive illness. DeLa Fuente JR. Psychiatric Annals 9:196–204, 1979.

A specific laboratory test for the diagnosis of melancholia. Carroll BJ, Feinberg M, Greden J, et al. Archives of General Psychiatry 38:15–22, 1981.

Secondary mania. Krauthammer C, Klerman GL. Archives of General Psychiatry 35:1333–1339, 1978.

Toward a Rational Pharmacotherapy of Depression. Stern SL, Rush AJ, Mendels J. American Journal of Psychiatry 137:545–552, 1980.

Psychological Factors

Mourning and Melancholia. Freud S. Collected Papers of Sigmund Freud 4:152–170, Hogarth Press, 1956.

The mechanism of depression. Bibring E. Affective Disorders (edited by P. Greenace). International Universities Press, 1953, pp 21–46.

Depression and the life cycle Lurie HJ. In Clinical Psychiatry for the Primary Physician, Roche, Nutley, NJ, 1976, pp 46–55.

Depression in the elderly. I. Relationship between depression, psychologic defense mechanisms and physical illness. Salzman C, Shader RI, Journal of the American Geriatrics Society 26:253–260, 1978.

Psychodynamics of depression: Implications for treatment. White RB, Davis HK, Cantrell WA. Depression: Clinical, Biological and Psychological Perspectives (edited by Usdin G). New York, Brunner/Mazel, 1977, pp 308–338.

Maladaptive cognitive structures in depression. Kovacs M, Beck AT. American Journal of Psychiatry 135:525–533, 1978.

Cognitive approaches to depression and suicide. Beck AT, Rush AJ. In Cognitive Defects in the Development of Mental Illness. edited by Serban G New York, Brunner/Mazel 1978, pp 235–257.

Sociocultural Factors

Environmental factors in affective disorders. Weissman MM. Hospital Practice 14:103–109, 1979.

PART

III

PERSONALITY DISORDERS

GEORGE ARANA, M.D., CAROL NADELSON, M.D.
AND FREDERICK GUGGENHEIM, M.D.

OVERVIEW

In order to understand disorders of personality, it is important first to consider the forces that mold normal personality development. Personality can be defined as those enduring and consistent attitudes, beliefs, values, and patterns of adaptation that distinguish one person from another. Personality development is influenced by a number of factors, including genetics, biochemistry, environment, society, and intrapsychic experience.

One of the earliest scientific inquiries into personality development was undertaken by Freud, who systematically explored the life histories of his neurologic patients. From his data he elaborated a theory of psychological development based on a concept of instinctual drives and conflicts engendered in the process of mediating these drives. He and subsequent theoreticians have viewed personality development as a stepwise occurrence. From infancy through childhood and adolescence, the individual passes through distinctly different stages, each with a particular set of psychological tasks to be mastered. Erikson and more recent authors have emphasized that this evolution continues into adulthood so that the individual has the capacity to change with time. Progress through successive stages may occur harmoniously, with the realization of personal potential, subjective satisfaction, and social adaptation; or there may be uneven growth of various personality components, with residues of difficulty from earlier stages that are carried into adult life.

PERSONALITY DEVELOPMENT AND EGO FUNCTIONS

Freud eventually conceptualized the components of mental functioning into a structural hypothesis that comprised *id, ego,* and *superego.* This theoretical organization provides a framework that is helpful in understanding unconscious aspects of personality. The id represents the instinctual aspect and the superego represents individual and societal moral values. These structural representations are mediated by the ego, which serves as the organizing executor. The ego represents perceptual, cognitive, and intellectual functions, utilizing mechanisms of adaptation and defense in negotiating between the external, real world and the individual's internal perceptions and experiences. Personality disorders evolve when there are major defects in ego functioning.

Among the most important ego functions is *reality testing.* This includes validating perceptions and the logical consistency of ideas, understanding of what is real or unreal, capacity to act in accordance with conscious judgments of reality, and differentiation of external events from internal perceptions. When a disorder of reality testing exists, there is some degree of distortion of thought, judgment, and perception often not perceived by the affected individual but generally apparent to others. This may range from a minor misinterpretation of a social interaction in normal individuals to blatant distortions that occur in delusions or hallucinations. Although there is some fluctuation of reality testing in most individuals, especially those in stressful situations, it occurs more profoundly and consistently in those people whom we judge to be mentally ill.

Another important ego function is the regulation and control of instinctual drives. Clearly, the individual must modulate the expression of certain drives (e.g., sexual and aggressive) commensurate with the need for gratification on the one hand and the limitations of reality on the other. It is not possible, after all, to allow full expression of drives and to live in a world with others whose needs differ and even conflict. The ability to think logically and objectively, the capacity to delay gratification, and the ability to exercise judgment by thinking out actions are all aspects of ego functioning. It is the absence of some of these characteristics that can be manifested in personality disorders.

Another aspect of ego functioning is reflected in relationships with others. Early in childhood, interactions are determined primarily by need gratification. As development proceeds, those providing gratification are gradually seen as separate and distinct individuals with their own needs and characteristics. The child then differentiates and forms a mental representation of the self as separate from others. This differentiation paves the way for identity formation and allows for the development of the capacity for empathy. In those individuals in whom, for whatever reason, this process did not occur or was disrupted, we see disorders of interpersonal interaction.

Each individual uses a number of adaptive strategies to cope with life events. These strategies range from mannerisms that avoid unpleasant situations and are under conscious control to defense mechanisms that are unconscious and enable the individual to ward off anxiety, often without objective awareness of a threat or challenge.

An example of a conscious coping strategy occurs with the hospital visitor who, when faced with a desperately ill patient, deliberately assumes a cheerful demeanor. Yet this same situation may cause other individuals to become so anxious that they utilize unconscious *ego defensive mechanisms*. They may develop physical symptoms (*somatization*), may insist on careful and elaborate explanations and avoid an emotional or affective dialogue (*intellectualization*); or may be unable to acknowledge the illness and even sincerely believe there was no cause for concern (*denial*).

Another example of a conscious coping strategy can be seen in the individual who must travel by air for the first time and is frightened. Fear may be acknowledged and conscious efforts made to alleviate the anxiety, perhaps by taking along several interesting books or by having a cocktail before boarding the airplane. If, however, the anxiety is greater than the individual can manage, he or she may employ unconscious mechanisms such as provoking an argument with the ticket agent about the choice of seating (*displacement*) or loudly discussing the "wonders and safety" of flying (*reaction formation*). Similarly, the individual may unknowingly become confused, dependent,

and helpless about minor details of travel that previously had been easily mastered (*regression*).

Although a person may employ individual patterns of response for ordinary life situations, when there is extreme stress, additional and alternative mechanisms may be necessary in order for the individual to cope adequately. For example, the person who characteristically is successful in utilizing an intellectual approach to problem solving may, in a threatening situation when failure is imminent, avoid responsibility and blame others for the failure (*rationalization*), an unusual response for this person. Another example is the individual who ordinarily handles pressure by being friendly and talkative but who may become withdrawn and unresponsive in a more threatening situation.

A person might also fail to comply with treatment recommendations when told of a serious illness, despite a previous record of compliance. This noncompliance can be understood if one views the specific nature of the distress and the anxiety generated by it. He or she may have been made overwhelmingly anxious by the news, and characteristic mechanisms were unable to contain the anxiety generated. Thus, regression to a mechanism used earlier in life (e.g., denial) may occur, which in turn impairs the individual's ability to acknowledge reality and employ good judgment. These mechanisms all evolve from early childhood and are reinforced or inhibited by a complex variety of factors during the course of development.

PERSONALITY TRAITS AND PERSONALITY DISORDERS

When a fixed, and at times obvious, personality trait becomes disabling, or when the trait leads to consistent difficulty in interpersonal relationships, it is called a personality disorder. Thus, one person who complains of personal obstacles in getting along with others, including family, teachers, peers, or friends, may seek help because of self-awareness. Someone else who seeks help may do so because of complaints from associates about his or her attitude and behavior. Two clinical examples illustrate the difference between the individual who copes with a stress in an adaptive way utilizing characteristic personality traits and the individual who manifests a personality disorder.

Mr. J is a computer programmer who has attained a prestigious position in his firm because of his mathematical, organizational skills and the reliability with which he performs. When his mother died, he attended her funeral, cried frequently alone and with family members, and returned to work after a two-week leave of absence. Within a month of her death, he was again functioning at work and at home as he had before her death, talking openly and appropriately about his loss, asking for support from friends as he did with other stresses, and reminiscing about details from her past.

Mr. S is a bright, capable accountant in a large firm. He frequently had verbal altercations with fellow employees when he felt they are not doing their work well or when he was criticized. He had threatened to fire an employee when she asked for a day off to attend an uncle's funeral. When his own mother died, he informed no one, "didn't have time" for the funeral, and showed no emotion privately or with his family. He became more verbally abusive with staff, his work performance deteriorated, and he became more distant from family members and acquaintances.

It is evident that, although both men experienced the same life event (death of a parent), Mr. J was more flexible and adaptable. He was able to function after a period of mourning, but did not become impaired in his home or work relations. By contrast, Mr. S fits the criteria for a personality disorder because he is inflexible; and his responses were maladaptive and led to functional impairment.

The major characteristics of personality disorders are (1) deeply ingrained, inflexible, and maladaptive behavior patterns that may become particularly apparent under stress; (2) sufficient distortion in perceiving the environment and one's self to cause impairment in adaptive functioning; and (3) subjective distress of variable intensity. Elements of both personality and personality disorders are generally seen in a wide range of personal and social settings. Specific characteristics of a particular personality disorder are recognizable by late adolescence or early adulthood.

CLINICAL TYPES
OF PERSONALITY DISORDERS

Personality disorders have been grouped into 11 different types: paranoid, histrionic, compulsive, antisocial, borderline, narcissistic, passive–aggressive, dependent, schizotypal, schizoid, avoidant, and atypical. We describe these various personality disorders by utilizing recent specific diagnostic criteria (DSM-III). In practice, characteristics of the various personalities do overlap somewhat. It is clinically useful, however, to distinguish types of disorders because this allows us

to understand better the style a person characteristically employs in a crisis and the behavior that others will observe and/or find difficult to tolerate. Clinical experience does make the differentiation of personality types somewhat easier, although when a person is in a frank crisis, stressing his or her coping abilities, it is usually not too difficult to see the predominant personality characteristics.

We wish to provide one other caveat about the diagnosis of personality disorders. Ordinarily, to make any medical diagnosis, one must apply these criteria: (1) reasonably predictable course or outcome, (2) fixed descriptive characteristics over time, (3) specific history and etiologic factors such as family history, (4) pathophysiology that can be described, and (5) treatment that is reliable and specific. But for personality disorders, items (3), (4), and (5) may be difficult to establish, because the state of our knowledge is not sufficient to lead beyond descriptive and dynamic classification. An analogy can be made with the diagnosis of fever a century ago. Fever used to be considered a diagnostic entity in and of itself and only later was it understood to be a physiological response to a wide range of stimuli. We have come to understand fever as a clinical sign, not a specific disease entity. At this time, personality disorders can be seen as descriptive of complex constellations of characteristics that are not necessarily tied to known specific causes or treatments.

Paranoid Personality Disorder

The essential feature of the paranoid personality disorder is a long-standing suspiciousness and mistrust of people. There is a tendency to blame others and to believe in their malicious intentions. People with this disorder are generally viewed as guarded, devious, and scheming. Paranoid individuals are overly concerned with the loyalty of others. They tend to be hypersensitive and easily offended and to assume a vigilant posture, seeking environmental clues to validate their suspicious thoughts, attitudes, or biases. A systematic history may reveal frequently shifting alliances with people. Although suspiciousness and mistrust may at times be appropriate and adaptive, a person afflicted with this particular disorder is generally unwilling to abandon suspicion, even when presented with noncontradictory evidence that suspicions are unwarranted. These individuals tend to be argumentative, excitable, and often unable to relax. They are quite critical of others, but have great difficulty accepting criticism of themselves. Although they may be seen as observant, energetic, ambitious, and capable, they also are often hostile, stubborn, defensive, and jealous. They avoid intimacy with others, causing those around them to feel a certain amount of uneasiness and fear. They may avoid participation in group activities unless they are in a dominant position. Occupational difficulties, particularly with authority figures or co-workers, are frequent. In more severe cases, the capacity to relate in a trusting fashion with others may be grossly impaired. These people use *projection* prominently as a defense mechanism.

Mr. A, a 43-year-old single farmer who lived alone, was seen in the emergency room with a black eye and several facial cuts. He gave a history of having had a fistfight with a neighbor because he believed that the neighbor was dumping garbage on his lawn. He stated that he had always mistrusted his neighbors because he believed they were jealous of him. He was convinced that they frequently trespassed on his property to destroy his crops. He kept a shotgun at his door to scare them away. He punched his neighbor earlier in the day, after he discovered him walking on an access road to the river. When his neighbor accused him of being hostile, suspicious, and "crazy", Mr A punched him and a fight ensued.

Histrionic Personality Disorder (Hysterical Personality)

These individuals often draw attention to themselves with exaggerated expression of emotions and exhibitionism. People with this disorder are often seen as reactive, shallow, superficial, or insincere. They are attention seeking and frequently manifest seductive behavior toward physicians and others meaningfully involved in their lives. Hence, these persons are often seen as vain, self-centered, immature, and emotionally unstable. Minor stimuli often give rise to excitable outbursts and may be a source of confusion to others.

The behavior of people with histrionic personality disorders is frequently misinterpreted. Even with a casual acquaintance it may run the gamut from impulsive displays of affection to sudden irrational and angry outbursts for seemingly minor incidents. Characteristically these individuals are initially warm, charming, and appealing in interpersonal relations. Although they are quick to form relationships, they may also rapidly become demanding, attention seeking, and inconsiderate. At other times, they may be described as dependent, helpless, and in need of reassurance. Their history often reveals that despite their overly sexualized approach to people, they have poor sexual judgment. Those with this disorder often

have a need for excitement that impairs impulse control and often makes sustained intellectual achievement difficult. They are often unable to be carefully analytic and lack the capacity to complete long tedious tasks.

Patients with histrionic personality disorders frequently are seen by physicians for physical symptoms, including abdominal pain, headaches, and other somatic problems. At times of more severe emotional stress, they may misinterpret reality and even experience illusions, i.e., "seeing or hearing" a deceased relative while looking at a photograph. It is also not unusual for those with a histrionic personality disorder to make suicidal gestures or attempts when disappointed.

Mr. B, a 29-year-old actor, called his physician to tell him that he had just taken an overdose of tranquilizers. He had taken ten Valium after an argument with his lover about his inability to make a commitment to her after an erratic two-year relationship. She accused him of being immature, self-centered, and insincere. He complained that she didn't understand him and that she was too demanding. When the argument escalated, she complained that his sexual performance was inadequate and that he was too dependent. Furthermore, she stated that she knew of his infidelity and thought he was being unfaithful to prove himself because he knew he wasn't a "real man." When she left his apartment, he impulsively took the pills and then called her. He called his physician after she refused to return.

Compulsive Personality Disorder

People with this personality disorder tend to be restricted, controlled, and inflexible. They have difficulty expressing warm and tender emotions, and their relationships tend to have a distant and formal quality. They are often preoccupied with trivial details. An example of this behavior is the individual who, having misplaced a short list of tasks, spends an inordinate amount of time looking for the list rather than taking a few moments to recreate the list and proceed with the work to be done. These people tend to become anxious when every detail of a task is not completed as they would like it to be, and they are insensitive to the feelings elicited in others by their behavior. Although efficiency and perfection are their goal, they seldom attain mastery. They seem to be constantly concerned with status, and they may insist that people submit to their way of doing things. Work and productivity are so important to them that pleasure and interpersonal relationships are often excluded. Because these individuals are plagued with an inordinate fear of making errors, decision making is often avoided or postponed. The necessity for making choices can cause extreme anxiety. These individuals are excessively conscientious, scrupulous, and judgmental of both themselves and others. They often are seen as stingy and parsimonious and become extremely uncomfortable in situations beyond their control, often reacting in an angry fashion. At times, however, they may be unable to express anger directly. They complain of their inability to express tender feelings. They may experience depressive affect when they feel unable to control their environment or are criticized by those with status or authority.

Mrs. C was a 37-year-old married mother of a 15-year-old son whom she brought to the Adolescent Medical Clinic complaining that he was unwilling to comply with even minimal requests to keep his room clean, dress neatly, perform his household chores in an organized fashion, or report on time for appointments. She wondered why he became so angry with her when she made requests of him and she was frightened that he was going to lose control. A careful history from both Mrs. C and her son, Tom, revealed that she was rigid, demanding, and inflexible. Tom described her as cold, preoccupied with order and cleanliness, and intolerant of any error or postponement. He complained that she expected everyone in the family to obey her orders instantly and to do things her way. When Mrs. C was interviewed, she appeared anxious and indecisive and struggled constantly to avoid any expression of anger or any other emotion. She revealed that she spent most of her time making certain that her house was spotless and that her family had exactly the proper diet and clothes, and she spent hours going over family budgets. She worried that they wouldn't have enough and was condemning those who didn't plan ahead or manage their lives more efficiently or righteously.

Antisocial Personality Disorder

The primary distinguishing features of antisocial personality disorder are (1) history of chronic antisocial behavior, in which the rights of others are violated, (2) appearance of such behavior before age 15 and persistence into adult life, and (3) failure to sustain consistent work or educational performance over a period of years. Violation of others' rights, including lying, stealing, fighting, truancy, and resisting authority, is often seen initially in childhood and continues into adolescence. Aggressive sexual behavior, excessive drinking, and the use of illicit drugs are also frequently seen. More flagrant behavioral problems, including criminality, tend to diminish after the age of 30. An almost universal feature of this disorder is a marked impairment in the capacity to sustain lasting, close, and responsible relationships with family, friends, or sexual partners. Often one sees signs of personal distress, which include complaints of tension, anxiety, inability to tolerate boredom, depressions, and the feeling (often correct) that others are hostile toward them. These interpersonal difficulties and dysphoria tend to persist into later adult life, even when more overt antisocial behavior is diminished. People with antisocial personality disorders often fail to become independent, self-supporting adults and may spend years in penal or medical institutions. The manifestations of certain aspects of this personality disorder in childhood often sufficiently interferes with education achievement, so that independently successful careers are rare.

There is some evidence to suggest that this disorder may have a genetic component, but conclusive data are not available. Clinically, what is usually apparent in this population is the absence of ordinary anxiety or guilt. Clinical investigations suggest that emotional deprivation at an early age and the lack of caring relationships or role models may be contributing factors. Because an important factor in predicting antisocial behavior is parental pathology, it is not yet clear how genetic and environmental factors interact etiologically.

Demographically, antisocial personalities are more commonly reported in the lower-class populations and in males. It may be that others, by virtue of status, position, or expectations, avoid being recognized as antisocial personality disorders. It has also been suggested that the class factor can be accounted for by the inability of these individuals to work constantly or effectively.

Mr. D, a 23-year-old man, was seen in the emergency room with a gunshot wound. He had been an alcoholic since the age of 16 and, in addition, had had several arrests and a history of conviction for selling illicit drugs. He was found by the police when an acquaintance called to reveal that he had been shot after cheating in a card game. He gave no permanent address, place of employment, or name of any available family member. His hospital chart revealed that he had been seen repeatedly since early childhood for a variety of problems, including knife wounds, needle abscesses, veneral disease, and alcoholism.

Borderline Personality Disorders

This particular personality disorder is a new diagnostic category in *DSM-III*, although the term has been used clinically for many years. The term "borderline" serves to define a group of patients who were originally described as having pathology that bordered on both the neuroses and the psychoses. Other diagnostic terms that have been used by different authors include pseudoneurotic schizophrenia, "as-if" personality, ambulatory schizophrenia, borderline states, and psychotic character.

These individuals manifest instability in a variety of areas, including behavior, mood, interpersonal relationships, identity, and self-image. The histories of people with borderline personality disorders are usually filled with impulsive and unpredictable behavior that may include self-mutilating or self-damaging acts in many areas of their lives, including overindulging in alcohol, gambling, and so on.

These patients may have a history of brief psychotic episodes, often related to stressful interpersonal relationships or alcohol or drug abuse. They frequently have not achieved either in school or work, despite apparent talent or ability. Their interpersonal relationships are intense and unstable, with marked shifts over time. Disturbances in relationships usually include devaluation or manipulation of others. They tend to limit emotional involvement with others and are characterized as demanding, clinging, and dependent. Intense anger is an important aspect of their relationships. They may vacillate rapidly and intensely for seemingly trivial reasons. They have difficulty tolerating loneliness, and they experience chronic feelings of emptiness and boredom. At times, there are brief periods of bizarre behavior or "odd thinking," which can approach delusional proportions. They tend to externalize; that is, blame their problems and their difficulties on an external, malevolent world. Indeed, their life histories are much more chaotic than their initial interview behavior would suggest. Although instability in mood, with marked shifts to intense affects such as anger and anxiety, is frequently reported, no one simple diagnostic feature is invariably present.

Ms. E, a 28-year-old single woman, was seen in the emergency room when she cut her wrists after she had lost her third job in as many months. She was an angry and vituperative woman who refused to speak with anyone but the senior attending physician because she didn't think anyone was competent. On examination, she was found to have multiple healed slash marks on both arms. She recounted to the physician the many injustices she had experienced and then told him that he was the only one who understood her, despite the fact that he had never met her before. The friend who brought her in described her as infantile, demanding, and erratic, a person who was an exceptionally talented artist, but who alienated everyone. She usually blamed other people or external events and was unable to take responsibility for these failures or to make efforts to ameliorate the situation. She was described as a "Dr. Jekyll and Mr. Hyde," a person who could be witty and engaging one moment and then suddenly become enraged for no apparent reason.

Narcissistic Personality Disorders

The primary distinguishing feature of narcissistic personality disorder is the person's sense of self-importance, of uniqueness that can at times attain grandiose proportions. These individuals appear to be self-absorbed and may harbor fantasies of achieving unlimited success in a variety of ways. If the goals they set for themselves are actually pursued, there is often a driven quality with little satisfaction, even when the goals are attained. These people are excessively concerned with appearances and constantly seek the admiration and attention of others. They are preoccupied with measurements of success and concerned about how they are regarded by others. In response to criticism, defeat, or disappointment they may react either with apathy and/or disinterest or with marked feelings of rage, inferiority, shame, humiliation, or emptiness. They lack the capacity for empathy, and their interpersonal relationships are shallow. They tend to vacillate between idealization and devaluation. They behave as if they were entitled to special favors, without assuming reciprocal responsibilities. When their wishes are not fulfilled, they react with surprise and anger.

Like Narcissus of Greek mythology, who fell in love with his own reflected image, these individuals frequently manifest painful self-consciousness, preoccupation with grooming and remaining youthful, and a chronic intense envy of others. Somatic complaints and preoccupation with aches and pains may be present from time to time. Because personal deficits, defeats, or injury to self-esteem are so painful in these individuals, one may see a great deal of rationalization or outright lying, frequently followed by a depressed mood. Short-lived psychotic episodes can be seen with these people, and a paranoid psychosis or a major depressive disorder can occur.

Mr. F, a 56-year-old attorney, requested a face lift and hair transplant from a plastic surgeon. He had recently married his fourth wife, a woman of 27, and he was concerned that she would lose interest in him because he was starting to "look middle aged." He was a tall, slim man who was preoccupied with physical fitness, dressed impeccably, and had an eternal suntan. He stated that his work kept him in the public eye and he had to maintain his image "at all costs." He revealed that he had not kept in touch with his children, who were all adults, because they reminded him that he was growing old.

Passive–Aggressive Personality Disorder

Those with passive–aggressive disorders generally are resistant to demands for activity or performance, both occupationally and socially. They procrastinate, "forget," or may be inefficient. They resent demands made on them to either maintain or improve their level of functioning. They are often late for appointments, and they persistently fail to perform certain tasks. The name of the disorder is based on the assumption that such individuals are passively expressing their hostility. They often lack self-confidence and have a pessimistic attitude toward the world, with little or no realization of their own obstructive and restrictive behavior pattern. Hence, it is no surprise that these people frequently experience transient though frequent depressions and have a high incidence of alcoholism.

Mrs. G, a 47-year-old laboratory technician, was fired from her job because her boss felt that she was "sabotaging" the research project, as she would "forget" to enter data, miss the time for obtaining samples, or fail to notify the lab chief when there was a technical problem that required intervention. She was seen in the Psychiatry Outpatient Department, because she complained of feeling unproductive and uncertain about her future. She reluctantly revealed that she had been angry and jealous because her boss, a younger woman, was successful and well recognized, while the patient had not been able to attain the recognition she felt she deserved.

Dependent Personality Disorders

People with dependent personality disorder frequently attempt to induce others to assume responsibility for them and to make their decisions. They may subordinate their needs to those of others and express unwillingness to make demands on others because they fear jeopardizing these relationships. They lack self-confidence, are fearful of abandonment, and, when alone for more than just a brief period of time, may feel helpless and experience intense anxiety. These individuals may become clinically depressed when faced with an interpersonal loss. Agoraphobic symptoms (see Part IV) are also not uncommon in those with dependent personality disorders.

Schizotypal Personality Disorders

This is a new diagnostic category in *DSM-III*. In the past, the term "schizoid personality" was often used to include individuals who would now be called schizotypal. The essential distinguishing features of schizotypal personality disorder are oddities of thinking, perception, communication, and behavior. The thought disturbance may appear to be mild, compared with frank schizophrenia, and is manifested by magical thinking, referential ideas, and/or paranoid thoughts. Distortions in perception may include illusions that recur and *depersonalization* or *derealization*, both of which may occur without an associated feeling of anxiety or panic attacks. These people often express concepts unclearly or in an odd fashion, but there are no loose associations or incoherence. Behaviorally, these persons may be isolated or constricted or show inappropriate affect in interactions with others. Some are prone to eccentric convictions.

Schizoid Personality Disorders

People with these disorders show little desire for social involvement and avoid close friendships. They are often insensitive and unempathetic to the feelings of others, and appear reserved, withdrawn, and seemingly detached from their environment. They lack the capacity to display warm feelings toward others. They appear to be indifferent to praise or criticism. They do not exhibit eccentricities of speech, behavior, or thought. It is important not to confuse self-absorption and excessive daydreaming seen in these persons with a thought disorder. Schizoid individuals may seem isolated and reclusive, but their capacity to recognize and test reality is intact. Some individuals with this disorder may attain a high level of occupational achievement, particularly in jobs requiring performance under conditions of social isolation and sensory deprivation.

There is a close association between this type of personality disorder and schizophrenia; and it is not unusual to elicit a strong family history of schizophrenic psychosis. Family and twin studies have shown that there is a relationship between schizoid (schizotypal) personalities and schizophrenia. Schizoid characteristics are often found in families of schizophrenics, and vice versa. In this particular disorder, there may be brief periods of bizarre behavior or oddities of thought that may approach delusional proportions. If brief psychotic episodes occur, other diagnoses such as *reactive psychosis*, schizophreniform disorder atypical psychosis, or paranoid state may be considered. If these episodes are prolonged enough or if there is evidence of repeated recurrences, then the diagnosis of schizophrenia should be strongly considered.

Avoidant Personality Disorder

The primary features of the avoidant personality disorder are hypersensitivity to rejection and excessive desire for closeness and acceptance. These individuals tend to be reluctant to enter into relationships because they fear rejection or humiliation. Their relationships are generally contingent upon unconditional approval. Although many of us are concerned about how we are viewed by others, those with avoidant personalities feel devastated by the slightest hint of disapproval. They are distressed by their lack of ability to socialize and to relate comfortably with others. They tend to be self-punitive and manifest low self-esteem. Depression and anxiety may become clinically evident, particularly at times when they perceive a rejection or feel criticized. They are often phobic about public speaking or public appearances.

Atypical, Mixed, or Other Personality Disorders

As with other diagnostic categories, this group includes individuals who do not meet the criteria for other personality disorder diagnoses, but may be masochistic, impulsive, or immature.

DIFFERENTIATING THE PERSONALITY DISORDERS

In making personality diagnoses, it is important to remember that personality traits are lifelong and not just recent changes. Thus, one should inquire about the duration of symptoms. The paranoia of a chronic amphetamine abuser (see Part VI) or the amphetamine abuser's inappropriate preoccupation with trivial details can mimic personality disorders.

Because a number of characteristics of the personality disorders do overlap, Table 1 organizes some of the signs and symptoms used in the evaluation of the potential personality disorder. It must be emphasized that few traits alone are diagnostic, but rather there is a spectrum of traits, with some overlap. For example, the cold, unemotional, and constricted fashion with which compulsive personalities control affect is also seen with the paranoid, schizoid, and introverted disorders. The compulsive disorder can be distinguished from the schizoid, schizotypal, and introverted disorders, since social isolation is generally not so apparent in the compulsive disorders, whereas it is

seen in the other two disorders mentioned. While the compulsive has a restricted ability to express feelings and is inappropriately preoccupied with trivial details, the paranoid is suspicious and distrustful of other individuals.

Isolated, detached persons often encounter difficulty with family, friends, and work relations. Three personality disorders include this trait as a major feature; thus it can become confusing. In the *DSM-III* nosology of personality disorders, "schizotypal personality" describes a certain group of patients who have difficulty in forming and maintaining social relationships and frequently have either family histories of schizophrenia or a progressive course that eventually is indistinguishable from schizophrenia. In attempting to separate the schizoid personality from the schizotypal personality, the main distinguishing feature is that the schizotypal disorder manifests certain eccentricities of communication and behavior that often appear very similar to the loose associations and the thought disorders commonly seen in schizophrenia. In the schizoid personality disorder, these eccentricities are not evident, although the inability to form social relationships, introversion, and bland or constricted affect are present. Although the schizotypal disorder shares poor response to criticism and social isolation characteristics with the avoidant disorder, the person with a schizotypal personality disorder has a constricted affect, whereas the avoidant person generally does manifest affect and, in fact, may be overly sensitive to life events. The schizoid personality has little desire for social interaction and relationships, whereas the avoidant personality is hypersensitive to rejection in social situations. Although desirous of relationships, he or she is unwilling to enter them without guarantees of uncritical acceptance. The capacity to be affectively appropriate, to tolerate criticism, and to control impulses makes the avoidant personality distinguishable from others.

It is important to remember that although a depressed individual may manifest some of these personality traits, he or she is suffering from depression, not a personality disorder. Time, course, and onset of the particular characteristics are important in distinguishing personality disorders from the depressive symptomology.

In paranoid schizophrenia, as opposed to the paranoid personality disorders, there are delusions, hallucinations, and a thought disorder. Although the antisocial personality disorder shares several features in common with the paranoid personality disorder (difficulty in forming close rela-

TABLE 1. Characteristics of Personality Disorders	Paranoid	Histrionic	Compulsive	Antisocial	Borderline	Narcissistic	Passive–Aggressive	Dependent	Schizotypal	Schizoid	Avoidant
Cold, unemotional, constricted, aloof	X		X						X	X	
Avoids contact with other people, social isolation									X	X	X
Difficulty controlling feelings of anger and temper outbursts		X		X	X	X					
Low opinion of self; many feelings of worthlessness and poor self esteem		X			X	X	X				X
Marked shifts in relationships with others; fluctuates from idealized to devalued		X			X	X					
Poor responses to criticism	X		X	X			X	X			X
Impulsivity: tendency to act when faced with strong affect, i.e., anger, sadness		X		X	X						
Exhibitionistic		X				X					
Lacking empathy		X			X	X					
Difficulty being alone					X						

tionships and poor work performance), the lifelong history of antisocial behavior is less often present in the paranoid disorder. The paranoid personality differs from the schizoid personality in that the schizoid personality does not manifest the hypersensitivity to criticism and the excitability seen with a paranoid personality disorder.

The manner in which people with passive–aggressive personalities deal with demands made on them for performances distinguishes this diagnostic category. Although poor response to criticism and demands is seen with a number of other personality disorders, other characteristics (such as social isolation, low self-esteem, inability to express affect) are not considered to be diagnostic of the passive–aggressive personality disorder. Rather, it is the passive manner of obstructing job performance or limiting the development of satisfying relationships that is the primary feature.

The borderline personality disorder is considered by many clinicians to be difficult to distinguish from the narcissistic, histrionic, and antisocial disorders. Indeed, individuals with all four of these disorders have difficulty with control, lack the capacity to empathize with others, and tend to be impulsive and exhibitionistic. We feel that the best criteria to use in differentiating among these various disorders is the quality of interpersonal relationships. The narcissistic person will engage in exploitative, interpersonal relationships with a sense of entitlement. The antisocial personality can also be difficult to distinguish from the narcissistic, but the impulsivity of the antisocial is usually more extreme and destructive. Furthermore, antisocial characteristics tend to be manifested before the age of 15. The histrionic person will be superficially warm, charming, and appealing, although self-absorbed, vain, and attention-seeking; the antisocial person seems relatively unburdened with guilt about his or her behavior and seems unbothered by violating the rights of others. Narcissistic people do not tend to manifest the degree of impulsivity seen in borderline personalities.

Impulsivity seems also to be a more pervasive symptom with a borderline personality and is often associated with inappropriate and intense anger. The borderline personality is more likely to be physically self-damaging and have difficulties with identity and self-image. The histrionic person may express emotions intensely, although they are perceived as shallow and superficial. These personality disorders are similar to the narcissistic personality in that they may seem to lack the capacity to empathize. One important difference is that the narcissistic person insists on being treated specially.

Clearly, it may be difficult to make the diagnosis of one disorder versus another, especially if characteristics of several diagnostic categories seem to be present. At times a mixed picture may be present, and a choice must be made to emphasize the predominant characteristics; for example, some people with a borderline personality may manifest passive–aggressive behavior.

DIFFERENTIAL DIAGNOSIS

A person with a psychosis may superficially appear to have a personality disorder. For example, a suspicious, frightened person may initially not talk freely and thus not demonstrate the disordered thinking and delusional ideas of reference seen in a paranoid schizophrenic. Similarly, an aloof, isolated person actively experiencing auditory hallucinations, might appear to be a schizotypal personality but may in fact be abusing drugs. A college student with a dramatic style who is outgoing and friendly and exhibits psychomotor acceleration may be experiencing the first manifestations of an affective disorder (major affective disorder, manic type) but be wrongly assessed as having merely a histrionic personality disorder.

Again, it is important to emphasize that personality characteristics outlined in this chapter apply to long-term functioning. The transient emergence of personality changes should alert the clinician to the possibility of some more serious type of functional or organic psychiatric disorder.

PERSONALITY DISORDERS WITH ORGANIC ETIOLOGIES

In assessing the patient who appears to have a personality disorder, it is important to determine the time of onset of symptoms, that is, a change in behavior. This may require the aid of family members and other observers.

An acute personality change, over a period of hours or days, is very likely to be the result of an organic process. In pursuing the history, the clinician should be particularly aware of the patient's work history, patterns of relationships, modes of relating with important people, and how these may have changed over the course of time. For example, a patient who has suffered a subdural hematoma will usually present a lethargic and somnolent picture and will have had a history of head trauma, although the presenting picture may be paranoia or hostility.

Many organic diseases can produce personality change without impairing cognition (the organic brain disorders are covered in Part VI). A brief list would include brain tumors, chronic barbiturate intoxication, the *Pickwickian syndrome* (CO_2 intoxication), and *endocrinopathies*, including *Cushing's* or *Addison's disease* or thyroid dysfunction, *insulinoma* with chronic *hypoglycemia*. Other diseases leading to personality changes that may present as personality disorders are encephalitis (e.g., herpes simplex), *steroid psychosis*, vitamin deficiencies, the *collagen diseases* including *systemic lupus erythematosus*, and the *slow virus syndrome (Jakob–Creutzfeldt disease)*.

The use and abuse of certain "street drugs" such as phencyclidine ("angel dust," PCP), LSD, cocaine, and amphetamines ("speed"), can mimic the symptoms of schizoid and paranoid personality disorders. These symptoms can persist up to weeks after the drugs have last been used. Although psychosis is a more typical presentation, chronic substance abuse can be mistaken for a personality disorder.

Of particular importance in the complete assessment of personality disorders is the group of patients afflicted with *temporal lobe epilepsy* (TLE). This is emphasized because it is often a diagnostic challenge. Temporal lobe epilepsy has a prevalence of 0.2% in the general population (schizophrenia has a prevalence of 1% in the general population) and can present with a range of personality characteristics, including circumstantiality, obsessionalism, extreme emotionality, religiosity, altered sexual interest, and minimal physical signs or symptoms. This diagnosis is important to make because TLE often can be treated successfully. Another treatable organic brain disease that can present as a personality disorder is normal pressure hydrocephalus (NPH). Still another dissembler is the *nondominant hemispheric lesion* (usually of the right hemisphere). Here the clinician may obtain a recent history of sudden outbursts of sadness or anger, clearly inconsistent with prior personality pattern. Another feature is minimization of illness that appears to be atypical for that individual. Personality disorders have also been described in *multiple sclerosis*. In such cases, alterations in personality are usually accompanied by intellectual and motoric deterioration. In some multiple sclerosis patients, depression or euphoria and denial of the disability incurred by the disease are persistent.

Finally, many individuals may manifest peculiar idiosyncracies or traits, but the diagnosis of a personality disorder must be made in those who have sufficient and significant impairment in both social and occupational effectiveness or who have a significant degree of subjective distress.

TREATMENT

Because of the inherent ambiguity in the nosology of the personality disorders, it is difficult to delineate specific effective treatments for each disorder. Moreover, because the etiology and course of these disorders are not well understood, and there is considerable overlap between the disorders, treatment outcome for each disorder is difficult to assess.

It is important that once an organic etiology is ruled out, a number of treatment approaches can be employed. Psychopharmacological treatment is often a short-term aid in symptom alleviation, but there is no definitive program for each specific personality disorder. Psychotherapeutic treatment approaches are most often employed, including supportive psychotherapy, *psychodynamic* psychotherapy, *psychoanalysis*, group and family therapy, and behavioral, cognitive, and gestalt therapy.

Generally, these psychotherapy modalities are variants of combinations of three basic theoretical perspectives. The psychoanalytic/psychodynamic approach is based on an intrapsychic model in which unconscious determinants and conflicts are viewed as important factors in symptom formation and affective expression. Although any one of the other therapies may be approached from a psychoanalytic/psychodynamic perspective, psychoanalysis and psychoanalytic psychotherapy are based on this theoretical underpinning.

Of the personality disorders outlined in this chapter, the schizoid, narcissistic, obsessive-compulsive, and histrionic are seen as most amenable to the psychoanalytic/psychodynamic approach. The system approach concentrates on the interactional network and interpersonal aspects of an individual's life. This theoretical construct forms the basis for supportive psychotherapy, group and family therapy, and cognitive therapy. Although these therapeutic modalities would be of use in any one of the personality disorders, they have been most useful in treating problems in interpersonal relations. Another broad category is the learning or behavioral therapies. They have been found to be most useful for treating compulsive, avoidant, and antisocial personalities, although these approaches may be useful for other disorders as well. There are contraindications reported for the use of various treatment techniques for individuals with one or another type of disorder, but there are no definitive or absolute indications or contraindications that are unequivocal. While some would state that psychoanalytic/psychodynamic approaches are contraindicated for borderline or schizotypal personality disorders, others have reported remarkable clinical success employing these techniques. The skill and flexibility of the therapist are of great importance. Further, most therapists working with patients with complex problems integrate approaches and, while their theoretical orientation or framework may be in a particular direction, the clinical work of skilled therapists may not be so markedly different as it would seem from their theoretical differences.

In choosing the appropriate therapeutic approach with any given personality disorder, it is of paramount importance that the individual's personal history and motivation for change be thoroughly evaluated. Thus, an avoidant personality who is terribly afraid of others, is brought to evaluation because of family pressures, and has little interest in change would probably not do well in group therapy. However, a similar person who seeks therapy because of an interest in personal learning and a desire to develop relationships may be a more appropriate patient for this modality.

When making a treatment recommendation, it is necessary for the physician to understand the individual's specific needs and expectations as well as past history and ability to cope with stress. Until more definitive data are available with regard to the etiology, pathogenesis, course, and treatment of personality disorders, a complete evaluation of each individual must serve as the prime focus, and a treatment plan formulated accordingly.

PERSONALITY TYPES IN MEDICAL MANAGEMENT

RALPH J. KAHANA AND GRETE L. BIBRING

In the course of our efforts to implement and study the integration of medicine and psychiatry within a general hospital, the diagnosis of personality structure has become an important element in the psychological management of the physically ill patient (G. Bibring, 1951, 1956; Dwyer & Zinberg, 1957; Kahana, 1959). We have found it convenient to delineate seven basic categories of personality types and attitudes: (1) the dependent, over-demanding personality; (2) the orderly, controlled personality; (3) the dramatizing, emotionally involved, captivating personality; (4) the long-suffering, self-sacrificing patient; (5) the guarded, querulous patient; (6) the patient with the feeling of superiority; (7) the patient who seems uninvolved and aloof. The first three types especially bear the direct imprint of specific developmental periods in childhood (S. Freud, 1905, 1908; Abraham, 1921, 1924, 1925). In the following four, the leading attitudes represent certain defensive reactions directed against impulses stemming from these early phases of development (Fenichel, 1945; A. Freud, 1946; S. Freud, 1905; Jones, 1913; Loewenstein, 1957; Reik, 1947). The above diagnostic categories do not designate personality disorders. They refer to the psychologically normal, well-functioning person and are especially applicable to the individual in any stressful, anxiety-producing situation. Physical illness invariably represents an emotional crisis which may be very intense but will be transient if well handled by the patient and the environment. A psychopathological diagnosis in a given case may be warranted if there is marked accentuation of character traits, neurotic or psychotic symptoms, serious difficulty in dealing adequately with social relationships, limited capacity for work, and even impaired ability to gain satisfaction and enjoyment in life.

As with much of our fundamental psychological knowledge, the recognition of personality structures has been derived in part from the study of the abnormal. These types and attitudes became familiar to psychiatrists first in their pathologically exaggerated forms, and were named respectively oral, compulsive, hysterical, masochistic, paranoid, narcissistic and schizoid personalities. We have not used the psychiatric terms because they seem to blur the important distinction between health and disease, but we shall include them parenthetically in the headings of the descriptive subtitles, to indicate the pathological correlates. These personalities are paradigms and, as with other models such as a "classical" example of a disease, few actual patients will represent one of them in pure culture. As we describe each category, we shall formulate briefly the meaning of physical illness to the particular kind of person in terms of his basic needs, the threat that he is trying to cope with, and the kind of defensive and adap-

EDITORS' COMMENTS:

THIS ARTICLE DESCRIBES RESPONSES AND BEHAVIORS COMMONLY OBSERVED IN A HOSPITAL SETTING DURING THE STRESS OF A MEDICAL–SURGICAL ILLNESS. ALTHOUGH THE ARTICLE ANTEDATES DSM-III-TYPE PERSONALITY DISORDERS, THE AUTHORS PROVIDE A CLEAR UNDERSTANDING OF THE PERSONALITY CHARACTERISTICS AND PSYCHODYNAMICS OF PATIENTS. THEY CLARIFY HOW THESE CHARACTERISTICS ARE AFFECTED BY ILLNESS, AND WHAT RESPONSES CAN BE ANTICIPATED WHEN ONE UNDERSTANDS THE PATIENT.

Reprinted from Psychiatry and Medical Practice in a General Hospital. New York, International University Press, Inc., pp. 108–123, 1964.

tive behavior that has become intensified under this stress. Some general inferences for medical psychotherapy—the employment of psychotherapeutic measures in medical management (G. L. Bibring, 1956; E. Bibring, 1954; Kahana, 1959) will be drawn.

THE DEPENDENT, OVERDEMANDING (ORAL) PERSONALITY

This type of person often impresses the physician with the urgent quality of all his requests. He seems to need special attention or an unusual amount of advice. He may reach out quickly and impulsively, putting himself in the hands of the doctor with an optimistic and naïve or self-assured expectation of limitless care. Even when he appears generous and concerned about others, he expects manifold repayment and becomes strongly resentful if this does not materialize. It becomes easily apparent that this sort of patient is very dependent upon others to protect him and to help him feel accepted and secure. His frustration tolerance is reduced, and unfulfilled needs may lead him to intense anger, depression, the feeling of helplessness, or apathy. If his formative childhood experiences were marked by feelings of disappointment, then revengeful, nagging, and demanding attitudes may prevail; the patient comes with a chip on his shoulder, expecting that the doctor will not make any effort to help him. The craving for satisfaction or stimulation through overeating, drinking, smoking, and taking medicine may be prominent, and a tendency toward addiction may be observed. These personality traits stem from the earliest period of childhood when the helpless infant's biological needs for food and protection become linked up with his growing awareness and interest in the outside world through the attention, affection, and care provided by his mother. For this patient, being given food or medicine or special consideration has persisted as an equivalent to being loved.

The Meaning of Illness

We may say that for this person the anxiety accompanying illness tends to be transformed into the wish for boundless and abundant care, and into a deep fear of being abandoned, helpless, and starving. Thus sickness presents the temptation to return to an early, blissfully secure, infantile state, but it is also perceived as the consequence of a lack of concern and protection on the part of others. In the struggle over these intense fears and wishes,

we may see any of the following responses, representing attempts to re-establish equilibrium: the patient may become extremely demanding or overdependent upon what his doctor prescribes; he may react strongly against his unconscious wishes and overindependently fight any need for care; he may become depressed, apathetic or withdrawn, perhaps feeling as small children often do, that if he suffers it must be because nobody loves him; he then may blame others for his discomfort in a complaining, vengeful, or spiteful way.

When the physician understands the meaning of illness he can decide to what extent it is possible to help the patient by attempting to satisfy his needs for special attention, whether or not the setting of certain limits is indicated, and how to facilitate or modify the patient's defensive efforts. Many elements of psychological management suggest themselves. Directly or implicitly, by word, action, or attitude, the doctors, nurses, and other medical attendants should convey their readiness to care for the patient as completely as possible. For the many acutely ill in whom dependent tendencies have become temporarily active, simple undemanding nursing care directed to physical comfort is not only a basic part of professional help, but is specifically important in meeting their psychological needs. If limits have to be set because the patient's demands have become excessive and self-perpetuating, great care must be exercised not to introduce them as if they were the expression of impatience or punitiveness. Setting of limits should not take the harsh form of a withdrawal of interest and consideration, but rather should be presented through thoughtful explanation. This patient may be willing to accept necessary restrictions if the doctor offers some form of concession as compensation. Such concessions may be of a minor nature, simply expressing the friendly interest of the physician, like a desired change in the diet, or helping his family to visit by providing transportation to the hospital, etc.

THE ORDERLY, CONTROLLED (COMPULSIVE) PERSONALITY

This person offers an example of excellent self-discipline. When under stress, he relies upon having as much knowledge as possible about his situation, not only as a basis for dealing with problems rationally, but also as his preferred way of handling his anxieties. Alongside of his logical approach, we can often observe a ritualistic tendency as a clue to diagnosis: he may keep to a set order of procedure even in small matters in daily life. The woman who spends a major amount of time eradicating the last speck of dust in her house, and the man who takes special pride in the exact fulfillment of obligations, including the most minute ones, are often of this type. This kind of patient tends to be remarkably orderly, tidy, punctual, conscientious, and preoccupied with right and wrong. With his rectitude and careful way of proceeding, we are not surprised to find that he can be quite obstinate. He places great value upon collecting and retaining possessions and is frugal in money matters. The formation of an orderly, controlled personality appears to be related to factors operative in the period from ages two to four years. Precocious development of motor and intellectual abilities and increased strength of aggressive impulses in the child play a part. Strong early insistence by the parents that the child be clean and good may have an intimidating effect, or the parents' excessive preoccupation with control of body functions and behavior may achieve a like result through intensifying the child's inner struggle between compliance and rebellion. Similarly, overindulgent disregard of the child's need to achieve a comfortable balance between expression and suppression of these tendencies may lead eventually to excessive and inflexible self-restraint. Early-maturing intellectual abilities are brought into the service of curbing impulsive behavior. Thinking tends to become a substitute for action, rather than a preparation and guide. Characteristically, impulses are warded off by the development of rigid opposite attitudes. The leading traits of orderliness, obstinacy, and frugality represent overcompensation against childhood tendencies to disorderliness, dirtiness, impulsively aggressive behavior, and pleasurable indulgence.

The Meaning of Illness

Sickness threatens the individual with loss of control over these impulses. It may impair or interfere with his capacity to master aggression and to satisfy his conscience through accomplishing "good" constructive hard work. He tries to cope with the danger by redoubled efforts to be responsible and orderly, and to suppress uncontrolled emotions. There is often an intensification of self-restraint, formalized behavior, and obstinacy so that the patient seems inflexible and opinionated. His increased striving for intellectual control, with the need to be certain that he understands and has taken into account every aspect of his problems, may lead to hesitation, doubting, and indecisiveness over the question of whether he knows all the

essential facts. At times we might be startled to see the breakthrough of disorderliness and anger, but generally his self-control predominates.

The orderly, controlled person usually finds the scientific medical approach a congenial one. He responds well to the precise and systematic efforts that characterize the doctor's careful, rational method of procedure in history-taking, physical diagnosis, laboratory studies, and treatment. He values highly the emphasis upon sympathetic efficiency and cleanliness in nursing care. In fact, these qualities are so important to him that he may evince unexpectedly strong disapproval of any lapse of routine or contradictory statement which he cannot fit into his logical framework. When his equilibrium becomes taxed under the stress of illness, perhaps leading to anxiety and intensification of characteristic reactions, an explicit therapeutic approach is indicated to facilitate his adaptation to the threatening situation. He should be informed methodically and in sufficient detail about his illness and the appropriate steps in diagnosis and therapy so that he can establish intellectual control over his anxiety. In doing this, one proceeds cautiously, carefully considering the risk of introducing new sources of anxiety, and not feeling bound to discuss all of the upsetting possibilities and unpleasant minutiae for the sake of "completeness." The patient's active participation in decisions is welcomed and, whenever it is feasible, he might be encouraged to carry out details of his actual medical care—for example, exercises or changing certain dressings, or carefully calculating his caloric intake. The physician will do well to give him recognition for his discernment, comprehension, sound reasoning, and high standards.

THE DRAMATIZING, EMOTIONALLY INVOLVED, CAPTIVATING (HYSTERICAL) PERSONALITY

The physician usually finds himself interested, charmed, fascinated, and challenged with this kind of person. However, at times he might feel mystified and suspect the patient of not really being sick, or even of malingering. The patient tends to react to the doctor in an eager, warm, very personal way, and to expect a similar response from him in return. He or she may be imaginative, dramatic, flighty, teasing or inviting, and characteristically strives for an intense, idealizing relationship with the doctor. This type of person may have an accentuated need to be noticed and admired as attractive and outstanding, and may show jealousy of the doctor's interest in any other patient. A man may repeatedly attempt to prove and even exaggerate his manliness and courage, especially before nurses and women doctors. In turn, with a male physician, a woman of this personality type may bring out in an inviting way her defenselessness and need for gallant support and protection. She will dress and make up in an attractive manner, notwithstanding rather severe physical conditions. This colorful, lively personality readily develops anxiety in connection with even minor medical procedures. The patient will avoid frightening situations if possible, but sometimes, in an attempt to overcome the fear, will rush into danger. A tendency toward denial or not remembering previous upsetting experiences may be apparent, so that the doctor may feel that this patient is not the most reliable informant. These personal traits are most typically derived from a period of development between three and six years of age, in which the child forms a strong attachment to the parent of the opposite sex. In his or her warm, colorful response, the adult of this type gives emotional expression to impulses stemming from this early affection. Guilt over hostile urges toward the parent of the same sex who is seen as a rival by the child, and fear of punishment and retaliation, form the basis for the later characteristic anxieties of the patient.

The Meaning of Illness

To the dramatizing, emotionally involved kind of person a sickness may feel like a personal defect; it means being weak and unattractive, unappreciated, and unsuccessful. It is often taken unconsciously as a punishment for forbidden childhood wishes. In men, the major fears are of bodily damage and loss of manly accomplishment and power: exertion of physical strength, competitiveness or pugnacity in order to deny these anxieties may dominate the picture, and amorous fantasies involving nurses or other attending women may be actively pursued. Women of this type feel threatened with the loss of their attractiveness: they may become flirtatious or dress up on the ward as for a special occasion. The struggle against anxiety in both men and women may be marked by increased efforts to gain admiration, dramatic bids for attention, or even an attitude of indifference to serious implications of disease if the illness is used by the patient to secure the attention and sympathy of the environment. Under intense anxiety, these reactions can go a step further and lead to a paradoxical condition in which the patient pushes for those very events that he fears the most. For instance, he may show an inappropriately light-hearted readiness to venture into a serious operation, without truly appreciating and accepting its necessity and consequences. Such "foolhardiness" in an otherwise intelligent and realistic person is reminiscent of the stunts of anxious adolescents who carelessly expose themselves to dangers in order to cope with anxiety by proving that they are not "chicken."

Since these patients seek appreciation of their attractiveness and courage, it would be an error for the doctor to be too reserved. At the same time the physician should remain aware of the patients' readiness for emotional involvement and anxiety; and should proceed with a measure of calmness and firmness to avoid stirring up these reactions. If anxieties are intense, reassuring explanations about the illness and the medical procedures will help the patient to distinguish reality from alarming fantasies. These discussions need not be as comprehensive and systematic as they should be with the orderly, controlled personality. It is often useful to allow the patient of this type a chance to discuss his fears repeatedly, if necessary, and in this way discharge some of his pent-up feelings.

THE LONG-SUFFERING, SELF-SACRIFICING (MASOCHISTIC) PATIENT

Physicians frequently see patients with a history of repeated suffering whether from illnesses, disappointments, or other adversities and failures. These people often regard their difficulties as a sign of bad luck. Upon closer examination of their experiences, we can discern that among those patients there is a group with a strong unconscious tendency to precipitate their own misfortunes—perhaps by placing themselves in difficult positions or by reacting too sensitively to the unpleasant aspects of life situations. They are inclined to disregard their own comfort and be of service to other people. Despite their apparent humility and modesty, we usually observe in such patients a tendency to display suffering in an exhibitionistic way. They evoke sympathy and praise from most people but also may arouse in them uneasiness and a guilty intolerance.

The desire to seek suffering is difficult to understand since it is contrary to the prevalent notion that pain can only be unpleasant. Though we cannot here do justice to the complexity of this attitude, it may be helpful to discuss this problem more extensively. The picture may become less puzzling if we consider the relation of pleasure to pain and the dynamic function of suffering and self-sacrifice. Pleasure and pain are often closely associated both physically and psychologically.

For example, we are familiar with the co-existence or fusion of pleasure and pain in athletic exertion and in bitter-sweet states of experience such as love-sickness or the adolescent Weltschmerz. In women, menstruation, intercourse, and childbirth are intimately associated with discomfort and yet also with the most deeply gratifying feminine experiences. Furthermore, as children we may have frequently encountered painful situations which were linked with satisfaction. Children repeatedly discover that when they become ill they can receive more than their usual share of love and attention from their parents. Beyond this, looking at the seeking of suffering from a dynamic point of view, we find in some individuals a search for punishment in order to expiate and relieve the pressure of a deep feeling of guilt. We are familiar with people who consciously or unconsciously believe that they do not deserve to succeed in life. They expect that when things go well something bad has to happen, and sometimes they bring about their setbacks, so that this suffering may temporarily atone and pacify the guilty worry in them. The extreme instance of this type of personality is exemplified in the martyr who finds glory and resolution of his guilt by achieving his social, political, or religious ideal through severe self-sacrifice and suffering. The co-existence of pain and satisfaction in the biological function of the woman, the young person with Weltschmerz, the child who is cherished and forgiven because he is ill, the person who atones unknowingly for guilt, and the martyr—all are models that demonstrate involuntary self-victimization.

Among the early experiences that appear to contribute to the development of this attitude we find severely repressive upbringing in which the child was made to feel excessively guilty, was not permitted to show anger even in a harmless manner, and was given corporal punishment, which in some children provokes excitement that is tinged with pleasure. An attachment to a parent who was aggressive toward the child may have shaped later relationships to important figures in life according to this pattern, or the child may have unconsciously modeled himself upon a suffering parent. In the youngster who felt especially favored and loved when he was sick, this satisfaction may take over as an end in itself and become established as a pattern that is carried throughout life.

The Meaning of Illness

The basic striving of this personality is to gain love, care and acceptance, although he feels too guilty and anxious to expect this without self-sacrifice and suffering. The dangers and discomforts of illness may be elaborated by the patient in intensified attitudes of submission and suffering, complaining, or self-effacement, and feeling martyred. For the doctor, the most frequently encountered form of this attitude is the childlike expectation, "you have to love me because I suffer so terribly." But when he tries to comfort a patient of this kind, perhaps a pitiably distressed elderly lady, he discovers a paradoxical phenomenon. He is confronted with a person who seems to work against his encouragement and above all to deny any improvement. As he offers helpful suggestions or comforting reassurance, her complaints increase. She disregards evidence of progress toward recovery and accentuates those aspects of her illness which have not improved. Very understandably, this may lead to feelings of disappointment and irritation on the part of the doctor if he does not recognize her reaction as fitting into a special pattern of behavior. When a person of this type says, "it's not easy, doctor," he is not asking for encouraging remarks but for acknowledgement of his pain and sacrifices. Accordingly, the doctor should express his appreciation of the difficulties of illness as they are experienced by this patient. The long-suffering, self-sacrificing person is better able to co-operate in a medical regimen out of a readiness to add to the "burden" that he must carry, than for the personal relief that health would bring to him. The physician may have to present the recovery to the patient as a special additional task, if possible for the benefit of others. For example, an older woman of this type who repeatedly refused a rehabilitating operation when it was urged as essential to preserve her well-being and comfort, was able to accept it only when it was pointed out that she could not continue to be of help to her children unless her physical condition was corrected.

THE GUARDED, QUERULOUS (PARANOID) PERSON

This patient is openly or covertly watchful of other persons, inclined to be suspicious of their intentions, or querulous and blameful of their motives. He may nurse grievances, especially a deep sense of having been let down by people. He particularly fears being placed in a vulnerable position in which he could be unexpectedly hurt or taken advantage of. Patients who consistently expect the worst are oversensitive to slights and to hints of negative feelings in other people. They easily feel oppressed and even persecuted and are likely to react with a self-righteous counter-attack, exaggerated out of all proportion to actual insults. This excessive sensitivity to criticism and expectation of being assaulted reflects a deeper concern with their own faults and weaknesses. They deal with their inner problems and self-reproaches in a very interesting way, by disclaiming them entirely as if they had no place within themselves, and reading them, with indignant disapproval, into the attitudes of other people. We can understand this kind of reaction in an adult better by referring back to the behavior of small children. In its simplest form, we see the youngster who hurts himself by running into a table and then blames the "bad, nasty table." At a somewhat older age, we may observe the little girl who, when chided for misbehaving, says with guilty defiance that her naughty doll did it, not she. An echo of this childhood cry of "I didn't do it—he did it" is found in those adults who have to get rid of whatever is painful, dangerous, or intolerable within themselves by attributing it to others. By thus freeing themselves from what seems unworthy, they both elevate their self-regard and perceive other people as threatening and bad. We are familiar with the individual of this type who does not want to acknowledge in himself impulses to infidelity but is hypersensitive and very critical when he has any possibility of finding and fighting these urges in his marital partner.

The Meaning of Illness

The guarded, querulous patient tends to blame others for his illness. During periods of sickness, his tensions and aggressive tendencies and his expectations of being harmed may be intensified. He becomes even more fearful, guarded, suspicious, quarrelsome and controlling of others. In medical management, it is essential to let this kind of person know, as far as foreseeable, the strategy of diagnosis and treatment so that his suspicions may be kept in abeyance. The frequent oversensitivity to slights of individuals of this type should be respected so as not to create a conflict between patient and doctor. A friendly and courteous attitude on the doctor's part, that avoids getting too close to or excessively involved with the patient, is often indicated. If the physician goes beyond this, there is the risk that the patient will feel he is either being forced or manipulated. Arguing with him or ignoring his suspicious attitude does not help, and if as his doctors we try to convince him that everyone has the best of intentions, he is unable to believe it and it might lead to further mistrust.

In the case of a man with these personality traits

who had undergone a very serious cancer operation and who complained bitterly about any inconvenience or irregularity in the hospital routine, we could observe two different reactions of the people attending him. Some were drawn into agreeing with him, sharing his irritation over the coldness of the food, the slowness of the nurses, and the inaccessibility of the doctors. This had the effect of increasing his acrimonious discontent. Others tried to point out how exaggerated his reproaches were, or, becoming provoked, told him in effect that he was asking for too much and was ungrateful for the care that he had been given. He responded with recriminations against them as well as undiminished anger at the hospital. We were able to lessen his preoccupation and mitigate his querulous response by taking a third approach. He was assured that we could appreciate how upsetting these inconveniences and delays can be for a person of his sensitivity who had gone through such a trying illness. By acknowledging and giving him full credit for his feelings as his way of perceiving and encountering the world—without disputing his complaints, but especially without reinforcing them—we could help him to detach himself and reduce the intensity of his reactions. Only then was it possible to take the next step: to appeal to his tolerance regarding these experiences in the hospital which, although very distressing to him, were less significant compared with the lifesaving surgery and rehabilitating postoperative care. Thus we were able to regain his co-operation.

THE PATIENT WITH THE FEELING OF SUPERIORITY (NARCISSISTIC)

Among our patients, we find people who have to see themselves as powerful and all-important. This need may lead to an attitude of self-confidence so exaggerated that a person of this type appears smug, vain or grandiose. Or his basic frame of mind may be covered by an artificial, patronizing humility. Frequently, associated characteristics include a kind of arrogance (he looks down on most other people), the tendency to surround himself with an aura of mysterious knowledge, and sometimes a fondness for holding forth—mainly in monologues. A considerable amount of every adult's interest centers around his own self. If this attitude is not excessive we speak of self-respect rather than a feeling of superiority. As we have discovered with so many exaggerated tendencies which serve the purpose of counteracting doubts, the patient who feels superior has an urgent need to surpass everyone else, coupled with an underlying uncertainty about his own transcendence. When he falls ill and must turn to a doctor, this person deems only the most eminent or senior physician worthy of serving him, choosing someone who will reinforce the sense of his own grandeur. Even in a large teaching hospital where he is cared for by a medical team, such a patient may only acknowledge that he is being treated by the Chief of Service. His attitude toward the younger physicians is frequently that of a benevolent supervisor who tolerantly aids them in their quest for education. In spite of his need for a doctor who has the utmost competence, the patient is bound at the same time to vie with him and outdo him. He may allow that he himself is not a medical expert (if this be the case), yet he might feel free to reject his doctor's counsel on the basis of his own conclusions and considerations which he believes to be of greater moment. This patient tends to search constantly for weaknesses in the doctor and is inclined to lose confidence in him, dwelling upon his faults and belittling him at the slightest provocation.

The Meaning of Illness

The person with the feeling of superiority is likely to react to a sickness as if it threatened his self-image of perfection and invulnerability. His characteristic behavior becomes intensified, often in the direction of a defensive grandiosity. Accordingly, he will feel most comfortable and secure if the doctor fulfills his need of being implicitly acknowledged as a person of achievement in his own right. Of course, this does not mean that the physician can or should deny his own expert knowledge and skill. In fact, this kind of person, in spite of all his effort to find weaknesses in the doctor, is at the same time deeply afraid of discovering that he might be in the hands of an incompetent physician.

THE PATIENT WHO SEEMS UNINVOLVED AND ALOOF (SCHIZOID)

This person gives an impression of remoteness, reserve, and lack of involvement with everyday events and concerns of people. His emotional expression may be reduced to a minimum and he may appear quiet, distant, seclusive, and unsociable. He may pursue his own way of life, seemingly with little need for emotional ties with others, appearing quite independent and not easily impressed. Beneath this surface such a person often is oversensitive, fragile, and lacking resilience, so that his inner equilibrium is too easily upset in the course of the ordinary difficulties of human relationships. His aloofness is a protective denial of these excessively painful experiences. The life history of such a person reflects solitary interests. He gravitates to noncompetitive jobs that require a minimum of contact with others. Within this group, we find eccentric persons engrossed individually with dietary and health fads, religious movements, and social improvement schemes. The aloof, eccentric patient may exhibit an unusual manner of dressing or behaving without concern for the reactions of conventional people.

We often find in the childhood history of this kind of patient that his earliest efforts to form a loving attachment to another person led to repeated disappointments, with the result that the child could invest feelings in others only in a tentative and limited way. This might be the consequence of repeated separations from mother, or of a lack of consistent responsive, empathic care by the environment. The infantile experience then is carried into the patient's later relationships, leading finally to the type of personality who impresses us as uninvolved and remote. There are also indications that constitutional factors may play an important role in the genesis of this kind of personality, especially in its most pronounced form.

The Meaning of Illness

The aloof person tries to remain undisturbed by life, seeking solace and satisfaction within himself. Illness intrudes into this system, threatening to upset this careful equilibrium. The patient frequently protects himself against this by intensifying his denial in proportion to the increase in underlying anxiety and thus seems to remain strikingly unperturbed and even more seclusive and distant than usual. Foremost in the psychological management of this patient, his "unsociability" has to be understood and accepted. We should make as few demands as possible upon him for personal involvement with others, yet he should not be permitted to withdraw completely. This may be achieved by trying to maintain a considerate interest in him, quietly and reassuringly, without requesting a reciprocal effort on his part.

CLINICAL APPLICATION OF PERSONALITY DIAGNOSIS

We have taken up only major aspects of personality diagnosis. Clinical experience reveals a wide vista of possible shades and combinations of characteristics in the make-up of different individuals. In practice, one must avoid the premature and rigid use of a diagnostic classification of personality since this involves the hazard of becoming limited in one's perception of the patient's structure. This will happen if "typing" a patient becomes a shortcut, replacing the natural development of a relationship and full observation of the distinguishing qualities of the person. Moreover, it is not always easy to establish quickly the correct personality diagnosis. The problem of perceiving the leading personality traits is complicated by the fact that in some degree everyone has passed through similar phases of early development and, therefore, in his adult personality tends to show an admixture of all modes of behavior. Nevertheless, each person has his particular means of adjustment and should be judged by his predominant psychological organization. But while the basic personality structure of an adult remains relatively stable, under special stress shifts between a variety of defenses and needs may occur (G. L. Bibring, 1961; Prange and Abse, 1957). With these pitfalls in mind, let us now take up a clinical example illustrating the task of managing flexibly the medical psychotherapy of a patient whose leading attitudes varied in the course of his illness.

A thirty-nine-year-old man with an acute, severe myocardial infarction, the fourth within nine years, was extremely apprehensive during his first days in the hospital.[1] Fully aware of the nature of his disease, he was terrified that he might die. Yet, despite his desperate desire to live, he frequently refused to rest or take medication. This handsome, physically powerful man regarded any request by the nurses as arbitrary and refused to be "commanded" by them. He was also aggressively seductive towards them. His previous pattern of reaction to illness suggested that a tendency toward hyperactivity might interfere with his recovery. Though he had been advised to return to only moderate physical activity after his earlier coronary thromboses, he had vigorously pursued water polo, handball and wrestling with his children. We discovered that these attitudes had a long history.

He had run away from home at the age of thirteen, shortly after his father had died of a malignant tumor. His flight had followed a quarrel in which he felt that his oldest brother had tried to order him around. He was a big youngster and passed himself off as sixteen or seventeen when he got a job with a traveling carnival. In subsequent years, he worked as a roustabout and rigger of amusement "rides," a bulldozer operator, a truckdriver and a

two-fisted bouncer in a penny arcade—nothing was too difficult for him to take on. In his marriage, he immediately established his position as the master of the household. Both in the home and at work, he felt that challenges and fights gave meaning to his life. He boasted about his manly prowess, yet, in listening to the account of his many successes, one had the definite impression that he exaggerated. All of this indicated his need to see himself as prepotent.

It was evident that this colorful, lively man had many features of the dramatizing, emotionally involved personality. Typically, he responded to his life-endangering illness as if it threatened his masculinity. Because he suffered from this anxiety and, therefore, might jeopardize himself by premature and excessive exercises, it was necessary to give immediate attention to help the patient re-establish his psychological equilibrium. It was found that he accepted the nurses' care with more comfort and appreciation when all medical recommendations were given to him personally, as far as possible, by his male doctor. At the same time it was considered essential to permit him to apply some initiative and strength. Thus, even while he had to remain strictly on bed rest, he was encouraged to carry out his own schedule of simple leg exercises and rest periods and to help in dietary planning. As an essential part of the therapeutic program, he did some light work with the occupational therapist. His physician repeatedly acknowledged the great discipline which the patient applied, and expressed his appreciation of the difficulties this illness may create for an active, vigorous man. Information about his illness was offered with the aim of reducing some of his uncertainty about the outcome of his condition, and to prepare him to cope with the illness in a more rational way. In responding to his questions about the future, emphasis was placed on his improved chances of survival with collateral coronary circulation, if he maintained his activities within limits under continued medical observation.

With this approach the patient was helped to make the shift from displaying his strength by muscular activity to exercising it through intelligent self-control. He became less quarrelsome and more optimistic, and was full of high praise for his house physician who had explained thoroughly some of the medical problems to him. However, as we have seen in similar cases, this patient who had dealt with the acute, critical and life-threatening situation by the protective mechanism of denying his weakness, in the convalescent period displayed different attitudes and needs in dealing with his underlying anxieties. This in turn required modification of the psychological management. When the patient returned home, he became very apprehensive whenever he went outside of the house. He had to lie down and complain to his wife that she did not realize how sick he was. He would ask whether he looked pale; his pulse seemed fast and weak to him. Pains occurred in his upper abdomen and chest which were not relieved by nitroglycerine but were helped by sedation. It was apparent that he needed special care and attention at this time in a dependent, anxious way. In response, his physician took a

---

[1]Dr. Arthur R. Kravitz and Dr. Robert E. Eisendrath have contributed their observations of this patient.

definitely protective attitude. He told the patient that his doctors were willing and able to take full responsibility for his treatment, and could be trusted and depended upon. With this assurance the patient's anxiety lessened. When he returned to work he felt better on the job than at home because he could be more active there and was less prone to yield to his dependent wishes. He was able to relinquish his bid for extra attention from his family and knew that he could be a well-functioning man in his own right. He came to the clinic less frequently, but kept a solid, confident relationship with his doctors and was able to adhere to the medical regimen.

SUMMARY

In a long-term program aimed at blending psychological understanding with medical practice in a general hospital, it has been found that a knowledge of personality structure is an important basis for the physician in order to employ appropriate psychotherapeutic principles in the management of physically ill patients. A paradigmatic classification of personalities is described that is useful as a guide for medical psychotherapy. It includes the following "types": the dependent, over-demanding personality; the orderly, controlled personality; the dramatizing, emotionally involved, captivating personality; the long-suffering, self-sacrificing patient; the guarded, querulous patient; the patient who feels superior; the patient who seems uninvolved and aloof. For each type a brief formulation is made of the essential psychological meaning of physical illness and inferences for medical management are drawn. The classification is particularly applicable to the normal personality under stress. A case illustrating medical psychotherapy is presented.

THE PARANOID PERSONALITY

RUSSELL NOYES, JOHN CLANCY, AND TERRY A. TRAVIS

Viewing the world about him as hostile and menacing, the paranoid individual uses characteristic traits to cope with that world and avoid a retreat into fantasy. On initial contact, the physician must be alert to the ways this patient reveals himself and subsequently must tactfully establish rapport to facilitate treatment.

The Greek word "paranoia," originally a general term for insanity, became the specific designation for a mental disorder characterized by persecutory delusions. "Paranoid," the adjective derived from it, applies to a spectrum of disorders typified by persecutory trends of thought. These range from the mild paranoid personality to severe paranoid schizophrenia, the latter representing a psychotic disorganization.

Falling on the mild end of the spectrum, the paranoid personality blends imperceptibly with normal behavior. It is characterized by ". . . pervasive and unwarranted suspiciousness hypersensitivity, and aloofness."[1] Because in their mildest form such traits are common occurrences, the diagnosis is generally reserved for persons whose interpersonal life is significantly disrupted as a result of them. Such traits represent the personality's attempt to cope with the world and avoid a retreat into fantasy. Individuals with such characteristics have little room in which to maneuver, however,

and under stress may lose contact with reality and regress into psychosis.

The paranoid individual views the world about him as hostile and menacing. He may have acquired this outlook early in life as a result of an insecure, mistrustful relationship with his parents. Within that troubled relationship, he may have avoided developing an image of himself as evil or worthless by using projection, a mental mechanism characteristic of this disorder. Projection is a process by which unacceptable impulses or traits are attributed to others. Blame for sexual or aggressive urges is transferred, with the result that they appear to emanate from others.

Having viewed his parents as rejecting and deceitful in early life, the paranoid generalizes this view and in adult life sees himself as surrounded by people with hurtful intentions. He is likewise prone to view the acute sense of inferiority and helplessness from which he suffers as being imposed on him from without. Since low self-esteem is painful, he blames others for it, saying, "I am not inferior but am treated as if I were."

Out of an expectation of emotional rejection, the paranoid increases his alertness to his interpersonal environment. His morbid sensitivity causes him to misinterpret the ambiguities of interpersonal interactions, and he displays "a remarkable genius for detecting in the ordinary run-of-life situations, just those tiny slights, inadvertencies or trifling disparagements which others overlook but which he builds up into crucial issues, not altogether imaginary but vastly overemphasized."[2] Everywhere he looks he sees persons cheating and stabbing one another in the back. Often one or more persons in his own life—spouse, employer, in-law, etc.—seem to be harassing or abusing him for reasons that are not entirely clear.

EDITORS' COMMENTS:

THIS BRIEF PAPER DESCRIBES THE CLINICAL PICTURE FOUND IN INDIVIDUALS WITH PARANOID PERSONALITY DISORDERS. THE AUTHORS OFFER PRACTICAL ADVICE ON APPROACHING THESE INDIVIDUALS.

Reprinted, with author revisions, from Postgraduate Medicine 55:141–146, 1974.

The paranoid's attitude toward the world is firmly implanted and his basic premise that it is threatening is practically unshakable. Believing as he does, he is alert and active in search of clues that confirm his belief.

There is more than a grain of truth to the paranoid's feelings that he is rejected, however, for out of a sense that the world is hostile, he presents to it a bitter, angry facade that invites the very rejection he fears. The rejection he evokes seems to benefit him in a pathologic way. It assists him in maintaining emotional distance from others and at the same time strengthens his conviction that people are untrustworthy. Although painful, this belief is familiar and therefore comforting.

While the paranoid maintains his distance, he nevertheless perceives himself as involved with those people who harass him. That people appear to go out of their way to do so suggests to him that he is somehow important to them. As a result, his feeling of self-worth is increased and his loneliness is assuaged.

The paranoid individual isolates himself from others as a result of his insecurity and self-doubt, characteristics that tend to keep him preoccupied with himself. Because of this self-preoccupation and a drive toward independence, his capacity to appreciate how others feel is poorly developed and he may brood over relationships. Similarly, the paranoid individual avoids dependence on others where he feels vulnerable and threatened. Since he trusts rather exclusively in himself, it is not surprising to find a compensatory development of his intellectual capacities. He is often meticulous, precise, and rational.

The following case summary illustrates the morbid sensitivity and social isolation of a paranoid individual. It portrays a painful life of conflict fueled by the patient's own projected anger.

CASE SUMMARY. A 26-year-old divorced man who was a moving-van driver consulted his physician regarding fatigue, insomnia, and abdominal distress. These symptoms developed after a breakup with a girl friend who he said had grown increasingly possessive of him. At times, he felt as if she were taking over his personality, but he was uncertain whether this was deliberate.

The breakup had caused him to doubt himself. He had lost motivation but described tremendous energy within himself that seemed without direction. As he described this, he doubled his fist and shook it in an angry gesture. He had been unable to sleep and doubted his ability to maintain emotional control.

This patient's parents were divorced when he was 4 years of age. He never knew his father and felt a lack of concern on the part of his mother. He never liked school and had had frequent fights and disagreements with classmates. He regarded himself as socially aloof and isolated from others because of his different views.

Following school, he began driving a truck. He felt a certain resentment and futility about this work; his boss seemed authoritarian to him and he felt he was being used.

His marriage of six years had been a failure from the start. Because his wife had been irresponsible and unfaithful, he had never gotten along with her. Although he denied ever having loved her, he could not help blaming himself when things did not work out. His bitterness toward her continued as a result of her behavior around the time of their divorce. At that time, it seemed as if she had followed his movements through a group of spies in an attempt to catch him at something.

He felt a bond with society's rebellious youth, although he had no friends among them. He felt society was restrictive and had robbed him of his freedom. He wondered whether to submit to its dictates or free himself to do as he pleased.

He accepted the recommendation that he see a psychiatrist, but because the consultant was authoritarian, he became aggressively accusatory and refused to see him again. A second psychiatrist found him serious and overly controlled. His eyes seemed unusually prominent and he looked fixedly, even suspiciously, at his interviewer. He reported that his mind was tremendously active and that he was forever questioning the motives of others.

He felt pressured by convention and the expectations of others to a point where it seemed to him that much of his behavior was controlled from outside sources. He described a feeling that periodically welled up within him that he had an important mission in life, in response to which he had the urge to drop everything and follow where it might lead.

INITIAL INTERVIEW

The paranoid individual may reveal himself on initial contact in a variety of ways. He is apt to show excessive concern regarding confidentiality and may insist on a need for secrecy. He may be guarded, vague, and evasive. At times, he may appear wary and may peer at the examiner as if questioning his motives. At other times, his eyes may dart from side to side or cast about the room in a searching fashion. He may be serious and lack a sense of humor.

The paranoid tends to be aggressive and from the initial contact may be argumentative and provocative. From the beginning, he may accuse the physician of mistreatment. For example, he may take offense at the physician's delay in seeing him. Beyond this, he may seem to pick a fight or reveal a typical chip-on-the-shoulder attitude, inquiring whether the physician intends to give him the same brush-off he experienced with his last physician. In the same provocative way he may challenge his physician's credentials.

Certain patterns appear repeatedly as the paranoid tells his story and outlines his history. The most significant of these is a theme of victimization. Because it pervades his life and preoccupies his mind, it emerges with little encouragement.

Disharmony in interpersonal relationships is characteristic and is often revealed in references to marriage, family, and employment. The conflict in which the paranoid individual finds himself often reaches a point of crisis, causing disruption of troubled relationships. Since intimacy is poorly tolerated, the patient often has a history of conflict in marriage or of divorce. The paranoid's defiance of authority leads to conflict with employers and to frequent job changes. While he is apt to view his employer as dictatorial, he becomes tyrannical himself in a position of authority.

The paranoid is socially isolated and aloof, but when he becomes involved with others, he is often jealous and rivalrous. He is a hypercritical person whose faultfinding ability is highly developed, yet his own sensitivity to criticism is extreme.

Certain problems arise in the initial contact with a paranoid patient. First, he may be vague and evasive of questions. Fearful of exposure and intimate contact, he adopts this means of keeping his distance. Because this restricts the exchange of meaningful information, the physician may find himself puzzled about the nature of the patient's visit. His symptoms may seem nebulous or ill-defined and his reasons for discontinuing previous treatment poorly understood. As rapport is established, evasiveness may diminish, but it is rarely responsive to impatient confrontation.

A second problem encountered is a filibuster. The physician may be confronted with ceaseless talking in place of fruitful history taking. The purpose of this troublesome interference is again the prevention of emotional closeness. By seizing control of the interview, the patient controls the degree of his emotional involvement. The problem may persist with the establishment of rapport. By then, the patient feels he must ward off rejection, which he does by "rejecting the interviewer first, using words to keep him at a distance, but at the same time hanging on by continuing to speak."[3]

To take a meaningful history, the physician must interrupt this filibuster in a way that does not alienate the patient. For example, he might say to the patient, "I would like to come back to what you are telling me, but first let me get some information that will be important to your treatment."

Third, as noted, anger may be expressed toward the physician. For example, in response to initial questions a patient might reply, "That information is all in my chart. I don't feel like going through it all again!" This type of statement is irritating but calls for a sympathetic response if rapport is to be established. One might reply that it must indeed be tiresome to repeat statements that have been made a number of times already. Finding the physician sympathetic and not defensive in the face of his anger, a patient may continue the interview, having vented his feelings.

A fourth problem occasionally encountered is the patient's reluctance to assume the patient role. Having come to the physician, he may proceed to deny that he needs treatment while at the same time speaking of additional symptoms or concerns. Once hospitalized, he may demand his release. For the paranoid, the acceptance of the patient role implies a humiliating loss of dignity. He feels exposed and vulnerable in this role. The physician should not be insistent that he remain in treatment. Instead, he might indicate to the patient that since he came to see the physician, he must have wondered what the physician could do for him. Realizing that he is free to leave but at the same time that the physician is interested in him, he may well remain for treatment.

PHYSICAL SYMPTOMS

The paranoid patient often has presenting physical symptoms that are without underlying pathology. Several interpretations of them are possible. First, his self-absorption leads to hypochondriasis. The energy and emotional investment that have been withdrawn from his interpersonal world are turned toward his body and its functioning. As a result, the sensations arriving from it become a focus of attention and take on significance. Such an individual may sense that his body, as well as his mind, is under attack. The fleeting thought that someone may have poisoned his food naturally colors his interpretation of indigestion.

The mechanism of projection may further contribute to somatic complaints. The paranoid individual may project onto his body a sense of impending personality decompensation. In so doing, he defends himself by saying, "It is not my mind that is coming apart, it is my body." Under these circumstances the sensations arriving from it are given ominous interpretation.

A paranoid person is lonely and fearful. He craves intimacy, although he fears it. Often part of his motivation in consulting a physician is this craving. He seeks the physician's interest, his benign concern, and the security of the physician-patient relationship, but in his seeking, he naturally presents medical complaints to which the physician can respond.

In times of crisis precipitated by the loss of a loved person or the forced assumption of a submissive role, somatic symptoms may accompany psychic ones. Such symptoms, including insomnia, weakness, fatigue, and irritability, represent early manifestations of personality decompensation.

Physical illness poses a crisis for the paranoid individual simply because he is forced to assume the patient role. In this submissive role he feels robbed of his isolation and independence; he feels acutely vulnerable and fears assault. Under these circumstances, his physician sees an exaggeration of paranoid traits. The patient may become belligerent, argumentative, and accusatory, and in so doing, he may alienate his physician or attending personnel. He may refuse to remain in the patient role and dismiss himself from the hospital or his physician's care.

PHYSICIAN-PATIENT RELATIONSHIP

The paranoid is a mistrustful, reluctant patient. Establishing rapport with this type of person is neither a gradual nor an ambiguous process. Usually he forces the physician to clarify the relationship at once. "He wants to know who is doing what to whom, and his intensity and anxiety usually demand a prompt answer."[4] It is imperative that the physician be scrupulously honest and that he state his position clearly.

Successful early encounters depend on the physician's response to the paranoid's hostility. "The best response to initial mistrust and verbal attack is sincere attentiveness to the patient but some disinterest in the content of the accusations."[4]

The paranoid often uses expressions of hostility to keep others at a distance; he seeks to hurt others before he gets hurt himself. Understanding this can be helpful. The physician should not argue or be drawn into conflict with a paranoid patient even though the patient's behavior often provokes such a response. Responding aggressively to the paranoid only leads to more intense expressions of hostility.

It is advisable to make the paranoid an active participant in his treatment to the greatest extent possible. Doing so allows him to preserve a sense of independence and, to the extent that it may be necessary, preserve emotional distance from his physician.

In dealing with this type of patient, the physician should respect his sensitivity. One should avoid humor, as it is readily misinterpreted.

Inappropriate reassurance casually given can foster mistrust and lead to deterioration of the physician-patient relationship. For the physician's own safety and sense of security, he should keep up-to-date, detailed, accurate records. He must realize that no matter how he conducts himself, the strain of maintaining rapport with a paranoid patient may exceed his tolerance and ingenuity, and disruption of the relationship may result in legal action taken against him.

MANAGEMENT

If the physician offers medication to a paranoid individual who is anxious or whose personality threatens decompensation, he should remember that this individual is frightened of drugs for two reasons. First, he is suspicious of anything that might control him. Second, the medication may induce physiological changes that alarm him because they lead him to feel that something is weakening his grip on reality. Antipsychotic medications such as chlorpromazine (Thorazine), 150 to 300 mg daily, or trifluoperazine hydrochloride (Stelazine), 5 to 10 mg, are the most appropriate in this situation.

A supportive, therapeutic approach to a paranoid patient may be taken with the specific objective of resolving the crisis that precipitated the patient's appearance for treatment.[5] Occasionally, the patient may be referred to a psychiatrist for this purpose. The latter may undertake the more ambitious objective of altering the paranoid's mode of thinking. A variety of approaches to this have been attempted, each aimed at convincing the paranoid patient that his suspicion and hostility are unwarranted, unnecessary, and self-defeating. After establishing some level of communication and a trusting relationship, the physician may give an indirect challenge to the patient's mode of thinking.[4] This involves assisting the patient to see that interpersonal interactions are often ambiguous and therefore subject to a variety of interpretations other than his usual personalized one. He may be assisted to see that he often elicits the negative behavior in others which he interprets as unprovoked. As a result, he may begin to view his problems as partly a matter of his own doing.

At times, it may be useful to instruct the paranoid individual to talk about subjects other than his preoccupation with abuse. This can help to enlarge his sphere of interest and increase his ties with the real world. Every effort should be made to reinforce realistic behavior and every encouragement given a patient to capitalize on his talents and strengthen areas of healthy functioning. The paranoid patient tends to be deficient in basic social skills and when he reveals naïveté in such matters, an effort may be made to enlighten him.

The physician needs to be reminded of the challenge to a harmonious physician-patient relationship that a paranoid patient presents. Because he is hostile, he may evoke rejection. Being hypersensitive, he is ready to pinpoint weakness in the physician or his approach, which makes the latter uncomfortable. Mistrustful of authority, he is particularly suspicious of and resistant to the physician's seeming attempts to control him. When he claims to be misunderstood, he often attempts to win the physician over to his way of thinking. In so doing, he threatens to disrupt the relationship.

Occasionally, a paranoid individual is successful in drawing his physician into conflict. Through long practice, he has become adept at provoking disharmony and the physician too often finds himself the object of this pathologic approach. Such conflicts are exhausting and benefit no one. The patient receives inadequate medical care and the physician is left with a sense of angry frustration.

SUMMARY

Characteristics of the paranoid personality include hypersensitivity, rigidity, unwarranted suspicion, jealousy, envy, excessive self-importance, and a tendency to blame others. On initial contact, the physician may find him guarded, vague, and evasive. Often physical symptoms are without underlying pathology. The paranoid patient is a challenge to a harmonious physician-patient relationship. The physician's response to his expressions of hostility should be sincere attentiveness mixed with disinterest in the content of the patient's accusations. Since the paranoid is reluctant to assume the patient role, he should be made an active participant in his treatment whenever possible.

Supported in part by Public Health Service grants MH 11396 and MH 05911 from the National Institute of Mental Health.

REFERENCES

1. Diagnostic and Statistical Manual of Mental Disorders. Ed 2. Washington, DC, American Psychiatric Association, 1968
2. Kolb LC: Noyes' Modern Clinical Psychiatry. Ed 7. Philadelphia, WB Saunders Company, 1968, p 403
3. MacKinnon RA, Michels R: The Psychiatric Interview in Clinical Practice. Philadelphia, WB Saunders Company, 1971
4. Swanson DW, Bohnert PJ, Smith JA: The Paranoid. Boston, Little, Brown and Company, 1970
5. Noyes R Jr, Clancy J, Travis TA: Personality disorders: An introduction. Postgrad Med 54:62, Oct 1973

THE OBSESSIVE STYLE

LEON SALZMAN

The human infant arrives in a state of absolute helplessness and total dependence upon his environment. Although his capacities to function independently enlarge as he matures physically and psychologically, he is never in full control of the forces which act upon him from the inside or the outside. In order to experience a minimum of security and a measure of certainty, man constructs a number of myths about his powers and skill in influencing these forces. Such techniques have been used since man developed a cortex capable of visualizing his own self. His structuralizing involved attempts to insure order and consistency in his universe and were often unreasonable. As they were rigidly held and had magical connotations, the devices could be called obsessive mechanisms.

In children these techniques consist of magical, repetitive acts which the child feels will prevent dangerous consequences from occurring if the rituals are carried out precisely. In adults such behavior is called superstitious and irrational; the magical quality involved is readily evident. The greater the extent of fear and uncertainty, the more prevalent will be the magical superstitions and

EDITORS' COMMENTS:

THIS PSYCHOANALYTIC DESCRIPTION DETAILS OBSESSIONAL MECHANISMS THOROUGHLY AND CLEARLY. WHILE EVERYONE HAS SOME NEED TO ACHIEVE CONTROL OVER THE INTERNAL AND EXTERNAL ENVIRONMENT, THE NEED FOR OMNISCIENCE AND OMNIPOTENCE PREVADES THE CLINICAL PICTURE OF INDIVIDUALS WITH OBSESSIVE STYLES AND IS AT TIMES ACCOMPANIED BY GRANDIOSITY, INDECISION, AND/OR RITUALS.

Reprinted, in condensed form, from The Obsessive Personality. New York, Jason Aronson, Inc., pp. 15–60, 1973.

rigid rules of behavior designed to control or master these uncertainties.

Obsessional mechanisms are omnipresent, but in some people they will be more pronounced and will characterize the major ways of dealing with their needs, therefore playing an integral part in their personality structure. Such people's behavior will be predictable and consistent in their reactions to various needs and circumstances. Yet, not all the characteristics of the obsessional way of life are present in all obsessional individuals. Nor will these tendencies always be adaptive or constructive. In the obsessive-compulsive neurosis such tendencies become extreme and maladaptive.

The primary dynamism in all instances will be manifested as an attempt to gain control over oneself and one's environment in order to avoid or overcome distressful feelings of helplessness. The concern about the possibility of losing control by being incompetent, insufficiently informed, or unable to reduce the risks of living produces the greatest amounts of anxiety. The realization of one's humanness—with its inherent limitations—is often the basis for considerable anxiety and obsessive attempts at greater control over one's living.

Fear of loss of control is commonly symbolized in the physical sense as losing control by fainting, by resorting to the extremes of shouting and screaming, or by engaging in other undisciplined activities. Phobias often develop around these situations, in which the person fears he will lose control of himself in giddiness, fainting, swaying feelings, collapsing, or possibly dying. The problem of control in the obsessive person is complicated by his tendency to deal in extremes, so that unless he feels he has total control he tends to experience total *lack* of control. He experiences the possibility of loss of control as so painfully humiliating, frightening, and dangerous that phobic avoidances are common.

THE NEED FOR OMNISCIENCE

To achieve control over one's living and to guarantee one's existence one must acquire a knowledge of all the possibilities that may occur. The striving for omniscience through emphasis on intellectuality is an integral part of the obsessive process and is a major goal. The obsessional can be comfortable only when he feels he knows everything or is engaged in the process of trying to know everything. He is convinced not only that this is absolutely necessary but also that often it is possible, even in the fact of his intellectual grasp of the impossibility of achieving the goal. He demands of himself that he be capable of anticipating his own reactions and the emotional responses of others by rational and logical means. He requires that he be able to control the uncontrollable. Thus he expects to know how he will be feeling several days hence so that he can plan properly. He expects his decisions or opinions to be acceptable to everyone, even those who disagree with him or do not know him. He expects to know in advance that his plans will be ideal and agreeable to all. Such expectations often serve to immobilize him and to prevent him from making any plans. He rationalizes the immobility by insisting that he wants only to plan most effectively and to suit everyone. He will say, "If it cannot be done perfectly, then why do it at all?" This has a flavor of righteous and conscientious living and is often rewarded with praise and support. The truth, however, is that it is not based on a moral injunction, but on a compelling need to guarantee the outcome of the endeavor—which is hardly ever possible. It is, in fact, compulsive behavior and not simply conscientious and responsible behavior.

When the compulsive is forced to act, he will often refuse to take full responsibility for the consequences, because he was not fully in accord with the plan and therefore should not be held accountable for the outcome. In this way the compulsive justifies any failure of his activities by placing blame on others who forced him to act.

The inability to relinquish or compromise, or to take a chance, impairs the effectiveness of the person's capacity for full and mature living. The person senses that there is something amiss in the way he organizes his living, but seems able to do very little about it. Instead, he justifies his behavior with intellectual and philosophical rationalizations. He prefers to present a picture of a thoughtful person who examines issues in depth, instead of acknowledging that his demands for omniscience make action and decision difficult.

Excursions Into Philosophy

Philosophizing can often provide the way to avoid action and to forego decision. While it may be a prelude to action, it often becomes a substitute for living rather than a design for better living. It avoids taking sides, which helps to sustain the aura of omniscience.

The obsessional insists upon arriving at ultimate truths in all matters. He claims a purity of intellectual pursuit in which he maintains that unless certainty can be established, final statements must be avoided. This is a defensive device, particularly when the certainty he demands is in areas in which the possibility of it is remote or unattainable and such a search may seriously impair the possibilities for real discovery.

Preoccupation with ultimate and total truths and abstract concepts of justice is often combined with a rigid set of standards. Exaggerated expectations of the behavior of others and supermoralistic requirements of one's own behavior often pose a caricature of human functioning so that the obsessional may insist upon truth under all circumstances—for example, without taking cognizance of the impossibility of establishing such criteria. It becomes truth for truth's sake alone, and not an honest awareness of the benefits to be derived from adhering to the truth. It is a slogan and a defense rather than a recognition of the virtue of integrity in human relationships. This applies also to his expressed goal of knowing all.

Because of his need to be decisive but never wrong, he is forced to take stands in which whatever he does must be correct. In practice this is very difficult—unless he can force others to approve his behavior no matter what choice is made. While he avoids direct and open negotiations, he demands that the relationship with him be intimate in spite of the absence of intimacy. He generally succeeds in such relationships for varying periods of time when the other person has something to gain from keeping the relationship intact. This is the case with one's wife, husband, friend, or relative, where the need to be considerate, gentle, or tolerant requires a variety of doubletalk that is pervasive even if it is not identified by the participants.

Rather than face an awareness of the impossibility of being omniscient and acknowledging his human limitations, the obsessional concludes that if only he knew more and tried harder he could achieve these goals. The solution is to become more perfect, and thus even more obsessional. In this respect obsessional living tends to stimulate the need for more obsessional defenses. This becomes one of the major burdens in therapy since the patient hopes to reduce his anxiety by improving his obsessional neurosis instead of abandoning it. The demands for omniscience, available only to the gods, prevent him from enjoying the rewards of limited potentialities that are available to humans. Even with a total understanding of all the relevant factors in an event he cannot take into account accidental circumstances and the indeterminacy which is an inescapable part of our physical universe. Such expectations lead to a futile impasse, and an enormous amount of time and energy is expended in fruitless efforts to overcome such obstacles.

The obsessional attempts to absorb every piece of information in the universe. Nothing seems irrelevant or unrelated to his interest, since every piece of information may have some value on some future occasion. In attempting to absorb it all he succeeds in absorbing less than he is capable of since his activities are laden with tension and uneasiness.

In the search for omniscience there is a singular incapacity to separate the relevant from the irrelevant since everything is considered relevant to the obsessional's global demands. This incapacity serves to impede any progress toward intensive exploration of one particular area. Unlike the obsessive, who is driven to such activity, the free researcher may be dedicated, but he is motivated more by the pleasure in his adventures than the decrease in anxiety. Even though there are no pure cultures of "free" or "compulsive" scientists or artists, such a distinction does provide some clues about creativity and productivity, which (although they may coexist), are not synonymous. The creativity of a genius need not derive from neurotic sources; more often it arises from curiosity and a capacity for originality and novelty that is anathema to the obsessive person.

Emotional Demands

The overestimation of one's thinking and knowing as a means of controlling oneself and the universe requires rigid control of one's emotions. All emotional responses must be either dampened, restrained, or completely denied. Since he approaches life in an intellectualized fashion, the obsessional tries to appear unmoved by disturbing or rewarding experiences. He tries to examine each situation as a rational event, insisting that only by putting emotional reactions aside can one be fair and accurate. Such an ideal goal, however, is rarely possible—man's emotional responses are mostly autonomic and beyond conscious control. Since intellectual reactions are entirely under control, it is not hard to understand why the obsessional person places such a great emphasis on intellectuality. Yet, he does not always use his intellectual resources to enlighten or clarify his living.

As he cannot always control his emotions, he may "get involved" or become committed to people or things too strongly to suit his protective needs. He would prefer to eliminate feelings entirely from his life; because he cannot achieve this end, he uses the technique of displacement—which characterizes obsessive behavior.

Displacement refers to the defense process by which strong feelings are attached to less significant or meaningless activities, thereby removing them from significant areas of living. In such circumstances, for example, a strong, unacceptable reaction may be displaced from a parent, child, or close friend onto some food fad, or distant relative, or political ideology. Such displacement is a means of isolating or distorting feelings and may give a bizarre appearance to an obsessional's behavior. He may appear to be uninvolved emotionally with significant people or events while grossly overinvolved with minutiae.

In the obsessional neuroses whatever emotional elements may be present appear to be attached to unessential or irrelevant issues in the person's life. In this way he is able to avoid a confrontation with his true feelings and become involved in areas of living which he can control, while appearing to be uninterested in those areas which he cannot control. He does not accept emotional responses, when they occur, as normal accompaniments to living. When they do occur they are justified by extensive rationalizations that make them appear to be reasonable and logical.

The efforts at controlling his emotions may result in a paucity of emotional displays, but they cannot eliminate the enormous ground swells of feeling which are stored up. These untapped emotional sources may periodically burst out, either in minor ways such as slips of the tongue, or other parapraxes, or in explosive, major eruptions. At times the obsessional is quite aware of the presence of these underground forces that he keeps under such strict control. He justifies his controlling behavior by pointing to the intensity of these feelings. He insists that he must keep his feelings in check because they are too explosive to be let out. At a certain point this undoubtedly becomes true, since the vicious circle that characterizes neurotic development allows for an accumulation of feelings because of a need to control one's feelings. After awhile the accumulation may be great enough so that the expression of such feelings might be excessive even if the stimulus were minimal.

What the obsessional really wishes to avoid, however, is the expression of any feelings—tender or hostile. The freer expression of tender feelings might actually stimulate positive responses from others, rather than rejection. For the obsessional such reactions might be more "involving" and thus more dangerous than hostile ones.

DOUBTING, PROCRASTINATION, AND INDECISION

A most effective way of supporting an illusion of infallibility and perfection is to avoid any challenges or tests which might expose one's deficiencies and errors. One can avoid a test or postpone the inevitable awareness of uncertainties through endless procrastination and indecision. When a decision can no longer be postponed, an element of doubt can then be introduced so that one need not be entirely responsible for the consequences of the decision. Such pervasive vacillating and indecision—accompanied by gnawing, inconclusive doubting—characterizes the obsessive state. At one time the disorder was known as mania de doute because doubt is often the most pronounced feature in the illness.

Unless one can be absolutely certain about one's choice or decision one stands the risk of being wrong. This, for the obsessional, is synonymous with being held weak, fallible, and defenseless. Until one can make a final, fully completed and perfect product, it is best to keep it from the view of others, lest they see the imperfections. Therefore, examination papers are held onto until the last possible moment in order to make changes, or manuscripts are not submitted until the final deadline date. Such delays are designed to put off the possibility of adverse judgment, but they are rationalized as a desire to do the finest job possible. Once a task is finished or a paper submitted, it is beyond correction and amplification. If completion is postponed until a deadline forces one to turn in a paper, one can rationalize by insisting that if only there were more time, any imperfec-

tions could have been corrected. In addition, the experience is used to support and justify more procrastination, as criticism may be the stimulus for considerable anxiety, which, in turn, will require more defensive patterns and more indecisiveness. It is the pervasive quality of this behavior which is so distressing, even in the most well-organized person. The indecisiveness may have disastrous consequences if no action is taken when action is required.

Decisions cannot be postponed indefinitely. Being forced by circumstances to make a choice, the obsessional may deny the deficiencies in it or become a partisan of it. He may behave as though he is entirely disinterested in such trivial matters and consider himself beyond criticism, joining his potential detractors by disparaging the choice he made and thus being unable to enjoy it. On the other hand, his rigid and unreasonable advocacy of his choice makes him incapable of recognizing its real defects and thereby avoiding the same error in the future. Any decision, minor or major, rarely gives him pleasure. It only serves to increase his anxieties and leave him wishing fervently that he could become more perfect.

Doubting, too, plays a role in the procrastinating. When one is forced to make a decision, one can always maintain that since he had doubts about it, he should therefore not be held fully accountable for the decision. Therefore, whatever the decision made, the obsessional feels that perhaps the alternative would have been better. The activity or issue is often lost sight of when the proper outcome becomes far more important than the activity itself. . . .

Doubting thus becomes a useful device in sustaining one's omniscience by not committing oneself without reservations and thereby risking a failure. By maintaining an atmosphere of doubt one can easily shift sides to come out with the correct position. Therefore, to avoid error, firm decisions should be avoided.

The obsessional's indecisiveness is also supported by an elaborate pseudo-pride in which he views himself as being objective, honest, and wishing only to examine all the issues involved in making a decision. This, of course, can prolong a decision indefinitely. However, the "examination" does not represent a valid quest but rather a compulsive need to avoid commitment and closure. It allows the obsessional to convey an atmosphere of open-minded flexibility in his desire to avoid quick judgments without an adequate exploration of the facts. It soon becomes evident, however, that what appears to be judicious scrutiny is really a compulsive need to keep the lines open for fear of making a decision.

Doubting, which serves to fortify the indecisiveness, often comes to play a most prominent role and overshadows all other elements in the obsessional's living. At times it may be so severe that the person doubts that he has really taken a breath or performed a task which, in fact, he may have completed only a moment ago. This may lead to the kind of behavior which has come to be the hallmark of compulsive behavior—compulsive hand-washing, a tendency to recheck doors to see that they were locked, and the like.

These well-described phenomena were presumed to be evidence of the person's hostile intentions toward others (e.g., in rechecking the locked door or turning off the gas). The hand-washing compulsion or the need to check up on one's mate was presumed to represent guilt feelings that were being dealt with by expiatory or undoing activities. While such factors may be present, it is clear that the element of doubt in these instances may be so pervasive as to cause the activities to be repeated endlessly and often in circumstances in which hostility plays no role whatsoever. The behavior represents an all-pervasive aura of doubt and uncertainty that does not permit the person to have any conviction of having completed a task; the rechecking is an attempt to achieve some degree of certainty about the matter.

Frequently the doubts about all aspects of living, including who one is and what one desires may paralyze all action. If one feels that his behavior, however trivial, may have disastrous consequences, it is understandable why action must be delayed or abandoned. The obsessional remains immobile and passive and abandons all pretense of making choices. He acts only when circumstances force him to, and then he feels the decision was made by default and not by choice. This allows him to disown the action if it is embarrassing to him. He blames fate or the circumstances that have denied him control of the behavior.

AMBIVALENCE

Ambivalence is a quality evident in all people. Everyone at one time or another will have mixed and at times opposite feelings toward the same person. In psychiatry, however, the term has taken on a special meaning. It was first used by Bleuler to describe the contradictory feelings noted in schizophrenia, in which the patient exhibited marked fluctuations in his feelings of love and hate, which may coexist in varying proportions toward the same person. Freud, too, was impressed with this phenomenon and explained it on the basis of unconscious feelings which are inconsistent with conscious ones. Freud assumed that when a person outwardly professed love but belied it by his actual behavior (which conveyed hate), his hateful feelings could be unconscious. Freud believed that marked ambivalence was the basis for severe conflict and personality disorganization, as in the neuroses and psychoses.

It is naive and idealistically visionary to conceive of absolute and unconditional feelings of love or trust toward another person in the realistic world of denials, frustrations, limitations, and disappointments. As the infant and child are required to conform to the requirements of the culture in which they live, discipline replaces permissiveness and demands are made of the child which he may not completely accept or enjoy. In addition, he inevitably faces some disappointments, disapprovals, and punishments—as well as rewards, satisfactions, and tenderness—from the significant people in his life. In this way ambiguous and mixed feelings of love, trust, hate, and distrust become tied up with the same person, without necessarily producing conflicts.

The obsessional, however, is unable to tolerate ambiguities and unpredictable responses. He has great difficulty with the ambivalent feelings he recognizes in himself and others. To be certain of how others feel about him, he must either have absolute power over the other or be unaware of the other's negative feelings. He could also be so committed to a relationship of love and trust with another that he might have no doubts about that person's feelings. Since the obsessional has great reluctance to commit himself fully, he finds himself trapped in a contradictory goal of trying to eliminate ambivalence but at the same time maintaining it; this produces great tension in his relations with others. He generally manages this dilemma by having immoderate views about people or things. In this way he may have extreme and absolute feelings but also be able to shift to the opposite extreme—thus managing to maintain ambivalent but absolute attitudes. He may even consider this a virtue and an example of his flexibility. However, it is really a way of not acknowledging ambivalences.

The obsessional cannot tolerate uncertainties; he views ambivalent feelings or tolerant attitudes as weak or dishonest. He has contempt for what he calls a compromise with deficiencies and demands of himself that he maintain firm, fixed attitudes without qualifications or reservations. Thus the awareness of ambivalent feelings leaves the obsessional feeling weak and threatened. When he notes such ambivalences his guilt and anxiety are related to the hostile elements in these feelings and to the self-derogatory attitudes which are then stimulated in him.

Ambivalence, ambiguity, and uncertainty are unavoidable ingredients in human existence. To function effectively and without undue anxiety one must recognize this existential fact. The obsessional who tries to overcome these issues through perfectionistic and superhuman achievements is doomed to fail. Closely related to the problem of ambivalence is its opposite—the tendency to think and feel in extremes or to react in an all-or-none manner. As the obsessional is concerned about this tendency, he justifies his demand for absolute control on the basis of preventing these extreme responses from occurring. The exaggerated feelings which he experiences are often the result of his incapacity to allow minimal reactions to be expressed. Since he lives in extremes, his expectation in relinquishing some control is to respond in the extreme, i.e., to feel completely out of control—and this is completely unacceptable to the obsessional (as it is for anyone else). The heart of the matter is whether human reactions and responses need to be "all or none." The obsessional views all situations and experiences only in extremes. Any compromise or acquiescence is viewed as weakness. He despises the indecisiveness in himself and insists that he must always be firm and definite. The pattern seems to derive from the desire to convey a picture of a firm, integrated, and positive person—which the obsessional wants very much to be.

In the atmosphere of all-or-none, tenderness cannot be given in a total sense as it is already viewed as a weakness and as giving in to someone else, which leaves one vulnerable. Like the other characteristics of the obsessional described above, these extremes do not occur all of the time. They are, however, sufficiently present to be consistent elements in the personality structure.

Further Attitudes and Symptoms

Much of the symptomatology of the obsessional state—such as the subject's meticulousness or sloppiness, dependent or independent attitudes, absoluteness or pervasive doubting—is related to the tendency to respond in extremes. Any in-between attitude is viewed as weakness. Being average or ordinary is contemptible, and mediocrity is the disgraceful acceptance of one's limitations. The obsessional therefore sees people as either exceptional or ordinary. There is no room for anything in-between.

When the obsessional is forced by circumstances to recognize his limitations and to acknowledge that he is, after all, a mortal human and not a superman, he may become quite depressed. Why does he react so violently to the notion that he is only human? On one level he does wish to be like everyone else, but on another level he has a need for absolute control and certainty—with guarantees that he be a superman. To him, an ordinary person is weak, helpless, unable to control the universe—someone who is pushed around and forced to yield to the control of others. The obsessional cannot acknowledge the fact that everything is not all black or white and that not everyone is either totally in control or controlled entirely by someone else. The obsessional equates normality with stupidity. For him, anything less than perfection is mediocrity, which is intolerable. He cannot recognize that acknowledging one's limitations enables one to achieve realistic goals, while he, on the other hand, with his extreme all-or-none philosophy, may have expansive but impossible goals which he then makes little effort to achieve. His goals usually remain on an idealized and verbalized level, mostly unrealized. His failure to achieve them is often rationalized as caused by the interference from others.

"Mediocre" is the derogatory label he applies to most hard-working, successful (or unsuccessful) people. Some other people are idealized, glamorized, and exaggerated far beyond the reality of the situation. These idealized images can rarely withstand close inspection, and when reality sets in, these persons are the ones who are treated with venom and exceptional bitterness.

To be acknowledged as a leader, beyond fear of danger or criticism, is rarely possible. Yet this is what the obsessional insists upon being, since he feels that some have achieved this (e.g., the President, a king, etc.) and therefore it should be available to him. Accidents of fate, birth, or genius do not exist; for him everything is possible. In spite of these professed beliefs, the obsessional is reluctant to take the initial steps toward or to assume any risks in arriving at these goals. While his demands are at one extreme, his willingness to accept the risks and challenges to achieve these goals are at the opposite one.

GRANDIOSITY

A significant outcome of the tendency to deal in extremes is the development of grandiose attitudes toward oneself. This is the obsessional's response to his attempts at omniscience and omnipotence. It is likely that he looks upon himself covertly as a superperson, even while he feels helpless and impotent. Because he sees himself as someone who is striving for perfection, or believes that he has already achieved it, he has a grandiose view of himself. This is not the result of a realistic appraisal of his capacities and capabilities but is an outgrowth of the high standards and impossible demands which he makes upon himself. It is his unwillingness to settle for anything less than the best which makes him feel superior to others and is frequently responsible for arrogant and contemptuous attitudes toward those who will settle for "second best."

In spite of his arrogance and grandiose contempt for others, he feels also that he is inferior to others—and therefore unsafe. His devotion to a task and his desire to know everything frequently result in achievements of great competence. Even under these circumstances, however, he remains dissatisfied and critical of his realistic achievements, which never seem able to satisfy his strivings for absolute perfection. The realistic basis for pride is lost in his own disparagement and disappointment and in his failure to achieve absolute success. This picture presents a difficult therapeutic problem because the obsessional esteem in the patient's neurotic achievements prevents the growth of valid esteem. He tends to belittle his small therapeutic gains and yearns only for superhuman, impossible achievements.

For the obsessional, always being in the right (exempt from criticism) is not a grandiose claim. It appears to be a reasonable expectation of someone who deserves it. He feels that his high ideals and exceptional standards merit only the highest rewards. Therefore, he should be free from criticism because he tries to be perfect—and he should not be criticized if he fails to attain perfection. Since this does not ordinarily occur, a great deal of resentment and grievance is felt by the obsessional. This pattern of grandiose development with its claims for exemption from human responsibility is the cause for many complications that occur in compulsive states—such as obesity, addictions, and kleptomania.

It is inevitable that the grandiosity of the obsessional will be challenged directly or indirectly by the notable successes and achievements of others in comparable age groups. This is particularly upsetting to the obsessional, as he can no longer deny such achievements. He will attribute others' successes to their being richer, more opportunistic than he, without his integrity, etc. He will maintain that he could have done as well if he had really wanted to, or if he had sacrificed his principles. More and more rationalizations are required as time goes by, as are more obsessional symptoms to overcome the realistic differences. The illusion of grandiosity is not maintained by realistic achievement but by a denial of the realistic limitations.

THE ANTISOCIAL PERSONALITY

C. ROBERT CLONINGER

Like alcoholism and schizophrenia, antisocial personality, or sociopathy, has a significant genetic component, albeit associated with major environmental influences. Diagnostic criteria, chief among them early onset, are helpful—but not necessarily predictive—in distinguishing the true sociopath from the criminal with no personality disorder. Characteristic medical problems associated with sociopathy are discussed.

The increase in crime over the past 10 to 15 years and the even more marked increase in public awareness of crime have helped to revive an old question among psychiatrist, psychologists, and sociologists: Is there such a thing as a "criminal personality"? The answer, on the basis of present data, is a heavily qualified "yes." There does seem to exist an identifiable personality type, the joint product of genetic and environmental factors, that is highly prone to criminal behavior. The type is that formerly known as psychopathy, later as sociopathy, but today most commonly as antisocial personality, though persons who possess it are still often called sociopaths for short.

EDITORS' COMMENTS:

THE AUTHOR IDENTIFIES THE ANTISOCIAL PERSONALITY ON THE BASIS OF A PERSONAL HISTORY CHARACTERIZED BY DISTURBANCES IN INTERPERSONAL RELATIONSHIPS THAT BEGIN EARLY AND REMAIN IN ADULT LIFE. PEOPLE WITH THIS DISORDER NEED NOT BE OVERT CRIMINALS, BUT THEIR LACK OF GENUINE EMPATHY PRODUCES A HISTORY OF INTERPERSONAL CONFLICT ON THE JOB, AT HOME, OR BOTH. SOCIOECONOMIC FACTORS, REARING PRACTICES, AND DATA FROM TWIN AND ADOPTION STUDIES ARE ALL CONSIDERED.

Reprinted from Hospital Practice 13:97–106, 1978. Figures by Albert Miller. Reproduced with permission.

As already noted, however, the bald statement that antisocial personality exists as a distinct entity requires important qualifications. Most significant, perhaps, is that it can at present be reliably diagnosed only in adult life, on the basis of the individual's behavior over a number of years. The diagnosis rests in part on the appearance of certain behavioral signs in early adolescence, but the majority of youths who display these signs do not become full-fledged sociopaths or, for that matter, criminals.

A second qualification is that while nearly all sociopaths are or become criminals (whether or not legally identified as such), not all criminals are sociopaths. In particular, the so-called white-collar criminal seldom if ever suffers from antisocial personality, and the same is probably true of the criminal bosses who run the "families," "syndicates," and "outfits" of organized crime, although there are few data about such individuals. The sociopath is much more likely to be found among the foot soldiers of crime than in its higher echelons, according to available anecdotal reports. Because of his impulsivity, the more severe sociopath is rarely acceptable for any long-term organized activity and usually functions sporadically and alone or with a few temporary associates.

The notion of a criminal type dates back at least to the late nineteenth century, when the Italian criminologist Cesare Lombroso claimed to have defined a "criminal physiognomy" by which potential or actual lawbreakers could be identified. The modern view of the criminal personality has nothing in common with this notion: antisocial personality is not diagnosed by the individual's appearance, which is in no way distinctive, but by his (occasionally, her) behavior. The diagnostic criteria, moreover, are purely operational. This

TABLE 1. Diagnostic Criteria for Antisocial Personality

A. Current age at least 18 and a history of continuous and chronic antisocial behavior in which the rights of others are violated

B. Onset before age 15, as indicated by a history of two or more of the following:

1. Truancy (at least five days per year for at least two years, not including the last year of school)
2. Expulsion from school
3. Delinquency (arrested or referred to juvenile court because of behavior)
4. Running away from parental or surrogate home at least twice
5. Persistent lying
6. Unusually early or aggressive sexual behavior
7. Unusually early drinking to excess or abuse of controlled substance(s) (not including marijuana)
8. Thefts
9. Vandalism
10. Required to repeat school grades or school performance (grades) markedly below what would be expected from known or estimated IQ
11. Chronic violation of rules at home and/or at school (except truancy)

C. At least three of the following since age 15:

1. Poor occupational performance over several years, as shown by one or more of the following:
   a. Frequent job changes (three or more jobs in five years not accounted for by nature of job or by economic or seasonal fluctuations)
   b. Significant unemployment (six months or more in 10 years, when work available and not otherwise occupied—e.g., in school, as housewife, in institution)
   c. Serious absenteeism from work (average three days or more a month, late or absent) not accounted for by illness

   Note: **poor academic performance for the last few years of school may substitute for this criterion in individuals who, because of their age or circumstances, have not had the opportunity to demonstrate occupational adjustment**

2. Three or more non-traffic arrests or a felony conviction.
3. Two or more divorces and/or separations (whether legally married or not)
4. Repeated physical fights or assaults (not required by job, or self-defense, or other cause)
5. Repeated thefts, whether caught or not
6. Illegal occupation (e.g., prostitution, pimping, selling drugs)
7. Repeated defaulting on debts or other major financial responsibilities (e.g., child support)
8. Traveling from place to place without a clear goal (e.g., a prearranged job) or clear idea when the travel would terminate

D. No period of five years or more without antisocial behavior between age 15 and onset of adult antisocial behavior, unless bedridden, confined in hospital or penal institution, or under treatment

E. Antisocial behavior is *not* symptomatic of severe mental retardation, schizophrenia, schizoaffective or paranoid disorder

means, in effect, that the disorder is defined by its diagnostic criteria. That is, the antisocial personality is identified on the basis of a particular type of personal history—and the antisocial person is defined as someone having such a history.

Broadly speaking, an antisocial personality suffers from severe, generalized disturbances in interpersonal relationships that begin no later than early adolescence (before age 15) and remain chronic (i.e., with few or no "remissions") into adult life. The precise diagnostic criteria, in their most recent revision, are listed in Table 1. Most of these are self-explanatory, but some warrant additional comment. Thus "unusually early or aggressive sexual behavior" (B-6) must naturally be judged in relation to the sexual standards of the social group to which the individual belongs, rather than those of the diagnostician. Beyond this, the kind of sexual activity encompassed here usually involves marked, even spectacular, promiscuity (several dozen sex partners in the course of a single year) coupled with the absence of significant emotional attachments to any of the partners and often with repeated veneral infection as well.

Concerning the "early" criteria as a whole, it is worth emphasizing that while satisfaction of these criteria is an essential condition for identifying antisocial personality, it is far from a sufficient condition. Taking an average population of young Americans, it is likely that at least 10% would satisfy the early criteria, yet the actual incidence of antisocial personality is no more than about 4%. The significance of the early criteria is merely that early onset appears to be an essential feature of the disease. An individual who in adult life adopts or drifts into the sort of life-style summarized in section B of the table (as is the case, for example, with not a few alcoholics) may be suffering from one or more of various character disorders, but he is not a sociopath.

Taking now the eight adult (post-age 15) criteria, it will be noted that four of them (C 2, 4, 5, 6) involve actual criminal behavior, whether or not detected or prosecuted, while of the remaining four, three (poor occupational performance, repeated defaulting on debts, aimless traveling) can be said to predispose toward later criminality if they do not coexist with it. Thus any individual satisfying even three of these eight criteria will very probably be a criminal already, if not, he will almost surely become one.

On the face of it, these adult criteria may seem to involve a degree of circular reasoning: the antisocial (criminal) personality is a person who is a criminal. Here two points should be made. The first is the criterion of early onset, already alluded to; the second is the nature of the "noncriminal" adult criteria (C 1, 3, 7, 8). All four of these either involve, or strongly predispose to, disturbances in one or both of two basic areas of interpersonal relations: occupational and familial. The antisocial personality, in other words, is not "only" a criminal (someone who has been, will be, or should be in trouble with the law), he will almost certainly at some point also be in trouble on the job (if he has a legitimate job) or at home or both.

The final criterion (E) requires that antisocial behavior not be a symptom of other major mental disorders. It is intended to exclude those individuals in whom antisocial behavior is in fact secondary to another identifiable psychiatric disorder. To look at this in another way, what we are saying is that the sociopath does not lack the intelligence to cope with the "normal" or "straight" world, nor are his perceptions of that world grossly distorted (e.g., by delusions or hallucinations). But if his deficiency or personality defect does not lie in the area of intelligence or perception, then just what is it that he does lack?

One consistent deficiency is in sensitivity to personal cues, a trait that can also be described as egocentricity or lack of empathy. The sociopath perceives other people only as objects to be manipulated for his own gratification and, as a corollary, is prone to blame them rather than himself if the desired gratification fails to materialize. Coupled with this is an inability to defer gratification to a normal degree as, of course, the rest of us are constantly forced to do. The sociopath reasons and makes decisions in terms of immediate consequences, but cannot or will not take into account possible later consequences. As a famous writer of detective stories put it, anybody can reason from A to B, and most people can reason from B to C; the criminal cannot take this second step.

These personality traits are hard to define precisely and hard to identify unless one has known the individual over a fairly prolonged period, which most people, including many physicians and psychologists, do not care to do for fairly obvious reasons. The sociopath may present a facade of sensitivity to others, but in retrospect this appears as merely a way of "conning" them, by telling them what they want to hear—as not a few mental health professionals have discovered to their chagrin. Likewise, the sociopath may show normal and even superior intelligence in dealing with an immediate situation, say, in devising a way of committing a crime. Only later does it become apparent (to others if not to him) that the immediate success implied a subsequent failure, say, being sent to jail. Because of the subjectivity and unreliability of available techniques for measuring such personality traits directly, the current criteria rely instead on overt behavior patterns that can be reliably assessed.

The diagnostic criteria cited are, in a sense, arbitrary, but so are those for many other psychiatric and medical conditions. We do not possess any biochemical or neurologic test for antisocial personality, any more than we do for schizophrenia and must therefore diagnose on the basis of what the patient does and has done rather than any organic signs and symptoms.

Nonetheless, the diagnosis of antisocial personality, based on the sort of objective criteria described, is at least as realiable as that of most other psychiatric disorders. The only important problem area concerns the differential diagnosis of sociopathy and alcoholism or other drug addiction, since many sociopaths are addicts or alcoholics, while many alcoholics and addicts show much the same antisocial behavior as sociopaths. The most useful pathognomonic feature here is probably early onset. The sociopath has engaged in clearly antisocial behavior (which may or may not include abuse of alcohol) before age 15, whereas the "primary" addict or alcoholic usually develops his addiction (which may or may not include antisocial behavior) in late adolescence or as an adult. As in some other areas of medicine, however, there exists a residuum of cases in which the conditions cannot be reliably distinguished.

Provided the diagnosis of antisocial personality is realiable, the prognosis can be summed up as bleak. Drugs appear to be of little value and in some cases can aggravate the problem by giving the patient added opportunities for drug abuse. Some studies have indicated a significant (though far from complete) correlation between hyperactivity in childhood and sociopathy in adult life, and since stimulants such as the amphetamines have shown some efficacy in treating hyperactivity, it was hoped that they would also alleviate antisocial personality. They did not. The anticonvulsant phenytoin (diphenylhydantoin) has also been tried, as the result of findings that sociopaths show a relatively high rate of EEG abnormalities, but again without results.

Nor has psychotherapy been any more successful. In the words of the late Samuel Yochelson, it produces "criminals with insight—but criminals nonetheless." A recent study describes a radically different approach to such individuals that involves confronting them with the kind of people they actually are—lying, inconsiderate, destructive to others and to themselves. The therapy pays little attention to the patient's feelings and emotions, which he commonly uses to manipulate others, but rather, according to a recent account (*Science* 199:511, Feb. 3, 1978), is "didactic, heavily concentrated on examination of thought processes, and unapologetically moralistic." This approach (as well as the extensive studies on which it is based) has been criticized on a number of grounds by some psychiatrists, and even its proponents concede that its efficacy cannot yet be reliably evaluated. Moreover, at best it involves "catching" the patient at a low point in his erratic life, one in which his antisocial life-style has generated intensely unpleasant consequences such as a stiff jail sentence or an alcoholic breakdown. Whether more extensive studies will prove this approach better than conventional ones remains to be seen; certainly it cannot be any worse.

Fortunately for themselves and for society, a substantial minority of sociopaths seem to move toward normality as they grow older. By age 35 or so, perhaps 40% will have ceased to manifest at least the more extreme forms of antisocial behavior and will have adjusted to something approaching normal living. (Somewhat the same thing, incidentally, occurs with many drug addicts.) Only a few of these people (perhaps one in four) will ever become "model citizens," with no more than normal difficulties in interpersonal relationships. The others are still atypically irritable, asocial, and self-centered. But they are coping after a fashion: working at some legitimate job, and probably have a reasonably stable marriage and family life. The majority of sociopaths, who do not achieve even partial remission, can be expected to spend the rest of their lives in and out of jail and on and off the welfare rolls, a pattern punctuated only by occasional episodes of free-spending prosperity when they manage to pull off a successful "job."

In the light of the present poor prognosis for the adult sociopath, with or without psychiatric intervention, the obvious question is whether prevention might be more successful. An answer must begin with examining the etiology of the condition so far as we understand it.

Given that antisocial personality is defined entirely in terms of social behavior, the condition would seem a prime candidate for classification as a purely environmental disorder. Rather surprisingly, however, a number of studies indicate that though environment undoubtedly plays an important role so do congenital (almost certainly genetic) factors.

This conclusion has emerged from studies of a type already discussed extensively in connection with genetic factors in schizophrenia and alcoholism (see L. L. Heston, Hospital Practice, June 1977; D. W. Goodwin, Hospital Practice, May 1978): measurements of concordance between twins, both mono- and dizygotic, and especially studies of "cross-adopted" children, those born to parents displaying a particular psychologic disorder but adopted by "normal" parents, and vice versa.

The findings for antisocial personality are much the same as for schizophrenia and alcoholism. Thus monozygotic twins show a higher rate of concordance for criminality (in one study, over 50% in males) than do dizygotic twins (22% in males) or other siblings. Likewise, the children of criminal or sociopathic parents show a relatively high incidence of the trait even when raised from infancy by normal adoptive parents.

Perhaps the most extensive and interesting study of the latter type was carried on in Denmark

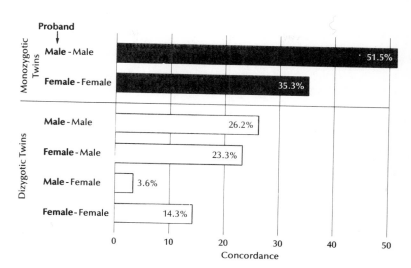

Although environment clearly is an influence on development of antisocial personality, twin studies show that genetic influences are also at work: concordance for the disorder is significantly greater in monozygotic twins of both sexes than in dizygotic twins.

(as were two other key genetic studies of alcoholism and schizophrenia, respectively). This investigation, it should be noted, did not concern antisocial personality as such but rather criminality. It was based upon police records of persons convicted of what would be equivalent to felony in America: robbery, rape, burglary, arson, manslaughter, aggravated assault, and the like. However, because of the extensive overlap between such criminals and sociopaths, the results seem clearly relevant to the etiology of the latter condition.

The Danish investigators found that when neither the biologic nor the adoptive parents had criminal records, the incidence of criminality in males was about 10%. This is considerably greater than the proportion for nonadopted individuals but is consistent with other findings on psychopathology in adopted children. If an adoptive parent, but neither biologic parent, was criminal, the incidence was only marginally greater, about 11%. If a biologic parent, but neither adoptive parent, was criminal, the incidence jumped to about 21%. Finally—and interestingly—if both a biologic and an adoptive were criminals, the incidence rose to around 36%.

The latter finding differs from those in alcoholism, in which alcoholism (or presumed alcoholism) in the adoptive parents did not increase the risk of alcholism in the male offspring of alcoholics. What the figures on criminality seem to mean is that being raised in a criminal family has little effect on development of criminality in adopted males unless a biologic parent was also criminal. In other words, the individual was at some presumed genetic risk of becoming a criminal.

Other studies have produced different figures, depending on the definitions of criminality or sociopathy used, but the relationships remain roughly the same. Similar findings have emerged from studies using a different methodology: retrospective rather than prospective. That is, if one examines a group of criminals or sociopaths who were adopted in early life and then checks out their adoptive and biologic families, one finds an abnormally high incidence of the condition only in the biologic relatives. The adoptive relatives show no more criminality or sociopathy than other groups of similar socioeconomic status.

The only exception to these findings that I know of is a Swedish study that found little increased risk of criminality even when the biologic parents were criminals. However, a close examination of the definitions employed indicates that the group studied consisted primarily of severe alcoholics rather than criminals per se (this applied to both the children and their parents). Consistent with the studies discussed by Goodwin, the data showed an association between alcoholism in the biologic parents and alcoholism in the children. The most plausible interpretation of these findings is that in the Swedish group criminality was mostly secondary to alcoholism and not to antisocial personality as defined earlier.

It is worth noting, incidentally, that other adoption and family studies have found no genetic or presumably genetic link between alcoholism and antisocial personality. That is, the relatives of alcoholics have a high incidence of alcoholism but not of sociopathy, while the relatives of sociopaths have a high incidence of sociopathy but not of alcoholism.

On the face of it, then, we have a strong case for

the existence of a genetic, or at least congenital, factor in antisocial personality. Some investigators have suggested that the factor may be congenital but not genetic: a mother who herself suffers from antisocial personality, they reason, would be less likely to take reasonable care of herself during pregnancy, so that the fetus would be at increased risk of sustaining some sort of (perhaps neurologic) intrauterine damage. This theory is difficult to disprove directly, but such data as we have give it little support. In families where the father is sociopathic but the mother is not, the risk of sociopathy in the offspring seems no less. Moreover, where it has been possible to check back, the mothers of sociopaths seem to have had no more than the normal incidence of complications in pregnancy or delivery.

There is one other aspect of antisocial personality that should be considered before further discussion of its etiology: its differential incidence in women and men. Male sociopaths are estimated to outnumber females by something like seven to one, a difference similar to that observed in alcoholics. There are two possible explanations for this difference, either or both of which may be correct. The first is the obvious one that in our culture (as in many others) males are encouraged to be assertive if not aggressive, whereas females are more commonly encouraged to be compliant and dependent—a type of personality that is obviously incompatible with sociopathy. The second is that something in the male's neurohormonal equipment, most obviously perhaps his secretion of testosterone, increases his predisposition to sociopathy.

A number of findings about sociopathy are relevant to this problem, although their precise significance remains uncertain at this writing. The first is that the incidence of antisocial personality within kinships, for both males and females, is consistent with the multifactorial model of disease. According to this model, such a condition is produced by many additive factors, relatively independent of one another, which may be genetic, environmental, or (usually) both. The patterns of incidence generated mathematically from the multifactorial model have been shown to apply to schizophrenia as well as to such organic conditions as cleft lip and congenital dislocation of the hip.

One of the postulates of the model is that when the condition differs in incidence between the sexes, the less frequently affected sex will have a higher incidence of the condition in his or her relatives. That is, the relatively immune sex has a higher "threshold," and more unfavorable factors must be present for the condition to become manifest. Thus, to the extent that the factors are genetic, members of the "immune" sex can be presumed to have inherited a higher concentration of unfavorable factors. This means that their relatives will be at specially high risk themselves. Antisocial personality conforms to this postulate. Female sociopaths tend to have more sociopathic relatives than do male sociopaths.

A second point is a curious inverse relationship between sociopathy and hysteria, specifically, the severe type of hysteria sometimes called Briquet's disorder. This is characterized by chronic polysymptomatic illness involving a complicated or dramatic history and many organ systems, with frequent hospitalization and surgery. As is well known, hysteria is far more common in women than in men, the difference in incidence being

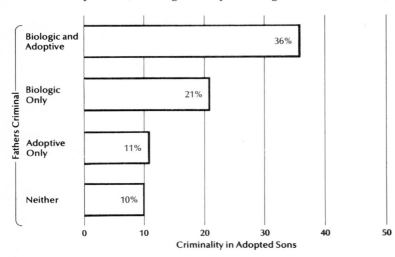

Being raised by a criminal adoptive father has little effect on a boy's potential criminality unless the biologic father is also a criminal. Conversely, a noncriminal adoptive home environment cannot counteract the genetic influence of a criminal biologic father.

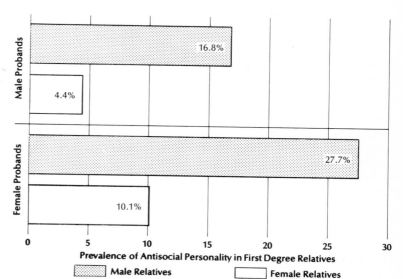

Incidence of antisocial personality within kinships is consistent (as is schizophrenia) with multifactorial inheritance. As model postulates, the less frequently affected sex has a higher prevalence of the disease in first degree relatives. For males, prevalence of sociopathy in general population was 3.3% in Denmark, for females, 0.9%.

Prevalence of Antisocial Personality in First Degree Relatives

☒ Male Relatives   □ Female Relatives

something like 20 to one. Like sociopathy, hysteria tends to run in families—and in the same families as sociopathy. In women with sociopathic "pedigrees," the incidence of Briquet's disorder is much higher than normal, and it is also not uncommon in male sociopaths. Putting it another way, the offspring of sociopaths or hysterics show an abnormally high incidence of hysteria and sociopathy combined, but the males are more likely to be sociopaths (with or without hysteria) and the females more likely to be hysterics (with or without sociopathy).

These findings suggest that some congenital predisposing factor, perhaps neurophysiologic, is shared by sociopathy and hysteria, and we shall consider the nature of this factor in a moment. The much higher incidence of hysteria in women, like the much higher incidence of sociopathy in men, may be due to social or hormonal factors or both.

That hormonal factors may play a part is suggested by many animal studies. In many mammalian species, injections of testosterone can induce aggressive behavior, which in most mammals is more common in males than in females. Sociopaths are, of course, typically aggressive, while hysterics are not.

On the other hand, hormonal pecularities do not seem to have any significance for the development of sociopathy per se. It is true that primate studies have shown correlations between male aggressiveness and dominance and serum testosterone levels, but under circumstances that leave us unsure which is cause and which effect. Is the animal aggressive because his testosterone levels are high or are the levels high because he is (for

other reasons) aggressive? In any case, studies of criminal populations have shown that their testosterone levels are no higher than those of normals.

Some recent studies suggest that sociopaths (and perhaps hysterics as well) may have a constitutionally high threshold for arousal of the autonomic nervous system. This might explain (among other things) the sociopath's typical search for "kicks" and the hysteric's addiction to self-dramatization, another form of kick. This may be coupled with a functional depression of certain inhibitory centers in the reticular activating system, which could explain the pathologic impulsiveness characteristic of both disorders. But these theories, like most other theories on the etiology of sociopathy, remain to be validated by further research.

Turning now to environmental factors, it appears that socioeconomic conditions play a substantial role. Sociopathy cuts across class lines. Even "in the best families," which presumably supply a near-optimal environment, its incidence is around 2%; this rises to nearly 10% in some slum populations. These differences are reflected in the different incidences in blacks and whites; 9% vs 3%. The difference is clearly not "racial" in the genetic sense: when populations are matched for socioeconomic status, the racial difference disappears.

The important question, from the standpoint of understanding and (one hopes) preventing sociopathy, is just what is meant by "socioeconomic factors" in this context. Poverty as such (a low material standard of living) does not seem to be the answer, but certain frequent concomitants of poverty may be. Some studies have singled out familial discord as a predisposing factor, and this is probably more common among the very poor, who are constantly faced with seemingly insoluble problems, than among the middle class. (It is also probably more common, of course, in families in which one or both parents are themselves sociopaths.) Other investigators have cited absence of the father and large numbers of siblings, both of which are also relatively common among the very poor. I regard these studies as suggestive rather than conclusive, but they are certainly plausible enough to warrant further investigation.

Much the same can be said of other aspects of the "culture of poverty" that could plausibly influence the development of sociopathy. For example, in populations where legitimate job opportunities are few and often unrewarding, many individuals have only feeble incentives to develop self-discipline and stable life patterns. Conversely, tendencies toward impulsiveness and manipulativeness can be reinforced by such illegitimate "opportunities" as pimping and drug pushing. Whether these and other socioeconomic and sociofamilial factors can by themselves engender sociopathy, i.e., in the absence of an inherited predisposition, is uncertain, but given such a predisposition they might well help to swing the balance. What we still don't know for certain is which of these factors are significant and what relative weight they exert.

One environmental factor that seems to have a clear bearing on sociopathy is the nature of the discipline received in childhood and adolescence. Several studies have shown that in a population of delinquent adolescents, those whose parents supply, or can be induced to supply, discipline that is both firm and consistent are at a much lower risk of becoming sociopaths in later life. Discipline need not and indeed should not be harsh or brutal, but neither should it be lax. Nor should it oscillate between strictness and laxity.

This disciplinary factor has, on the one hand, an obvious relationship to the culture of poverty per se: in families where the father is absent and the mother quite possibly working, the chances that a child will receive consistent and firm discipline are rather poor. On the other hand, the quality of discipline has an equally clear relationship to the hereditary factor: sociopaths are no more likely to exert consistent and firm discipline on their children than they do or have done on themselves.

Nonetheless, the matter of discipline is worth stressing if only because it seems to be about the only "handle" we now have on preventing sociopathy. If the parents of a delinquent child are themselves reasonably normal, and such people do produce sociopathic offspring, they need to be counseled to supply the appropriate type of discipline if they are not doing so already. At least in the milder and younger cases, this may prove an effective alternative to referring the child to a psychiatrist. Indeed, it is probably safe to say that few children of any kind would fail to benefit from discipline of this type!

In conclusion, I should like to say something about the sociopath or potential sociopath as patient, not mainly from the standpoint of the psychiatrist but rather from that of the family or primary physician. Sociopaths are unquestionably very peculiar people, but they do get sick, become depressed, or sustain injuries just like anyone else. The conscientious clinician, though he may find them difficult and quite possibly unpleasant patients, has no alternative but to treat these patients as best he can.

The first peculiarity in the medical history of the sociopath or potential sociopath is likely to appear around age four or five, in the shape of an upsurge in traumas produced by fighting, sometimes even requiring hospitalization. Of course most boys and some girls get into fights now and then, but those prone to antisocial personality get into more fights and more violent ones. This peak in traumatic injuries drops during the early school years, in which the school apparently supplies enough structure and discipline to control all but the most extreme cases. The traumas plus other medical conditions, such as complications of alcoholism and drug abuse, show up again as the child moves into puberty.

At this point, the physician may well want to discuss the case with the parents, with particular reference to their employing the type of consistent, firm discipline I have already discussed. If this fails to solve the problem, or if the parents themselves lack the ability to cope, the child should be referred to a psychiatrist or clinical psychologist. Such a specialist may decide that little can be done in any event, but he should be given the opportunity to make that determination or to recommend alternative or additional modes of treatment. (We might note in passing that the more severe the child's antisocial behavior in adolescence, the worse the prognosis.)

As an adult, the sociopath is an unsatisfactory patient for either the specialist or the primary physician. To the mental health specialist, he poses an almost insoluble problem in treatment.

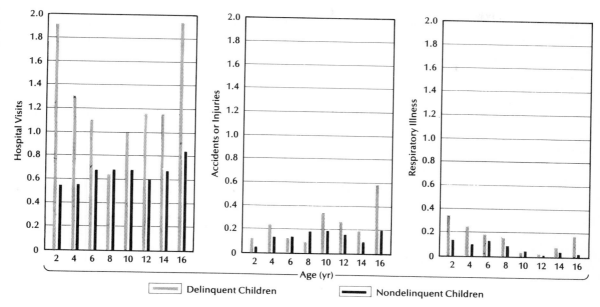

Delinquent Children   Nondelinquent Children

To the primary physician, he poses certain special problems in management as summarized below.

Though the common stereotype of the sociopath portrays him as wholly cold and unfeeling, a sizable number in fact come to a physician complaining of anxiety, insomnia, or "nerves," especially when under some sort of environmental pressure. The usual means of dealing with such symptoms, sedative drugs of some sort, is complicated here by the sociopath's tendency to drug abuse and eventual dependence. The physician should therefore avoid drugs with a high dependence potential, notably, the barbiturates and methaqualone. Flurazepam (as a hypnotic) and diazepam and chlordiazepoxide (as tranquilizers) have a much lower potential for physiologic dependency, though, of course, all three can be abused, as can most psychotropic compounds. In any case, the patient should never be given a refillable prescription and should be monitored periodically. It is also desirable to change the drug occasionally.

The low level of cooperation that the physician can expect from the sociopathic patient makes him (or her) a difficult individual to deal with. Often the best the doctor can do in prescribing medication or some other regimen is to lay extra stress on the relationship between following instruction exactly and relief of the patient's complaint. Unfortunately, follow-up is often difficult because the patient may well lie about how conscientiously he has in fact been following instructions. Here, as in some other clinical situations, the doctor can only do his best and hope for the best.

Striking differences were found between delinquent and nondelinquent children in study by Lewis and Shanok at Yale. Delinquent children suffer more trauma (even more respiratory illness) than do nondelinquent children from early infancy on. School discipline may be responsible for improvement around age six; puberty coincides with the later upsurge.

Rather surprisingly, one of the most common presenting complaints of sociopaths is attempted suicide. As noted in an earlier article in this series (see G. E. Murphy, "Suicide and Attempted Suicide," Hospital Practice, November 1977) attempted or pseudosuicide is much more common in women as a group, while completed suicide is most common in men. In the male sociopath, however, true suicides are rare, while attempted suicides, which of course mesh neatly with his generally manipulative personality, are common. However, since even an attempted suicide may, if repeated, prove inadvertently successful, such individuals should be referred to a specialist.

Hysteria, which, as noted, is especially common in female sociopaths presents another set of problems. When the physician suspects hysteria, the diagnosis can often be strengthened by some inquiry into the patient's life-style, especially for signs of the sort of disorganized, impulsive existence that the sociopath is prone to. In such cases, decisions about hospitalization, surgery, or the prescription of drugs should be made primarily on the basis of physical signs rather than the patient's subjective complaints.

In any event, it is desirable to take a few minutes

TABLE 2. A Comparison of the Parental Home Experience of Male and Female Sociopaths

Home Experience	% Male Sociopaths (n = 58)	% Female Sociopaths (n = 28)	Significance Level (P value)
Parents divorced or separated	48	64	NS
Subject reared in:			
Foster home or orphanage	12	21	NS
Home of relative or friend	29	39	NS
Parents' or surrogates' behavior:			
Not a steady worker	3	11	NS
Heavy drinking	38	64	.05
Physical cruelty	5	21	.05
Absent from home*	28	54	.05
Jailed	10	39	.01
Neglected	12	39	.01

*Duration greater than three months and not due to ill health.

to discuss what is going on in the patient's life, rather than going directly to writing a prescription or undertaking further diagnostic tests. Hysterics usually consult a doctor when they are under some kind of pressure, and sometimes simply talking about the pressure will provide enough support to relieve the symptoms, at least temporarily. If not, referral to a psychiatrist is probably the best solution.

All in all, the antisocial personality presents almost as difficult and intractable a problem to the physician as he (or she) does to society in general. Medically, we can do little for his underlying disorder and often less than we would like for the ailments he shares with the rest of the population.

Given the pronounced socioeconomic component in antisocial personality, the most effective prophylactic measures may well prove to be socioeconomic, for example, supplying the unemployed with reasonably rewarding jobs rather than handouts. Such measures would hardly abolish sociopathy or the crime it engenders, but they might well reduce its incidence. Considering that it costs something like $30,000 a year to keep a criminal in jail, prevention might well prove more economical than treatment as the history of medicine has repeatedly demonstrated.

SELECTED READING

Guze SB: Criminality and Psychiatric Disorders. Oxford University Press, New York, 1976

Cloninger CR, Reich T, Guze SB: The multifactorial model of disease transmission: 2. Sex difference in the familial transmission of sociopathy (antisocial personality). Br J Psychiatry 127:11, 1975

Martin R, Cloninger CR, Guze SB: Female criminality and the prediction of recidivism: a prospective six-year follow-up. Arch Gen Psychiatry 35:207, 1978

Cloninger CR: The link between hysteria and sociopathy. Psychiatric Diagnosis: Exploration of Biological Predictors. Akiskal HS, Webb WL (Eds). Spectrum, Inc., New York, 1978, pp 189–218.

Hare RD, Shallings D (Eds): Psychopathic Behavior. John Wiley and Sons, New York, 1978

SOCIOPATHY AS A HUMAN PROCESS:
A VIEWPOINT

GEORGE E. VAILLANT

Case histories of narcotic addicts who also were impris-oned for felony were selected to illustrate some underly-ing dynamics of Cleckley's so-called psychopath and some principles useful in their management. Often in outpatient settings, such individuals seem to be without anxiety, unable to experience depression, and without motivation for recovery; but in inpatient settings, such deficits appear illusory. Once such chronically socio-pathic individuals are prevented from "running," their resemblance to individuals with severe but thoroughly "human" and comprehensible personality disorders be-comes evident.

In treatment, external controls are important. It is vital both to appreciate the contagion of the psychopath's invisible anxiety and to provide such indi-viduals with alternative defenses with which to mitigate their depression. Finally, sociopaths must be realisti-cally, but not punitively, confronted with the conse-quences of their behavior.

The sociopathic character disorders are a confus-ing area of psychiatry. One reason for confusion is that in an outpatient setting the management of these disorders produces therapeutic frustration. This frustration blurs our perception of important clinical realities, and the defensive maneuvers of the sociopath become wrongly interpreted as signs

EDITORS' COMMENTS:

THE DEFENSIVE ARMOR OF SOCIOPATHS IS COMPARED WITH THE CHARACTER STRUCTURE OF NEUROTIC OUTPATIENTS. THE AUTHOR USES CASE HISTORIES TO ILLUSTRATE THE IMMATURE DEFENSES OF SOCIOPATHS AND CONCLUDES THAT UNDER FAVOR-ABLE CIRCUMSTANCES, THEY CAN BE HELPED TO MA-TURE.

Reprinted from Archives of General Psychiatry 32:178–183, 1975. Copyright 1975, American Medical Association.

of that incurable entity, the psychopath. These signs include an apparent absence of anxiety, an apparent lack of motivation for change, and an apparent inability to feel depression.[1] This pejora-tive term, psychopath, is accurate only insofar as it describes the back of a patient fleeing therapy. If a psychiatrist sees the same patient in a prison hos-pital, he may doubt that such a disorder exists. For then he sees sociopaths face-to-face, and they are human. He is able to do what Edward Glover suggested 50 years ago; he can "apply to the spe-cial problems of anti-social behavior the principles established by Freud to mental function as a whole."[2]

What I am suggesting is that when the psychia-trist is protected from therapeutic frustration, when control is established and flight is not possi-ble, the stigmata of psychopathy disappear. This report will be an effort to examine why in the eyes of most psychiatrists the outpatient sociopath may appear incorrigible, inhuman, unfeeling, guiltless, and unable to learn from experience; and yet in a prison hospital, the sociopath is fully human. I shall try to demonstrate that Cleckley's psycho-path, immortalized in the *Mask of Sanity*,[3] is a mythical beast.

To illustrate that our textbook conceptions of the psychopath are illusions, I have chosen three narcotic addicts. All had extensive criminal rec-ords; all were sent against their will to the US Pub-lic Health Service Hospital at Lexington, Ky. All demonstrated an absence of anxiety, an absence of motivation to change, and an absence of overt de-pression. But, once immobilized, they became in-distinguishable from Otto Kernberg's "border-line" patients[4] and Elizabeth Zetzel's "primitive hysterics"[5] that are familiar to most psychiatric teaching units. Such patients do not appear psychologically healthy, but they appear neither alien nor untreatable. Over a period of time, seemingly organic and immutable deficits emerge as dynamic and understandable defense mechanisms.

ABSENCE OF ANXIETY

An apparent absence of anxiety is a clinical hallmark that sets the real sociopath apart from most psychiatric outpatients. One reason that sociopaths conceal anxiety is that their parents often experienced great difficulty tolerating tension in others. They often used inappropriate means to relieve or to obscure anxiety in their children. The sociopath may confide to the psychiatrist that he had a "normal" family but that he was a "bad seed." He maintains that his parents (unlike the wicked fairy-tale stepparents who allegedly bring up neurotics) gave him "everything" he wanted. He often blames society for his behavior, but not his parents. His parents willingly corroborate the story. In the *Mask of Sanity,* Cleckley provides us with innumerable examples of wicked children and noble parents.[3] The psychopath seems the very antithesis of the fairy-tale hero.

An unsolicited letter from a woman whom I had never seen provided a vivid illustration of what may lie beneath parental innocence:

Dear Sir: My son is a dope addict and because he no longer knows the truth himself, I don't know how long it has lasted. I do know that I cannot continue the way I've been doing; I have no resources left.... I have about 30 pawn tickets on which I cannot even pay the interest. Every time I renew things, he'd hock them again. He had been arrested a total of five times, dismissed from all cases. The lawyers and the bail cost me about $1,500. [In short, she paid $1,500 to shield him from the normal consequences of his behavior.] When he was working he made $60 a week. He was supposed to pay me $12 a week but I seldom got it.... Now he has started selling off my books, and, as I've already weeded these down to bare essentials in the interest of space, this makes me very nervous [not angry but nervous]. One example of how dissipated this is he says he sold his camera for $5. His camera was a Brownie and complete with case was a $10.50 Christmas gift from me. [How difficult it was for her to decide to whom the camera really belonged!]

He is inarticulate and quarrels quickly and finds fault. He writes like a child and misspells words. He's losing his hair in front and has lost a tooth on the upper right. He is thin. I've lost my social career also. I have not had my hair fixed for a year—doing it myself. I have not bought any new clothes, and the getups I wear to school are a disgrace ... no one even wants to walk to the door with me. I know I am an 'indulgent' mother, but what can I do? I don't want to let him go. I see these jungle addicts in the house, and I know that I am the buffer which is keeping him from looking like them.

One example of how bad off I am is that every month I have one or two bounced checks, and the bank charges me $4 because of my poor record ... what I am trying to say is that I have $288, that is all I have left until September 15 when we go back to school. [The parents of sociopaths seem more in need of parental care than their children.] Nevertheless, in one way or another, my son gets the money from me.... Last week he promised if I would give him $15 on Tuesday and Wednesday, he would go to the hospital on Thursday. I got up at 5:30 a.m. on Thursday and Friday, but he didn't want to go; and as we had such a terrible heat spell, I can't blame him. At night, I lock my door and barred the door and jammed the lamp against it besides. Occasionally, he frightens me. [Although reluctant to let her son experience anxiety, she subtly amplifies her own secret fears.] Other times he seems so young and helpless. He is 22 and he is beautiful. Please tell me what to do.

The sociopath is supposed to be unable to postpone gratification; but in a family matrix intolerant of anxiety, postponement of gratification is difficult to learn. The letter demonstrates that it is never clear who is dependent on whom and who needs the help. The son's delinquency frightens his mother, but rather than oppose it, she conceals it. When she calls for help, she writes to a physician whom she has never seen and who is 700 miles away.

As the sociopath matures, he is not without anxiety; but it remains invisible to many observers—including judges and psychiatrists. Why? Neither the explanation that he cannot feel it nor the more sophisticated explanation that his anxiety is defended against by the ego mechanism of acting out is entirely satisfactory.

There are two other reasons that his anxiety is invisible. First, there are times that the sociopath makes his anxiety very clear to us; but at such times, our empathic response may blind us to it. By this I mean that the sociopath elicits from physicians and social workers the same response that he elicited from his parents. We behave as if to ask him to bear his anxiety would be too cruel, too disruptive, too sadistic, too authoritarian. Instead, we, too respond by distorting the very reality that would help him to learn that anxiety is acceptable—both to himself and to others. Too seldom therapists are able to say to sociopaths, "I am sorry that you are feeling bad, but I think that you can manage the feeling."

Second, we are often blind to the sociopath's anxiety because we cannot bear it or because the sociopath has managed to transfer his anxiety to us. The resulting staff apprehension then serves to make the patient unreachable, unfeeling, incurable, and unaware that the staff anxiety that surrounds him was originally his own. (The situation is analogous to that of the well-defended Kraepelinian psychiatrist; he calls the acute schizophrenic's affect "flat" when, in fact, the affect is one of stark terror.)

Consider the following example of concealed anxiety in a sociopath:

CASE 1. I was informed by several upset senior staff members that an unmanageable and notorious "psychopath" had returned to the US Public Health Service Hospital at Lexington, Ky, for the tenth time. He was reported to be on the admission ward out of control and holding the security staff at bay with a broom handle. It was with conscious fear that I learned that this unseen man was to be transferred to the psychiatric unit where I worked. I was anxious.

Once transfer was effected, I realized my fears were without substance. Confined to the isolation room and stripped to his shorts, he countered my anxiety with tranquility and charm. With injured innocence, he asked, "How can I regain my self-respect if I'm not given some clothes and let out of seclusion?" His behavior was beyond reproach; his privileges were soon returned, and so he left the unit.

A year later he returned. After having been refused medication, he had cut his wrists. It was at this point that I reviewed his chart, started to talk to him, and for the first time saw him in human dimensions. From suburban New York, he was the only child of middle-class, and apparently long-suffering parents. Only during his fifth admission to Lexington was it learned that his mother was secretly addicted to meperidine hydrochloride (Demerol) and that his father was an alcoholic. But his social history is not what is most pertinent. Rather more remarkable was the covert staff anxiety that was disclosed by his hospital record during this, his tenth admission. The Lexington medical staff was highly sophisticated to inappropriate demands for medication; but in one year, this known psychopath received the following results from laboratory procedures: six urinalyses—all normal; two urine cultures—no growth; ten different blood chemistry evaluations—all normal; an electrocardiogram; three roentgenograms of the chest and one of the skull; two gallbladder examinations; two gastrointestinal series; a barium enema; and a spinal tap—all of which were normal. At no time had he been organically ill.

Although he had never had a fever or evidence of an infection, he received penicillin. Although the patient was in a hospital that virtually never gave narcotics, even to patients with painful illness, he had received phenobarbital, codeine, pentobarbital (Nembutal), methadone hydrochloride, and chloral hydrate—all after his withdrawal period was completed. He also received 34 other medicines including meprobamate, imipramine hydrochloride, chlorpromazine, methamphetamine hydrochloride, chlordiazepoxide hydrochloride, and hydroxyzine hydrochloride.

There is little question that the staff response to this patient was unique. Nevertheless, he serves as an example of the difficulty that even sophisticated staff had in recognizing his anxiety, tolerating it or believing that he should tolerate it. The irrational therapeutic response he evoked had not become conscious in anyone's mind and, during the year, had been diffused among a large number of people.

Significantly, this tenth admission was his first imprisonment; it was the first time he ever had been made to stay in one place. Shortly after his second visit to the psychiatric unit, he built up a relationship in psychotherapy with one of the staff. Through this relationship, he learned to tell the physician on night duty, "I don't want any medicine—I just want to talk." (Admittedly, non-sociopathic patients can often learn to do this within a few days of hospitalization.) Once this lesson was learned, once his anxiety was conscious, he required—and received—no additional drugs. He caused the staff less anxiety; but he was able to show them more of his own. Previously, the patient had been unable to postpone gratification, but this was partly because nobody really tolerated his distress when he did so.

This man not only defended against anxiety with drug-seeking behavior, but he also manifested clear conversion symptoms. Psychiatrists, however, conceive of sociopathy and hysteria as two different syndromes and fail to recognize conversion in the sociopath. The hysteric is a woman; she is not out of control, and is immensely human. We see her conversion symptoms as a defensive process, and we perceive her distress behind these defenses. We believe her to be treatable. In contrast, the sociopath is usually a man and his physicians perceive him to be out of control. His defenses are invisible and his conversion symptoms are seen as conscious, hostile manipulation rather than unconscious efforts to conceal anxiety. Unfortunately, unrecognized defenses can seem to psychiatrists like deliberate offense; the psychiatrists defend themselves. Human beings are labeled "psychopaths."

LACK OF MOTIVATION

Sociopaths have a second hallmark that makes them appear inhuman: supposedly, they lack motivation for change. Sociopaths are supposed not to learn from experience. Often psychiatrists who have successfully banished the pejorative terms psychopath and sociopath from their vocabularies, replace the terms with "passive-dependent" or "inadequate personality." In such cases, the psychiatrist perceives the distress but shrinks from the seemingly overwhelming oral, passive, and receptive qualities of these individuals. His own helplessness may be projected onto the patient. At this juncture, it is well to recall two things. First, adolescents sometimes seem unable to learn from experience, yet this is a temporary artifact of one stage of development. Second, if individuals respond to an unconscious fantasy or impulse, this is different from being unable to learn. Sociopaths are more adolescent than ineducable.

CASE 2. A 30-year-old black addict prisoner received the admission diagnosis of passive-dependent character disorder; his behavior over the preceding four years was consistent with the diagnosis. He had grown up in New Orleans. His father, a pullman porter, had always made an adequate living, but he was an extremely ineffectual man. At 8 years, the patient was a better carpenter than his father. In order that his father might resemble the fathers of his friends, he used to daydream that his father would spank him. His mother, the family disciplinarian, was also the patient's chief competitor in arguments and power struggles. But he could remember his mother forbidding him to do only one thing—to play the trumpet. When he reached adolescence, his uncle gave him a trumpet; he took it up with a vengeance. He experimented briefly with meperidine, but never became addicted.

He took five years of college training in music and band teaching. He also became a successful jazz musician. However, when he reached the point where he was performing well-applauded trumpet solos, he abruptly gave up the instrument. There was no reason except, "I was not as good as other people thought I was." For the same reason, he turned down a well-paying job with the Chicago Department of Education.

Two years after giving up the trumpet, he had an affair with a "flashy woman." After she had canceled a date, the patient, unaware of any resentment, developed an overwhelming, inexplicable urge to take meperidine. He rapidly became addicted and four years later came to Lexington as a prisoner. He had no insight into his problems and wanted psychotherapy to relieve his functional gastric bloating and, magically, to cure his addiction.

Many months later he began to speak about his love of the trumpet and said that he gave it up because, "I was afraid of becoming addicted to it. I was afraid that I would

only be able to play the trumpet and be interested in nothing else." His fantasies about drugs became more explicit. He felt that marihuana was harmful. Although marihuana improved his trumpet playing, it made him think that he was too powerful. It might lead him to become "wild" and to drive his car too fast. In contrast, he felt that heroin was helpful to society and should be legalized. Heroin just made him drowsy and obtunded his sexual drive. When he got angry now, he got severe "ulcer" pains; these pains could be relieved with heroin. Only at the end of treatment was he able to talk tentatively about the anger he felt toward whites—especially policemen. [Ten years before he had belonged to CORE, but after he gave up the trumpet, he had also lost his interest in civil rights.] Any acknowledgment of negative transference toward me or resentment of his mother was assiduously avoided.

Throughout, it was difficult to mobilize this man's motivation for treatment. Had he not been in prison, he would never have kept his appointments. Yet after a year of psychotherapy, it was clear that beneath his "passive-dependent" camouflage there lurked a fairly competent individual who went to extraordinary pains lest some of his competence become visible to others. It is not that sociopaths do not feel; they feel, but fear lest they feel too much. For them recovery becomes synonymous with unconsciously forbidden sexual and aggressive competence. It is dangerous at 8 years to be a better carpenter than your father.

CASE 3. Another Lexington patient had wished two years before her imprisonment to put her illegitimate baby up for adoption. Instead, her mother insisted on keeping it. The patient remembered watching in silent rage while her mother triumphantly passed her daughter's baby off to the mother's friends as her own. A year later, the patient married a drug addict. During this period she wrested her child away from her mother and brought the child to live with her. The mother was furious and the patient felt extremely guilty at depriving her mother of the child. At this point she became addicted. When she was imprisoned, her mother regained control of the child.

Initially, the patient's anxiety over resumption of this struggle once she left prison was invisible. Instead, the patient tried to avoid help and preferred to deny herself parole than to return to this conflict. The details of her dilemma and the fact that at age 10 years her father had repeatedly sexually molested her came out only after months in therapy that she, too, would have fled had she not been in prison. In the setting of a prison hospital, however, this woman's lack of interest in "getting well" became dynamically understandable.

Perhaps the following vignette sums up the point of this section. Because the above patient deprecated her low self-image still further whenever her own strengths became evident, I asked her if she remembered how the ugly duckling story had ended. Without hesitating, the patient recounted the story as follows: The ugly duckling had been all black; the other ducks went off and left the ugly duckling all alone—end of story.

THE INABILITY TO EXPERIENCE DEPRESSION

The third hallmark of the sociopath is his apparent inability to experience depression and his inability to acknowledge that others matter to him. But it may be as preposterous to ignore depression in the sociopath who vehemently denies its existence, as it would be to ignore sexuality in the hysteric who feigns lack of interest in the subject.

CASE 4. A 25-year-old prostitute was sentenced to Lexington for five years for drug peddling. She was the daughter of a strict, middle-class, Christian Scientist family. Since age 16 years, the patient had been incorrigibly delinquent, and at first she seemed the very model of the classical psychopath.

Only after a year of imprisonment at Lexington and after many weeks of psychotherapy was depression more than an intellectual concept to this woman. Only gradually were another set of facts obtained. When the patient was an infant, her mother, unable to accept the responsibility of parenthood, had delegated her daughter's care to others. Like Arthur Miller's fatherless Willy Loman, the patient grew up feeling "kind of temporary" about herself. One day she finally protested to me, "You inject sadness into me." Until that time she had hidden behind a private rose-colored version of Christian Science or behind angry, childlike dissatisfactions that lifted too rapidly to resemble clinical depression.

After several months of therapy, and following a rather friendly hour the time before, she began to speak about her fears of intimacy; then, feeling anxious, she drew into herself and said, "I guess I am destined to be lonely." Two months later, on an occasion when she was denying that she felt any warmth or intimacy toward me, she spoke of herself as an IBM machine. She declared that I was seeing her only because "You were assigned to me." I wondered about her reluctance to consider the alternative formulation that she was human and that I might have chosen to work with her. She answered, "You are confusing and upsetting me. If you go on, I will stop therapy." During the next hour she was silent for the entire hour except to ask who solved the riddle of the sphinx; then, she described the sphinx as "a woman who ate everyone who was wrong." When I asked, "Do you mean that you're afraid of devouring people that you care about?" the patient retorted, "An astute observation, but what can you do about it?" During the next hour she spoke of getting close to her family; "I don't believe other people have feelings or emotions. When I see that they do, I push them away." On one occasion she became

upset at a compliment and said, "The danger of intimacy with people is that people will depend on you; and, then, you may hurt them and let them down. . . . It is not nice to punish those who love you."

She handled separation in the following dissociative manner. She canceled the hour before I went away on vacation. She then wrote me an exceedingly cheerful postcard that ended with, "I have put my neurosis on the shelf till you get back." When I returned, like a good sociopath, she spent two appointments demanding tranquilizing drugs and then skipped the next appointment.

Near the expiration of her sentence, she said, "Of course, I'm fond of you. You listen like a parent and you're a good teacher." She skipped the next session. When she returned, she said, "Can you give me any reason why I should continue with therapy?" When I suggested that at this point one purpose of continuing was in order to say goodbye, she declared, "I never said goodbye to anybody!" She spent the next two sessions in angry manipulation and vituperation, and canceled all future appointments. She let a year go by; then, safely distant from my by several hundred miles, began to write. For five years she continued to write me sensible, warm, and often appropriately depressed letters. She did not return to drug use.

Glover has said of sociopaths:

In addition to his incapacity to form deep personal attachments and his penchant to cause suffering to those who are attached to him, the psychopath is essentially a non-conformist, who in his reaction to society combines hostility with a sense of grievance.[2(p128)]

But the sociopath's "incapacity" represents defensive process, not inability. Close relationships arouse anxiety in them. Terrified of their own dependency, of their very real "grievances," and of their fantasies of mutual destruction, they either flee relationships or destroy them.

As the above case history illustrates, the depression of sociopaths resembles that of bereaved children. Bowlby has suggested that mourning in childhood is characterized by a persistent and unconscious yearning to recover the lost object.[6] The persistent crime and polydrug abuse of the sociopath represents a similar quest. Bowlby tells us that in lieu of depression, bereaved children, like sociopaths, exhibit intense and persistent anger that is expressed as reproach toward various objects including the self. However, Bowlby notes that such anger, if misunderstood, seems often "pointless enough to the outsider." Finally, sociopaths, like children, often employ "secret" anodynes to make loss unreal and overt grief unnecessary. Their need for secrecy is based on the fact that "to confess to another belief that the loved object is still alive is plainly to court the danger of disillusion." These defensive maneuvers then, serve to hide the child's and the sociopath's depression from our psychiatric view. The painstaking controlled studies of the Gluecks' have established beyond reasonable doubt that the sociopath usually was a neglected (ie, bereaved) child[7] and that for this reason, serious delinquency (unlike most psychiatric conditions) can be prospectively predicted by age 6 years.[8]

In conclusion, I would like to recapitulate certain themes that were present in the above case histories. All had lacked a benevolent, sustained relationship with the same-sexed parent. All were afraid of intimacy and of assuming responsibility for it. None could believe that others could tolerate their anxiety, and all devoutly feared responsibility for achieving success by open competition. They could neither identify with authority nor accept its criticism. Finally, their persistent, seemingly mindless delinquencies made symbolic sense if interpreted dynamically—as one might interpret misbehavior in a dream or in a child's play therapy. In short, psychopaths are neither born that way nor incapable of change. I believe that their "incomprehensible" behavior is a product of a well-defended ego and of a strict, albeit primitive, conscience.

THE EGO MECHANISMS OF SOCIOPATHY

If the ego of the psychopath is not inadequate and if his superego is not absent, what are the underlying dynamics of the psychopath that make him or her seem so inhuman? Certainly, they employ very different styles of defense from neurotic outpatients. The classical defenses that underlie the neuroses are as distressing to the owner and as insignificant to the observer as a run in a stocking or a stone in one's shoe (ie, repression, isolation, reaction formation, displacement, and dissociation).[9] The defense mechanisms that underlie sociopathy seem as harmless to the owner and as unbearably gross to the observer as a strong cigar in a crowded elevator (ie, denial through fantasy, projection, turning against the self, hypochondriasis, and acting out). Because nobody likes them, these latter defenses are less well understood. Therapists have difficulty feeling sympathetic toward delinquent, prejudiced, passive-aggressive, and hypochondriacal individuals. Except in children, we are apt to call such defenses sins, not coping behavior.

Nevertheless, before the defensive armor of the sociopath is viewed as too different from our own,

consider those hopeless character disorders—adolescents. They, too, make extensive use of the sociopath's defenses. They use mood-altering drugs without moderation and see others, not themselves, as out of step. Their physical complaints are often imaginary; so are many of their most passionate loves. No other age group is so passive-aggressive or so masochistic. Yet adolescence is a self-limiting disease! Thus, it becomes possible to view the ego mechanisms that underlie drug addiction, paranoia, hypochondriasis, eccentricity, and masochism as immature defenses.[9] True, we are unable to cajole, psychoanalyze, or beat somebody out of adolescence. They need to grow out of it slowly—with a little help from their peers. If we can wait 15 to 20 years, it becomes possible to demonstrate that intractable delinquents and addicts also remit.[10,11]

Although we build walls (concrete or social) to protect ourselves from sociopaths, our efforts to save ourselves are in vain. The more we punish them, the less they learn. This aspect of sociopaths is maddening and defies logic. However, Bowlby might remind us that it does not do much good to beat a bereaved child.[6]

There is also a second explanatory facet to the seeming illogic of sociopathy. Can you imagine a hypochondriac, an exhibitionist, or a paranoiac existing alone on a desert island? Of course not. These seemingly immutable character traits exist only in the presence of other people. In brief, immature defenses are not always the incurable bad habits that they appear on the surface. Sometimes, they are a means of making a painful truce with people whom we can neither live with or without.

If neurotic defenses are more often the modes with which we cope with instincts, immature defenses are most often the ways we cope with people.[12] In adult life, projection, hypochondriasis, fantasy, and masochism perpetuate a subtle process that we usually acknowledge only between mother and infant and perhaps between lovers—namely, a merging of personal boundaries. A cherished or a loathed person may suddenly cause pain within a hypochondriac's body. In prejudice the obnoxious trait of a parent, inadvertently absorbed in childhood, may be projected onto some hapless minority group. The promiscuous daydreams of a minister become mysteriously acted out by his delinquent daughter. In *The Glass Menagerie* the fragile animals of Laura's fantasy came suddenly to life—inside her mind.

Put another way, if our inner worlds include relatively constant people toward whom we have relatively unambivalent feelings, in real life, our external relationships remain relatively assured, loving, autonomous, and well-demarcated. However, the interpersonal relationships of sociopaths remain perpetually murky and entangled. In an effort to preserve an illusion of interpersonal constancy, immature defenses permit ambivalent mental representations of other people—especially of parents—to be conveniently "split" (into good and bad) or moved about, and reapportioned. Just as neurotic mechanisms (eg, displacement, isolation, and dissociation) transpose feelings, immature mechanisms magically maneuver feelings and their objects.

If we fail to understand the defensive process, we take the sociopath's defenses personally and condemn them. Perhaps one reason that we often label immature defenses perverse is that, once touched, we rarely can divorce ourselves completely. One reason immature defenses are so taboo is because they are contagious. In the presence of a drug addict, liberals become prejudiced; the masochist elicits our own latent sadism, and the malingerer our passive-aggression. When baited by their adolescent children, even the most reasonable and staid parents become hopelessly involved and utterly unreasonable. And yet the process by which this all happens is obscure and, if noticed, quite mysterious to an outsider. This phenomenon does much to account for the inhumanity of man to man that is seen throughout much of our criminal justice system. But there is no culprit. Only anticipation and understanding will allow therapists to disentangle themselves from the defenses of the sociopath.

TREATMENT

One conclusion of this report is that the dynamics of the so-called psychopath differ little from those of Kernberg's so-called borderline.[4] Nevertheless, conventional psychiatric management is not the answer to effective treatment.

1. Before treatment can begin with a sociopath, the therapist must find some way of dealing with the patient's self-destructive behavior. Be it via parole, commitment to a prison hospital, or the ideological grip of Synanon, real control over behavior is a sine qua non of treatment. Sociopaths are too immature for the therapist to suggest that a given behavior is self-detrimental and then to stand by helpless when they do it. Not only do sociopaths interpret such helplessness as lack of concern, but also unchecked, self-detrimental behavior scares the therapist. Although voluntary outpatient therapy may foster autonomy, this ad-

vantage is for naught if the therapist becomes so frightened that he is defensively blind to the human qualities of his patient. Therefore, it is no accident that we find the borderline imprisoned by suicide precautions in psychiatric teaching hospitals and the psychopath repeatedly locked up in maximum security institutions.

2. Control is important not only to prevent self-destruction but also to overcome the sociopath's fears of intimacy. His wish to run from the pain of honest human encounter and from tenderness must be frustrated. He must be immobilized long enough for him to be perceived as human. The challenge to psychiatry, however, is to separate control from punishment and to separate help and confrontation from social isolation and retribution. Possible models include sustained employment enforced through parole, halfway house residence enforced by probation, "addiction" to methadone clinics, or the kind of therapeutic community behind bars that Kiger has devised for sociopaths at the Utah State Hospital.[13] All seem vastly preferable to jails or psychiatric hospitalization, per se. In every case the hope of freedom is preferable to the threat of imprisonment. Sociopaths should work for liberty, not pay for past mistakes.

3. Too vigorous intervention or protection from harm can be as bad as too little. Sociopaths are made worse by good defense lawyers. Their anxiety should not be controlled. But it is not always easy to remember that acute anxiety, like untreated insomnia, is a self-limiting, nonfatal illness. The only way that the therapist can show the sociopath that anxiety is bearable is by bearing it with him and by not trying to alleviate it. The therapist must recognize that his wish to control the sociopath's anxiety (whether by psychotropic drugs or by solitary confinement), is countertransference. In fact, the therapist's own anxiety can be openly acknowledged to the sociopathic patient. Brought up to believe that anxiety is too dreadful to be borne and too awful to confess, the sociopath is reassured that someone can be anxious and yet in control.

4. Sociopaths, like children, deny their depression and repress parental neglect. The therapist must learn to put little trust in their childhood histories as initially given.

5. From the start, the therapist must accurately assess each of the sociopath's defenses. To relabel the "sociopath" as "borderline"—as is currently fashionable—will obscure differential diagnosis and lead to perceiving defenses as immutable or as attacks on the therapist. No defense, however, can

be abruptly altered or abandoned without an acceptable substitute. Successful treatment demands that the therapist try to help the patient develop a substitute for each defense. For example, addicts give up addiction bit by bit; their abstinence is achieved via a process analogous to mourning. Countless criminals have replaced acting out with reaction formation and projection with altruism.

6. Interpretation of defenses like projection, denial through fantasy, masochism, or major acting out is rarely effective. Besides substitution, confrontration is the best way to breach immature defenses.

7. Finally, one-to-one therapeutic relationships are rarely adequate to change the sociopath. A therapist—even five times a week—is not enough to satisfy an orphan. At the start of the recovery process, only the church, self-help residential treatment, and addicting drugs provide relief for a sociopath's pain; they all work 24 hours a day. Conventional psychotherapy is most effective in helping people who have received too much or the wrong sort of parental attention. Only group membership or caring for others, or both, can eventually provide adults with parenting that they never received.

The paths out of sociopathy are like the paths out of drug addiction[14] and adolescence. These are usually quite independent of formal therapy and are derived from peer identifications. Membership in altruistic but revolutionary movements like Black Panthers, in self-help groups like Alcoholics Anonymous and Synanon, or even marriage to a person as needy as themselves are all more useful than intensive psychotherapy. A compulsory but real job, outside of prison, offers more than vocational counseling or prison trade schools.[14] The therapeutic community at the maximum security ward of the Utah State Hospital, where the inmates hold the keys both to the outside and to the seclusion rooms,[13] offer more than programs that try to transform psychopaths into patients.

Why? Sociopaths know only too well that they have harmed others; they can meaningfully identify only with people who feel as guilty as themselves. They can abandon their defenses against grief only in the presence of people equally bereaved. Only acceptance by peers can circumvent the sociopath's profound fear that he may be pitied. Only acceptance by "recovered" peers can restore his defective self-esteem. Finally, the psychopath needs to absorb more of other people than one person, no matter how loving, can ever provide. Sociopaths need to find groups to which they can belong with pride.

This investigation was supported in part by the Grant Foundation, New York, and National Institute of Mental Health grants MH-10361 and MH-38798.

This report was published with permission from the *Massachusetts Journal of Mental Health*, Boston.

NONPROPRIETARY NAME AND TRADEMARKS OF DRUGS

Chlorpromazine—*Chlor-PZ, Cromedazine, Thorazine.*

REFERENCES

1. Cleckley HM: Psychopathic states, in Arieti S (ed): American Handbook of Psychiatry. New York, Basic Books, 1959, pp 567–588.
2. Glover E: The Roots of Crime. New York, International Universities Press, 1960.
3. Cleckley HM: Mask of Sanity. St. Louis, CV Mosby Co, 1941.
4. Kernberg O: The treatment of patients with borderline personality organization. Int J Psychoanal 49:600–619, 1968.
5. Zetzel E: The so-called good hysteric, in The Capacity for Emotional Growth. London, Hogarth, 1970, pp 229–245.
6. Bowlby J: Pathological mourning and childhood mourning. J Am Psychoanal Assoc 11:500–541, 1963.
7. Glueck S, Glueck E: Unraveling Juvenile Delinquency. Cambridge, Mass, Harvard University Press, 1950.
8. Glueck S, Glueck E: Toward a Typology of Juvenile Offenders. New York, Grune & Stratton Inc, 1970.
9. Vaillant GE: Theoretical hierarchy of adaptive ego mechanisms. Arch Gen Psychiary 24:107–118, 1971.
10. Vaillant GE: A 20-year follow-up of New York narcotic addicts. Arch Gen Psychiatry 29:237–241, 1973.
11. Glueck S, Glueck E: Criminal Careers in Retrospect, New York, Commonwealth Fund, 1943.
12. Freud A: The Ego and the Mechanisms of Defense. London, Hogarth Press, 1937.
13. Kiger RS: Treatment of the psychopath in the therapeutic community. Hosp Community Psychiatry 18:191–196, 1967.
14. Vaillant GE: A 12-year follow-up of New York narcotic addicts: IV. Some characteristics and determinants of abstinence. Am J Psychiatry 123:573–584, 1966.

DEFINING BORDERLINE PATIENTS:
AN OVERVIEW

JOHN G. GUNDERSON AND MARGARET T. SINGER

This review of the descriptive literature on borderline patients indicates that accounts of such patients vary depending upon who is describing them, in what context, how the samples are selected, and what data are collected. The authors identify six features that provide a rational means for diagnosing borderline patients during an initial interview: the presence of intense affect, usually depressive or hostile; a history of impulsive behavior; a certain social adaptiveness; brief psychotic experiences; loose thinking in unstructured situations; and relationships that vacillate between transient superficiality and intense dependency. Reliable identification of these patients will permit better treatment planning and clinical research.

In 1953 Knight noted that the term "borderline" was applied to patients who could not be classified in other ways, i.e., as psychotic or neurotic, hence making it something of a wastebasket diagnosis (1). No doubt much of the dissatisfaction with recognizing such a category, whether it is termed borderline or any of its alternative labels, stems from the wish to keep schizophrenia as a clearly distinct disorder. Yet despite this objection, its use has steadily expanded.

Stern (2) was the first to use the term borderline, but the real parentage for this unwanted category is traceable to the "as-if" personality described by Deutsch (3), the ambulatory schizophrenia of Zilboorg (4), and the latent schizophrenia as introduced and developed by Rorschach (5), Bleuler (6), and Federn (7). Latent schizophrenia was sanctioned by Bleuler in 1911 to classify persons whose conventional social behavior he felt concealed underlying schizophrenia. Ambulatory schizophrenia was subsequently offered by Zilboorg in 1941 to combat the therapeutic nihilism that clinicans felt the latent schizophrenia label implied. Deutsch's article on the "as-if" personality described persons whose superficial social appropriateness masqueraded highly disturbed personal relationships.

Before and even after Knight's paper popularized the term borderline, many other names were suggested and then silently retired in favor of the ever-widening use of this term. Among these are preschizophrenia (8), schizophrenic character (9), abortive schizophrenia (10), pseudopsychopathic schizophrenia (11), psychotic character (12), subclinical schizophrenia (13), borderland (14, 15), and occult schizophrenia (16).

The most serious competition in the nomenclature has come from the term pseudoneurotic schizophrenia. This term was particularly popular in New York because of the local influence of its originators, Hoch and Polatin and associates (17, 18). Hoch urged replacing the term borderline with pseudoneurotic schizophrenia, which defined a specific psychopathological condition characterized by the combination of panneurosis, pananxiety, and pansexuality together with symptoms of schizophrenia. The broadening of the concept of schizophrenia which followed in New York may be responsible for a discrepancy in diagnostic habits between New Yorkers and other American psychiatrists as well as the British (19). Yet this

EDITORS' COMMENTS:

THE AUTHORS DESCRIBE THE BORDERLINE SYNDROME, WITH SPECIAL ATTENTION TO EGO FUNCTIONS. THEY NOTE THE REMARKABLE CONTRAST IN SYMPTOMS AND BEHAVIOR BETWEEN BORDERLINE PATIENTS WHO VOLUNTARILY SEEK TREATMENT AND BORDERLINE PATIENTS WHO ARE HOSPITALIZED.

term, too, has given way in the most recent APA diagnostic manual (20).

Although the use of the term borderline has become more common, disagreement over its definition has not subsided but has merely been displaced and camouflaged. Many who accept this term now disagree about whether it refers to borderline patient (21), state (22), personality organization (23, 24), character (25), pattern (26), schizophrenia (27, 28), condition (29), or syndrome (30). The increasing frequency of "borderline" patients (31–36), the greatly expanding literature, and the existing confusion about diagnosis and treatment make it imperative that some method for defining the patient group be devised that is replicable and from which research can proceed and conclusions can be generalized. In this paper we will attempt to survey the major relevant descriptive accounts of the borderline and to chronicle the common and discriminating features of these accounts.

Before we expand on these descriptive accounts, certain features about the literature itself should be noted. Since Knight's pivotal article appeared, there has been a large and still expanding descriptive literature on the borderline patient. There were approximately 25 articles on borderline patients up to 1955, and that number has doubled in the past 10 years. Nevertheless, there remains a confusing overlap and discrepancy among authors in their descriptive attempts to define borderline patients. While most authors pay lip service to the previous literature, they proceed to describe borderline patients anew without noting how their descriptions add to or simply repeat earlier contributions. It is not clear whether this provincialism stems from an unfamiliarity or an unspoken dissatisfaction with the existing literature.

In this article we will discuss the major descriptive accounts of the borderline syndrome. Clearly, not all of the writings are of equal importance. The work of some authors is extremely well known and widely quoted, while others' work is obscure and/or limited to a single publication. Certain writers attribute every imaginable trait to borderline patients, while others are quite selective in their descriptions. Furthermore, some authors expand or contract their definitions of borderline patients in later publications. In addition, some descriptive accounts are secondary or preliminary to a discussion of other issues, e.g., psychodynamics (37, 38), theory (27, 38), treatment (21, 31–33, 36, 37, 39–42), testing technique (43, 44), and schizophrenia (45). Yet in many the descriptive accounts are the primary goal of the paper (12, 17, 23, 29, 30, 46–49). Among the latter, only Grinker and as-

sociates (30) have undertaken a prospective and systematic collection of observations and data analysis.

Nevertheless, each of the authors cited has attempted to articulate his conceptualization of borderline patients and in so doing has implied either his agreement or disagreement with others. Taken in their entirety, these various views reflect the present clinical opinion about these patients. Any attempt by researchers to reliably define borderline patients should encompass these major clinical impressions. In this review, the most common and distinguishing characteristics will be identified, and a rational guide for standardizing clinical criteria for diagnosing borderline patients will be offered.

METHODOLOGICAL PROBLEMS

There are essentially three types of descriptive accounts: symptomatic and behavioral observations, psychodynamic formulations, and psychological test findings. Although these sources of descriptive data are parallel, they seldom seem touched or influenced by each other's proximity. This independence, or ignoring of other sources, arises in part from the different contexts in which the observations are made and reported. Symptom and behavior observations tend to be published in the psychiatric literature and are the purview of clinical researchers and of those involved in residential treatment. Psychodynamic formulations frequent the psychoanalytic literature and usually are developed within individual psychotherapeutic office practice. Finally, the psychological literature contains the accounts made of the borderline patient by psychologists who have administered controlled clinical testing procedures. In addition, the independence of these three groups no doubt grows out of a traditional suspicion each group holds for each other's methodologies. In any event, the psychologist tends to focus upon intrapsychic structure, the psychoanalyst upon theory and therapy, and the general psychiatrist upon diagnosis, prognosis, and outcome.

Clearly, the amount of structure provided by a setting in which the borderline phenomenology is observed will influence how these patients are described. For example, clinicians using psychoanalytic techniques and psychologists using the Rorschach test agree in emphasizing the major ego defects and primitive intrapsychic mechanisms and thinking found in these patients. Yet clinicians observing these patients in structured hospital settings or evaluating them with structured interview techniques emphasize their stable personality features and interpersonal patterns. Certainly the broad agreement among authors from all persuasions (4, 21, 22, 27, 29, 31–33, 35, 37, 39–41, 43, 50, 51) about the borderline patient's proclivity for regression in unstructured settings draws attention to the critical need to define the context in which the observations and descriptions of the borderline patient are being made. This propensity to regress when structure is low becomes an important and perhaps pathognomonic criterion for defining any sample of borderline persons.

The circumstances that lead the borderline person and his evaluator to meet are also important. For example, there appears to be a remarkable contrast between borderline outpatients voluntarily seeking treatment and borderline inpatients, who may be referred by others for treatment. A comparison of the observations made by Hoch and Cattell (17) with those made by Grinker and associates (30), the only authors whose descriptive data were collected in a systematic manner, sheds light on the influence of sample selection upon the conclusions reached about borderline patients.

Both research groups viewed schizophrenia as a distinct pathological condition and selected borderline patients who were free of overt schizophrenic symptomatology, such as clear-cut delusions and hallucinations, on the basis of their history and mental status examination. Hoch and Cattell further limited their sample to patients who presented mainly severe psychoneurotic symptoms, but who, on closer evaluation in psychoanalytic therapy and eventually in hospitals, revealed primary signs of schizophrenia in their thinking, feelings, and physiological functioning. Grinker and associates, on the other hand, selected patients on the basis of good functioning between hospitalizations and the presence of an ego-alien quality to any psychotic behavior. The diagnosis of borderline was made on outpatients, who were then hospitalized for participation in a prospective study. Thus Grinker and associates chose as their sample subjects with good premorbid features, and hospitalization was not a clinical necessity but rather for research purposes. It is not surprising, then, that their sample showed rare psychotic phenomena and developed virtually no schizophrenia during a five-year follow-up (52). In contrast, slightly more than one-fourth of Hoch and Cattell's hospitalized population later developed manifest schizophrenia (53).

It is clear that the initial selection of samples influenced the conclusion that Grinker and associates reached that borderlines and schizophrenics have separate and distinct disorders while Hoch and Cattell concluded that their patients were a subgroup of schizophrenics. It is somewhat like packing a suitcase and then being surprised later to find what is in it when it is opened.[1] Most authors choose to regard borderline patients as a group somewhere between, and perhaps including, both of these extremes. Thus the need for hospitalization is a critical variable in comparing samples. Borderline patients who are referred for hospitalization because of severe symptoms would be expected to be more disordered than those functioning as outpatients.

In summary, we have cited four major variables to be considered in any descriptive account of borderline patients: who is describing them, the methods used to collect descriptive data, the context in which the patients were observed, and how the sample was selected. Each has an important impact on the resulting description of borderline patients.

What follows is a selective review of the literature covering three major descriptive conceptualizations of the borderline: first, the literature on symptoms and behavior; second, the psychological test literature; and third, the analytic literature as it views ego functioning.

SYMPTOMS AND BEHAVIOR

In the descriptive behavioral and symptom literature for borderlines, a number of characteristics are repeatedly mentioned that can be grouped under the general headings of affect, behavior, and psychosis. Among the studies that have considered the behavior and symptoms of borderlines, the study by Grinker and associates (30) deserves special citation as the only prospective, systematic one. Despite the slanted selection of patients in that sample, the findings must be considered as the marker against which all other reports should be measured. It is thus of special value to compare the findings of Grinker and associates with those other descriptions based on purely clinical impressions.

---

[1]Grinker and associates noted that Hoch and Cattell tended to include more clearly schizophrenic symptoms in their later definitions of pseudoneurotic patients. Dyrud (32) has commented that Grinker and associates may have too readily dismissed the relationship between borderline and schizophrenic patients.

Affect

Of the four prevailing characteristics that Grinker and associates found in their borderline patients, two were qualities of affect.

1. *Anger.* "Expressed more or less directly to a variety of targets, anger seems to constitute the main or only affect that the borderline patient experiences" (30, p. 90). The expression of this anger—or the defenses against it—are a major discriminating feature used to identify four separate subgroups of borderline patients.

2. *Depression.* "Not the typical guilt-laden, self-accusatory, remorseful 'end-of-the-rope' type, but more a loneliness as the subjects realize their predicament of being unable to commit themselves in a world of transacting individuals" (30, p. 91). Grinker and associates pointed out that this depression was not present in their healthiest borderline group, which suffered instead from a clinging, childlike, anaclitic depression.

These conclusions by Grinker and associates are given substantial albeit inconsistent support by others. Some authors have noted the prevalence of anger but do not mention depression (21, 33), and vice versa (17, 36, 54). It seems likely that the confusion over the qualities of affect is traceable to at least two major sources. First, there is confusion about whether one is describing affects the patient presents with, affects that are covert, or affects that emerge in treatment. Second, as some authors have noted, the borderline patient's anger and depression have peculiar qualities.

How these two sources of confusion influence the descriptions of borderline affects becomes apparent when one examines some of the statements about depression in the literature. For example, there are frequent qualifying phrases used by those clinicians who note a predominance of depression. Cary (29) has noted that the borderline patient is characterized by a "sense of futility and pervasive feelings of loneliness and isolation" that he says do not constitute a "true" depression. Hoch and Cattell (17) stated that they found frequent secondary depressions due to the persistent illness in their pseudoneurotic patients, but that primary depressions were infrequent. Kernberg (23) noted the prevalence of depressive-masochistic character traits in some of his borderline patients but differentiated these from depressive symptoms. Further, he advised that depression "as a symptom should not be used directly as

an indicator of borderline personality organization" but suggested that only severe depression approaching psychosis in the form of "ego depersonalization" should be a presumptive indicator for a diagnosis of borderline personality. Gruenewald (55) commented that there is often a "covert" depression that emerges later. Chessick (56) described a chronic "existential despair" in borderline patients.

Anger is less controversial than depression. Many authors have noted a prevailing anger in borderline patients. This one feature seems to have been used progressively to discriminate borderlines from the original description of the "as if" personality (3, 30) and from "schizoid" personalities (29), where withdrawal from frustration is considered more characteristic. One author (57) felt that the borderline patient's anger is so prominent that he suggested changing the name to "choleric." Despite the apparent agreement about the prevalence of anger, such a broad range of behaviors is cited as being "angry" that a high degree of inference may be required. Some examples are hostility (50), rage reactions (31, 49), acting out (3), self-destructiveness (23, 31, 33, 58), detachment (59), mutism (33, 57), and demandingness (29, 57). Several authors have said that anger is not a presenting theme but one that emerges in the course of treatment (42, 50, 59). Kernberg (23) and Meza (57) speculated about excessive aggressive drive, while Modell (38) saw the anger as "mostly defensive."

In contrast, several authors have regarded anxiety as the typical affect shown by their parents. Hoch and Cattell (17) gave this anxiety the status of a "defining secondary diagnostic symptom." Although others (23, 32, 41, 47, 49) have also commented on anxiety in borderline patients, it is difficult in most instances to know if they are describing a symptomatic problem among borderlines or are making an inference based on a theoretical role given anxiety in personality theories.

Finally, another term frequently applied to borderline patients is anhedonia (32). In fact, there is considerable agreement that they lack a capacity for pleasure and rarely experience truly satisfied feelings. Their anhedonia has been discussed in terms of borderline dysphoria, unhappiness (47, 60), anguish (56), and lack of tenderness (3, 38).

In summary, the affective state of borderline patients is characterized by the prominence of anger and depression plus varying degrees of anxiety and anhedonia. If a generalization can be made, it is that these patients are not flat in their affect tone; they tend, in fact, to experience intense and variable affects, although this does not seem to include the experience of pleasure.

Behavior

Much of the literature on the treatment of borderline patients describes behavior during therapy, especially during hospitalization. Here we are interested in those behaviors which characterize borderline patients when they come for evaluation and that would therefore be used as criteria for making the diagnosis of borderline and in planning treatment. This is an important issue, since there may be a typical and highly distressing behavioral regression following hospitalization whose active prevention may be required from the start (21, 29, 31, 33, 35, 50, 61). Within the repertoire of hospital behaviors, such acts as window breaking, wrist slashing (31, 33, 58), and repeated overdosing (50, 62) emerge as quite specific to this kind of patient.

One historical factor, which led psychoanalysts to the conception of and interest in borderline patients as a distinct entity, was the discovery that many patients who by their histories and demeanors seemed relatively healthy underwent regressions on the couch. This disparity between good social behavior and poor intrapsychic structure has been mentioned repeatedly by both analysts (18, 48, 63, 64) and psychologists (28, 60, 65). What is meant by good social behavior seems to be good appearance and manners combined with superficial interpersonal relationships, and—more surprisingly—good functioning at work (12, 36, 42, 48, 60, 66, 67). The latter is surprising because this impression is noted almost in passing by many writers despite its apparent conflict with the behavioral record the patients have elsewhere in their lives. Schmideberg (47) took exception to this view. She described her borderline patients as marginal and transient in their work histories and cited their "sense of entitlement" as a source of their work problems. Grinker and associates summarized their follow-up data by saying, "Although gainfully employed and largely self-sufficient economically, the facts, suggest that the group was occupationally and academically static at a fairly low level" (30, p. 132). Frosch (12, 66) noted that a borderline person may have a surprisingly stable work record when he is employed in a highly structured environment.

The characteristic most frequently and consistently ascribed to the behavior of borderline patients is that of impulsive and self-destructive acts.

"Self-destructive" is used here to indicate a broad range of behaviors whose result is self-destructive although their intent or purpose is not. Examples include sexual promiscuity and perversions in search of affection (56, 68), self-mutilation with the goal of object manipulation (58, 61) or establishing self-identity (66), and addiction in search of escape (15, 32). Generally, borderline patients do not regard these behaviors as self-destructive, self-degradative, or guilt provoking. Although relatively little of the literature on borderline patients has dealt with actual suicide, repeated suicidal gestures and threats have been noted (50, 54, 57) and specific manipulative behavior attributed to such patients (69, 70).

Diverse sexual problems are attributed to borderline persons, but there is little agreement on their prevalence. Certain authors have noted a preoccupation with sex (17), and others have described polymorphous perverse sexuality (17, 23, 35, 46). Some authors (3, 12) have even included within the borderline category most persons with specific sexual deviances. Greenson (35) noted a "prominence of organ pleasures at the expense of object relations" among this group. Several authors (17, 41, 42) believe that these behaviors reflect a basic confusion in the sexual identity of the individuals.

The presence of obvious behavioral disturbances in a variety of spheres including drug use and sexual deviance often causes the borderline diagnosis to overlap with various character problem diagnoses in which chronic acting-out patterns such as antisocial, addictive, alcoholic, and homosexual behavior are seen. Because of this, Kernberg (71) has argued for a new classification of character types based upon what he believes are more fundamental personality features than behavior. He and many others have included a number of specific character disorders within the broader diagnostic category of borderline syndrome (21, 38, 41, 46, 47, 54, 68). Jan Frank (35) has suggested that various acting-out behaviors provide outlets for many persons now diagnosed as borderline who previously would have become overtly schizophrenic. He and others (71, 72) believe that inadequate impulse control is the dominant ego defect in these persons.

One concludes that in considering the behavioral evidence for the diagnosis of borderline, a clinician should not be deterred by the presence of a stable work history or superficial social adequacy but should examine other areas, where he may often find evidence of impulsive sexual, drug-taking, or other activities whose results are self-destructive even though the patient's intent or purpose is not.

Psychosis

While there has been general agreement that borderline syndrome is a stable personality disorder (12, 23, 30, 33, 38, 39, 47), there is also widespread recognition that a number of these patients may develop psychotic symptoms (1, 17, 36, 39, 45, 46, 49, 51, 66, 73). Indeed, as indicated earlier, the borderline person's capacity to develop regressive psychotic symptoms may be a pathognomonic feature. Weiner would seem to concur with this conclusion in his review of the literature (28). However, there is a consensus that when psychoses do occur, they have the following differential features: 1) stress related (21, 23, 36, 43, 49, 68), 2) reversible (21, 30, 41, 49), 3) transient (12, 15, 30, 49), 4) ego-alien (1, 12, 30), and 5) unsystematized (23, 29, 30, 43, 45, 60, 74). Numerous authors have used some or all of these features to differentiate borderline psychoses from the psychoses of schizophrenia and other disorders (21, 23, 29, 30, 38, 45, 54, 66). Thus there is general agreement as to absence of stable or clear delusions or hallucinations, with only a few dissenting opinions (17, 33). Some authors have postulated that the borderline's psychoses occur in response to intolerable rage (29, 30, 41, 73).

Interestingly, despite the consensus about the vulnerability of certain borderline persons to psychotic-like episodes and regressions, only a few authors have viewed this as an essential feature of the borderline syndrome (1, 12, 45, 73, 75). Most authors have hastened to note that the occurrence of psychoses is the exception, not the rule (23, 29–31, 39, 46, 76). A few have taken a determined position that psychoses do not occur at all in borderline persons (33, 50, 63). At the opposite extreme, Hoch and Cattell (53) found that the psychoses in their sample of pseudoneurotic schizophrenic patients were not necessarily transient and reversible. A more recent report (77) suggested that the psychoses of this group cannot be differentiated from those of schizophrenics, and another (46) reported that they are brief and rare. This last report would thereby place pseudoneurotic schizophrenia within the mainstream of thought about psychoses among borderline persons.

There have also been widespread references to the similarity between the psychotic thought processes of borderline and schizophrenic persons.

Some borderline persons demonstrate fears of being controlled (17), ideas of reference (38), externalization (1, 56), and other paranoid tendencies (12, 23, 56). Some writers have noted that they have vividly loose associations and other symptoms of formal thought disorder. For example, Knight (1) stated that loose associations can be detected by use of the Rorschach test and free-associative interviews. On the other hand, Grinker and associates (30) emphasized that they found no looseness of associations. (However, they did not use projective tests of free-associative interviews in their assessment of their patients.) Hoch and Cattell (17) took an intermediate position, stating that "approximate" or "parallel" associations are frequent. Thus there is little agreement among clinicians about the presence of thought disturbances in borderline persons. Some say there are none (23, 30), while others say there are many (1, 47, 50, 65, 73). It is clear that these differences result from problems in defining and assessing thought disorder as well as from the methodological problems cited earlier.

Some authors have underscored the frequent occurrence of disturbed states of consciousness. These peculiar ego states, which were first described by Deutsch (3), have been variously categorized as depersonalization, dissociation, and derealization (23, 29, 36, 45, 61, 66). They have been called borderline "states," to be differentiated from borderline "personalities." These states are seen as responses to anxiety (66), depression (23), and rage (29) and as prepsychotic experiences (3).

Separate from the purely clinical literature already summarized, a literature grew in the 1960s that recognized a vulnerability among borderline persons to psychoses when exposed to pharmacological stress, namely, that produced by marijuana (78), LSD (68, 79), and mescaline (68). These reports suggest that the borderline person is unique in his sensitivity to pharmacological stress. This special sensitivity or vulnerability seems to support Schmideberg's often quoted characterization of the borderline personality as "stably unstable" (47).

From the many foregoing clinical reports, which vary in their positions on whether psychoses occur among the borderline group, a series of clinical questions arise: Do all borderline persons have a vulnerability to psychosis even if they are not psychotic when assessed? Are most borderline persons free from psychosis throughout their life despite such a vulnerability? Clinicians are uncertain and divided over these issues. Grinker and associates (30) contended that psychoses occur in only one subgroup of borderline persons. Equally important, they are the only authors who have attempted to identify subgroups of borderlines who they contend will not develop psychoses. Other authors have implied or hinted that many or even most borderline persons could develop psychoses, given properly stressful circumstances. Parallel issues concerning the extent and type of their reality testing and the nature and type of their cognitive style will be considered in a later section of this paper.

To conclude, reports in the clinical literature generally agree that an undetermined number of borderline persons do develop psychoses in stressful situations. Moreover, when such psychoses occur, they are characterized by their limited symptoms and limited duration. There are, however, few actuarial data on the prevalence of vulnerability to psychosis among borderline persons. Some authors have suggested that dissociative states may be quite marked in these patients.

INTRAPSYCHIC PHENOMENA

The psychological test literature devoted to characterizing borderline patients has generally been in agreement that they demonstrate ordinary reasoning and responses to structured tests such as the Wechsler Adult Intelligence Scale (WAIS), but that less structured tests such as the Rorschach reveal deviant thought and communication processes (27, 28, 43, 60, 74, 80–83). As in the clinical literature, most articles on which this conclusion is based are impressionistic. Their many methodological issues require attention before this broadly held viewpoint is accepted (6). The seminal contributions were made by Rorschach, Rapaport and associates, and Schafer, with subsequent authors generally being content to add confirmatory evidence.

Rorschach (5) and later Rapaport and associates (8) used the terms "fabulizing, combinatory, and confabulated" thinking to describe the propensities of borderline persons to overspecify secondary elaborations of their associations and to combine and reason oddly. They are prone to reason circumstantially rather than logically. Their separate perceptions tend to become intermingled and related simply because they occur close together in time or space. Borderline persons read more affective elaboration into their perceptions than others can validate, i.e., they tend to add too much and too specific affective material to simple perceptions. Other persons then have trouble accepting this affective meaning, although they might accept the same basic percept that the borderline person sees.

Rorschach, in 1921 (5), was the first to call attention to some seemingly adequately functioning persons whose responses to inkblot tests resembled those given by schizophrenic patients. He applied the term latent schizophrenic to those persons who had average surface behavior but Rorschach test features in common with schizophrenics, such as self-references, belief in the reality of the cards, scattered attention, variability in quality of ideas, and absurd and abstract associations.

It was Rapaport and associates (8) who first described the borderline person's intact performance on the WAIS and a pervasively odd Rorschach record; this has subsequently become an almost axiomatic diagnostic rule for later writers presenting single case studies. Although these authors defined two groups of what they called preschizophrenics, namely, the coarctated group and the overideational group, it has been largely the overideational borderline patient who is referred for psychological testing and upon whom subsequent literature has concentrated. Stone and Dellis (74) reiterated Rorschach's observation about the disparity between social functioning and thinking. They went on to confirm in a prospective study (74) Rapaport and associates' finding of a discrepancy between the Rorschach test and the WAIS in their evidence for pathology in borderline patients.

Schafer (82) introduced a third distinguishing feature about the disturbed thinking of borderline patients when he suggested that they are more comfortable about their bizarre and distorted thinking than are schizophrenics. Although Schafer's finding seems to differ from the general impression in the clinical literature that psychoses are ego-dystonic, it was later repeated in a report by Fisher (60).

In an interesting report DeSlullitel and Sorribas (84) compared the Rorschach test results of normal subjects, borderline persons, and creative artists. They found that the negative unpleasant content within "fabulized combination" responses by borderline persons distinguished them from the creative artists, who presented positive content within similar types of responses.

Gruenewald (55) reported on psychological test batteries given to 10 of Grinker and associates' original 51 borderlines five or more years after their discharge. She noted that based solely on test results, 2 would have been diagnosed as schizophrenic. However, when these data were combined with other information, the results were consistent with the borderline diagnosis and fit within the subgroups Grinker and associates had derived. She noted that "maladaptive primary process manifestations" were sometimes present in thought content and organization. Unfortunately, she made no mention of any discrepant functioning on individual tests.

In summary, borderline persons are believed to connect unrelated percepts illogically, overelaborate on the affective meaning of percepts, and give circumstantial and unpleasant associations to the Rorschach inkblots. This disturbed thinking may be more flamboyant and more ego-syntonic than that found among schizophrenic persons. Yet such borderline persons are reported to function adequately on the WAIS, showing few or none of the ideational deviances.

EGO FUNCTIONS

There are various ways to assess and classify ego functions. Thus it is difficult to select from the literature comparable descriptions of specific ego-function characteristics of borderline persons. However, two functions do emerge as particularly relevant to this group, namely, reality testing and interpersonal relationships. While the latter remains almost solely within the purview of clinical impressions, several approaches to evaluating reality testing have been made.

Reality Testing

Any discussion of psychosis is based upon the concept of reality testing. Frosch (12, 40) has stated that an intactness in reality testing differentiates borderline persons from schizophrenics. Distinguishing among reality testing, sense of reality, and relationship to reality, he concluded that borderline and psychotic persons share a poor sense of reality and relationship to reality, but that the borderline person can test out his experiences whereas the psychotic cannot. In a panel report on the "as if" personality, a similar conclusion was reached about this subgroup of borderline persons (85). This position is akin to the frequent comments of several authors that borderline persons, when compared to schizophrenics, have more distance from their psychotic experiences and regard the episodes as ego-alien or ego-dystonic. Zetzel (21) added a twist to Frosch's viewpoint by stating that it is the capacity to reverse impaired reality testing, given a good situation (in treatment), that

distinguishes borderline persons from schizophrenics.

A number of authors seem to agree with Frosch that reality testing is generally maintained in borderline persons (23, 30, 85). Wolberg (85) has stated that the reality distortions that do occur are defensive in nature and that the borderline person's actual perception of reality is always extant. However, Kernberg (51) has noted that "under special circumstances—severe stress, regression induced by alcohol or drugs, or transference psychosis"—they may lose this capacity. Kernberg and others have noted that these patients are prone to develop psychotic transference reactions. Of course, unless this feature is cited in the patient's history, it would not be of use in an initial diagnostic evaluation. Authors using psychological tests have assigned relatively greater importance to the vulnerability of the borderline person's reality testing to stress (31, 43, 60). Knight (1) noted the borderline person's inability to distinguish between dreaming experiences and reality. Hoch and Cattell (53) later drew a similar conclusion about the impairment in reality testing in their group of pseudoneurotic schizophrenic patients.

A number of authors have emphasized that reality testing should not be viewed as a phenomenon that one has or does not have but, rather, that there is a spectrum of reality testing (1, 16, 38, 50). Modell (38) and others (21, 23) have discussed the borderline person's reality testing problems in the context of self-object differentiation. Modell noted,

> The testing of reality depends upon the fact that in the ego's growth a distinction has been made between self and object . . . there are degrees of alteration of this function of testing reality that correlate with the degree to which self and object can be differentiated . . . the borderline transference is based on a transitional object relation where there is some self-object discrimination, but where this discrimination is imperfect. (38, p. 228)[2]

Such a graded view of reality testing helps to reconcile certain discrepancies noted earlier among authors who have presented contradictory views of reality testing in borderline persons.

As Hurvich (86) has pointed out, there is a need for quantifiable measurements of this ego function, which could be used to evaluate whether and to what extent impairment exists. Although

---

[2]Burnham (61) has suggested that borderline patients frequently have pets or toy animals.

Grinker and associates (30) included "relation to reality" as one of the seven ego functions they intended to evaluate in their borderline patients, they did not include any instruments to measure this directly. Their evaluation was based on behavior that was generally labeled as "positive" or "negative" and upon ratings of perception devised from global judgments of the patient's awareness of self, others, time, events, and things. These assessments did not give any consideration to latent vulnerability to disruptions in reality testing. Further, their validity as reflections of reality testing is not always obvious. Grinker and associates seemed aware of these problems and did not draw any definite conclusions about the relationship to reality and the capacity for reality testing in their sample. Until instruments or methods of measuring reality testing are developed, the literature on borderline persons will continue to reflect the ambiguity of the concept and clinical impressions will be subject to the unstated and therefore unknown biases of the researchers.

At this time the consensus is that there is a definite impairment of reality testing in borderline persons, but it is not as severe as that in psychotic persons and, under most circumstances, is not apparent.

Interpersonal Relationships

A number of authors have pointed to borderline patients' style of relatedness as the most distinguishing diagnostic feature of this group. Zetzel (21) said that for the borderline patient in particular, "the kind of doctor-patient relationship that is established may prove to be a crucial factor in reaching a definitive diagnostic evaluation." This relationship is best illustrated by the following observations.

A frequently cited feature of the borderline patient's object relationships is a predictable superficiality and transiency (30, 32, 60, 87). Fisher (60) suggested that "superficiality in relationships" distinguishes borderline patients as a group from neurotic patients. Knight alluded to this somewhat differently by noting, "Other ego functions, such as conventional (but superficial) adaptation to the environment and superficial maintenance of object relationships, may exhibit varying degrees of intactness" (1, p. 6). This echoes the observation made earlier about the borderline person's surprising capacity for adequate social functioning but adds that this apparent behavioral normality may depend on superficiality. Dyrud (32) commented that case material cited by Grinker and others

demonstrates more than anything else the remarkably short sequences of interactive behavior that these patients are capable of maintaining.

This quality of superficiality and transiency is supported and explained in some measure by the original formulations of the "as if" personality by Deutsch (3). Deutsch described the borderline person's interpersonal relationships as "plastic" and "mimicry." She stated that the "essential characteristic is that outwardly he conducts his life as if he possessed a complete and sensitive emotional capacity." Eventually, the absence of real emotional responsiveness leads to repeated dissolution of relationships. This disparity between adequate superficial relatedness and inadequate internal relatedness has been used to characterize borderline patients more generally (29, 30, 48–50, 60, 80). It may be attributable to a lack of coherent self-identity, which Grinker and associates (30) found in their sample and which other authors have also noted (1, 21, 23, 45, 49, 56, 66).

In contrast to the recurrent theme that borderline persons' interpersonal relationships are superficial and transient is the claim that they are prone to form intense, clinging relationships. Adler (31) stated that their "readiness to form rapid, intense, engulfing relationships" is what differentiates them from schizoid and schizophrenic persons. Similarly, Modell (38) stated, "My principal reason for considering this group homogeneous is that they develop a consistent and primitive form of object relationships in the transference." Grinker and associates (30) referred to this when they cited as one of the four identifying characteristics of borderlines "a defect in affectional relationships. These are anaclitic, dependent, or complementary, but rarely reciprocal." These accounts of borderline persons' intense relationships are underscored by the consensus that their initial relationships with therapists are dependent and demanding (12, 21, 23, 29, 31, 38, 50, 76). In addition, many authors have noted that the intense therapeutic relationship is characteristically devaluative and manipulative (21, 31, 38, 50, 57). The emergence of such angry behaviors may in turn lead to the repeated disruption of such close relationships (49, 50, 57). These qualities of the borderline person's close relationships may not be immediately discernible. Houck (50) pointed out that this initial deception can lead to later problems for unsuspecting therapists.

Thus in their everyday relationships borderline persons relate in a fairly normal but superficial and transient manner, while in their close relationships they become intense, dependent, and manipulative. In any event, these individuals are actively involved with other people and are not particularly socially withdrawn.

SUMMARY

In this paper we have surveyed the large literature of descriptive accounts of borderline patients. Within the major variations in these accounts we have attempted to identify certain themes and prevailing clinical impressions. We have discussed the four methodological issues that significantly influence the resulting descriptive accounts. Taking these methodological issues into account, we have identified a number of features that most of the authors believe seem to characterize most borderline persons. These features are as follows:

1. *The presence of intense affect.* It is usually of a strongly hostile or depressed nature. The absence of flatness and pleasure and the presence of depersonalization may be useful in differential diagnosis.
2. *A history of impulsive behavior.* This may take many forms, including both episodic acts (e.g., self-mutilation, overdose of drugs) and more chronic behavior patterns (e.g., drug dependency, promiscuity). Often the result of these behaviors is self-destructive although their purpose is not.
3. *Social adaptiveness.* This may be manifested as good achievement in school or work, appropriate appearance and manners, and strong social awareness. However, this apparent strength may reflect a disturbed identity masked by mimicry, a form of rapid and superficial identification with others.
4. *Brief psychotic experiences.* These are likely to have a paranoid quality. It is felt that this potential is present even in the absence of such experiences. The psychoses may become evident during drug use or in unstructured situations and relationships.
5. *Psychological testing performance.* Borderline persons give bizarre, dereistic, illogical, or primitive responses on unstructured tests such as the Rorschach, but not on more structured tests such as the WAIS.
6. *Interpersonal relationships.* Characteristically, these vacillate between transient, superficial relationships and intense, dependent relationships that are marred by devaluation, manipulation, and demandingness.

These six features provide a rational basis for diagnosing borderline patients. The criteria can be readily assessed during an initial evaluation. Further research is under way to evaluate the relative frequency and discriminating value of each of these features. From these studies a reliable system of diagnostic criteria can develop. It is hoped that such prestated and standardized means of identifying borderline patients will permit better treatment planning and clinical research on these patients to proceed.

REFERENCES

1. Knight R: Borderline states. Bull Menninger Clin 17:1–12, 1953
2. Stern A: Psychoanalytic investigation of and therapy in the borderline group of neuroses. Psychoanal Q 7:467–489, 1938
3. Deutsch H: Some forms of emotional disturbance and their relationship to schizophrenia. Psychoanal Q 11:301–321, 1942
4. Zilboorg G: Ambulatory schizophrenia. Psychiatry 4:149–155, 1941
5. Rorschach H: Psychodiagnostics (1921), 5th ed. Bern, Hans Huber, 1942, pp 120–121, 155–158
6. Bleuler E: Dementia Praecox, or the Group of Schizophrenias (1911). Translated by Zinkin J. New York, International Universities Press, 1950, p 239
7. Federn P: Ego Psychology and the Psychoses. New York, Basic Books, 1952, pp 166–183
8. Rapaport D, Gill M, Schafer R: The Thematic Apperception Test, in Diagnostic Psychological Testing, vol 2. Chicago, Year Book Publishers, 1946, pp 395–459
9. Schafer R: The Clinical Application of Psychological Tests. New York, International Universities Press, 1948, pp 218–223
10. Mayer W: Remarks on abortive cases of schizophrenia. J Nerv Ment Dis 112:539–542, 1950
11. Dunaif S, Hoch PH: Pseudopsychopathic schizophrenia, in Psychiatry and the Law. Edited by Hoch PH, Zubin J, New York, Grune & Stratton, 1955, pp 169–195
12. Frosch J: The psychotic character: clinical psychiatric considerations. Psychiatr Q 38:81–96, 1964
13. Peterson DR: The diagnosis of subclinical schizophrenia. J Consult Psychol 18:198–200, 1954
14. Clark LP: Some practical remarks upon the use of modified psychoanalysis in the treatment of borderland neuroses and psychoses. Psychoanal Rev 6:306–308, 1919
15. Chessick R: The psychotherapy of borderland patients. Am J Psychother 20:600–614, 1966
16. Stern A: Psychoanalytic therapy in the borderline neuroses. Psychoanal Q 14:190–198, 1945
17. Hoch P, Cattell J: The diagnosis of pseudoneurotic schizophrenia. Psychiatr Q 33:17–43, 1959
18. Hock P, Polatin P: Pseudoneurotic forms of schizophrenia. Psychiatr Q 23:248–276, 1949
19. Kuriansky J, Deming W, Gurland B: On trends in the diagnosis of schizophrenia. Am J Psychiatry 131:402–408, 1974

20. American Psychiatric Association: Diagnostic and Statistical Manual of Mental Disorders, 2nd ed. Washington, DC, APA, 1968

21. Zetzel E: A developmental approach to the borderline patient. Am J Psychiatry 128:867–871, 1971

22. Weinshel EM: Panel report: severe regressive states during analysis. J Am Psychoanal Assoc 14:538–568, 1966

23. Kernberg O: Borderline personality organization. J Am Psychoanal Assoc 15:641–685, 1967

24. Kernberg O: Prognostic considerations regarding borderline personality organization. J Am Psychoanal Assoc 19:595–635, 1971

25. Giovacchini PL: Character disorders: with special reference to the borderline state. International Journal of Psychoanalytic Psychotherapy 2(1):7–20, 1973

26. Millon T: Pathological personalities of moderate severity: borderline patterns, in Modern Psychopathology. Philadelphia, WB Saunders Co, 1969, pp 302–337

27. McCully RS: Certain theoretical considerations in relation to borderline schizophrenia and the Rorschach. Journal of Projective Techniques 26:404–418, 1962

28. Weiner IB: Borderline and pseudoneurotic schizophrenia, in Psychodiagnosis in Schizophrenia. New York, John Wiley & Sons, 1966, pp 398–430

29. Cary GL: The borderline condition: a structural dynamic viewpoint. Psychoanal Rev 59:33–54, 1972

30. Grinker RR, Werble B, Drye R: The Borderline Syndrome: A Behavioral Study of Ego Functions. New York, Basic Books, 1968

31. Adler G: Hospital treatment of borderline patients. Am J Psychiatry 130:32–35, 1973

32. Dyrud JE: The treatment of the borderline syndrome, in Modern Psychiatry and Clinical Research. Edited by Offer D, Freedman D. New York, Basic Books, 1972, pp 159–173

33. Friedman HJ: Some problems of inpatient management with borderline patients. Am J Psychiatry 126:299–304, 1969

34. Schimel JL, Salzman L, Chodoff P, et al: Changing styles in psychiatric syndromes: a symposium. Am J Psychiatry 130:146–155, 1973

35. Rangell L: The borderline case (panel report). J Am Psychoanal Assoc 3:285–298, 1955

36. Arnstein RL: The borderline patient in the college setting, in Psychosocial Problems of College Men. Edited by Wedge BM. New Haven, Conn, Yale University Press, 1958, pp 173–199

37. Blum HP: Borderline regression. International Journal of Psychoanalytic Psychotherapy 1(1):46–59, 1972

38. Modell A: Primitive object relationships and the predisposition to schizophrenia. Int J Psychoanal 44:282–292, 1963

39. Chessick RD: Use of the couch in psychotherapy of borderlines. Arch Gen Psychiatry 25:306–313, 1971

40. Frosch J: Technique in regard to some specific ego defects in the treatment of borderline patients. Psychiatr Q 45:216–220, 1971

41. Wolberg A: The psychoanalytic treatment of the borderline patient in the individual and the group setting, in Topical Problems of Psychotherapy. Edited by Hulse J. New York, S Karger, 1960, pp 174–197

42. Rosner S: Problems of working through with borderline patients. Psychotherapy: Therapy, Research, and Practice 6:43–45, 1969

43. Shapiro D: Special problems in testing borderline psychotics. Journal of Projective Techniques 18:387–394, 1954

44. Stern A: Transference in borderline neuroses. Psychoanal Q 17:527–528, 1948

45. Kety SS, Rosenthal D, Wender PH, et al: The types and prevalence of mental illness in the biological and adoptive families of adopted schizophrenics, in The Transmission of Schizophrenia. Edited by Rosenthal D, Kety SS. New York, Pergamon Press, 1968, pp 345–362

46. Godbey AL, Guerra JR: Pseudoneurotic schizophrenia. Journal of the Florida Medical Association 57(4):17–20, 1970

47. Schmideberg M: The borderline patient, in American Handbook of Psychiatry, vol 1. Edited by Arieti S. New York, Basic Books, 1959, pp 398–416

48. Wolberg A: The Borderline Patient. New York, Intercontinental Medical Book Corp, 1973

49. Pfeiffer E: Borderline states. Dis Nerv Syst 35:212–219, 1974

50. Houck JH: The intractable female patient. Am J Psychiatry 129:27–31, 1972

51. Kernberg O: The treatment of patients with borderline personality organization. Int J Psychoanal 49:600–619, 1968

52. Werble B: Second follow-up study of borderline patients. Arch Gen Psychiatry 23:3–7, 1970

53. Hock P, Cattell J: The course and outcome of pseudoneurotic schizophrenias. Am J Psychiatry 119:106–115, 1962

54. Chessick RD: The borderline patient, in How Psychotherapy Heals. New York, Science House, 1969, pp 144–160

55. Gruenewald D: A psychologist's view of the borderline syndrome. Arch Gen Psychiatry 23:180–184, 1970

56. Chessick RD: Externalization and existential anguish in the borderline patient. Arch Gen Psychiatry 27:764–770, 1972

57. Meza C: El Colerico. Mexico City, Mortiz, 1970

58. Grunebaum H, Klerman G: Wrist slashing. Am J Psychiatry 124:524–534, 1967

59. Wolberg A: The "borderline patient." Am J Psychother 6:694–701, 1952

60. Fisher S: Some observations suggested by the Rorschach test concerning "the ambulatory schizophrenic." Psychiatr Q 29 (suppl 1):81–89, 1955

61. Burnham DL: The special-problem patient: victim or agent of splitting? Psychiatry 29:105–122, 1966

62. Havens L: Some difficulties in giving schizophrenic and borderline patients medication. Psychiatry 31:44–50, 1968

63. Bellak L (ed): Schizophrenia: A Review of the Syndrome. New York, Logos, 1958, pp 55–56

64. Bychowski G: The problem of latent psychosis. J Am Psychoanal Assoc 1:484–503, 1953

65. Weiner H: Diagnosis and symptomatology, in Schizophrenia: A Review of the Syndrome. Edited by Bellak L. New York, Logos, 1958, pp 107–173

66. Frosch J: Psychoanalytic considerations of psychotic character. J Am Psychoanal Assoc 18:24–50, 1970

67. Little M: Transference in borderline states. Int J Psychoanal 47:476–495, 1966

68. Denber H: Mescaline and LSD: therapeutic implications of the drug-induced state. Dis Nerv Syst 30(Feb suppl):23–27, 1969

69. Jensen V, Petty T: The fantasy of being saved in suicide. Psychoanal Q 27:327–339, 1958

70. Sifneos PE: Manipulative suicide. Psychiatr Q 40:525–537, 1966

71. Kernberg O: A psychoanalytic classification of character pathology. J Am Psychoanal Assoc 18:800–822, 1970

72. Eisenstein VW: Differential psychotherapy of borderline states. Psychiatr Q 25:379–401, 1951

73. Willett AB, Jones FD, Morgan DW, et al: The borderline syndrome: an operational definition. Read at the 126th annual meeting of the American Psychiatric Association, Honolulu, Hawaii, May 7–11, 1973

74. Stone HK, Dellis NP: An exploratory investigation into the levels hypothesis. Journal of Projective Techniques 24:33–44, 1960

75. Miller MH: The borderline psychotic patient. Ann Intern Med 46:736–743, 1957

76. Schmideberg M: The treatment of psychopaths and borderline patients. Am J Psychother 1:45–70, 1947

77. Weingarten LL, Korn S: Psychological test findings on pseudoneurotic schizophrenics. Arch Gen Psychiatry 17:448–454, 1967

78. Heiman E: Marijuana precipitated psychoses in patients evacuated to CONNUS. US Army Medical Bulletin 40(9):75–77, 1968

79. Laurie P (ed): LSD applied, in Drugs: Medical, Psychological and Social Facts. Baltimore, Penguin Books, 1967, pp 112–130

80. Forer BR: The latency of latent schizophrenia. Journal of Projective Techniques 14:297–302, 1950

81. Mercer M, Wright SC: Diagnostic testing in a case of latent schizophrenia. Journal of Projective Techniques 14:287–296, 1950

82. Schafer R: Psychoanalytic Interpretation in Rorschach Testing. New York, Grune & Stratton, 1954, pp 66–67

83. Zucker LJ: The psychology of latent schizophrenia: based on Rorschach studies. Am J Psychother 6:44–62, 1952

84. DeSlullitel SI, Sorribas E: The Rorschach test in research on artists. Rosario, Argentina, 1973 (unpublished paper)

85. Weiss J: Clinical and theoretical aspects of "as if" characters (panel report). J Am Psychoanal Assoc 14:569–590, 1966

86. Hurvich M: On the concept of reality testing. Int J Psychoanal 51:299–312, 1970

87. Knight R: Management and psychotherapy of the borderline schizophrenic patient, in Psychoanalytic Psychiatry and Psychology. Edited by Knight R, Friedman CR. New York, International Universities Press, 1954, pp 110–122

THE PSYCHODYNAMICS AND DEVELOPMENTAL PSYCHOLOGY OF THE BORDERLINE PATIENT: A REVIEW OF THE LITERATURE

EDWARD R. SHAPIRO

The author reviews the psychodynamics and developmental psychology of the borderline patient as described in the literature on intensive therapy, early mother-child interaction, and family interaction. Focusing on the borderline patient's characteristic difficulties in intimate relationships, he describes the patient's use of splitting and projective identification as seen in the characteristic transference-countertransference interaction in intensive therapy. These primitive defensive mechanisms, which are also utilized by family members, appear to contribute to a failure of empathic responses both during the child's early development and in the family interactions during his adolescence. The author concludes that conceptual attempts to relate adult and child phenomena, although highly speculative, create new and useful perspectives for the treatment of the borderline patient.

There is a growing body of work on the dynamics and developmental psychology of the borderline patient. The literature springs from three main sources: observations of the transference-countertransference interaction in intensive psychotherapy or analysis, observation of the preverbal infant in interaction with his mother, and study of the family in interaction. Despite the active controversy about the nondefinitive boundaries of the diagnostic classification of borderlines (1–3) and the continual attempts to reach better descriptive diagnoses (4), clinicians have found the increasing clarity about the underlying dynamic and developmental issues of great use in working psychotherapeutically with these patients and in understanding and putting into perspective the tensions that develop in the work.

In this paper I will survey the major relevant literature and attempt to synthesize the current understanding of the many dynamic and developmental issues involved. The literature is large and is filled with highly condensed metapsychological abstractions which represent attempts to make sense of subtle and complex data. I will attempt, when possible, to translate these concepts into clinical language without doing unnecessary violence to the complexity of the thinking.

The focus of the review will be on the borderline patient's characteristic difficulties in intimate relationships (5). There are specific elements in borderline psychopathology that engage both family members and therapists in unique ways. I will attempt to trace these observations as they have been elaborated in both the dynamic and the developmental literature.

CONTRIBUTIONS OF DESCRIPTIVE AND PSYCHOLOGICAL STUDIES

Although the attempt to apply a descriptive analysis to the presence and frequency of symptoms and to the observable abnormal behavior of the borderline patient is important (2, 4, 6), it may be misleading. Many of the characteristic behavioral and symptomatic responses of these patients seem to appear only at times of stress, while

EDITORS' COMMENTS:

THE AUTHOR REVIEWS PSYCHOANALYTICALLY ORIENTED FINDINGS, WITH PARTICULAR ATTENTION TO EARLY RELATIONSHIPS. ONE REMNANT OF EARLY SYMBIOTIC INTERACTION IS THE INTERPERSONAL USE OF PROJECTIVE IDENTIFICATION, WHICH CAN BE SEEN IN THE PATIENT–THERAPIST INTERACTION.

Reprinted from The American Journal of Psychiatry 135:1305–1315, 1978. Copyright 1978, the American Psychiatric Association. Reprinted by permission.

at other times the patients may be relatively asymptomatic (7). Nonetheless, certain findings from descriptive studies and from review of psychological test reports are congruent with dynamic observations from intensive therapy.

Gunderson (4) and Grinker and Werble (6) found the most discriminating data in their descriptive studies to be in the observation of the difficulties borderline patients have in interpersonal relationships, particularly in terms of their pervasive sense of aloneness and their tendency to see difficulties as emanating from outside themselves. Gunderson[1] suggested from his data that these attributes, as well as an inability to acknowledge wants and to discriminate them from needs, are "core conflicts" in borderline patients.

On unstructured projective tests that provide the opportunity for regressive responses, borderline patients reveal evidence of primary process thinking (7), a strong tendency to add too much and too specific affect to simple perceptions, and a propensity to produce these peculiar responses without concern or embarrassment. Margaret Singer's review of series of test reports (8) revealed that these responses do not occur on more structured tests, suggesting that these patients can utilize an external organizing structure to support their thinking. This finding has been corroborated by repeated clinical observations (2, 9–11). Melvin Singer (12) suggested the presence of a cognitive disturbance in which these patients fail to structure, delay, detour, and check their impulses and affects through "cognitive binding" (i.e., through contemplation, fantasy, reflection, and symbol formation).

These findings suggest that borderline pathology is related to difficulties in the management of impulse and affect, which is perceived most characteristically in interpersonal relationships and emerges most clearly in relatively unstructured settings. The intensive, relatively unstructured therapeutic relationship, then, is an ideal setting in which to study in detail the elements of the disorder.

TRANSFERENCE DEVELOPMENT AND PROBLEMS

The response of borderline patients in intensive therapy is characteristically marked by gross fluctuations in perception, thinking, and feeling about themselves and the therapist, without awareness

---

[1]Gunderson JG: Discriminating characteristics of borderlines and their families (unpublished paper, 1977).

of the contradictions (13, 14). Margaret Singer (8) found this tolerance and bland acceptance of contradictory thoughts a unique attribute of these patients.

Kernberg (7) described the borderline patient as having little capacity for realistic appraisal of others and, in the absence of a relationship, as experiencing others as distant objects to whom he can compliantly adapt. In therapy borderline patients present narrow, rigid, unmodulated affects (15) and show little ability to tolerate guilt, concern, or internalized depressive affect (16, 17). They have difficulty in discriminating and reporting body sensations and emotions (13) and manifest little capacity for anxiety or frustration tolerance, delay, or impulse control (7). Their unpleasant affects readily escalate to panic without triggering reliable defensive operations (18), and they manifest a profound sense of identity diffusion, with little sense of inner continuity from past to present to future (15). Unlike the majority of psychotic patients, they are capable of higher level defenses and good reality testing in many situations, but they are likely to regress to transient psychotic states under stress or within the transference relationship, readily developing fantasies of extreme neediness, destruction, and abandonment (7, 19).

The transference of the borderline patient has been described as immediate, intense, and chaotic, only gradually developing over time into discernible patterns (7, 15). Modell (20–22) described the patient's diagnostic transference response to the therapist as similar to the infant's response to the "transitional object" (e.g., blanket or teddy bear). He suggested that although the patient recognized the therapist as existing outside the patient (as is not the case in the transference of many psychotic patients), the quality of this perceived existence is determined by processes arising within the patient. Although neurotic patients also attribute certain qualities of their own to a therapist, they seem to have the capacity to recognize the origins of these perceptions within themselves, while borderline patients do not (5).

The transference response described by Modell is seen most clearly in the borderline patient's difficulty in asking the therapist for help in a way that would imply an acknowledgment that the therapist as a separate person might reasonably refuse or be unable to respond to the request. For the borderline patient, to consider the possibility of the therapist's refusal is to become aware of anxious, rage-filled fantasies of abandonment that are perceived as potentially arising from the therapist.

To avoid these fantasies, the patient does not ask directly for help. Instead, he either angrily demands a response or overtly ignores the therapist in the session while maintaining an illusion of comfort from the therapist's response. This response is seen as similar to the child's response to his blanket.

Winnicott (23) described the child's blanket as something that possesses attributes of its own (warmth, texture, something "not me") yet is not allowed to change unless changed by the child. It is "used" by the child—both loved and mutilated—and must survive both (24). As in the therapeutic relationship described by Modell, the blanket is not "asked" for help. It is, instead, symbolically placed as a protective shield between the child and the dangers of the outside world; the child is comforted by it. Several authors (23, 25–27) have described the relationship with the transitional object as representing a phase in the child's gradual separation from his mother, a gradual disengagement in which the blanket partly represents his mother (and the child) and partly represents the outside world. Abelin (28) described the father as occupying this position during the child's separation-individuation period.

In the early stages of therapy, some borderline patients use inanimate objects, animals, or certain fantasies as transitional ways of relating to the therapist, metaphorically putting these objects between them and the therapist both to protect them from a dangerous intimacy and simultaneously to allow a relationship to exist (25, 26).

Borderline patients demonstrate their characteristic unmodified, polarized responses in the therapeutic relationship (15, 22). They have magical expectations from therapy, often anticipating improvement without their own active participation. They may experience the therapist as benevolent but demonstrate the constant fear that he or she will be transformed into the opposite. Under stress, they may experience the therapist as attacking and may fear that they will be dominated, controlled, or abandoned by him (19, 29). In the latter experiences they feel alone, helpless, and needy and appear unable to maintain a reliable sense that the therapist remains with them in a caring way (19). Because of these tensions, they present the manifest conflict of extreme dependence and intense fear of closeness, the solution to which appears to be a constant preoccupation with maintaining the "proper" distance from the therapist in order to regulate their anxiety about both distance and closeness.

EGO DEFENSES

The use of specific primitive ego defenses has been described as characteristic of the borderline patient in intimate relationships. Kernberg (7, 30), in describing the borderline patient's disjointed, contrasting behaviors and fantasies in intensive therapy, suggested that there is an underlying pattern of sharply polarized fantasied relationships that is "activated" in the transference. The polarization of these fantasies is determined by the defensive maneuver labeled "splitting." Kernberg suggested that borderline patients' core difficulty lies in their inability to bring together and integrate loving and hating aspects of both their self-image and their image of another person. Kernberg's observation was that these patients cannot sustain a sense that they care for the person who frustrates them. Kernberg saw this characteristic failure in the achievement and tolerance of ambivalence and in the modification of affects as diagnostic. He suggested that loving fantasied relationships and hating ones are internally "split" for the borderline patient to prevent the anxiety that would result if they were experienced simultaneously. These positive or negative stereotyped fantasies are activated in a relationship depending on the degree of gratification or frustration perceived by the patient. In a gratifying relationship, the patient develops positive fantasies, with the negative ones dissociated or "split off" and therefore unavailable. When frustrated, the patient elaborates negative fantasies and loses all memory of the positive relationship.

Other authors (1, 4, 13, 31, 32) have been less comfortable with the idea of splitting as a primary mechanism for borderline patients. Most, however, acknowledge the patient's failure to integrate and modify impulses and affects as an important characteristic.

Splitting as a defense is to be distinguished from denial, which is the disavowal of whole percepts and the substitution of a wish-fulfilling fantasy, and repression, which is the repulsion of mental content from consciousness due to a linkage of that content with a conflicted memory (33). In splitting, the positive and negative fantasied relationships remain alternatively in consciousness with the complementary side dissociated.

Defensive splitting also contributes to the patient's alternating view of the therapist as omnipotent and devalued. In these responses to the therapist, the patient experiences no real dependency on him in the sense of love or concern. Instead, the patient experiences a sudden shift from total need to total devaluation (7).

A second major defense of borderline patients, often associated with both splitting and transitional relatedness, is that of projective identification (7, 34–38). This defense involves the dissociation of uncomfortable aspects of the personality (elements of impulse, self-image, or superego) and the projection of them onto another person, resulting in an identification with the other person because of having attributed qualities of the self to him. Included in this intrapsychic and interpersonal mechanism, particularly for borderline patients, is the unconscious attempt to evoke feelings or behavior in the other that conform with the projection and the willingness (conscious or not) of the recipient of these projections to accept these attributes as part of himself (32).

The person using this defense is selectively inattentive to the real aspects of the other that may contradict or invalidate the projection (39). In addition, the other (now seen as possessing the disavowed characteristics) is consciously identified as unlike the self (36), while an unconscious relationship is sustained in which the projected attribute can be vicariously experienced.

This defense differs from projection in that the individual maintains some contact with that which is projected. The projections are not simply placed onto another; an unconscious attempt is made to develop a relationship with the other and to involve him as a collusive partner in conforming to the way in which he is perceived (37, 40).

Projective identification is a defense used along a spectrum of psychopathology from normal to psychotic. The severity of the pathology is determined by the content of the projection, the capacity of the subject to test reality and to differentiate himself from another person, and the intensity of the subject's defensive need to avoid conflict by disavowing a dystonic aspect of himself. Depending on the interaction of these factors, projective identification can endow a relationhip with emphatic qualities or create a delusional distortion and give a binding quality to the interaction (38).

Of central importance in the borderline patient's use of this defense are its consequences in terms of a weakening of his or her ego functioning. Klein (34) noted that projection of aggressive aspects of the self may result in a loss of attributes important for the development of power, potency, strength, and knowledge. Kernberg (30) suggested that the resultant failure of integration leads to incomplete development of internalized standards (e.g., guilt and internal delay of impulses) and other internal "structures" (18).

Similarly, according to Klein (34), the chronic

projection of positive aspects of the self (as seen in primitive idealization) may result in extreme dependency, loneliness, fear of parting, and fear of the loss of the capacity to love. Kernberg (7) suggested that the borderline patient's use of idealization in its primitive form involves no regard for the real person who is idealized but represents a use of the other as a "thing"—an "all positive" magical protection in a dangerous world (3, 7).

The borderline patient has been described as having a peculiar "empathy" for the unconscious impulses of other people (41, 42) and as having little or no ability to recognize the mature defenses, reaction formations, or other adaptive ego functions manifested by the other person in his struggle with these impulses (7, 43). This intuitive sensitivity allows for a powerful coercive use of projective identification because there is often some degree of perceptual accuracy in the projection that touches a conflicted area of the recipient. When frustrated and projecting their anger in therapy, for instance, borderline patients may utilize this intuition to provoke a response in such a way as to justify their distrust and may then destroy, devalue, or reject all the therapist has to offer (44).

COUNTERTRANSFERENCE

The use of these primitive defenses contributes to the transference-countertransference difficulties often seen in intensive treatment. Many authors have described the powerful countertransference responses evoked by the borderline patient (11, 13, 14, 19, 20, 22, 45). Unlike the more gradually developed, complex, empathic understanding that characterizes his or her response to neurotic patients, the therapist's response to the borderline patient's transference appears to be more rapid, intense, and stereotyped. Different therapists discover similar responses to these patients; the response seems less related to specific problems of the therapist's past and more to the patient's poorly integrated impulses (7).

Because of their defensive inability to integrate loving and angry aspects of the same internal image, borderline patients are inordinately sensitive to minor frustrations in treatment. In the face of such frustrations, their characteristic response is to withdraw all affectively positive perceptions of the therapist and reinvest them elsewhere. At this point, patients "lose" all memory of positive experiences with the therapist and feel abandoned. Through the mechanism of projective identification, they experience the therapist as attacking and rejecting and respond defensively to control their now projected rage (46). Their defensive response may include rage, devaluation, withdrawal, or paranoid thinking and an inability to call up the previously experienced image of a comforting therapist (19).

If the therapist exposed to these raw affective interchanges undergoes an "emphathic regression" (7) in an attempt to keep in touch with the patient, he may become vulnerable to countertransference guilt and anxiety. Many therapists who have devoted their lives to healing are concerned at some level about their capacity to hurt, which borderline patients unconsciously sense. In his introspective attempt to understand the patient, the therapist might find a punitive aspect of himself at whom the patient might "accurately" be angry. Such a counteridentification might evoke guilt in the therapist which, when perceived by the patient, would validate the patient's projection, making it difficult for the therapist to work on it collaboratively with the patient as a projection (46, 47). This blurring of ego boundaries between patient and therapist might contribute to the familiar regressive transference psychosis in which patients' reality testing is lost, their unmodified rage and guilt increase, and they experience the therapist as a reincarnation of the fantasied early frustrating parent.

Similarly, the unexpected and uncontrolled intensity of the patient's rage may make the therapist vulnerable to his own anxiety, which is potentially disruptive to the therapeutic work. Such anxiety in the therapist could be related to the possible loss of the relationship with the patient (with specific countertransference implications) or the need to manage his own hatred and need to retaliate (45, 48). In response to these countertransference feelings, Kernberg (7) suggested that otherwise sophisticated therapists may at times experience an almost masochistic submission to the patient's aggression, disproportionate doubts in their own capacity, and exaggerated fears of criticism by third parties.

In their description of the therapeutic task with borderline patients, several authors have discussed the need for the therapist to withstand these unmodified affects without withdrawal or retaliation. The therapeutic position is characterized as the provision of a "holding environment" (49), a response that includes the need 1) to reflect, absorb, transform, and feed back the patient's responses (7), 2) to maintain contact, concern, and emotional availability (50), 3) to set limits for the patient to help him or her manage internal and external stimuli, and 4) to accept the patient's ambivalence with continuing concern (19). This description of the therapeutic response in situations in which interpretation appears to have no effect (51) has its parallels in the developmental observations described below.

OBJECT RELATIONS THEORY

Much of the data derived from the above observations has been used by theorists in the development of object relations theory (7, 21, 33, 52–55). The basic assumption behind this theory is that one can understand the relationships between people through an examination of the internal images they have of one another. In the healthiest people, these images correspond rather accurately to the reality of the other person and are continually reshaped and reworked as new information is perceived and integrated. In less psychologically healthy people, the images are stereotyped, rigid, and relatively unchanged by new information. The theory proposes a model for the developmental shaping of these images as the child begins to separate the image of himself from that of his mother. Anna Freud (56) characterized this developmental line as proceeding from dependency to emotional self-reliance to adult relationships.

According to the theory, there are at least three major developmental tasks in this progression: 1) self-object differentiation, 2) the integration of loving and hating images and the development of object constancy, and 3) the further integration of these images into flexible psychic structures (for example, superego and ego ideal).

These ideas are based primarily on clinical observations of transference relationships with psychotic, borderline, and neurotic patients and are inferentially related to early child development. Self-object differentiation refers to the child's capacity to separate intrapsychically the boundaries of his own experience from his experience of his mother. Failure in this task is presumably seen in psychotic patients who have difficulty in recognizing the therapist's independent existence. The attainment of object constancy (or the "depressive position")(16, 34) is a consequence of the child's capacity to recognize himself simultaneously as both loving and hating in response to the image of another who is both gratifying and frustrating. Accomplishment of this task presumably allows the child to tolerate and master separation and loss by being able to maintain a comforting image of the mother (a "constant object image") despite her frustrating the child by her absence (11, 56). Further, the capacity to acknowledge angry feelings toward the image of a loved person leads to the development of the capacity for reality testing and the capacity to tolerate guilt, concern, and "internalized depression" (11, 56). "Internalized depression" in this sense refers to an experience of mourning and regret over lost "good" internal images, rather than the more primitive sense of impotent rage and defeat by external forces (7). Failure in this achievement of object constancy is presumably characteristic of borderline patients who have mastered self-object differentiation but cannot tolerate separation or ambivalence without regression.

This object relations view of borderline pathology is of interest in that it suggests a basis for the failure of object constancy. Presumably, the child must have a strong enough image of his positive relationship with his mother to be able to tolerate the integration of his images of negative interactions with his mother without being overwhelmed. Kernberg (7, 30) suggested that this failure of integration and the persistence of splitting is due to excessive aggression, either constitutional or from excessive or chronic early environmental frustration.

Horner (57) described the person who has mastered these tasks as "a separate individual who has a firm sense of self and other, who is able to relate to others as whole persons rather than simply need satisfiers, who can tolerate ambivalence . . . and who has the ability to sustain his own narcissistic equilibrium from resources within the self." Further integration, modification, and "depersonification" of these internalized relationships evolves into such psychic structures as superego and ego ideal (7, 30).

DEVELOPMENTAL PSYCHOLOGY

Many psychoanalytically oriented researchers who study preverbal infant development focus their attention on the intimate mother-child relationship, an area of particular interest to the student of borderline psychopathology. The literature, however, is filled with warnings about the dangers of direct extrapolation from infant observations to adult phenomena (58–61). Since the infant has a unique cognitive apparatus with little capacity for conscious memory and verbal symbolization, it has been suggested that the child observer's inferences are likely to be distorted by "retrospective falsifications and adultomorphic errors in empathy" (62). Several observers (63, 64)

have suggested that the closest one can get to preverbal experience in the adult patient is that which is filtered through the fantasies of the oedipal period, when the child's mental and verbal capacities begin to approximate more closely those of the adult. Theodore Shapiro (64) warned of the danger of the "great oralizing fallacy," which suggests that the first year of life so determines what follows that its stamp is irreparable. He offered the alternative hypothesis that each developmental stage presents a new opportunity for mental reorganization that allows earlier experiences to become less toxic.

Others (34, 54, 65) have argued that the very crudeness of the infant's mental apparatus and his crucial, all-encompassing internal struggle to differentiate himself from a symbiotic unity with the mother contain such a core, global, organizing experience that its traces must be seen (particularly if unsuccessful) in subsequent stages. At the very least, the metaphors derived from this struggle seem to be applicable to repetitive dynamic issues with which the borderline patient struggles.

As described above, the clearest, most comprehensive formulation about the relationship between borderline psychopathology and developmental psychology is that of Kernberg (30) and the object relations theorists (54). Kernberg suggested that borderline pathology is a consequence of a developmental failure occurring after self-object differentiation but before the development of object constancy. He described this failure as marked by a continuing defensive use of splitting, with resultant limitations in the capacity to test reality, to tolerate anxiety and frustration, and to sustain a stable, integrated relationship with an underlying attitude of basic trust (7, 46).

This formulation is apparently applicable to a large number of borderline patients, but it has been questioned by some authors, who have found two discernible groups or at least two different qualities of experience within the borderline population. These two qualities are variously described as schizoid versus aggressive (19), constricted versus expansive (12), compliant versus aggressive (13), obsessive ("as-if," "false self") versus hysterical (66), and "those who have given up" versus "those who are still searching" (3). Although Kernberg's formulation appears to apply to the second group in each of these pairs, it does not seem adequately to describe members of the first group, with their distant, "pseudoautonomous" functioning and their difficulty in engaging the other in anything but a compliant manner (13). Clearer formulations about both groups emerge from the developmental data of the symbiotic and separation-individuation periods (ages 0–3), when the issues of intrapsychic separation and the development of formed images first appear.

Symbiotic Period

Mahler (6) described the symbiotic period as extending from the second month (when the infant begins tactilely and visually to explore the mother) to the fifth month (when the infant begins to explore beyond the mother). She defined this period as characterized by the infant's acting as though his internal experience of himself and his mother were joined by a common boundary with no recognition of separateness.

During this period the tasks of the mother are to satisfy the infant's needs, to buffer and modify the stimuli he receives (both internal and external), and in effect to act as an auxiliary ego. Preparation for these tasks is facilitated by a regression in the mother (49, 68) that increases her empathy, reawakens fantasies of her own childhood experiences, and helps develop her capacity to provide a "holding environment" (49) in which the infant's "absolute need for empathy" is met.

Mahler (67) described the "mutual cuing" that must take place between infant and mother for normal symbiosis to take place. The infant's contribution to this interaction requires attributes of both perceptual ability (i.e., the capacity to receive and seek nurturance and attachment and to link patterns of experience) and stimulus sensitivity (i.e., sensitivity to touch and visual responses). The mother's tasks require her recognition and acceptance of her own infantile impulses, with a resultant continuing empathic responsiveness to similar impulses in her child.

Unacknowledged conflict in the mother in interaction over time with specific attributes of the child may result in an empathic failure that interferes with this "optimal symbiosis." Some authors (39, 42, 57, 69–71) have suggested that in such situations the infant may prematurely inhibit his dependency on his mother in order to respond to her defensive needs, a response that may result in premature ego development. Failure in the mother-child interaction during this period has been suggested as the origin of pathology for the first quality of experience within the borderline spectrum (i.e., the "pseudoautonomous" complaint, detached response).

If, for example, because of unconscious conflict about her own needs, the mother disavows them, sees them as "bad," and projects them onto her child, she may persistently withdrawn from or be relatively unresponsive to the child's actual needs because of the confusion with hers (projective identification). Several authors have suggested that such chronic nonresponsiveness is experienced by the child as a meaningless interruption, resulting in his eventual detachment (39, 70, 71) and formation of a "false self" (51) in which the child compliantly adapts to his mother's needs with relative abandonment of his own, since they represent a threat to a mother whom the child absolutely needs and who is relatively immune to his feedback (70).

This detached self is the consequence of a premature severing of the symbiotic tie before any internalization of maternal functions can occur. It leaves the child with a sense of detachment (72), a profound emptiness, and an undeveloped potential for the direct and personal experience of living (70). It is a distancing maneuver, presumably developed by the child to ward off the negative experience of the mother's chronic empathic failure and misinterpretation. The pseudoself is that which validates the mother's projection (70). According to Friedman (70), Winnicott suggested that the failure of interpretation in the therapy of patients with such false self-organization is due to their perception of the interpretation as another "act of attribution" by a nonempathic parent.

Separation-Individuation

Mahler and associates (27) divided the separation-individuation period (5 months–3 years) into four subphases: 1) differentiation (5–8 months), 2) "practicing" (8–16 months), 3) rapprochement (16–25 months), and 4) object constancy (25 months–3 years). Within this period the child's task is to emerge gradually from the symbiotic unit and to develop increasing autonomy both internally and externally. Successful completion of this developmental period results in the capacity for frustration tolerance, the mastery of separation anxiety, and the maintenance of self-esteem.

It is during these subphases of separation-individuation that the issues central to the dynamics of borderline psychopathology first appear. It is here that the conflict between the push for autonomy and the wish to unite is for the first time apparent in the behavior of the child.

During the differentiation subphase (5–8 months), the child remains anchored to the mother but develops an increasing alertness, an outer orientation, and finally, a social smile that increasingly focuses on the mother (59, 73). In her absence the child gets restless and unhappy, but he smiles on her return. This fact suggests the initial development of "recognition memory": the ability for perception to revive a memory trace (73, 74).

At 8 months the infant develops "stranger anxiety." Mahler and associates (27) observed that if there is a good symbiotic period the infant reacts to strangers with curiosity and wonderment; if it is less good the infant demonstrates more anxiety. These observations are congruent with Kernberg's formulation (30) that a greater quantity of frustration during symbiosis would threaten the infant's loving experiences, resulting in a prolonged defensive splitting and projection of fearsome negative experience onto the "stranger."

In the "practicing" subphase (5–16 months), the infant develops the capacity for locomotion with an exuberance and excitement that temporarily enables him to ignore the presence of his mother. Exhausted by autonomous movements, the infant periodically returns to the mother for "emotional refueling" (27), a brief contact that rapidly enables the infant to restore his or her energy and momentum. During this subphase there is evidence that the child begins to notice and tolerate his mother's departure, since he tones down his activities ("low keyedness") in her absence (27).

Kernberg (7, 30) suggested that the child begins to be able to differentiate between positive images of himself and his mother during this period; similar self-object differentiation within images of negative experiences occur somewhat later. He suggested, however, that this differentiation of images is still tentative at this point and vulnerable to "regressive refusion" at times of stress.

The rapproachement subphase (16–25 months) is the period during which the conflict between autonomy and reunion is demonstrated most clearly in the child's behavior and response. Even the language of the descriptions evokes images familiar to therapists of borderline patients. It is in this phase that the toddler's behavior indicates a sense of increased separateness, loneliness, helplessness, a constant concern with the mother's presence, and increased separation and stranger anxiety. It is during this period, according to Kernberg (7, 30), that the child develops firm boundaries between the experience of himself and that of his mother. The infant now responds to more than a refueling place, he responds to her.

Observers of the child in this subphase have described the toddler's active interest in his mother's presence and his developing need for her

to share actively in his autonomous achievements. Mahler (58) noted two normal patterns: shadowing of the mother and darting away expecting to be swept up in her arms. Inferred from this behavior is both the wish for reunion and the fear of engulfment.

In children who have difficulties during this subphase, Mahler (58) observed increased aggressive behavior manifested by rapidly alternating clinging to and repudiation of the mother. McDevitt (73) noted that the less a child can assert himself pleasurably in independent play, the greater the frequency of aggressive clinging and repudiation. The implication of these observations is that significant conflict is precipitated in the mother-child relationship if their interaction does not support the child's developmental move toward autonomy.

With the development of the capacity for "representational thought" (75) and symbolization, the toddler develops the use of transitional objects and begins to use his relationship with his father more significantly as a way to mediate the shift from the exclusive tie with his mother toward autonomy (28).

At about 18 months the infant develops the capacity both to retain the memory of a concrete object after it has disappeared ("object permanence") and to evoke the image of the mother in her absence ("evocative memory")(74, 75). Throughout most of rapprochement, although the image of the mother appears to occur to the child, it does not seem to persist during her absence, suggesting an incomplete internalization of the mother's caring functions and a persisting reliance on her actual presence. Kernberg (7, 30) suggested that when the child is frustrated by his mother's departure, he is overwhelmed with rage and his comforting image of the loving relationship with her is threatened. To preserve this comforting fantasy, the child dissociates it and sees himself as a "bad" child abandoned by an angry mother. The child then experiences profound separation anxiety in the form of hopelessness and a negative sense of self, with complete loss of the "good" images.

The task of the mother during this subphase is to tolerate sufficiently her own wishes for dependency and autonomy so that she can respond in a stable empathic way to corresponding wishes in her child without seeing them as "bad" or dangerous and responding with retaliation or withdrawal (49, 76). Mahler and associates (76) described two kinds of empathic failure. One group of mothers who had difficulties in tolerating their own dependency responded with hurt and anger to their child's clinging by saying in effect, "A minute ago you didn't want me, now I don't want you." Presumably, this response would evoke anxiety in the child about his wishes for nurturance. A second group of mothers with conflicts about autonomy responded to the child's autonomous moves with, "You think you can manage on your own, well go ahead." This response threatens the child with abandonment and inhibits his freedom to explore because of the reactive fantasy: "If I grow up, I'll be all alone."

The implication drawn from these observations is that this kind of chronic withdrawal represents the mother's defensive inability to distinguish between her own unresolved needs (for the child's response to her) and her recognition of the needs of her child for autonomy and support. This defensive response from the mother is contributed to by her own conflicts and by the increased aggressiveness of her 2-year-old during the anal period.

Adler (44) described the "good enough mother" (49) of this subphase as one who is not afraid of her own or her child's anger and can be firm when she needs to frustrate. She has confidence in her basic goodness and a capacity to care without having to retaliate for old hurts. The descriptions of Mahler and associates (27) indicate that there is a broad spectrum of "good enough" mothering responses. Typical failures in the interaction between mother and child, then, are likely to represent chronic empathic insensitivity from mothers at the ends of this spectrum in interaction with particularly sensitive infants.

Toward the end of rapprochement, the child's cognitive apparatus sufficiently matures so that he can notice that the same mother both gratifies and frustrates. Winnicott (24) suggested that if the mother can "contain" the child's aggression (by nonanxious, firm limit setting) while continuing to provide love and understanding, she will demonstrate to him that she is not created or changed by his impulses and that she is separate from him and not a creation of his projections. Such a response allows the child to develop a relationship with her as a real and autonomous person and helps the child to tolerate his anger and put it in perspective by allowing him to recognize that it cannot destroy his loving mother (by turning her into a bad, angry, or anxious mother). In addition, the mother's response will help strengthen the child's conviction in the strength of his good self-image and that of his mother and will decrease the child's fear of his own aggressive tendencies (7).

Alternatively, if the mother, because of unacknowledged conflict revived by the interaction, retaliates for her infant's aggression or withdraws from his demands, she will confirm his fear of aggressive fantasies, making it difficult for him subsequently to integrate them. Responding to the withdrawal, the infant generates increased rage and greater demands (e.g., clinging), which contributes to a spiraling crisis in their interaction and an intensification of the infant's need for defensive splitting and projection, the phenomena characteristic of borderline patients.

With successful negotiation of rapprochement the child develops the capacity for ambivalence and object constancy (27, 74). The ambivalently held image of the mother is more stable in the face of frustration, providing the infant an inner sense of comfort and contributing to his or her capacity to experience guilt, concern, depression, and increasing anxiety tolerance. The infant's image of himself now begins to develop increasing complexity, affects are modulated, ego control of impulses is increased, and there is a clearer sense of self and others. Observers of the child during this subphase (59, 73) have noted that with this development there is a shift from self-centered, demanding, clinging behaviors to more mature expressions of affection, trust, confidence, regard for the interests and feelings of others, cooperation, sharing, making sacrifices, and offering gifts.

Latency

The relative absence of clinical descriptions of borderline phenomena in the literature of the latency period (ages 6–10) suggests a relative decrease in symptomatic behavior during this period. Chiland and Lebovici (77), however, described the two borderline qualities of inhibition and excitability as emerging in some children during latency in response to the disciplinary and learning requirements of school. These children were described as rejecting attempts at communication and refusing to carry out tasks. Despite high learning performance, they were described as exploding periodically in rage. The authors commented on the characteristic contrast between good intellectual development and poor relationship modalities in these children that marked their "developmental disharmony." Again, in these descriptions, the two types of borderline presentation were seen: cold, detached, and removed versus subject to unpredictable outbursts of rage. The authors also commented on the probable use of projective identification by these children, noting that "the interlocutor himself feels the whole burden of anxiety."

Adolescence

Several authors (65, 78, 79) have perceived a recapitulation of the dynamic themes of separation-individuation during the adolescence of the borderline child, a period when borderline symptomatology often becomes apparent. With my colleagues at NIMH (78, 79) I observed a family group regression that occurs during the adolescence of the borderline patient in which family members respond with retaliation or withdrawal to autonomous or dependent behaviors of the adolescent. The conflict between the striving for autonomy and the fulfillment of dependency needs revived in adolescence is inadequately resolved in these families because of a regressive, shared use of projective identification (38) in which the adolescent becomes the bearer of disavowed aspects of the parents. In some families the child's dependent wishes are seen as devouring demands from which the family members withdraw. This withdrawal often represents parental anxiety about their own wishes to be given to, which they cannot acknowledge. In other families, the adolescent's autonomous strivings are interpreted as a hateful abandonment of the family, which the parents cannot accept. In these families parental strivings for autonomy are disavowed, seen as bad, and projected onto the adolescent, resulting in a defensive inability to respond to the adolescent's autonomous development with the necessary support.

Masterson and Rinsley (65, 80) described the latter group in terms of the adolescent's "abandonment depression," which is defended against by splitting, acting out, and other pathological maneuvers. They viewed as the "basic dynamic theme" of the borderline patient that "the borderline mother withdraws emotional supplies at her child's efforts to separate and individuate." This is a characteristic phenomenon observed by several authors (42, 78). The consequence of this maternal withdrawal in the face of separation is that the child is torn between the engulfment of symbiosis if he moves toward his mother and the experience of loss and abandonment if he moves away. Zinner and my study of the families of these patients in interaction (78) revealed that this retaliatory withdrawal of supplies is a shared family dynamic that is only one element in a family regression involving all family members.

The borderline adolescent's alienation, aggressive responses, and inadequately structured self-image (81) contribute to this family turmoil, but parental contributions are also significant. Our analysis of family interactions (79) revealed that these parents depend heavily on projective identification for their own defensive organization and that in this process there is considerable collusion from the child. We also observed a blurring of parental capacity to experience themselves as separate from the particular child in the areas of conflict and an idiosyncratic but often overlapping content of parental projections involving disavowed wishes for dependency or autonomous strivings (78, 79).

Although Masterson (82) found the parents of the borderline patient to be borderline themselves, this finding does not agree with our observations of significant variability in parental psychopathology (79) or with the observations of Margaret Singer (8) who found that 84% of the borderline patients had normal or neurotic parents according to psychological tests. Although some authors (6, 65)[1] have discussed these parents in descriptive terms (i.e., "ineffectual, passive father," "intrusive, dependent mother"), other authors (78, 79, 83) have described a more dynamic, shifting tension between parent and child.

The latter observers illustrated how family members' use of primitive defenses may be encapsulated in response to issues involving certain offspring. In interaction with siblings or the outside world, they may use more advanced ego defenses and greater maturity but may regress to fixation points relating to deficient resolution of symbiosis and identity formation in relation to the designated borderline child. Singer and Wynne (83) commented on the discrepancy between the severity of the disturbance when family members interact compared with the relatively mild disturbance each family member shows individually. They suggested that in attempting to understand the family pathology it is insufficient to look only at the individual parent in relation to the individual child. Their data and ours (78, 79, 83) indicate that there are contributions from the entire family group that affect the nature of the developmental interference.

DISCUSSION

The continuing study of the psychopathology of the borderline patient has inevitably led to an increased interest in and examination of a two-person psychology. The remnants of early symbiotic interaction seen in the interpersonal use of projective identification by the borderline patient are evident in the patient-therapist interaction, the mother-child response, and the family life of the borderline adolescent. In contrast to the complex fantasy life of the neurotic patient, with his more differentiated and articulated presentation of intrapsychic conflict (usually involving triadic fantasies), the borderline patient presents more stereotyped, primitive difficulties, frequently communicated nonverbally. Often the key to a comprehension of these difficulties lies in the affects and reactive fantasies of the caretaker (e.g., therapist or mother).

The growing experience in intensive work with such patients has led to a closer study of countertransference phenomena (7, 30), the setting or "framework" of the therapeutic interaction (21, 84), the nature of the "holding environment" (10, 46, 50, 62), the components and complexities of empathy and its failures (10, 24, 36–40, 44, 48, 57, 62, 71, 79), and the unconscious communicative process involved in family interaction (78, 79, 83). In addition, the nature of psychological defense has been reevaluated.

Although Klein (34, 35) focused her study of projective identification on the nature of the child's internal fantasies, more recent work has focused on the collaborative nature of this defense (38, 39, 70, 78, 79, 84, 85). Much of this work supports the idea that there is an entire range of interpersonal defenses in which the collaboration of a particular other is required to maintain defensive equilibrium.

Certainly, unconscious conflict in the mother, externalized in her relationship with the infant, appears to be related in some way to difficulties in the process of "adequate symbiosis" as well as in the carefully choreographed movements required for normal separation-individuation. Unconscious fantasy and the defensive collaborative use of particular family members to represent disavowed aspects of inner conflict in the family of the borderline adolescent seem to be a significant impediment to development. It remains to be seen how these family interactions affect the environmental matrix in which the infant's earliest sense of self develops. This question remains a relatively unexplored frontier of developmental theory.

Although there remains significant controversy about the applicability of child observation to adult phenomena as well as serious debate about the possibility of recreating elements of the relationship between infant and mother in the therapeutic situation (86), conceptual attempts to make these comparisons have produced fascinating new insights. The delineation of the therapist's

"holding" function, of his task of "containing" the patient's affects and projections, and of the hazard of his own projections interfering with the therapeutic process (46, 84, 85) have all emerged in part from this study of the borderline patient and his development. All seem in some way to have relevance to the developing understanding of the complex preverbal interaction between infantile impulses and human environmental responses from which personality evolves.

The increasing overlap of the observations, formulations, and inferences derived from the three different areas of study reviewed above suggests at least an approximation to reality that future follow-up studies should address. The data from the current studies have already made an important contribution to the therapist's ability to listen better to particular elements of these patient's productions, to develop more accurate empathic responses, and to provide borderline patients with some coherent organization for their chaotic experience.

The author would like to thank Drs. Leon Shapiro, Shervert Frazier, Roger Shapiro, Susan Abelson, and Peter Panzarino, and Diane Englund, A.C.S.W., for their helpful comments on an earlier draft of this paper.

REFERENCES

1. Mack JE (ed): Borderline States in Psychiatry. New York, Grune & Stratton, 1975, pp 135–138
2. Gunderson JG, Singer MT: Defining borderline patients: an overview. Am J Psychiatry 132:1–10, 1975
3. Grinker RR: The borderline syndrome: a phenomenological view, in Borderline Personality Disorders, Edited by Hartocollis P. New York, International Universities Press, 1977
4. Gunderson JG: Characteristics of borderlines. Ibid
5. Zetzel ER: The so-called good hysteric (1968), in The Capacity for Emotional Growth. By Zetzel ER. New York, International Universities Press, 1970
6. Grinker RR, Werble B: The Borderline Patient. New York, Jason Aronson, 1977
7. Kernberg OF: Borderline Conditions and Pathological Narcissism. New York, Jason Aronson, 1975
8. Singer MT: The borderline diagnosis and psychological tests: review and research, in Borderline Personality Disorders. Edited by Hartocollis P. New York, International Universities Press, 1977
9. Grinker RR, Werble B, Drye R: The Borderline Syndrome: A Behavioral Study of Ego Functions. New York, Basic Books, 1968
10. Adler G: Hospital treatment of borderline patients. Am J Psychiatry 130:32–36, 1973
11. Zetzel ER: A developmental approach to the borderline patient. Am J Psychiatry 128:867–871, 1971
12. Singer M: The borderline delinquent: the interlock-

ing of intrapsychic and interactional determinants. Int Rev Psychoanal 2:249–440, 1975

13. Robbins MD: Borderline personality organization: the need for a new theory. J Am Psychoanal Assoc 24:831–853, 1976

14. Kernberg OF: Transference and countertransference in the treatment of borderline patients. Journal of the National Association of Private Psychiatric Hospitals 7:14–24, 1975

15. Kernberg OF: Structural change and its impediments, in Borderline Personality Disorders. Edited by Hartocollis P. New York, International Universities Press, 1977

16. Winnicott DW: The depressive position in normal emotional development, in Collected Papers: Through Pediatrics to Psychoanalysis. By Winnicott DW. New York, Basic Books, 1958

17. Zetzel ER: On the incapacity to bear depression (1965), in The Capacity for Emotional Growth. By Zetzel ER. New York, International Universities Press, 1970

18. Pine F: On the concept "borderline" in children: a clinical essay. Psychoanal Study Child 29:341–368, 1974

19. Adler G: The usefulness of the "borderline" concept in psychotherapy, in Borderline States in Psychiatry. Edited by Mack JE. New York, Grune & Stratton, 1975

20. Modell AH: Primitive object relationship and the predisposition to schizophrenia. Int J Psychoanal 44:282–291, 1963

21. Modell AH: Object Love and Reality. New York, International Universities Press, 1968

22. Modell AH: A narcissistic defense against affects and the illusion of self sufficiency. Int J psychoanal 56:275–282, 1975

23. Winnicott DW: Transitional objects and transitional phenomena, in Collected Papers. By Winnicott DW. London, Tavistock Publications, 1958

24. Winnicott DW: The use of an object. Int J Psychoanal 41:585–594, 1969

25. Volkan VD: Primitive Internalized Object Relations. New York, International Universities Press, 1976

26. Fintzy RT: Vicissitudes of a transitional object in a borderline child. Int J Psychoanal 52:107–114, 1971

27. Mahler MS, Pine F, Bergman A: The Psychological Birth of the Human Infant. New York, Basic Books, 1975

28. Abelin EL: The role of the father in the separation-individuation process, in Separation-Individuation: Essays in Honor of Margaret S Mahler. Edited by McDevitt JB,Settlage CF. New York, International Universities Press, 1971

29. Lewis AB: Perception of self in borderline states. Am J Psychiatry 124:1491–1498, 1968

30. Kernberg OF: Object-Relations Theory and Clinical Psychoanalysis. New York, Jason Aronson, 1976

31. Heimann P: Comment on Dr Kernberg's paper. Int J Psychoanal 47:254–260, 1966

32. Pruyser P: What splits in "splitting." Bull Menninger Clin 39:1–46, 1975

33. Lichtenberg J, Slap H: Notes on the concept of splitting and the defense mechanism of the splitting of

representations. J Am Psychoanal Assoc 21:772–787, 1973

34. Klein M: Notes on some schizoid mechanisms. Int J Psychoanal 27:99–110, 1946

35. Klein M: On identification, in New Directions in Psychoanalysis. By Klein M. New York, Basic Books, 1955

36. Novick J, Kelly K: Projection and externalization. Psychoanal Study Child 24:69–95, 1970

37. Malin A, Grotstein JS: Projective identification in the therapeutic process. Int J Psychoanal 47:26–31, 1966

38. Zinner J, Shapiro R: Projective identification as a mode of perception and behavior in families of adolescents. Int J Psychoanal 53:523–530, 1972

39. Brodey WM: On the dynamics of narcissism: I. Externalization and early ego development. Psychoanal Study Child 20:165–193, 1965

40. Laing RD: The Self and Others: Further Studies in Sanity and Madness. Chicago, Quadrangle, 1962

41. Krohn A: Borderline "empathy" and differentiation of object relations: a contribution to the psychology of object relations. Int J Psychoanal Psychother 3:142–165, 1974

42. Carter L, Rinsley DB: Vicissitudes of "empathy" in a borderline adolescent. Int Rev Psychoanal 4:317–326, 1977

43. Fast I, Chethik M: Some aspects of object relationships in borderline children. Int J Psychoanal 53:485–497, 1972

44. Adler G: Helplessness in the helpers. Br J Med Psychol 45:315–326, 1972

45. Maltsberger JT, Buie DH: Countertransference hate in the treatment of suicidal patients. Arch Gen Psychiatry 30:625–633, 1974

46. Shapiro ER, Shapiro RL, Zinner J, et al: The borderline ego and the working alliance: indications for family and individual treatment in adolescence. Int J Psychoanal 58:77–87, 1977

47. Grinberg L: On a specific aspect of countertransference due to the patient's projective identification. Int J Psychoanal 43:436–440, 1962

48. Winnicott DW: Hate in the countertransference. Int J Psychoanal 30:69–74, 1949

49. Winnicott DW: The theory of the parent-infant relationship. Int J Psychoanal 41:585–595, 1960

50. Kernberg OF: Technical considerations in the treatment of borderline personality organization. J Am Psychoanal Assoc 24:795–829, 1976

51. Winnicott DW: Ego distortion in terms of the true and false self, in The Maturational Processes and the Facilitating Environment. By Winnicott DW. New York, International Universities Press, 1965

52. Guntrip H: Schizoid Phenomena, Object Relations and the Self. New York, International Universities Press, 1969

53. Jacobson E: The Self and the Object World. New York, International Universities Press, 1964

54. Blanck G, Blanck R: Ego Psychology: Theory and Practice. New York, Columbia University Press, 1974

55. Gedo JE, Goldberg A: Models of the Mind. Chicago, University of Chicago Press, 1973

56. Freud A: Normality and Pathology in Childhood. New York, International Universities Press, 1965

57. Horner AH: Early object relations and the concept of depression. Int Rev Psychoanal 1:337–340, 1974

58. Mahler MS: A study of the separation-individuation process and its possible application to borderline phenomena in the psychoanalytic situation. Psychoanal Study Child 26:403–424, 1971

59. Winestine MC: The experience of separation-individuation in infancy and its reverberations through the course of life: I. Infancy and childhood. J Am Psychoanal Assoc 21:135–154, 1973

60. Balint M: The Basic Fault. London, Tavistock, 1968

61. Settlage CF: The psychoanalytic understanding of narcissistic and borderline personality disorders: advances in developmental theory. J Am Psychoanal Assoc 25:805–834, 1977

62. Kohut H: The Analysis of the Self. New York, International Universities Press, 1971

63. Thiel JH, Treurniet N: Panel on "the implications of recent advances in the knowledge of child development for the treatment of adults." Int J Psychoanal 57:429–440, 1976

64. Shapiro T: Oedipal distortions in severe character pathologies: developmental and theoretical considerations. Psychoanal Q 46:559–579, 1977

65. Masterson JF: Treatment of the Borderline Adolescent: A Developmental Approach. New York, John Wiley & Sons, 1972

66. Meissner WW: Some aspects of the diagnostic differences between borderline conditions and psychosis. Presented at an academic conference, McLean Hospital, Belmont, Mass, Dec 2, 1977

67. Mahler MS: On Human Symbiosis and the Vicissitudes of Individuation. New York, International Universities Press, 1968

68. Benedek T: Parenthood as a developmental phase. J Am Psychoanal Assoc 7:389–417, 1959

69. Deutsch H: Some forms of emotional disturbance and their relationship to schizophrenia. Psychoanal Q 11:301–321, 1942

70. Friedman LJ: Current psychoanalytic object relations theory and its clinical implications. Int J Psychoanal 56:137–146, 1975

71. Khan MMR: The concept of cumulative trauma. Psychoanal Study Child 18:286–306, 1963

72. Bowlby J: Attachment and Loss, vol 2: Separation. New York, Basic Books, 1973

73. McDevitt JB: Separation-individuation and object constancy. J Am Psychoanal Assoc 23:713–742, 1975

74. Fraiberg S: Libidinal object constancy and mental representation. Psychoanal Study Child 24:9–47, 1969

75. Piaget J: The Psychology of Intelligence. London, Routledge & Kegan Paul, 1947

76. Mahler MS, Pine F, Bergman A: The mother's reaction to her toddler's drive for individuation, in Parenthood. Edited by Anthony EJ, Benedek T. Boston, Little, Brown and Co, 1970

77. Chiland C, Lebovici S: Borderline or prepsychotic conditions in childhood—a French point of view, in Borderline Personality Disorders. Edited by Hartocollis P. New York, International Universities Press, 1977

78. Zinner J, Shapiro ER: Splitting in families of borderline adolescents, in Borderline States in Psychiatry. Edited by Mack JE. New York, Grune & Stratton, 1975

79. Shapiro ER, Zinner J, Shapiro RL, et al: The influence of family experience on borderline personality development. Int Rev Psychoanal 2:399–411, 1975

80. Masterson SJ, Rinsley DB: The borderline syndrome: the role of the mother in the genesis and psychic structure of the borderline personality. Int J Psychoanal 56:163–177, 1975

81. Giovacchini PL: The adolescent process and character formation: clinical aspects. Adolescent Psychiatry 2:269–284, 1973

82. Masterson JF: The splitting mechanism of the borderline adolescent: developmental and clinical aspects, in Borderline States in Psychiatry. Edited by Mack JE. New York, Grune & Stratton, 1975

83. Singer MT, Wynne LC: Thought disorder and family relations of schizophrenics: IV. Results and implications. Arch Gen Psychiatry 12:201–212, 1965

84. Langs R: The Bipersonal Field. New York, Jason Aronson, 1976

85. Bion WR: Elements of Psychoanalysis. New York. Basic Books, 1963

86. Fleming J: Some observations on object constancy in the psychoanalysis of adults. J Am Psychoanal Assoc 23:843–859, 1975

DEPENDENCY:
NORMAL AND PATHOLOGICAL

JOHN C. NEMIAH

Dependency is not necessarily a pathological need, but becomes so when it is increased at the expense of other psychological factors. Mental health is a proper balance among the various psychological forces that constitute personality.

One restless and troubled night before the walls of Troy, Agamemnon, the leader of the Greeks, was unable to sleep. Concerned over the perilous position of his troops, he went to the tent of wise old Nestor to share his anxiety. In the course of their discussion Nestor could not refrain from a caustic comment about Agamemnon's younger brother, Menelaus, for being asleep at such a critical time and leaving all the work to Agamemnon. The latter, while informing Nestor that he had just found Menelaus up and about, none-the-less implicitly agreed with Nestor's criticism in these words: "Sir, another time I should urge you to chide him, for he is often lax and unwilling to be active—not that he hesitates out of fear or because of stupidity, but because he looks to me and waits for my prompting."

In the 2800 years that have elapsed since Homer's portrayal of Agamemnon's gentle disapproval of his brother's reliance upon him, the attitude toward dependency has changed little, if at all. We respect and admire the strong and self-reliant, and pity, even scorn, the weak and depen-

dent person. In the field of medicine this attitude is particularly evident in the current concepts of dependency and dependency needs, which are invoked (especially in the theories of psychosomatic medicine) to explain the genesis of symptoms and the pathological reactions to illness and injury. The tacit assumption seems to be that dependency (and the passive attitude that often accompanies it) is pathological, and the term "passive-dependent character" used to describe patients is often invective rather than a diagnosis. Our reaction as physicians to our patients' dependency needs is an important and complex problem; our focus here, however, must be limited to the nature of dependency itself, and to its place in man's psychological functioning.

REPRESENTATIVE CASES

Let us begin our investigation by examining two patients. Although each of these brief descriptions is that of an individual person, it represents a type of behavior pattern repeatedly observed by the psychiatrist and his colleagues.

1. M.S., a man of 42, lives with his mother. He has never married, preferring not to leave home. He has not worked for 10 years, ever since the time of a hermorrhoidectomy. His mother supports both of them by working as a cleaning woman, and in addition takes care of her house and her son, making his meals, cleaning his room and doing his laundry. Occasionally he will help around the house if she is sick or will run errands for her to get the groceries, but in recent years because of phobias he has not like straying far from home alone—in fact, he feels comfortable going places only when his mother accompanies him.

2. A.N., a man of 41, married and the father of an adolescent son, prides himself on his strength and indepen-

Reprinted from Journal of the Kentucky State Medical Association 61:415–419, 1963.

dence. He has always been a self-reliant person. Even as a boy he had a paper route and did odd jobs to make his own spending money so that he would not have to ask his parents for help. He left home at 16 to work full time in order to "be on his own," and now as an adult, he always seeks out the hardest, most challenging kinds of work, volunteering for jobs that no one else dares attempt, or for tasks that other men have tried and failed.

He works long hours (often 12 to 14 hours a day) and refused to take time off from work for vacations or for minor illnesses; furthermore, he is proud that he always does a conscientious job, giving his employers all or more than they require. He never likes to ask for help, and although always willing to lend a hand to someone else in need, he insists on "doing for himself" whenever he wants anything. He will not borrow money or things, and "does without" if he can't get whatever he wants for himself and by himself. He never confides his problems in anyone else, and on one occasion, when unemployed during a depression, he refused to take governmental relief, considering it "charity"; he preferred to starve if "he could not make his own way".

At first glance there is a world of difference between these two men, the one still living in the shelter of his mother's bosom, the other striking out courageously on his own. There should be little disagreement that the term "dependent" applies to M.S., and it is apparent that he is dependent to a pathological degree. Most men of 42, even if they have not married and assumed the responsibility of supporting a family, are at least working and providing for themselves. It is unusual to find a grown man, whose physical capacities are intact, so needful of his mother's presence that he has to have her with him when he ventures away from the house; and it is a rare man who would allow his mother to provide his sustenance and look after his physical needs. This is behavior characteristic of a two-year-old, not a forty-two-year old.

A.N., on the contrary, seems to live his life at the other end of the spectrum. He is strong, courageous, conscientious and self-reliant. Even the words used to describe him carry overtones of worth that lead one to admire him. And indeed the qualities so evident in him are of value to himself and to society. They have enabled him from an early age to have the things he wants—things that he might not have obtained had he relied on others to give them to him. They allow him to provide well for his family, and to achieve a certain amount of success and reputation in his work. They endow him with attributes that make him valued by others—employers like him for his skill, his initiative and his faithful conscientiousness. His friends like him for his honesty, and his altruistic helpfulness. In short, A.N. seems to be an ideal man.

INDEPENDENCE AS DEFENSE

A little reflection, however, raises the suspicion that there are flaws in the strengths so obvious in A.N. and others like him. There appears to be something exaggerated in his stance of strength—he is too set on showing no sign of dependence, of incapacity, of weakness. If one talks to the relatives or close friends of such people one's suspicions are confirmed: Those who know them well complain that they are "too independent," that they keep too much to themselves. They are, furthermore, often emotionally aloof; they will not allow others to help or to direct, even when the situation is entirely appropriate, or even demands it.

As physicians dealing with such people we soon discover the difficulties which their behavior as patients poses for our adequate management of their illnesses: Out of fear of showing weakness they hide serious symptoms, and compromise our diagnostic operations. They find it hard, if not impossible, to take orders even when these are necessary for the recovery of their health. They are often quite unable to remain inactive for the period required to heal a lesion—they leave the hospital against medical advice and return to strenuous work completely against the dictates of medical judgment. In short, characteristics of behavior that ordinarily are assets become liabilities when they are seriously ill.

What is more, if such people fall victim to a serious and crippling illness or injury that despite all their drive to activity forces them for long periods of time to remain invalided, one finds paradoxical behavior patterns emerging: They become excessively demanding of other people (doctors, nurses, families and others on whom they are forced to rely). They become dependent on others to a degree far in excess of the limitations to activity posed by their physical infirmities. And even when their physical lesions are healed so that they are ready to return to work and to resume their former life of activity, they persist in their passive and dependent behavior, complaining of symptoms, demanding help and support from others, refusing to do anything for themselves. They suffer from what is clinically termed a regressive reaction, and are now as totally helpless as they once were totally self-reliant. With their symptoms as an excuse, they have become as dependent and ineffective as our patient M.S.

If one explores the psychological structure of such patients, one discovers an interesting fact: Over and above its intrinsic value, their behavior pattern of independence serves a defensive function. Such people are so frightened by the idea of in any way being dependent on others that they lean over backward to be entirely the opposite—totally self-reliant. Although they appear to have had no dependency needs before becoming sick or injured, these needs become obvious once they are incapacitated. The incapacity does not simply create the needs—it uncovers and unleashes them. For the needs have always been there as a part of the patient's total personality structure; they have, however, been rendered inoperative and have been kept out of the patient's conscious awareness by his defensive reaction formation of excessive self-reliance and independence. Once they appear in the open around the focus of the symptoms of an injury or illness (which renders their usual defences of activity inoperative and invites the dependency needs into overt, conscious expression) the intensity and strength of the needs becomes apparent.

UNIVERSALITY OF DEPENDENCY

Such observations of patients' psychological functioning tell us something of importance: Dependency is a universal human phenomenon. It is not in itself an abnormal or pathological need, but becomes so only when it has certain quantitative and qualitative characteristics.

No one is concerned over the total helplessness and dependency of the infant on his mother for every aspect of his physical and emotional needs. As the child develops, a drive (which appears to be a basic human impulse) toward activity and independent self-reliance makes its appearance. The child wants to do things for himself—to feed himself, dress himself, and often to do things beyond his abilities. The child's determination is often intense, and touching to observe—as one little boy said when his father remarked, "Shall I help you?" in the face of his struggle to do something obviously beyond his skills, "No! I help me!" And even as the child's capacities to take care of his physical needs have matured and developed, he still needs the love and emotional support of his parents. None of us ever outgrows these needs, no matter how effective and strong we become as adults. There are always times when we need concrete help for something beyond our capacities (the help of a doctor's special skills when we are sick, for example), and all of us need the love and emotional support of family and friends, especially in times of trouble. Such human dependence of one person on another is not pathological.

It becomes pathological in at least two ways. In the first place the intense dependency needs characteristic of the infant may persist, and (for a variety of reasons) the drive to autonomy may fail to develop. As the person grows into physical adulthood, his dependency becomes excessive, and is almost untempered by a weak drive toward self-reliance that has remained underdeveloped. On the other hand, a child may early in life develop a fear and mistrust of depending on others—again for a variety of reasons, one important factor being a failure on the part of others adequately to care for his needs. He tends more and more to rely on himself, excessively and prematurely, and the unsatisfied dependency needs, though increasingly pushed beneath the surface, remain potentially strong, just because they have not been adequately gratified.

In each of these cases, one aspect of the growing person's personality has been developed at the expense of the other. In the one, as exemplified by M.S., the dependency needs flourish and autonomy remains stunted; in the other, as seen in A.N., autonomy develops at the expense of the dependency needs. Although on the surface, each of these types of persons seems totally different from one another, they are seen, when one examines their character structure, to have certain features in common. And each of them has an unbalanced character structure, as contrasted with the normal person in whom dependency and autonomy have reached a more equitable equilibrium. The concept of a balance of the elements of personality structure is an important one, and we shall return to it later. But first we must examine one other factor that frequently adds to the problems that exist in patients with the personality difficulties we have been discussing.

THE REGRESSIVE REACTION

In the patient who suffers a regressive reaction, there is another paradoxical contrast beside that between his former strength and his present helplessness: Despite his dependent, demanding, often querulous behavior, he still thinks of himself as being essentially a strong, self-reliant person, and is convinced that he would be active now if it were not for his symptoms, on which he blames all his difficulties. Even though his actions belie him, he stoutly maintains that he wants to be active and self-reliant. ("I'd go to work tomorrow, Doc, if it weren't for these pains" is his repeated refrain.) In other words, his goal, his ideal of behavior for himself remains the same as it was before his injury occurred or his sickness began. What is more, recognizing how much his present state of invalidism falls short of his ideal, he often becomes quite depressed over the loss of his independence and chides himself for his weakness—not realizing how much of his predicament stems from the underlying dependency needs, of which he still remains unconscious. Furthermore, if we focus on his ideals for himself, we find that they are exceedingly lofty, demanding and uncompromising—he cannot and will not knowingly lower his standards of behavior under any circumstances, and his conscience pricks him sternly if he feels he has in any way fallen short of his ideals.

Superficially, the overtly dependent person, like M.S. would appear to have no such lofty ideals, and yet as one explores the psychological structure of this group of people, one finds that they, too, frequently have excessively high standards for achievement—goals of excellence, strength and perfection that are often way beyond their real capabilities. The obvious behavioral difference between them and the overtly independent group of people may be understood in part as follows: The latter feel capable of achieving their ideals and are often able to live up to their self-imposed standards for long periods of time. The former, on the contrary, are convinced from the start that they have not the capacity to gain their ideal goal—in the very act of trying to reach it, they are insecure, self-doubting, and convinced that their attempts can only end in failure. To obviate the pain of the anxiety and depression that accompanies this desperate insecurity they reach out to others for help and for reassurance—reassurance in the form of praise, of encouragement, of understanding, of forgiveness, of a sign that others still like them despite their shortcomings. A large share of their dependence on others is attributable to this insecurity of theirs in the face of their demanding ideals.

Although the problem of the difference in the response of these two groups to their ideals is an important one, it cannot concern us here. Our purpose in focusing on the nature of their ideals is to observe that for both groups they are excessively high, demanding, uncompromising and inflexible, and the self-judgment of individuals of both types is excessively severe when they feel they have not lived up to their self-imposed standards. Because of the rigidity of these standards, they are often forced into actions that are beyond their skills and physical capacities, or that are even harmful for the functioning of the organism as a whole. Or they are prevented from expressing and satisfying instinctual demands that are both pleasurable and beneficial. They become the victim of the tyrannical rule of one aspect of their total psychological functioning. Once again we are observing an imbalance in the individual's personality structure, resulting from the excessive development and strength of one part of it (in this case, the superego with its ego ideals and conscience), which makes its demands on the individual at the expense of the other parts of the structure.

NORMAL BALANCE

In the normal person there is a better balance of the functioning parts. In the face of an illness, for example, he is able to accept the dependency imposed on him by his incapacity, and to utilize the benefits of the dependent state to achieve his ultimate recovery and rehabilitation. By the same token, when he is physically able to return to activity, he does not cling to dependency, but is able to return to a state of self-reliance and strength.

There is a flexibility in his personality structure that enables him to adapt to circumstances as they require. Even in health there is a free give-and-take between himself and others, that permits him comfortably to rely on others when he needs them and to do things for himself and for others when he is able. So too, his goals, his ideals and his conscience show a flexibility and adaptability—not that he is a hypocrite or an opportunist, but his goals are realistic as measured by his capabilities and skills, his ideals are a guiding principle for important decisions in his relationships with others without tyrannically imposing their standards where they are inappropriate, and his conscience, though a loyal guide and an often painful goad, does not cripple him with excessive or unduly prolonged sanctions.

The key words in our discussion here are "balance" and "proportion"; and it is our thesis that in the psychologically healthy person the parts of his psychological structure are in equitable balance. This does not mean that he is without inner conflict or strife, but that there is a just proportion of psychological functions in an equilibrium which permits him to adapt realistically to his environment and to make the fullest use of his human capacities.

As concepts, these are neither new nor strange to us, for we are accustomed to conceive of the various functions of the healthy physical body as operating within the boundaries of a homeostatic equilibrium. Our purpose here is to apply the idea of balance and proportion to the psychological as well as the physical functioning of the human being. In this framework, as we postulated earlier, dependency is not in itself a pathological human need. It becomes a pathological force only if its strength is excessive in proportion to other psychological functions, or if its expression is too greatly curtailed by psychological agencies that have become overgrown at the expense of dependency itself, throwing the psychological organism into an unhealthy imbalance.

The Greeks had a word—or better—a phrase, for it: "Meden agan"—"Nothing in excess." And this, perhaps better than any other, expresses a basic and guiding concept for mental health.

SUGGESTED READINGS

General

The DSM-III personality disorders sections: A commentary. Frances A. American Journal of Psychiatry 137:1050–1054, 1980.

Psychopathic personality. In Clinical Psychopathology. Schneider K. (translated by Hamilton MW). New York, Grune & Stratton, 1959, pp 15–37.

Ther paranoid condition revisited. Janosko REM. Psychiatry Digest 38:17–25, 1977.

Paranoia and paranoid: A historical prospective. Lewis A. Psychological Medicine 1:2–12, 1970.

The hysterical personality: A controlled study. Slavney PR, McHugh PR. Archives of General Psychiatry 30:325–329, 1974.

Psychopathic personality: A most elusive category. Lewis A. Psychological Medicine 4:133–140, 1974.

The Mask of Sanity. Cleckley H. St. Louis, C.V. Mosby, 1955.

The borderline patient: A comparative analysis of four sets of diagnostic criteria. Perry JC, Klerman GL. Archives of General Psychiatry 35:141–150, 1978.

Passive aggressive personality disorder: A search for a syndrome. Small IF, Small JG, Alig VB, Moore DF. American Journal of Psychiatry 126:973–983, 1970.

Biological Factors

Heredity and character disorders. Rainer, JD American Journal of Psychotherapy 33:6–16, 1979.

Cerebral lateralization and personality style. Smokler IA, Shevrin H. Archives of General Psychiatry 36:949–954, 1979.

Some neurophysiologic aspects of individual behavior. Betz B. American Journal of Psychiatry 136:1251–1256, 1979.

Lithium carbonate in emotionally unstable character disorders. Rifkin A, Quitkin F, Carillo C, Blumberg AJ, Klein DF. Archives of General Psychiatry 27:519–523, 1972.

Genetic studies of antisocial personality and related disorders. Crowe RR. In Critical Issues in Psychiatric Diagnosis (edited by Spitzer RL, Klein DF). New York, Raven Press, 1978.

Psychological Factors

A diagnostic framework. Bursten B. International Journal of Psychoanalysis 5:15–30, 1978.

The diagnosis of hysteria: An overview. Chodoff P. American Journal of Psychiatry 131:1073–1078, 1974.

The so-called good hysteric. Zetzel E. International Journal of Psychoanalysis 49:229–245, 1968.

Hysterical personality: A reevaluation. Easser BE, Lesser SR. Psychoanalytic Quarterly 34:390–405, 1965.

Borderline Conditions and Pathological Narcissism. Kernberg O. New York, Jason Aaronson, 1975.

Thoughts on narcissism and narcissistic rage. Kohut H. Psychoanalytic Study of the Child 27:360–400, 1972.

Borderline personality organization: The need for a new theory. Robbins MD. Journal of American Psychoanalytic Association 24:831–854, 1976.

The borderline syndrome: The role of the mother and the genesis and psychic structure of the borderline personality. Masterson JE, Ringlsey DB. International Journal of Psychoanalysis 56:163–167, 1975.

Some narcissistic personality types. Bursten B. International Journal of Psychoanalysis 54:287–300, 1973.

The schizoid maneuver. Silverberg WV. Psychiatry 10:383–393, 1947.

Sociocultural Factors

Implications of sex differences in prevalence of antisocial personality, alcoholism, and criminality for familiar transition. Cloninger CR, Christainsen KO, Riech T, Gottesman II. Archives of General Psychiatry 35:945–951, 1978.

IV
ANXIETY DISORDERS

OVERVIEW

Normal anxiety can be a biologically protective symptom. It is an unpleasant feeling of apprehension accompanied by sensations of bodily discomfort. Anxiety differs from fear, because fear is a reaction to a specific external threat, whereas anxiety is usually not. Anxiety may be precipitated by future threats and/or emotional conflict.

Developmentally, anxiety is an alerting signal. It arouses the infant to activity in the face of separation, loss of love, or threat to physical comfort. It is stimulated by the possibility that bodily damage, pain, or punishment will occur. Anxiety also occurs in the course of ordinary life experiences with change and growth.

Anxiety can be a symptom in almost any psychiatric disorder. For example, with severe episodic depression, anxiety often accompanies guilt and may take the form of intense agitation. In the early phases of a schizophrenic disorder, anxiety appears as bewilderment about powerful and inexplicable perceptions. In paranoid states, persecutory delusions may lead not only to anxiety but even to panic. In organic conditions such as the *delirium* caused by toxic-metabolic disturbances, severe anxiety is often accompanied by terrifying visual hallucinations and delusions which may wax and wane with the ability of the individual to sustain clear thinking. The level of anxiety may be independent of the social setting.

Severe anxiety in the absence of other psychiatric disorders is called an anxiety disorder, of which there are three different types: the phobic disorders, the anxiety states, and the post-traumatic stress disorders. Included among the phobic disorders are: (1) agoraphobia, fear of being alone or in public places from which escape might be difficult; (2) social phobia, avoidance of social situations, which might include scrutiny of others; and (3) simple phobia, fear of an object or situation that has specific meaning for the individual.

Included under anxiety states are: (1) panic disorder, three panic attacks within a three-week period of time other than during marked physical exertion or life-threatening situations; (2) generalized anxiety, persistent anxiety; and (3) obsessive compulsive disorder, involving extreme obsessions or compulsions.

Post-traumatic stress disorders follow a recognizable, realistic stress and may involve re-experiencing of trauma and other symptoms. These may be acute, chronic, or delayed.

CLINICAL FORMS

When intense anxiety is associated with fear of some ordinary neutral object or situation such as height or elevators, it is defined as a phobic disorder. When an individual is away from the phobic situation, or not thinking of it, he or she may well be very comfortable. But when faced with a phobic object, the individual abruptly develops a rapid heart beat, weakness, shortness of breath, and feelings of extreme fright.

A **phobic disorder** appears to be an avoidance technique by which one attempts magically to control dangerous and undesirable impulses or situations. A person with a phobia deals with massive anxiety by substituting or displacing some or all of that anxiety onto a relatively more neutral, commonplace object or situation such as heights, closed spaces, elevators, buses, dangerous weapons, stage appearances, or social gatherings. Multiple phobias are also common.

Phobias may also be symbolic. For example, fear of a horse may represent fear of an overpowering or uncontrollable person. The object of a phobia may also appear to be rather incidental, woven around another situation. For example, fear of the cold may occur after a person has been mugged on the street on a cold day.

Phobias must be distinguished from other avoidant tendencies. Certain objects or experiences are avoided on the basis of prior unpleasant experiences. For example, a rider may avoid remounting a horse for several months after a jarring fall. Brief avoidance reactions are commonplace, specific, and literal. They diminish over the course of weeks or months and are generally devoid of unconscious symbolic meaning. Phobias involve perceived dangers to the psyche, whereas avoidance responses relate to actual physical dangers. There is considerable variation in the severity of both phobias and avoidant reactions: some are mild and of little consequence; some are so severe as to force individuals to change their life-styles.

Amongst the **anxiety states,** those with panic disorder have the greatest experience of fright. When an attack of acute anxiety occurs, seemingly spontaneously and not in an actual life-threatening situation, it is called a panic disorder. Often people with panic disorders experience terrifying episodes that may last for many hours, several times a week. These episodes may be so intense that each time the individual is convinced that he or she is either dying or "going crazy" and may precipitate multiple visits to the hospital emergency room for a presumptive heart attack or for severe air hunger (hyperventilation attacks). The repetition of frantic help seeking may indeed become disruptive to family and friends.

Episodes of mild to severe panic may also appear in such diverse medical conditions as *cardiac arrhythmias, angina pectoris, hypoglycemia, thyrotoxicosis, pheochromocytoma, pulmonary embolism,* asthma, *hyperventilation, caffeinism,* "bad trips" from hallucinogens, abrupt withdrawal from certain psychoactive medications, and *psychomotor epilepsy.*

Panic attacks are more acute and intense than generalized anxiety disorders, which are usually of low to moderate severity and are often present most or all of the time. Sometimes anxiety may sweep over a group of people for no apparent reason. At times, anxiety may accompany or follow the onset of a severe medical illness. In order to merit a psychiatric diagnosis of generalized anxiety disorder, the condition cannot be accounted for by a known physical disorder and it must have been present for more than a month.

Symptoms of a generalized anxiety disorder are both psychological and somatic. The individual will manifest, and sometimes complain of, free-floating anxiety, which is usually not attributed by the sufferer to any specific situation or event; rather, it appears to occur spontaneously and uncontrollably. Indeed, the disorder itself may emerge after some major episode of conflict or stress, or it may show up spontaneously. The intensity of the felt anxiety may vary from "mild tension" and "nervousness" to a long-standing "dread" and "panic." The individual with a generalized anxiety disorder may be so apprehensive that he or she is no longer thinking rationally and effectively. Typically, this patient has a preoccupation with memory lapse or fear of impending insanity in the face of a good memory with clear recall. The patient's constant need for reassurance about mental functions may be so insistent and repetitious that he or she becomes a burden to family, friends, and others. Such an individual may then be pejoratively labeled as "sick" or "neurotic," often without recognition of the need for skilled help. Other psychological symptoms seen in people with generalized anxiety disorders include episodes of mild or severe depression, depersonalization, and derealization.

Many patients with anxiety disorders seek help not for their anxiety but for complications such as depression or alcoholism. Others experience somatic symptoms which lead them to consult an internist or a family physician. The more frequent somatic symptoms in such patients relate to the cardiorespiratory system. Typical complaints are palpitations, labored breathing, and smothering sensations. Additionally, there may be signs of pallor, cold hands and feet, sweating, goose pimples, dry mouth, pupillary dilatation, and daytime urinary frequency.

In some patients gastrointestinal complaints may predominate, with abdominal cramping, diarrhea, constipation, nausea, "butterflies," a sinking feeling in the stomach, belching, flatus, and difficulty swallowing. Finally, other somatic symptoms include restlessness, listlessness, fatigue, insomnia, headaches, muscular aches, impotence, and frigidity. People with generalized anxiety disorders often feel helpless about understanding the nature of their problem and avoiding their uncomfortable feelings. By contrast, people with phobias may have some similar physical symptoms but are aware of the type of situation precipitating their distress, and often are able to take steps to circumvent their symptoms.

Another type of anxiety disorder takes the **obsessive compulsive** form, with preoccupations and/or ritualistic behaviors that are understood as a means of controlling or undoing aggressive or sexual impulses that would otherwise produce an unacceptable level of anxiety. Doubting, indecision, and compulsive acts are utilized to displace anxiety onto nonessential rather than essential, anxiety-provoking issues. Additionally, two other ways that obsessive compulsives ward off anxiety are a relentless search for knowledge and the avoidance of personal commitment. These meticulous, overly intellectualizing people work to keep everything under control. They may recognize the senselessness of the obsession or compulsion, but they experience an internal pressure to continue.

Post-traumatic stress disorders occur after severe life experiences that are generally outside the range of usual human experiences, including combat, rape, a severe automobile accident, or other assaults. Subsequent to any shocking event, those affected may experience recurrent frightening dreams or recollections of the event and/or may suddenly feel as if the event were about to happen again for a number of months. Relevant to making a psychiatric diagnosis of post-traumatic stress disorders, the individual does not function as well as before. This may merely take the form of a constriction of affect, a feeling of detachment, or psychic numbing, or there may be diminished interest in one or more usually important activities. Moreover, the individual will usually experience exaggerated startle responses, fitful sleeping, recurrent nightmares, mild memory impairment, and difficulty in concentrating. If others have perished or have been severely injured, there may be guilt about survival. People with this disorder tend to avoid activities that stimulate recollections of the traumatic event. Although many of these post-stress disorders come on shortly after the trauma itself, occasionally there is a latency of months or even years before symptoms emerge.

EPIDEMIOLOGY AND CLINICAL COURSE

Anxiety disorders afflict about 4% of the population and are often described by terms such as "nerves," "nervous," "neurotic." Women more frequently receive diagnoses of phobic and panic disorders. Generalized anxiety and obsessive compulsive disorders appear to be evenly distributed among men and women. Formal demographic and epidemiologic data, however, have not yet been extensively gathered nor differences in incidence understood.

These conditions often begin in young adults,

but the age range may be between 10 and 40 years of age. Often there will be an abrupt onset following a psychologically disruptive event.

Anxiety disorders are often chronic, with an intermittent fluctuating or episodic course. For about one-third of affected individuals, the condition will be continuous and lifelong. In schools or camps there will occasionally be an epidemic of generalized anxiety for one to two weeks, which then clears and leaves no residual symptoms. A psychiatric diagnosis can be made only if the symptoms have persisted for at least a month.

The most significant phobia is *agoraphobia*, a fear of going out or of being outside the house. This phobia often begins when individuals are in their 20s. Other phobias, e.g., fears of animals, trains, elevators, seem to start a decade later. Many simple phobias disappear spontaneously after a few months. Severe phobias that are untreated and last longer than a year seldom remit spontaneously before later life. A fluctuating course of illness is certainly not rare. Agoraphobia may last for many years. As long as the sufferer is inside the house, or is accompanied outside the house, he or she may be symptom free.

Patients with obsessive compulsive disorders usually have a variety of nervous symptoms as children and obsessive traits prior to the emergence of this illness.

Panic disorders seem to be episodic and often chronic, but little is known about their natural history.

ETIOLOGY

Clinicians for many years have been impressed that anxiety responses "run" in families, and that veterinarians have been able to breed strains of "nervous" animals. These include dogs that spontaneously develop specific avoidance reactions; rats that squeal, race around, and defecate when presented with slight environmental changes; and "nervous" behaving mice that have a decreased number of *cerebellar Purkinje cells*, which may be involved in the inhibition of anxiety responses.

Despite considerable research into the etiology of the anxiety disorder, no clear-cut and widely accepted underlying biochemical mechanism has yet emerged as a "front runner." Yet there have certainly been a number of tantalizing leads. For example, injections of *epinephrine* (a neurohormone discharged from the adrenal medulla during stress and under the direct control of the *midbrain*) produce symptoms that clinically mimic anxiety reactions. Epinephrine also produces an elevation of serum lactic acid, and people with anxiety disorders often have elevated lactic acid levels. In some experimental settings, lactic acid, but not placebo infusions, have precipitated strong anxiety reactions in susceptible subjects.

Another but perhaps unrelated lead concerns the blockade of a specific set of central nervous system *neuronal receptors*. Propranolol, which blocks *beta-adrenergic receptors*, is a useful therapeutic agent for a small segment of patients with anxiety disorders.

More recently the *anxiolytic* (anxiety-reducing) benzodiazepines (including Valium and Librium) have been discovered to have specific receptors on certain neurons. Unevenly distributed in the central nervous system, these receptors are found in highest concentration in the cerebral cortex, *cerebellum*, and *amygdala*, but only rarely in the midbrain. The benzodiazepine receptors differ in location and affinity from receptors for dopamine, norepinephrine, *acetylcholine*, or gamma-aminobutyric acid (GABA). Moreover, 14 other putative endogenous neurotransmitters seem to exhibit no affinity for this binding site. Caffeine and theophylline, plus two naturally occuring purines, inosine and hypoxanthine, may be inhibitors at this binding site. Researchers hope to determine whether stress increases, and relaxation therapy decreases, the number of benzodiazepine binding sites. It may be that the anxiolytic properties of the benzodiazepine function by enhancing GABA activity, since this neurotransmitter dampens or inhibits certain central nervous system activity. The possibility exists that the central nervous system has built in not only endogenous opiates but also endogenous calming substances—and their relative lack in those people with anxiety disorders leads to their symptom formation.

On a psychodynamic level, anxiety has been seen as an unconscious attempt to prevent the conscious emergence of unacceptable impulses or feelings. While the psychological and physiological determinants are clearly intertwined, few definitive data are available on this process and the mechanisms that may be operating.

TREATMENT

Patients with anxiety disorders rarely need psychiatric hospitalization and they rarely commit suicide. The milder disorders of short duration are often treated with supportive and/or insight-oriented psychotherapy or psychoanalysis with or without psychoactive medication. Psychotherapy may help the patient to recognize anxiety-producing precipitants and determinants. In turn, this recognition can increase the likelihood of the patient's gaining control over aspects of his or her life.

Anxiolytic drugs such as the benzodiazepines can be effective in treating generalized anxiety disorder. Particularly useful are diazepam (Valium), chlordiazepoxide (Librium), oxazepam (Serax), chlorazepate (Tranxene), and alprazolam (Zanax). The beta-blocker propranolol (Inderol) helps some patients, especially those performers, such as musicians, who have performance anxiety; but propranolol is not helpful in allaying anticipatory anxiety.

Drug dependence or even alcohol addiction can occasionally result if anxiety-ridden patients begin self-medication with benzodiazepines when symptomatic relief is inadequate. Occasionally, for some of the anxiety disorders of moderate or marked severity, when the individual is "falling apart" and depressed, a brief course of a neuroleptic such as thioridazine (Mellaril) may be indicated. Patients with panic disorder may need intermittent quick relief with rapid-action anxiolytics, perhaps given intravenously. It is also necessary for someone to give verbal reassurance and to stay with the patient until the terrifying attack subsides. Sometimes the long-term administration of a monoamine oxidase inhibitor or a tricyclic antidepressant may provide relief.

For agoraphobia and for phobias characterized by spontaneous panic attacks, the use of an antidepressant of the tricyclic or the monoamine oxidase group may be helpful, even when depression is not particularly prominent. Obsessive compulsives often develop depressions, which may be treated with psychotherapy or psychoanalysis and/or antidepressant medication.

As with medication, the role of psychotherapy or psychoanalysis cannot be readily generalized. For the patient with an anxiety disorder, these modalities can effect change. Intrapsychic conflict resolution, help or encouragement in achieving significant social or work-related changes, and facilitation of identity integration can all help to lower anxiety levels. With patients who cannot or do not wish to invest in an intense process or to make major personal changes, intermittent therapy can often be a source of comfort and relief.

Behavior therapy has been useful for patients with simple phobias and for those with some severe obsessive or compulsive disorders. In addition, reassurance, conflict resolution by way of insight-oriented psychotherapy, and even hypnosis have all been successful in rapidly restoring the individual to a functional state.

THE RAPE VICTIM:
PSYCHODYNAMIC CONSIDERATIONS

MALKAH T. NOTMAN AND CAROL C. NADELSON

Rape challenges a woman's ability to maintain her defenses and thus arouses feelings of guilt, anxiety, and inadequacy. Women's individual responses are determined by life stage considerations as well as their defensive structures: concerns about separation-individuation may be aroused in the young woman; a divorced or separated woman may find her credibility questioned; older women's fears of sexual inadequacy may be compounded. In counseling, the victim's previous adjustment should be assessed, she should be given support and reassurance, and specific considerations related to her life circumstances should be acknowledged and dealt with.

The experiences that we call rape range from surprise attacks with threats of death or mutilation to insistence on sexual intercourse in a social encounter where sexual contact is unexpected or not agreed upon. Consent is crucial to the definition of rape. The importance of mutual consent is often overlooked and misinterpreted; many people assume that certain social communications imply willingness for a sexual relationship. Although men, women, and children are raped, the majority of rape victims are women: this paper will focus on understanding rape as a psychological stress for the woman victim.

Burgess and Holmstrom (1) divided the rape

EDITORS' COMMENTS:

THE ARTICLE REVIEWS STRESS RESPONSE AND DE-
SCRIBES WAYS OF DEALING WITH A PARTICULAR
TRAUMA. THERE IS A CLINICAL DISCUSSION OF
POST-TRAUMATIC STRESS DISORDERS THAT ARE
ACUTE, CHRONIC, AND DELAYED.

victims they studied into three groups: 1) victims of forcible completed or attempted rape, 2) victims who were "accessories" because of inability to consent, and 3) victims of sexually stressful situations where the encounter went beyond the woman's expectations and ability to exercise control. Despite the different circumstances, the intrapsychic experiences of rape victims in all categories have much in common.

The rape victim usually has had an overwhelmingly frightening experience in which she fears for her life and pays for her freedom in the sexual act. Generally, this experience heightens a woman's sense of helplessness, intensifies conflicts about dependence and independence, and generates self-criticism and guilt that devalue her as a person and interfere with trusting relationships, particularly with men. Other important consequences of the situation are difficulty handling anger and aggression and persistent feelings of vulnerability. Each rape victim responds to and integrates the experience differently depending on her age, life situation, the circumstances of the rape, her specific personality style, and the responses of those from whom she seeks support.

RAPE AS A STRESS

Rape can be viewed as a crisis situation in which a traumatic external event breaks the balance between internal ego adaptation and the environment. Since it is an interaction between an extreme environmental stimulus and the adaptive capacity of the victim, rape is similar to other situations described in the literature on stress, including community disasters (2, 3), war (4–7), surgical procedures (8, 9), etc. The unexpectedness of the catastrophe and the variability of victims' resources for coping with an experience that may be viewed as life-threatening are critical factors in rape, as in other crisis situations.

Although there are cultural and personality style differences, descriptions of stress reactions generally define four stages, which vary in intensity and duration (10). These responses, listed below, are also found in rape victims.

1. *Anticipatory or Threat Phase.* In this stage, anxiety facilitates perception of potentially dangerous situations so that they can be avoided. Most people protect themselves with a combination of defenses that maintain an illusion of invulnerability, with enough reality perception to allow them to protect themselves from real danger. When a potential stress is planned (i.e., elective surgery), an individual can protect his/her ego integrity by strengthening those defenses which will ward off feelings of helplessness.

2. *Impact Phase.* Varying degress of disintegration may occur in a previously well-adapted person during this second phase, depending on the degree of trauma and the adaptive capacity of the individual. There may be major physiological reactions, including vasomotor and sensorial shifts. Tyhurst (2) reported on the extremes of fire and flood victims' reactions, which ranged from "cool and collected" to "inappropriate" responses, with "states of confusion, paralyzing anxiety, inability to move out of bed, hysterical crying, or screaming." The majority of these victims showed variable but less extreme responses—they were "stunned and bewildered" and demonstrated restricted attention and other fear responses, such as automatic or stereotypical behavior. This picture is also seen in rape victims.

3. *Posttraumatic or "Recoil" Phase.* Emotional expression, self-awareness, memory, and behavioral control are gradually regained in the recoil phase. However, perspective may continue to be limited and dependency feelings are increased. The individual perceives adaptive and maladaptive responses in him/herself and may question his/her reactions. A positive or negative view of one's ability to cope may affect the course of resolution of the trauma and future capacity to respond to stress, and self-esteem may be enhanced or damaged.

Group support during this phase enables the victim to feel less isolated and helpless. Obviously, the rape victim, who is usually alone during the attack, can only hope for support later. Women

are often disappointed by the failure of family, friends, and the community to validate their experience.

Janis (9), in his study of surgical trauma patients, noted that any threat that cannot be influenced by the individual's own behavior may be unconsciously perceived in the same way as were childhood threats of parental punishment for bad behavior. This results in attempts to control anger and aggression in order to avoid provoking "punishment." The absence of overt anger is also a very prominent finding in rape victims.

4. *Posttraumatic Reconstitution Phase.* A process occurs during this phase that may alter future life adjustment. The loss of self-reassuring mechanisms that had fostered a sense of invulnerability may result in a decrease in self-esteem. The victim then blames him/herself for lack of perception or attention to danger. Kardiner and Spiegel (11) studied war stress and stated, "As soon as fear is directed inward in the form of questioning the individual resources to cope with external danger, or toward the group in the form of questioning its ability to be a protective extension of the individual, then a new and more serious danger situation is created." Maladaptive responses have been reported in the war neuroses of World War II (12), in which the individual develops mechanisms that are protective against further exposure to trauma but are psychologically costly and may involve loss of pride and self-esteem (13).

The rape trauma syndrome described by Burgess and Holmstrom (1) can be considered a form of stress reaction that can lead to traumatic neurosis. They reported an acute disorganizational phase with behavioral, somatic, and psychological manifestations and a long-term reorganizational phase with variable components depending on the ego strength, social networks, and specific experiences of the victim. They focused on the violent life-threatening aspects of the crime. Two types of response they noted are: "the expressed style," in which the victim is emotional and visibly upset, and the "controlled style," in which denial and reaction-formation seem to be the most prominent defenses. They also described feelings of shock and disbelief in many victims and the prevalence of guilt and self-blame in the initial phase. The reconstitution phase varies considerably with each individual: however, the patterns of response appear to be similar to those reported in the other types of stress reactions we have discussed.

THE DYNAMICS OF THE RESPONSE TO RAPE

The important considerations in understanding the dynamics of women's responses to rape are 1) affects, 2) unconscious fantasies, and 3) adaptive and defensive ego styles.

Anger

A striking phenomenon in rape victims is the initial display of fear, anxiety, guilt, and shame—but little direct anger. There are several probable reasons for this.

1. Since rape may evoke memories of childhood threats of punishment for misdeeds (9), the victim may feel that she is being punished or is in some way responsible. Her anger may be repressed and experienced as guilt and shame, despite her concomitant feelings of helplessness and vulnerability. Most of the angry feelings appear later in recurrent nightmares, explosive outbursts, and displacement of anger as the woman attempts to master the assault.

2. Expression of aggression in women has been highly conflictual because of cultural restrictions and expectations of passivity and greater compliance for women. Women have often tended toward a masochistic orientation, in which anger is transformed into culturally supported patterns of self-blame. Identification with the aggressor, a mechanism that serves as an attempt to gain mastery, may also make it difficult to acknowledge anger toward the rapist.

3. The socially reinforced suppression of aggression in women has a possible adaptive function, since women are usually smaller and physically weaker than men. Therefore, not responding with a counterattack may prove beneficial. This is an important consideration in understanding the concept of consent. In the past, legal expectations included evidence of force or a struggle in order to establish rape. Current laws accept threat of force as sufficient, recognizing that a woman may submit in fear rather than risk fighting and being overcome.

Guilt and Shame

Despite the varying circumstances of rape and the different degrees of violence, surprise, and degradation involved, guilt and shame are virtually universal. The tendency to blame the victim, thereby assigning responsibility for her, fosters guilt and prevents her from adequately working through the crisis. It is common for a rape victim to feel that she

should have handled the situation differently, regardless of the appropriateness of her actual response. Concerns about the amount of activity or passivity that might have prevented the attack or the rape are frequent. The assumption is that the woman should or could have handled the situation better, that her unconscious wishes perhaps prevented more appropriate assessment and more adaptive behavior.

The guilt of the victim is further increased by focusing on the sexual rather than the violent aspect of the experience. Although aggression is most prominent in the victim's perception, society regards rape as sexual. Since long-standing sexual taboos still persist for many people, even an unwilling participant in a sexual act is accused and depreciated. The popular adage that advises the woman who cannot avoid rape to "relax and enjoy it" misconstrues the attack as a sexual experience. In reality, the rape experience is depersonalizing and dehumanizing. The woman is often a faceless object for the rapist's expression of hostility, and the victim feels degraded and used. Furthermore, since women are expected to exert impulse control in sexual encounters, the rape victim's sense of failure in setting limits, impossible though this may have been, contributes to her guilt.

Unconscious Fantasies

The question of unconscious wishes translated into provocation of a rape must be seriously considered. While undoubtedly there are unconscious fantasies in which rape plays a part, and some women do have fantasies in which submission to a stronger man may be linked with forbidden oedipal wishes, on the conscious level the woman knows she is submitting because any other behavior would result in real danger to her life. However, this is not so clearly differentiated in the unconscious. The universality of rape fantasies certainly does not make every woman a willing victim—or every man a rapist. The unconscious fantasy does not picture the actual violence of the experience.

An individual's defensive organization usually protects him/her from acting out such fantasies. However, if the defensive barrier breaks down and unconscious destructive, aggressive, or masochistic wishes gain expression, anxiety over the loss of control combines with guilt regarding the impulses. Rape involves an overwhelming confrontation with another individual's sadism and aggression and one's own vulnerability. This challenges the woman's confidence in her ability to maintain her defenses and controls.

Many women feel some ambivalence toward men as a result of past developmental experiences. Women expect men to be their protectors and providers, as well as relating to them sexually. Men may also be seen as potential aggressors and exploiters, and the experience of rape confronts the woman with this violent potential. The betrayal by the supposed protector who turns aggressor has a profound effect. Almost all rape victims say they trust men less after the rape. All men may be suspect, and all are potentially on trial. Uncertainty about one's ability to control the environment reverberates with concerns about the ability to control and care for oneself.

Men's Responses to Rape

It is important to consider the responses of men who participate in discussions about rape. They often feel indignation and sometimes identify with both the victim and aggressor. They may feel their masculinity is violated by both the attack on a woman who is felt to "belong" to them and by their own helplessness deriving in part from early feminine identification as well as from their actual failure to have prevented the attack. This may be particularly threatening to men who need to reject any latent feminine components of their own personalities and may lead to a defensive identification with the rapist in an attempt to escape the anxiety of their own sense of vulnerability. Some men have difficulty coping with the impulse for revenge, which would reestablish their sense of control and the ability to protect "their" women.

A man whose daughter, girlfriend, or wife has been raped may react by becoming overprotective, partly as a result of his sense of guilt for not having been protective enough. However, it may also evolve as a defensive means of handling his anger at the attacker of "his" woman and at the woman for having allowed herself to get in this position. A complex series of feelings about his own sexual impulses may be evoked, and a man may find himself unable to be supportive or helpful to the woman after the rape, despite a previously close relationship. He may have difficulty with his own rape fantasies, his concerns about "used merchandise," and even the breakthrough of homosexual impulses. He may withdraw from the woman as a result of this anxiety. The woman who is deprived of support from a man who is important to her is particularly vulnerable to adverse reactions after a rape. The man may be unaware that he is not supportive, since denial operates to minimize the experience so it can be forgotten.

LIFE STAGE CONSIDERATIONS

It is difficult for anyone to predict how he/she will actually behave in a crisis. In the state of panic evoked during a rape, most women think about how to behave to avoid being physically injured or killed. Some talk, some resist, and others become passive, depending on their assessment of what is going on and their past styles of managing stress (14). There are, however, some specific issues related to age and life stage.

The Young Single Woman

The single woman between the ages of 17 and 24 is the most frequently reported rape victim. She is vulnerable often by virtue of being alone and inexperienced. Her relations with men have frequently been limited to the trusted, caring figures of her childhood or the young men she dated in high school. She enters the adult world with little sophistication in some of the nuances of human interaction, and she may easily become involved in an unwelcome sexual encounter. In this age group, the frequency with which rape victims report prior knowledge of the rapist is striking, and this is often the reason for a victim's refusal to prosecute. A young woman may have been raped by a date, an old friend, or even an ex-husband, and she oftens reproaches herself because she should have "known better" or been more active in preventing the rape.

As was discussed earlier, feelings of shame and guilt are prevalent regardless of the circumstances of the rape; coupled with the victim's sense of vulnerability, these feelings color the victim's future relationships with men. This is especially true for the very young woman who may have had her first sexual experience in the context of violence and degradation.

The experience of rape may revive concerns about separation and independence. A young woman's sense of adequacy is challenged when she asks, "Can I really take care of myself?" Parents, friends, and relatives often respond with an offer to involve themselves in taking care of her again. Although the offers may be supportive and reassuring, they may also foster regression and prevent mastery of the stress and conflict evoked by the experience.

Problems for the younger rape victim also affect her perception of and tolerance for gynecological examination. She may have suffered physical trauma, she is susceptible to venereal disease, and she may become pregnant. An examination is indicated, but it may be perceived, especially by an inexperienced or severely traumatized woman, as another rape. She is concerned about the intactness and integrity of her body and wants reassurance. However, she may have difficulty dealing with the necessary procedures if they stimulate memories of the original rape experience.

The Divorced or Separated Woman

The divorced or separated woman is in a particularly difficult position because she is more likely to be blamed and have her credibility questioned. Her lifestyle, morality, and character are frequently questioned. Her apparent sexual availability makes her seem more approachable sexually. She may experience the rape as a confirmation of her feelings of inadequacy, and she is especially likely to feel enormous guilt that can lead to failure to obtain aid or to report the crime. Her ability to function independently is challenged. If she has children, she may worry about her ability to protect and care for them, and others will probably raise questions about her adequacy as a mother. The woman with children must deal with the problem of what, how, and when to tell them about the rape. If the event is known in the community, its implications for her and her children may be difficult to manage.

The Middle-Aged Woman

For the middle-aged married woman, issues of her ability to have control and her concerns about independence are particularly important. She is often in a period of critical reassessment of her life role, particularly in the face of changed relationships to her grown-up children. Husbands in their own midlife crises are often less responsive and supportive to their wives' sexual and emotional needs.

There is a common misconception that a woman, married or single, who is past her most sexually active period has less to lose than a younger woman. One cannot quantify the self-devaluation, feelings of worthlessness, and shame in any woman—especially a woman who may already be concerned about her sexual adequacy.

ATTITUDES OF PROFESSIONALS

Until recently, many psychiatrists felt that rape was not a psychiatric issue and that psychiatrists had little to offer the rape victim. They often shared the view that the victim "asked for it," and she was seen as acting out her unconscious fantasies and therefore was not a "true victim." Thus the woman who had been raped did not receive the empathy and understanding usually extended to people in a crisis. There is also the common belief that many accusations of rape are false. We have not found this to be true in the majority of cases seen at the Rape Crisis Intervention Program at Beth Israel Hospital, nor have others in this field with whom we have spoken.

Professionals have shared the image of the rape victim as a young, sexually attractive woman who in some way exposes herself to an avoidable danger or uses the accusation of rape to save herself from criticism. This view of rape implies that it happens only to marginal people, who collude in some way, and this idea fulfills several functions. It protects the individual who accepts the view from anxiety about his/her feelings of vulnerability. It is also another way to deny that rape occurs and that its incidence is increasing. This defensive position is further expressed by the focus on the sexual aspect of rape. If it is sexual, then one can think that the victim and the rapist were both seeking sexual gratification. The professional is thus protected from any sense of guilt or responsibility.

In our own experience in the development of a rape crisis progran at Beth Israel, we saw a change of attitudes in participating professionals. An increase in interest results in recognition of the crisis nature of the experience and increased dignity for the individual victim.

CONSEQUENCES OF RAPE

Attention to the long-term effects of rape is important. It is difficult to predict all the long-term needs of the rape victim, since the working out of the trauma proceeds in many different ways. The feelings aroused may lead to behavior that seems out of character and would be puzzling if it were not for the rape. Some of the issues that reemerge in some women at a later time are 1) mistrust of men, with consequent avoidance or hesitation; 2) a variety of sexual disturbances; 3) phobic reactions to situations that are reminiscent of the rape; and 4) anxiety and depression, often precipitated by seemingly unrelated events that in some small details bring back the original trauma.

COUNSELING CONSIDERATIONS

Counseling of rape victims should involve an assessment of previous adjustment, including stress tolerance and adaptive resources. In addition, it is also important to learn whom in her environment the victim views as supportive and to attempt to involve these people if possible.

The woman in this situation needs support and reassurance about the way in which she handled the encounter and her efforts to cope afterward, even if she seems volatile, disorganized, or guilty. Negative countertransference feelings may be evoked if she displaces her anger onto those who are attempting to help, e.g., friends, doctors, or the police. It is important that she have the opportunity for constructive catharsis with a caring and empathic person. The counselor's patience may be tested by the victim's repetitive retelling of the story. The counselor may need to be available frequently for the more overtly upset rape victim. The more subdued victim may need to be encouraged to communicate and should be offered the opportunity for future counseling.

Each woman presents special considerations and requires the acknowledgment and support of the counselor in verbalizing and working through the complex problems she faces. The young woman needs help in confronting her family, her relationships with men, and her feelings about her sexuality; the woman with children must deal with her communication with them; and the older woman may have to face her sexual anxiety more openly.

REFERENCES

1. Burgess AW, Holmstrom LL: Rape trauma syndrome. Am J Psychiatry 131:981–986, 1974

2. Tyhurst JS: Individual reactions to community disaster: the habitual history of psychiatric phenomena. Am J Psychiatry 107:764–769, 1951

3. Lindemann E: Symptomatology and management of acute grief. Am J Psychiatry 101:141–156, 1944

4. Glover E: Notes on the psychological effects of war conditions on the civilian population: I. The Munich crisis. Int J Psychoanal 22:132–146, 1941

5. Glover E: Notes on the psychological effects of war conditions on the civilian population: III. The blitz. Int J Psychoanal 23:17–37, 1942

6. Schmideberg M: Some observations on individual reactions to air raids. Int J Psychoanal 23:146–176, 1942

7. Rado S: Pathodynamics and treatment of traumatic war neurosis (traumatophobia). Psychosom Med 4:362–369, 1942

8. Deutsch H: Some psychoanalytic observations in surgery. Psychosom Med 4:105–115, 1942

9. Janis IL: Psychological Stress. New York, John Wiley & Sons, 1958

10. Weiss RJ, Payson HE: Gross stress reaction, in Comprehensive Textbook of Psychiatry. Edited by Freedman AM, Kaplan HI. Baltimore, Williams & Wilkins Co, 1967, pp 1027–1031

11. Kardiner A, Spiegel H: War Stress and Neurotic Illness. New York, PB Hocher, 1941

12. Kardiner A: The Traumatic Neuroses of War. Psychosomatic Medicine Monograph II–III. Washington, DC, National Research Council, 1941

13. Grinker R, Spiegel J: Men Under Stress. Philadelphia, Blakiston, 1945

14. Burgess AW, Holmstrom LL: Coping behavior of the rape victim. Am J Psychiatry 133:413–418, 1976

THE BIOCHEMISTRY OF ANXIETY

FERRIS N. PITTS Jr.

Patients with anxiety neurosis show an excessive rise in lactate, a normal metabolic product. A double-blind experiment has shown that anxiety symptoms and attacks can be induced by infusions of lactate.

The patient feels very sick. He is tired and apprehensive, his heart pounds and his breathing is labored. From time to time he is overcome by fright and the conviction that he is seriously ill or even about to die. Still, his doctor says: "There is nothing wrong with you." This is a description of someone with an anxiety neurosis, a chronic disorder that affects perhaps 5 percent of the U.S. population. Most physicians have been unable to recognize it, let alone treat it; its cause has seemed to be obscure and somehow "psychogenic." Yet in our laboratory at the Washington University School of Medicine we have been able to produce the symptoms of anxiety neurosis and even acute anxiety attacks in susceptible patients by chemical means: we administer enough lactate, a normal product of cell metabolism, to raise the blood lactate level about as high as it is in strenuous physi-cal exercise or other heavy physiological stress. This is the first time anxiety attacks have been produced in any group by any specific stimulus. Our findings have led us to a tentative hypothesis about the biochemical mechanism that gives rise to anxiety symptoms and also seem to explain a new method of treating this hitherto intractable condition.

Anxiety neurosis is a chronic familial illness characterized by feelings of tenseness and apprehension, breathlessness and shortness of breath, palpitation, nervousness, irritability, chest pain and chest discomfort, easy tiring, dizziness, numbness and tingling of the skin, trembling and faintness—and by acute anxiety attacks: abrupt spells of intense fear of impending doom that come on without any apparently appropriate stimulus. The attacks are associated with symptoms of smothering and palpitation and often result in fear of heart attack, cancer, insanity or some other grave disorder. The condition most often arises between the ages of 15 and 35; the symptoms persist with fluctuating intensity for many years without in any way reducing longevity or increasing susceptibility to other diseases. The symptoms are frightening and the fatigue is intense, and so the anxiety neurotic quickly seeks medical attention.

Physical examination reveals no abnormality; laboratory tests are usually normal. The physician is faced with treating an individual who has many subjective physical complaints and great fear of serious illness but who gives no evidence of such illness. Quite probably the physician, who has received little or no training in recognizing the various psychiatric conditions on the basis of reported symptoms, does not even know what questions to ask in order to define the disorder. Most physicians either send these patients away after telling

EDITORS' COMMENTS:

THE BLOOD OF MANY PEOPLE WITH ANXIETY DISORDERS CONTAINS CONSIDERABLY MORE OF THE METABOLIC BREAKDOWN PRODUCT, LACTATE, THAN IS FOUND IN NORMALS. IT IS STILL UNCLEAR, HOWEVER, IF THESE RESULTS ARE RELATED TO THE GENESIS OF ANXIETY. THIS PAPER PRESENTS IN SIMPLE TERMS A MODEL OF HOW AN INVESTIGATOR CAN PROCEED FROM THE PHASE OF HYPOTHESIS GENERATION TO HYPOTHESIS TESTING.

Reprinted from Scientific American 220:69–75, 1969. Copyright © 1969, by Scientific American, Inc. All rights reserved.

them there is nothing wrong or prescribe a sedative, and then forget the whole matter or blame the patient by labeling him a "crock"—medical slang for a neurotic complainer.

The patient is nonetheless certain that his symptoms signal a distressing condition; he comes to believe his disease is either so serious that the doctor cannot tell him the truth or so early in its course as to be unrecognizable. Naturally the patient often seeks other medical opinions, and the

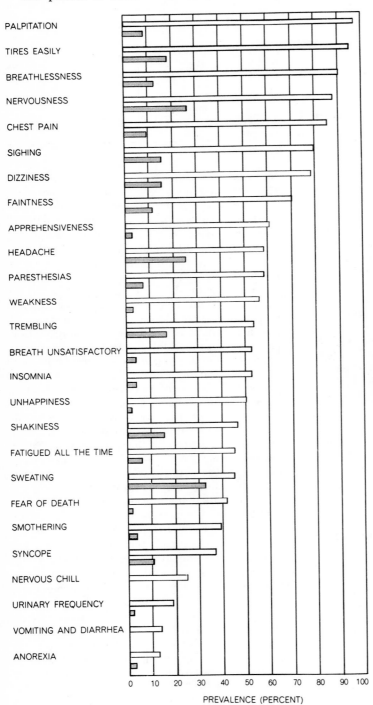

FIGURE 1. Symptoms of anxiety neurosis among 60 patients (*white area*) and 102 controls (*dotted area*) were reported by Mandel E. Cohen and Paul Dudley White of the Harvard Medical School. Paresthesia is tingling skin, syncope is fainting and anorexia is loss of appetite.

more active and determined the patient is the more doctors he sees. Family physicians and internists are consulted about breathlessness and heart palpitations, ophthalmologists about blurred vision, neurologists about dizziness and numbness, otolaryngologists about "a lump in the throat" and psychiatrists about the subjective anxiety and its behavioral consequences. Psychotherapy has little effect on the symptoms of anxiety neurosis, although it may influence the patient to accept his condition.

The mutual frustration of physicians and patients over anxiety neurosis is common because the magnitude of the problem is so great. The 10 million Americans with the disease outnumber by 40 to one the 250,000 practicing physicians. The high prevalence of the disorder, together with the fact that anxiety neurotics see physicians frequently, accounts for the fact that between 10 and 30 percent of the patients of most general practitioners and internists have anxiety neurosis.

The disorder has had many names. The first written description was given by Alfred Stillé, a Civil War military surgeon, in 1863; he called it "palpitation of the heart." Some of the other terms suggested have been muscular exhaustion of the heart, nervous exhaustion, neurasthenia, irritable heart and neurasthenia with abortive and larval anxious-state, effort syndrome and neurocirculatory asthenia; the term anxiety neurosis was introduced in 1895 by Sigmund Freud. Early clinical descriptions were sketchy and imprecise, but in 1871 Jacob M. DaCosta listed nearly all the symptoms in a report on more than 300 cases seen in a Union Army hospital during the Civil War. DaCosta pointed out that the disorder could not be new because he had located complete case reports of the syndrome in British army records from the Crimean War and incomplete descriptions in other military hospital records from campaigns in the preceding two centuries. He emphasized that although the disorder had been recognized and defined by military surgeons evaluating soldiers unable to take the field, it was not caused by military life, since most soldiers had developed the disorder before joining the army and many civilian patients also exhibited it. DaCosta was also the first to demonstrate the familial nature of anxiety neurosis, and described a pair of affected twins. As a result of his report (which was remarkably rigorous in organization and content, even compared with many papers published in medical journals today) the disorder was long known as DaCosta's syndrome. In many ways that is still the best term, since it is the only one that does not imply the cause is known or implicate any one organ system.

Figure 2. Blood lactate was measured by Cohen and White in anxiety neurosis patients and in normal controls before and after moderate exercise (walking on a treadmill) and heavy exercise (running on a treadmill). When results are plotted for each subject, it is clear that the lactate level was significantly higher in patients than it was in controls after the walk (*left*) and, for the same duration of running, after the run (*right*). Mean values are 21 for controls and 44.6 for patients (*left*), .6 for controls and 1.48 for patients (*right*).

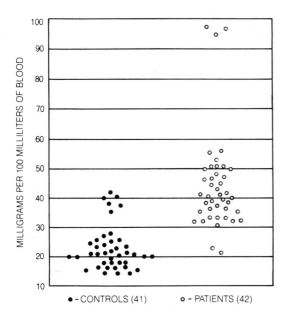

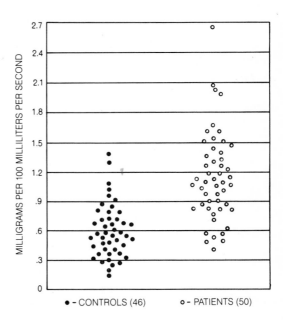

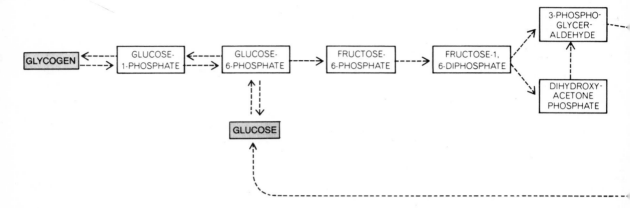

FIGURE 3. Lactate is the end product of anaerobic glycolysis, the process by which glucose (or glycogen, its storage form) is broken down by cells in the absence of oxygen, as in the case of muscle cells during exercise. This occurs in a number of steps, each catalyzed by a different glycolytic enzyme, with energy extracted along the way. The lactate diffuses into the blood, is carried to the liver and there reconverted to glucose. When oxygen is available, pyruvate is oxidized to carbon dioxide and water through aerobic respiration.

Physicians disagree as to how many distinct conditions are described by the various diagnostic terms and how the terms overlap and interrelate. The fact is that it seems impossible to differentiate DaCosta's syndrome from neurocirculatory asthenia or either of them from anxiety neurosis or any other of the terms. The standards for the diagnosis of anxiety neurosis have been the least stringent, but if one does a systematic psychiatric examination of a person labeled an anxiety neurotic (for whatever reason) and is able to rule out the presence of other psychiatric conditions, the patient will report enough of the symptoms associated with neurocirculatory asthenia to justify that diagnosis also. In short, although the symptoms of anxiety neurosis are subjective and the disorder may represent a group of symptoms caused by several different specific factors or diseases, we still have no reliable way of subclassifying the group of patients with anxiety neurosis on any clinical grounds. The symptoms characteristic of anxiety neurosis (see Figure 1) are also seen, in different percentage distributions, in many

psychiatric conditions and in the course of many medical conditions. It is important for physicians to learn the complex differential diagnosis of anxiety symptoms if each patient is to be given the best treatment.

The familial nature of anxiety neurosis was demonstrated some years ago in a systematic study by Paul Dudley White and his colleagues at the Harvard Medical School. They found that the incidence of the disorder in a random control sampling of the general population was 4.7 percent, but that among relatives of patients it was several times higher. With one parent affected, 48.6 percent of the children suffered from anxiety neurosis; with two parents affected, 61.9 percent of the children suffered from the disorder. With neither parent affected but with one child suffering from anxiety neurosis, 27.9 percent of the other children in the family were affected, whereas the incidence among children in the general population sample was about 4 percent. These data demonstrated that some kind of associational factors operate in the transmission of anxiety neurosis and suggested that the factors are hereditary, but the number of subjects was too small to establish the precise type of transmission.

Most studies among civilians reveal an excess of women with anxiety neurosis, with about two female patients for every male. The Harvard group's family study showed that the deficit of males is probably only apparent; when the number of males in a family who were alcoholics and also had anxiety symptoms was added to the number

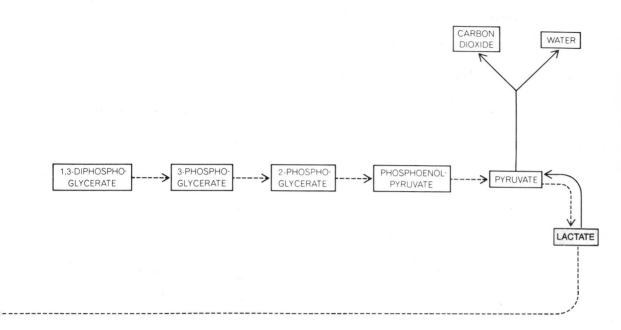

with anxiety symptoms alone, the sum equaled the number of females with anxiety symptoms. In other words, alcoholism may often be symptomatic of anxiety neurosis in men, and when it is, the alcoholism makes it difficult to diagnose anxiety neurosis.

Some of the symptoms of anxiety neurosis resemble those produced by physical exertion, and indeed most patients report that physical activity can bring on or intensify their symptoms. These facts led medical investigators to evaluate various physical functions in anxiety neurotics. They found that, compared with normal controls, anxiety neurotics react sooner to increasing levels of noise, light or heat. They cannot maintain a strong handgrip as long. Their breathing rate increases more in response to discomfort (a tightening blood-pressure cuff, for example). They sigh more and breathe faster when carbon dioxide is added to the air they are inhaling. In response to light exercise they show more of an increase in pulse and breathing rates, utilize inspired oxygen less efficiently and develop a higher level of lactic acid in the blood.

The rise in lactic acid (or lactate, to speak of the ionic form of the substance) has been of particular interest. Lactate is the end product of anaerobic glycolysis, the process by which cells break down glucose (or glycogen, its storage form) and extract energy from it. When muscle cells do work, they convert large quantities of glycogen to lactic acid, some of which is subsequently oxidized to carbon dioxide and water but most of which diffuses into

the blood and is eventually resynthesized into glucose in the liver. A rise in blood lactate is therefore a normal result of exercise. It has been shown, by four investigations in four countries over the past 25 years, that the rise in blood lactate with exercise is excessive in anxiety neurotics. The effect was first noted by White and Mandel E. Cohen at Harvard (see Figure 2). It was independently confirmed by Maxwell S. Jones of the Mill Hill Emergency Hospital in London, by Eino Linko of the University of Turku in Finland and by Alf G. M. Holmgren and his associates at the Royal Caroline Institute in Stockholm. The appearance of anxiety symptoms evoked in patients by the exercise appeared to be concomitant with the extremely rapid rise in lactate; nonpatients serving as controls did not develop anxiety symptoms with exercise and showed only the expected normal increase in lactate. In the anxiety neurotics the rise in lactate (per unit of work per unit of time) was about what is seen in patients with such serious medical conditions as arteriosclerotic or rheumatic heart disease.

It occurred to me that perhaps the lactate ion itself could produce anxiety attacks in susceptible people. We conducted a pilot study of nine patients and in two of the controls typical anxiety attacks developed with lactate infusions that were sufficient to raise the venous lactate level to between 12 and 15 millimoles per liter, a range that is normally attained only with maximum muscular exertion or after the administration of adrenalin. Such attacks did not develop in patients or controls with either of two control infusions.

236

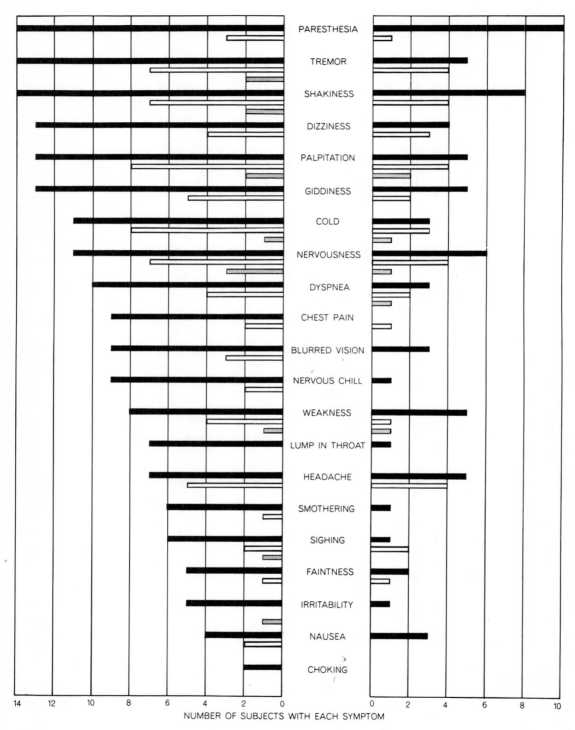

FIGURE 4. Anxiety symptoms were produced in anxiety neurosis patients (*left*) and in nonpatients (*right*) as shown here. The bars indicate the number of subjects who reported each symptom during the infusion of lactate (*black area*), lactate with added calcium (*white area*) and glucose in salt solution (*dotted area*). The lactate produced paresthesia in all the subjects. The other symptoms were produced significantly more often in the patients than in the nonpatients by the lactate but not by either of the two control infusions.

We went on then to perform a more elaborate double-bind experiment. On the basis of rigid criteria we selected a group of 14 patients who could definitely be classified as anxiety neurotics, and we picked a carefully matched group of 10 normal subjects to serve as controls. Each of the 24 subjects received 10 milliliters per kilogram of body weight (about half to three-quarters of a quart) of each of three experimental solutions by intravenous infusion at three experimental sessions five to 10 days apart, with the various solutions administered in carefully randomized order. The experimenter, my colleague James N. McClure, Jr., at that time was unaware of the contents of each infusion, the medical history of the subjects or the purpose of the experiment. He gave the infusion, recorded the subject's behavior and comments and took blood and urine samples. Then the subjects were questioned intensively about their symptoms.

The three infusions were solutions of sodium lactate, of sodium lactate with added calcium and of glucose in sodium chloride. The control solution of sodium lactate with calcium was selected for a specific reason. It had seemed to me that many of the symptoms of anxiety neurosis were identical with those seen in hypocalcemia, a condition in which the level of calcium ions in the blood is low. The lactate ion has a weak but definite ability to complex with ionized calcium, binding it into a physiologically inactive form. It seemed possible, therefore, that the excess lactate in anxiety neurotics might operate by binding calcium, which plays an important role in the transmission of nerve impulses. The calcium in my control infusion was about enough to saturate the binding capacity of the added lactate, so that the lactate would presumably leave the calcium level in the subjects' blood and tissue fluids unaltered. The second control solution, glucose, was chosen simply because its normal metabolic destiny is lactate and it would therefore not introduce any new biochemical effect.

After his third session each subject was asked to rate the three infusions in order of the severity of their effects. McClure, the "blind" observer, did the same thing for each of the subjects. All 24 subjects were able in effect to identify the three solutions, reporting that the sodium lactate had caused the most symptoms, the glucose very few symptoms or none at all and the sodium lactate with added calcium an intermediate number of symptoms. This result had a high statistical significance: the probability that the 24 subjects would correctly rank all three solutions by chance was one in 10,000. McClure did almost as well. He correctly ranked all three solutions for 11 of the 14 patients and for seven of the 10 controls, a performance that would be achieved by chance only five times in 10,000 trials. (His only error was in reversing the two lactate solutions in three members of each group.)

The most striking outcome of the experiment was that the infusions produced anxiety attacks. This is the first time, to my knowledge, that such a result has been achieved with a chemical, physiological or psychological stimulus. Thirteen of the 14 patients and two of the 10 controls had typical acute anxiety attacks during the lactate infusion. (The difference was statistically significant, showing that patients have a characteristic response to lactate.) The anxiety neurotics likened the effect of the lactate to their "worst attacks." One commented: "Heart pounding, mouth dry, vision blurred, dizzy, headache, and all just like my sick spells, even breathing tight and like mint." Another reported: "Have palpitations, tightness-lump in throat, trouble breathing, shuddering sensation all over, can't stop shaking feeling, hard to focus my eyes and things are blurred, I'm very apprehensive and jumpy, this all began with this experiment." None of the subjects in either group had such attacks with either of the control infusions. In other words, the addition of calcium did markedly reduce the effect of the lactate on the anxiety neurotics.

When individual anxiety symptoms are considered, the results again show a strong effect of lactate, a mitigating effect of calcium and a difference in the response of patients and controls to lactate (see Figure 4). It is noteworthy that with the lactate infusion all subjects in both groups experienced paresthesia, a numbness and tingling of the skin that is usually caused by a low level of calcium in the tissues. With the lactate-plus-calcium infusion only a small minority of the subjects reported paresthesia, and none of them did with the glucose infusion. Significantly more patients than controls reported experiencing nearly all the other symptoms with lactate, but with the two control infusions there was no significant difference in the extent to which each symptom was reportedly by the two groups. These observations hold true for the cumulative total of symptoms as well as the individual reports. Of the 294 possible symptoms (21 symptoms for each of 14 subjects), the anxiety neurosis patients reported experiencing 190, or 64.6 percent, during lactate infusion, 25.5 percent with lactate plus calcium and 4.4 percent with glucose. Of 210 possible symptoms, the control subjects reported experiencing 34.3 percent during lactate infusion, 17.1 with lactate plus calcium and 2.9 percent with glucose. Analysis of these figures shows that the anxiety neurotics developed significantly more symptoms than the controls did with lactate but not with the control infusions.

There were marked aftereffects—significant symptoms lasting more than 24 hours—from the lactate infusion in patients but not in controls; there were no marked aftereffects for either group from the control infusion. One patient reported, for example: "I was sick, weak and dizzy for several days and couldn't get out of bed to go to school the next day. I was still very weak two days later and gradually recovered over several days."

Let me summarize the findings. A 20-minute infusion of lactate into a patient with anxiety neurosis reliably produced an anxiety attack that began within a minute or two after the infusion was started, decreased rapidly after the infusion but was often followed by from one to three days of exhaustion and heightened anxiety symptoms. Such patients did not have anxiety attacks and had many fewer individual symptoms when calcium was added to the lactate infusion. Patients had almost no symptoms when they were infused with glucose in saline solution. Nonpatient controls had many fewer and less severe symptoms in response to lactate; they had only a few symptoms in response to lactate with calcium and almost none with glucose. The patient group differed from the controls significantly only in the case of the lactate infusion. Clearly the patients were responding to a specific effect of the lactate, not to any psychological aspects of intravenous infusion.

Our conclusion is that a high concentration of lactate ion can produce some anxiety symptoms in almost anyone, that it regularly produces anxiety attacks in patients but not in controls, and that calcium ion largely prevents the symptoms in both patients and controls. Together with earlier findings on abnormal lactate metabolism in anxiety neurotics, we believe, our experiments demonstrate that the lactate ion may operate in a very specific way to produce naturally occurring anxiety symptoms. We have developed a theory, which is still in a preliminary stage, that anxiety symptoms may ultimately be expressed through a common biochemical mechanism: the complexing of calcium ions by lactate ions. If this binding occurs in the intercellular fluid at the surface of excitable membranes such as nerve endings, an excess of lactate could interfere with the normal functioning of calcium in transmitting nerve impulses.

What is the source of the excess lactate? The difference between patients and nonpatients is not one of lactate "tolerance," or ability to clear lactate from the blood; in all our subjects the excess lactate from the infusions was removed normally by the liver in 60 to 90 minutes. According to our theory, anxiety symptoms could occur in normal people under stress as a consequence of excess lactate production resulting from an increased flow of adrenalin, which is known to stimulate anxiety symptoms as well as to step up lactate production. The anxiety neurotic would be someone particularly subject to this mechanism because of chronic overproduction of adrenalin, overactivity of the central nervous system, a defect in metabolism resulting in excess lactate production, a defect in calcium metabolism or a combination of these conditions.

Such a mechanism is still far from being clearly established, but the theory is entirely compatible with a new and apparently effective treatment for anxiety neurosis. Adrenalin steps up lactate production by acting on metabolic receptor sites on the cell surface to activate the cell's glycolytic enzyme system. A new drug, an adrenalin analogue called propranolol, has recently become available that blocks these metabolic sites and also sites (the β-adrenergic receptors) at which adrenalin exerts its nerve-stimulating effect. In the past two years investigators in London and in South Africa have conducted double-blind experiments in which propranolol is alternated with an ineffective placebo and have shown that propranolol can reduce or eliminate anxiety symptoms.

We have, then, evidence of the biochemical physiology of the anxiety symptoms that are characteristic of anxiety neurosis; we also have a seemingly effective and possibly specific treatment, a treatment that the new knowledge of the biochemistry of anxiety would lead one to expect to be effective. Much further work needs to be done to answer some important questions. Does the infusion of lactate cause anxiety symptoms and attacks in various other groups of patients characterized by anxiety or is there more than one mechanism for expressing these symptoms? Does adrenalin infusion produce anxiety symptoms in anxiety neurotics and other anxious patients and, if so, is the production of anxiety correlated with the production of blood lactate? Can propranolol block anxiety symptoms that have been produced in susceptible patients by the infusion of lactate or adrenalin?

BENZODIAZEPINES:
BEHAVIORAL AND NEUROCHEMICAL MECHANISMS

LARRY STEIN, JAMES D. BELLUZZI AND C. DAVID WISE

The therapeutic effects of benzodiazepines in psychoneurosis may depend in part on their ability to release or disinhibit a patient's anxiety-suppressed gratification-seeking behavior. Benzodiazepines may disinhibit behavior by reducing the activity of serotonin (and possibly acetylcholine) neurons in the brain's "punishment" system. Reduction of serotonin transmission may be due to a facilitation of γ-aminobutyric acid (GABA)-mediated presynaptic inhibition at the serotonin nerve terminal.

Behavior in mania and other psychotic states often has an uncontrolled or compulsive character. Neuroleptic phenothiazines and butyrophenones seem to be useful in these conditions because they help to control an excessively strong impulse to act. By contrast, the tendency to act (especially to attain sexual or other gratification) in some neurotic disorders seems too weak; it is as though the neurotic individual's behavior were excessively inhibited by anxiety or fear of punishment. Benzodiazepines may be therapeutic in these disorders because by their punishment-lessening actions they allow suppressed behavior to be released from inhibition.

These clinical impressions of different and even opposite actions of phenothiazines and benzodiazepines are fully supported by psychopharmacological studies in animals (see table 1). In general, phenothiazines and butyrophenones weaken all forms of operant behavior, regardless of the type of reinforcement (appetitive or aversive) that maintains the behavior (1). On the other hand, characteristic effects of the benzodiazepines are best demonstrated when a strong tendency to respond is suppressed by punishment or nonreward. In moderate doses, the drugs increase the rate of occurrence of the previously suppressed behavior selectively, providing a valuable model for their antianxiety actions (1).

In this paper we will describe our attempts to relate the behavioral effects of benzodiazepines and related tranquilizers (barbiturates, meprobamate) to their effects on monoamine turnover in the brain (2–5). Specifically, we will review the evidence suggesting that tranquilizers may exert their punishment-lessening effects at least in part by a reduction of central serotonin activity (6, 7). At high doses, benzodiazepines also exert depressant effects that seem to be separable from their anxiolytic effects and that may depend at least in part on a reduction in central catecholamine activity (6, 7). Finally, we will report some preliminary tests of the idea that benzodiazepines may regulate monoamine turnover by a primary action on γ-aminobutyric acid (GABA) neurons (8–10).

RAT CONFLICT TEST

The anxiety-reducing and depressant effects of tranquilizers can be measured in animals by the conflict test of Geller and Seifter (11). In this test, hungry rats perform a lever-press response to obtain a sweetened milk reward at infrequent and variable intervals. Approximately every 15 min-

Reprinted from The American Journal of Psychiatry 134:665–669, 1977. Copyright 1977, the American Psychiatric Association. Reprinted by permission.

TABLE 1. Operant Schedules Based on Appetitive and Aversive Reinforcement (1)

Schedule	Procedure	Effect of schedule on response rate	Drug of choice*
Appetitive schedules			
Positive reinforcement	Reward produced by response	Facilitation	Chlorpromazine or haloperidol
Extinction	Reward withheld after response	Suppression	Benzodiazepines
Aversive schedules			
Avoidance	Punishment avoided by response	Facilitation	Chlorpromazine or haloperidol
Punishment (conflict)	Punishment produced by response	Suppression	Benzodiazepines

*Drug of choice indicates the pharmacological treatment that most selectively blocks the behavioral effect of the schedule. Note that the drugs do not discriminate between schedules on the basis of their appetitive or aversive character; rather, they discriminate between schedules on the basis of their behavior effects (facilitation versus suppression).

utes, a tone announces that a punishment schedule has been programmed for 3 minutes' duration; at this time every response is rewarded with milk but is also punished with a brief electrical shock to the feet. Adjustment of shock intensity permits any degree of behavioral suppression in well-trained animals. Drug-induced increases in the rate of punished responses are taken as an index of anxiety-reducing activity, and significant decreases in the rate of nonpunished responses are taken as an index of depressant activity.

Geller and associates (11–13) and Cook and associates (14, 15) studied the effects of different psychotherapeutic drugs in the rat conflict test. In general, a substantial release of punished behavior is produced only by benzodiazepines and related tranquilizers; furthermore, the potency of these compounds in the rat conflict test accurately predicts their clinical potency (14, 15). Neuroleptic phenothiazines and butyrophenones do not have punishment-lessening activity and often cause a further suppression of punished behavior (12, 14). Stimulant drugs of the amphetamine type also decrease the frequency of punished behavior (11, 14). Even morphine, a powerful analgesic, fails to disinhibit punished behavior in this test (13, 15). This observation and the fact that a well-trained animal will usually cease to respond at the onset of the warning stimulus and before any painful shocks are delivered make it clear that it is not pain itself but the threat or fear of pain that suppresses conflict behavior.

BENZODIAZEPINES AND BRAIN NOREPINEPHRINE

If the punishment-lessening effects of benzodiazepines depend on a reduction of central norepinephrine activity, other agents that reduce such activity ought also to exert a punishment-lessening effect. As already indicated, phenothiazine derivatives such as chlorpromazine exert strong central catecholamine-blocking effects but do not release punished behavior from suppression.

Since phenothiazines also antagonize other neurotransmitter actions, the relatively selective α-noradrenergic antagonist phentolamine and the β-noradrenergic antagonist propranolol were used in further tests (6, 7, 16). Both antagonists failed to release punishment-suppressed behavior in the rat conflict test. Intraventricular injections of 20–100 μg of propranolol had no obvious effect, but intraventricular injections of 5–10 μg of phentolamine strongly suppressed both punished and nonpunished behaviors (16). These experiments do not support the idea that disinhibitory effects of tranquilizers depend on noradrenergic blockade. On the contrary, they suggest that α-noradrenergic blockade causes suppression of behavior.

Experiments with (−)-norepinephrine support this idea (7). Intraventricular injections of the transmitter produced large increases in the rate of punished responses (7); indeed, the punishment-lessening activity of norepinephrine administered intraventricularly compared favorably with that of the benzodiazepines administered systemically. Neurochemical specificity is suggested because (+)-norepinephrine and dopamine produced only negligible effects. Intraventricular injections of norepinephrine increased rather than decreased the punishment-lessening activity of systemically administered benzodiazepines (7); this finding again contradicts the idea that the disinhibitory effects of tranquilizers depend on a reduction of noradrenergic activity. At the same time, norepinephrine antagonized the depressant effect of oxazepam on nonpunished behavior (7); this supports the suggestion that the depressant action of benzodiazepines may be mediated at least in part by reduction of noradrenergic activity.

BENZODIAZEPINES AND BRAIN SEROTONIN

If reduction of serotonin rather than norepinephrine turnover is involved in the punishment-lessening activity of benzodiazepines, antagonists of serotonin or inhibitors of its synthesis should counteract the suppressive effects of punishment. This seems to be the case. Graeff and Schoenfeld (17) observed very large increases in the punished response rates of pigeons after intramuscular injection of the serotonin antagonists methysergide and D-2-bromolysergic acid diethylamide (BOL-148); they reported that the effect "was of the same magnitude as that produced by chlordiazepoxide, diazepam, and nitrazepam." Stein and associates (7) also obtained punishment-lessening effects with methysergide in the rat conflict test, and both Geller and associates (18) and Cook and Sepinwall (15) observed a similar effect with the serotonin antagonist cinanserin.

There are also reports of large releases of punishment-suppressed behavior after administration of the serotonin-synthesis inhibitor p-chlorophenylalanine (PCPA) (16, 19, 20). The time courses of behavioral release and of serotonin depletion after PCPA injection coincide closely, and repletion of serotonin by administration of its precursor 5-hydroxytryptophan reverses the punishment-lessening effect of PCPA (16, 20).

Finally, Stein and associates (21) obtained a profound, if transitory, release of punished behavior in the rat conflict test after a single intraventricular administration of 100 μg of 5,6-dihydroxytryptamine, a drug that destroys serotonin-containing terminals in the brain (22). The punishment-lessening effects of 5,6-dihydroxytryptamine peaked on the second day after the injection but virtually disappeared by the fourth day.

It may be noteworthy in this regard that Baumgarten and associates (22) found a significant recovery of serotonin in pons-medulla, hypothalamus, and septum 4 days after a single 75-μg intracisternal injection of 5,6-dihydroxytryptamine, although serotonin levels seemed permanently depleted in spinal cord and neocortex. The punishment-lessening effects of 5,6-dihydroxytryptamine in the conflict test were relatively selective. Although the unpunished response rate was significantly depressed on the day of the injection, it had recovered almost fully to normal by the second day, when punished behavior was maximally disinhibited.

Consistent with these findings, elevation of the concentration of serotonin in the brain by combined administration of 5-hydroxytryptophan and an inhibitor of monoamine oxidase causes suppression of food-rewarded behavior in the pigeon (23). Furthermore, the long-lasting serotonin agonist α-methyltryptamine suppresses punished and nonpunished behaviors in the pigeon (17) and the rat (7). These findings with serotonin agonists, antagonists, PCPA, and 5,6-dihydroxytryptamine support the possible existence of a behaviorally suppressive serotonin "punishment" system whose activity may be decreased by benzodiazepines and other anxiety-reducing agents.

Stein and associates (7) tried to antagonize the punishment-lessening action of oxazepam by intraventricular administration of serotonin. Eight rats received intraventricular injections of either 5 μg of serotonin hydrochloride, 5 μg of (−)-norepinephrine hydrochloride, or 10 μl of Ringer-Locke solution immediately before receiving intraperitoneal injections of 10 mg/kg of oxazepam. All rats received all drug combinations in different sequences during 10 days of testing. In six of the eight rats serotonin decreased the anxiety-reducing action of oxazepam, but in seven of the eight rats (−)-norepinephrine increased the anxiety-reducing effect of the tranquilizer. These findings, together with those already described, form a consistent body of evidence implicating serotonin systems in the anxiety-reducing actions of benzodiazepines (see appendix 1).

EFFECTS OF REPEATED DOSES OF OXAZEPAM ON MONOAMINE TURNOVER

The hypothesis that benzodiazepines act on different monoamine systems to exert their anxiety-reducing and depressant effects contains as a corollary the implication that these effects are distinct. This inference is supported by studies in animals and man demonstrating that the two actions of benzodiazepines follow different courses during chronic administration. The depressant action rapidly undergoes tolerance after a few doses (24), but the anxiety-reducing action fails to show tolerance and may even increase with repeated doses (25). If the behavioral effects were mediated by reductions in norepinephrine and serotonin turnover, respectively, it should be possible to show that benzodiazepine-induced decreases in serotonin turnover will persist with repeated doses but the decrease in norepinephrine turnover will undergo tolerance.

Wise and associates (6) compared the effects of single doses of oxazepam with six repeated doses of oxazepam on the turnover (rate of disappearance) of ^{14}C-serotonin and ^{3}H-norepinephrine in the midbrain-hindbrain region of rat brain. In animals treated with a single dose of oxazepam, significant elevations relative to those of control animals given saline were found in the concentration of both radioisotopes. In rats treated with repeated doses of oxazepam there was a significant increase only in the concentration of ^{14}C-serotonin. Thus a decrease in norepinephrine turnover in the midbrain-hindbrain region was no longer detectable after six doses of oxazepam, although serotonin turnover was still substantially reduced. As noted, in the conflict test the depressant effect of this dose of oxazepam also disappears after six daily injections, whereas its anxiety-reducing effect persists and even is potentiated. This potentiation possibly reflects an increasingly favorable norepinephrine/serotonin turnover ratio that develops with repeated doses of oxazepam.

BENZODIAZEPINES AND BRAIN GABA

Although the foregoing data implicate central serotonin neurons in the anxiety-reducing actions of benzodiazepines, they leave open the question of whether these neurons are affected directly or indirectly by the drugs. A number of investigators have suggested that benzodiazepines may exert a primary action on GABA-containing neurons,

some of which may in turn regulate transmission at monoaminergic synapses; therefore, the tranquilizers may affect serotonin systems only indirectly (8–10). According to one version of this idea, benzodiazepines may increase the release of GABA at the serotonin nerve ending; this would cause a reduction in the release of serotonin by presynaptic inhibition.

As a preliminary test of this suggestion Stein and associates (21) gave rats with stabilized performances in the conflict test daily doses of 15 mg/kg of oxazepam 10 minutes before the start of experimental sessions. Consistent with previous work (25), the punishment-lessening effects of the benzodiazepines increased sharply and then leveled off after three or four doses. On subsequent days, 1–4 mg/kg of the GABA antagonist picrotoxin was administered 10 minutes after the oxazepam dose in an attempt to reverse the anxiety-reducing effect of the tranquilizer. The glycine antagonist strychnine (1–4 mg/kg) was also tested against oxazepam in the same series of experiments as a test of the suggestion (26) that benzodiazepines may activate glycine to exert their anxiety-reducing effects.

Both drugs were active against oxazepam, although picrotoxin had a somewhat greater and more selective effect. At an optimal dose of 2 mg/kg, picrotoxin significantly reduced the punishment-lessening effect of oxazepam without disturbing rates of unpunished response (see table 2). Strychnine also antagonized oxazepam's disinhibitory effect on punished behavior, but the antagonism was accompanied by a parallel reduction

TABLE 2. Picrotoxin and Strychnine Effects in Oxazepam-Reversal Experiments (21)

		Responses (percent of oxazepam alone)			
		Punished		Unpunished	
Treatment	Number of rats tested	Mean	SEM	Mean	SEM
Picrotoxin					
1 mg/kg	11	80.9	18.5	128.8	23.4
2 mg/kg	19	34.8	8.7*	92.3	9.8
4 mg/kg	8	25.0	8.4*	44.0	19.3**
Strychnine					
1 mg/kg	11	136.6	33.8	147.9	21.8
2 mg/kg	19	73.7	17.7	81.1	8.2**
4 mg/kg	9	35.0	17.8***	30.0	15.2***

*The difference from 100% of oxazepam alone is significant (p < .001).
**The difference from 100% of oxazepam alone is significant (p < .05).
***The difference from 100% of oxazepam alone is significant (p < .01).

of the rate of unpunished behavior. Interestingly, at the lowest dose tested, both picrotoxin and strychnine tended to increase the rate of unpunished responses.

The results with picrotoxin are quite consistent with the idea that GABA systems may be implicated in the anxiety-reducing action of benzodiazepines. The results with strychnine are more ambiguous. Although one cannot rule out the possibility that glycine-containing neurons may also be involved in the therapeutic action of tranquilizers, it is equally likely that the oxazepam reversal was produced by some general response-depressant effect of strychnine.

REFERENCES

1. Margules DL, Stein L: Neuroleptics vs tranquilizers: evidence from animal studies of mode and site of action, in Neuro-Psychopharmacology. Edited by Brill H, Cole JO, Deniker P, et al. Amsterdam, Excerpta Medica, 1967, pp 108–120

2. Corrodi H, Fuxe K, Hokfelt T: The effect of some psychoactive drugs on central monoamine neurons. Eur J Pharmacol 1:363–368, 1967

3. Taylor KM, Laverty R: The effect of chlordiazepoxide, diazepam and nitrazepam on catecholamine metabolism in regions of the rat brain. Eur J Pharmacol 8:296–301, 1969

4. Chase TN, Katz RI, Kopin IJ: Effect of diazepam on fate of intracisternally injected serotonin-C^{14}. Neuropharmacology 9:103–108, 1970

5. Corrodi H, Fuxe K, Lidbrink P, et al: Minor tranquilizers, stress and central catecholamine neurons. Brain Res 29:1–16, 1971

6. Wise CD, Berger BD, Stein L: Benzodiazepines: anxiety-reducing activity by reduction of serotonin turnover in the brain. Science 177:180–183, 1972

7. Stein L, Wise CD, Berger BD: Antianxiety action of benzodiazepines: decrease in activity of serotonin neurons in the punishment system, in The Benzodiazepines. Edited by Garattini S. New York, Raven Press, 1973, pp 299–326

8. Polc P, Mohler H, Haefely W: The effect of diazepam on spinal cord activities: possible sites and mechanisms of action. Naunyn Schmiedebergs Arch Pharmacol 284:319–337, 1974

9. Costa E, Buidotti A, Mao CC, et al: Evidence for the involvement of GABA in the action of benzodiazepines: studies on rat cerebellum, in Mechanism of Action of Benzodiazepines. Edited by Costa E, Greengard P. New York, Raven Press, 1975, pp 113–130

10. Haefely W, Kulcsár A, Mohler H, et al: Possible involvement of GABA in the central actions of benzodiazepines. Ibid, pp 131–151

11. Geller I, Seifter J: The effects of meprobamate, barbiturates, d-amphetamine and promazine on experimentally induced conflict in the rat. Psychopharmacologia 1:482–492, 1960

12. Geller I, Kulak JT Jr, Seifter J: The effects of chlordiazepoxide and chlorpromazine on a punishment discrimination. Psychopharmacologia 3:374–385, 1962

13. Geller I, Bachman E, Seifter J: Effects of reserpine and morphine on behavior suppressed by punishment. Life Sci 4:226–231, 1963

14. Cook L, Davidson AB: Effects of behaviorally active drugs in a conflict-punishment procedure in rats, in The Benzodiazepines. Edited by Garattini S. New York, Raven Press, 1973, pp 327–345

15. Cook L, Sepinwall J: Behavioral analysis of the effects and mechanisms of action of benzodiazepines, in Mechanism of Action of Benzodiazepines. Edited by Costa E, Greengard P. New York, Raven Press, 1975, pp 1–28

16. Wise CD, Berger BD, Stein L: Evidence of α-noradrenergic reward receptors and serotonergic punishment receptors in the rat brain. Biol Psychiatry 6:3–21, 1973

17. Graeff FG, Schoenfeld RI: Tryptaminergic mechanisms in punished and nonpunished behavior. J Pharmacol Exp Ther 173:277–283, 1970

18. Geller I, Hartmann RJ, Croy DJ, et al: Attenuation of conflict behavior with cinanserin, a serotonin antagonist: reversal of the effect with 5-hydroxytryptophan and alpha-methyltryptamine. Res Commun Chem Pathol Pharmacol 7:165–174, 1974

19. Robichaud RC, Sledge KL: The effects of p-chlorophenylalanine on experimentally induced conflict in the rat. Life Sci 8:965–969, 1969

20. Geller I, Blum K: The effects of 5-HT on para-chlorophenylalanine (p-CPA) attenuation of "conflict" behavior. Eur J Pharmacol 9:319–324, 1970

21. Stein L, Wise CD, Belluzzi JD: Effects of benzodiazepines on central serotonergic mechanisms, in Mechanism of Action of Benzodiazepines. Edited by Costa E, Greengard P. New York, Raven Press, 1975, pp 29–44

22. Baumgarten HG, Bjorklund A, Lachenmayer L, et al: Long-lasting selective depletion of brain serotonin by 5,6-dihydroxytryptamine. Acta Physiol Scand Supplement 373, 1971, pp 1–15

23. Aprison MH, Ferster CB: Neurochemical correlates of behavior: II. Correlation of brain monoamine oxidase activity with behavioral changes after iproniazid and 5-hydroxytryptophan. J. Neurochem 6:350–357, 1961

24. Goldberg ME, Manian AA, Efron DH: A comparative study of certain pharmacological responses following acute and chronic administration of chlordiazepoxide. Life Sci 6:481–491, 1967

25. Margules DL, Stein L: Increase of "antianxiety" activity and tolerance of behavioral depression during chronic administration of oxazepam. Psychopharmacologia 13:74–80, 1968

26. Young AB, Zukin SR, Snyder SH: Interaction of benzodiazepines with central nervous system glycine receptors: possible mechanism of action. Proc Natl Acad Sci USA 71:2246–2250, 1974

APPENDIX 1

Evidence Linking Benzodiazepines to Brain Serotonin (5-HT)

1. Benzodiazepines reduce 5-HT turnover.

2. Benzodiazepine antipunishment effects are mimicked by:
   a. 5-HT antagonists (methysergide, cinanserin, BOL-248)
   b. 5-HT synthesis inhibition (PCPA)
   c. 5-HT nerve terminal damage (5,6-dihydroxytryptamine).

3. Punishment effects are intensified by:
   a. 5-HT agonists (α-methyltryptamine)
   b. 5-HT precursor (5-hydroxytryptophan plus MAO inhibitor)
   c. 5-HT (administered in lateral ventricle)
   d. Carbachol activation of 5-HT cells in dorsal raphe nucleus.

4. Benzodiazepine effects are antagonized by 5-HT but are potentiated by norepinephrine.

OBSESSIONS AND PHOBIAS

LEON SALZMAN

Phobias are intimately related to the obsessive-compulsive state and are operationally and dynamically similar to it. Both phobics and obsessives are energetically engaged in maintaining control over living, but the phobic attempts this through a total avoidance of the kind of situation that might put him out of control.

The literature on the etiology and therapy of the phobias is very extensive. Freud's original formulation was that the phobia is an attempt to deal with anxiety by substitution and by displacement of anxieties which are alien to the ego. The phobia relates to objects which have unconscious symbolic meanings and which represent regressions to earlier infantile fears and anxieties. Freud felt that the object always symbolized some sexual anxiety and that every phobia, therefore, was invested with some element of sexual symbolism. This formula has remained unchanged, as is obvious from the literature, which consists of abundant case histories, all of them in support of this notion. For the most part, no attempts have been made to extend Freud's original views. It was also believed that the phobia generally represents specific anxieties. For example, street phobias represent unconscious fantasies of prostitution, or a phobia of heights might represent competitive ambitions to be in a superior position. The phobia in these terms is

thus an avoidance reaction which deals with specific infantile anxieties. Psychoanalysis was considered the treatment of choice and the literature merely reaffirms these views.

In 1955 Lief (13) suggested that the phobic object may be unrelated to the inner anxiety or conflict in any way other than by simply representing the sensory context in which the critical situation occurred and at which time the phobia originally began. Other authors (e.g., Arieti [2]) suggest that phobias are expressions of the general tendency to concretize and that abstract anxiety-provoking situations and relations are often concretized as fear.

In spite of Freud's clear statement about the psychology of the phobic state, almost all descriptions of obsessive-compulsive disorders include phobic manifestations, and vice versa. Both types of illness are often described together under a single heading, or else, as in case descriptions, the symptoms are invariably seen as occurring alongside one another. A brief excerpt from Freud's "Interpretation of Dreams" (12) paraphrases this situation so well that I would like to quote it.

> On another occasion I had an opportunity of obtaining a deep insight into the unconscious mind of a young man whose life was made almost impossible by an obsessional neurosis. He was unable to go out into the street because he was tortured by the fear that he would kill everyone he met. He spent his days in preparing his alibi in case he might be charged with one of the murders committed in the town. It is unnecessary to add that he was a man of equally high morals and education. The analysis (which, incidentally, led to his recovery) showed that the basis of this distressing obsession was an impulse to murder his somewhat

Reprinted, in condensed form, with permission from CONTEMPORARY PSYCHOANALYSIS, journal of the William Alanson White Institute and the William Alanson White Psychoanalytic Society, New York, Vol. II; No. 1, 1965, pages 1–25.

over-severe father. This impulse, to his astonishment, had been consciously expressed when he was seven years old, but it had, of course, originated much earlier in his childhood. After his father's painful illness and death, the patient's obsessional self-reproaches appeared—he was in his thirty-first year at the time—taking the shape of a phobia transferred on to strangers. A person, he felt, who was capable of wanting to push his own father over a precipice from the top of a mountain was not to be trusted to respect the lives of those less closely related to him; he was quite right to shut himself up in his room.

Freud might have added in this case that the phobia was a device which served to guarantee as well as to generate the control necessary to obviate the dangers involved in the young man's going out into the streets. From the description, we get the feeling that Freud considered the obsessions and the phobias as two parts of a single phenomenon in which the only distinction was semantic.

In this instance, the obsessional preoccupations and ritualistic behavior of the patient were a means of controlling his aggressive impulses, which had their unconscious roots in his hatred of his father. Both the phobic and obsessive devices were attempts at controlling dangerous and undesirable impulses.

□ □ □

While the theory I am putting forth is not novel, it has not been sufficiently emphasized in the literature.

Clarification of the dynamic role that phobias play in mediating anxiety in their relationship to obsessions has many significant implications for therapy. The widespread belief that the phobia attempts to deal with aggressive or sexual impulses needs to be amplified by the recognition that the phobia can deal with any potential threat to the individual's capacity to control himself.

Phobias, like obsessions, frequently develop around the need to defend oneself against tender impulses, or the potential threats against feelings of pride or self-esteem. Loss of control and the attendant humiliating and threatening consequences are aspects of both the phobic and obsessive processes; the threat of loss of control typically does not involve dangerous or hostile feelings against another person. Rather, the fear of losing control is in terms of being humiliated and feeling worthless and insignificant because of such weakness. It is the public display of inade-

quacy and imperfection, rather than violence, which is feared in the loss of control. The striking and dramatic examples illustrated by my excerpt from Freud do occur, but are decidedly in the minority.

The phobia, by an absolute injunction, prevents an individual from confronting any situation, place, or person which produces a magnitude of anxiety that threatens to put him temporarily out of control. It is a ritualized avoidance reaction which attempts, like all rituals, to exert some control over nature through the agency of magic. The phobia is a ritual of "no-doing," or inaction. The obsessive-compulsive syndrome, with its characteristic rituals of behaving or thinking, is likewise an attempt to control and influence the environment. It, however, is a ritual of doing.

The ritual, as practiced in the cultural context of religions is, in both its primitive and more sophisticated sense, an attempt to exercise control over nature through divine or superhuman agents. The ritual is designed to influence these forces in one's favor and to have them do one's bidding. Through ignorance and the inevitable limitations of human capacities, man attempts to control aspects of his living over which his strength and intelligence have no effect. As his understanding of himself and of nature grows, his need for ritual diminishes. Rituals, totems and taboos are the social and cultural analogues of the obsessions and phobias, as Freud declared in "Totem and Taboo" (11).

In order to have some frame of reference at this point, I would like to describe briefly some elements of the obsessive-compulsive state before returning to an examination of the phobias. The preoccupation with the nonessential, or distraction from the essential—that is, the displacement—is a characteristic controlling device in these disorders and accounts for much of the symptomatology. The attempts at omnipotence are also desperate devices aimed at controlling the environment and guaranteeing the future. The meticulousness, overintellectualized interests, and efforts toward omniscience are other evidences of this same need to control.

Extremely important, also, is a variety of the obsessive's operations which serve to avoid his making a commitment; this avoidance of commitment is also a means of exerting control. For the obsessional individual, uncertainty, dilatory behavior, perfectionistic drives, and emotional isolation are techniques for avoidance of commitment which, he hopes, will protect him from making an error or losing control, which, in turn, would cause him to feel humiliated. He remains in control only to the extent that he does not make any final choice, and unless he knows everything that will allow him to predict the consequences of the choice. Control, and particularly, control over the future, is the essence of the dynamics of the obsessive syndrome. The dreaded sense of humiliation results from another element—from the awareness that he is a mere mortal, imperfect, and like all other humans. This recognition is intolerable, since the obsessional individual feels he will be swallowed up, overwhelmed, inundated and completely lost unless he can maintain a constant state of vigilant control over all his living.

It is in this respect that the phobic individual is strikingly similar to the obsessional. He, too, is energetically engaged in maintaining control over living, but through an absolute avoidance of the kind of situation which may put him out of control.

The phobic kind of avoidance must be clearly distinguished from other avoidance tendencies which are very prominent in nature. In the typical conditioned responses of man and animals, certain objects or experiences are avoided on the basis of a prior unpleasant experience. These avoidance reactions are specific, literal, and devoid of any content other than the anticipated pain or displeasure based on a previous experience and reinforced by subsequent experiences. This is an example of the learning process in which we utilize our past experiences to protect our future existence. It is a physiological response and part of the inherent interest of the organism in preserving its integrity. Such responses may be reflected in nature, or secondarily conditioned. A single experience with a cactus plant, or a whiff of ammonia, may serve to produce a strong avoidance reaction. Similarly food reactions and other sensory experiences may condition the individual against further contacts.

John Dollard and N. E. Miller, in a chapter on phobias in their book, *Personality and Psychotherapy* (3), give a typical example of an avoidance reaction which is described as if it were a phobia. They cite the case of a pilot who, during a mission, underwent severe danger and was exposed to intense fear-provoking stimuli. As a consequence, he developed extreme anxiety when he approached a plane, looked at a plane, or even thought about flying. The authors call this a phobic response. However, the phobia is a more complicated phenomenon involving symbolism, and deals with psychic dangers as opposed to ac-

tual physical dangers. Therefore, the pilot's reaction should be called an avoidance response.

In this connection, the distinction between fear and anxiety, and the distinction between the satisfaction of physiologic needs as opposed to security needs is useful. This distinction derives from interpersonal theory and is spelled out by Sullivan in his *Conceptions of Modern Psychiatry* (14). Sullivan made this distinction based on the recognition that there is a qualitative difference between the physiologic needs and the psychologic needs, manifested particularly in the consequences following deprivation of these respective categories of needs. These most useful distinctions are applicable in many situations and particularly in the technical process of therapy, which emphasizes the elucidation of anxiety and its roots in interpersonal relationships. I believe the distinction between the simple avoidance reaction and the phobia is comparable to that between fear and anxiety.

The pilot's reaction in the above instance was based on an actual danger in a situation which provoked enough uneasiness to cause him to refuse to confront the same situation again. If this avoidance reaction were to generalize to other situations, such as fear of heights or elevators, it could then be called a phobia, since it would involve symbolic transformations and psychic elements. This often occurs when the realistic avoidance reaction produces a sense of shame or humiliation and begins to involve psychic defensive reactions as well as physiologic ones. To illustrate such a transition from a realistic avoidance reaction to a phobia: The avoidance of deep water when one is a poor swimmer and has recently had to be rescued from drowning is not a water phobia. However, if such an experience were to produce a total avoidance of bathing, and spread to situations in which breathing might be interfered with, it would obviously no longer be a simple avoidance reaction but rather a phobia. While the phobia always includes the avoidance reaction, it is, nevertheless, something more. The additional dimension of the psychic involvement, over and above the purely somatic response, comprises the distinction between the simple avoidance reaction and the phobic state.

The notion of unconscious versus conscious knowledge of the issues involved, could also be used to distinguish between phobias and avoidance reactions. This distinction, however, is not entirely adequate since the phobia may exist even when there is clear knowledge of all the relevant factors. The establishment of the distinction between avoidance reaction and phobia, though difficult, is essential, since the response to therapy is markedly different in each category. The case of the pilot described by Dollard and Miller, and many other so-called phobias, have a very high rate of cure since they can often be quickly influenced by conditioning or relearning techniques. True phobias may shift but are extremely difficult to resolve, even with extensive psychotherapy. If the so-called easy cures in some of the described cases are reexamined it may be found that they fit more accurately into the category of simple avoidance reactions.

Phobias may appear without there having been any prior precipitating event as well as under circumstances where the relationship of displeasure or anxiety in connection with the object or event is either unclear or contradictory. One can understand the avoidance of cactus, or of airplanes after a dangerous flight, but not the avoidance of elevators, or open spaces, or the other varieties of phobia present in man. The phobia cannot be comprehended on rational grounds, even though rational explanations might be made for its existence. Characteristically, the phobia is not specific to a particular element, but is generalized to include a total event or situation. In addition, the phobia tends to involve similar objects or situations; for example, a phobia of elevators may also include narrow spaces or mechanical objects which are not connected to the outside or other noticeable escape routes. In other words, the phobia involves an idea or some aspect of experience which revolves around an object and which is symbolized through the object, rather than actually involving the object in and of itself. It is the symbolic significance implicit in the phobia which distinguishes it most clearly from simple avoidance reactions.

The confusion created by a failure to distinguish the simple avoidance reaction from phobias is compounded by the tendency to use the terms fear, phobia and anxiety as synonymous. This unfortunate and unscientific semantic muddle prevents a clear delineation of the phobic state. Fear, which is defined by Webster as a painful emotion marked by alarm, awe, or anticipation of danger, is obviously not synonymous with phobia, which is defined as an irrational or persistent fear of a particular object or objects. Fear can be present with or without a phobia, while a phobia invariably contains as one of its elements the experience of fear. Fear is not a phobia, even though Hinsie, in his *Psychiatric Dictionary*, defines 211 phobias in

terms of fear only. The definitions range from fear of air, animals, anything new, to fear of weakness, wind, women, work, and writing. These names are an exercise in the application of Latin to psychiatric nosology and offer nothing new to the comprehension of the phenomenon of the phobic state. Anything and everything may become a phobic object. Indeed, a significant characteristic of the phobic state is the tendency for phobias to spread. A phobia which involves large groups of objects may gradually include smaller and smaller groups, so that ultimately the individual can function only when he is alone. Clues as to what underlies the selection of or spread to a particular object as the seeming source of the phobic symptom may be difficult to ascertain. For example, in stage fright (the phobic state surrounding public appearances) the issue is not a particular place, event, or specific fear, but rather the broad spectrum of feeling that one is under scrutiny by a critical or unfriendly audience. This could apply to theaters, parties, or luncheons with just one or two people. The apprehension is not of physical danger, but of being humiliated, laughed at, or making a fool of oneself by inadequate or uncontrolled behavior, in spite of genuine competence or the actual friendliness of a given audience. The individual's pride system is at stake and his perfectionistic demands are endangered.

It is at this point that the transition between an obsessional state, in the usual sense of the obsessive-compulsive individual, to the phobic state grounded in the obsessional state, can be discerned. When the obsessional, with his need to control his world in order to guarantee his security, is faced with situations in which he fears he will be out of control, a certain way of dealing with the possibility is to avoid such situations permanently—i.e., the phobic state.

One clue to the spread of a phobia often lies in the similarity of situations or objects. For example, a phobia of enclosed spaces may begin with an avoidance of elevators, spread to small rooms of any type, and ultimately to auditoriums, theaters, and so on.

The spread is also determined by the symbolic meaning of the anxiety, for instance, that related to the closed space, which may in turn refer to the difficulty in getting out quickly when anxiety supervenes. Thus the phobia of elevators may also, in addition to involving enclosed spaces, involve any situation in which escape is difficult, such as airplanes once they are in flight, sitting in the middle of a long row of seats, or sitting in a large crowd. The latter anxiety may be obviated by sitting in an aisle seat in a theatre as a partial solution to the difficulty. The anxiety of being confined to the elevator even for seconds or of being unable to get through a crowd immediately involves the inability to take the consequences of ordinary living, where it is often necessary to wait a moment before doing as one wishes. The phobic person demands immediate and absolute relief, whether in the form of a tranquilizer or some other measure providing instant relief. Like an overindulged child, his needs must be fulfilled at once. The phobia is a way of making certain of this fulfillment, since life becomes organized in such a fashion as to guarantee that one will not have to endure a state of discomfort.

Inevitably, once such a phobia begins, continued public exposures tend to draw in more and more items and situations. A writing phobia in a young woman became manifest in a bank setting, soon spread to an inability to sign her name in department stores and restaurants, and finally took the form of a phobia about holding a drinking glass or any item in her hand which would reveal her tremors and uneasiness. The tremors were of psychological origin and the result of tension which involved all her activities. Being unable to accept any deficiency or evidence of not being completely in control, she began to avoid any situation in which she might manifest some uneasiness. The spread of the phobia reduced the chances of exposing her deficiencies and lack of control, but it also limited her dealings with others to the point that she could eat only in the presence of her immediate family.

It is apparent then, that phobias can develop around an infinite variety of situations or objects. In order to treat phobias which are attached to such situations, it is necessary to determine the factors which produce the phobic response. The term school phobia, for example, generally implies a fear of or resistance to going to school. It gives us no clue as to whether the phobic object is the school bus, driver, teacher, desk, other pupils, or the inability to leave Mother for any period of time. For a clearer understanding of the phobic process, it is imperative to recognize that in speaking of a school phobia, one does not describe the specific condition, but rather a generalized situation in which the specific operates. A greater semantic and descriptive precision will add immeasurably to the understanding of phobias, as it has to other psychological problems.

At the time when it was believed that each phobia had a separate etiology and dynamic function, elaborate classification of over 211 phobias was justified (1). It will be recalled that Freud adopted this view of the phobic state even though he contributed to a greater understanding of it by recognizing that the phobia was a symbolic representation. The symbolism, he believed, always concerned an unacceptable aggressive or sexual impulse. He considered the phobic situation or object to be specific to these dynamics, regardless of the personality or previous experience of the patient.

More recently the theory of phobias has assumed a less specific etiology. When an individual has a great anxiety about his hostile or aggressive feelings toward another person, it is not surprising that his phobia might involve dangerous weapons, or access to the hated person, or the presence of circumstances that would prevent a loss of control which might endanger the hated individual. The symbolic significance of the phobia may be the same even when the phobic objects are very different. The phobic object, itself, may have symbolic significance within the context of the phobic dynamism, but it does not imply a specific etiology.

Dr. Harold Lief, in a paper which bears out my view of the origin of the phobic state (13), has further contributed to the theory that phobias have less specific etiology. He points out that the phobic object may be related to inner conflict, but may also have nothing to do with this state. The phobia begins in some sensory context of a critical anxiety; the symbolic associations may or may not be invested with original unconscious sources of anxiety. Lief points out that the phobic object is distinctly related to the sensory context of the critical anxiety situation and does not, in itself, constitute the symbolism or the significance of the underlying anxiety.

I believe that all phobias have the same dynamic and functional significance. The particular content and setting are largely accidental and have only secondary significance. That is, the phobic object or situation is an accidental or coincidental accompaniment of a severe state of anxiety at a time when the individual has experienced the possibility of losing control. The content of the phobia is then woven around that situation which presented itself when the anxiety occurred. The fact that certain situations—such as heights, elevators, closed spaces, dangerous weapons, stage appearances or social gatherings—are conducive to setting off severe anxieties about loss of control accounts for their high incidence in the phobic states.

In therapy, analyzing why one selects a specific

phobic object is secondary. What must be analyzed and clarified is the dread of losing control which first manifested itself in a crowded vehicle or a high place where, for some reason, the person experienced panic or severe anxiety. The analysis of this anxiety about losing control then resolves itself in the analysis of the basic character structure of which this problem forms the hard core. This is the obsessive-compulsive character structure.

☐ ☐ ☐

Phobias invariably occur in obsessional characters, either as part of an obsession-compulsive neurosis, where they may play only a minimal role, or the phobia may be the prominent symptom in an individual, where the obsessional way of life is secondary. The presence of the phobia, I believe, indicates that the obsessional mechanism is not serving its purpose sufficiently well; consequently, the phobic state intervenes to guarantee the avoidance of, and thus absolute control in, seriously threatened areas. The relationship of obsessional states to phobias offers four clinical possibilities:

obsessional state without phobias
obsessional state with mild phobic symptomatology
obsessional state with moderate phobic symptomatology
obsessional state with severe phobic symptomatology.

1. In the obsessional state without phobic symptomatology, one finds the classical obsessional disorders, which may be characterized by doubting, indecision, or compulsive acts. Phobic avoidance symptoms have not crystallized out of the matrix of the general distracting and avoiding tendencies of the obsessional mechanism. While there is considerable anxiety about engaging in any activity or initiating any project, there is no specific bar or obstacle aside from the generalized unwillingness to commit oneself. The reluctance to make decisions or to select alternatives often presents a picture of an individual who avoids involvements, but these avoidance reactions are not yet organized to absolutely prevent involvement.

Under these circumstances, the obsessional patterns are apparently sufficiently potent and successful in warding off severe anxiety attacks without there being the necessity of imposing absolute safeguards in the form of phobias. This does not mean that the individual is healthier or even that he functions more efficiently. It does imply

that the obsessional technique is capable of exerting enough control to make other techniques unnecessary. However, this may mean that the obsessive is ultimately less effective than the phobic individual, since it may be more efficient to isolate only one area of living and close it off to further experiencing while maintaining relatively healthy functioning in all other areas than it is to succumb to the generally inhibiting and depressive effect of obsessional doubting and indecisiveness, which minimizes all involvements.

2. In the category of obsessive states with mild phobic symptomatology are the obsessive-compulsive neuroses in which there are one or several phobic problems, all secondary to the main issue. The phobias frequently relate to the content of the obsessions or the compulsions; in one instance, where the obsessional preoccupation involved murder, there was a marked phobia regarding knives or guns. In other instances the phobias involve the issue of losing control in a particular area where the individual may have had an experience in which this control was endangered.

In these instances the phobias do not occupy a central role in the therapy and may often go unnoticed as part of the patient's problem. Therapy revolves around the obsessive-compulsive problem and the phobia frequently disappears without there having been any focal attention paid to it.

3. Obsessive state with moderate phobic symptomatology describes the group in which the phobic manifestations of the individual's difficulties often predominate, and the emphasis of therapy for such patients would be on the phobic problems rather than the underlying obsessional state. More often than not, it is the phobia which forces the individual into therapy, since he has either overlooked or resisted any inquiries into his obsessional problems. Such patients are often categorized as phobic. They then prove very resistant to hypnosis, conditioning, or other therapies designed exclusively to alter the phobic manifestations. At such times, one can see the very close relationship of phobia to the obsessional state. Several case histories will illustrate this point.

Case one involves a lawyer who came to therapy for what was described as a phobia involving court appearances. While defending a client, he experienced a sudden, rapid rise in pulse, with a fear of fainting, and was forced to leave the courtroom and terminate his relationship with the case. Following this incident, he avoided all court appearances. In the above-described episode, the patient thought he was having a heart attack, and for a great many years was obsessionally preoccupied with his cardiac state. In addition to the courtroom phobia, he also had phobias about bridges, enclosed spaces, and tunnels of all sorts. As time went on he developed a speaking phobia whenever he was called upon to give a prepared address. However, if he were called upon unexpectedly, he could function very well and could speak quite persuasively.

Prior to the fainting spell, he had experienced other difficulties in his law practice, since he always had to have a perfect case. He would therefore prepare with exceptional thoroughness, a practice which his associates found annoying, unnecessary and excessive. His life was organized around being a dedicated man of integrity who was beyond reproach in both his private and professional life. In his legal work he assumed total responsibility for the fate of his clients and their problems. He had great difficulty distinguishing between doing the best he could for his clients and the need to win every single case. It was essential that everyone think highly of him, and many people did, since his successes managed to far outweigh his defeats.

The fainting attack had occurred when the opposing counsel introduced an argument which the patient had not anticipated. He therefore was taken unawares in a situation in which he felt he was expected to be prepared and in control. He immediately became very tense, excited, and extremely restless. His pulse became very rapid; he felt a sudden pain in his chest and collapsed. It is interesting to note that the argument which caused this reaction was neither significant nor crucial to the ultimate outcome of the case, but since it was unexpected, it could not be dealt with in an ideal and perfect fashion.

The patient's phobias are characteristically those of control. Since he could never be certain, and could not achieve absolute clarity and wisdom in every situation, his phobias allow him to avoid the challenge to, and discovery of, his human frailties and weaknesses. Yet he feels weak and cowardly for avoiding these situations that characterize his profession. This feeling is easily dissipated by fantasying that, but for the phobias, he would achieve the hero role and perform perfectly. This patient has recognized many times that if he knew precisely how the case would proceed, or how he would perform at a speaking engagement, he would have no difficulty at all. The problem arises when he cannot be assured that all will go well and that he will not go blank and stutter, faint, or have a heart attack. This patient's problems arise directly out of his obsessional difficulties and are closely related to them. As the obsessional problems have gradually been clarified, many of the phobias have been entirely resolved, others have shown marked improvement, and still others have remained unchanged.

Case two is that of a 45-year-old female whose major problem was a writing phobia which had its beginnings when she had to sign her name to a contract in the presence of other people. On that occasion she was in the spotlight and began to get uneasy about the possibility of losing her composure and shaking visibly. This would have been utterly humiliating for her. By pleading illness she was able to avoid the actual trial, but thereafter she could not sign her name at banks, department stores, or even at home in the presence of strangers or friends. Her pride prevented her from informing anyone except her husband and one close friend about her incapacity. The major focus in this phobia is the issue of displaying a tremor which would betray her nervousness. The writing phobia gradually extended to a phobia about socializing wherever drinks were to be served. This included luncheons, teas, dinners, etc. Her social life became very restricted and the agitation and preoccupation in anticipation of such engagements became very great. The phobias served a vital purpose in her life, but were entirely unacceptable to her; she felt ashamed and disappointed in herself for not being able to overcome these weaknesses. She was a very bright person who could not tolerate any situation in which she was second-best or less well-informed than another. Socializing was difficult aside from the tremors, since she never knew in advance whether she would measure up to her own standards with all the people she might encounter. She felt that she must know everything or others would find her dull and uninteresting. Her emphasis was entirely on intellectual achievement and though she recognized the impossibility of competing with everyone about everything, she actually expected this of herself. She recognized that she demanded the impossible of herself, yet felt that anything less than this was unacceptable. To be less than perfect meant that one was ordinary, and this was humiliating. While she wanted her phobias eliminated, she did not wish to alter her perfectionistic goals and her omniscient requirements. The phobias directly intervened at times when she felt or was in danger of appearing human, and therefore limited and imperfect. Her obsessional problems were manifest not only in her demands for perfection, control, guarantees of the future, but in specific matters as well, such as her meticulous concern for her own person and affairs, and her obsessional ruminations and preoccupations.

4. Obsessional state with major phobic symptomatology is the category in which one finds the phobic condition so much in the forefront that the underlying obsessive-compulsive patterns are frequently either hidden or remain in the background. It is these situations which led to the separate categorization of phobic states, since they would appear to be the sole psychic deviations which require special notice and handling. The content of the phobias may be varied and diffuse and, at times, gives no clues to the underlying obsessive-compulsive state which is invariably present.

For example, a particularly severe phobia about animals prevented a very prosperous business man from entering any house or establishment unless he was assured that there were no animals on the premises. This phobia was closely related to a dirt phobia which necessitated washing his hands dozens of times during the day, and changing his clothes three or four times a day. The phobic issues were so incapacitating that the compulsive handwashing ritual was considered secondary and unimportant. These phobias alternated with other strong phobic reactions to particular places and things, but essentially the problem centered around the issue of germs, dirt and other noxious elements which he was compelled to guard against because of the potential danger to his health. This man was very successful as an entrepreneur and go-getter who managed very large financial deals without seeking help from anyone except banks. He felt that he could trust no one and that others would inevitably let him down. He was a lone operator who was convinced of his own invincible capacity, but was afraid, at every moment, that he might not be able to meet his financial obligations and would lose everything in one sudden stroke. He was in a constant state of tension, preoccupied with ways of guaranteeing his next payments and making certain of his future. He could enjoy neither his money nor his possessions because of his constant concern as to whether they would be there tomorrow. Every restaurant bill, charity drive, or legitimate demand was scrutinized with great care to guard against being victimized. Objectively, his financial situation was extremely secure, but he directed all his efforts to making sure that tomorrow would be exactly like today, though there was no possible way to achieve this certainty. He displayed no interest in his tendencies towards omnipotence and omniscience. He saw the whole difficulty as a peculiarity of his phobias, which he wanted eliminated.

While the phobic problem was certainly central, both in his thoughts and in the limitations in his living, the obsessional difficulties were clearly in the background. The phobias expressed his insistence on a purity and perfection that was impossible to achieve, since he demanded to know from one second to another that he was devoid of germs and other noxious elements that were all-pervasive. His extensive handwashing was designed to achieve this purpose and to guarantee his health. The animal phobia represented a focused concern about preventing the passage of germs and organisms from the animal hosts. Any contact, even the most remote, would require a washing and a change of clothes. This was an extreme form of control in the sense of dictating to the world what contacts he should make and what should be kept out of his range. It was often apparent that the germ phobia was a device to distract him from his greater concern, which was the need to be financially sound, so as to demonstrate to the world and, particularly, to his father, that he was invincible and unassailable. To fail meant that he would be totally rejected and expelled from the human race.

When we examine the phobias from an adaptational as well as a motivational point of view, it is clear that they are excellent techniques of defense against anxiety. The anxiety is clearly related to personality characteristics which are in danger of being exposed or destroyed. Phobias may involve covert hostilities or fears of being weak and dependent, or they may cover the entire range of human conflict. The underlying character structure which is organized to maintain a rigid control against exposure or acknowledgment is the obsessive-compulsive dynamism which is ideally set up to serve this purpose. Under those circumstances where the obsessive-compulsive dynamism is not sufficiently intact, the absolute avoidance mechanism of the phobia guarantees against such an exposure by never permitting the situation to develop. Consequently, the phobia becomes a technique for absolute control, and unless it becomes too diffuse or widespread, it serves its purpose well. It is, however, qualitatively different from the simple avoidance reactions which serve the same purpose of protecting the individual from a known source of danger as a result of previous experience with it. The phobia arises in response to a severe and critical anxiety attack in which some psychological need, defense, or conflict is brought dangerously near to being exposed or going out of control, and is a symptom of an underlying disorder, not a syndrome in itself.

The setting or sensory accompaniments determine the phobic object in which the real danger may or may not be symbolically represented. The phobic object may then be entirely accidental or coincidental, and may involve the sensorium in an auditory, kinesthetic, as well as in a visual sense. The symbolism and setting frequently combine and the spread of the phobia is determined either by sensory contiguity or by the symbolic associations possible in the new setting. The phobia is, in essence, an avoidance technique established through the defensive capacities of the human psyche to prevent the destruction of the integrity of the organism. However, it is a neurotic integration which is being maintained and, consequently, symbolism and other devices to represent both unconscious and out-of-awareness needs and conflicts are essential.

The recognition of the phobic origin from an obsessive-compulsive disorder makes it clear that the ultimate resolution of the phobia rests with the necessity of clarifying the obsessive-compulsive difficulty.

REFERENCES

1. Alexander, F., Fundamentals of Psychoanalysis (New York: Norton Co., 1948).
2. Arieti, S., "A Reexamination of the Phobic Symptom and of Symbolism in Psychopathology." Amer. J. Psychiat., 118:2, 1961.
3. Dollard, J. and Miller, N. E., Personality and Psychotherapy (New York: McGraw-Hill, 1950).

4. Fenichel, O., The Psychoanalytic Theory of Neurosis (New York: W. W. Norton Co., 1945).

5. "Remarks on Common Phobias," Psychoanal. Quart., 13:313, 1944.

6. Freud, S., Standard Edition of the Complete Psychological Works of Sigmund Freud, Vol. III (London: Hogarth Press, 1962, pp. 71–87).

7. Freud, S., Analysis of a Phobia in a Five-Year-old Boy (1909), Vol. X. Standard Edition (London: Hogarth Press, 1955, pp. 5–153).

8. Freud, S., From the History of an Infantile Neurosis (1918), Vol. XVII, Standard Edition London: (Hogarth Press, 1955, pp. 7–123).

9. Freud, S., Introductory Lectures on Psycho-Analysis (1916–17), Vol. XVI, Standard Edition (London: Hogarth Press, 1963, Lecture XXV, pp. 392–412).

10. Freud, S., Inhibitions, Symptoms and Anxiety (1925–1926), Vol. XX, Standard Edition (London: Hogarth Press, 1959, pp. 87–157).

11. Freud, S., Totem and Taboo (1913–1914), Vol. XIII, Standard Edition (London: Hogarth Press, 1955, Essay II, sections 2 and 3 (c) and Essay III, sections 3 and 4).

12. Freud, S., Interpretation of Dreams (1900), Vol. IV, Standard Edition (London: Hogarth Press, p. 260).

13. Lief, H., "Sensory Association in the Selection of Phobic Objects," Psychiat., 18:331–338, 1955.

14. Sullivan, H. S., Conceptions of Modern Psychiatry (New York: Norton Co., 1953).

SUGGESTED READINGS

General

Anxiety states (anxiety neuroses). Marks I, Lader M. Journal of Nervous and Mental Disease 156:3–18, 1973.

Severe social anxiety. Nichols KA. British Journal of Medical Psychology 47:301–306, 1974.

National history of obsessional neurosis. Kringlen E. Seminars in Psychiatry 2:403–419, 1970.

Obsessive compulsive disorders: A review of the literature. Salzman L, Thaler FH. American Journal of Psychiatry 138:286–296, 1981.

Agoraphobic syndrome (phobic anxiety states). Marks I. Archives of General Psychiatry 23:538–553, 1970.

Mitral valve prolapse syndrome in agoraphobic patients. Kantor JS, Zitrin CM, Zeldis SM. American Journal of Psychiatry 137:4, 1980.

Signs and symptoms of posttraumatic stress disorder. Horowitz MJ, Wilner N, Kaltreider N, Alvarez W. Archives of General Psychiatry 37:85–92, 1980.

Individual reactions to community disaster. The natural history of psychiatric phenomena. Tyhurst JS, American Journal of Psychiatry 107:764–769, 1951.

Gross stress reaction. Weiss RJ, Payson HE. In Comprehensive Textbook of Psychiatry (edited by Freeman AM, Kaplan HI). Baltimore, Williams & Wilkins, pp 1027–1031.

Biological Factors

The evidence for genetic components in the neuroses. Miner G. Archives of General Psychiatry 29:111–118, 1973.

Genetics and the future of psychoanalysis. Rainer, JD. Journal of Nervous and Mental Disease 167:721–725, 1979.

Familial anthropophobia in pointer dogs? Dykman RA, Murphee OD, Reese WG. Archives of General Psychiatry 36:988–1000, 1979.

A familial study of anxiety disorders. Crowe RR, Pauls DL, Slymen MS, Noyes R. Archives of General Psychiatry 37:77–79, 1980.

Receptors for the age of anxiety: Pharmacology of benzodiazepines. Tallman JF. Science 207:274–281, 1980.

Brain mechanisms associated with therapeutic actions of benzodiazepines: Focus on neurotransmitters. Snyder S, Enna S, Young A. American Journal of Psychiatry 134:662–664, 1977.

Amitriptyline therapy of obsessive–compulsive neurosis. Snyder S. Journal of Clinical Psychiatry 41:286–289, 1980.

The neurophysiological basis of anxiety: A hypothesis. Gellhorn E. Perspectives in Biology and Medicine 8:488–514, 1965.

Psychological Factors

Behavioral theories: Pathological patterns. Etiology of human neuroses. Wolpe J. In Theories of Psychopathology and Personality (edited by Millon T.) Philadelphia, W. B. Saunders, 1973, pp 319–337.

A clinical contribution to the psychopathology of war neuroses. Rosenberg E. International Journal of Psychoanalysis 24:32–41, 1943.

Nosophobia and hypochondiasis in medical students. Schwartzman E. Journal of Nervous and Mental Disease 139:147–152, 1964.

PART

V

SOMATOFORM DISORDERS

OVERVIEW

Individuals with somatoform disorders usually present first to their physician with symptoms suggestive of organic physical illness. Further evaluation reveals no demonstrable physical disorder to explain the symptoms. Patients with somatoform disorders consistently have physical complaints that tend to be exacerbated during times of life crisis. Nonetheless, these patients may not be aware of any relationship of stress to symptom formation. Another important feature in this disorder is that the intensity of somatic complaints often decrease, even if only temporarily, when there is support from a concerned physician or other significant person.

Although they are often unaware of the impact of their style of approach, patients with somatoform disorder usually elicit attention or assistance by exaggerating or dramatizing the severity of their somatic symptoms while often appearing somewhat indifferent in a way that seems, to the observer, to be inappropriate to the symptom. Thus, the patient may complacently complain of "paralysis." Since emergence and perpetuation of symptoms are not under conscious control, persons with somatoform disorders should not be seen as imposters. Often the gratification they seek (secondary gain) may be apparent, but at other times the meaning of the symptom and its gain are not immediately obvious. Thus, a person with a somatoform disorder and an early childhood history of deprivation may seek caretaking, but those who are not aware of this history might be perplexed by the apparent self-destructive aspects of assuming the sick role.

The somatoform disorders represent a new diagnostic grouping encompassing frequently misinterpreted or loosely used concepts such as *hysteria*, *hysterical neurosis*, *Briquet's hysteria*, *hypochondriacal neurosis*, and *psychogenic pain*. An important feature of this diagnostic entity is that the operational criteria do not refer to the underlying personality type (dramatic, histrionic, hysterical), which once confounded the diagnosis.

There are five different types of somatoform disorders in *DSM-III*: somatization disorder, conversion disorder, psychogenic pain disorder, hypochondriacal disorder, and atypical somatoform disorder.

Somatization disorder is characterized by a dramatic, vague, and complicated medical history in which symptoms have a psychogenic etiology. An individual may have had many hospitalizations without clear-cut medical or surgical diagnosis and without positive pathological findings for a number of vague complaints. The patient's focus is on physical discomfort(s) rather than on the meaning or the possible health care implications of symptoms.

Conversion disorder formally was called conversion hysteria or hysterical neurosis, conversion type. Physical functioning of some sensory organ or bodily part is impaired because of psychogenic factors, for example, paralysis of both lower limbs with no consistent specific lesion, disease, or objective neurological finding. Conversion reactions can occur in a variety of other mental disorders, but when it is the only or predominant disturbance, it is called a conversion disorder.

In psychogenic pain disorder, severe physical pain may be present without known physical cause or relation to psychogenic factor. For example, a person with extremity pain not following a neurogenic pattern of disturbance may have psychogenically determined pain.

Hypochondriacal disorder is characterized by the patient's unrealistic evaluation of physical signs or symptoms. The individual is bothered more by the implications of the symptoms than by the pain or discomfort itself and becomes convinced that he or she has a serious disease, perhaps one that has not yet manifested itself in a way that facilitates medical diagnosis. For example, the hypochondriac may feel that he/she has undetected cancer. Patients with this disorder remain steadfastly unreassured by normal evaluations ("negative work-ups") and often see many physicians. Thus, emphasis is not so much on present discomfort as it is on the meaning of symptoms for secure functioning in the future.

Atypical somatoform disorder represents those disorders with bodily preoccupation that do not meet this specific criteria for the other somatoform disorders. One of the atypical somatoform disorders, called dysmorphophobia, is an intense preoccupation with, and dislike or distortion of, body image; for example, the person with a small facial scar who believes that his or her entire physical appearance is grossly marred.

Somatic symptoms are often found in people with other mental disorders. For example, people with schizophrenia may have bizarre notions about specific parts of their bodies, and they may experience tactile or other somatic hallucinations. Patients with major episodic depressive disorders experience vegetative symptoms, including anorexia, constipation, dry mouth, and muscular aches and pains. At times they may have somatic delusions, e.g., "My body is rotting!" These people may first consult a cardiologist or a gastroenterologist because of their system-specific somatic complaints.

With the somatoform disorders, at first a psychogenic etiology may not seem to be apparent because somatic symptoms appear compelling and overt evidence of mental illness is not apparent. The patient usually presents symptoms in such a way as to point to a physical illness, and the relationship of physical distress to life stress does not emerge clearly from the patient's history. This may be further complicated if the patient forgets or unconsciously represses that he or she had the same or similar physical symptoms during another period of psychosocial difficulties. It may become necessary to consult old chart notes and family members to obtain the necessary relevant past history.

Physicians are often tempted to use the diagnosis of somatoform disorder when a patient's illness is otherwise inexplicable. Thus many patients who eventually develop multisystem, polysymptomatic medical illnesses are initially incorrectly suspected of having a somatoform disorder. Illnesses most likely to be confused with somatoform disorder include *systemic lupus erythematosus, acute intermittent porphyria, multiple sclerosis, myasthenia gravis,* and some of the neurological degenerative conditions, particularly those that present with intermittent symptoms.

SOMATIZATION DISORDER

Somatization disorder is a chronic polysymptomatic condition most often diagnosed in women. It begins in adolescence or in young adulthood and is characterized by the occurrence of multiple somatic complaints leading to repeated requests for medical care. Despite extensive examinations and often multiple invasive diagnostic and even surgical procedures, no clear-cut organ pathology can account for the diverse somatic complaints. Although fluctuations in severity of symptoms occur, spontaneous remission is rare, and it is unusual for these patients to be out of contact with a physician for longer than a year.

Essential symptoms include headaches, fatigue, fainting, palpitations, nausea, vomiting, menstrual and sexual difficulties, abdominal pain, bowel trouble, and conversion reactions. Anxiety and depression are accessory symptoms often associated with these somatization disorders. Indeed, affective symptoms may initially dominate the clinical picture. For example, a patient with multiple somatic complaints may come to the attention of the physician after making a suicide gesture.

Another accessory feature is extensive interpersonal conflict. There may be a history of truancy, lying, fighting, poor work record, and marital difficulties. Hallucinations are another accessory symptom sometimes seen in somatization disorder, often taking the form of hearing one's name called aloud. These hallucinations are usually transient rather than persistent, and they are not accompanied by other manifestations of thought disorder. Although the usual type of personality seen in patients with somatization disorder is the histrionic type (see Part III), this is not a necessary diagnostic feature.

The three operational criteria for the diagnosis of somatization disorder are:

1. Symptoms of unexplained physical illness commence by age 20
2. The necessary information for making the diagnosis is readily elicited in the course of taking a medical history. Somatic symptoms must

have been of sufficient severity that the patient actually took medication (other than aspirin), saw a physician, or altered his or her life-style
3. Symptoms are widespread, involving many organ systems without demonstrable pathology.

In order to develop a homogeneous population for research purposes, to better understand this nosological entity, *DSM-III* criteria require for women 14 and for men at least 12 of the more than 30 possible symptoms, listed below by functional groups:

1. Sickly: The individual believes that "sickly" describes the general state of health for a good part of his or her life.
2. Conversion symptoms: Included are difficulties swallowing (dysphagia); difficulties speaking audibly (*aphonia*); double vision (dyplopia); blindness (amblyopia); blurred vision; deafness; trouble walking or standing (astasia abasia); paralysis or muscle weakness (paresis); urinary retention or difficulty urinating; memory loss (*amnesia*); fainting or loss of consciousness; seizures; dizziness.
3. Gastrointestinal symptoms: Included are a considerable amount of abdominal pain; nausea and vomiting spells (except during pregnancy); bloating; marked food intolerance from a variety of foods; diarrhea.
4. Cardiopulmonary symptoms: Included are frequent shortness of breath (dyspnea), palpitations, and chest pain.
5. Psychosexual symptoms: For the major part of the individual's life after opportunities for sexual activity are possible he or she has sexual indifference, lack of sexual pleasure, or actual physical pain during intercourse (dyspareunia).
6. Pain: In the back, joints, extremities, during urination, in the genital area (except during intercourse), or other pains (except headaches).
7. Female reproductive symptoms: The patient herself judges that she has the following symptoms more frequently or more severely than most women: *dysmenorrhea*, menstrual irregularities, excessive bleeding, or severe vomiting either throughout pregnancy or else causing hospitalization during pregnancy.

CONVERSION DISORDER

In this disorder, the patient has a loss or alteration of some sort of motor power or sensory modality that would seem to represent a calamity of major proportions. Yet, in the face of such a deficit, many

of these patients seem surprisingly calm, almost indifferent (*la belle indifference*).

The best known case of conversion disorder is Joseph Breuer's celebrated case of Anna O. She was a bright and articulate 21-year-old woman who developed a number of somatic symptoms including a paralyzed right arm and leg, impaired eyesight, nausea, mental confusion, delirium, and a changed personality. The illness resembled no known neurological condition, and no organic cause could be determined. With hypnosis she was able to recall the onset of her symptoms and ventilate feelings, which led to a disappearance of her ailments. Dr. Breuer's concept and its formulation led to the idea that there could be an emotional cause for these somatic symptoms, symptoms amenable to a "talking cure."

In order to establish the diagnosis firmly, the clinician needs to understand how psychological factors are involved in symptom formation. For example, the temporal relationship between a psychologically painful occurrence and the symptom must be demonstrated. The clinician must also be able to understand the specific meaning, symbolic or practical, of the symptom choice. Similarly, it is necessary to comprehend why the symptom is necessary in the resolution of a conflict or the avoidance of some noxious situation. The net result of the disability of a conversion disorder is an avoidance of an unpleasant consequence or a gain in some form of support otherwise not forthcoming. Somatic symptoms occur by means of unconscious mechanisms, out of the awareness of the afflicted individual. Thus the person with paralysis may not be aware that he or she may unconsciously prefer this condition to the stress induced by being mobile and responsible for one's own care.

Clinicians are often tempted to make the diagnosis of conversion disorder when they cannot find an organic basis, a medical cause, for a symptom. It is important to remember that unexplained physical complaints or dysfunctions are not necessarily conversion disorders. One large series with a long follow-up revealed that 25% of all those with symptoms originally diagnosed as a conversion disorder eventually turned out to have a medical disorder that caused the symptoms.

PSYCHOGENIC PAIN DISORDER

Severe and prolonged pain can be the dominant or only clinical feature of a disorder that has an emotional etiology. Pain is, after all, based on a self-perception. Interpreting a complaint is made even more complicated for the physician by the fact that each person has an idiosyncratic threshold for pain. Although most chronic pain disorders have some organic basis, there clearly are patients who do not have a detectable peripheral or central lesion to account for their painful sufferings.

One characteristic of psychogenic pain is that the localization of the pain sensation does not follow a pattern normally associated with known neurological lesions (it does not follow a neurological distribution) and no evidence of any lesion can be found. But psychogenic pain can be diagnosed in patients who do have peripheral lesions when the complaint grossly exceeds the degree of suffering expected from such a lesion.

To substantiate the diagnosis of psychogenic pain, it is important to have a clear understanding of the psychological factors in its etiology. The same criteria operate as in conversion disorders; that is, there must be a temporal relationship between a psychologically traumatic event and the occurrence of the pain, or the pain must enable the individual to avoid some activity or responsibility that is noxious. Alternatively, the pain may enable the individual to obtain what might not otherwise be forthcoming from significant others (secondary gain). For example, the prospect of high financial compensation following a painful, prolonged disability may in some cases have unconscious motivation for the perpetuation of symptoms until after the settlement has been made (compensation neurosis). Finally, to make the diagnosis, there must be no other mental or physical disorder that can account for the pain. A conversion disorder with pain as a predominant feature by definition is called psychogenic pain.

The reasons leading to the selection of pain as a protective or manipulative symptom rather than some other bodily complaint are not always clear. It is, however, not at all rare for a patient with psychogenic pain to have a childhood history of severe corporal punishment and/or other physically painful experiences at an early age.

Patients with chronic pain from any cause may feel alienated and embittered when they do not receive medical help. They may feel that they are entitled to have special privileges because of the extent of their suffering. Patients with psychogenic pain generally tend to be more manipulative and demanding in their use of symptoms than those whose pain derives from organic factors. Not infrequently, they abuse narcotics and even become addicted. They tend to focus on the intensity of their distress, at times to the exclusion of the meaning of the pain or even of factors that might be relevant to better understanding the pain's onset and etiology.

HYPOCHONDRIACAL DISORDER

The term "hypochondriasis" is derived from the Greek word "hypochondrium," which literally means "under the rib cage." It implies a condition that (like tissue under the rib cage) is not palpable, one in which there is no detectable abnormality on careful physical examination. No doubt the ancient physicians were impressed by patients who alleged they had derangements of the abdominal (or other) organs, yet on long-term follow-up failed to develop evidence of any physical ailment.

The condition is found equally in men and women. It is a chronic disorder that begins for some in adolescence, but for most it begins later in life, typically for men in their 30s and for women in their 40s. Development of hypochondriacal symptoms in the elderly is often part of a depressive disorder, while in teenagers, hypochondriasis may be the harbinger of schizophrenia. At any rate, the diagnosis of a hypochondriacal disorder is made only in the absence of other serious mental disorders.

The prognosis for cure of hypochondriacal disorders is not good, although remissions do occur. Fears or beliefs about one disease may fade, but all too often they recur or are replaced by a focus on another disease. Characteristically, the hypochondriac is tense, restless, or depressed and claims that this inner turmoil stems from pressures or fear of some sort of physical disease. Usually, however, such an individual is able to carry on most everyday work responsibilities, but there is some impairment in work, social, or recreational capacity.

Many people occasionally have complaints about mild physical symptoms, symptoms that may or may not be associated with a physical ailment or even a transient fear concerning an illness that they read about in the newspaper. Or perhaps they briefly relate some physical sensation to a fatal disease that recently afflicted a friend or family member. But the person with a hypochondriacal disorder has a prolonged and somewhat disabling fear or belief that persists despite multiple medical reassurances.

So insistent are hypochondriacs about some undetected and dreadful disease process, and so persistent are they in their search for the ailments' cause, that the physician often becomes alienated and even irritated with the patient's tenacious resistance to reassurance. These patients believe that they have an abnormality, which the doctor, because of ineptitude, has failed to detect. Indeed, one complication of this disorder is that the physician may fail to diagnose an intermittent physical problem because he believes the patient to be a "crock" or malingerer. New and different complaints can be dismissed by the physician as "more of the same." Another complication of the condition relates to the unnecessary diagnostic procedures that are often performed. Many hypochondriacs have repeated *laparotomies* (exploratory surgical procedures), without positive pathological findings. It is not unusual for some hypochondriacs to become "doctor shoppers." They are often overmedicated with a wide variety of drugs, especially anxiolytic agents, which are usually ineffective, because these patients do not want medication for anxiety, but rather contact with the physician.

The hypochondriacs' somatic experiences, behaviors, and emotional reactions differ in intensity and/or amount from those expected from patients of similar age and background. Their preoccupation with internal physical events may actually be abetted by an increased awareness of a normal heartbeat or a normal bowel *peristalsis,* a mild nonproductive cough, or a nonmalignant type of mole. These somatic preoccupations emerge in the face of a vivid imagination and a psychosocial stressor, such as loss of control, lowered self-esteem, loneliness, or increased sense of personal responsibility.

ATYPICAL SOMATOFORM DISORDER

Preoccupation with self is not necessarily pathological. In a healthy sense, it implies appropriate self-care and concern, a sense of pride, a positive feeling. Taken to extremes, however, pathological narcissism shuts out the relationship between the self and others and precludes the establishment of the feelings and experiences related to living, loving, and working. When self-preoccupation takes the form of overconcern with a trivial physical defect, it is termed dysmorphophobia. This and other emotional disorders with predominant somatic symptoms that do not meet the exacting criteria for the other somatoform disorders have been lumped together under the "catch-all" term of atypical somatoform disorder.

Thus, the individual with an atypical somatoform disorder may be a person who "somatizes" a great deal, especially during times of high tension, when emotional reserves have been called on, and defenses are stretched. Such a person knows that he or she has "dis-ease," and may develop new, or troublesome old, physical symptoms. The deflection of attention away from psychological matters and onto bodily dysfunction may lessen the individual's perceived anxiety level, although it rarely eliminates it.

In a similar fashion, if a man says that his life is a social disaster because the bridge of his nose has a hump, or if a woman says that no one can love her because she is 15 pounds overweight, the mechanisms are parallel. The individual blames social failures, even self-loathing, on a physical attribute whose outward appearance is merely magnified. The self-loathing that develops would appear to be related to the defect, but in reality it is a displacement of feelings that were already present, onto something concrete and particular rather than something diffuse and related to one's most central and vulnerable aspect, one's self.

EPIDEMIOLOGY

No definitive survey of the epidemiology of somatoform disorders exist, as this is a new diagnostic entity, but there are some relevant studies on some of the previously standardized diagnostic groupings. Based on interviews of patients hospitalized for nonpsychiatric conditions (e.g., childbirth), it is estimated that somatization disorder afflicts some 2% of women aged 15 to 35. Indeed, people with the somatoform disorders are rarely if ever seen on the psychiatric inpatient service, although they are often seen in physicians' offices and not infrequently on the surgical service. Conversion disorder may be found in 2–5% of admissions to a general hospital. Hypochondriacal disorders represent about 1% of all admissions to psychiatric inpatient and outpatient services. Most physicians would estimate that a higher proportion of their patients are hypochondriacs or have somatization disorder because of the dogged persistence that those patients have for medical care and/or the colorful presentation that they may use to draw attention to themselves.

The somatoform disorders comprise one part of what is often considered to be the psychoneuroses or the neuroses, distressing (*ego-dystonic*) mental disorders with anxiety as a core. These neuroses are often expressed as such or converted (conversion disorder, psychogenic pain disorder), somatized (hypochondriacal disorder, somatization disorder), displaced (phobias, obsessions, and compulsions), or *dissociated* (*fugue states*).

ETIOLOGY

Why do some people express their distress through physical rather than emotional symptoms? The answer to this question is complex and probably multifaceted. A neurophysiological mechanism has been proposed to account for some of the manifestations of the somatoform disorders. Just as the amoeba tends to accommodate (discount noxious repetitious stimuli so as to be alert to some new menace or stimulus in the environment), so certain individuals may superficially discount or repress painful experiences or memories while remaining more alert and attentive to new threats from the environment. Hence, it could be that the individual with a somatoform disorder is one who represses (accommodates) some of the anxiety and other emotional feelings about an unresolved, bothersome psychosocial conflict, keeping it out of awareness. Thus, when a new crisis arises, the individual remains clear headed about what to do and is not flooded with a surfeit of feelings. New tensions when they arise are reflected and displaced in a bodily rather than an emotional sphere.

The pattern of somatizing seems to be familial. Clinicians working with families have noted that some members who both fear and disdain emotional disorders tend to experience their psychic distress in somatic rather than emotional ways. On an unconscious level, as discussed above, perhaps this "solution" is more acceptable to them. Sociologists and anthropologists report that different cultures value and use pain and the presentation of physical illness in different ways. Moreover, the presentation of physical symptoms varies with the psychosocial setting. Finally, the attribution of symptoms to benign or malevolent factors also relates to the social field. Thus the type and prevalence of somatoform disorders may vary considerably in different cultures.

TREATMENT

Because many patients with somatoform disorders vigorously deny an emotional component to their disorder, especially early in the course of their illness, the offer of referral for traditional psychotherapy to these patients may be misinterpreted as a rejection by the treating physician. Often these patients fear that the physical suffering

that has been clearly experienced will be doubted. Moreover, because the mechanism or *repression* is an active, ongoing process that serves the purpose of keeping threatening material out of awareness, any interaction that might threaten the self is to be avoided or attacked. An insight-oriented type of psychotherapy is usually not sought out by patients who somatize their emotional distress.

What these individuals want and seek most is relief of their physical anguish. They also wish emotional support to be prompt and attentive. They want a listener who is willing to hear their repetitive grievances and sometimes offer a word of encouragement or advice. They need some means of conflict resolution, and often this is no easy task. They do respond positively to gentle assistance in rearranging their disordered family dynamics. They also respond favorably when they are helped to accept a difficult loss. Finally, some of these patients can be supported in obtaining another goal other than the sick role and gradually giving up their symptoms, as a therapeutic alliance is slowly built.

For the treatment of conversion disorders, a variety of methods have been used successfully: psychoanalysis, supportive and insight-oriented psychotherapy, *behavior therapy*, and family therapy. Many conversion disorders appear to be self-limited, and therapy of various sorts may hasten recovery. If in addition therapy can effect some type of lasting resolution of the specific conflict, then the likelihood of the patient's subsequently developing other conversion disorders is lessened. For some, however, this illness is not so benign, because they cling tenaciously to their developed symptoms. They may develop permanent physical complications of their conversion disorder, such as contractures of their muscles and tendons.

The role of psychoactive medication in the somatoform disorders is complex. Hypochondriacal patients may see the offer of medication as the way of quieting them, or of cutting down on the frequency of clinic or office visits. Actually, hypochondriacs tend to develop exacerbations of symptoms when medication is offered. For patients with psychogenic pain, antidepressant or neuroleptic medications may, for reasons that are unclear, dramatically relieve the pain. For those patients with somatoform disorders who develop secondary but major affective disorders, tricyclic antidepressants can be helpful. Finally, active medication seems to have no role in the treatment of those with conversion disorders or dysmorphophobia.

SOMATIC EXPRESSIONS AND CONSEQUENCES OF CONVERSION REACTIONS

ARTHUR H. SCHMALE, JR.

There has been confusion in the literature as to what should be included as well as excluded under the heading of somatic conversion reactions. This presentation will attempt to delineate what is most useful in understanding what a conversion symptom is, how the body may react to it, and what somatic complications may occur in response to the symptom. Finally, I will discuss the ways in which the process can be differentiated from other psychologic syndromes with somatic complaints, that is, psychophysiologic reactions, hypochondriasis, and somatic delusions.

CONVERSION REACTIONS

Conversion reactions are a favorite form of reaction in those individuals with a hysterical character structure and, indeed, explain why at one time all conversion reactions were called hysterical conversions. The grandes hysteries with their dramatic flare for acting-out genital sexual reminiscences with convulsions, faints, amnesias, paralyses, and pains are fairly easily recognized. Clinical experience, however, has made it clear that the somatic conversion process can occur as an isolated symptom and in someone other than a woman with a rural, primitive, or mystical background and with a repressed, phallic sexual conflict.[1]

The conversion process is an intrapsychic process which involves a conflict, usually thought of in terms of an instinctual drive and a defense against the drive, which threatens to become conscious. The conversion symptom represents a shifting of the unconscious elements of the conflict to a form of body language. The shift to body language usually occurs in a setting in which the body is involved or is threatened to become involved in an activity which may be symbolically related to the conflict. Thus, there is a threat that the conflict will become conscious. For example, a woman was in the process of "stabbing" potatoes in an oven with a cooking fork when her arm and hand became "paralyzed." Of importance to the understanding of the use of the words "stabbing" and "paralyzed" was the fact that her husband had just returned home. He was late, and as he entered the kitchen she was immediately aware of his having violated his pledge never to drink again. To indicate how strongly she had felt about his drinking, on a previous occasion she had vowed that the marriage would all be over if he drank again. The "paralysis" defended against the act of "stabbing" which symbolically expressed her aggressive wish which threatened to break through.

As a psychic symptom formation the conversion symptom is of the same order of compromise as are other neurotic symptoms, such as phobias and compulsions. As such all may develop from conflicts first occurring during the pregenital period of development as well as from the genital. The symptom may appear at any time of life and may be associated with a wide variety of psychopathologic conditions.[2]

EDITORS' COMMENTS:

THE CONVERSION OF PSYCHIC STRESS INTO SOMATIC SYMPTOMS IS DISCUSSED BY A CLINICIAN WITH EXTENSIVE EXPERIENCE IN FOLLOWING MEDICAL AND SURGICAL PATIENTS WITH CONVERSION DISORDERS.

Reprinted with permission from the NEW YORK STATE JOURNAL OF MEDICINE, copyright by the Medical Society of the State of New York, Vol. 69, pp. 1878–1883, 1969.

Somatic conversion reactions may occur as isolated episodes at times of acute and extreme psychologic stress in individuals not considered psychologically maladjusted. Such symptoms commonly develop during grief.

CASE 1. In a group of 12 "normal, healthy" women, who were under study during a time their husbands were dying of cancer, 3 developed a symptom similar to what they observed their husbands were experiencing. The symptoms of chest pain, hoarseness, and weakness of the right arm and leg, respectively, were similar to those experienced by their husbands with cancer. The conversion symptoms came at a time when the husbands were making more demands for care than these women could meet. None of these women had had conversion symptoms in the past; and even though they considered it an extremely inopportune time to get sick, all of them were judged to have been psychologically relieved by the appearance of a somatic symptom which allowed them to ask for help. With the onset of the symptom, all 3 considered themselves ill and sought medical advice. All 3 reported they had reached the end of their psychologic endurance in trying to please and care for their dying husbands. There was nothing more they could do to make their husbands more comfortable and less symptomatic. In one way or another all 3 expressed the fleeting awareness of conflict over the wish that it would all be over soon. In each case the conflict over the wish was symbolized by the appearance of a symptom indicating an identification with the suffering of the dying spouse. The symbolic suffering protected them from having to take any further responsibility or action as far as it concerned the suffering object. The symbolic suffering thus served to protect them from a conscious awareness of their aggressive wishes toward their husbands.

Some investigators have emphasized that the somatic conversion symptoms in such circumstances also serve as a punishment for the underlying guilt associated with the wish. From my own observations the protective or defensive quality of the compromise symptom is dynamically more important than the punishment aspect.

As indicated by the previous examples, conversion reactions are marked by their sudden onset. There are, however, long-standing unconscious antecedents which threaten to emerge as a result of an event, idea, or fantasy which suddenly threatens to bring the conflict into consciousness. The following two examples illustrate how an acute event threatened to bring long-standing sibling rivalry out into the open.

CASE 2. A twelve-year-old boy suddenly became unable to speak at a time when his brother, two years younger, fell from the back of a truck on which they both had just hitched a ride. The inability to speak lasted for almost a week.

CASE 3. A second example is that of a twenty-two-year-old Italian athlete, who had recently started his own construction company and challenged his younger brother to a brick-laying race to prove his superiority. As he neared the end of the race and suddenly realized he was going to lose, he fainted.

Both these individuals became patients and were studied extensively in the hospital without discovering any somatic disorder to explain their symptoms. Details of their aggressive wishes toward their siblings were well documented, and in both cases the conversion reaction served as a protection against a forbidden wish.

The twelve-year-old boy (Case 2) thought he saw his brother "starting to slip and wanted to warn him" but found he could not speak. He also had not wanted his brother to tag along with him in the first place. On repeated previous occasions he had "difficulty in getting rid of the brat."

The loss of consciousness for the contractor (Case 3) was face-saving in that he recalled a fleeting thought just before he fainted which was, "I will never be able to face him (my brother) again." As it turned out, the younger brother was willing to accept the idea that his older and stronger brother would have won if he had not fainted.

The question of the type of bodily functions which can be represented in a conversion reaction has been discussed previously in an article coauthored with Engel.[3] Our view extends that of the commonly held one which has followed the thinking of Alexander.[4] Alexander and others restrict conversion reactions to the voluntary neuromuscular or sensory perceptive systems "with a switching of energy from psychic to somatic innervation and discharge."[2] Our focus emphasizes the completely intrapsychic nature of the conversion symptom. There is no somatic innervation or discharge. There is no mysterious leap from the mind to the body.[5] The conversion symptom represents a stored mental representation of bodily functioning. In effect any reminiscence of activity of any part or system of the individual's body or the observations of the actual or fantasied bodily functioning of other individuals, which has reached mental representation and has been stored as a memory trace, can be utilized as a conversion symptom. Thus, the somatic conversion symptom is a reactivation of a memory of somatic functioning and is not primarily concerned with the voluntary nervous system and its sensory or motor functioning, or even the autonomic nervous system for that matter.

Memories or fantasies of symptoms, such as

feeling nauseated, breathless, feverish, or injured, may occur as conversion symptoms as well as feelings of pain, paralysis, anesthesia, and blindness. Any actual or fantasied bodily activity or inactivity can serve as a conversion symptom if it satisfies the dynamic requirements of a compromise symptom formation. The specific description of the symptom will frequently indicate in a symbolic way the general determinants of the underlying conflict, for example, such expressions as "I suddenly felt nauseated when I saw him trying to kiss another woman"; "Father always had difficulty breathing when he was displeased with me"; "I have been so feverish that I cannot even be a good wife to him"; "I tried to prevent the baby from falling, and suddenly I felt like I had been injured instead of the baby."

SOMATIC EXPRESSIONS

It is important to differentiate the somatic reaction, which may follow the conversion symptom, and to recognize it as separate and distinct from the conversion process. For example, there may be a somatic response of vomiting to a conversion feeling of nausea, hyperventilation in response to breathlessness, and a localized inflammatory reaction in response to a fantasied local injury. From these physiologic responses it is not difficult to see how a pathologic complication may result if these reactions continue for any length of time. For example, as a result of vomiting a loss of gastric fluid and electrolytes may occur; with hyperventilation, hypocapnia, respiratory alkalosis, and tetany may result; and a localized inflammatory response may lead to vasodilatation, edema, hemorrhage, and the release of proteolytic enzymes.[6]

As one considers these actual somatic complications that occur in response to somatic conversion symptoms one is reminded of the somatic changes that have been reported with experimental hypnotic suggestions of injury.[7,8] Such suggestions as injury to the skin may produce vesicles or urticaria,[9] suggestions of injury to the respiratory tract have produced wheezing or coughing,[10] and suggestion of the ingestion of spoiled food has led to nausea and vomiting.[11]

The somatic changes that occur with hypnotic suggestion of injury demonstrate how an intrapsychic idea of a change in somatic state can lead to somatic reactions which are normally associated with actual changes in somatic functioning. The extent of the actual tissue reactions, which may occur in response to a hypnotic suggestion or a somatic conversion reaction, may be determined by a biologic predisposition to disease or tissue changes related to previously experienced disease.

The hypnotic suggestion as well as the conversion reaction is not directly related to and in no way causes the tissue reaction of the disease which may ensue, but the conversion reaction may determine the time of onset and the site at which a lesion may appear or recur. Let me illustrate again from the study of "healthy" grieving women how the site of a conversion symptom may become the area in which a somatic disease process is first identified.

CASE 4. The very first evidence of rheumatoid arthritis developed in a forty-year-old woman in the ring finger of her left hand within days after the sudden onset of pain in the area of this finger covered by her wedding ring. The pain first occurred as she was getting ready for bed, and as she opened the medicine cabinet in the bathroom. This was the medicine cabinet in which she kept a bottle of sleeping pills. In another context she reported that her husband earlier the same day in a moment of desperation, related to his progressive downhill course from cancer, had said he could not continue on in this manner and suggested he might as well commit suicide by taking a handful of sleeping pills. She had thought at the time of his comment that maybe she should hide the pills but then did nothing and forgot about the threat.

On later reconstruction of what happened that evening when she actually saw the pill bottle, it became obvious that her long-standing ambivalent relationship with her husband was acutely reinforced by her struggles over whether she should hide the pills and thus prevent his possibly doing away with himself or to "put him out of his misery . . . and to be single once again." She did not hide the pills because she had told herself it was highly unlikely that he would do such a thing. It was in this chronologic sequence that the pain in the wedding ring finger appeared which symbolized her acute conflict over her ambivalence toward her husband.

She was only vaguely aware of this discomfort over the next several days, until it suddenly became worse when she attempted to bowl. In discussing her having gone bowling with a group of girl friends, she indicated she had had mixed feelings about going. On the one hand she felt she should not leave her ailing husband, but on the other she felt she just had to get out of the house and away from him. Following this she noticed morning stiffness and swelling in the proximal joint of this finger, and over the next several months she had similar difficulty with her left wrist and her right knee.

This is not an unusual story of a progression from a conversion symptom to a somatic disease state. If one can get the details of the initial symptom and appreciate the symbolic dynamics involved, the antecedent psychic diagnosis can be made. More often than not the busy practitioner does not have the time or appreciate the psychodynamic importance of an isolated symptom which may appear in a particular location and at a particular period in time, especially if the symptom occurs shortly before an actual somatic disease or disease episode may have its "apparent" onset. Observations of an isolated antecedent conversion symptom have been made with the onset or exacerbation of a number of the so-called psychosomatic diseases as well as with a number of other diseases, such as multiple sclerosis,[12] herpes simplex,[13] erythrocyte autosensitization,[14] and even carcinoma.[15]

Here, again, I must emphasize my theoretical position that the somatic conversion reaction in no way causes the disease or is necessary for disease onset. The conversion symptom represents an intrapsychic symptom which is given in the mind's eye a bodily location, and the brain interprets or reacts to the symptom as if it actually existed in the particular location fantasied. In an ingenious set of hypnotic experiments, Seitz[16] demonstrated that psychodynamically equivalent symptoms could be substituted for an initially experienced somatic conversion symptom.

The subsequent somatic changes represent a somatic response or reaction to the conversion symptom. These somatic responses can run the gamut from atrophy and changes related to sensory-motor disuse to somatic activity based on the central nervous system's reaction to the conversion symptom as if it were a currently experienced somatic symptom. How the fantasied symptom can take priority over the perceptual data coming in from the peripheral somatic apparatuses is under study by such investigators as Hernandez-Peon,[17] Pribram,[18] and Melzack.[19] Melzack and coworkers propose a gate control system wherein peripheral as well as central nervous system influences determine when and how a sensory input is experienced.

OTHER PSYCHIC SYNDROMES

To return to the somatic conversion symptom, it is important to be able to make a differentiation from the other psychic syndromes with somatic symptom expressions, namely, psychophysiologic reactions, hypochondriasis, and somatic delusions. When one is forced to go through such a differential diagnostic process, one has to keep in mind the specific criteria for each, and thus one avoids making a diagnosis on the basis of exclusion alone. By this I mean the diagnosis should be made on the basis of positive criteria and not only because all the other diagnostic possibilities have been elimi-

nated. This, of course, also includes a differentiation from primary somatic disease and the symptoms which originate in the soma.

In contrast to conversion symptoms, psychophysiologic symptoms are actual perceptions of somatic reactions. These somatic reactions are developmentally related to the biological activities which ordinarily prepare the body for fight-flight or conservation-withdrawal as a means of homeostatic control.[20] They become symptoms when there is a decision not to fight, flee, or withdraw, and yet the wish to do so remains. Physiologic preparation is undertaken as if the act was to occur. Any one or a combination of symptoms may occur with extremes of pulse rate, sweating, urine secretion, bowel activity, and respiratory and blood pressure changes. These symptoms of arousal or withdrawal are mediated through endocrine as well as autonomic nervous system pathways. Frequently these reactions are called emotional reactions or somatic concomitants of anxiety, fear, anger, guilt, shame, sadness, or feelings of depression. Such expressions as "cold with fear," "muscles ached from anger," "blushed with shame," and "tears of joy" all reflect an awareness of the somatic changes associated with emotional reactions. The symptoms which occur are actually somatic and do not represent psychic compromise symptoms symbolizing a repressed conflict. The repeated activation or continuation of a psychophysiologically determined symptom may interfere with the function of one or another organ by producing an acute overload or increase the rate of wear and tear on the organ, so that structural or disease changes may occur. Alexander's[4] vegetative neuroses and Wolff's[9] defensive or offensive adaptive reaction patterns fit under the diagnostic heading of psychophysiologic reactions as does neurasthenia, "actual" neuroses, and the giving up-given up complex.[21]

In a similar way hypochondriacal symptoms do not directly and symbolically represent intrapsychic conflict. the functioning or malfunctioning of a body part may be secondarily focused on by the mental apparatus as a means of defense against the possibilities of acting out a forbidden wish. There is a displacement of the need for intrapsychic control onto bodily functioning with a resulting exaggerated preoccupation with the control of bodily functioning. Thus, there is an increase of attention, a preoccupation with particular somatic functioning, such as, bowel elimination, breathing, seeing, hearing, maintaining balance, muscle strength, and so on, to avoid the threat of losing control and in turn self esteem. The patient with such somatic preoccupation can usually find others who are willing to share in his preoccupation, namely, physician, family, and friends, and thus a great deal of secondary gain is derived from the symptom.

Somatic delusions represent a direct, primitive, and symbolic expression of intrapsychic disorganization. The somatic delusional symptom is not a remembered or fantasied perception of bodily functioning but a direct symbolic expression of a primitive idea of disintegration. The body itself or one body part may be imagined to be set against the rest of the body, the mind, or the external world. Such expressions as the intestines have grown shut, the white cells are eating up the red cells, the skin is being penetrated by submicroscopic organisms, the brain is split into many pieces, an odor is being given off that will destroy others, are all somatic expressions classified as somatic delusions. Although somatic delusions may appear as acute and isolated symptoms, particularly at times of life-threatening procedures, such as open heart surgery, they are more commonly seen as part of a generalized psychotic reaction, that is, psychotic depressions or paranoid schizophrenic reactions.

Thus, it can be seen that a symptom such as nausea, breathlessness, and pain can be a somatic symptom, a conversion symptom, a somatic reaction to a conversion symptom, a psychophysiologic symptom, a hypochondriacal symptom, or even a delusional symptom at times and, indeed, the symptom expression may change from representing one level of reaction to another depending on the intrapsychic needs, psychic defenses available, and the somatic predispositions of the individual.

Those who claim that conversion reactions are unconsciously simulated illnesses which act as self-deceptive enactments of sick roles as a means to tolerate personal inadequacies are pejoratively saying psychic maladaptation should not be included with somatic maladaptation in a classification of disease.[22,23] Such a "sick role only" theory also ignores the somatic changes which occur in response to conversion symptoms. Finally, whatever we define as disease in the last analysis is relative to what is perceived as changes in health, changes which are perceived by not only the physician, who tries to categorize what he observes, but more directly by the individual who actually experiences the disease.[19]

REFERENCES

1. Chodoff, P., and Lyons, H.: Hysteria, the hysterical personality and "hysterical conversion. Am. J. Psychiat. 114:734 (1958).

2. Rangell, L.: The nature of conversion. J. Am. Psychiat. 7:632 (1959).

3. Engel, G. L., and Schmale, A.: Psychoanalytic theory of somatic disorder: conversion, specificity and disease onset situation, ibid. 14:344 (Apr.) 1967.

4. Alexander, F.: Psychosomatic Medicine, New York. W. W. Norton & Co. Inc., 1950, p. 39.

5. Cobb, S. et al.: Is the term "mysterious leap" warranted, in Deutsch, F., Ed.: On the Mysterious Leap from the Mind to the Body: A workshop Study on the Theory of Conversion, New York. International University Press, Inc., 1959, chap. 2, p. 11.

6. Chapman, L. F., Goodell, H., and Wolff, H. G.: Augmentation of the inflammatory reaction by activity of the central nervous system. A.M.A. Arch. Neurol. 1:557 (1959).

7. Barber, T. X.: Physiological effects of "hypnosis," Psychol. Bull. 58:390 (1961).

8. Idem: Physiological effects of "hypnotic suggestions": A critical review of recent research (1960–64), ibid. 63:201 (1965).

9. Wolff, H. G.: Stress and Disease, Springfield, Illinois, Charles C Thomas, 1953, p. 128.

10. Dekker, E., Van Vollenhoven, E., and During, J.: Further experiments on the origin of asthmatic wheezing. Fotschr. Psychosom. Med. 1:240 (1960).

11. Cleghorn, R. A., and Brown, W. T.: Psychogenesis of emesis, Canad. Psychiat. A. J. 9:299 (1964).

12. Langworthy, O. R.: Relation of personality problems to onset and progress of multiple sclerosis, A.M.A. Arch. Neurol. & Psychiat. 59:13 (1948).

13. Blank, H., and Brody, M. W.: Recurrent herpes simplex, Psychosom. Med. 12:254 (1950).

14. Ratnoff, O. D., and Agle, D. P.: Psychogenic purpura: A reevaluation of the syndrome of autoerythrocyte sensitization. Medicine 47:475 (Nov.) 1968.

15. Ludwig, A. O.: The role of identification in the conversion process in Deutsch, F., Ed.: On the Mysterious Leap from the Mind to the Body: A Workshop Study on the Theory of Conversion, New York. International University Press, Inc., 1959, chap. 7, p. 105.

16. Seitz, P. F.: Experiments in the substitution of symptoms by hypnosis, Psychosom. Med. 15:405 (1953).

17. Hernandez-Peon, R.: Psychiatric implications of neurophysiological research, Bull. Menninger Clin 28:165 (1964).

18. Pribram, K. H.: Emotion: steps toward a neuropsychological theory, in Glass, D. C., Ed.: Neurophysiology and Emotion, New York, The Rockefeller University Press, 1967, p. 3.

19. Melzack, R.: Brain mechanisms and emotion, in ibid., p. 60.

20. Engel, G. L.: Psychological Development in Health and Disease, Philadelphia, W. B. Saunders Company, 1962, p. 392.

21. Schmale, A. H., and Engel, G. L.: The giving up-given up complex illustrated on film, Arch. Gen. Psychiat. 17:135 (Aug.) 1967.

22. Szasz, T. S.: The Myth of Mental Illness, New York, Hoeber Medical Division, Harper & Row, Inc., 1961.

23. Rogers, D. A., and Ziegler, F. J.: Cognitive process and conversion reactions. J. Nerv. & Ment. Dis. 144:155 (Mar.) 1967.

NEW CONCEPTS OF CHRONIC PAIN
AND THEIR IMPLICATIONS

JOHN M. LUCE, TROY L. THOMPSON II, CARL J. GETTO,
and RICHARD L. BYYNY

When chronic pain fails to respond to therapy, the approach often has been based on outmoded concepts of the nature of pain. The current unified pain theory takes into account recent biochemical advances and can serve as a basis for more effective diagnostic and therapeutic approaches. Various treatment modalities are reviewed in the context of the psychology as well as the physiology of severe intractable pain.

In 1973, Marks and Sachar of the Psychiatric Liaison Division of Montefiore Hospital, New York City, reported on 37 medical inpatients whom they had been asked to evaluate because of apparently exaggerated responses to pain. Instead of emotional factors being the cause of these responses, as one might have expected them to report, the psychiatrists found that virtually every one of the patients was being undertreated with narcotics by the house staff. Marks and Sachar then surveyed the hospital physicians and found that, although all of them aimed for complete pain relief, only 25% would use enough meperidine to achieve this endpoint in a hypothetical case of myocardial infarction. Thirty-three percent of the house staff overestimated the duration of action of meperidine, 27% exaggerated its addiction potential, and 77% underestimated the likelihood of meperidine withdrawal. Finally, a full 21% of the

EDITORS' COMMENTS:

PAIN IS NOT SIMPLY A STIMULUS–RESPONSE PHENOMENON, BUT INVOLVES COMPLEX BIOCHEMICAL AND PHYSIOLOGICAL PROCESSES. THE ROLE OF CATECHOLAMINES, ENDORPHINS, AND NARCOTICS IS DISCUSSED.

Reprinted from Hospital Practice 14:113–123, 1979. Figures by Carol Donner. Reproduced with permission.

physicians stated that they would not increase the dose of meperidine in terminal cancer patients, while 14% preferred to reduce drug dosages or give placebos.

Although Marks and Sachar suggested that faulty pharmacologic information and overconcern with addiction were the major reasons for undertreatment with narcotics, they also acknowledged that for many physicians these drugs have an emotional stigma that interferes with their rational use. Many factors account for this irrationality, but it most often stems from misconceptions about the nature of pain. The most basic of these misconceptions is that pain is a uniformly experienced and biologically purposeful sensation that should be proportional to tissue injury; the corollary to this view is that patients who do not manifest such injury do not have "real" pain. But what is "real" pain? This is the question we will seek to address here, with a view to presenting a unified theory that can serve as a basis for better diagnostic and therapeutic approaches to pain management.

PAIN IN HISTORY

The oldest interpretation of pain is that it is a price paid for offending the gods. This interpretation is evident in the roots of the word itself, which come from the Latin poene and the Greek poine meaning penalty or punishment. The concept of pain as punishment is reflected in the Greek myth of Prometheus, who gave man knowledge in the form of fire and suffered the wrath of Zeus as a result. Similarly, in the Biblical story of the Creation, man is banished from the Garden of Eden after eating from the Tree of Knowledge and is exposed ever after to illness and pain.

Most Western faiths continue to value pain as a sign of atonement, but from its inception science has sought a more rational view of suffering. Among the first investigators to study pain was Aristotle, who considered it not a sensation but a feeling. Aristotle classified pain as a "passion of the soul" rather than as one of the primary senses. He placed the seat of feelings in the heart and believed that its beating gave rise to sentiments, a notion that is reflected in the origins of our word emotion—the latin ex motus, meaning from motion.

The next major explanation of pain was the "specificity theory," which holds that the experience of pain is proportional to a pain stimulus. This theory first was postulated by Descartes, who argued that pain arises because a form of physical energy such as fire evokes vibrations in the skin that in turn activate a thread connected to the pineal gland, favored by Descartes over the heart as the locus of the soul. This formulation underwent little change until the 19th century, when Müller

FIGURE 1. Specificity theory of pain holds that peripheral nerves carry stimuli from pain receptors to the spinal cord, where they ascend in Lissauer's tract to connect with secondary neurons. These, in turn, cross the cord and ascend via the lateral spinothalamic tract to the thalamus, from which other fibers project to the cerebral cortex and other areas of the brain.

declared that the quality of a sensation depends not on the form of physical energy that initiates the sensory process but upon the properties of the nerve receptor that is stimulated and of the brain area in which the nerve terminates. The search for these receptors led to the discovery of free nerve endings, to which in 1894 Von Frey attributed the reception of pain.

Today the free nerve endings are called nociceptors and are thought to be activated by mechanical deformation and extremes of temperature. They are linked with two types of peripheral nerve fibers: large, myelinated A fibers, which conduct impulses rapidly and are associated with sharp pain sensation; and small unmyelinated C fibers, which transmit more slowly and are associated with dull pain. These fibers arise from cell bodies in the dorsal root ganglion and subserve cutaneous areas called dermatomes. The fibers from each dermatome enter the spinal cord in Lissauer's tract, where they synapse with other neurons. The secondary nerves in turn cross the thalamus, from which other fibers project to the cerebral cortex and perhaps to the limbic area and the reticular activating system (see Figure 1).

In this classic pathway, pain assumes the status of a primary sensation. Pain experience is seen as a direct communication from skin to brain in which the quality of experience is determined entirely at the level of the peripheral pain receptor. As a re-

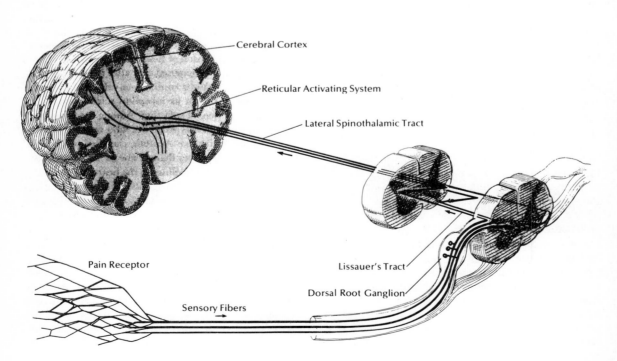

Cerebral Cortex

Reticular Activating System

Lateral Spinothalamic Tract

Pain Receptor

Sensory Fibers

Lissauer's Tract

Dorsal Root Ganglion

sult, a painful stimulus must evoke a proportional pain response if all parts of the pathway are competent, and the easiest way to prevent such a response is to interrupt the pathway. Many interruptive techniques have been developed, including analgesic nerve blocks and such neurosurgical procedures as neurectomy, sympathectomy, rhizotomy, cordotomy, thalamotomy, and frontal lobectomy. Yet, although these techniques have benefited many patients, they are not uniformly successful. For example, neurectomy and rhizotomy may eliminate one form of pain only to be followed by another. And although stereotactic ablation of thalamic nuclei may lead to diminution of pain sensations and retention of other sensory modalities in some patients, in others it may produce a loss of every sensation save pain.

Another limitation of these therapeutic approaches and of the specificity theory that underlies them is that they are not applicable in certain pain states, such as causalgia, neuralgia, and phantom limb pain, which may follow injury to the peripheral nervous system. Although these states differ somewhat, they all may involve spontaneous pain episodes in which no stimulus can be demonstrated. Some examples are the application of light stimuli to certain trigger zones, which can cause severe pain at the site of injury that may spread to other areas of the body; autonomic and motor dysfunction; and a phenomenon called pain summation in which continual mild stimuli such as low heat may not be felt for several minutes but thereafter produce excruciating distress. Finally, these pain states are similar in that they may respond to techniques that modulate sensory input to the peripheral nerve, such as injections of local anesthetics and counterstimulation with cold water over a prolonged period.

THE PATTERN THEORY OF PAIN

The realization that pain is not simply a stimulus-response phenomenon has prompted investigators to propose improvements on the specificity theory. One such improvement is the "pattern theory," which holds that pain is determined not only by stimulus intensity but also by central summation. This theory first was proposed in 1896 by Goldscheider, who suggested that the summation seen in states like causalgia is caused by the additive effects of sensory inputs in the dorsal horn cell. In 1943, Livingston stated that the stimulation of sensory nerves that occurs subsequent to peripheral nerve injury initiates activity in reverberating circuits in the spinal cord's internuncial

pools. This activity also may cause spontaneous pain or may be intensified by non-noxious stimuli after an initial insult. The abnormal activity also may stimulate adjacent neurons in the spinal cord, causing autonomic and motor dysfunction and providing further sensory input that helps establish a vicious circle of pain (see Figure 2).

The major advantage of pattern theory is that it accounts for the fact that pain can occur long after an initial injury and in the absence of apparent stimulation. The theory also potentially explains the effectiveness in treating peripheral nervous system pain of phenytoin, carbamazepine, and other analeptics, which are said to suppress the spinal cord's reverberating circuits. Yet, although pattern theory overcomes some objections that have been raised with the specificity theory, both theories concentrate on the peripheral reception and pathway transmission of painful stimuli to the exclusion of central mechanisms. They overemphasize sensation and underemphasize perception in the experience of pain.

The importance of perception in pain experience is best illustrated by those individuals who sustain injury and yet do not suffer pain. Such people include Indian fakirs and other professional pain endurers, women undergoing natural childbirth, and persons with congenital pain insensitivity who have normal nervous systems and are aware of every sensation except pain. Beecher has cited a number of such patients in his writings and also has reported on 215 soldiers on the Anzio beachhead during World War II, only 32% of whom requested narcotics despite their severe wounds. Their behavior contrasts with that of 150 civilian surgical patients with lesser injuries, 83% of whom wanted pain medication. Beecher attributed the differences between these two groups to the fact that to the soldiers injury was a ticket home, whereas to the civilians it implied underlying illness. He also noted that in these and other clinical situations, there is little correlation between pain experience and the extent of tissue injury.

Just as some people sustain injury but do not suffer, so do others suffer without obvious injury. Among these are psychiatric patients, such as schizophrenics, for whom pain may be an hallucination; hysterics, who may experience paralyses and other forms of painful conversion reactions; patients with grief reactions, who seem to deny the loss of other people by assuming their suffering; depressed persons, who may dwell on their pain to the exclusion of other feelings; and hypochondriacs, with their habitual overconcern for somatic

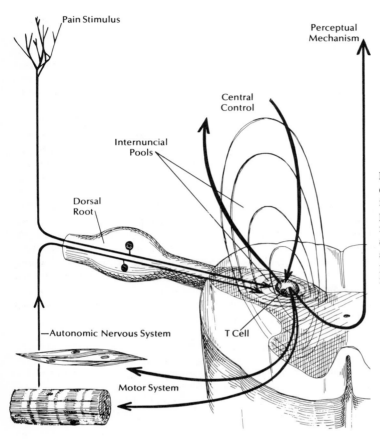

Pain Stimulus

Perceptual Mechanism

Central Control

Internuncial Pools

Dorsal Root

—Autonomic Nervous System

T Cell

Motor System

FIGURE 2. According to the pattern theory of pain, intense stimulation initiates activity in reverberating circuits in internuncial pools within the spinal cord. This activity may stimulate adjacent neurons, causing autonomic and motor dysfunction, and spread via special transmission (T) cells to perceptual and central control mechanisms in the brain.

ills. Other persons in whom pain often appears disproportionate to their injury are called "pain-prone patients" by Engel, "low-back losers" by Sternbach, and *les hommes douloureux* by Szasz. Most of these chronic pain patients do not fit into traditional psychiatric categories, yet they often exhibit the so-called neurotic triad of hysteria, depression, and hypochondriasis on the Minnesota Multiphasic Personality Inventory. Although their pain does not appear to serve a biologic purpose, it does provide an all-consuming preoccupation and a focus for their lives.

Several interpretations have been offered for the distress of chronic pain patients, most of which center around the unconscious pursuit of secondary gain. Yet whatever gain exists for these people, pain probably has psychodynamic significance for everyone. For example, pain may have sexual overtones or may be linked with punishment, in keeping with traditional religious interpretations. It also may be a way of justifying failure or of establishing object relationships. In part, the psychodynamics of pain may be mediated by such neuropsychologic factors as anxiety and arousal. Age, sex, and other demographic factors

also have been implicated in pain behaviors, as have socioeconomic level and religious and cultural background. In sum, pain perception is the product of multiple inputs, and any theory that purports to account for all forms of distress must accentuate the importance of central mechanisms in the experience of pain.

GATE CONTROL THEORY OF PAIN

Currently, the most comprehensive explanation of pain is the "gate control theory," which was authored in 1965 by Melzack and Wall. This theory proposes that a neural mechanism in the dorsal horns of the spinal cord acts like a gate that can increase or decrease the flow of nerve impulses from the peripheral to the central nervous system and thereby modulate pain perception. The degree of modulation is determined by the relative activity in the inhibitory A fibers and the facilitatory C fibers and by descending influences from the brain. The special gating mechanism seems to be located in the substantia gelatinosa, where it impinges upon specialized transmission of T cells.

The T cells are activated as the gate is opened, and when the activity of the cells exceeds a certain level, a so-called action system is set in motion, causing pain (see Figure 3).

The gate control theory can be used to explain all the pain states covered by the specificity and pattern theories. For example, the apparently spontaneous pain seen in postherpetic neuralgia and other peripheral nerve injuries is said by Melzack to occur because selective degeneration of the A fibers by the herpes virus allows the C fibers to open the spinal gating mechanism. This provides a situation in which successive stimuli cause an intense barrage of nerve impulses and hence central summation. Trigger zone pain also may be related to the open gate. The role of the autonomic nervous system in certain pain states is explained by the fact that the fibers from sympathetic ganglia impinge upon the same spinal cord cells that receive cutaneous inputs and thereby participate in gating activities.

Even more important, the gate control theory takes full account of central mechanisms in pain. Level of arousal is thought to be one factor that impinges upon the T cell, which sends and receives impulses to the reticular activating system. Anxiety also becomes an important pain determinant, as do other emotions and past experiences that, by helping to open or close the gate, influence pain perception. Pain is a balance between peripheral and central factors, according to Melzack. A person therefore can have pain without tissue injury or can be injured and not experience pain.

Finally, the gate control theory can be employed to justify the success or failure of traditional pain approaches and also to rationalize new types of therapy. Nerve blocks and neurosurgical techniques that interrupt the classic pain pathway can be said to succeed when they disrupt more facilitatory than inhibitory inputs and to fail when they do not. At the same time, local anesthetic infusions, which are useful in phantom limb patients, may decrease the number of nerve impulses that reach the T cell, while counterstimulation may work by increasing the input from inhibitory A fibers and thereby overcome the contribution of facilitatory C fibers. This theory of counterstimulation has been used to explain the efficacy of transcutaneous nerve stimulation and acupuncture in treating some patients. Another new technique of proved effectiveness is biofeedback, which allows patients to monitor and ultimately control autonomic nervous system activity.

However, for all its usefulness, the gate control

FIGURE 3. Gate control theory of pain is based on concept that large-diameter inhibitory A fibers and small-diameter facilitatory C fibers influence a special gating mechanism in the substantia gelatinosa, as do central mechanisms. The gating mechanism in turn impinges on the special transmission (T) cells, which are activated as the gate is opened. When the activity of the T cells exceeds a certain level, an action system is set in motion, causing pain perception and autonomic and motor responses.

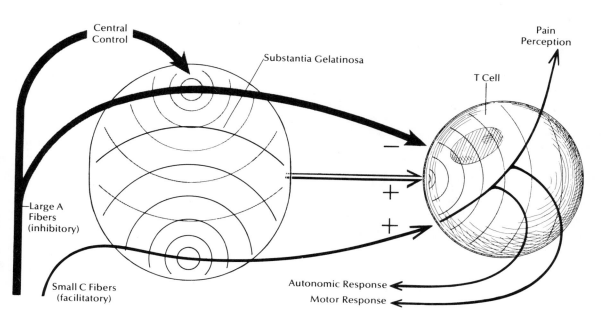

theory remains only a theory. The T cell, which is so essential to the model, has never been demonstrated, and all that gate control theory proponents can legitimately claim is that some sort of modulation seems to occur in or near the dorsal horn cell. Furthermore, although central pain mechanisms are vital to the theory, they never have been elucidated. The brain thus remains a black box, and because no neuroanatomic explanation has proved totally satisfactory, investigators increasingly are looking for biochemical answers to the puzzle of pain.

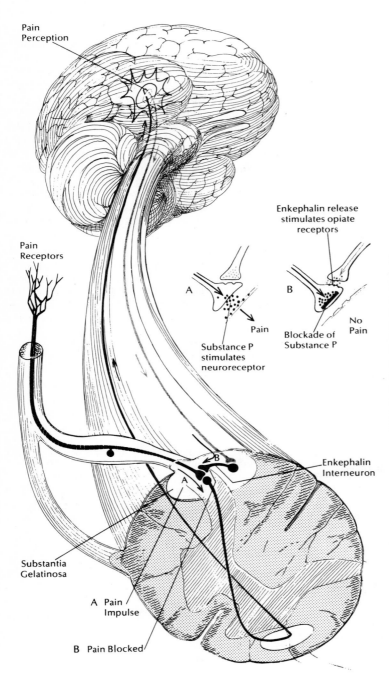

Pain Perception

Pain Receptors

Enkephalin release stimulates opiate receptors

A

B

Pain

No Pain

Substance P stimulates neuroreceptor

Blockade of Substance P

Enkephalin Interneuron

Substantia Gelatinosa

A Pain Impulse

B Pain Blocked

FIGURE 4. Current biochemical theory of pain stresses role of brain opiate receptors and endogenous opioids. Presence of specific binding sites in the limbic system and in substantia gelatinosa suggests that endogenous narcotics are active in both brain and spinal cord. Details (A and B) hypothesize how endogenous narcotics may operate to block pain perception. Intrinsic and extrinsic discrepancies in neurotransmissions are held to account for individual differences in psychophysiologic response to painful stimuli.

BIOCHEMICAL THEORIES OF PAIN

One line of biochemical investigation originally focused on the possibility that pain receptors function as chemoreceptors. Subsequently this idea was abandoned, yet many researchers now believe that although true chemoreceptors do not exist, substances like histamine and prostaglandin, which are released from injured tissue, may lower the threshold of the nociceptors and thereby contribute to pain reception. Indeed, this theory currently is invoked to explain the action of acetyl-salicylic acid and other prostaglandin inhibitors in reducing pain.

Another biochemical theory points to the role of biogenic amines in the pain process. Interest in this area originally was stimulated by the fact that anxiety, which is associated with high catecholamine levels, reduces pain tolerance in most individuals. As a result, the benzodiazepines and other antianxiety drugs now are used for some chronic pain patients. Tricyclic antidepressants, which are thought to increase brain catecholamine levels, also are prescribed for pain patients, although this practice is explained in terms of restoring cortical inhibition rather than by the catecholamine theory. Another concept is that pain is caused by an imbalance of dopaminergic and serotoninergic influences in the neurotransmission of pain.

The most current biochemical theory of pain stresses the potential significance of brain opiate receptors and endogenous opioids. The presence of such receptors has long been suspected, since opiate agonists share chemical similarities, are stereospecific, and can be converted into antagonists such as naloxone by only a slight modification of their molecular structure. Yet demonstration of the receptors proved difficult until Snyder located specific high affinity—binding sites in the limbic system and in the substantia gelatinosa, suggesting that exogenous narcotics are active in both the brain and the spinal cord.

The next step in the discovery of endogenous opioids revolved around the realization that the opiate receptors might be associated with natural morphine-like substances in the brain. Such substances were identified by Hughes and Kosterlitz and independently by Snyder in the area of the opiate receptors; they were called enkephalins from the Greek word for in the head. Next Goldstein isolated comparable substances from pituitary extracts that then were found to match a segment of the hormone beta-lipotropin that was originally described in 1965 by Li (see R. Guillemin, "Beta-Lipotropin and Endorphins: Implications of Current Knowledge," HP, November 1978). Li subsequently named his peptide betaendorphin for endogenous morphine. Since the pituitary is outside the central nervous system, the biologic function of pituitary endorphin is not well understood, but Snyder believes that the enkephalins serve as neurotransmitters that help determine the emotional response to pain (see Figure 4).

Although the true clinical significance of this information has yet to be determined, there is no lack of speculation on the subject. Pomeranz, for example, has demonstrated that acupuncture analgesia can be blocked by naloxone and has hypothesized that acupuncture works by inducing the brain to release endogenous opioids rather than through an effect on the spinal gating mechanism. Snyder, meanwhile, has stated that the discovery of endogenous opioids may explain such phenomena as narcotic tolerance and withdrawal. In brief, he believes that the opiate receptors are exposed to a certain basal level of enkephalin under resting conditions. When exogenous narcotics bind to the receptors, they potentiate the effects of enkephalin and thereby cause pain relief. After prolonged treatment with narcotics, however, the receptors become overloaded and signal the brain to stop releasing enkephalin. When this occurs, the receptors are exposed only to exogenous narcotics and become tolerant. Then when the narcotic is not administered, the receptors lack any substrate, and the patient undergoes withdrawal.

A UNIFIED THEORY OF PAIN

Although Snyder's explanations are as yet unproved, when combined with traditional theories they provide a unified approach to the understanding of pain. In this scheme, pain is seen as a result of peripheral sensation and central perception. The perception process appears to impinge upon sensation either at the spinal cord, as gate control theory would have it, or at a higher level in the central nervous system. Whatever location is involved, pain perception probably is modulated by enkephalins and/or similar substances that function as neurotransmitters. Pain intensity, therefore, is determined both by the level of endogenous enkephalins and exogenous opioids and by the amount and availability of enkephalin-binding sites. Thus, intrinsic and extrinsic discrepancies in neurotransmissions account for individual differences in the complex psychophysiologic experiences we call pain.

PAIN AS A CHRONIC DISEASE

Whether this unified theory holds or not, biochemical investigators should enable us some day to quantify and objectify pain. For the moment, how-

FIGURE 5. When specific interventions have failed to ameliorate chronic pain, neurodestructive procedures such as cordotomy (*top left*) or rhizotomy (*top right*) may be indicated to interrupt reception or transmission of pain impulses. If these or other such procedures are unsuccessful, an attempt may be made to alter pain perception by modulation of sensory input, as with acupuncture (bottom left), transcutaneous stimulation of peripheral nerves (bottom right), hypnosis, or biofeedback.

ever, pain still should be approached as a subjective, unmeasurable experience that is determined in large part by psychologic factors. Furthermore, since emotions play a major role in the pain of most people, patient care can best be served by taking all pain seriously rather than by thinking in terms of "organic" or "psychogenic" pain. This is particularly true of chronic pain, which feeds upon itself and is associated with depression and physical disability regardless of its origin.

One distinction that is useful, however, is that of Foley and Posner, who divide patients into groups, those with so-called benign chronic pain, which lacks a physical explanation, and those suffering the "malignant" pain of cancer and other

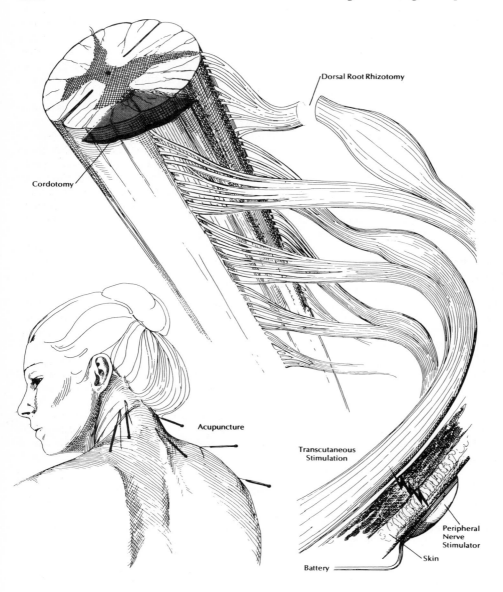

Dorsal Root Rhizotomy

Cordotomy

Acupuncture

Transcutaneous Stimulation

Peripheral Nerve Stimulator

Skin

Battery

forms of chronic illness. Foley and Posner do this not as a value judgment but to remind clinicians that the latter group of patients appear to be less psychologically crippled by their pain and to respond better to analgesic agents and neurodestructive procedures, whereas the former are likely to do better with psychotropic drugs and psychotherapy. Yet despite this difference, in many cases of malignant pain and in most chronic benign conditions, pain assumes a disease status. Although this disease often can and should be managed initially by the general physician, he eventually may benefit from the evaluation and therapeutic service of pain clinics and other multidisciplinary agencies.

The basic diagnostic approach that should be taken by pain clinics and general physicians alike is to pursue the specific cause or causes for pain in all patients and, if unsuccessful, to give the patient a diagnosis of chronic pain of unknown etiology. This approach should allow clinicians to avoid dismissing the pain as merely psychogenic and to maintain a continuous search for a neoplasm or other form of occult organic illness; such illness is found in as many as 10% of the patients referred to pain clinics, reminding us of the difficulty in separating benign from malignant pain. At the same time, clinicians should seek those psychiatric conditions like schizophrenia, hysteria, and depression that may present as chronic pain and aggravate the suffering of patients. And, since pain patients often abuse alcohol and other licit and illicit agents, clinicians should be aware of how drugs can complicate the pain posture and be prepared to diagnose and treat drug withdrawal.

From a treatment standpoint, clinicians should seek to ameliorate underlying medical and surgical conditions with proved, specific interventions before employing a more general, empiric approach to therapy. For example, in patients with angina, nitrates and beta-adrenergic antagonists or coronary artery bypass surgery are usually more appropriate than narcotic analgesia. Similarly, surgical debulking, radiation therapy, or antineoplastic agents may be the best therapy for some cancer patients, whereas others who no longer respond to these measures may profit from cordotomy, rhizotomy, and other neurodestructive procedures that attempt to interrupt the reception or transmission of pain.

When destructive procedures fail or are not indicated, patients may profit from nondestructive methods designed to modulate sensory input and alter pain perception. Modulation techniques include acupuncture and transcutaneous stimulation, which often benefit people with degenerative arthritis and low back pain as well as peripheral nerve injuries. Among the procedures directed at altering pain perception are hypnosis and biofeedback, which may be helpful in patients with ill-defined disorders as well as such specific complaints as tension headaches and myofascial syndromes (see Figure 5).

In addition to these techniques, the clinician has at his disposal a variety of drugs with specific effects and indications. Among these are tricyclic compounds that are used for carotodynia, atypical facial pain, and migraine prophylaxis because of their vasocontrictive properties. As previously noted, phenytoin, carbamazepine, and other analeptic drugs are employed in the treatment of various peripheral pain states, including trigeminal neuralgia. Oxyphenbutazone and indomethacin also are recommended for inflammatory arthritis pain, and corticosteroids and Δ-9-tetrahydrocannabinol are used in some terminal patients for their appetite-stimulating properties.

GUIDELINES FOR THE USE OF ANALGESIC AGENTS

Analgesic drugs generally should be employed in pain patients only when more specific measures have been exhausted. However, when they are used, analgesics should be given in doses and at intervals sufficient enough to control pain without causing undue side effects. Treatment should begin with a mild non-narcotic agent. Aspirin, given in doses of 650 mg every four to six hours, remains the most effective mild analgesic and the standard of comparison for all other drugs despite the gastrointestinal toxicity. Para-aminophenol or phenacetin may be used as a substitute in patients who do not tolerate salicylates, although its use is associated with methemoglobinemia, sulfhemoglobinemia, and interstitial nephritis. Acetaminophen also is equivalent to aspirin as a analgesic, although it lacks anti-inflammatory properties.

If non-narcotics do not provide adequate relief, weak narcotics with low addiction potential may be added. The idea of addition rather than substitution should be stressed, since drugs like the salicylates probably act peripherally and thereby synergize with the centrally active narcotics. Codeine is the most widely used mild narcotic and can be given in a dosage of 32 mg or more every four to six hours by mouth for several months with little risk of physical dependence, although tolerance to codeine does develop, and the drug may cause nausea. Propoxyphene, 65 mg of which is equianalgesic with 32 mg of oral codeine, also has limited addiction potential in low doses, although its advantages over aspirin are debatable. A third mild narcotic is pantazocine, 30 mg of which is equivalent to 32 mg of oral codeine. Although originally advertised as being nonaddicting, as have most narcotics, pentazocine is both an agonist that can cause physical dependence and an antagonist that, when given to patients receiving other narcotics, can precipitate withdrawal. In addition, it often causes hallucination and dysphoria, especially in high doses.

If the analgesics cited are not enough, patients can be given even more potent narcotics with high addiction potential. Ten milligrams of morphine administered intramuscularly every three to four hours is the prototype preparation for severe pain and is the equivalent of 120 mg of intramuscular codeine, 240 mg of propoxyphene, 60 mg of pentazocine, 100 mg of meperidine, 15 mg of oxycodone, 1.5 mg of hydromorphone, and 10 mg of methadone. The same pain relief can be achieved with 30 mg of morphine given by mouth, which is equianalgesic with 200 mg of oral codeine, 180 mg of pentazocine, 300 mg of meperidine, 20 mg of oxycodone, 7.5 mg of hydromorphone, and 20 mg of methadone. Although meperidine and oxycodone may be useful because of their short onset and duration of action in some patients, most benefit more from longer-acting drugs like hydromorphone and methadone, which do not need to be given so frequently, are not associated with rapidly rising and falling blood levels, and are less likely to cause psychologic dependence. The gastrointestinal toxicity produced by most narcotics can be reduced by mixing them with antiemetics, as is done with the Brompton mixture. Similarly, the sedating effects of narcotics can be counteracted by combining them with a stimulant like dextroamphetamine, which seems to have some analgesic properties of its own.

PSYCHOTROPIC AGENTS

Although many patients with chronic malignant pain may require strong analgesics, they and most patients with benign pain may be aided by psychotropic agents used either alone or as adjuvants to other forms of drug therapy. In addition to the stimulants already mentioned, these agents include the benzodiazepines and other antianxiety agents, phenothiazines, and tricyclic antidepressants. Antianxiety drugs like diazepam may help some pain patients, particularly those with associated muscle spasm, but they may harm others by amplifying their depression. The phenothiazines also are reported to be helpful in some anxious patients and may potentiate analgesics. However, these possible benefits must be weighed against such side effects as sedation, hypotension, urinary retention, and Parkinsonism.

The tricyclic antidepressants are perhaps the most logical agents for pain patients, many of whom are either depressed initially or become depressed because of their pain. The drugs indeed may assuage anxiety and depression alike in such persons; in addition, they may improve sleep if given at bedtime and are said to possess analgesic properties. Unfortunately, however, the efficacy of the tricyclics has yet to be fully demonstrated despite their wide use in treating pain patients. Pending such demonstration, patients with chronic pain, especially those with vegetative symptoms, probably should be given a trial of approximately 150 mg of imipramine or amitriptyline per day over at least a three-week period unless arrhythmias or anticholinergic side effects preclude their use.

PSYCHOLOGIC PERSPECTIVES IN TREATMENT OF CHRONIC PAIN

It cannot be emphasized enough that no therapeutic maneuvers, not even psychotropic drug therapy, will succeed if attention is not paid to psychologic factors. This is not only because such factors may precede chronic pain in some instances but also because the chronicity of pain provides ample opportunity for learned behavior. As Fordyce has emphasized, patients communicate their pain by certain actions, such as tears and grimaces, which become reinforced if they are positively rewarded. Such rewards may include concern from a spouse, financial reward from an insurance company, or assistance from a clinician. Clinicians also may reward pain behavior by giving patients drugs only when they hurt, by seeing patients exclusively during exacerbations, or by advising patients to work until they suffer. As a result, patients learn that they can obtain relief, attention, and rest only if they have pain.

To avoid such learning, Fordyce and others advocate a deconditioning process in which patients receive more reward for healthy than for pain behavior. Instead of giving drugs on a prn basis, for example, clinicians are urged to administer them around the clock, perhaps in a vehicle like cherry syrup that can mask the active ingredients and influence patients to think about something other than their next pill. Clinicians also should see pain patients regularly, should not spread out appointments when patients feel better, and should focus on subjects other than the patients' distress.

Finally, clinicians should urge patients to work to predetermined quotas rather than to tolerance, so that they will not associate rest from work with pain. Since activity is inversely related to depression, patients should be helped by drugs and physical therapy to become more active. They also may profit from keeping charts or diaries that reinforce progress by comparing "up" and "down" time.

Unfortunately, some patients do not improve despite these and other methods. Yet physicians should not interpret this as failure or abandon either patients with malignant pain whose cancer is unchecked or patients with benign pain who prefer a sick role. Supportive care is a great comfort to patients with malignant pain, who should be as free of pain as they desire. At the same time, great service can be provided to patients with chronic benign pain who seem to cling to their suffering like "an old friend," as Penman has noted. Simply by offering another form of unconditional support, clinicians can limit the pain of such people, help them avoid hospitalization, and lessen the money spent on their disability compensation and health care.

SELECTED READING

Marks RM, Sachar EJ: Undertreatment of medical inpatients with narcotic analgesics. Ann Intern Med 78:173, 1973

Melzack R: The Puzzle of Pain, Basic Books, New York, 1973

Foley KM, Posner JB: Pain. American Academy of Neurology, Review Book, 1978, pp 199–217

Livingston WK: What is pain? Sci Am 196:59, 1943

Sternbach RA: Pain Patients. Academic Press, New York, 1974

Szasz T: Pain and Pleasure. Basic Books, New York, 1957

Melzack R, Wall PD: Pain mechanisms: a new theory. Science 150:971, 1965

Snyder SH: Opiate receptors and internal opiates. Sci Am 236(3):44, 1977

Halpern LM: Analgesic drugs in the management of pain. Arch Surg 112:861, 1977

Fordyce WE: An operant conditioning method for managing chronic pain. Postgrad Med 57(6):123, 1973

"PSYCHOGENIC" PAIN
AND THE PAIN-PRONE PATIENT

GEORGE L. ENGEL

In the past fifteen years, at two university medical centers, I have studied a large number of patients with pain. The great majority of these patients were seen in my role as a medical attending physician on the medical wards, teaching students and house officers, and as such included the usual variety of diagnosed and undiagnosed painful disorders ordinarily encountered on a medical service. A few patients were referred to me by colleagues who knew of my interest in pain. In addition, I have had random opportunities to observe the appearance and disappearance of pain during the course of psychoanalysis of patients with neuroses and psychosomatic disorders. The views about pain presented in this paper have evolved out of this clinical experience.

THE THEORETICAL PROBLEM

Pain is a cardinal manifestation of illness, and the relief of pain is probably the most common demand made by the patient upon the physician. In spite of this importance of pain, it is astonishing how little we understand pain, but how confident we are of our knowledge of pain. Perhaps familiarity breeds contempt. Every physician has his own personal experience with pain and it began long before he ever became a physician. This is in con-

Reprinted from the American Journal of Medicine 26:899–918, 1959.

trast to other complaints which we learn about only while studying medicine. The medical student, when asked what pain is, feels at once that pain is something familiar, although he may have great difficulty defining it in scientific terms. What he means is that he himself has experienced pain and hence "knows" what pain is. When he is taught that there are pain receptors, pain fibers, pain pathways, and a center for pain perception, his concept of pain becomes scientific. To the comfortable familiarity that comes from personal experience are now added these simple "facts" and from this a relatively simple concept of pain is constructed. Pain is the sensation which arises when pain receptors are stimulated and it is transmitted via its own fibers and pathways to the thalamus where it is perceived or experienced. The more thoughtful student usually notes that whatever is transmitted from the periphery must also somehow or other be perceived in consciousness, otherwise it is not pain. He may also note that people seem to respond differently to whatever it is that they perceive as pain. This insight then leads to the familiar formulation that pain has two components—the original sensation and the reaction to the sensation. There the matter usually rests. When a patient complains of pain, it is taken for granted that pain end organs somewhere in the body are being stimulated, presumably by a pathological process. That this often proves to be the case provides repeated and comforting support to those who hold this centripetal point of view. When no such explanation is found, it is assumed that a pathological process is there nonetheless but simply has not yet been discovered. Rarely this too proves to be so. Or it is postulated that something is affecting the nerves ("neuralgia"), or the nerve pathways, or even the thalamus, producing so-called "central" pain. If no other explanation is forthcoming, the patient is told in one way or another that his pain is "imaginary," often meaning that the physician does not believe it exists, in spite of the most tangible evidence that the patient is suffering just as intensely as the person who has a visible and palpable painful lesion. In more recent years the term "psychogenic" pain has come into use and is generally applied by exclusion to those instances in which no other cause of pain can be demonstrated. For many this is a vague and mysterious concept since the commonly accepted concept of pain provides no room for such a notion. How can there be pain if pain end organs are not being stimulated?

I emphasize these points because unless you can relinquish the notion that pain must originate in peripheral receptors and nowhere else, it is virtually impossible to understand what is referred to as "psychogenic" pain. Perhaps we need to ask first: What is pain? A definition of pain is elusive at best, if possible at all. As observers we cannot even recognize pain. Indeed, pain can only be experienced and for our information about pain we are totally dependent upon the report of the person experiencing it. As Szasz has pointed out, pain falls into the category of private data—experience which cannot be simultaneously shared and reported by anyone other than the person experiencing it. (1). It can only be reported. This is different from some varieties of experience, such as vision or hearing where what impinges on the sense organs can also be experienced by other observers and hence some consensus can be achieved as to what was seen or heard. Hence we have had no difficulty in discovering that occasionally persons may report seeing or hearing things in the absence of recognizable visual or auditory stimulation. One thinks at once of the hallucinations of psychotic people. However we should not overlook the fact that visual and auditory experiences in the absence of the corresponding peripheral stimulation are part of our daily life. Our dreams, for example, are predominantly and at times brilliantly visual in character—perhaps less often auditory. Some persons have a capacity for vivid visual and auditory imagery during the waking state. During complete sensory deprivation, including pitch darkness, there may be brilliant visual hallucinations (2). A variety of chemicals, e.g., mescaline and lysergic acid, characteristically produce visual images (3). Penfield has reported on the auditory experiences in temporal lobe epilepsy and during direct brain stimulation (4). I make these points to emphasize that when it

is possible to verify the presence or absence of a peripheral source of stimulation in studying sensory experiences, we have no difficulty in identifying a host of examples in which no peripheral stimulation takes place and yet the person clearly experiences sensation. Arguing by analogy alone, I contend that the same must also hold true for pain.

What significance, then, are we to attach to the undoubted fact that there are pain pathways and that pain can be invoked by stimulation of parts of the body that are so innervated? Certainly it makes clear that in whatever manner we may conceptualize pain, one way in which it can be evoked is by appropriate stimulation of this peripheral sensory system. This does not justify the additional, usually inferred postulate that pain can result only from the stimulation of such pathways. But it does permit us to study and to identify characteristics of pain which are dependent on the neurophysiological characteristics of the peripheral system, an important consideration since this enables us to identify a pain process originating in muscle as compared to skin, for example. The peripheral distribution of pain-sensitive receptors has another importance in terms of how the individual's concept of pain develops. Pain belongs to the systems concerned with protecting the body from injury. We may assume that from birth on the individual builds up a library, so to speak, of pain experiences, originating from the variety of peripheral painful stimulations which he experiences during the course of his life. As we will show later, these are importantly concerned with the person's over-all development. Thus, from the developmental side we presume that the capacity to experience pain in the first place develops from numerous peripherally induced experiences but thereafter pain experience, like visual or auditory experience, may occur without the corresponding stimulation of the end organ.

There are still other reasons that compel us to question the purely centripetal concept of pain. We have already noted that only the sufferer knows whether or not he has pain and we may then ask: How does he know? Obviously consciousness and attention are necessary. Actually, the most successful technics for relieving pain, namely, general anesthesia and hypnosis, are not directed to pain per se but to consciousness and/or to attention. We know that the grievously wounded soldier in the heat of battle may experience no pain until the action is over.

Now, how do we know "pain" when it reaches our attention? We know it only by its quality and from this point on language fails us. It is completely impossible to describe pain accurately. We can describe it only in terms of experiences which evoke pain. Thus we may describe it as "sharp," thinking of a cut or a quick blow; or "dull," thinking of some slow pressure; as "burning," "tearing," or like a "pin-prick" or "toothache," and so forth. Obviously these are not descriptions of pain—these are descriptions of circumstances under which pain actually was experienced, or our imagination of how it would feel were something of this sort to be experienced. The man with a coronary occlusion may say it feels like his chest is being crushed, even though he may never have experienced actual compression of the chest and were he to experience it he would discover that it did not resemble his pain of coronary occlusion at all.

When we scrutinize more carefully the identifying quality of pain we note that it includes an affective tone. Pain is never neutral. It is usually unpleasant, but it may also be pleasant, if only in a relative sense. This effective quality brings pain into a very central position in terms of psychic development and function. Thus pain acquires special meanings for the individual as follows:

(1) Pain warns of damage to or loss of parts of the body, and is part of the system for protection of the body from injury. It is, therefore, intimately concerned with learning about the environment and its dangers on the one hand, and about the body and its limitations on the other. We presume that what causes pain and the part that hurts are permanently registered in the central nervous system. We may, therefore, speak of "pain memories"* and of a "body pain image," the latter referring to parts of the body which have been sites of pain in the past.

(2) In terms of development, pain is very much involved in human relationships (object relations). From infancy, pain leads to crying and to a response from the mother or some other close person. The association of pain → crying → comforting by a loved person → relief of pain, is an important determinant of tender love relations and helps to explain the "sweet pleasure" of pain. It is not the pain that is pleasurable, but the anticipation of reunion with a love object and the relief of the pain

that are enjoyed. Certain individuals function as if the pain is worth the price.

(3) Fairly early in childhood, pain and punishment become linked. Indeed, in many languages the two words spring from the same root. This establishes another kind of communication between the child and adults, namely, pain is inflicted when one is "bad." Pain thus not only may come to signal that one really is "bad," and thereby become a signal for guilt, but also pain may become an important medium for expiation of guilt. Some children as well as adults welcome pain if it means expiation and forgiveness and, hence, reunion with the loved one. If pain serves to relieve guilt, pleasure in a relative sense is again involved.

(4) Pain also early becomes closely associated with aggression and power. The child quickly discovers the effects of inflicting pain on others and on himself. We will learn how by suffering pain one may control one's own aggression. The pleasure of the aggression is retained, but one's self is taken as the target.

(5) Closely related to the preceding is the connection between pain and real, threatened or fantasied loss of loved persons. Especially when there is also guilt for aggressive feelings toward such persons, pain may provide a psychic means of expiation. Further, as Szasz points out, the patient succeeds in reducing the feeling of loss by experiencing a pain in his own body which he then substitutes for the lost person (1). He suffers more from the pain than the loss, so to speak. Later we will see how the patient's ideas of pain actually or presumably experienced by the lost person will determine the location of the patient's pain. The psychic logic of this is revealed in our language when we speak of a "painful loss."

(6) Pain may also be associated with sexual feelings. We know that at the height of sexual excitement pain may not only be mutually inflicted but actually enjoyed. When this becomes the dominant feature of the sexual activity, we recognize it as a perversion, sado-masochism. We will also discover some persons who prefer to experience pain rather than have sexual experience, the latter existing only at the level of unconscious fantasy.

When we examine the full gamut of circumstances, from the simple peripheral stimulus to the complex psychological components, we must acknowledge that pain in final analysis is a psychic phenomenon. The two-component concept of pain, which speaks of the pain sensation and the reaction to pain, is misleading because it implies that pain can originate only from a "pain" receptor. Gooddy goes so far as to say: "There can be no

---

*One is not able to re-experience a pain at will, but one may have memories about the pain. This is true of affects in general. Hence, the term "pain memories" refers to the ideational complexes, conscious and unconscious, associated with past pain experiences, stimulation of which may later give rise to pain. This pain is not the "old" pain anymore than the joy evoked by certain memories is the same joy that was felt on the occasion of the original joyous experience.

pathways nor nerve endings for pain. The notion of pathways for pain is but a figment of the observer's mind." (5). Instead he suggests that disordered patterns (rate, amplitude, time and space) in nerves or neural centers provide the neurophysiological conditions which may be experienced as pain, but they do not by themselves account for pain. Certain characteristics of the impulse patterns may influence the quality of pain, but they will not in themselves determine that it be pain. This certainly is consistent with the clinical observation that one can identify qualities associated with colic, for example, as differentiated from a toothache, qualities which arise from the properties of the particular anatomical system giving rise to the disordered impulse patterns. Thus such patterns originating in the periphery contribute certain qualities to the pain and determine where the patient locates the pain, but the total pain experienced is always a psychic phenomenon.

This brings us then to "psychogenic" pain. While the pain experience is only and always a psychic phenomenon, it is nonetheless of both practical and theoretical importance to know whether or not what is being experienced as pain includes disordered patterns originating in nerve endings, just as we need to know whether or not a visual experience originated from light waves striking the retina. But the fact of a peripheral process does not necessarily mean pain, for we know that pathological changes may be associated with the most excruciating pain in one person and with little or no pain in another. By hypnosis, or with placebos, we may eliminate or induce pain without modifying to the slightest the nature of the pathological lesion (6,7). The practical clinical problem really has to do with how the individual experiences pain. Clinical observation reveals that there are people who seem to experience pain with unusual intensity and frequency. With peripheral lesions they seem to suffer more pain than most people do, but often they suffer pain without any peripheral process. Among such patients the presence or absence of a peripheral disorder is not well correlated with the presence or absence of pain. Indeed we often find that the discovery of the lesion and its removal or cure does not alleviate the pain, which may persist or even recur at a later date. In other words, there are certain individuals, whom we shall call "pain-prone," among whom psychic factors play the primary role in the genesis of pain, in the absence as well as in the presence of peripheral lesions.

Clinical psychologic studies of many pain-prone persons have by now provided us with a fairly good understanding of the determinants of this susceptibility to suffer pain (1,8–13). The key comes through understanding how pain may yield pleasure. It is pleasure in a relative sense, that is, in place of something even more distressing. Beginning from a primitive protective system, pain evolves into a complex psychic mechanism, part of the system whereby man maintains himself in his environment. Both as a warning system and as a mechanism of defense, pain helps to avoid or ward off even more unpleasant feeling states or experiences and may even offer the means whereby certain gratifications can be achieved, albeit at a price. If we can understand this adaptive role of pain in the psychic economy, we can begin to comprehend how it is that certain persons actually seek pain, even to the extent of creating it as a purely psychic experience if no peripheral stimulus is available to evoke it.

THE CLINICAL PROBLEM

Let us now examine pain in terms of the problem as it is actually encountered by the physician, namely, a patient seeks medical aid because he is suffering from pain. I propose that we approach each patient with the following questions in mind.

(1) Are there pathological processes affecting nerve endings and leading to disordered patterns in nerve pathways which are being experienced as pain? (2) If such processes are present, can the character of the pain experience reported by the patient be fully, partially, or not at all accounted for by the distinctive characteristics of the peripheral pathological process? (3) How are psychological processes operating to determine the ultimate character of the pain experience for the patient and the manner of its communication to the physician?

All three questions are pertinent with every patient, although circumstances as well as patients differ in respect to how much attention each question requires before our problem is solved. They acknowledge the principle that a peripheral factor may or may not be operating and that when it is operating it may not fully account for the pain experience. Further, they permit us to explore in more practical clinical terms the precise criteria which should enable us to make accurate interpretations. For example, if a man complains of epigastric pain, neither a normal gastrointestinal x-ray series nor one showing some irritability of the duodenal cap will, by itself, provide the explanation for the pain. The patient may or may not have a duodenal ulcer, and if he has a duodenal ulcer this may or may not account for the pain which he experiences. When we examine what is called the typical "ulcer pain" we realize that there are distinctive characteristics of the pain associated with duodenal ulcer which we can recognize as the qualities conferred upon the total pain experience by the type of the disordered impulses arising in the nerve endings in the region of the ulcer. It is these qualities which permit us to identify duodenal ulcer as compared to biliary colic. Our first concern, then, must be with how the patient describes his pain.

The Description of the Pain

The peripheral signature. The relatively good concordance among individuals as to the kinds of pain associated with particular pathological processes gives us our first clue as to what differentiates the peripheral contribution to pain experience from the rest of the pain experience. Gooddy spoke of "disordered patterns," referring to rate, amplitude, time and space, and we immediately recognize that what enables us to identify a particular pain experience as being associated with myocardial ischemia, or renal colic, or a perirectal abscess, or a bone metastasis, concerns how the specific anatomic and physiologic characteristics of the diseased part gives rise to these disordered "patterns" (5). Wolff's meticulous study and demonstration of the varieties of pain evoked by stimulation of various parts of the head provides an excellent demonstration of the consistency of the signature conferred on the pain experience by anatomical and physiological factors (14). With a stone in the ureter, we can predict with a high degree of confidence where the patient will locate the pain and we will recognize in the colicky character of the pain the rhythmic contractions of the ureter in its attempt to pass the stone. Further, once we understand the anatomy and physiology of the structure involved we can also predict that certain movements, postures and behaviors of the patient are chosen because they are associated with pain amelioration, while others are avoided because they are associated with the intensification of the pain.* While this is common

---

*In the two person field we may also note that certain movements, postures and behaviors are utilized by the patient with pain because of their value in communicating to others the need for help.

knowledge, I stress it because the precise elucidation of such correlations between anatomical and physiological characteristics on the one hand, and pain experience on the other hand, provides the most certain evidence that processes originating in the periphery are initiating a particular pain experience. Conversely, deviation from these understandable anatomical and physiological principles should immediately caution the physician that peripheral disordered patterns either play no role or their influence is being obscured by other factors. The patient, for example, with acute myocardial infarction who continues to experience the same pain unremittingly for a week arouses our suspicion. Does this indicate a further extension of the infarct? This is an unlikely possibility and would have to be established by means other than the pain itself. Could it be that pain that originated in relationship to the myocardial infarct now has established an existence independent of the changes taking place in the myocardium? Finally, could it be that the pain never was related to the myocardial infarct, but rather to something else which again may or may not be affecting nerve endings? The incongruity between the pain characteristics as described by the patient and the known pathophysiological and pathoanatomical processes is in itself sufficient grounds to question the accuracy of the interpretation which explains all on the presence of the allegedly demonstrated peripheral disorder. Here I would warn especially against the commonplace practice of describing such situations simply in terms of the pain being "atypical."

The individual psychic signature. As we listen to the patient's account of his pain, we first attempt to detect and identify pain qualities associated with stimuli arising from the periphery, as just described. All the other features of the pain description are understandable in terms of what we might call the individual's "psychic signature," as contrasted to the "peripheral signature." What are some of the varieties of pain description that are not understandable in terms of a peripheral process, even when the latter is present? I have already mentioned discrepancies in respect to what would be predicted from anatomy and physiology. We need to pay attention to pain location in terms of the patient's concept of his body image as contrasted to pain location determined by the distribution of nerves. For example, the patient who locates his pain in the region of the left nipple or the apex beat may at some point indicate concern about heart disease. The doctor should consider the possibility that some idea about heart disease accounts for the location of the pain, although not for the pain itself, rather than the pain giving rise to the idea of heart disease. Actually, patients with heart pain often prefer to explain the pain on the basis of something non-cardiac, such as indigestion.

Patients' private concepts of how their bodies function may influence their description of pain. For example, the person who entertains an autointoxication theory may get pain relief from cathartics or colonic irrigations, such relief not indicating in any way colonic disease. The intensity of pain reported by patients is a highly individual matter. Clinical experience is a useful guide but, in general, gross deviations in either direction inform us more of the psychic state of the individual than of the existence or nature of a peripheral lesion. Libman's test for pain sensitivity by styloid pressure is a useful way of evaluating quickly how a patient deals with a painful peripheral stimulation (15).

In general, the more complex the ideation and the imagery involved in the pain description, the more complex are the psychic processes involved in the final pain experience. In part this is a matter of reality testing. When the pain experience is initiated from the periphery and this is the primary factor responsible for its presence, and when the function of the pain is to signal to the patient damage or injury to a part of his body and nothing else, the pain description is likely to be economical and relatively uncomplicated. Terms such as "sharp," "dull," "aching," "throbbing," and the like are relatively easily applied and the relationship to physiological processes relatively easily identified by the patient. On the other hand, vague descriptions as well as more elaborate imagery are reflections of the degree to which the pain is entering in psychic function in a more complicated fashion, now serving purposes far beyond the simple nociceptive function. While the patient almost always initially presents his complaint as a pain, an ache, a headache, a backache or some such symptom, request for elaboration will sometimes, but not necessarily, bring out a vague description, as "a sensation," "an unpleasant feeling," "I just can't describe it"; or descriptions such as "being jabbed with an icepick," "burning like a red-hot coal," "bruised and torn," "like my face is being eaten up," "electric shocks burning me," and "just too horrible to describe." Or "headache" may become "a sort of pressure as if the top of my head would come off." A backache may become "a pull-

ing or drawing as if the cords of my back were being pulled at." Sensations described as boring, gnawing, biting, penetrating, crawling, twisting and tearing are particularly meaningful. Now these varieties of description are extremely valuable in identifying the presence or absence of a peripheral process. In general, however, while we can be fairly confident of a peripheral lesion when the description is not only crisp and economical but also concordant with anatomical and physiological processes, we cannot conclude that the patient who gives us the more complex, the vague, or the vivid type of description does not have a peripheral lesion. Such descriptions reflect the characteristics of the individual and if he is suffering from a peripheral lesion, the disordered patterns arising from it are subjected to the most complex psychic distortion and elaboration so that at times the peripheral qualities may be totally obscured.

This now brings us to explore *who* are the patients disposed to use pain in this fashion and under what circumstances do they do so. For convenience we shall refer to them as the "pain-prone patients."

The Pain-Prone Patients

For the most part these patients repeatedly or chronically suffer from one or another painful disability, sometimes with and sometimes without any recognizable peripheral change. There are also patients who may have only a single or occasional episode of pain, among whom essentially the same psychic mechanisms are operative. Such patients by no means constitute a homogeneous group and yet they have many features in common. By recognizing and understanding the clinical expressions of the psychodynamic processes underlying this type of psychic function of pain, the physician will be able to recognize the patient who uses pain in this fashion and hence more correctly interpret each pain experience for which he is consulted.

The choice of pain as symptom. Pain as punishment. I mention this component first because clinical observation leads me to conclude that guilt, conscious or unconscious, is an invariable factor in the choice of pain as the symptom, as compared to other types of body sensations. Clinically we should expect to find either a long-term background of guilt and/or an immediate guilt-provoking situation precipitating pain. The clinical characteristics of the chronically guilt-ridden person are not difficult to recognize, if one appreciates the role of penitence, atonement, self-denial and self-depreciation as means of self-inflicted punishment to ease the feeling of guilt. The patient who uses pain as a means of self-punishment and atonement almost always manifests other psychological and behavioral devices which serve the same purpose, and their recognition will alert the physician to the likelihood that this patient is indeed using pain in this fashion.

Some of these individuals are chronically depressive, pessimistic and gloomy people whose guilty, self-depreciating attitudes are readily apparent from the moment they walk into your office. They seem to have had no joy or enthusiasm for life and, indeed, some seem to have suffered the most extraordinary number and variety of defeats, humiliations and unpleasant experiences. You may first be inclined to pass this off as a consequence of the pain they are suffering or as just a matter of bad luck. But it quickly becomes apparent that many of these difficult situations have either been solicited by the patient or simply not avoided. They drift into situations or submit to relationships in which they are hurt, beaten, defeated, humiliated and, to our astonishment, seem not to learn from experience; for no sooner out of one bad spot they are in another in spite of the most obvious danger signals. At the same time they conspicuously fail to exploit situations which should lead to successes and, indeed, when success is thrust upon them they do badly. This provides the clearest proof that these characteristics are not the result of the pain, for we note often that it is just when life is treating them worst, when circumstances are the hardest that their physical health is likely to be at its best and they are free of pain. Paradoxically, when things improve, when success is imminent, then a painful symptom may develop. Unconsciously they do not believe that they deserve success or happiness, and feel that they must pay a price for it. A common kind of statement is, "When I was having such a hard time, I felt good; but now, just when I should be able finally to enjoy myself, this terrible pain has to come." Even though they complain of the pain, for them the pain is almost a comfort or an old friend. It is an adjustment, a way of adaptation acquired through psychic experience. We are often struck by the disparity between the intensity of the pain and suffering they describe and their general appearance of well-being. Some patients may describe a terrible pain with so little evidence of current suffering that you may be surprised to discover that they are speaking of a present pain. This stoical behavior may express the need to see oneself and be seen as

a martyr who tolerates suffering. Other patients display intense suffering, behavior which also has psychic determinants, including a need to appear as the suffering person, to be pitied, or to be succored. Some patients seem to experience a secret joy in their pain while others appear literally to be persecuted by it. Many of these patients are unusually tolerant of pain inflicted upon them by nature or by the physician in the course of examination and treatment. In their histories we discover an extraordinary number of injuries and operations and more than the usual number of painful illnesses and pains, the latter usually described in medical jargon as "pleurisy," "kidney attacks," "sinus," "lumbago," "appendicitis," and the like. Careful history will usually render doubtful that such terms actually correspond with the diagnosis in more than a few instances. We soon realize that what many of the patients solicit from us is the infliction of further pain, usually in the form of surgery or painful diagnostic or therapeutic measures. Treatment that is not painful or a hardship may be rejected. Physicians may be surprised at how well these patients tolerate painful procedures. Indeed, the patient who is very fearful of such painful procedures is not likely to be found among this group at all.

The following cases are illustrative:

A sixty-one year old man had suffered intense pain intermittently for twenty-five years in the region of the right ear. This pain had lasted for several days at a time and was described as "raw and burning." The patient's mother had died when he was seven and a half years old. His father and stepmother had treated him harshly, and "boxing the ears" was a frequent punishment from both, a procedure to which he had submitted passively, although his younger brother had not. Characteristic of this man was that he had allowed himself to be struck by his father until his twenty-first birthday, feeling that he had no right to protest until he was legally an adult. However, he did not leave home until he was twenty-six years old and up to that time had contributed the major share of his earnings to his father. Face pain began about this time.

Although of superior intelligence, he had done heavy manual labor for many years. Later he had gone into business with a partner. The business was a success, but his partner had soon cheated him of all the profits and he had ended up losing everything. Like other events in his life, he had accepted this without a struggle.

Six years before examination, he had suffered a myocardial infarction and since then had experienced severe angina pectoris decubitus. The face pain became less severe from that time on.

A fifty-three year old unmarried school teacher had had severe dysmenorrhea and headaches since the age of eighteen. At various times in her life she had had severe pains in her head, cheeks, teeth, abdomen, back, legs and hips. The low back pain had been described as "like a raging toothache—sometimes like something is moving or crawling down my legs." She described a fantastic career of suffering, of which the following sequence is typical:

She had worked hard for almost thirty years, depriving herself of all comforts in order to build herself a house in which to retire. In the meantime she lived with an old woman who suffered from senile dementia and who made excessive demands. Finally the long-awaited day arrived and she moved into her new home. She soon began to feel guilty enjoying this all by herself, so she advertised for a roomer. She took in a young couple with two small children who soon spread out to occupy the whole house, the patient retiring to a single bedroom. When the new tenants complained that she interfered with their privacy, she had obligingly moved out, sold them the furniture at a loss, rented them the house for a ridiculously small sum and had returned to live with the senile lady.

With many of these patients we will be struck by the dramatic fashion in which they describe both the hardships of their lives and the extent of their suffering from pain, illness, and the slings and arrows of misfortune. Indeed, this very dramatic quality and the relish with which they recount the story, often an almost unbelievable one, should immediately alert the physician that this is a person for whom pain and suffering are unconscious sources of gratification.

A forty-four year old woman had a host of painful symptoms beginning in adolescence. At various times they included "appendicitis," "arthritis," "pleurisy," "kidney colic," "heart" pain, face pain, back pain, headaches and pains in the extremities. She had had fourteen major and minor operations and at least five painful injuries. Everything in her life was described in dramatic terms. The patient's relation to her mother had been a very ambivalent one, while towards her father she had felt most affectionate as a child. She had especially enjoyed resting her face on his shoulder. She recalled an occasion when she was twelve years old when her mother had had severe pain in the face due to a tooth infection. Although she was extremely frightened of the dark, she ran a considerable distance at night to get a doctor.

Early in childhood she felt her mother favored her four siblings. She deliberately provoked her mother by misbehaving and when her father came home from work she expected to be punished and indeed often was. This was actually a pleasurable experience because, after the spanking, her father would hold her on his lap and fondle her. She had many fears in childhood and would find these an excuse to jump into her father's bed for comfort. When she first began to menstruate she thought she was bleeding to death. When she was twenty-two years old she married a boy she hardly knew and her life with him

was a nightmare. They lived with his mother who treated her as a servant. He drank, beat her, and openly brought prostitutes to the house and required his wife to wait on them. Occasionally she would leave her husband for a few months at a time but she always returned. At these times she lived with her well-to-do physician brother and his wife where she functioned essentially as a servant. When her father and later her mother became ill, she undertook the complete responsibility of their care.

Her father died in her arms when she was thirty. Following his death the mother became depressed, and this depression lasted several years. The patient undertook her care and never left her alone. The first and only time the patient went out, her mother took the opportunity to commit suicide by throwing herself in front of a train. The body was badly mutilated and no one was permitted to see it. The patient repeatedly attempted to reassure herself that her mother's face had escaped mutilation. After her mother's death she finally brought herself to divorce her husband. At the age of forty she married a sixty-year old man. Commenting on this marriage, the patient stated that she would be content to settle for ten years of happiness. She called her husband "Daddy." No sooner had she entered what she called the first happy period in her life, when she quarreled with her sister-in-law and physician brother. Then the face pain developed which already had robbed her of the first four of her hoped-for ten years of happiness.

The development and backgrounds of the pain-vulnerable patients. For practical clinical purposes it is usually not necessary to elucidate all the factors predisposing to these developments. Suffice it to say that we often find that aggression, suffering and pain played an important role in early family relationships. These may include: (1) Parents, one or both of whom were physically or verbally abusive to each other and/or to the child. (2) One brutal parent and one submissive parent, the former sometimes an alcoholic father. (3) A parent who punished frequently but then suffered remorse and overcompensated with a rare display of affection, so that the child became accustomed to the sequence, pain and suffering gain love. (4) A parent who was cold and distant but who responded more when the child was ill or suffering pain, even to the point that the child invited injury to elicit a response from the parent. (5) The child who had a parent or other close figure who suffered illness or pain for which he came to feel in some way responsible and guilty, most commonly because of aggressive impulses, acts or fantasies. (6) The child who was aggressive or hurting until some event suddenly forced an abandonment of such behavior, usually with much guilt. (7) The child who deflected the aggression of a parent away from the other parent or a sibling onto himself, usually an early manifestation of guilt. Some of these backgrounds are illustrated in the following excerpts of the histories of pain-prone patients. It is consistent with their psychological characteristics that these patients readily provide the physician with such information if only he indicates his interest to hear it. This eagerness to tell of such distressing life experiences is in itself of diagnostic value, and it is not of crucial importance whether such descriptions are factual or fanciful. In either event, the fact and manner of telling betrays the wish of the patient to present himself as long-suffering and abused.

A thirty-two year old married woman had cruel, impulsive parents. The father was a chronic alcoholic and the mother unpredictable and sadistic. She had vivid memories of being hit hard across the face and back by both parents. Mother would slap her face suddenly and without warning as insurance against future misdeeds. When the patient was seven, all of mother's teeth were extracted; the patient remembers the severe face pain suffered by the mother.

A thirty-four year old married woman witnessed the death, by accidental burning, of her two year old sister when she was five. This little girl's clothes caught fire from a wood stove and her face was badly burned. Later the parents separated and she was placed with an older couple. The foster mother frequently beat her about the face and head and pulled her hair. The patient said, "I often think of her when I have my pains."

A twenty-seven year old married mother had pain in the head, face and eyes. As a child she frequently witnessed her brutal, alcoholic father slap her mother across the face. Her sister, seven years younger, was born blind in one eye. The patient blamed the father for this and also accused him of preventing the girl from receiving proper medical attention. She herself undertook to obtain this care for her sister at the expense of great personal hardship.

A forty-one year old unmarried woman, a school teacher, had severe sharp pain involving the entire left half of the face and head. Since childhood she had always maintained the strictest control over the expression of any aggression. As a child, however, she had had a reputation of being a little "spitfire." This period came to a close when, in a fit of anger, she threw a pair of scissors which stuck in the left cheek of her little cousin. The mother warned her that retaliation in kind would befall little girls who throw things and put people's eyes out. From that time on she never actively expressed aggression externally.

Alternating with the face pain had been back pain. When she was sixteen her father was killed in a mine accident. That day he had awakened with a backache and although his wife urged him to stay home and rest, he went to work and as a consequence was killed.

Under what circumstances does the pain occur? Many of these people have had repeated episodes of pain, so that this question has two aspects: when did the patient first have pain and when did each episode occur? Quite a number have had their first significant painful syndromes in adolescence. This is especially so among women patients whose story may begin with painful menarche, dysmenorrhea, or headaches, especially premenstrual. A very important clinical finding is the history of "appendicitis" and appendectomy. These episodes do not fit the usual clinical picture of acute appendicitis, but usually involve chronic or intermittent abdominal pain of quite varied nature and severity, sometimes associated with a variety of other symptoms. Such attacks usually begin in the age range fourteen to eighteen years, eventually leading to appendectomy. When surgical records are available we find the appendix reported as "normal" or "chronic appendicitis." Curiously, this pain usually disappears after surgery, although it may soon be replaced by other pains often related by the patient and some physicians to the scar or to adhesions. This "appendix" syndrome is much more common among girls than boys and its presence in the past history provides a valuable clue for the interpretation of later pains (16).

The onset of pain syndromes in adolescence also reflects the important psychological changes occurring in this period of life and especially the sexual conflicts that may be involved in the genesis of pain. Both guilt about sexual impulses and an unconscious sado-masochistic concept of sex are important. Pain may occur in lieu of or may prevent sexual activity, and hence under circumstances in which sexual impulses might be aroused, in fact or in fantasy. Frigidity, dyspareunia and varieties of impotence are common accompaniments. Or the patient may enjoy some sexual pleasure if he is hurt (masochism). Along these same lines we may discover painful, mutilating and destructive concepts of pregnancy and labor, among men as well as among women.

We may now consider some of the circumstances under which individual episodes of pain may occur, remembering that this may also include pain precipitated by unconsciously motivated accidents or injuries. While our discussion so far has focussed on the patients with the most pronounced pain vulnerability, we should keep in mind that there are also persons among whom the specific psychodynamic constellation conducive to pain may be activated on only a few occasions in their lives.

(1) When external circumstances fail to satisfy the unconscious need to suffer. We have already commented on the patient in whom pain develops when things begin to go well. These are always individuals with an exaggerated need to suffer who may remain relatively pain-free as long as external circumstances make life difficult. When the environment does not treat them harshly enough or they cannot get it to do so, it seems almost as if they inflict pain upon themselves.

A forty-five year old woman had at various times abdominal pain ("chronic appendicitis"), back pain, and finally severe pain in the left side of the jaw, left ear and left side of the temple. She described the latter as "like a jab with an icepick." Although she came from a wealthy and socially prominent family, at the age of twenty-five she married a ne'er-do-well who cruelly mistreated her. She was humiliated by the divorce three years later. She remarried twelve years later and although this was a good marriage it was marred by a series of distressing deaths, injuries and illnesses in her family. In spite of the fact that small children irritated her, she adopted two little boys in rapid succession when she was over forty years old. She was always getting sick. Her face pain began just at a time when things finally seemed to be going well for the first time, and after she had consented to allow her paralyzed mother-in-law, whose care she had undertaken at great personal sacrifice for many years, to go to a nursing home.

A thirty-two year old woman married to a brutal, alcoholic man who frequently beat her and the children, and who provided for her most inadequately, struggled hard to maintain herself. She began to suffer a series of painful disabilities when her husband underwent a religious conversion, gave up drinking, and became the model of a conscientious and considerate husband and father. Just when she had everything to live for, her pain prevented her from enjoying it.

Such precipitating circumstances are easily overlooked if the physician fails to recognize that for certain persons, success and good fortune are stressful in that they mobilize intolerable feelings of guilt (17,18). These persons really feel that they do not deserve happiness or success and they must suffer to achieve it.

(2) As a response to a real, threatened, or fantasied loss. Following the death or any permanent loss of a loved person, or during the period of anticipation of such a loss, the survivor may develop pain during the period of mourning and sometimes on anniversaries of the mourning. Szasz has pointed out how the mourner may take a part of his own body as a love object in place of the lost person and by experiencing pain in this part, symbolically assure himself of its continued presence (1). He designates pain as an affect that warns of the danger or threat of loss of a body part. I agree with this formulation but find it incomplete, for it does not sufficiently include the affect of guilt. While following the loss of a loved person one becomes more self-centered and sometimes more aware of body sensations (or also at times less aware), this is not experienced as pain by the sufferer unless there is also a strong element of guilt, most often related to ambivalence toward the lost person. In a study of patients with ulcerative colitis we observed that if a relationship with a love object was threatened by some overt or unconscious aggressive act or fantasy and the patient responded with guilt, then pain (usually headache) developed; if the patient responded with feelings of despair, helplessness or hopelessness, activation of the colitis was the more usual response (19).

A classic illustration of pain in response to a sudden loss is illustrated in the following case:

A forty-two year old woman had a brief attack of sharp pain in the left anterior chest. In the interview she almost immediately began to speak of how upset she had been since the shotgun murder of her brother-in-law one week earlier. He was shot in the left side of the chest. His body was taken South for burial, but she had to remain home to care for the children. She cried when thinking or speaking of this event. She greatly admired and was very fond of this man who was a stable and successful man in the community. In contrast, her husband (the victim's brother) was irresponsible and abusive. In fact, exactly one year earlier, while drinking, he brutally beat her and then threatened to shoot her with a shotgun. She averted this by clutching her infant to her chest and jumping out the (ground floor) window. She preferred charges against him and he was currently on probation. Further interview strongly indicated a guilty wish that the victim had been the husband rather than his brother.

While many episodes of pain occur in direct relationship to the loss of a loved person, as in this case, many more occur in relation to threatened losses, anniversaries of losses, or fantasied losses. Thus we may find pain developing in relationship to the illness or impending departure of important family members or friends, where the patient responds with, or had previously experienced aggressive feelings toward such persons. Or the patient may experience the loss or its anniversary as a painful reminder of guilt, and actually suffer with it in the form of pain.

(3) When guilt is evoked by intense aggressive or forbidden sexual feeling. There are some individuals for whom any expression of aggression is unacceptable and even the threat or possibility that aggression might be expressed provokes guilt.

Some of these persons instead experience pain, sometimes without any aggression being expressed and sometimes remorsefully after it has been expressed. After the pain develops, the provoking situation may be forgotten or only vaguely remembered or the patient may recall it remorsefully, consciously accepting the pain as a punishment and as a warning against future expressions of aggression. Some patients observe that their pains occur when they do not control themselves.

A thirty-two year old woman, who also had had ulcerative colitis, was compulsively clean and always kept close rein on any expression of aggression. Her two and a half year old son defecated in his crib and smeared the feces. She became furious and immediately spanked him. A few hours later a severe headache developed. She felt remorseful for her outbreak of temper and resolved not to do so again. The headache was considered a deserved punishment.

When the provoking situation involves sexual impulses, these, in contrast to the aggressive impulses, are almost always at an unconscious level and must be inferred by the examiner. In general, they involve situations which might normally be expected to be sexually exciting, but are not so recognized by these patients, who instead experience pain; or more subtle situations in which the precipitating stimulus has special symbolic meaning to the individual, generally reminiscent of some childhood sexual conflict. Pains so experienced follow the classic model of the hysterical conversion mechanism, in which the pain simultaneously expresses symbolically the forbidden impulse and at the same time successfully prevents it being acted upon. When the conversion symptom is pain, we find that along with the sexual impulse there is always a strong aggressive component and guilt. The sexual fantasy is a sado-masochistic one.

A twenty-six year old woman with a variety of hysterical manifestations had several episodes of pain and burning at the end of urination. The urine examination was always negative but she referred to it as "my cystitis." One episode occurred during her first year of marriage. Her husband proved less capable sexually than she hoped for and she felt both frustrated and angry. As a child the bathroom was the scene of many sexual fantasies and of masturbation, which included poking things in and around the urethra. These symptoms recurred briefly during the course of psychoanalysis when her husband had a severe case of flu and was sexually inattentive for several weeks. She developed fleeting sexual fantasies about the analyst and then her "cystitis" recurred. The painful dysuria promptly disappeared when these transference sexual feelings were brought up during the analytic hour and connected with the childhood fantasies and masturbatory activities.

The location of the pain. The patient usually describes the pain as occurring in some part of his body, whether it originates there or not. When no peripheral factor is operating, the patient still assigns a location to the pain. This choice of site of the pain is determined by one or more of the following:

(1) *A peripherally provoked pain experienced by the patient sometime in the past.* In essence, the patient revives unconsciously a past pain experience and by mechanisms not understood suffers again from pain of the same character and in the same location as the original pain. This may be the pain of a past injury, an operation, or any physical disorder which had occurred at a time when the pain could fulfill, directly or indirectly, a psychic regulating role for the patient. It may have been punishment or it may have been the vehicle whereby a relationship was re-established. Some postoperative and post-traumatic pain syndromes are of this sort.

A young man had repeated bouts of severe searing shocks of pain in the right side of his forehead. These came on with explosive suddenness, sometimes associated with a sensation of flashing light and staggering, and were followed by a dull, throbbing pain of growing intensity.

When he was twelve years old he prepared a home-made bomb, one of numerous aggressive act unconsciously directed toward his stern and punitive father. The bomb exploded prematurely and he suffered a depressed skull fracture as well as the loss of several fingers of his left hand. He felt extremely guilty and considered the accident a deserved punishment. The location and character of the head pain exactly duplicated the original accident. The pain characteristically occurred in settings in which anger toward authority figures was blocked by guilt. Sometimes he could terminate the pain by an attack of blind destructive fury against some inanimate object, such as a piece of furniture.

The widest variety of painful disorders in the past may provide the basis for future pain experiences and a careful history often will uncover the original painful incident as well as the psychological factors operating at the time. When the current pain, which may be described in terms identical with the original pain, is not also accompanied by the appropriate physical or laboratory findings, especially when this occurs in a person with the other characteristics of the "pain-prone" population, the diagnosis is strongly suggested. This is illustrated by the patient with ear pain who in the past had otitis media; the patient with throat pain who once had a peritonsillar abscess; the patient with painful dysuria and frequency and normal urine who once had acute cystitis.

(2) *A pain actually experienced by someone else or a pain the patient imagined or wished the other person experienced.* This is perhaps the most common and the most important determinant of the site of the pain. It involves several important psychologic mechanisms. First of all, the other person is important to the patient and is one with whom the patient is in some (usually unconscious) conflict or from whom he has been or may be separated. Secondly, it involves the psychic mechanism of identification, meaning that the patient unconsciously becomes like the other person, notably in terms of suffering like him. We have already mentioned real, threatened or fantasied losses and guilt for forbidden impulses as precipitating factors. We can now add that the location of pain may be determined by the real or fantasied location of pain in the other person(s). It must be emphasized that this is unconscious. The patient is unaware of a connection between his pain and the pain of the other person and if directly questioned will never consciously make the connection, although he may unconsciously reveal it by word or gesture. On the other hand, if the physician meticulously explores the history of pain and illness of all the important persons in the patient's life he will usually uncover without much difficulty the model for the patient's pain. To do this the patient is asked to describe the symptoms of each person, paying particular attention to the patient's idea of the pain.

A forty-two year old man complained of severe stabbing pain in the region of the left nipple. This occurred while he was out hunting and just taking aim at a buck deer. He felt fearful, had difficulty breathing, became lightheaded and collapsed. The patient's father had died of a "heart attack" the previous fall. The medical student who took the history assumed that the patient knew his father's pain had been substernal. When asked where his father's pain was the patient said, "I don't know," but he pointed to the region of his own pain.

Sometimes we know the other person's illness to be painless, only to discover the patient thought otherwise. Thus edema of the ankles may be assumed to be painful, or dyspnea may be thought to be an expression of pain. In such cases the patient may describe the pain he believed the other person to have suffered in the same terms he used to describe his own pain. There is little chance of over-looking such relations if one always gets the patient's description. One may even ask, "What did you imagine it was like?" The cases already noted have provided a number of examples of this mechanism. The following cases offer additional data.

A forty-one year old unmarried woman, a teacher, lived with and took care of her ailing mother for many years until her death one month before the beginning of the patient's face pain. She slept in the same bed as her mother. On the night of her mother's death she had awakened to find that the right side of her mother's face was drawn and a short time later it became blue. She was breathing heavily and the patient believed her to be suffering great pain. She called for help but when unable to secure any climbed back into bed only to realize that her mother was dead.

She had been engaged to a man for many years but had not married because she could not leave her mother. However, upon her mother's death, she first felt emancipated, and bought a house, but then pain developed in the right side of her face and because of it she gave up both her home and fiancé. She expressed remorse at her feelings of emancipation after her mother's death and consciously considered the pain as punishment, a sign that she was being inconsiderate of her mother's memory.

A forty-seven year old married woman had experienced strong guilt when her only daughter was born twenty-two years ago with a cleft palate and harelip. She felt that this was the result of her husband's practice of coitus interruptus. When her doctor implied that this might have resulted from clumsy attempts at abortion, she said, "That was just like a slap in the face to me." The patient's mother also had indicated by innuendo that she believed her daughter was in some way responsible for the baby's defect. The mother suffered from erysipelas of the face fifteen years ago and the patient took care of her. The mother has had face pain from time to time since then. The patient's face pain began one month after the daughter underwent the first of a long series of plastic operations on her face. The patient commented, "I am doing the suffering for her." The patient imagined that her daughter suffered great pain from these procedures, although actually this was not so.

In this last case we note how the choice of location may be overdetermined, here involving not only the daughter's facial deformity and operations, but also the "slap in the face" and mother's erysipelas and face pain.

A thirty-one year old married woman had severe pain in the right side of the neck and throat radiating into the shoulder, right eye and cheek. This had developed while she was taking care of her mother who had suddenly acquired erysipelas of the face. It began while the patient was undergoing treatment from the chiropractor who was taking care of her mother and who had recommended a chiropractic treatment as a prophylactic measure. When asked what part of her mother's face was involved by the erysipelas, the patient was unable to recall, but placed her hand over the painful area of her own face.

Among other symptoms, a twenty-three year old married woman had severe throbbing pain in the temporal regions radiating into the eyes. Her soldier husband had been injured in combat. He had sent her a photograph of himself in which he had cut out the left eye with scissors, indicating that this was the extent of his injury. The patient's symptoms began a week later. It developed that just before he went overseas she had learned that he had been involved in an extramarital affair. She was so angry that she struck him violently in the eye, knocking him down. Under pentothal hypnosis she told how much she wanted him punished. "I wanted him to get as much hurt as I was. I hoped he would get his leg or his foot, or his privates shot off." While he was overseas she had a brief affair, over which she felt very guilty. It was shortly after her lover had left her that she received the news of the husband's injury and the photograph. She was tremendously concerned at his possible retaliation for her infidelity and her pain began when she received word that he was being shipped home.

Sometimes the site of the pain is determined by a conscious or unconscious wish that the other person suffer pain. This may have appeared only as a fleeting thought or may not have been associated with the person at all. This is illustrative of the intrapsychic operation of lex talionis, the patient inflicting on himself exactly what he wished on the other person.

We can understand these determinants of pain location in terms of the importance of object relations (interpersonal relations) in the maintenance of health and of psychic balance. They are expressions par excellence of attempts to maintain object relations, albeit at a price. It is as if the patient says, "If I can't continue to have this relationship and get from it what I want and need, I will become like him in some way." This is a generally used mechanism to deal with a real or threatened loss, but in these cases, mainly because of guilt and the role of pain in past relationships, the patient experiences the object's pain, real or fantasied. By such a psychic experience of pain the patient simultaneously denies the intensity of the loss and atones for his guilt.

Psychiatric diagnosis. While similar psychodynamic features may operate, these patients do not constitute a homogeneous group in terms of psychiatric nosology.

(1) *Conversion hysteria.* The largest number of these patients satisfy the requirements for the diagnosis of conversion hysteria and their histories usually reveal many other conversion symptoms, such as globus, fainting, aphonia, sensory or motor disturbances. They manifest the relative indifference to or exaggerated display of symptoms, as well as the dramatic, exhibitionistic, seductive or shy behavior so common among hysteric persons. They are suggestible and may have intense emotional involvements with the physician, often associated with dramatic remissions and relapses of symptoms. To varying degrees they may have been involved in acting out behavior, including drinking, use of drugs, and sexual promiscuity. The men patients are often relatively passive and have feminine identification, usually with the mother. A peculiarly intense interest and preoccupation with hunting, especially solitary hunting has, in my experience, been a common finding among the men. The hysterical patients with pain generally differ from those without pain in the prominence of sadistic and masochistic elements in their sexual developments, usually with pronounced guilt.

The following case is a classic example of conversion hysteria with pain as a prominent manifestation. It is presented in detail because patients with conversion hysteria constitute the largest percentage of the pain-prone population and a thorough study of this case protocol will be richly rewarding in illustrating the characteristic features of hysterical patients with pain. Interpretative comments, in brackets, call attention to some of the characteristic features of psychogenic pain and the pain-prone patient discussed in the body of this paper.

A twenty-seven year old married woman, a singer by profession, had suffered from pain in her face and head for many years. She was first seen in February 1945. She felt she could distinguish at least three kinds of pain. At about the age of eleven or twelve she began to have attacks of pain in the right side of the face. This pain became extremely severe during a pregnancy which ended in a spontaneous abortion at three months in October 1944. The attacks usually began as a dull ache over the right eye, and rapidly progressed to a severe throbbing pain involving the entire right side of the head and face, and radiating into the neck and shoulder. This was associated with tearing of the right eye, stuffiness of the right nostril, and at times flushing and hyperesthesia of the right side of the face. The pain was made worse by movement and noise, and when severe was associated with nausea and vomiting. Such attacks lasted a day or more.

A second type of face pain consisted of sudden brief shooting pain of moderate intensity involving the right cheek and followed by a dull aching pain. This pain had been present intermittently for about a year.

The third pain was of several years' duration and consisted of a sudden sharp, burning pain arising at the angle of the right jaw, radiating into the teeth, along the ramus, and into the ear. This pain generally came on when she was about to eat. It was associated with increased salivation. Generally it lasted several minutes and then subsided, permitting the patient to go on with her meal. She was examined for salivary duct calculus but none was found. Detailed examination, including neurologic, roentgen and dental study, revealed no abnormalities.

At first the patient stated that her general health was and always had been good and that if it were not for the face pain she would be entirely well. It soon became evident that this was not so. She also suffered from attacks of nausea and vomiting; she was "sensitive" to many food items which induced nausea, vomiting and urticaria a few minutes after ingestion and sometimes simply on sight; she had attacks of bloating and swelling of the abdomen; she had shaking chills, with chattering of the teeth; and a subjective feeling of great coldness, during which her hands and feet would blanch and become icy cold; she had attacks of breathlessness, dizziness, and numbness and tingling, during which she occasionally lost consciousness; paroxysms of cough occurred which could not be explained on the basis of any respiratory tract disease, although she had had two to three attacks of rather typical bronchial asthma in her life; she had dyspareunia and was totally frigid; she suffered with urinary frequency and urgency. [Other hysterical conversion symptoms.]

The patient, an only child, was born in Chicago in 1918. Both parents were exceedingly neurotic persons. The mother was a successful business woman at the time of her marriage, although it was rumored that her success was partially accounted for by being the mistress of her employer. Unable to get him to marry her, she impulsively married her present husband as a spiteful gesture. He at this time was a rather inconsequential but handsome man, who so far had been quite unsuccessful in establishing himself as a business man. His wife paid his debts, set him up in business and thereafter never permitted him to forget her role. For a period he was quite successful, but in 1928 he lost all his money and went heavily in debt. Since then he has held only small jobs and tends to use alcohol to a considerable degree. [Aggressive, controlling mother; relatively passive father.]

The patient felt the parents' marriage to be entirely devoid of any love or affection. They quarrelled frequently and violently. The patient always felt in the middle. She recalled one occasion when her mother threw a hammer at her father, and another occasion when he hit her mother with an ash tray. Not infrequently she had witnessed them strike each other in the face during quarrels. [Prominence of aggression in early family relations.] During such scenes the little girl felt she had to separate the two combatants "lest the quarrel end in murder." She consciously directed the parents' anger toward herself in order to avoid their hurting each other. On one occasion she scratched her father's face to "bring him to his senses." [As child, deflects aggression to herself.]

The patient said the mother avoided any sexual contact with father and besides she believed he was impotent anyway. "Mother could scare anyone into impotency." She was not born until the parents had been married nine years, when they were thirty-five years old. The mother carried on a constant harangue against her father. She repeatedly warned the patient to have nothing to do with men and especially to avoid sexual contact. Even after the patient's marriage mother continued to urge her to have a separate bedroom as she herself had. [Mother's hostility to men and fear of sex.]

In 1938 the father was discovered to have cancer of the urinary bladder. The mother openly taunted him with the diagnosis and expressed pleasure that she would now be free of him. [Mother's sadism.] A subtotal cystectomy was performed and the father recovered, although he was left with frequency of urination. More recently the father had had a heart condition and was short of breath. [Factors in patient's "choice" of respiratory and urinary symptoms.]

During the early contacts with the patient she was most bitter toward her mother, whom she described as argumentative, domineering, nasty and hypercritical, with no love for her. After such attacks on the mother, however, the patient would have the impulse to call her on the phone, and then would feel remorseful because her mother seemed more kind and interested than she had described her to be. [Hostility to mother, guilt, and submission.] On the other hand, she first described her father as "sweet and nice." He had beautiful curly hair and he would let his little daughter play hairdresser and fuss with his hair for hours. Later on, statements changed and she said he was "wish-washy, inconsistent, and an opportunist," that he "always disappointed me." "My dream castle is nothing but a backwoods shed," was her comment after a visit from father. [Disappointment with father.]

As a little girl she had tried to get close to her father, but her mother would never permit this. Mother would either make fun of any show of affection between the two or would fly into a rage and accuse them of conspiring against her. On many occasions the mother threatened to leave home and when father and daughter begged her to stay, she ridiculed them. Several times the mother spent all day in a movie to simulate such a threat. [Mother's sadism.] The little girl was heartbroken. Father always dealt with mother's threats by giving in. He wanted peace at any price.

The patient described herself as a difficult child to take care of. She devised various technics to provoke or exasperate her mother. One was to hide her mother's prized possessions, tell her she had hidden them but not where. This generally led to a spanking. [Patient's use of pain and punishment as way of relating to mother.]

At a very early age she demonstrated unusual ability in singing. The mother had a "magnificant voice" and cultivated her little daughter's talent, functioning for a period as her teacher. When she was nine she won a singing contest and made her debut with a nationally known symphony orchestra. Following the concert her mother pointed out that Mozart had made his debut at an earlier age. [Mother's depreciating and rivalrous attitudes.] Thereafter the patient concentrated on her singing, studied with well known teachers, and made several public appearances. She progressed rapidly in school, finishing high school at fifteen, and college at twenty. For a while in college she lost interest in a career as a singer; but after graduation she joined a light opera company which toured the country. She often had the leading soprano role and received good press notices. Her mother, however, always depreciated her performances.

Her early sexual education was very strict. Her mother depreciated all things sexual, and warned the child against any sexual activity. She kept her from wearing attractive or feminine clothing, opposed her fixing her hair, and insisted that she wear glasses although she had no need for them. In high school and college she was known as "Prudence Prim." Her mother would not permit her to go out alone until she was twenty-one years old, saying only bad girls went out. She was not permitted to live away from home. In early adolescence she fought hard to get away and mother let her go to boarding school. After a few months mother brought her home because she thought she was having too good a time. [Mother's depreciation of femininity and sexuality. The patient submits.] Her menses began at eleven, two weeks after an auto accident (which will be described in detail later). Although she had been told about menses, she thought they were the result of the accident.

The patient was married in August 1942. She had not previously gone out with many men, although she enjoyed their company on an intellectual basis. She liked to be with a group of men on a "man to man basis." She had had no sexual experience until marriage. [Patient's masculine identification and sexual inhibitions.] She had gone with her husband about two months when they became engaged; they were married six months later. He was in the army at that time and stationed near Boston awaiting embarkation. Immediately after the ceremony coughing and wheezing developed which became so severe over the course of the next two weeks that she felt compelled to go home to Chicago. [Asthma in response to first real separation from mother.] As she stepped from the train and was met by her mother her asthma ceased and did not recur. The next day her husband was shipped overseas and she felt guilty that she was not there to see him off.

The patient worked in a war plant during her husband's absence and held a rather responsible position. She lived with her parents. In the fall of 1943 her husband returned to the United States to convalesce from an attack of pleurisy and she joined him. In June 1944 she

became pregnant and felt disgusted in spite of the fact that she had been trying to get pregnant for several months and was beginning to worry about sterility. During the pregnancy she had a great deal of nausea and vomiting and almost continuous severe head and face pain. She remained very active and "heaved furniture around." [Patient's self-destructive behavior.] Three months later she aborted while visiting her mother. She first felt very panicky and then became somewhat depressed. [Guilt.] She had the thought that she had not long to live and that her husband would be unhappy if she died. She behaved provocatively toward him and deliberately irritated him. ". . . so that he would hate me and would not miss me and could remarry." Several times she made the gesture of packing her bags and leaving. At other times she provoked the neighbors, sometimes by her singing, and she often got herself into unhappy situations with tradespeople and friends. [She provokes attacks on herself.]

During the period of therapy there occurred a number of experiences during sleep which her husband wrote down and brought in for discussion. The patient had complete amnesia for these experiences but was able to bring important associations. Two such episodes were particularly revealing.

(1) One night she said while asleep, "He hit me in the face with a buckle. I was a naughty girl." This recalled an incident at age four. She had been naughty and mother insisted that father punish her. He was undressing. As he pulled his belt from his pants he suddenly struck her violently in the face with the buckle end. [Determinants of the face as location of pain.] "I remember hating him violently after that." Once, at eighteen, during a violent quarrel between the parents, the patient thought, "If he hits me, I would murder him." Just before her husband was discharged from the army she impulsively threw all his belts into an incinerator. They made her feel very uncomfortable, but as she watched them burn she had a happy feeling of triumph. This reminded her that mother had often used father's belt to strike her. [Unconscious association between father and husband. Aggression and guilt.]

Later she brought up that on two occasions she had provoked her husband to the extent that he had slapped her face. A severe exacerbation of face pain resulted on both occasions.

(2) The most dramatic episode concerned the auto accident to which she had briefly alluded in the first interview. At the time she merely said that she had been in an auto accident at age eleven, and that she suffered a fractured kneecap and was in a cast for a year. She did not mention any injury suffered by mother. [First face pain began when the patient was eleven or twelve.]

While asleep the patient tossed restlessly and began talking. [Reliving a traumatic episode.] "I know he didn't have any lights on. He turned them on after he got to the middle of the street. We never start to cross the street without looking." She cried out in pain, "My knee, my knee! That morphine makes me see the lights all over again. That car is rolling mother down the street and it isn't going to stop. I can't stand that car rolling her. I see her face full of blood. The eye is cut. She is dead. My face, my face, my face hurts.'' [Injury to mother's face as determinant of site of pain.] The patient beat on the bed. She awakened and appeared terrified. "I have to get up and see if I can walk." She struggled with her husband to get up, but was unable to. Her teeth chattered violently and she had a shaking chill at this point. "I am cold like I was sitting in the snow that night." The husband observed: "She was breathing rapidly and her arms and legs were icy cold. There was decided swelling of the right cheek which was red and hot over the area of pain. I sensed this temperature change by contrasting the two sides of the face. She writhed, clutched, and gasped, so intense was the pain. A cold object pressed against the pain area produced a shocking feeling in the face. "Light hurt her eyes." In referring to the shortness of breath the patient commented, "It feels as if someone is sitting on my chest." [Origin of other conversion symptoms.]

The patient was then able to describe the accident in more detail. It occurred in a suburban district at night where it was quite deserted. It was a cold wintry night, 13°F. below zero with snow on the ground. Mother and daughter stepped from the streetcar and started to cross the street. Suddenly they realized a car without lights was bearing down on them. Just before striking, the headlights were turned on and glared in their eyes. Mother raised her hand to protect her face. She was struck by the car and dragged a half a block. The patient was knocked to her knees and found herself alone in the dark sitting in the snow. She screamed; she felt alone and deserted. She shivered with the cold and it seemed endless before anyone picked her up. When she saw her mother, her face looked "like someone had beaten it with a hammer." Mother was coughing up blood. The patient was brought to a hospital where she received morphine and had repetitive frightening dreams of the accident. Her mother, who recovered quickly, brought violets, which remain the patient's favorite flower. The patient remained in a cast for a year and was taken care of at home by her mother. She described this as a not unhappy time. "I was completely helpless. Whenever I have been ill, mother has been good to me." [Love from mother when she suffered.]

(2) *Depression*. Another group of patients suffers predominantly from depression. The generally depressed appearance, the retarded or agitated behavior, the content of speech, the expressed affects of sadness, guilt and shame, all identify the depression and this is usually documented by history. Some patients, it will be found have had previous episodes of depression without pain and some are the chronically gloomy and depressive characters already described. A common error by the physician is to assume that the patient is depressed because he has pain. Investigation will usually make clear that the experience of pain serves to attenuate the guilt and shame of the de-

pression. Indeed, in some instances the pain is clearly protecting the patient from more intense depression and even suicide. This group of patients in particular may become addicted to drugs.

(3) *Hypochondriasis*. The hypochondriacal patient experiences and communicates his pain or other body sensations in a distinctive way. One quickly notes its peculiarly intense and persistent quality. It may not be as severe as it is inescapable, annoying and bedeviling, and the patient is made desperate by the pain. As the physician listens to the patient's description he immediately notes the urgency with which the patient seeks relief and his tremendous concern as to what the pain means. He often seems more concerned with the interpretation of the pain, is it cancer or some terrible infection, than with the pain per se, and he is little or not at all reassured by the doctor's examinations. There is often a distinct quality of being persecuted by the pain. At the same time it will be found that the patient lavishes all varieties of attention and care on the painful part, somewhat in contrast to the relative indifference of the hysteric patient or the long-suffering attitude of the depressive patient. Some of these patients are prepsychotic.

(4) *Schizophrenia*. Closely related to the hypochondriacal patients are those who are psychotic and whose pain represents a delusion. Many of these patients are not recognized as psychotic simply because their complaint is pain. But the alert physician will note the following qualities. The patient truly feels persecuted by his pain and he seeks help with a desperation that is impressive. It is not so much that it is painful as that it is unrelenting, annoying and inescapable. The description of the pain include bizarre ideas which are expressed as vivid analogies or as actualities. A pregnant woman had pain in the lower part of her abdomen. She ascribed this to being poked by the erect penis of her unborn child who she knew was a boy. Little further inquiry was needed to establish the diagnosis of schizophrenia. Patients express convictions that certain extraordinary changes have taken place in their bodies, the very bizarreness of which makes their delusional quality evident. A fifty-five year old man with repeated attacks of abdominal pain said with conviction that his intestines were "twisted like a mop" and had to be untwisted, and begged for surgery. He also was convinced that there was some strange object in his abdomen, perhaps left in during previous surgery. Such patients usually manifest other paranoid qualities, including suspicious accusations against other physicians as being responsible for the pain. Or they may ascribe

the pain to various outside influences, including rays and vibrations. A very important clinical point is the patient's tendency to associate the pain with nasal or rectal difficulties. Indeed these patients often first approach otolaryngologists or proctologists, or they may have sought treatment with colonic or nasal irrigations. The diagnosis will rarely be overlooked if the patient is given sufficient opportunity to present his explanation for the pain. This usually proves to be a complicated delusional concept.

It is perhaps important to mention here that often the schizophrenic patient either experiences no pain or does not complain of it when an ordinary painful disorder develops. An acute coronary occlusion or a perforated appendix may be entirely silent as far as the observer is concerned. Actually, pain is experienced in a delusional fashion by the schizophrenic relatively infrequently.

SUMMARY

The general principles formulated in this paper may be summarized as follows:

1. What is experienced and reported as pain is a psychological phenomenon. Pain does not come into being without the operation of the psychic mechanisms which give rise to its identifiable qualities and which permit its perception. In neurophysiological terms this also means there is no pain without the participation of higher nervous centers.

2. Developmentally, however, pain evolves from patterns of impulses arising from peripheral receptors which are part of the basic biologic nocioceptive system for the protection of the organism from injury. The psychic experience, pain, develops phylogenetically and ontogenetically from what was originally only a reflex organization. This may be compared to the necessity for functioning eyes and ears to receive light and sound waves before the complex psychic experiences of seeing and hearing can evolve.

3. Once the psychic organization necessary for pain has evolved, the experience, pain, no longer requires peripheral stimulation to be provoked, just as visual and auditory sensations (hallucinations) may occur without sense organ input. When such are projected outside the mind (in contrast to a painful thought or a painful frame of mind) they are felt as being in some part of the body and are to the patient indistinguishable from pain arising in the periphery.

4. Since the experience, pain, and the sensory experiences from which it evolves are part of the biologic equipment whereby the individual learns about the environment and about his body, and since this has a special function as a warning or indicator of damage to body parts, pain plays an important role in the total psychologic development of the individual. Indeed, pain, along with other affects, comes to occupy a key position in the regulation of the total psychic economy. We discover that in the course of the child's development, pain and relief of pain enter into the formation of interpersonal (object) relations and into the concepts of good and bad, reward and punishment, success and failure. Pain becomes par excellence a means of assuaging guilt and thereby influences object relationships.

5. From the clinical viewpoint we discover that disordered neural patterns originating in the periphery confer certain qualities on the pain experience that permit the physician to recognize their presence and hence make a presumptive diagnosis of an organic lesion.

6. Clinical psychological studies of all varieties of patients with pain reveal that some individuals are more prone than others to use pain as a psychic regulator, whether the pain includes a peripheral source of stimulation or not. These pain-prone individuals usually show some or all of the following features:

1. A prominance of conscious and unconscious guilt, with pain serving as a relatively satisfactory means of atonement.
2. A background that tends to predispose to the use of pain for such purposes.
3. A history of suffering and defeat and intolerance of success (masochistic character structure). A propensity to solicit pain, as evidenced by the large number of painful injuries, operations and treatments.
4. A strong aggressive drive which is not fulfilled, pain being experienced instead.
5. Development of pain as a replacement for a loss at times when a relationship is threatened or lost.
6. A tendency toward a sado-masochistic type of sexual development, with some episodes of pain occurring in settings of conflict over sexual impulses.
7. A location of pain determined by unconscious identification with a love object, the pain being either one suffered by the patient himself when in some conflict with the object or a pain suffered by the object in fact or in the patient's fantasy.
8. Psychiatric diagnoses include conversion hys-

teria, depression, hypochondriasis and para-noid schizophrenia, or mixtures of these. Some patients with pain do not fit into any distinct nosologic category.

CONCLUSION

I would like to close with a historical note. It is astonishing how little discussions of pain in stan-dard textbooks of medicine have changed in a hundred years. In a textbook published in 1858 Wood discusses pain in terms which differ only in details from what appears in Harrison's "Princi-ples of Internal Medicine" published in 1954 (20,21). These details mainly concern more recent knowledge about the anatomy and physiology of nerve pathways. In both sources it is taken for granted that pain arises from the periphery or in the nerves themselves. The most modern explana-tion of chronic pain is that "recurring painful stimuli from the periphery set up reverberating circuits related to the central activating system which influence, and are in turn influenced by the cerebral cortex so that there may develop a syn-drome or chronic pain" (22). In all these writings, psychological processes are relegated to a purely subsidiary role, such as reinforcing the reverberat-ing circuit, or are simply dismissed by saying that the neurotic (or, in 1858, the "nervous") patient is less tolerant of or has a lower threshold for pain, clearly a cultural prejudice for which there is no scientific evidence. It is all the more remarkable that this state of affairs should continue to exist when, as early as 1895, Breuer and Freud in "Studies on Hysteria" published detailed case his-tories demonstrating convincingly pain as a psychogenic manifestation (8). In contrast to much of Freud's later writings, this early work includes a wealth of case material. The modern physician, regardless of his knowledge of or attitudes toward psychoanalysis, will find it richly rewarding to read these case histories, for in them he can learn for himself the nature of the data and observations which permitted Freud to discover how pain may develop as a purely psychic phenomenon. Freud himself was not primarily interested in pain, but it happened that among many of these patients pain was a common and prominent manifestation, as were a great number of other somatic symptoms which also proved to represent hysterical conver-sions. Indeed, one might be justified in saying that psychoanalysis came into being through the clarification of the mechanism of some of these mysterious pain syndromes.

This leads to an interesting question, namely, how is it that this contribution to the understand-ing of pain has had so little influence on medicine in general, even on psychoanalysis. I believe the explanation is to be found in the peculiarities of medical practice. Freud began his practice as a neurologist and, in Vienna in the 1880's, undiag-nosed pains were considered to be forms of neuralgia, an affection of nerves, concerning which the neurologist was the expert. As long as Freud was known primarily as a neurologist and his technic was not recognized as a form of psychotherapy, many such patients were referred to him and most went willingly enough. As he evolved into a psychoanalyst and the technic of treatment became increasingly recognized as a psychological one, there must have occurred a change in the categories of patients who were con-sidered suitable for referral. Further, patients with conversion hysteria, who suffer primarily from somatic symptoms, are reluctant to seek psycho-logical help. In general, they regard their symp-toms as organic in origin, a belief in which they are often supported by their physicians. The pain patients in particular are among the most re-luctant to accept a psychiatric referral and to par-ticipate in psychotherapy if they do so. As time went on, Freud's practice consisted more and more of patients with the classic neuroses and with few exceptions this trend away from patients with somatic symptoms, including conversion hysteria, has continued to date. It is of interest in this respect that in Freud's early works, pain is referred to fre-quently, but later on one rarely finds any mention of pain. In the current scene, the analyst or psychi-atrist is rarely consulted directly by a patient be-cause of pain and only infrequently are such pa-tients referred, and when they are many do not accept the referral. Thus the analyst and psychia-trist have had little opportunity to study this prob-lem, which remains as common and difficult as ever. A large percentage of patients who consult physicians of all types belong to the group of "pain-prone" patients and are seeking help for painful disorders such as I have described in this paper.

This brings me also the technic of investigation of these patients. Again, let me refer back to the original case histories of Breuer and Freud. These patients were not psychoanalyzed in the sense that we now understand the term. Every physician is free to rediscover for himself what Freud discov-ered about pain if he follows two simple princi-ples: permit the patients to talk freely and take seriously what the patient says. If, in addition, he has some understanding of the psychic function of pain as I have outlined it in this paper, he will have no difficulty in confirming the observations of Freud as well as of those who followed him. This is not the place to discuss *in extenso* the technic of medical interview. Suffice it to say that an interview technic which permits the patient to speak of himself, his family, and his relationships as well as of his symptoms, which does not force a separation between what is regarded as organic and what is regarded as psychological or social, will be tremendously productive in clarifying the patient's illness. We have learned now that when one knows what one is looking for, this can be accomplished in a remarkably brief time. I have seen some patients in whom the basic dynamics of the pain, including an explanation of the choice of the pain and its location, could be worked out in as little time as thirty minutes; with a great number of patients an hour's interview will suffice. But even when more interview time than this is required, this is more economical in time and expense for both the physician and the patient than the currently traditional technic of "ruling out organic disease" and attempting to establish a diagnosis by exclusion. Such interminable diagnostic procedures may not only be a waste of time and money but may also render virtually impossible the establishment of correct diagnosis simply because the patient himself becomes increasingly oriented towards this type of approach and less spontaneous in revealing personal and psychological data which the physician, by his approach and behavior, has made him feel are completely out of place. Needless to say, the physician whose technic of interview does not permit the patient spontaneously to reveal personal and psychological data along with his symptoms will not succeed in confirming the observations reported in this paper. But neither, for that matter, will the physician who uses only Sabouraud's medium to examine urethral discharges succeed in confirming the relationship between the gonococcus and some cases of gonorrhea. As in all matters scientific, the application of the appropriate method is indispensable.

Supported in part by a grant from the Foundations Fund for Research in Psychiatry.

REFERENCES

1. Szasz, T. Pain and Pleasure. New York, 1957. Basic Books.
2. Solomon, P., Leiderman, P. H., Mendelson, J. and Wexler, D. Sensory deprivation. A review. Am. J. Psychiat., 114: 357, 1957.
3. Osmond, H. A review of the clinical effects of psychotomimetic agents. Ann. New York Acad. Sc., 66: 418, 1957.
4. Penfield, W. and Jasper, H. Epilepsy and the Functional Anatomy of the Human Brain. Boston, 1954. Little, Brown & Co.
5. Gooddy, W. On the nature of pain. Brain, 80: 118, 1957.
6. Rosen, H. The hypnotic and hypnotherapeutic control of severe pain. Am. J. Psychiatr., 107: 917, 1951.
7. Beecher, H. K. Limiting factors in experimental pain. J. Chronic Dis., 4: 11, 1956.
8. Breuer, J. and Freud, S. Studies on Hysteria (1895). Standard edition complete psychological works of Freud, S. London, 1955. Hogarth Press.
9. Schilder, P. The Image and Appearance of the Human Body. London, 1935. Kegan Paul, Trench, Trubner & Co.
10. Engel, G. L. Primary atypical facial neuralgia. An hysterical conversion symptom. Psychosom. Med., 13: 375, 1951.
11. Rangell, L. Psychiatric aspects of pain. Psychosom. Med., 15: 22, 1953.
12. Kolb, L. C. The Painful Phantom. Psychology, Physiology, and Treatment. American Lecture Series. Springfield, Ill., 1954. Charles C Thomas.
13. Hart, H. Displacement guilt and pain. Psychoanalyt. Rev., 34: 259, 1957.
14. Wolff, H. G. Headache and Other Head Pain. New York, 1948. Oxford University Press.
15. Libman, E. Observations on individual sensitiveness to pain with special reference to abdominal disorders. J. A. M. A., 102: 335, 1934.
16. Eisele, C. W., Slee, V. N. and Hoffman, R. G. Can the practice of internal medicine be evaluated? Ann. Int. Med., 44: 144, 1956.
17. Freud, S. Analysis. Terminable and Interminable (1937). In: Collected Works, vol. 5. London, 1950. Hogarth Press.
18. Schuster, D. On the fear of success. Psychiat. Quart., 29: 412–420, 1955.
19. Engel, G. L. Studies of ulcerative colitis. IV. The significance of headaches. Psychosom. Med., 18: 334, 1956.
20. Wood, G. B. A Treatise on the Practice of Medicine. Philadelphia, 1858. J. B. Lippincott & Co.
21. Harrison, T. R. Principles of Internal Medicine, 2nd ed. New York, 1954. Blakiston.
22. Von Hagen, K. O. Chronic intolerable pain. J. A. M. A., 165: 773, 1957.

SURGERY-PRONENESS:
A REVIEW AND CLINICAL ASSESSMENT

RICHARD A. DeVAUL and LOUIS A. FAILLACE

The authors review the psychiatric literature on patients who undergo repeated, often ill-advised surgery for pain relief, and report on their own clinical study, which shows that many polysurgery patients have similar social and medical histories as well as common aspects of clinical presentation that identify them as a subgroup of chronic pain patients. Identifying surgery-prone patients and redefining their illness as chronic rather than acute can help reduce the incidence of unnecessary surgery.

The tendency of certain patients to undergo numerous surgical procedures, many of which seem ill-advised in retrospect, is common enough to be a recognizable clinical phenomenon, known as surgery-proneness. The medical history of the surgery-prone patient is characterized by repeated operations for the same symptom, usually pain, with unsatisfactory results. Not infrequently, the patient ends up with the designation of "permanently disabled."

The increase in unnecessary surgery in the United States has resulted partly from the demands of such patients, combined with the compliance of their physicians, who fail to see the un-derlying emotional problems. When individuals seek surgery to escape from overwhelming life burdens, they need support both in dealing with their difficulties and in understanding how they have evaded them in the past.

Our experience as liaison psychiatrists on a surgery service and in a multidisciplinary pain service demonstrated the clinical need to identify patients at high risk for unnecessary surgery so that we could break the chain of unsuccessful procedures in individuals reporting increasing pain. A controlled retrospective study of 23 polysurgery patients, close clinical evaluation of approximately 250 additional patients, and a review of the psychiatric literature form the basis for our present assessment of the surgery-prone patient.

LITERATURE

The psychiatric literature offers three types of explanation for surgery proneness: (1) psychodynamic analyses, (2) investigations associating psychogenic pain and numerous surgical procedures, and (3) studies on the incidence of polysurgery among psychoneurotic patients. (In another type of literature, investigators, unconcerned by and large with patient characteristics, look at the epidemiologic and health care delivery aspects of the problem.[1-8])

Menninger[9] theorized that the unconscious motivation to undergo surgery is the expression of a masochistic need to suffer. Surgery, according to Menninger, allows this group of patients to sacrifice a part of the body in order to avoid actual suicide, and to shift responsibility to the surgeon, whose "surgical sadism" is accessory to the patient's masochism. In addition, at the time of surgery and during the recovery period, pa-

EDITORS' COMMENTS:

NOT ALL PATIENTS WHO HAVE MULTIPLE SURGICAL EXPLORATIONS HAVE PSYCHOGENIC PAIN; AND NOT ALL PATIENTS WITH PSYCHOGENIC PAIN HAVE MULTIPLE OPERATIONS. THE AUTHORS GIVE PROFILES OF TYPICAL PRESENTATIONS AND HISTORIES OF SURGERY-PRONE PATIENTS, TO FACILITATE IDENTIFYING SUCH PATIENTS, AND REDUCING THE INCIDENCE OF SURGERY PERFORMED FOR PSYCHOLOGICAL RATHER THAN MEDICAL PROBLEMS.

Reprinted from Psychosomatics 21:295–299, 1980.

tients usually receive the solicitude of important others in their lives and can avoid adult responsibilities.

Wahl and Golden,[10] reporting on 16 polysurgery patients, stressed a pervading unconscious guilt common among them as well as a severe deprivation of dependency gratification during childhood. Many of these patients had virtually no childhood because they had to assume adult responsibilities very early in life. Periods of childhood illness, however, brought rare parental attention and respite from work. Family members had a relatively high incidence of illness and surgery. Further, the surgery (type and timing) experienced by the surgery-prone patients sometimes coincided with that experienced earlier by their parents.

Several contemporary analytic writers, including Chertok,[11] Jelliffe,[12] Menninger, Greenacre,[13] and Engel,[14,15] have noted that patients with psychogenic pain are at high risk for unnecessary surgical procedures. In two studies of such patients, Engel, like Menninger, concluded that a masochistic character structure is the underlying determinant of what he termed the "pain-prone personality." In his patients, masochism seemed to be the product of early experiences with punitive or abusive parents. Engel outlined a characteristic medical history of individuals susceptible to psychogenic pain.

Studying patients with persistent pain, Merskey[16,17] found, as Chertok, Engel, and others had, that as a group these patients had had much more surgery than individuals in a control group. Further, he pointed out that most of the procedures had been performed in response to complaints of pain and not other symptoms.

Additional psychiatric research indicates that psychoneurotic patients have more operations than do healthy or organically ill controls.[18,19] In their ongoing efforts to derive and test a clinical definition of hysteria, Cohen and associates[20] compared the number of surgeries in two subgroups of psychoneurotic patients—the anxiety neurosis and hysteria subgroups. The investigators hypothesized that the hysteria subgroup by itself may account for the excessive operations documented in psychoneurotic patients.

Thus, evidence shows that persons with masochistic characters, unconscious guilt, pain-prone personalities, psychogenic pain, and psychoneurotic disturbances, particularly hysteria, may be at greater than average risk for unnecessary surgery.

CLINICAL EVALUATION

In a recent paper[21] we reported on a study designed to yield a medical profile for the identification of the surgery-prone patient. Because undergoing many operations is the only objective measure of surgery-proneness, we defined polysurgery for the purposes of our study as five or more major surgical procedures, neither diagnostic nor pregnancy-terminating. We identified 23 psychiatric consultation patients whose reports of five or more operations were substantiated by physicians on hospital records. These patients were matched for age, sex, marital status, and type of insurance (to control for the ability to finance surgery) with other consultation patients who did not meet polysurgery criteria.

Hospital records of all patients were examined for clinical characteristics that might differentiate between the two groups. The polysurgery group had a mean of 9.8 operations, the control group, a mean of 1.0 operations. Seventeen polysurgery patients were diagnosed as having hysteria (using Feighner's[22] criteria), and 18 were diagnosed as having pain-prone personalities (using Engel's profile). Of the control patients, six were considered as having hysteria and one was diagnosed as having a pain-prone personality. Drug use by the index group was 3.7 times as great as that of the control group.[23] Although individuals in both groups had received recommendations for psychiatric intervention with similar frequency, compliance was significantly better in controls.

The anticipated medical profile for proneness to surgery did indeed emerge, with these salient characteristics: (1) history of childhood abuse and deprivation, (2) family history of repeated surgery, (3) history of pain-related operations, especially for similar pains, and (4) many physician contacts with disappointing therapeutic results. All the surgery-prone patients were seeking care for persistent pain that previous treatment had not relieved, and which, they urgently insisted, had an organic cause. They denied having personal, social or marital problems, and demanded alleviation of their pain.

PATIENT CHARACTERISTICS

The problem of repeated, medically unnecessary surgery can best be understood as a need on the part of the patient to define the pain problem as an acute illness, despite a history of chronic pain that is, at least in part, emotionally determined. In this section we will describe more fully the characteristics associated with the surgery-prone patient.

Surgery for Persistent Pain

In clinically evaluating more than 270 patients, we found that repeated surgical procedures were performed to relieve pain, not to alleviate other symptoms. This corroborates the opinions in the literature described earlier.[11,14-17,20] Our finding also suggests that polysurgery patients comprise a subset of chronic pain patients. Two clinical patterns appear to set this subgroup apart from chronic pain patients who avoid repeated operations. One pattern conforms to Engel's description of the pain-prone masochistic personality and to Whal and Golden's[10] outline of social history. Emotionally deprived children from large families begin to experience illness and undergo surgery at an early age, learning to exploit illness as an occasion for exemption from responsibility. Frequently there is a family history of illnesses and surgical procedures that the patient seems to be repeating. Individuals who fall into this grouping are very often intolerant of success and develop pain or illness precisely when life seems most crisis-free.

A second pattern that emerges in the surgery-prone subset of persistent pain patients appears to be situational. Members of this group usually have had a major operation in early adulthood with either slow recovery or non-recovery, leading to repeated surgery. During their unsuccessful recovery periods, these patients often seem to face severe problems of living. Perhaps they begin to see responsibilities as undesirable, if not overwhelming.

Illness Insistence

Despite the long duration of the pain complaints, all polysurgery patients in our study group insisted that they were acutely, organically ill, and that it was the physician's job to cure the pain. They asserted a willingness to cooperate in any medical or surgical intervention aimed at their pain relief. The high incidence of emergency room treatment they received reflects their persuasiveness.

According to social role theory,[24] once a physician declares a person sick, the individual accepts the implicit duties and privileges of the sick patient's role—i.e., wanting to get well, seeking medical help, and cooperating with medical manage-

ment plans. During the period of acute illness, patients are expected to be passive and to transfer responsibility for their illness to the physician. Thus, designating a patient as acutely ill sanctions his or her exemption from adult responsibilities. But, while an acute condition is temporary, requiring extreme changes in obligations, a chronic condition calls for the patient to assume an adjusted normal role. We believe that the insistence on acute illness by polysurgery patients is an attempt on their part to be granted sick role status and, with it, to be declared exempt from adult role responsibilities.

Long-standing Regression

Polysurgery patients present in various stages of regression, displaying an increase in egocentricity, reduced scope of interest, preoccupation with their bodies, increase in dependency, and demanding, manipulative insistence on attention. And the physicians on whom chronic pain patients become dependent may perpetuate their regression. Prolonged or severe regression seriously hampers the patient's ability to cope with chronic illness and to return to normal social functioning. A few polysurgery patients under our care were able to return to work with no other treatment than the redefinition of their problem as chronic.

Polysurgery patients, like other chronic pain patients, frequently show elevated scores on all the scales of neurosis on the Minnesota Multiphasic Personality Inventory (MMPI), and physicians often diagnose them as having hypochondriasis, depression, or personality disorders. We think these elevations reflect regression secondary to assumption of the role of acutely ill patient. The scores do not differentiate between psychogenic and organically caused pain, and do not correlate well with response to surgery.[25-27] This supports our finding that psychiatric and psychological testing is unreliable for the purpose of prognosis for rehabilitation of regressed, surgery-prone patients. But once patients become mobilized and overcome regression, diagnosis and prognosis can be made more accurately.

Gaining Physician's Cooperation

In our study, most of the primary physicians suspected that their patients had emotional problems, but felt obligated to rule out organic disease. The training of contemporary physicians to be deliverers of acute care makes them particularly vulnerable to the surgery-prone patient's presentation. Patient's effective mimicking of acute illness, their deteriorating conditions, and intensified pleas for new treatment convince many physicians to give "emergency" treatment—a step many later regret.

When emergency room or other primary treatment fails, chronic pain patients are likely to seek surgery. After surgery fails, the frustrated surgeon may refer the patient for psychiatric consultation. Psychiatric treatment usually is not acceptable to the patient, nor is it likely to relieve the pain. When consulted, psychiatrists should explain their diagnosis of chronic pain to the referring surgeon and give recommendations for management. The surgeon can then substantiate the diagnosis on the basis of personal experience with the patient, and will be less likely to consider surgery again for the same problem. We recommend that the surgeon confront patients with the chronic nature of their pain problems, and state a willingness to cooperate in management. Referral to a pain clinic is a feasible option.

In sum, the risk of excessive surgery is increased by the chronic, emotional nature of the patient's pain, the patient's desire to assume the role of an acutely sick individual, and the physician's wish to relieve pain. However, in the absence of objective findings, pain is an exceedingly unreliable criterion for surgery. The evaluating physician or surgeon must investigate closely the duration of the pain as well as the medical histories of the patients and their family members.

MANAGEMENT

Treatment strategies for chronic pain patients are applicable to surgery-prone patients, a subgroup of the chronic pain group. Based on our experience with surgery-prone patients, we suggest several principles for management.[28–30]

The medical examination should include a thorough history and comprehensive physical workup to detect surgery proneness, to satisfy the patient that a careful attempt has been made to identify an organic etiology of the pain, and to rule out any illness unrelated to the pain. (The ability of pain- and surgery-prone patients to focus attention on the urgent need for pain relief can cause physicians to overlook other illnesses.)

Redefining the Problem

Physicians who complete the medical evaluation and find no objective signs of pathology or mechanical dysfunction should report just that to the patient and redefine the problem as a chronic one. The patient should be told how chronic and acute pain differ, and how the diagnosis of chronic pain was determined. The physician can point out that seeking continued treatment for acute pain is one option, while stressing that it has already proven unsuccessful. The alternative and suggested approach is to have the patient develop control of his or her perception of the pain.

Sometimes patients reject the redefinition of their problem and return to the referring physician for further "treatment" of acute pain. However, many patients are willing to try the newly suggested approach. If patients are dependent on narcotic medication, or if the referring physician does not wish to administer the suggested treatment regimen, we recommend referral to a multidisciplinary chronic pain service. In any case, the evaluator should give the referring physician the diagnosis and the suggestions for management that follow.

Assurance of Support

Primary physicians must make clear at the outset that they will continue to see the surgery-prone patient regardless of the pain. Regular appointments should be scheduled and intermediate goals set for the patient's return to a normal life, with any necessary adjustments. The primary goal now becomes rehabilitation with minimal disability, not treatment of pain.

Dealing with Regression

Occupancy of the acutely sick patient's role leads to regression, which may be reversed by redefining the problem, as urged above. The patient with chronic pain should no longer be permitted passive and helpless behavior. Second, subacute pain treatments, which are ineffective and impede successful social functioning, should be discontinued. Specifically, the physician should stop administering narcotic medication (an inpatient withdrawal regimen is often effective) as well as tranquilizers and sedatives, which frequently lead to secondary depression. Antidepressants should be considered, since they not only alleviate secondary depression but may also raise the pain threshold.[31,32]

A final attack on regression should be made by remobilizing the patient. Inactivity leads to poor physical condition and intolerance of exercise. A program of light general exercise, or specific rehabilitative exercises if indicated, may also be helpful in drawing the patient out of the disabled role.

Family Involvement

The problem must be redefined for family members or caretakers as well as for the patient. The privileges of being acutely ill—such as relinquishing social and family duties, receiving pain medication on demand, and being waited on—should not be allowed or reinforced. Instead, caretakers or family members should reward appropriate behavior, insist that the patient take medication only as prescribed, rather than on demand, and encourage the increased activity and resumption of duties outlined by the physician. Satisfactory change of the patient's role to a more normal one without the cooperation of the persons with whom he or she lives is improbable, if not impossible.

Individualized Management

When all the steps described so far have been taken, the physician can plan individualized management strategies. Patients with lifelong histories of pain and suffering who seem to be masochistic may have a psychological need to continue suffering with their pain symptoms, and their goals may have to be modest. Social functioning of such patients sometimes improves if they regard their pain as a burden they must bear, and their improvement as a difficult task to be performed for the benefit of important others in their lives. Several authors have suggested specific management techniques for use with these patients.[33,34]

The strategies of crisis intervention, which begin with identification of the patient's problems and circumstances, may be applied. While psychotherapy as treatment for the pain itself is doomed to failure, counseling (psychiatric, social, economic) can lighten the burden that has forced these people into the sick role. At the same time, the physician can use methods that have been found effective for controlling pain perception. Relaxation therapy, hypnosis, and biofeedback monitoring have been used successfully and have the advantage of giving patients some sense of power over their own pain perception.

Conclusion

The surgery-prone patient is predisposed to adopt the role of patient in order to resolve an inability to handle adult responsibilities. The risk for surgery per se is a function of development (severe childhood circumstances, family medical history) and a susceptibility to persistent pain. Profiles of typical presentations and histories of surgery-prone patients make identifying them easy and reduce the incidence of surgery performed for persistent pain complaints.

REFERENCES

1. Doyle JC: Unnecessary ovariectomies: Study based on removal of 704 normal ovaries from 546 patients. JAMA 148:1105–1111, 1952.
2. Doyle JC: Unnecessary hysterectomies: Study of 6,248 operations in 35 hospitals during 1948. JAMA 151:360–365, 1953.
3. Bunker JP: Surgical manpower: A comparison of operations and surgeons in the United States and Wales. N. Engl J Med 282:135–144, 1970.
4. Bunker JP, Brown BW Jr: The physician-patient as an informed consumer of surgical services. N Engl J Med 290:1051–1055, 1974.
5. Lewis CE: Variations in the incidence of surgery. N Engl J Med 281:880–884, 1969.
6. Perkoff GT, Ballinger WF, Turner JK: Lack of effect of an experimental prepaid group practice on utilization of surgical care. Surgery 77:619–623, 1975.
7. McCarthy EG, Widmer GW: Effects of screening by consultants on recommended elective surgical procedures. N Engl J Med 291:1331–1335, 1974.
8. Bunker JP, Wennberg JE: Operation rates, mortality statistics, and the quality of life. N Engl J Med 289:1249–1251, 1973.
9. Menninger KA: Polysurgery and polysurgical addiction. Psychoanal Q 3:173–199, 1934.
10. Wahl CW, Golden JS: The psychodynamics of the polysurgical patient: Report of sixteen patients. Psychosomatics 8:65–72, 1966.
11. Chertok L: Mania operative: Surgical addiction. Psychiatr Med 3:105–118, 1972.
12. Jelliffe SE: The death instinct in somatic and psychopathology. Psychoanal Rev 20:121–132, 1933.
13. Greenacre P: Surgical addiction—A case illustration. Psychosom Med 1:325–328, 1939.
14. Engel GL: Primary atypical facial neuralgia. An hysterical conversion symptom. Psychosom Med 13:375–396, 1951.
15. Engel GL: Psychogenic pain and the pain-prone patient. Am J Med 26:899–918, 1959.
16. Merskey H: The characteristics of persistent pain in psychological illness. J Psychosom Res 9:291–299, 1965.
17. Merskey H: Psychiatric patients with persistent pain. J Psychosom Res 9:299–309, 1965.
18. Bennett AE, Semrad EV: Common errors in diagnosis and treatment of the psychoneurotic patient: A study of 100 case histories. Nebr Med J 21:90–92, 1936.
19. Ulett PC, Gildea EF: Survey of surgical procedures in psychoneurotic women. JAMA 143:960–963, 1950.

20. Cohen ME, Robins E, Purtell JJ, et al: Excessive surgery in hysteria. JAMA 151:977–986, 1953.

21. DeVaul RA, Faillace LA: Persistent pain and illness insistence: A medical profile of proneness to surgery. Am J Surg 135:828–833, 1978.

22. Feighner JP, Robins E, Guze SB: Diagnostic criteria for use in psychiatric research. Arch Gen Psychiatry 26:57–63, 1972.

23. DeVaul RA, Hall RCW, Faillace LA: Drug use by the polysurgical patient Am J Psychiatry 135:682–685, 1978.

24. Parsons T: The Social System. New York, The Free Press, 1951, pp 428–479.

25. Sternbach RA: Pain Patients, Traits and Treatment. New York, Academic Press, 1974.

26. Erickson DL, Michaelson MA, Acharya A: Patient selection for implantable stimulating devices, in Bonica JJ, Albe-Fessard D (eds): Advances in Pain Research and Therapy. New York, Raven Press, 1976, vol 1, pp 479–482.

27. Waring EM, Weisz GM, Stewart SI: Predictive factors in the treatment of low back pain by surgical intervention, in Bonica JJ, Albe-Fessard D (eds): Ad-vances in Pain Research and Therapy. New York, Raven Press, 1976, vol 1, pp 939–952.

28. DeVaul RA, Zisook S: Chronic pain: The psychiatrist's role. Psychosomatics 19:417–421, 1978.

29. DeVaul RA, Zisook S, Lorimor R: Patients with chronic pain. Med J St Joseph Hosp 12:59–63, 1977.

30. DeVaul RA, Zisook S, Stuart JH: Patients with psychogenic pain. J Fam Pract 4:53–55, 1977.

31. Singh G, Verma HC: Drug treatment of chronic intractable pain in patients referred to a psychiatric clinic. J Indian Med Assoc 56:341–345, 1971.

32. Beaver WT, Walenstein SP, Houde RW, et al: A comparison of analgesic effects of methodtrimeprazine and morphine in patients with cancer. Clin Pharmacol Ther 7:436–446, 1966.

33. Fordyce WE, et al: Operant conditioning in the treatment of chronic pain. Arch Phys Med Rehabil 54:399–408, 1973.

34. Kahana RJ, Bebring GL: Personality types in medical management, in Zinberg NE (ed): Psychiatry and Medical Practice in a General Hospital. New York, International Universities Press, 1964, pp 108–123.

HYPOCHONDRIACAL NEUROSIS

E. JAMES McCRANIE

Although hypochondriasis is recognized as a specific neurosis, no definitive syndrome has been delineated descriptively or psychodynamically. The term has become a grab bag for a variety of poorly defined medical and psychiatric problems. Patients are too often labeled as "crocks" and not considered amenable to help. A clearer delineation of hypochondriasis, on both descriptive and psychodynamic levels, can provide the basis for better and more appropriate treatment.

Hypochondriacal neurosis is briefly described in official psychiatric nomenclature as "... an unrealistic interpretation of physical signs or sensations as abnormal, leading to preoccupation with the fear or belief of having a serious disease."[1] For a fuller and more accurate description, three aspects of the somatic representation provide useful information: the nature of the patient's symptoms, his response to diagnosis and treatment, and his general medical history.

The hypochondriacal patient tends to use medical terms to describe his symptoms. He often complains of having a disease, rather than a specific symptom, and he describes his symptoms in terms of this disease. A headache is described as migrainous, for example, or a backache as rheumatic. The patient also has a predilection for anatomic terms. He refers to low back pain as "sacroiliac"; chest pain as "substernal." When pressed for specific sensory or physical descriptions, he may become vague.

The thrust of the communication is, "Doctor, I have a terrible disease. Please diagnose and treat it." This suggests strongly that the preoccupation is not with the soma on a concrete, sensory level, but rather with the idea of having a somatic disease.

REACTION TO DIAGNOSIS

The patient's reaction to diagnosis and treatment is even more revealing. If he is told there is nothing wrong, he feels disappointed. If a positive diagnosis is made and treatment is prescribed, he feels good, sometimes even elated. Hypochondriacal anxiety is not, therefore, a fear of having diseased organs. Rather, the patient wants or needs to have a disease, and part of his anxiety is a fear that his somatic claims will be rejected.

The full flavor of hypochondria is best realized by a careful medical history. By the time he sees a psychiatrist, the patient has usually had an extensive and frustrating medical experience. He has probably seen many physicians, had several diagnoses, and received a variety of medical and surgical treatments. Although he most likely has been told more than once that there is nothing wrong with him, a disappointing diagnosis, he does not give up. If one disease is ruled out, he adopts another.

The elation the patient feels when a positive diagnosis is made requires close analysis. On one level, the patient feels vindicated, particularly if

Reprinted, with revisions, from: Psychosomatics 20:11–15, 1979.

his somatic claims had previously been rejected or challenged. On a deeper level, he feels good because the disease provides a plausible and acceptable explanation of his inadequacies and failures. The patient probably had sought a diagnosis as a medical sanction for a sick-role type of adjustment. On a still deeper level, the diagnosis provides a combination of relief and hope: relief that what is wrong with the self has finally been discovered and anticipation that it can be cured medically.

At this level, the patient is particularly pleased when surgery is prescribed, not because he has a masochistic need to be cut or hurt, but because surgery is perceived as definitive and corrective. The elation does not last long, however. After surgery, disillusionment sets in with the realization that nothing has really changed. Again, however, the patient does not give up. Old symptoms return or new ones develop, and the endless search for a diagnosis and cure is resumed.

TYPES OF HYPOCHONDRIA

Based on these considerations, we can differentiate two types of hypochondria: the ambitious and the sick-role type. In the ambitious type, the patient is satisfied only with a definitive diagnosis and treatment. Tentative or equivocal diagnoses are nearly as disappointing as negative ones. The patient is not likely to cooperate for long, if at all, with symptomatic treatment. If medication is prescribed, he is apt, after a half-hearted trial, to relegate it to his already well-stocked cabinet of unused pills.

In the sick-role type of hypochondria, the patient is satisfied with any diagnosis and treatment that provides medical sanction for a sick role. He does not expect, or even desire, to be cured, and so he prefers long-term symptomatic treatment to more definitive treatment. He cannot, however, just relax and be sick. He works at it, making frequent visits to the physician and faithfully taking an ample supply of prescribed pills.

SYMPTOM FORMATION

Since the primary theme of hypochondriacal communication is, "There is something wrong with me," it is proposed that the somatic symptom serves as a symbolic representation of low self-esteem. The mechanism of symptom formation is a simple displacement of the feeling that there is something wrong with the self from the psyche to the soma. The transformation of an amorphous feeling into a somatic disease enables the patient to define and communicate his problem in a concrete form.

Since the purpose of expressing the problem is to get something done about it, the ultimate function of the symptom is resolution. In the ambitious type of hypochondria, the goal of resolution is the complete elimination or correction of what is wrong with the self. In the sick-role type, the goal is to use the somatic symptom as an explanation of worthlessness and as a substitute technique of coping with helplessness.

PSYCHODYNAMICS

The hypochondriacal patient's life is characterized by chronic anxiety and recurrent depression, activated by repetitive frustrations of basic intake and self-protective needs. The frustration of intake needs consists of the deprivation of love and acceptance, goods and services. The frustration of self-protective needs consists of being imposed on, taken advantage of, dominated and controlled, or directly abused by others. The frustrations are real and painful, but they are neurotic because they are caused by the patient's own maladaptive personality functioning.

The patient is deprived because he fails to express himself effectively or to ask for what he wants and needs. He is used and abused because he fails to effectively say no or otherwise deal with the aggression of others.

These coping difficulties are derived from a general inhibition of normal self-expression and self-assertive behavior, motivated by anxiety derived from low self-esteem and feelings of worthlessness and helplessness; and the lack of effective techniques of asking and saying no, a lack that results in a real functional helplessness.

The low self-esteem and functional helplessness constitute a core neurosis that arises in response to frustrations of needs experienced during the patient's developmental years and subsequently becomes ingrained in his personality. In adulthood, it produces frustrations similar to those imposed in childhood by parents and others. This adaptational model of neurotic illness has been described more fully in previou papers.[2-4]

Usually the hypochondriacal patient has little or no insight into the connection between his frustrations and his maladaptive functioning. Instead, he attributes deprivation and mistreatment by others to their not liking him because he is somehow unacceptable. Since feelings of unacceptability are a basic component of core feelings of worthlessness, low self-esteem becomes the focus of all the patient's problems in living. He comes to feel that all his frustrations result from there being something wrong with him, and believes satisfaction in living would come if whatever is wrong could be corrected or removed.

To find a focus for his feelings of worthlessness, the patient tries to discover exactly what is wrong. A variety of physical and personality characteristics, imagined or real, may be focused on and become the symbol of all that feels wrong with the self. Over time, the patient has probably decided on and discarded many foci before he adopts physical hypochondria. Somatic disease is a particularly useful focus because medical sanction and treatment are available and because it provides a socially acceptable rationale for inadequacies.

DIFFERENTIAL DIAGNOSIS

Differential diagnosis involves distinguishing hypochondria from other types of somatic preoccupations and symptoms as well as from organic disease. Hypochondriacal preoccupation with the soma differs from normal concerns about the body in two ways. First, normal anxiety is focused on actual somatic integrity and functioning, whereas hypochondriacal anxiety is focused on the idea of having a disease. Second, normal anxiety is relieved by appropriate medical reassurance and treatment, whereas hypochondriacal anxiety is not.

Hypochondriacal preoccupation with the soma differs from that often seen early in schizophrenia in that the schizophrenic preoccupation is focused on actual somatic feelings and sensations, albeit sometimes distorted, whereas the hypochondriacal focus is an obsessional idea that has little or no relationship to somatic reality. Moreover, the schizophrenic patient does not view his concern as a medical problem or seek medical care on his own accord. Conversion hysteria is the somatic neurosis most likely to be confused with hypochondriasis. However, conversion symptoms involving a loss of function differ from hypochondriasis as follows. First, the focus in conversion symptoms, such as paralysis or blindness, is on the loss of function per se, not on the loss as a symptom of a disease. In contrast, hypochondriacal symptoms rarely consist of specific functional losses, unless the loss is a cardinal characteristic of and supports the diagnosis of a disease. Second, the conversion patient is seemingly indifferent about the symptom and does not seek or even want medical intervention unless monetary compensation is involved and medical sanction is necessary to val-

idate a legal claim. The hypochondriacal patient, in contrast, clamors for both medical diagnosis and treatment.

Conversion pain differs from hypochondriacal complaints of pain as follows. First, in conversion pain there is a communication of real misery and suffering, although the pain has more an affective than a sensory quality; in hypochondria, the pain complaint, like other symptoms, is used primarily to support the diagnosis of a disease and in itself does not contain a strong affective component. Second, the primary affective accompaniment of conversion pain is depression; of hypochondria, anxiety. Third, although the conversion pain patient, like the hypochondriac, actively seeks medical intervention, his goal is symptomatic relief of the pain rather than the establishment of a disease diagnosis and a treatment regimen.

Hypochondriasis is frequently superimposed on organic conditions. Characteristics that suggest a hypochondriacal overlay in patients with an organic disease include overdramatization of the illness; complaints or disability disproportionate to the organic pathology; use of the illness as a technique of coping (e.g., to get attention or avoid responsibility); failure of symptoms to respond to appropriate therapy; dissatisfaction with appropriate treatment and realistic improvement; and a push for overdiagnosis and treatment. If the differentiation is not made, there is a serious risk of either neglecting or overtreating the organic disease.

DISCUSSION

The most widely accepted interpretation of hypochondria is based on the psychoanalytically derived hypothesis that neurotic symptoms are compromise solutions of unconscious conflict. Hypochondriasis, as stated by Altman,[5] "serves the ego function of conflict resolution by allowing these patients to express impulses, primarily dependency and anger, without loss of self-esteem." The defensive function served by the somatization is the expiation of guilt about anger and dependency, through masochistic suffering.

There are theoretical and practical difficulties with this interpretation. The primary theoretical problem derives from the psychoanalytic interpretation of depression as a defensive technique of handling guilt about unconscious content. While there is an underlying depressive core in hypochondriasis, as there is in all neuroses, the depressive pain is a primary reaction to need frustration, rather than a secondary defensive maneuver. The depressive misery that characterizes the life histories of hypochondriacal patients results from painful frustrations rather than from a masochistic need to suffer.

The practical difficulty with this interpretation is its uselessness in dealing with the hypochondriacal patient; even its proponents almost universally agree that hypochondriasis is not amenable to definitive psychotherapy. Thus, Altman[5] says clearly, "He [the psychiatrist] must understand that the appropriate approach to the patient is a supportive, sustaining one, rather than an attempt to promote insight or use confrontation."

Another interpretation that relates somatization to depression is based on the concept of "masked depression." Dorfman[6] holds that in hypochondria the symptom is a defense against depression through the displacement of depressive affect onto somatic concerns. This interpretation differs from the author's in two important ways. First, in the content of what is displaced to the soma and, second, in the function served by the symptom.

In hypochondria, it is not depressive affect itself that is displaced to the soma, but rather feelings of low self-esteem perceived as there being something wrong with the self. Since low self-esteem is a crucial component of pathologic depression, this distinction might be considered academic. It is important to maintain the distinction, however, because feelings of low self-esteem are more crucial in the dynamics of depression than is the affective response, and hypochondria is an attempt to deal with low self-esteem rather than depressive affect per se. As long as the patient hopes that his hypochondriacal solution is viable, the depressive response is held in abeyance, or "masked."

Thus, the symptom might be considered a defense against depression. But it actually has more ambitious functions, because it represents an attempt to resolve the core neurosis that produces frustrations that activate depression. It is aimed, therefore, at eliminating depression rather than hiding or "masking" it. When depressive affect is displaced to the soma, the resulting somatic pain should be labeled conversion pain, rather than hypochondria.[4]

TREATMENT

Recognizing that the somatic symptom is a positive, albeit symbolic, attempt to communicate and resolve a real problem provides a common ground on which to proceed. It also gives direction and clues for uncovering the symbolic meaning of the symptom and the critical components of the underlying neurosis that the symptom is attempting to resolve. Positive acceptance of, interest in, and use of the somatic communication puts the patient at ease to talk freely, removes much of his defensiveness, and helps establish a therapeutic relationship.

In definitive psychotherapy, the first task is to work through the somatic fixation and transpose the patient's perception and communication of his problem back to the psychic arena. Two directions are possible. First is gradually detaching the feeling that something is wrong with the self from the somatic displacement through a detailed exploration of the hypochondriacal experience. By emphasizing the feeling at the expense of its somatic attachments, the central role of this feeling in all of the patient's hypochondriacal episodes is exposed. This approach works best for patients with some intellectual sophistication and introspection.

In less sophisticated patients, a more direct approach may be taken. By examining the patient's interactions with medical personnel and others and his frustrations in these situations, characteristic neurotic attitudes and coping patterns can be elicited. Once delineated, the transposition to how the interactions operate in everyday life is made.

The next task is to help the patient understand the reasons for his misery. His neurotic attitudes and coping patterns are delineated to show him that his frustrations lie in his defective personality functioning, not in some defect in his human nature.

The final goal is resolution. This involves helping the patient to acquire a more comfortable and secure self-concept and to learn more effective techniques of coping with legitimate need satisfaction. Success depends on the therapist's skill, the patient's personality assets, and the environment in which coping occurs. These variables may make complete resolution impossible. In some cases, the only realistic goal is to make the sick-role type of adaptation more comfortable for the patient and less burdensome to other people.

Although the nonpsychiatric physician cannot be expected to do intensive psychotherapy, understanding hypochondria will enable him to manage his hypochondriacal patients more effectively. With a little insight and guidance, some patients may come to grips with their neurosis without intensive therapy. Others will learn to function better, lessening the intensity and scope of the sick role as a coping mechanism. If nothing more, the recognition that the patient is making a valiant, albeit misguided, attempt to resolve real misery and suffering should prevent the physician from dismissing him as a "crock." This will lessen the possibility of psychologically damaging the patient by rejection and hostility and will make a successful psychiatric referral more likely. Finally, knowledge and understanding will reduce the likelihood of overtreatment of minor or nonexistent somatic conditions.

REFERENCES

1. Diagnostic and Statistical Manual of Mental Disorders III. Washington, D.C., American Psychiatric Association, 1980.

2. McCranie EJ: The neurotic process. Psychiatr Q 44:422–434, 1970.

3. McCranie EJ: Depression, anxiety, and hostility. Psychiatr Q 45:117–133, 1971.

4. McCranie EJ: Conversion pain. Psychiatr Q 47:246–257, 1973.

5. Altman N: Hypochondriasis, in Strain JJ, Grossman S (eds): Psychological Care of the Medically Ill. New York, Appleton-Century-Crofts, 1975.

6. Dorfman W: Hypochondriasis as a defense against depression. Psychosomatics 9:248–251, 1968.

SUGGESTED READINGS

General

The problem patient: Evaluation and care of medical patients with psychosocial disturbances. Drossman DA. Annals of Internal Medicine 88:366–372, 1976.

Hysteria: Studies of Diagnostic Outcome, and Prevalance. Woodruff RA, Clayton PJ, Guze SB. Journal of the American Medical Association 215:425–428, 1971.

Diagnosis of conversion reactions: Predictive value of psychiatric criteria. Raskin M, Talbott JA, Meyerson AT. Journal of the American Medical Association 197:530–534, 1966.

Charcot and hysteria. Havens LL. Journal of Nervous and Mental Disease 141:505–516, 1966.

Cognitive performance and conversion hysteria. Bendefeldt F, Miller LL, Ludwig AN. Archives of General Psychiatry 23:1250–1253, 1976.

Medical and psychological characteristics of "crocks." Lipsitt DR. Psychiatry in Medicine 1:15–25, 1970.

The hypochondriac. Socarides C. Physician's World, pp 56–60, 1974.

Psychiatric considerations in pain. Blumer D. In The Spine (edited by Rothmen R, Simeone FA) Philadelphia, W. B. Saunders 1975, pp 871–906.

Dysmorphophobia: Symptom of disease? Andreasen NC, Bardach J. American Journal of Psychiatry 134:673–676, 1977.

Biological Factors

Are there precursors to repression? Aleksandrowicz D. Journal of Nervous and Mental Disease 164:191–197, 1977.

Hysteria: A neurobiological theory. Ludwig A. Archives of General Psychiatry 27:771–777, 1972.

Attention in hysteria: A study of Janet's hypothesis by means of habituation and arousal measures. Horvath T, Friedman J, Meares R. America Journal of Psychiatry 137:217–220, 1980.

Neurological disease and hysteria—The differential diagnosis. Zigler DK. International Journal of Neuropsychiatry 3:388–396, 1967.

Psychological Factors

Fraulein Anna O. Breuer J, Freud S. Studies on Hysteria (translated by Brill AA). Boston, Beacon Press, 1964, pp 14–32.

Conversion symptoms. Engel G. In Signs and Symptoms: Applied Pathologic Pysiology and Clinical Interpretation, 5th ed (edited by MacBryde CM, Blacklow RS). Philadelphia, Lippincott, 1970, pp 650–668.

Conversion: Fact or chimera. Nemiah JC. Psychiatry in Medicine 5:443–448, 1974.

Multiple sclerosis and hysteria. Kaplan LR, Nadelson T. The Journal of the American Medical Association 243:2418–2421, 1980.

Polysurgery and polysurgical addiction. Menninger KA. Psychoanalytic Quarterly 3:173–199, 1934.

Primary atypical facial neuralgia: An hysterical conversion symptom. Engel GL. Psychosomatic Medicine 13:375–395, 1951.

Sociocultural Factors

Pain as abnormal illness behavior. Pilowsky I. Journal of Human Stress 4:22–27, 1978.

Culture and symptoms—An analysis of patients' presenting complaints. Zola I. American Sociological Review 31:615–630, 1966.

Social psychological factors affecting the presentation of bodily complaints. Mechanic D. New England Journal of Medicine 286:1132–1139, 1972.

Pain transactions. Sternback R. In Pain Patients, Traits and Treatments. New York, Academic Press, 1974, pp 52–78.

PART

VI
ORGANIC BRAIN DISORDERS

OVERVIEW

It is important to differentiate organic from functional psychoses. Functional psychoses include schizoprenic disorders, affective disorders, brief reactive psychoses, and *dissociative disorders* (including *multiple personalities* and amnesia) for which a specific organic etiology has not been defined. Organic brain disorders, by contrast, are caused by neurological or medical conditions that can be detected or verified by physical findings and/or laboratory examination. A careful search will reveal either a toxic metabolic defect or a visible abnormality of brain structure. This impaired brain function disrupts an individual's usual ability to handle complex tasks and relationships.

The presence of *organicity* (an organic brain disorder) rests upon defects of five interrelated mental functions that can be demonstrated during mental status examinations: (1) diminished cognition—inability to solve problems and think abstractly; (2) deficient orientation—lack of awareness of specifics of location, time, and identity of people; (3) poor memory—inability to remember recent events as well as some of those in the distant past; (4) impaired affect—unstable emotional responses that are shallow and labile; and (5) lessened judgment—inability to make informed judgments and to have insight into events including, for example, the reasons for the present hospitalization.

Although defects need not be present in all five spheres, the more global (generalized, widespread) the impairment, the easier it is to make the diagnosis on clinical grounds. Certain confirmatory procedures can be used to clarify and substantiate diagnosis. For example, psychological testing with design copying (Bender Gestalt) and block arrangement can reveal visual–motor (e.g., eye–hand) incoordination, common in cerebral insufficiency. The presence of slow, high-amplitude wave forms, in the *electroencephalogram* (EEG) is also characteristic of most cases of organic brain disorder.

Neurological signs and symptoms that suggest organicity include a coarse tremor, slurred (or *dysarthric*) speech, ataxic gait, and somnolence; muscular rigidity; pathological *reflexes* such as *snout*, *grasp*, suck, and *glabellar*; and motor perseveration. Medical signs in a distraught patient that might suggest organicity include fever, jaundice, skin rash, and odd breath smell (alcohol, acetone, uremic odor).

For many patients, the emergence of organicity is the first clue to an urgent need for hospitalization for some type of medical disorder. Casual evaluation, however, may not bring out evidence of an organic brain disorder, especially when it is long-standing or chronic, because routine and usual social functioning may be preserved in people with organic brain disorders of even moderate severity. Open-ended interviewing (nonstructured, nondirective) may be helpful diagnostically, since this requires the patient to draw more on his or her own resources, thus revealing impaired associations or memory deficits that may not have been apparent in a more structured, predictable encounter. Customary social amenities may superficially cover up profound deficits of cognitive function if there is no mental obtundation, gross confusion, or preoccupation with delusions or hallucinations.

The three major important types of organic mental disorders are delirium, dementia, and the amnestic syndrome. *Delirium* is an acute and fluctuating behavioral syndrome that often begins abruptly, even dramatically, with a clouding of consciousness, disorientation, shortened attention span, and perceptual disturbances (misconceptions of sensory input, with simple misinterpretations, illusions, or even hallucinations). These symptoms develop when neurons in some of the primitive areas of the brain, including the *brain stem*, midbrain and *limbic system*, are temporarily (and usually reversibly) affected.

Dementia is another syndrome of intellectual and memory impairment, with slow onset and less fluctuation in course. Because its duration is longer, it affords the individual more opportunity to adjust gradually to a diminished capacity. Dementia is found especially, although not only, among the elderly, and usually results from irreversible neuronal changes that involve the *cerebral cortex*.

The third major type of organic mental disorder is the *amnestic syndrome*. In contrast to those with delirium and other types of chronic brain syndrome, people afflicted with this chronic condition usually retain their intellectual ability, but they have a severe memory defect, especially for recent events. Additionally, those with the amnestic syndrome lack the ability to form new memories. Associated with the amnestic syndrome are *lesions* in specific parts of a subcortical midbrain area. Thiamine-depleted severe alcoholics are particularly vulnerable to this disorder.

DELIRIUM

Clinical Picture

The casual observer's first inkling of delirium may come from the patient's manifesting nonspecific symptoms: anxiety, depression, irritability, difficulty in concentration, forgetfulness, nightmares, or incoherent speech. Sometimes these early symptoms are missed, and the first indication that the patient is "not right" occurs when someone observes the patient talking with animation to an area of the room in which no one is present. Another typical presentation may be "sundowning" (confusion at night) and wandering. Indeed, disturbed sleep with restlessness or total insomnia for one or two nights may be the first indication of an impending delirium.

Disability in three spheres—attention, memory, and orientation—is necessary for the diagnosis of delirium. The attention span may be measured in seconds instead of minutes as it had previously been. No longer can the individual sustain interest in a topic of conversation, pursue a thought pattern to its conclusion, or perform sustained work. Simple calculations become difficult.

Problems with memory present a second major defect for the delirious patient. There is repeated inability to recollect recent or current events. Especially affected is *short-term memory*, including occurrences within the day, hour, or even the past minute. Events during the past months are sometimes more vividly recalled than those of the past day, and even former rather than current telephone numbers and addresses are remembered.

A third major deficit in delirium is disorientation. This results from difficulty in focusing mental efforts and in laying down new memories. Usually we are alert to the facts of our surroundings; we orient ourselves to place automatically and, with a little more conscious effort, we orient ourselves to time. Minor errors in the day or date of the month, especially when someone is sick and hospitalized, should not receive undue emphasis. The persistent inability to recall the month or year correctly, especially if the proper answer has been offered recently, is characteristic of delirium. The individual may also recurrently fail to identify correctly the name of the city or the hospital in which he or she is located.

In addition to these primary cognitive impairments, there may also be secondary disturbances, such as disturbances of mood; poor sleep or persistent wakefulness; change in the usual speed of bodily movement (psychomotor retardation or acceleration); and disturbed perception. Additionally, gross disruption of the processing of input data and abnormal brain activity may produce transient visual hallucinations. Severely disordered interpretation of sensory input may lead to illusions. Strong affective responses, often unrelated to current or even recent life situations, may occur. Usually the affects are those of terror or depression, but occasionally there may be a strong oceanic peaceful feeling. Delusions occur, presumably as a way of accounting for the unusual set of incoherent mental messages experienced by the patient, such as disordered sensory input, strong dysphoric (unpleasant) feeling states, and inadequate cognitive processing of the whole bewildering experience. Impulse control and modulation of emotions, the "fine tuning" of the cognitive–emotional system, are impaired. As a consequence of these deficits, insight, judgment, and the ability to care for oneself are all compromised. Indeed, some patients with profound delirium, or dementia, may be so disoriented and lacking in insight and impulse control that they may manifest extremes of aggressive behavior by disrobing, playing with feces, or even masturbating in public.

Paradoxically, when an agitated delirious patient spontaneously becomes calm, this may presage a worsening of the underlying medical condition, as the individual becomes torporous and then fades into coma. Another and more frequent cause of change in the mental state in the delirious patient is the characteristic waxing and waning of symptoms that occur during the course of the day and night.

Medical Findings

Laboratory reports usually indicate some abnormality in patients with delirium. For example, there may be a lack of glucose, oxygen, vitamin B_{12}, niacin, thiamin, or folic acid in body fluids. There may also be a deficit or a surfeit of electrolytes (calcium, sodium, magnesium) or endogenous hormones or metabolites (thyroxine, urea, carbon dioxide).

Medical conditions at times associated with delirium can be life threatening. Examples are hypertensive or anoxic encephalopathy and liver and kidney failure. Relative or absolute sensory deprivation can also produce or exacerbate delirium in some patients, as can fever. A brain tumor or a *subdural hematoma* may cause delirium because of pressure obstructing distribution of nutrients to cortical neurons. Acute brain syndromes can also be associated with *cerebral edema* from such causes as head trauma, encephalitis, or *neurosyphyllis*.

Medications can cause or aggravate delirium. A drug that is clinically therapeutic in small concentrations may cause a *toxic psychosis* in excess; examples are digitalis and some drugs with much anticholinergic activity. In susceptible elderly persons, atropine eye drops can cause an *anticholinergic psychosis*. Central nervous system depressants such as alcohol can also cause delirium. In large or larger than prescribed doses, *hypnotic medication* such as the barbiturates (amytal, phenobarbital), and methaqualone (Quaalude), or *anxiolytic agents* such as meprobamate (Miltown, Equanil) or the benzodiazepines (Librium, Valium, Serax) can also cause an acute organic brain disorder. Emotionally unstable and sensation-seeking individuals sometimes take these sedative–hypnotic agents in excess to produce a delirious state for their pleasure (substance abuse).

After prolonged use, acute withdrawal from some of these delirium-producing medications may itself produce a delirium. This occurs because the brain responds to the sudden lack of the central nervous system depressant with rebound hyperexcitability, producing a delirious state that can last for a week. During this rebound-type of delirium, a tremor may appear, often followed by convulsions. When an abstinence syndrome is associated with chronic alcohol excess and then acute withdrawal, the rebound delirium is called *delirium tremens* (DTs). Unlike most other acute organic brain syndromes, delirium tremens and some other abstinence syndromes are associated with *tachycardia*, elevated blood pressure, tremor and fever, and an EEG pattern of rapid activity. Often there is the sensation of *formication* (a tactile hallucination of ants crawling over the skin) and feelings of panic, in addition to the usual findings in delirium. Untreated, full-blown DTs have an astonishingly high mortality rate, ranging from 15 to 30% in some series.

The incidence of delirium varies considerably with the population studied. For example, almost all patients undergoing open heart surgery with cardiac bypass became at least temporarily delirious sometime after they awake from anesthesia. The longer the operation has required the patient's blood to be circulated through the external cardiopulmonary oxygenation pump, the more likely delirium is to occur, often with some mild neurological signs. Renal dialysis patients often have some delirium related to accumulation of toxic metabolic products and/or inadequate replacement of trace electrolytes.

Delirium also may occur in patients undergoing ophthalmological surgery necessitating the patching of both eyes simultaneously (black patch psychosis). In the intensive care unit (ICU), about one-third of all patients become delirious. Some of these patients with the ICU syndrome have no detectable biochemical disturbance. They usually recover from their delirium within hours of transfer from the sensory-depriving, monotonous environment of the ICU and back to a less sterile, more homelike environment repleat with more obvious external cues such as light and dark periods, outside visitors, clocks, and calendars. Patients with the ICU syndrome often seem to respond well to contact and support from family and friends.

Delirium is much more common in the elderly than in the young. At some time during hospitalization, at least one-third of all patients over 65 become delirious. Among those elderly Americans thought to be hopelessly demented, it is estimated that 10–20% (300,000 people) actually have a treatable, remediable organic brain syndrome that is an undetected, untreated delirious condition erroneously written off as dementia.

DEMENTIA

Dementia is usually a permanent disorder caused by gradual neuronal degeneration and atrophy of the cerebral cortex. Clinically, demented people are less likely to be psychotic and less likely to appear to be acutely physically ill than people who are delirious. The demented person is usually not obtunded or extremely restless, except in the later end stages of the disorder. Finally, clinical observation clearly indicates that demented patients are less likely to admit to having cognitive disturbances than delirious patients.

After a delirious patient has an organic brain disorder for about three weeks, he or she often learns to avoid referring to topical areas that demonstrate poor cognitive function. Thus, when asked the date, the delirious patient may respond defensively, "You must think I'm crazy"; or matter-of-factly, "I never read the newspapers anymore, so I don't know"; or with humor, "I'll tell you that if you tell me which way stairs go, up or down!"

In contrast to delirium, dementia usually has an insidious onset, often beginning with a variety of ill-defined somatic complaints without demonstrable bodily pathology. A demented person may suffer a gradual decline in cognitive ability over months or years, while social responses may superficially appear to remain intact. To those who know the patient well, he or she may "just not be himself (herself)." Changes in initiative, caring and creativity, along with a new moodiness or emotional instability, may be agonizing to the family. Often the physician is asked to see the patient after a gradual increase in emotional lability and temper outbursts, socially embarrassing behavior, or even suspiciousness.

Essential for the diagnosis of dementia are two features: first, a deterioration of previously acquired intellectual abilities leading to some social or work-related impairment; and second, poor memory, especially for recent events. In addition, there is often an impairment in abstract thinking that can be demonstrated in the mental status examination. Concrete interpretation of proverbs occurs: "People who live in glass houses shouldn't throw stones" is interpreted literally and not symbolically; or the patient is unable to give an example of what is similar about two items of the same class (e.g., a cat and a mouse). There may also be difficulty in copying patterns, naming objects, performing calculations, or following instructions.

Finally, there may be an impairment of judgment and impulse control and a change in the basic personality style, usually in the direction of overemphasis of a previous trait. For example, an individual may become more suspicious, compulsive, or orderly than previously. Furthermore, the individual may have trouble comprehending or thinking about a particular topic or outlining a plan of action as he or she had previously been able to do. Relatives or friends may be able to see the gradual evolution of changes. Sometimes, however, certain mental capacities may be relatively intact and others almost absent, according to the type and the location of ongoing pathological processes.

Although there are a variety of obscure and rare dementias (some of which may be due to *slow reacting viruses*, (e.g., Jakob–Creutzfeldt disease)), the two most frequent types are Alzheimer's (idiopathic *senile*) *dementia* and *multi-infarct* (small stroke) dementia. The former type is the most common of the dementias and occurs more often in women than in men. It is accompanied by some personality deterioration. The multi-infarct dementia is seen more often in men than in women. In multi-infarct dementia, the personality and previous intellectual assets of the individual tend to be better preserved until a relatively advanced stage. In *Alzheimer's disease* there is a gradual but progressive deterioration, as neurons, especially in frontal and temporal lobes, are replaced by *neurofibrillary tangles*, senile plaques, and *granulovacular degeneration* in much greater frequency than is the case in normal aging. In contrast, the dementias associated with vascular disease show a stepwise, stuttering deterioration with a loss of cognitive and some motor functioning. At autopsy, spotty areas of infarction may be seen in many areas of the brain.

Some of the other dementias are caused by once reversible medical conditions that have over time eventually produced irreparable damage. Finally, there are two types of long-lasting organic brain syndromes that are not often considered in most physicians' differential diagnosis, yet they can be treated successfully: Normal pressure *hydrocephalus* and depressive *pseudodementia*.

Normal pressure hydrocephalus in the elderly is caused by an increasing resistance to outflow of cerebral spinal fluid from the ventricles. This syndrome is associated with a triad of dementia, *ataxia*, and urinary incontinence.

The second type of reversible, long-lasting syndrome with marked organic features is called depressive pseudodementia. The affected individual shows deterioration of personality, psychomotor retardation, apathy, disorientation, perseveration, disturbed sleep and global cognitive deficits. Careful history-taking reveals that the "dementia" has not been progressive over months to years, but only a few weeks or months in duration and is associated with feelings of sadness. This condition can be fatal if undetected because of self-neglect or even suicide. It is important that the clinician attempt to make contact with both the patient and family so that depressive features and vegetative symptoms can be documented.

Most people with dementias are elderly. More than 10% of people over age 65 have some type of organic brain disorder that interferes with their functioning. Among those confined to nursing homes, 50–75% have been reported to have some type of dementia. It is important to note, however, that depression and other reversible conditions may be mistaken for dementia when a careful examination is not done. Follow-up on patients with diagnosed delirium or dementia in a general hospital reveals a rather gloomy prognosis: half are dead within four years, including one of six under the age of 50 and a great majority of those over that age. Of those who survive the initial hospitalization, more than half are left with some type of residual dementia, so that one of five survivors ends up in a psychiatric facility for custodial care or behavioral management.

AMNESTIC SYNDROME

Amnestic syndrome is a specific and readily identifiable type of chronic organic brain disorder. In this condition, a localized anatomic lesion of the medial dorsal nuclei of the *diencephalon* is associated with one specific type of cognitive impairment. People with the amnestic syndrome have a clear state of consciousness. They retain the ability to reason clearly and think abstractly, but their *short-term memory* is impaired; that is, they cannot remember an event that took place several minutes ago. Curiously, people with this disorder still have good immediate recall, so that they can repeat back four or six numbers correctly, but they cannot remember that they did this an hour later.

The profundity of memory loss for events in the past minute, hour, or even in some cases, the past decade, is seriously incapacitating. The inability to form new memory traces makes the task of orientation to place and time difficult unless there are immediate visual cues available (identifying signs). Often accompanying this type of defect is the tendency to *confabulate* (filling in actual memory gaps by imaginary or dimly recollected experience in response to clues from the immediate environment). These confabulations may be interlaced with partial recalled memories of past events. Thus, the patient who has been hospitalized on a chronic ward continuously for the past year may respond affirmatively when asked by the examiner: "Didn't we meet last night in the hotel bar?" The term "amnestic confabulatory syndrome" is descriptive, with *Korsakoff's syndrome* a common eponym for this phenomenon.

Some amnesias are of psychogenic origin; for example, painful anxiety-provoking experiences can be kept out of conscious awareness by one's not remembering. When functional or psychogenic amnesia is severe, as in a *fugue state*, the individual takes flight and forgets what has recently happened, often even who he or she is. People with organic amnesias may be disoriented to place and time, but they are rarely disoriented to person unless there is a marked clouding of consciousness or there are very clear-cut positive neurological findings including gross impairment of intellectual functioning. Selective amnesias for inconvenient items are usually psychogenic, whereas amnesia for unrelated details of an experience is usually organic in etiology. A patchy amnesia with memory for a few isolated events during a period of confusion is typical of the organic amnesia associated with delirium.

Although head trauma and carbon monoxide poisoning can cause lesions of the medial dorsal *nucleus*, the vast majority of people with the amnestic syndrome are thiamine-depleted alcoholics. Generally there is a pattern of steady heavy drinking for months or years with inadequate food intake. Initial episodes of the amnestic syndrome are often prolonged; months to a year are required for recovery. Many subjects have repetitive amnestic episodes along with their alcoholism so that instead of complete recovery, they are eventually left permanently impaired.

Because alcoholism is much more common in men than in women (four to one), one would predict that more men than women have the amnestic syndrome. This is true, but the ratio of men to women is only 1.7:1. The amnestic syndrome is rare before age 35 and seems to be rather evenly spread over the ages through 70, with some overrepresentation in the fifth and sixth decades. It is not, however, a syndrome that is seen frequently, except in metropolitan hospitals caring for large alcoholic populations.

TREATMENT

The cardinal principle in treating people with organicity is to search for remediable causes. The most obvious and easiest cause of reversible organicity is medication. Prescriptions and over-the-counter drugs that are well tolerated in the general population may produce a striking delirium in the elderly, even in those who previously showed no overt signs of dementia. Many times the acutely delirious elderly patient can be returned to an independent life-style a few days or a few weeks after administration of the delirium-producing agents is stopped.

The second important principle in treating people with organicity is protection from accidental falls. Confused patients, especially the elderly, may have difficulty in navigating familiar places and certainly will need assistance with new environments, since organicity implies difficulty with new learning, short-term memory deficits, visual motor incoordination, and poor logical deductive thinking. If hallucinations are present, they may be distracting. Those with organicity are prone to see illusions, including architectural details that don't exist, stairs outside an open window, planks across an open pit. Moreover, threatening hallucinations (e.g., a fiendish murderer) may make the organically impaired person wish to chance jumping out a window rather than face certain dismemberment.

To provide physical protection, good lighting at night is important. A lighted bedside lamp, plus a bed that is not too high off the floor or side rails on the bed may all have some prophylactic value.

Although restraints may be needed to prevent the beclouded individual from wandering around aimlessly in a fog and falling, it is far more preferable to have a family member or a staff person sit with such a person during times of maximal confusion, especially at night.

When the patient with organicity is agitated, neuroleptics may be indicated. These medications do not change the fundamental cognitive defect, of course, but their use may decrease abnormal anxiety levels. At times patients' paralyzing fears, delusional systems, and/or irritability may prevent them from using effectively whatever cognitive resources have been preserved. Night wandering can be decreased or eliminated by the use of non-delirium-producing hypnotic agents such as chlopromazine (Thorazine) in very low doses.

Many times crisis intervention and social supports can allow a patient with a mild to moderate dementia to continue to live in his or her own neighborhood.

A final principle to consider in treating the patient with gross cognitive impairment is the preservation of respect for the individual. Granted, in severely impaired patients this may be difficult. When the patient disrobes, smears feces, and strikes out in fear or rage, the clinician may find it difficult to be kindly and understanding. However, brusque treatment only further dehumanizes the patient, accelerating the downward spiral. And even the severly demented patient will on occasion have a few moments of clarity.

Firm kindness and kind firmness, structure, and occasionally low doses of neuroleptic medications such as haloperidol (Haldol) can assist the organic patient. Knowledge of the specific cognitive deficits can alert staff and family as to what are appropriate levels of expectation for that particular patient.

THE PSYCHIATRIST
IN THE SURGICAL INTENSIVE CARE UNIT:
POSTOPERATIVE DELIRIUM

THEODORE NADELSON

Delirium has been defined as a condition of cerebral insufficiency consisting of impairment of cognitive processes, with a characteristic slowing of the electroencephalographic pattern. Present also is a global "clouding" of consciousness, resulting from a potentially reversible impairment of ability to maintain attention. In these states there is usually a simultaneous diminution of the ability to think, perceive, and remember. Although drowsiness may be a part of this state, patients can be awake and yet delirious, with diminished consciousness of their surroundings.

Postoperative delirium is seen more often in patients over 50 years of age, in those who are "vigilant" or overalert, and in those undergoing more complex surgery. Adverse influences in the postoperative period are certain drugs and the psychological stresses engendered by the ICU environment. Appropriate management obtains from attention to the impact of the strange environment on the patient.

The psychiatrist who first rounded on a surgical intensive care unit (SICU) probably was asked to see a postoperative patient who "seemed to develop schizophrenia overnight." The task of distinguishing between schizophrenia and delirium in the SICU has remained a challenge, as has the etiologic understanding and the management of such cases.

Reprinted, with author revisions,* from Archives of Surgery 111:113–117, 1976. Copyright 1976, American Medical Association.
*Revision of October 11, 1980, based on Dr. Nadelson's comments of August 18, 1980.

Postoperative delirium has held the interest of investigators from the fields of surgery, medicine, and psychiatry. In approaching the multiconvergence of forces leading to delirium, we address etiologic factors, diagnostic problems, and prophylactic principles that also have application to other problem areas of psychological disequilibrium. An additional impetus to better understanding and treating patients with postoperative delirium is that these patients tend to have less successful surgical outcome.

A number of features distinguish postoperative delirium from the acute functional psychoses of schizophrenia disorders and affective disorders even for the person not specifically trained in psychological observation. The patient with delirium is usually more motorically restless than the patient with a functional psychosis, and the delirious patient's mental set is more haphazard: a tangle of confusion, shifting thoughts and feelings, and unpredictable agitation. The difference between functional psychosis and delirium is perhaps easier to discern for the psychiatric clinician with an ear atuned to the nuance in cadence and content of usual and unusual communication: the patient with a functional psychosis tends to be persistently bizarre, whereas the patient with the acute delirium tends to be more fragmented and is more often frightened.

The psychologically oriented clinician can usually tell on first approach that the postoperative patient in the SICU does not have a schizophrenic disorder. People rarely emerge into full-blown functional psychosis with no previous history of emotional difficulties. Also, when the delirious patient is interviewed, it becomes clear that there is primarily a difficulty of attention accompanied by a memory deficit. The distortions of patients with functional psychosis, although at variance with normally perceived reality, usually have some internally consistent ideas, fixed delusional percepts around which communication is centered. Such patients are, for example, persecuted by the FBI or by a relative; there is a more constant structure to their ideas. The mode or agent of attack is more or less predictable and remembered from one moment to the next and over long periods of time.

Patients with postoperative delirium do not have "fixed ideas." Thus, the initial impression of "organicity" comes from the fleeting nature of the ideas, plus the inability to remember what has happened. They do not know or remember who the doctor is, where they are, and so on. Such patients are often disoriented in all modes when the delirium is extreme, not knowing where they are or what year it is (1). The degree of disorientation is variable, as is the amount of restlessness, which can range from mild to extreme agitation. Still, severely disturbed thinking may unpredictably be followed by a transient clear period. For example, a postcardiotomy patient in a delirium suddenly appeared concerned, then frightened. He looked at his interviewer, relaxed somewhat, seemed puzzled, and then said, "I think I was just crazy for a moment." He had experienced a transient visual hallucination.

The hallucinations are more often visual in such acute confusional states (as opposed to the auditory hallucinatory experiences of schizophrenic patients) (1,2). The total experience is almost always frightening and can be termed paranoid. Paranoid thinking is an inevitable accompaniment of such confusional states. The premorbid character exerts no influence on this phenomenon. There are ideas of reference attached to the hallucinations and delusions. Inevitably all personnel are seen by the patient as focused on him or her, laughing at helplessness or discussing death. The internal phenomenology of such a patient (recalled later) is similar to a dream. The paranoid ideas can be seen as a way of organizing evanescent images and feelings in a state of deficient memory, unpredictability, fear, and helplessness; they are the "last defense" of the self-perceiving ego which imposes some form of explanation on the otherwise unexplainable.

"Organicity," as a clinical manifestation, can be conjectured as occurring in parallel with the disordered physiology of neuronal activity. Functional psychotic states have more "order" and tend to last longer and to remit, when they do, more slowly.

Delirium with agitation usually manifests itself on the third to seventh postoperative day and often lasts only from 24 to 48 hours (3,4). Nevertheless, the experience is often terrifying and unforgettable (5). A longer duration of 14.7 days (average) has been reported in 57% of 139 patients who survived heart surgery (6,7). Indeed, disorientation has been reported to last as long as a month before clearing (8).

There is usually a lucid interval of two or three days after surgery before delirium ensues (9). Some authors make a distinction between delirium that occurs after the lucid interval and another condition with a different cause, early organic brain syndrome, which is present from the outset postoperatively. This latter type of organic brain syndrome is perhaps less influenced by factors within the SICU environment and does not seem to remit spontaneously. However, it may be that a lucid or clear interval is merely the result of less-than-intensive observation of the mental state by the staff because of the demand for strict observation of other seemingly more important parameters of acute patient care. Thus, the lucid interval is probably best viewed as the time period before manifestations of florid psychological/cognitive symptoms are noted.

CAUSE OF POSTOPERATIVE DELIRIUM SYNDROME

The cause of the postoperative delirium syndrome has been viewed variously as biochemically[10] or psychologically[11,12] derived. The syndrome emerges from interaction of a number of specifiable factors. The first set of factors includes the variables present prior to surgery. The second set of factors includes procedures and manipulations intrinsic to the operative procedure. The third set of factors includes both drugs used postoperatively and those variables that reside within the SICU milieu itself.

Preoperative Factors Associated With Delirium

The preoperative factors include those that are usually expected to decrease the ability to withstand stress. Increasing age of over 50 years notably increases the risk. Senile patients may show a deterioration of postoperative psychological functioning without a lucid interval.[9]

Viewpoints regarding the influence of gross preoperative psychological aberrations (psychosis or family history of psychosis) vary, and it is difficult to assess this factor. However, personality styles or modes of coping, with less than usual flexibility under stress, are seen to correlate with delirium postoperatively.[13] Patients with depression functional psychosomatic disease, sleep disturbance, or history of habitual drug use have generally less than average coping ability.

Preoperative modes of psychological "coping" or "flexibility" are also important in overall surgical success. In this regard, denial often has been regarded as a maladaptive psychological defense mechanism, correlating with general postoperative psychological complications and increased morbidity and mortality. It is suggested that the physician approach avoidance actively before surgery.[14–16] Others contest this position.[5,17,18] For the psychotherapist a "breakthrough" in the patient's denial is usually followed by anxiety, which may herald a positive change and emotional reintegration. In our experience most patients who are physically ill deny the extent of their illness or the intensity of their feeling about it in varying degrees. Some degree of denial is normal and functions as a positive psychological defensive posture. It has been found by others that a coping style termed "avoidance" (of knowledge or awareness of the medical condition) leads to more rapid postoperative recovery than does "vigilance" (over alertness to the threatening aspects of upcoming surgery).[19] Most physicians, we have found, have more difficulty in establishing an alliance with patients who are vigilant, questioning, and suspicious than with those who deny, but are accepting of the physicians good intentions and skill. Denial of a steadfast, unwavering sort, however, often presents a problem for the staff in that it makes it difficult to establish a mutual or cooperative relationship with the patient.

General interest in preoperative psychological characteristics has been in the direction of prediction of postoperative psychiatric complications such as delirium.[9,17] but also in extended psychological effects. The surgeon's particular interest in this subject may be more specifically focused on whether or not knowledge of preoperative personality characteristics should be among the factors to be considered in surgical risk and prognosis. Difference in scores on a battery of psychological and intellectual tests were found to have predictive value in distinguishing survivors and nonsurvivors in cardiac surgery.[20] It is suggested that it may be possible, with such information, to ameliorate the degree of risk for some patients.

Operative Factors Associated With Delirium

Type of Procedure. An incidence of 1,250 "mental disorders" (without specification of the clinical findings) was reported in all surgical patients in 1910.[21] An overall incidence of psychiatric problems was reported, loosely encompassing delirium or psychosis, which ranges from 0 to 60%. In a random sampling of 200 general surgical patients, delirium was found in 78%.[22] Some procedures characteristically eventuate in affective disturbance; hysterectomy particularly is indicted.[23] Eye operations show a higher incidence of postoperative psychiatric states than other nonthoracic surgery.[16,24,25] It is difficult to assess independence of variables; for example, the age of the patient may be highly correlated with the type of procedure, as in cataract surgery.

Cardiotomy generally has exceeded other surgical procedures in the incidence of postoperative psychiatric complications, including the major ones of delirium, but also the incidence of the rarer psychosis. The predominance of articles written exclusively on psychiatric aspects of treatment of the surgical heart patients attests to that. Before 1963, incidence of such complications ranged from 5% to 17%.[6] After 1963, an increase has been reported, ranging from 38% to 61%[26,27] and occasionally higher for all behavioral disorders including delirium. Delirium is reported in one article at 57% of 139 surviving patients.[28] More recent studies point to decreasing incidence of postcardiotomy delirium.[9,29]

Complexity of Procedure. It was first suggested that there was a causal relationship between mitral valve procedures per se and the postoperative psychiatric complications that followed.[6] As numbers of intracardiac procedures increased, it became clear that the abnormality could be causally linked, at least in part, to physiological stresses induced by the operation.

As procedures on the heart developed from closed-heart, "finger fracture" valvulotomy to more complicated operations involving cardiopulmonary bypass and hypothermia (with attendant longer hours of operation and anesthesia time), the incidence of psychological complications increased. The increasing complexity of newer procedures and technical improvement brought into play the following factors: (1) greater manipulation of life processes, ie, longer anesthesia and bypass time, with greater numbers of drugs in larger amounts and hypothermia, and (2) operations on older, sicker patients.

In patients subjected to anesthesia time longer than eight hours and bypass time exceeding four hours, there is a 75% incidence of postoperative delirium.[28] It is not clear what the underlying physiological factors are; it has been suggested that at least one of the conditions present in long operations is decreased brain perfusion or hypoxia or both. Anoxia resulting from decreased circulating volume has been correlated with postoperative delirium.[30] Patients who receive transfusion of more than 2 units of blood had a higher incidence of such psychiatric symptoms. However, patients receiving no blood had a higher incidence of symptoms than those receiving up to 10 units. A similar situation is found in the use of hypothermia; hypothermia of a few degrees below 37 C correlated with a low incidence of psychiatric complications than did an absence of hypothermia, and with a much lower incidence than chilling of the patient below 27 C.[28] Embolization from use of silicones in the bypass apparatus or from antifoam agents also have been suggested as a cause of decreased brain circulation.[6] Disturbance of blood gases, hypoxia, hypocapnia, and hypercapnia, are known to cause confusion or psychotic behavior.[10] Agents such as succinylcholine chloride have been implicated in abnormal psychological states.[31] Although one could assume as well that decreased cardiac output would also be associated with abnormal psychological states, it has been found paradoxically that hallucinations occur with a rapid rise in cardiac output and never when the output is falling.[7] High cardiac output is not always associated with hallucinations, however.

One of the more interesting and compelling physiological explanations is in research on catecholamine activity. Catecholamine levels are measured at their highest after open-heart surgery and during the time of the usual occurrence of psychiatric symptoms of delirium.[6,32] Hypoxia may be a stimulus to increased epinephrine secretion, and adrenochromes may be produced from epinephrine through abnormal metabolic pathways in some patients on a purely hereditary basis, or released by direct oxygenation of blood in the bypass apparatus. The observed phenomenon of children's "immunity" to postoperative psychosis may be due to differences in need or in ability to metabolize amines.[26,28] The effect of phenothiazines on postoperative delirium stands in partial support of the "amine theory" as well, since phenothiazines are known to block amine synthesis. There is still some difficulty in disentangling cause from effect; it can be speculated as to whether increase in circulating amines proceeds from a psychological state or vice versa.

In the past five years, however, a decreased incidence of postcardiotomy delirium has been found.[9,29] The operative factors seen as responsible for the change are decreased operative-anesthesia-pump time. As ease with cardiotomy techniques increases more complicated cases are performed faster. Other factors responsible are better preoperative psychological preparation and greater attention to psychological issues in the SICU postoperatively, which often occurs when the staff becomes more expert in technical matters.

Postoperative Factors Associated With Delirium

Drugs. Most of the drugs used after surgery are potential factors in the induction of depression, anxiety, delirium, or psychosis in a predisposed patient. Many of the side-effects of such drugs are well-known and documented, perhaps especially so in the case of barbiturate use, notorious for causing or aggravating post-operative delirium. Ironically, the barbiturates are often given for an acute sleep disorder, which is often the first postoperative sign of impending delirium.

Anticholinergic drugs (atropine, scopolamine, and related compounds), antitussives, anti-Parkinson agents, drugs to control cardiac output and rhythm, the tricyclic antidepressants, and antihistamines may not be recognized as potential causes of untoward psychological effects. Some of these drugs may be used after surgery to provide relief of symptoms; all are said to be capable of promoting major psychological disturbance.[10] Corticosteroids have definite dose-related psychological effects. Patients taking steroids (or withdrawing from them) show degrees of aberration ranging through mild euphoria to delirium and hallucinations.

The SICU Environment. The environment of the SICU itself has long been indicted as a factor in delirium. The first impression of the SICU relates to the intensity of illumination, visibility of patients, and movements of the staff. Sleeping and dreaming, which impose order on the day and perhaps integrate emotional experience,[33] are often disturbed. Patients frequently experience a distorted sense of expansion and contraction of time. Such a perception arises from fatigue, lack of sleep, or pain with its "minutes-into-hours" phenomenon, and anxiety and depression. There may be no calendar or clock for reference, or the patient may not be able to see it. Perception, dulled by pain, weakness, or beginning toxic delirium is further dulled by the limitation imposed by the environment. It was found in a medical intensive care unit that half of the patients had lost their time sense.[34] Personnel change frequently, and the patient often cannot establish a trusting relationship.

ease of medical progress." Conn Med 30:633–636, 1966.

12. Nahum LH: Madness in the recovery room from open heart surgery or "They kept waking me up." Conn Med 29:771, 1965.

13. Morse RM, Litin EH: Postoperative delirium: A study of etiologic factors. Am J Psychiatry 126:388–395, 1969.

14. Deutsch H: Some psychoanalytic observations in surgery. Psychosom Med 4:105–115, 1942.

15. Dlin BM, Fischer HK, Huddell B: Psychological adaption to pacemaker and open heart surgery. Arch Gen Psychiatry 19:599–610, 1968.

16. Linn L, Kahn RL, Coles R, et al: Patterns of behavior disturbances following cataract extraction. Am J Psychiatry 110:281–289, 1953.

17. Gilberstadt H, Sako Y: Intellectual and personality changes following open heart surgery. Arch Gen Psychiatry 16:210–214, 1967.

18. Kennedy JA, Bakst H: The influence of emotions on the outcome of cardiac surgery: A predictive study. NY Acad Med 42:811–845, 1966.

19. Cohen F, Lazarus RS: Active coping processes, coping dispositions and recovery from surgery. Psychosom Med 35:375–389, 1973.

20. Kilpatrick DG, Miller WC, Allain AN, et al: The use of psychological test data to predict open-heart surgery outcome: A prospective study. Psychosom Med 37:62–73, 1975.

21. Da Costa JC: The diagnosis of postoperative insanity. Surg Gynecol Obstet 11:577–584, 1910.

22. Titchener JL, Zwerling I, Gottschalk L, et al: Psychosis in surgical patients. Surg Gynecol Obstet 102:59–65, 1956.

23. Lazaras HR, Hagens JH: Prevention of psychosis following open heart surgery. Am J Psychiatry 124:1190–1195, 1968.

24. Knox SJ: Severe psychiatric disorders in postoperative period: Five year survey of Belfast Hospitals. J Ment Sci 107:1078, 1961.

25. Weisman AD, Hackett TP: Psychosis after eye surgery: Establishment of a specific doctor-patient relationship and treatment of "black patch" delirium. N Engl J Med 258:1284–1289, 1958.

26. Egerton N, Kay JH: Psychological disturbances associated with open heart surgery. Br J Psychiatry 110:433–439, 1964.

27. Kornfield DS, Zimberg S, Malm JR: Psychiatric complications of open heart surgery. N Engl J Med 273:287–292, 1965.

28. Blachly PH, Starr A: Postcardiotomy delirium. Am J Psychiatry 121:371–375, 1965.

29. Layne HR, Yudofsky SC: Postoperative psychosis in cardiotomy patients: The role of organic and psychiatric factors. N Engl J Med 284:518–520, 1971.

30. Fox JM, Rizzo NO, Clifford S: Psychological observations of patients undergoing mitral surgery. Psychosom Med 16:186–208, 1954.

31. Meyer E, Mendelson M: Psychiatric consultation with patients on medical and surgical wards: Patterns and processes. Psychiatry 24:197, 1961.

32. Sensenback W, Madison L, Eisenberg S: Cerebral hemodynamic and metabolic studies in patients with congestive heart failure: I. Observations in lucid subjects. Circulation 2:697–708, 1960.

33. Greenberg R, Pearlman C, Fingar R, et al: The effects of dream deprivation: Implications for a theory of the psychological function of dreaming. Br J Psychol 43:1, 1970.

34. Hackett TP, Cassom NH, Wishne HA: The coronary care unit: An appraisal of its psychological hazards. N Engl J Med 279:365–370, 1968.

35. Sos J, Cassem NH: Managing postoperative agitation. Drug Therapy, March, 1980, pp 103–106.

Death is a constant presence and threat. It occurs often in the SICU, and patients are bound to be aware of it, often despite the efforts of the staff to screen them from it. It figures in their fantasies despite denial either of its presence or of the intensity of its emotional impact.

TREATMENT

Neuroleptics, including phenothiazines, are effective against postoperative delirium. There is often a reluctance to use these potent agents because of potential hypotensive side-effects. In one study, however, the major hypotensive effect of phenothiazines in postoperative delirium was found to be minimal. Phenothiazines may be used safely in treatment of postoperative delirium if the initial dose of chlorpromazine does not exceed 25 mg given intramuscularly and if there is careful monitoring. If this dose is tolerated, additional doses may be used from five to six hours thereafter until abnormal behavior remits. The hypotensive effect does not seem to be dose related. Trifluoperazine hydrochloride is less sedating, may have a lesser hypotensive effect, and is suggested as a possible alternative treatment in doses of 2 mg, four times daily.

Haloperidol, a butyrophenone derivative, in tablets, 2 mg given two to four times a day, is an effective medication against psychosis, with a wide dose range of therapeutic efficacy and a minimal risk of hypotensive side-effects. Haloperidol has also been used, if the patient's agitation hinders treatment, as an intravenous injection, with a dose range of 1 to 30 mg. The usual rate of administration is 10 mg/minute, but it can be given faster. Tranquilization occurs usually after 10 minutes (35). Barbiturates, other sedatives, and benzodiazepines such as Valium should be avoided in the delirious patient, as they often aggravate the clinical condition.

Supportive psychological treatment in the SICU is often effective and less dangerous than drug treatment. Moreover, most symptoms remit without intervention after a relatively short period of time. There is often an insistence on the part of medical personnel to *control* the patient either by medication or physical restraint. Such mutual agitation usually has "feedback" characteristics. If there is calm in the face of the patient's delirium, and acceptance of such behavior without necessity for immediate control, staff members can quietly and firmly control such behavior, often without use of medication (and its side-effects), and usu-

ally without physical restraints. Calm on the part of the staff can be promoted by open discussion of the stresses induced by the aberrant behavior. The attitude of the nursing personnel toward such psychological issues has been important in our experience. The patient should not be placed in restraints unless absolutely necessary, and then only when a staff member can be close to him. Group discussions with the unit psychiatrist allows for ventilation, sharing, and understanding of staff feelings.

The question certainly can be raised in some cases as to whether factors within the environment are responsible for symptoms or their remission. With many patients a persuasive cause-effect relationship has been demonstrated.

For example, a request for a psychiatric consultation was made for a 56-year-old man with a postmyocardial infarct and described as "agitated, delirious, and combative." When first seen he was in bed in a single, windowless room, in physical restraints, struggling, and inappropriate in his responses. His room was next to the medication station where two nurses were talking. His door was ajar, and the room was half illuminated.

The psychiatric consultant spoke to the patient by name, removed the restraints, turned the room lights on to full illumination. The psychiatrist continued to talk with the patient loudly and clearly. The patient's responses became increasingly appropriate. Personnel were advised to be as definite with the patient as possible, to leave the room door either fully open or fully closed, and not to talk outside of his door. A calendar and clock were provided. The patient exhibited no further delirium.

CONCLUSIONS

Delirium, from a psychological perspective, is an overmagnification of the usual behavior/psychological maneuvers, with particular use of those defenses lowest on the adaptive hierarchy (denial, isolation, projection, and delusion). It then is both a last ditch defense and also a deterioration of defenses. (It is analogous on the behavioral level to the biological phenomenon of anaphylaxis.) The usual feeling of being in touch with reality and with one's own feelings depends both on intactness of internal regulatory mechanisms and external constancies embedded in the "average expectable environment." Internal controls emerge from (1) neurologically based perceptual mechanisms (innate and learned), (2) cognitive mechanisms, and (3) affectual controls derived from parental and societal training and reinforcement. These internal controls are known as ego functions. The average expectable environment is one of more or less usual stimulus input. There is continuous interaction between an individual's ego functions and the environment. Certain actions of the person are reinforced by the environment (and particularly by the people within it) other actions are tolerated, and still others are unacceptable. The physical environment "reinforces" or "condemns" acts (playing with fire often leads to pain), as does society. The individual affects his environment too, by changing it to his needs and accepting or rejecting aspects of it.

The adult patient in the SICU is in a state of more than usual dependence on his environment. He is forced both by illness and the passivity necessitated by treatment to abdicate the usual decision-making processes. This position of enforced passivity usually leads to relinquishing many of the adult psychological functions. With a normative internal state the person can recognize an environment as "strange." An aberrant event can be "put in place" as unique. With the regressive pull enforced by his extreme passivity and with physiological shifts altering perception and cognition, the patient often cannot distinguish an event as strange; he feels strange in the face of stimuli that are not immediately understandable. The environment also engenders fatigue and reduces sleeping and dreaming. (There is sometimes a dramatic termination of delirium after a long, restful sleep, somewhat like recovery from delirium tremens.[28]) It is also a strange, constricted milieu without the usual props to reality; cycles of the day are disturbed and the interaction with other people is unusual. In states of fatigue and with anxiety related to death and dying, induced both by a heightened state of internal vigilance and the strangeness of the environment, unexpected events will trip a massive psychological response in the direction of retreat from reality. Physiological shifts have altered the internal regulatory mechanism so that it can no longer perform the usual function of distinguishing external fact from internal fantasy. The external environment in the SICU does not contain the more usual expectable clues for reality testing, and madness may result.

This model can be of practical help in dealing with all patients in the SICU. A good assumption is that all patients have a potential for psychological problems (including delirium) as the internal and external factors for keeping reality in focus undergo change; such changes are a certainty for intensive care patients. Most of the patients in the SICU will have delusional states in varying degrees while on the unit. Personnel should attempt to keep the external environment unambiguous, and remain patient and human in the face of the patient's unavoidable shifts in internal controls. Calendars (with large type and pull-off pages) and clocks in clear view (perhaps with digital readings) are helpful. Most important is the staff's awareness of the terror the patient feels when disoriented. Such awareness may soften staff annoyance when the patient asks sequential redundant questions. Repetition is always necessary to establish and maintain contact. The sense of a benign environment is essential for the patient. Such attitudes and actions on the part of the staff operate to reduce and to limit delirious states. On occasion, when necessary, the internal state may be directly changed by use of psychoactive medication.

Nonproprietary Name and Trademarks of Drug

Chlorpromazine—*Chlor-PZ, Cromedazine, Promachel, Thorzine.*

REFERENCES

1. Muncie W: Postoperative states of excitement. Arch Neurol 32:681–703, 1934.
2. Engel GL, Romano J: Delirium: A syndrome of cerebral insufficiency. Chronic Dis 9:260–277, 1959.
3. Lipowski ZJ: Delirium: Clouding of consciousness and confusion. J Nerv Ment Dis 145:227–255, 1967.
4. Hackett TP, Weisman AD: Psychiatric management of operative syndromes: II. Psychodynamic factors in formulation and management. Psychosom Med 22:256–372, 1960.
5. Abram HS: Adaptation to open heart surgery: A psychiatric study of response to threat of death. Am J Psychiatry 122:659–667, 1965.
6. Hazan SJ: Psychiatric complications following cardiac surgery: I. A review article. J Thorac Cardiovasc Surg 51:307–318, 1966.
7. Blachly PH, Kloster FE: Relation of cardiac output to postcardiotomy delirium. J Thorac Cardiovasc Surg 52:422–427, 1966.
8. Blachly PH, Starr A: Treatment of delirium with phenothiazine drugs following open heart surgery. Dis Nerv Syst 27:107–110, 1966.
9. Heller SS, Frank KA, Malm JR, et al: Psychiatric complications of open heart surgery. N Engl J Med 283:1015–1019, 1970.
10. Altschule MD: Postoperative psychosis: A biochemical disorder. Med Counterpoint, 1969, pp 23–27.
11. McKegney FP: The intensive care syndrome: The definition, treatment and prevention of a new "dis-

rival. He refused medication and permitted a physical examination only after considerable persuasion. A left intracapsular cataract extraction was performed on the following day, and bilateral patches were applied. On the 1st postoperative day, believing that he was being experimented upon and confined against his will, he repeatedly removed the bandages and insisted on being sent home. He had to be heavily sedated and restrained. The psychiatric consultant found him to be thrashing about in bed, disoriented in time and place and shouting to be released. Communicating with him was a major problem because he spoke poor English. After he was moved to a private room and his family arrived, he became oriented and less agitated. However, he removed the bandages as soon as his arms were released.

From his wife it was learned that he enjoyed reminiscing about the time he had spent in the Italian army. Using her as interpreter, the psychiatrist encouraged him to recount this period of his life. His favorite story had to do with taking the mess wagon to the front lines. It infuriated him to think that everyone considered a mess sergeant's life to be soft and safe. Just the contrary was true, he asserted, because frequently he had to serve food during an artillery barrage. After this hazardous duty, he had always derived great pleasure from returning to camp and eating a huge meal with his favorite beverage, wine mixed with coffee. On the following day the therapist arrived for lunch bringing Italian sausage, bread and a bottle of wine. This impressed the wife, who quickly communicated her excitement to the patient. The wine and coffee were mixed, and during the course of the meal it was explained how we were actually trying to help him by keeping the bandages on his eyes and why he had to remain in the hospital. After he had finished eating, the wrist restraints were not applied. Throughout the remainder of his stay in the hospital, he continued to be cantankerous and obstinate, but his behavior no longer presented a serious threat to his recovery.

CASE 2. A 72-year-old woman with a bilateral retinal detachment was flown in from a distant city. Once on the ward, she was disoriented and confused and insisted on going home to prepare a meal for her family. Her husband was able to calm her and eventually succeeded in properly orienting her. He reported that during the previous year his wife had demonstrated progressive memory loss, increasing irritability and withdrawal. She was oriented and friendly when the psychiatrist arrived that evening but remained confused in that she could not believe she had come so far in such a short time. During the course of the examination, it was discovered that she came from a city close to where the psychiatrist was born. This was immediately revealed, and she was urged to talk about the changes that had taken place since the examiner had been there. She did this with animation and enthusiasm. Comparisons were made between Boston and her home town to impress upon her the fact of her present location. The details of the physical environment and of the operation were explained as well as the postoperative care.

On the following morning she was operated upon, and was seen again that afternoon by the psychiatrist. Although he continued to encourage her to talk about his native city, he took every opportunity to remind her where she was and what had happened. On the 1st postoperative day she suddenly became restless and again insisted on getting out of bed and going home to prepare a meal for some guests. The presence of her husband seemed to support her belief that she was in her own home. When the psychiatrist arrived and identified himself, she seemed confused for a moment but then remembered who he was and allowed herself to be conducted back to bed. After a brief conversation in which the previous comparisons between Boston and her city were recalled, she regained orientation and appeared much more relaxed. During the next few days she was constantly attended by some member of her family. Nevertheless, she had recurrent confusion during convalescence. These episodes were always dispelled by reminders of the doctor's identity and this, in turn, established her spatial orientation.

CASE 3. An 86-year-old woman with acute glaucoma was admitted to the hospital for bilateral iridectomy. The examining physician found her to be disoriented in time and place, unco-operative and hostile. She refused to enter the hospital unless her husband could room in. Even after this was arranged, she would not allow her eyes to be medicated and stubbornly resisted all attempts to help her. The consulting psychiatrist discovered a thin, wiry but healthy-appearing woman who looked younger than her age. She had been totally unprepared for the sudden admission and was both confused and angry. For months she had denied failing vision and had come to the clinic only at the urging of her husband, who had noticed that she could no longer get around the house without bumping into furniture. This was the 1st time she had ever been a hospital patient, a fact that made the situation even more frightening for her. Through the 1st interview she constantly threatened to sign out but seemed, in spite of this, to become calmer after repeated explanations had been given.

It was found that she was an avid horticulturist who stated that she had one of the neatest gardens in her city. Furthermore, she took pride in being what she called a "stubborn Yankee from Nantucket." A few hours after the initial interview, the therapist returned with a small bouquet of carnations. Although unable to see, she identified them by the fragrance. Because she was afraid of being alone, her husband was included in the ensuing conversation. This consisted of a general discussion about gardening as well as an explanation about the surgical procedure that was going to take place. By this time, she was completely oriented and far more co-operative. The thought of having both eyes covered frightened her, whereupon it was suggested that her "Yankee strength of will" would see her through. On the following day, she was operated upon, and the psychiatrist visited her that afternoon with another bouquet of carnations. After smelling the flowers she addressed the doctor by name and expressed satisfaction that the operation had gone well. She was oriented, not confused, and offered no problem to the nurses. Over the next 2 days she was seen 4 times, with conversations along the original lines, interspersed with explanations about why the medicines had been changed and what was happening around her. At 1 point, when she complained bitterly about the patches, her "Yankee strength of will" was reemphasized. The postoperative course was uneventful.

CASE 4. A 70-year-old laundryman was admitted to the hospital for corrective surgery because of a corneal ulceration. Seven years previously, a squamous-cell carcinoma had been removed from the right eyelid. In the intervening years, several other operations were performed for contracted scars. Since the most recent procedure he had been confused and disoriented.

He was apathetic and retarded. His attitude was one of profound hopelessness. In the 3 years since the death of his wife his depression had deepened, and his isolation increased. He withdrew from his usual habits and lived alone. There were several periods of agitation and confusion in which he lost track of time and restlessly paced the floor for hours.

He could not realize that the ulcer threatened his vision. Despite all explanation, he maintained that cosmetic surgery was pointless in a man his age. With considerable difficulty, he was encouraged into giving an account of his life. From this, the doctor discovered 2 significant topics, which he used therapeutically. After being a confirmed alcoholic for over 20 years, the patient, without assistance, had been able to stop drinking. Also, by initiative and enterprise, he had founded a successful laundry business. He was praised for both these accomplishments. A special point was emphasized about resisting alcohol, in that it had been an exceptional achievement for a man to cure himself, on his own. The patient was both surprised and pleased. At this point, the doctor reviewed the course of the eye disease and again emphasized the patient's capacity for perseverance despite physical hardships and personal loss. In the 4 interviews before operation a standard technic was used: ego support, encouragement, praise for past accomplishments and repeated explanations that the aim of surgery was to preserve vision rather than to improve appearance.

After the operation, it was arranged to have a member of the family present both day and night. The psychiatrist visited the patient twice daily. For the first 2 days he remained oriented, co-operative and reasonably cheerful. On the 3rd day he became agitated and restless. Despite protests by his daughter and the nurse, he left his bed and paced the ward, loudly demanding immediate removal of the bandages. When the doctor arrived he agreed to return to bed. The patient was then reminded of a previous conversation in which the present action had been anticipated and discussed. Again the doctor stressed the fact that anyone who had had the courage and stamina to give up whiskey could hold on another

day in the present discomfort. The reasons why it was necessary were repeated, and he was praised for having held on so long. During the course of this talk he visibly relaxed and agreed to keep trying. On the following day the patch was removed from the intact eye, and the remainder of the hospital course was uneventful.

CASE 5. An 80-year-old widow was admitted to the hospital for an intracapsular-cataract extraction. After a similar operation some years previously, she had had an episode of delirium. At that time, she had been a severe management problem, with both visual and auditory hallucinations, paranoia and hyperactivity that had to be controlled by heavy sedation.

The patient was a thin, fragile woman who was more apprehensive about becoming delirious than she was about the operation. She remembered the previous delirium as being a time when she "misbehaved" and described it as "living in a nightmare." It was explained that we hoped to prevent a recurrence and that there was every likelihood we would succeed. It then became apparent that she looked upon her past postoperative behavior as evidence that she was becoming senile. At this point she was complimented on her vigor and alertness and was told that the chance of senility seemed remote. Since the operation was scheduled for the following morning, the psychiatrist returned that evening to have tea with the patient. In his search for a topic of common interest, he found that her father had been born in Ireland, as had the therapist's. The conversation was shifted into this area with active participation on the part of the doctor. When she again expressed concern about becoming senile, he explained that senility was a disease and not just the process of aging. Furthermore, it was pointed out that postoperative delirium occurred in very young people also. She was complimented on her ability to tell stories about the old country in terms of her good memory, facility with words and mimicry, all of which made senility seem very unlikely as a future prospect. She was told that we would stand by her through the ordeal of patching and at the 1st sign of uneasiness, day or night, we could be reached and would see her through. Masks were applied after the operation on the next morning. Over the course of 36 hours she was seen twice a day and presented no sign of confusion or disorientation. The therapist initiated each conversation with some remark about Ireland and, as well as reassuring her, described in detail what was happening on the ward. Throughout the 10-day postoperative course, there was no evidence of delirium.

CASE 6. A 57-year-old Cuban businessman with bilateral retinal separation became confused during the 1st hospital night. He suddenly awoke from a dream in which he was aboard a ship in Boston harbor. Thinking that he was still in his cabin and was late in disembarking, he began making frantic efforts to clothe himself. After being discovered by a nurse, he was persuaded back into bed, where he spent a sleepless night. During the next morning he was seen by the psychiatrist, who

PSYCHOSIS AFTER EYE SURGERY:
ESTABLISHMENT OF A SPECIFIC DOCTOR-PATIENT RELATION IN THE PREVENTION AND TREATMENT OF "BLACK-PATCH DELIRIUM"

AVERY D. WEISMAN AND THOMAS P. HACKETT

Few physicians would dispute the importance of the doctor-patient relation in facilitating recovery from an illness. Although the factors involved in this relation in psychiatry apply equally to patients with medical and surgical disorders, only rarely have internists or surgeons made conscious efforts to establish an appropriate therapeutic relation in advance. Instead, the absence of precise knowledge has led to vague recommendations for "good," "supporting" or "friendly" relations without specific instructions how this may be accomplished. Often, it is after the fact that the doctor decides that his relation has been appropriate and therapeutically advantageous.

Certain eye patients who enter a strange environment to undergo an anxiety-producing, damaging operation with temporary loss of vision may have postoperative delirium. Linn and his colleagues[1] report some form of delirium in 95 per cent of their patients, and a severe disturbance in 65 per cent. The occurrence of psychotic disturbances with bilateral masking indicates that ego functions and reality testing are impaired in these patients. The term "reality testing" refers to the ego functions that describe and evaluate the context of various levels of experience. The processes that integrate perceptual schemata, conceptual fields, symbolic forms and logical systems provide an intellectual basis for the corroboration of different kinds of experience, ranging from the perception of everyday objects to the validation of logical hypotheses.[2] This paper proposes that a specific doctor-patient relation that selectively fortifies the ego functions and supplements reality testing may help to relieve and prevent postoperative delirium in patients with bilateral bandaging.

Although the term "cataract delirium" has been generally used to describe these reactions, the cataract is much less important than the masking since the condition may occur in any patient when bilateral bandages are employed. The term black-patch delirium recognizes this fact and is a descriptive diagnosis sometimes used by ophthalmologists even though it has not, to our knowledge, been mentioned in the literature.

The clinical picture of black-patch delirium resembles other forms of postoperative delirium except that the precipitating factor is the total deprivation of vision. Disorientation in time and place, restlessness, suspiciousness, hyperactivity, anxiety and irritability are its most common features. However, mania, delusions, auditory and visual hallucinations, hypochondriacal complaints and paranoid ideas often replace the milder manifestations. Suicidal attempts have been reported, and, in senile patients, the delirium sometimes persists for days and weeks after the patches have been removed. Although most frequently beginning on the evening of the second postoperative day, the delirium may occur as soon as the patient returns from the operating room, or as long as a week after the bandages have been applied.[3] Despite the fact that both eyes are covered, the delirium is apt to be

EDITORS' COMMENTS:

THIS ARTICLE WAS WRITTEN BEFORE NEUROLEPTICS WERE READILY USED IN A MEDICAL SETTING. THE AUTHORS FOCUS ON THE IMPORTANCE OF INTERPERSONAL RELATIONSHIPS IN THE PATIENT WHO IS AT RISK FOR DELIRIUM. CLINICAL EXAMPLES ELUCIDATE METHODS FOR BOLSTERING PATIENTS' DIMINISHED CAPACITY FOR PROCESSING CONFUSING, PAINFUL, AND UNFAMILIAR ENVIRONMENTAL STIMULI.

Reprinted with permission from The New England Journal of Medicine, Vol. 258, pages 1284–1289, June 26, 1958.

most severe at night. This is the time when a hush falls on the ward, and auditory cues, which may have been responsible for alerting and orienting the patient during the day, are replaced by silence, with an occasional whispered conversation and the soft, sporadic sounds of the night. Under these circumstances, somewhat analogous to sensory deprivation,[4] misinterpretations may become delusions and anxiety may become panic. If no one is present to speak with the patient, his impaired reality testing does not prevent the confusion, disorientation and anxiety from developing into delirium.

Delirium may be considered an adaptation of a vulnerable patient to severe psychic stress. A typical pattern of adaptive activity consists of denial of illness. For example, the patient may attempt to remove the bandages and to leave his bed. Some patients often claim that nothing is wrong with them and that they are being restrained against their will and are being experimented upon. Fortunately, despite violent protests, physical and verbal, patients rarely damage the operated eye,[5] as if they want only to recover their visual cues, rather than to impair their sight. Another common form of denial is the delusion of being in the familiar surroundings of home or work. The disorientation in time, as in other forms of delirium, refers to a period when the patient was functioning effectively.[6] Symptoms of displacement may also develop. Instead of complaining of eye pain or blindness, the patient becomes preoccupied with constipation, back pain or headache, which he insists are the reasons for being in the hospital and which must be taken care of immediately.

As with other postoperative forms of delirium, the elderly patient is more susceptible than the young. A history of alcoholism has been thought to be an important factor, especially in the earlier literature.[7] Foreign patients who have a limited command of English are more likely than the native born to isolate themselves[8] and to misinterpret perceptions because their reality testing on a verbal level is impaired. Some authors, who believe that the premorbid personality is a significant factor, claim that the more "suspicious and childish" patients are more apt to become delirious after surgery.[6] All these conditions were present in our cases.

Various methods of treatment for delirium have been recommended, most of which are based on the use of sedatives. However, the use of sedatives or tranquilizers alone has been unsatisfactory unless they are administered in hypnotic doses. Moreover, these drugs interfere with higher-level reality testing and may increase the delirium. Without doubt, one of the most effective means of relieving delirium is simply to remove the bandage from the unoperated eye.[9] This improves both the patient's perception and his capacity to test reality. Often, however, the unoperated eye has diminished vision or is involved in the same pathologic process for which the patching was originally applied. Although investigators concur that psychologic factors must also be regulated, the manner in which this may be systematically achieved has not been described. Some physicians stress the necessity of having "sympathetic" nurses in constant attendance during the early postoperative course; others advise that the family should care for the patient during the period of bilateral patching. Both these suggestions are important but are often not sufficient, as our cases show. Experienced ophthalmologists have observed that private patients are less likely than ward patients to have black-patch delirium. Possibly, this is a function of the more personal doctor-patient relation that is cultivated in private practice. In the early literature, there are reports of surgeons who performed cataract extractions in the home,[10] followed by frequent postoperative visits. Without benefit of statistics, the frequency of delirium is said to have decreased under these circumstances. What this information demonstrates is that, to compensate for a patient's impaired ability to test reality, a reliable, personal relation must be established. This may be obtained through the physical presence of the family, through familiarity of the surroundings or through the constant attention of a physician whose identity has been firmly defined.

CASE MATERIAL

The present series consists of 6 patients, 3 men and 3 women, ranging in age from fifty-seven to eighty-six years, who entered the hospital for various kinds of eye surgery involving bilateral patching. Because they were considered likely to have postoperative delirium, a psychiatric consultation was requested. Three patients were confused, disoriented and uncooperative at the time of admission. Two patients had a previous history of postoperative delirium, and 1 had a chronic dissociative reaction consisting of somnambulism and pavor nocturnus.

CASE 1. A 78-year-old Italian workman was admitted to the hospital for treatment of bilateral cataracts. Although oriented, he was unco-operative from the moment of ar-

2. Weisman, A. D. Reality sense and reality testing. Behavioral Sc. (in press).

3. Boyd, D. A., Jr., and Morris, M. A. Delirium associated with cataract extraction. J. Indiana M. A. 34:130–135, 1941.

4. Solomon, P., Leiderman, P. H., Mendelson, J., and Wexler, D. Sensory deprivation: review. Am. J. Psychiat. 114:357–363, 1957.

5. Thomas, F. C. Delirium following cataract operations. Kentucky M. J. 24:134–143, 1926.

6. Coles, R. S., and Linn, L. Behavior disturbances related to cataract extraction. Eye, Ear, Nose & Throat Monthly 35:111–113, 1956.

7. Brownell, M. E. Cataract delirium. J. Michigan M. Soc. 16:282, 1917.

8. Cobb, S., and McDermott, N. T. Postoperative psychoses. M. Clin. North America 22:569–576, 1938.

9. Greenwood, A. Mental disturbances following operations for cataract. J.A.M.A. 91:1713–1716, 1928.

10. Bailey, F. W. Cataract operations performed upon patients in their own beds. J. Iowa M. Soc. 18:8–10, 1928.

11. Weisman, A. D. Doctor-patient relationship: its role in therapy. Am. Pract. & Digest. Treat. 1:1144–1151, 1950.

12. Kinross-Wright, V. Chlorpromazine in psychiatric disorders. M. Clin. North America 41:295–306, 1957.

found him to be an affable and intelligent person with a history of somnambulism and nightmares going back into early childhood. Since these usually occurred during times of stress, the patient was concerned lest they appear after the operation, with resulting damage to his eyes. Sedation of any kind seemed only to aggravate the condition. Although it had been arranged for his wife to remain in his room, this added little comfort because her presence had not previously prevented the nightmares and sleepwalking. The patient believed that sleepwalking was based on a serious mental disease. Since this was not borne out in the examination, he was reassured and encouraged to talk about his vivid dreams. They were actually unique productions, many of them having the quality of better-class English motion-picture thrillers. The therapist treated them as creative productions rather than ominous signs of a mental disorder and suggested that they would make good material for scripts. In short, they were made light of, and their deeper connotations totally ignored. The patient was delighted. Throughout the rest of the hospital course, which included two eye operations with patching, he did not walk in his sleep and no longer dreamed.

DISCUSSION

The effect of what is called therapy in medicine is frequently due as much to the personal transactions between doctor and patient as to the specific treatments.[11] Some of the factors in the doctor-patient relation arise from the patient; others come from the doctor. Along with his illness and a variety of personal and medical needs, the patient brings to the relation the entire range of his past experience and emotional conflicts. The physician, because of his unique background and personal qualities, as well as his social manner and method of expression, also contributes to the relation. The interaction of all these factors determines the quality of the doctor-patient relation.

The purpose of the conventional type of psychotherapeutic relation is to create an atmosphere in which the patient's conflicts may be objectively evaluated. The psychiatrist is, for this reason, an interested but detached observer who keeps his personal involvement at a minimum. Aside from a careful display of interest and inquiry, he usually follows the patient's lead in discussing various topics that will clarify conflicts.

In this study, the goal of therapy was not the relief of psychiatric symptoms by the systematic investigation of conflict but the prevention and treatment of delirium by correction of faulty reality testing.[2] This was brought about in three ways. A specific type of doctor-patient relation, in which the therapist could be accepted as an ally in mastering the stress of the operation and of the mask-

ing, was fostered. He supplemented the patient's impaired vision by providing auditory, gustatory, tactile and olfactory perceptual cues. By repeated explanations, encouragement and description, he also supplied a conceptual framework to accompany the accessory perceptual reorientation. Finally, the doctor supported the functions of reality testing by concentrating on an area of the patient's life in which the ego had operated at maximum efficiency.

All the patients were recognized as being vulnerable to psychic stress, and in several, in fact, psychotic symptoms had already developed at the time of the first psychiatric interview. At this initial stage, the doctor made every effort to identify himself as a distinct personality. He explained the unfamiliar procedures to the apprehensive patient, and emphasized the necessity of bilateral masking. Because the patient was confused, these explanations frequently had to be repeated. When the patient could not see, the doctor punctiliously described the physical surroundings. In this way, the patient became familiar with the hospital environment, and was provided with a frame of reference for all perceptions.

After the first contact, the psychiatrist then attempted to discover, as quickly as possible, an area of mutual interest that he could share with the patient. He was interested in finding a period in the patient's life when he had functioned effectively. In some patients, the sphere of efficient function concerned a hobby; in others, it consisted merely of pleasant recollections of early life, and in still others, it was a period of stress that had been overcome. Thus, the doctor discussed gardening with one patient, army life with another, the familiar surroundings of her native state with a third, and the conquest of alcoholism with a fourth. Whenever possible, the doctor did not hesitate to introduce pertinent observations of his own that served to clarify and substantiate the patient's sometimes hesitant remarks.

These shared interests cannot, of course, be discovered in advance, since few patients will spontaneously participate in the search. Consequently, during the interviews, the doctor displayed enthusiasm, persistence and often considerable ingenuity in seeking out the significant areas. The specific topic was unimportant, except as it recalled past activities in which the patient had functioned well. By the deliberate recollection of accomplishments, the patient was assisted in appraising the helpless, threatening confusion of the present in terms of a happy or successful past. Through sharing the patient's interest, the physician was no longer a stranger. When attention faltered or delirious symptoms recurred, he actively reminded the patient of their previous discussions of former achievements, interests or successes. Disorientation was often corrected merely by reference to familiar emotional and conceptual landmarks. The therapy was based on the hypothesis that if the doctor became an active collaborator in recapturing the period when reality evaluation was at an optimum, the patient might also be able to reorient himself with respect to the damaged perceptions, misinterpretations, uncertainty and fear associated with the current illness.

Loss of vision, temporary or permanent, actual or threatened, may evoke delirium by depriving a precariously adjusted patient of an important source of reality testing. In some patients delirium may develop by mere application of eye patches, independent of the operation. As Linn and his associates[1] reported, removal of the masks may not relieve the delirium or restore adequate reality testing in certain patients. Such observations indicate that reality testing depends on the integrity of several levels of mental function. Although perceptual cues are essential, this is not enough. It is necessary that perceptions be organized on an intact conceptual framework, and that the various symbolic forms by which the patient recognizes his world and communicates with his fellow man be accessible.[2] By realizing the range of reality testing, the doctor tried to "speak the patient's language" on every level.

Another method of fortifying the patient's reality testing consisted of providing supplementary perceptual cues through other sensory channels. Mere talk often supplied enough auditory substitutes for the visual lack. In Case 1, the doctor, by sharing spicy Italian food with the patient, substituted familiar gustatory perceptions for the neutral taste of hospital food. With Case 2 the physician provided a means of spatial reorientation on a conceptual level by speaking to the patient of her home town, with which he was familiar. Olfactory perceptions in the form of daily bouquets were helpful to Case 3, an elderly woman who had taken pride in her flower garden. In 2 other patients, reality testing was fortified at the higher level of symbolic forms, abstract thought and reasoning. Case 5 was afraid of the insidious effect of old age. She believed that a previous episode of delirium was proof that she was becoming senile. The doctor, recognizing her fear of illness, assured her that old age did not necessarily entail senility. He then admired her ability to recount amusing recollections of an Irish girlhood, thereby reinterpreting the current experience in conceptual terms that she could

understand. Case 6 was afraid that a psychosis would develop because of his chronic nightmares and his intense anxiety in facing the operation. The doctor reinterpreted the significance of the nightmares, dismissing them lightly and indicating that their content reminded him of colorful motion-picture scripts. Because this patient had traveled widely, the doctor asserted that it was rich material of his life rather than mental impairment that accounted for the vivid dreams. The information was thus integrated into a more acceptable conceptual structure. In neither Case 5 nor Case 6 did delirium develop. Apart from his eye disorder, Case 4 was suffering from a moderately severe depression. He was afraid of the delirium of which he already had some forewarning. By his constant reassuring presence, the psychiatrist himself was an orienting focus for reality testing, and on several occasions he was able to correct misinterpretations in the process of developing.

These observations are by no means original. Similar methods have been used for many years in the management of cataract delirium in patients with bilateral patches. It has long been recognized that a friendly nursing staff, the presence of the family and the understanding support of the doctor will forestall delirium. With these patients, however, the therapeutic relation was not based on empirical generalities but on psychodynamic principles of ego function and reality testing. In this way, the various factors that comprise the doctor-patient relation were selectively controlled. Recent workers have reported the value of drugs in treating acute toxic psychoses.[12] The use or omission of drugs in this series neither prevented nor relieved the delirium. Drugs may calm the hyperactive patient, but, because reality testing is not corrected, the course of the delirium is unchanged.

CONCLUSIONS

Black-patch delirium occurs most frequently in patients who are particularly predisposed to impaired reality testing. It is a faulty adaptation to the psychic stress of visual deprivation and loss of familiar perceptual and conceptual cues. A specific type of doctor-patient relation may be used to compensate for the deficit in reality testing and thus to relieve or prevent the delirium.

REFERENCES

1. Linn, L., et al. Patterns of behavior disturbance following cataract extraction. Am. J. Psychiat. 110:281–289, 1953.

likely to complain of somatic or affectual discomforts that point to other diagnoses. Even patients with moderately advanced disease may conceal their dysfunction quite skillfully by using well-preserved social skills. Often, only family members or close friends can provide the physician with the correct perspective, and they are not always consulted when complaints strongly suggest a systemic or affectual disorder. Unless the physician asks for tbe specific information required in a thorough mental status examination, the diagnosis can easily be missed until a crisis arises (25).

Diagnosing dementia when it is *not* present arises from another source. The patient who appears demented and is not, i.e., has pseudodementia (26–28), will surely be asked questions appropriate to investigate the possibility of organic brain disease, and answers usually are consistent with such a diagnosis. These diagnostic errors arise because the physician fails to heed the patient's behavior sufficiently; the behavior usually suggests a level of brain function incompatible with the severity of dysfunction revealed by mental status evaluation. Another source of error in these situations is unwarranted reliance on ancillary diagnostic procedures, especially psychological testing (29) and computerized cranial tomography (CT scan) (30). Dementia remains a clinical syndrome that must be established by clinical evaluation.

Etiology of Chronic Brain Syndromes

Most physicians in the past manifested little enthusiasm for the exacting process necessary to identify the specific disorders underlying the chronic brain syndromes. It has been assumed that most chronic dementing disorders, especially those in the elderly, are due to arteriosclerotic cerebrovascular disease, and most patients are almost automatically assigned this diagnosis. Further, precise diagnosis is often regarded as an unprofitable exercise that is unlikely to lead to fruitful therapeutic intervention, and the prognosis in these disorders has been considered uniformly poor. These assumptions should be examined.

Vascular disease. Do the facts support the assumption that most chronic brain disease results from arteriosclerotic cerebrovascular disorders? Although evidence to the contrary is not absolutely incontrovertible, there are significant data questioning the assumption from both clinical and pathological sources.

The most telling evidence is from the careful clinicopathological studies of Tomlinson and associates (31). In a study of 50 successive demented elderly patients coming to autopsy, they found that Alzheimer's disease accounted for 50% of the cases, contributed equally with infarction in 8%, and possibly played some role in 10%. Cerebral changes due to arteriosclerosis, on the other hand, accounted definitely for only 12%, probably for an additional 6%, contributed equally with Alzheimer's disease in 8%, and possibly played some role in 10%. Thus in this study, which is the finest available, degenerative diseases played a far more important role in the genesis of dementia than did vascular disease. This finding has been corroborated in three recent clinical studies (22, 32, 33) of patients presenting symptoms and signs of dementia (see table 1). In only 8% of these patients was vascular disease identified as the cause of dementia; 51% were diagnosed as having atrophy of unknown causes, almost certainly presenile or senile Alzheimer's disease in most cases.

It is unjustified to assume that most dementia in the elderly results from vascular disease. Although the mental status evaluation cannot differentiate chronic brain disease due to multiple cerebral softenings from that due to the degenerative disorders, there is a significant body of evidence suggesting that other clinical features can lead to accurate differentiation. Based on his extensive experience with cerebrovascular disease, Fisher (34) said that dementia due to cerebral infarction is usually manifested by abrupt onset, stuttering course, and symptoms and signs of focal neurological dysfunction. According to Fisher, slowly progressive dementia (in the absence of acute episodes and focal neurological signs and symptoms) rarely results from cerebrovascular disease, except in the patient with prolonged, sustained hyperten-

TABLE 1. Summary of Diagnoses in Three Reported Series of 222 Patients Fully Evaluated for Dementia*

Diagnosis	Number	Percent
Atrophy of unknown cause	113	51
Vascular disease	17	8
Normal pressure hydrocephalus	14	6
Dementia in alcoholics	13	6
Intracranial masses	12	5
Huntington's chorea	10	5
Depression	9	4
Drug toxicity	7	3
Dementia (uncertain)	7	3
Other**	20	9

*See references 22, 32, and 33.
**Other diagnoses, each seen in 1% or less of the 222 patients, were as follows: Creutzfeldt-Jakob disease, posttraumatic, thyroid disease, postencephalitic, psychiatric disease, neurosyphilis, amyotrophic lateral sclerosis, postsubarachnoid hemorrhage, Parkinson's disease, pernicious anemia, liver failure, and epilepsy.

sion. Paulson and Perrine (35) observed that vascular disease could be demonstrated only in rare cases as the cause of "chronic brain syndromes" diagnosed in patients chronically hospitalized in public institutions. In a clinicopathologic correlation, Birkett (36) demonstrated that although psychological features could not differentiate multi-infarct dementia from that due to degenerative processes, a sudden onset plus focal neurological symptoms or signs strongly indicated cerebrovascular disease.

Hachinski and coworkers (37) devised an ischemia score that they used clinically to differentiate "primary degenerative dementia" from "multi-infarct dementia." Patients were given two points for each of the following features: abrupt onset, fluctuating course, history of strokes, focal neurological symptoms, and focal neurological signs; and one point for each of the following: stepwise deterioration, nocturnal confusion, relative preservation of personality, depression, somatic complaints, emotional incontinence, history of hypertension, and evidence of associated atherosclerosis. Applying this score to their small group of patients, they found two distinct groups: those with scores more than seven having multi-infarct dementia and those with less than seven having primary degenerative dementia. Use of this score merits further clinical evaluation.

Because the pattern of clinical dysfunction seen in cerebrovascular disease with secondary dementia can usually be distinguished readily from that of Alzheimer's disease and other degenerative processes, there is no longer any justification for indiscriminately ascribing most dementias to vascular disease.

The value of accurate diagnosis. It is inaccurate to assume that exact clinical diagnosis in the chronic brain syndromes is unprofitable in terms of the lack of potentially beneficial treatment for the disorders so identified. As is noted in table 1 a definite disease diagnosis was reached in approximately half of the cases reported in three studies of patients with a primary diagnosis of dementia (22, 32, 33), and a diagnosis of Alzheimer's disease could have been justified in most of those identified as "atrophy of unknown cause." More important, diligent investigation uncovered numerous disorders that required medical treatment. Potentially correctable disorders requiring definitive treatment included depression, drug toxicity, normal pressure hydrocephalus, benign intracranial masses, mania, thyroid disease, pernicious anemia, epilepsy, and hepatic failure. Such diagnoses were found in 15% of the 222 patients. Non-correctable disorders requiring intervention, found in 20%–25% of these patients, included multi-infarct dementia with hypertension, malignant brain tumors, alcoholism, normal pressure hydrocephalus, neurosyphilis, and Huntington's chorea.

Even when treatment cannot reverse the pathologic process entirely, treatment of hypertension, palliative treatment for malignant brain tumors or normal pressure hydrocephalus, withdrawal from alcohol, arrest of neurosyphilis, and genetic counseling for families with Huntington's chorea are important. In summary, thorough diagnostic evaluation can be expected to identify disorders with specific therapeutic implications in 30%–50% of patients thought to be demented. The search for etiology in dementia can no longer be regarded as a luxury.

Appropriate Diagnostic Evaluation

What constitutes an adequate medical evaluation for patients suspected of having chronic brain disease? No answer is applicable to all patients. The questions that the physician is seeking to answer through the evaluation are, however, applicable to all patients. Is the patient's dysfunction due to organic brain disease? If so, does the dysfunction result from a disorder involving a limited (focal) segment of the brain or involving the brain tissue diffusely? What is the nature of the disease process involving the brain tissue? In general, the physician seeks to answer these questions sequentially. Even when the last question cannot be answered with certainty, the physician must be sure that the chronic brain dysfunction is not due to easily recognizable treatable diseases. The psychiatrist should both ask and seek to answer these questions for patients who are referred for psychiatric evaluation and treatment. Certainly, a neurologist may be consulted, but generally I believe this should be done only when the psychiatrist is unable to answer these questions satisfactorily after making sophisticated use of the diagnostic tools available. I think the psychiatrist should be the specialist best trained to meld the organic and the functional aspects of the patient's problems and that he or she should grasp this responsibility.

The tools at the physician's disposal are the history, clinical observations (i.e., medical and neurologic examinations, mental status examination, psychiatric interview), and ancillary diagnostic procedures. The application of the history and clinical observations to the diagnostic process is dealt with in detail elsewhere (38). Here I shall

CHRONIC BRAIN DISEASE:
AN OVERVIEW

CHARLES E. WELLS

The author discusses the current state of clinical and pathological knowledge regarding chronic brain disease, focusing particularly on the dementias. His review of clinical studies deals with diagnostic issues and methods, etiology, and treatment. More basic research on brain alterations with aging, their relation to clinical manifestations of dementia, and studies of specific disorders are also reviewed. These disorders have been receiving increasing attention from psychiatrists, who are becoming more aware of the importance of organic cerebral factors in their patients' complaints. The need to understand the chronic brain diseases and their appropriate diagnosis and treatment will continue to grow as the proportion of older individuals in our society increases.

Concern for patients with chronic brain disease has grown among psychiatrists and other physicians in recent years, in part because these disorders have increased in absolute number in our society, which has a steadily increasing population of individuals over 65. Katzman and Karasu (1) estimated, for example, that the senile form of Alzheimer's disease now ranks as the fourth or fifth most common cause of death in the United States. These disorders are also diseases of medical progress. Sweet and associates (2) reported the development of dementia in one-third of patients with Parkinson's disease who were followed for 6 years during treatment with L-dopa. The authors suggested that this reflected "prolongation of the course of the illness" by treatment, which allowed emergence of the dementia.

Another reason for this growing interest in chronic cerebral disease is that psychiatrists have become more sensitively attuned to the importance of organic cerebral factors in the genesis of many of their patients' complaints. This changed perspective has resulted in several books (3–9) that deal (depending on the professional identity of the authors) with behavioral neurology or with organic psychiatry. A prominent neurologist, N. Geschwind, was recently quoted in a national publication (10) as estimating that perhaps 40% of chronically hospitalized psychiatric patients suffer primarily from unrecognized "physical" brain disorders. Whether or not this unsubstantiated guess is accurate, psychiatrists must develop expertise in the recognition and treatment of organic brain disorders. They must also be able to answer questions about the likelihood of physical disorders playing a significant role in a patient's symptoms.

Another aspect of this topic that deserves mention, even if only in passing, is the importance of the organic integrity of the brain for successful human adaptation. A corollary to this is the importance of organic integrity of the brain in the psychiatric treatment of patients with problems in adaptation. Even mild or barely perceptible organic brain disease may lead to impairment in a person's ability to learn, work, or achieve satisfying social relationships, as is evidenced by several recent reports on minimal brain damage in adults

Reprinted from the American Journal of Psychiatry 135:1–12, 1978. Copyright 1978, the American Psychiatric Association. Reprinted by permission.

(11–15). Furthermore, most common and accepted modes of psychiatric treatment, from psychoanalysis to pharmacotherapy, generally presuppose (implicitly if not explicitly) organic intactness of the cerebral structures.

I shall not attempt to cover herein all the varieties of organic brain disorders encountered in a population of psychiatric patients. This overview will be limited to the current state of clinical and pathological knowledge about those chronic brain diseases generally regarded as degenerative and primarily affecting diffusely and symmetrically the cerebral hemispheres, i.e., the dementias. In the first section I shall deal largely with clinical studies; in the second, with more basic investigations.

CLINICAL STUDIES

Recognition of Organic Disease

The description of the organic brain syndromes provided in *DSM-II* (16) is clear and straightforward, giving the impression that their recognition and diagnosis might be equally so. These disorders are described as being manifested by impairment in orientation, memory, intellectual functions, and judgment, and by lability and shallowness of affect. Although these symptoms are indeed classic for moderately advanced dementing diseases, they may be far from evident when the disorder is mild and in its early stages. Thus, they may not be recognized at a stage when treatment could be most effective. On the other hand, not every patient with this classic pentad of symptoms has dementia, and clinical experience suggests that pseudodementias are not uncommon. What evidence do we have that diagnostic errors occur with significant frequency?

I have found no reliable figures indicating how often physicians fail to recognize and diagnose organic brain disorders when they are present. Large-scale population studies fail to provide this information, since they deal with many persons who have no contact with medical services. In a survey of 200 patients over 65 years of age who were on the lists of three Edinburgh general practitioners, Williamson and associates (17) identified 55 patients with some degree of dementia, only 7 of whom were known by their practitioners to be demented. However, not all of these listed patients made regular visits to their physicians, so that no exact data were provided as to how often the physician failed to recognize an identifiable dementia. Despite ample anecdotal evidence of psychiatrists and other physicians overlooking intracranial disease (18), accurate information on the frequency of such missed diagnoses is lacking. Anecdotal descriptions often highlight rarities.

There is, on the other hand, reliable evidence to demonstrate that dementia is overdiagnosed, i.e., functional disorders are misdiagnosed as organic, especially in the elderly. In a study comparing psychiatric diagnoses given to patients over 65 in three cities, Duckworth and Ross (19) found that organic brain disorders were diagnosed with more than 50% greater frequency in New York than in either Toronto or London. Although variations in patient populations might account for some of the difference, it is more likely that the figures indicate that in New York elderly patients with affective disorders were labeled as demented, whereas in Great Britain, where Roth (20) and his group have emphasized the importance of recognizing functional disorders in the aged, patients with affective disorders were more likely to be labeled correctly.

Nott and Fleminger (21) reported on a followup of 35 patients diagnosed as having presenile dementia at Guy's Hospital in London. The initial diagnosis was confirmed by progressive deterioration in only 15 (43%). In a study of 106 consecutive patients (all screened by a consultant psychiatrist, neurologist, or both before admission) hospitalized for thorough neurological investigation of the cause of their dementia (22), the diagnosis of dementia could not be corroborated in 19 (18%). Specific functional disorders (largely depression) were identified in 10 patients. In a follow-up study of 18 patients previously diagnosed as having Alzheimer's disease after exhaustive neurological evaluation (23) Lijtmaer and associates (24) found 1 patient who had shown remarkable improvement and who was therefore presumed to have had a "pseudodementia due to depression."

The conclusion is inescapable that diagnostic errors, both of omission and commission, are not rare, even when patients are evaluated carefully by well-trained psychiatrists and neurologists. What are the sources of these errors?

An entirely satisfactory explanation is lacking. I suspect that errors of omission and commission in the diagnosis of organic brain disease arise from different sources. Failure to recognize cerebral disease when it is present to a significant degree probably occurs most commonly simply because the physician fails to ask the significant questions. As Arie (25) observed, "The important thing is to ask the questions, and never simply to assume the answers...." Patients with dementia seldom complain specifically of its characteristic symptoms. Early in the course of disease, patients are cal dysfunction. A similar but less exact relationship was demonstrated between the number of neurofibrillary tangles and neuropsychological loss. These findings have now been confirmed independently (52). In the minority of the Newcastle group's subjects who manifested significant ischemic cerebral softening, a rough correlation between the mass of infarcted tissue and the severity of dementia was also identified.

Thus there is a well-documented body of evidence relating brain morphologic alterations to clinical dementia. Dementia has been related quantitatively to tissue loss, density of senile plaques and neurofibrillary tangles, and mass of ischemic softening. Of the "normal" changes of age, only neuronal loss has not yet been quantitatively related to the severity of dementia, probably because the complexity and tedium of manual techniques for counting have precluded thorough study. Computerized counting will soon fill in this lacuna in our knowledge.

Tomlinson (45) observed that the three major variables in brain morphology with aging—new structural elements, neuronal loss, and ischemic softening—are also the three major variables in most instances of dementia. I suspect, as does Tomlinson, that if these three aspects of morphologic change are quantitatively evaluated there will be few instances in which dementia cannot be explained on morphologic grounds. My current view is that the clinical diagnosis of dementia should be seriously questioned when thorough morphologic study does not acount for the clinical picture. Pseudodementias are too common and too accurate in their mimicry of true dementia to permit diagnostic complacency. Also, delirium may be easily misdiagnosed as dementia, especially in the elderly, in whom the diagnosis of dementia is often accepted too quickly and uncritically.

Alzheimer's Disease

This disease is characterized by the presence of senile plaques, neurofibrillary tangles, and granulovacuolar degenerative changes in greater numbers and in different anatomic sites from those found in normal subjects. Semantic confusion still surrounds this disorder. When dementia begins in the presenile period due to these pathognomonic morphologic changes, the disorder is uniformly labeled Alzheimer's disease. When dementia occurs with the same morphologic changes in the elderly, it may be labeled Alzheimer's disease, senile dementia, or senile dementia Alzheimer's

type. Although some clinical and morphologic differences between the presenile and the senile forms can be identified, most authorities consider the morphologic changes identical (45), and the disorder is labeled Alzheimer's disease in this paper regardless of age of onset. Significant progress has been made in recent years in elucidating the nature of the specific morphologic changes.

Senile plaques. Senile plaques are microscopic lesions with a central amyloid core surrounded by a less densely staining fibrillary or granular zone. In Alzheimer's disease, some patients may not have a single uninvolved cortical field on microscopic examination; in severe cases, senile plaques may involve half the cortex. They are particularly dense in the amygdaloid complex, hippocampus, subiculum, and hippocampal gyrus. Electron microscopy (53–58) has shown the plaque to consist of abnormal neurites, defined by Terry (59) as unmyelinated axons or dendrites, which may be difficult to distinguish from each other. Dozens of these abnormal neuritic processes may be present in one plaque. Although amyloid can be found in virtually all plaques, ultrastructural studies (60) have shown that nerve terminal abnormalities precede amyloid deposition. Thus, it appears unlikely that amyloid is responsible for plaque formation; it is more likely that amyloid deposition is a secondary event.

Experimental production of senile plaques has proved difficult. In animals surviving for long periods after aluminum administration (60, 61), plaque-like neuritic structures have been observed, but they lack the amyloid core characteristic of the human lesion. When the transmissible disease scrapie (*vide infra*) is induced in mice, plaques with ultrastructural components identical to those in the human lesion are found (62, 63). However, such plaques are not characteristic in sheep, the usual hosts for this disease. Nonetheless, the identification of an animal model for plaques resembling human senile plaques is an important development.

Neurofibrillary degeneration. Neurofibrillary tangles, usually visible only in medium and large neurons, consist of changed intraneuronal fibrils that have become thickened, twisted, and distorted within the neuronal perikaryon. They are found in large numbers throughout the cortex in Alzheimer's disease, especially in the amygdaloid, subiculum, and hippocampal gyri.

Ultrastructural studies (58, 64, 65) have shown these tangles to consist of massive proliferation of intracytoplasmic material, either paired helical filaments or twisted tubules of predictable size and configuration. They may be the manifestation of an abnormal protein, which has been partially characterized (66).

Neurofibrillary tangles are also prominent in the parkinsonism-dementia complex that is seen in Guamanians, in progressive supranuclear palsy, and in the dementia seen in some boxers (45). In none of these disorders are senile plaques characteristic, which shows that the two lesions characteristic of Alzheimer's disease do not occur together invariably. Therefore, it is probable that they result from different pathologic mechanisms. The sites of major involvement by neurofibrillary tangles are different in these disorders than in Alzheimer's disease, and although the tangles in the Guam parkinsonism-dementia complex are indistinguishable morphologically from those in Alzheimer's disease, those in progressive supranuclear palsy are distinctly different.

Aluminum salts (60, 61), colchicine (67), vinblastine, and vincristine (68, 69) administered intracerebrally or into CSF produce neurofibrillary tangles, but the resulting tubules are straight and easily distinguished by electron microscopy from those of Alzheimer's disease. A few twisted tubules have been observed in cases of tetraethyl lead intoxication (70).

Granulovacuolar degeneration and Hirano bodies are often more pronounced in Alzheimer's disease than in normal old age, but quantitative studies are less exact for these structures.

Relation to vascular disease. No predictable relationship has been demonstrated between cerebrovascular disease and plaque formation or Alzheimer's disease (71). A type of amyloid angiopathy has been described (72) that is present to some degree not infrequently in Alzheimer's disease. The vascular amyloid substance has been described as extending to and continuous with the core of the plaques in some cases. Alzheimer's disease may be severe without these congophilic vascular changes, and amyloid deposition appears to be a secondary event in senile plaque formation. Most authorities agree that vascular disease should not be implicated etiologically in Alzheimer's disease (45).

Down's syndrome and Alzheimer's disease. Pathologic changes characteristic of Alzheimer's disease are present, usually to a striking degree, in virtually every patient with Down's syndrome (mongolism) who lives beyond 35 to 40 years of age (73, 74). The changes are absent in patients who die young. The morphology of the senile plaques and neurofibrillary tangles in these patients is indistinguishable by electron microscopy from that in Alzheimer's disease without mongolism (75, 76). The predictable occurrence of these changes in patients known to have chromosomal abnormalities opens many investigative avenues.

The role of aluminum. The production of neurofibrillary tangles and plaques by administration of aluminum to experimental animals (60, 61) has resulted in speculation about its possible role in human Alzheimer's disease. Elevated aluminum content has been reported in some areas of the cortex in Alzheimer's disease (77). The increased aluminum was found by Crapper and coworkers (77) in areas where neurofibrillary tangles but not senile plaques were prominent. On the other hand, Terry and Peña (60) failed to localize aluminum in human neurofibrillary tangles, and Duckett (78) reported localization of aluminum in senile plaques. The best that can be said at present is that the role, if any, of aluminum in human Alzheimer's disease is uncertain.

Huntington's Chorea

Recent studies on Huntington's chorea have centered on biochemical changes; morphologic abnormalities have been shown to be nonspecific aside from their distribution. Reduced levels of GABA were found in the basal ganglia but not in the cortex of brains from patients with Huntington's chorea (79), and reduced concentrations of the GABA-synthesizing enzyme glutamic acid decarboxylase were later demonstrated in the same areas (80). This suggests that GABA-mimetic drugs might alleviate the movement disorder in Huntington's chorea (81), but it provides no explanation for the mentative changes. Terry (82) has also pointed out that the enzyme defect may merely reflect—and not explain—neuronal loss.

Stahl and Swanson (83) reported the presence of an abnormal protein with high molecular weight in the striatum in advanced cases of the disorder, and Iqbal and associates (84) described isolation of abnormal amounts of three histone-like compounds in the cytoplasm of neuronal somas isolated from brains of patients who had Huntington's chorea. Abnormalities of protein synthesis would better explain the neuronal loss, and confirmation of these protein changes is awaited with interest.

deal only with the choice of ancillary diagnostic techniques, a topic often approached with uncertainty by physicians who do not regularly see patients requiring thorough evaluation for organic brain disease.

The basic aim is to employ the smallest number of ancillary diagnostic studies possible that will afford diagnostic accuracy. When there is reason on the basis of history and clinical observations to suspect a specific etiology (e.g., hypothyroidism), a single laboratory determination may be sufficient to establish the diagnosis. More often, patients do not present clues that point toward any specific disease, and a more comprehensive search must be undertaken. I have suggested (38) the following procedures as a basic routine diagnostic battery in patients thought to have organic brain disease.

1. Urinalysis
2. Chest X ray
3. Blood studies
    a. complete blood count
    b. serological test for syphilis
    c. standard metabolic screening battery
    d. serum thyroxine by column (CT_4)
    e. vitamin B_{12} and folate levels
4. CT scan

Use of this basic test battery would have permitted accurate diagnosis in all the patients described in the three series mentioned earlier (22, 32, 33). Not all of these tests are required in all patients, since a diagnosis might be reached through selected tests without the need to use them all. When the diagnosis is uncertain, however, it is difficult to justify a less thorough laboratory evaluation.

The CT scan may require description. This is a new technique for radiologic imaging that is based on the different capacity of various tissues for absorption of photons (39–42). The cranium is scanned by X-ray beams in a series of contiguous slices. A narrow X-ray beam is transmitted across the cranium, and detectors on the opposite side of the head record the photons transmitted. For each cranial plane studied, the brain is irradiated around its circumference from 180 points, each marking $2°$ of the circle. A computer compiles and assembles the information and transmits it in a form suitable for imaging. A cathode ray tube displays the varying X-ray absorption patterns within the cranium for each plane studied, and the image is recorded photographically. The photograph is in many ways similar to the image obtained by pneumoencephalography.

CT scanning is quick, safe, and painless, and it provides much detail of intracranial structures. In centers where it is available the technique has largely replaced pneumoencephalography and to a lesser extent cranial angiography (42). It is most helpful when there is a large difference between the absorption values of diseased tissue and normal tissue, and it has proved especially helpful in the detection and definition of cerebral infarctions, intracranial masses, hydrocephalic conditions, and cerebral atrophy.

There are many instances in which additional diagnostic procedures should be ordered, depending on the specific clinical problem encountered. Psychological testing (29) and EEGs (43) are examples of potentially valuable or even necessary procedures, but their routine use appears unjustifiable in terms of both expense and diagnostic yield.

Treatment

As in all medicine, treatment is most efficacious when there is a specific remedy for the specific disease causing the clinical syndrome. As has been noted previously, thorough study of patients with organic brain syndromes leads to the identification of a number of treatable, although not always reversible, disorders. Unfortunately, 50% or more of these disorders do not have specific remedies. Most of these patients (e.g., those with Alzheimer's disease. Pick's disease, or Huntington's chorea) suffer a variety of symptoms not unlike those encountered in nonorganic patients. Fear, anxiety, depression, elation, agitation, apathy, insomnia, and a host of other symptoms are common, and relief or palliation is as essential here as in patients with functional disorders. Therapeutic tools for symptomatic treatment of these organic disorders include supportive psychotherapy, environmental manipulation, pharmacotherapy, and family counseling, all of which are useful or even essential (38). However, in the absence of intact neural structures, symptomatic results are often less impressive than those achieved in patients with structurally normal brains, and symptomatic treatment obviously cannot reverse progressive disease processes.

STUDIES UNDERLYING CURRENT UNDERSTANDING OF CHRONIC BRAIN DISORDERS

Much work in the past few years has been devoted to understanding the pathophysiologic mechanisms underlying the obscure dementing disorders for which no specific treatment is available. In this section I shall turn to more basic investigations designed to bolster our knowledge of fundamental pathophysiologic processes in dementia and our understanding of their clinical expression.

Brain Alterations with Aging

Pathologists have long recognized that the weight of the human brain decreases in late-middle and old age and that some concomitant ventricular enlargement and cortical convolutional shrinkage may occur (44). Recently, more specific cellular aspects of aging have been quantified (45).

New structural elements. Four structural elements—senile plaques, neurofibrillary tangles, granulovacuolar degeneration, and Hirano bodies—commonly appear in the human brain with aging. Because senile plaques and neurofibrillary tangles play major roles in the cerebral dysfunction seen in varied degenerative diseases, their presence in the brains of intellectually normal elderly subjects raises questions as to their functional implications.

Senile plaques appear in middle age and gradually increase with age; they are found in approximately 70% of all people over 65. However, the number of plaques is limited in most intellectually normal old people (44). Neurofibrillary tangles also occur with increasing frequency in the hippocampus and subiculum with aging, but their number remains small in the neocortex. Tomlinson (45) stated that "no normal old subject ever shows large numbers of neurofibrillary tangles in the neocortex. . . . " Granulovacuolar degeneration, largely involving cells in the hippocampus and subiculum, and Hirano bodies also appear in increasing numbers in the normally functioning elderly population.

Neuronal loss. Quantitative assessment of neuron populations is tedious, and changes with age in neuron populations have been established for only a few cell groups, with conflicting results. Newer automatic techniques have shown that over the life span there is a considerable loss of neurons in certain areas of the cerebral cortex, even in subjects well preserved intellectually (45). However, not all cell populations are subject to such attrition with age.

Ischemic lesions. There is pathologic evidence of cerebral infarction in approximately 50% of normal subjects over 65 who retain normal in-

tellect, but the volume of infarcted tissue rarely exceeds 50 ml in these subjects.

Structural Brain Alterations and Clinical Manifestations of Dementia

If the brain of an elderly subject with normal intellectual function sometimes demonstrates shrinkage, senile plaques, neurofibrillary tangles, granulovacuolar degeneration, loss of cortical neurons, and ischemic softening, what is the evidence that the clinical syndrome of dementia is due to morphologic changes in brain tissue? This is a perplexing problem, since observed morphologic changes may not always be sufficient to account for dementia and morphologic alterations can be found in the absence of dementia. Such occasional discrepancies led Rothschild (46, 47) to propose that the basic personality structure of certain people rendered them vulnerable to the emergence of dementia in the presence of morphologic changes. Subsequent studies using diverse investigative techniques have helped to resolve much of this problem.

Chapman and Wolff (48) provided the first quantitative data in human subjects. Using complex neuropsychological techniques, they studied the "highest integrative functions" in a large series of patients who had lost measurable amounts of brain tissue through neurosurgical intervention. They demonstrated that the severity of integrative loss was directly related to the quantity of brain tissue lost. The same group used these techniques to study other patients with diffuse cerebral degenerative processes, measuring cerebral atrophy by pneumoencephalograms (49). Again, they found that the loss of neuropsychological function closely paralleled the extent of brain tissue loss. Willanger and colleagues (50) used similar techniques to study psychological deficits in a large sample with brain tissue loss as demonstrated by detailed pneumoencephalography, and they reached essentially the same conclusions. All of these studies found that the greater the tissue loss, the greater the psychological impairment.

The Newcastle-upon-Tyne group approached the same problem from a different perspective. They carefully assessed psychological functioning of both normal and demented elderly persons and sought to relate these findings to the microscopic cerebral alterations found in those coming to autopsy (31, 44, 45, 51). In general, they found a direct relationship between the number of senile plaques identified through quantitative counts of the cerebral cortex and the severity of psychologi-

PML is caused by cerebral infection with viruses that commonly infect humans but are not known to cause disease in immunologically competent hosts (120, 121). Electron microscopy of brains of patients who died of PML revealed papovavirus-like particles (122), and a new papovavirus (JC virus) was subsequently isolated from an affected brain (123). The JC virus has now been isolated from most human cases studied, but at least one other virus has also been implicated (124).

Unconventional agents causing chronic brain infection. In 1957, Gajdusek and Zigas (125) described a subacute cerebellar disease called kuru in New Guinea natives, and Gajdusek thereby began a series of studies for which he was awarded the Nobel Prize in medicine in 1976. Two years after this initial report, Hadlow (126) noted the resemblance between kuru and scrapie. In the same year Klatzo and associates (127) described the neuropathology of kuru and remarked on its resemblance to Creutzfeldt-Jakob disease. There was then no evidence that any of these diseases was transmissible, and the absence of clinical signs of inflammation made a viral etiology appear unlikely. However, in 1966 Gajdusek and colleagues (128) reported the experimental transmission of kuru to chimpanzees (from brain of diseased patient to animal brain), and in 1968 this group reported experimental transmission of Creutzfeldt-Jakob disease to the same animals (129). Since then, both disorders have been transmitted on many occasions to a variety of lower animals. The period between inoculation and the onset of clinical signs is always many months (130).

Creutzfeldt-Jakob disease (131, 132), which usually begins in the fifth and sixth decades, is marked clinically by a progressive dementia accompanied by a host of neurologic signs, commonly including myoclonic jerking. Patients usually become severely demented in less than 6 months and survive less than a year after onset. As many as 10% of the cases may be familial, most consistent with an autosomal dominant inheritance. EEGs (43) often show characteristic (but not pathognomonic) recurrent high-amplitude sharp and slow forms. The disease is characterized pathologically by a striking neuronal loss, astrocytosis, and cytoplasmic vacuolation, but marked variation in pathology from case to case has been described.

The transmissible agent that causes Creutzfeldt-Jakob disease is a replicable, filterable particle, but it differs from conventional viruses in several respects (130). It possesses considerable resistance to inactivation by heat, ultraviolet and ionizing radiation, proteases, nucleases, and formalin. Recognizable viral particles cannot be detected by electron microscopy. The transmissible agent does not evoke virus-like inflammatory responses in the brain or CSF, nor is any antibody response recognizable in the host. The agent has not been identified in blood or other body fluids. Evidence for direct transmission from person to person is scanty, but there has been one report of probable transmission through a corneal graft (133) and two reports of the disease occurring in husband and wife (130).

Many divergent observations converge to fuel speculation about the pathogenesis of Creutzefeldt-Jakob disease. There is much evidence that genetic factors are important in the expression of the disease, but there can be no question that it is also transmissible. How is an apparently hereditary disease also transmissible by injection of diseased tissue? If these disorders are due to an infectious agent, cannot a method of treatment be developed, as has been done with so many other contagious diseases? Inoculation of scrapie-injected brain into mice results in plaques indistinguishable by electron microscopy from those in Alzheimer's disease. Is it possible, then, that Alzheimer's disease is also due to a transmissible agent? Numerous attempts to transmit Alzheimer's disease by inoculation of affected brain to brains of experimental animals have failed, but so-called familial Alzheimer's disease has twice been transmitted to lower animals (130). Does this represent a different form of Alzheimer's disease or a variant of Creutzfeldt-Jakob disease, which is so often familial? Are other chronic neuropsychiatric disorders due to similar transmissible agents, the transmissible nature of the disorders never having been suspected because of the absence of clinical and pathological signs of inflammation?

COMMENT

We possess more questions than answers just now, but the fact that so many questions are being asked proves that the chronic brain diseases are no longer the neglected backwaters of neuropsychiatry. The importance of these disorders, in both numerical and personal terms, is being recognized increasingly and is reflected in the advances already made. As detailed above, many patients with dementia have specifically treatable disorders, and exacting diagnostic study is now a necessity. Unfortunately, many, probably most, of these patients have disorders for which no specific treatment exists. So far, advances in the study of these disorders have been most notable in the areas of neuropathology and neurochemistry; they have not yet led to effective treatment for the most common and most devastating diseases. Nevertheless, the recognition and investigation of these disorders as *diseases* and not as inevitable concomitants of aging should be a harbinger of improved treatment, perhaps even of prevention or cure.

REFERENCES

1. Katzman R, Karasu TB: Differential diagnosis of dementia, in Neurological and Sensory Disorders in the Elderly. Edited by Fields WS. New York, Stratton Intercontinental Medical Book Corp, 1975, pp 103–134

2. Sweet RD, McDowell FH, Feigenson JS, et al: Mental symptoms in Parkinson's disease during chronic treatment with levodopa. Neurology 26:305–310, 1976

3. Wolstenholme GEW, O'Connor J (eds): Alzheimer's Disease and Related Conditions: A Ciba Foundation Symposium. London, J & A Churchill, 1970

4. Pearce J, Miller E: Clinical Aspects of Dementia. London, Balliere Tindall, 1973

5. Pincus JH, Tucker GJ: Behavioral Neurology. New York, Oxford University Press, 1974

6. Slaby AE, Wyatt RJ: Dementia in the Presenium. Springfield, Ill, Charles C Thomas, 1974

7. Benson DF, Blumer D (eds): Psychiatric Aspects of Neurological Disease, New York, Grune & Stratton, 1975

8. Smith WL, Kinsbourne M (eds): Aging and Dementia. New York, Spectrum Publications, 1977

9. Wells CE (ed): Dementia, 2nd ed. Philadelphia, FA Davis Co, 1977

10. Clark M, Gosnell M: The brain prober. Newsweek, Dec 20, 1976, p 54

11. Hartocollis P: The syndrome of minimal brain dysfunction in young adult patients. Bull Menninger Clin 32:102–114, 1968

12. Quitkin F, Klein DF: Two behavioral syndromes in young adults related to possible minimal brain dysfunction. J Psychiatr Res 7:131–142, 1969

13. Shelley EM, Riester A: Syndrome of minimal brain damage in young adults. Dis Nerv Syst 33:335–338, 1972

14. Mann HB, Greenspan SI: The identification and treatment of adult brain dysfunction. Am J Psychiatry 133:1013–1017, 1976

15. Wood DR, Reimherr FW, Wender PH, et al: Diagnosis and treatment of minimal brain dysfunction in adults. Arch Gen Psychiatry 33:1453–1460, 1976

16. American Psychiatric Association: Diagnostic and Statistical Manual of Mental Disorders, 2nd ed. Washington, DC, APA, 1968, p 22

17. Williamson J, Stokoe IH, Gray S, et al: Old people at home: their unreported needs. Lancet 1:1117–1120, 1964

18. Malamud N: Organic brain disease mistaken for psychiatric disorder: a clinicopathological study, in Psychiatric Aspects of Neurologic Disease. Edited by Benson DF, Blumer D. New York, Grune & Stratton, 1975, pp 287–305

19. Duckworth, GS, Ross H: Diagnostic differences in psychogeriatric patients in Toronto, New York and London, England. Can Med. Assoc J 112:847–851, 1975

20. Roth M: The natural history of mental disorder in old age. J Ment Sci 101:281–301, 1955

21. Nott PN, Fleminger JJ: Presenile dementia: the difficulties of early diagnosis. Acta Psychiatr Scand 51:210–217, 1975

22. Marsden CD, Harrison MJG: Outcome of investigation of patients with presenile dementia. Br Med J 2:249–252, 1972

23. Coblentz JM, Mattis S, Zingesser LH, et al: Presenile dementia: clinical aspects and evaluation of cerebrospinal fluid dynamics. Arch Neurol 29:299–308, 1973

24. Lijtmaer H, Fuld PA, Katzman R: Prevalence and malignancy of Alzheimer disease (ltr to ed). Arch Neurol 33:304, 1976

25. Arie T: Dementia in the elderly: diagnosis and assessment. Br Med J 4:540–543, 1973

26. Kiloh LG: Pseudo-dementia. Acta Psychiatr Scand 37:336–351, 1961

27. Post F: Dementia, depression, and pseudodementia, in Psychiatric Aspects of Neurologic Disease. Edited by Benson DF, Blumer D. New York, Grune & Stratton, 1975, pp 99–120

28. Wells CE: Dementia, pseudodementia, and dementia praecox, in Phenomenology and Treatment of Schizophrenia. Edited by Fann WE. New York, Spectrum Publication (in press)

29. Wells CE, Buchanan DC: The clinical use of psychological testing in evaluation for dementia, in Dementia, 2nd ed. Edited by Wells CE. Philadelphia, FA Davis Co, 1977, pp 189–204

30. Wells CE, Duncan GW: Danger of overreliance on computerized cranial tomography. Am J. Psychiatry 134:811–813, 1977

31. Tomlinson BE, Blessed G, Roth M: Observations on the brains of demented old people. J Neurol Sci 11:205–242, 1970

32. Katzman R: Personal communication, June 2, 1975

33. Freemon FR: Evaluation of patients with progressive intellectual deterioration. Arch Neurol 33:658–659, 1976.

34. Fisher CM: Dementia in cerebral vascular disease, in Transactions of the Sixth Congress on Cerebral Vascular Diseases. Edited by Toole JF, Siekert RG, Whisnant JP. New York, Grune & Stratton, 1968, pp. 232–236

35. Paulson GW, Perrine G Jr: Cerebral vascular disease in mental hospitals. Ibid., pp 237–241

36. Birkett DP: The psychiatric differentiation of senility and arteriosclerosis. Br J Psychiatry 120:321–325, 1972

37. Hachinski VC, Iliff LD, Zilhka E, et al: Cerebral blood flow in dementia. Arch Neurol 32:632–637, 1975

Normal Pressure Hydrocephalus (NPH)

A signal advance was the recognition that disorders of CSF absorption can produce a characteristic clinical triad of gait disturbance, incontinence, and dementia without elevation of CSF pressure. Since the description of this clinical syndrome by Hakim and Adams (85) and associates (86) in 1965, almost a thousand cases have been reported (87), and even this number does not adequately reflect the attention accorded the disorder in clinical and laboratory investigations. The recognition of NPH has been especially important because some patients have recovered after neurosurgical shunting procedures performed to relieve the postulated disturbance in CSF absorption. The syndrome usually occurs when there is obstruction in the flow of CSF over the convexities of the cerebral hemispheres, and CSF absorption through the usual pathways at the superior sagittal sinus is impaired.

Although the syndrome is usually classified among the dementias (88), gait disturbance is often the earliest and most prominent manifestation. The impairment takes many forms—spastic, ataxic, spastic-ataxic, or apraxic—and may be confused with Parkinson's disease. Urinary (rarely fecal) incontinence and dementia, usually mild, are common late-stage phenomena. To these symptoms, almost any other neurological abnormalities may be added. Patients are usually slow and withdrawn, although examples of paranoid and aggressive behavior have been recorded (89, 90). Depression is frequent and sometimes severe (91).

NPH is divided etiologically into secondary and primary groups. Approximately two-thirds of the reported cases (87) fall into the secondary group, i.e., secondary to identified intracranial diseases that interfere with spinal fluid circulation and absorption. The most common precursors of NPH are subarachnoid hemorrhage and cerebral trauma; infections, tumors, and preceding intracranial surgery are seen less often. The other group is identified as primary or idiopathic, i.e., no other disease process has been recognized. Detailed clinical and pathological study of this group sometimes reveals Parkinson's disease, Alzheimer's disease, or hypertensive disease, but the cause of the absorptive defect often remains obscure. Most cases in this primary group are unexplained.

Ancillary diagnostic procedures often help in reaching the correct diagnosis but are never diagnostic in themselves (42). Pneumoencephalograms demonstrate enlarged lateral ventricles (particularly the anterior portions), widened basilar cisterns, and absence of air in the subarachnoid spaces over the hemispheres. The CT scan (42, 92) usually shows similar changes, although cerebral atrophic changes (not present in primary NPH) may be demonstrated in areas where air cannot pass by pneumoencephalography. Thus the CT scan has become the most valuable technical aid in the diagnosis of NPH. Isotope cisternography reveals stasis of radioactive materials in the ventricles and impaired CSF absorption over the convexities of the hemispheres. Impairment of CSF absorption has also been demonstrated by the infusion manometric test (93) and by slowed isotope transfer from CSF to blood (94), although neither of these techniques is common in clinical practice today.

Although the pathogenesis of NPH is not completely understood, it appears likely that for a variety of reasons the normal pathways for CSF absorption over the hemispheres are blocked, leading to a transient increase in CSF pressure and to ventricular enlargement. CSF is produced through a secretory process that is not dependent on CSF pressure, so that in cases of obstruction alternative routes for CSF absorption must develop quickly, a process that probably occurs largely through the thinned ependymal walls of the ventricles (95–97). With the development of these alternative pathways, the CSF pressure returns to normal. Ventricular stasis is believed to be a late-stage phenomenon (98). Although the course of events is reasonably certain, just how these changes result in the clinical syndrome remains uncertain. Greitz (99) suggested that the reversible clinical syndrome might result from impaired cerebral blood flow due to ventricular distention. Greitz and coworkers (100) and Mathew and associates (101) have reported the reduction of cerebral blood flow in patients with NPH. The Mathew group observed the greatest reduction in the area of brain supplied by the anterior cerebral arteries, an anatomical distribution that could explain both ataxia and incontinence.

Neurosurgical shunting procedures to relieve the obstruction to CSF absorption are the treatment of choice for NPH. Unfortunately, results are far from predictable, and mortality and morbidity remain uncomfortably high. Improvement has been reported in approximately 55% of all patients treated surgically, with better results in the secondary group (65% improved) than in the primary or idiopathic group (41% improved) (87). It is also generally agreed that results are better in those patients whose clinical pattern conforms most closely to the classical triad. No ancillary diagnostic procedures have been proved to predict accurately the outcome of surgery.

The reason for improvement after surgery remains unknown. Improvement does not depend on the presence of ventricular stasis before surgery or on reduction in ventricular size after surgery (87). Cerebral blood flow has been reported to increase after insertion of CSF shunts, suggesting that improvement results from increased perfusion of brain (100). The same studies suggested that the extent of clinical improvement might vary directly with the extent of increase in cerebral perfusion. It has been proposed (101) that an increase in cerebral blood flow after removal of spinal fluid before surgery might predict clinical improvement after surgery, but adequate study in a sufficient number of patients is lacking and should be pursued. Changes in cerebral blood flow after shunting might explain the clinical improvement reported after surgery in some patients with NPH associated with Alzheimer's disease (102) and hypertension (103), but results of shunting in these patients are usually disappointing (87).

Dementia Due to Transmissible Agents

Acute and subacute intracranial infectious processes have long been recognized as causes of dementia. They usually concern the psychiatrist most when the disorder has an acute onset and is not accompanied by clinical signs to suggest cerebral inflammation. Herpes simplex encephalitis is a prime example of acute brain infection that often appears clinically as an acute psychosis and is easily confused with schizophrenia and other acute functional psychoses. Recently, interest among neuropsychiatrists has focused less on these acute infectious processes than on chronic, progressive neurologic disorders that result from transmissible agents.

Recognition that disorders of this type occur in humans has resulted from animal studies. Visna is a chronic brain disease in sheep that is caused by a conventional virus. Subacute sclerosing panencephalitis (SSPE), progressive rubella encephalitis, and progressive multifocal leukoencephalopathy (PML) have been recognized as similar disorders in man. Scrapie, a chronic brain disease occurring naturally in sheep, results from an unconventional transmissible agent. Kuru and Creutzfeldt-Jakob disease have been discovered to be similar human disorders. This topic has been reviewed recently by Roos and Johnson (104).

Conventional viruses causing chronic brain disease. The chronic disorders described below are strikingly different clinically from ordinary viral infections. There is a considerable body of evidence attributing this difference either to abnormalities in the virus replicative cycle or to abnormalities in the hosts' immune responses.

SSPE is a chronic dementing disorder with prominent myoclonic jerks common late in its course (105, 106). It usually begins between the ages of 2 and 21, although later onset has been reported. There is often a history of measles infection before the age of 2, with a 2–10 year gap between the primary infection and the onset of SSPE. Death usually occurs 1–3 years after onset.

The relationship between SSPE and measles was revealed through a series of observations. Patients were found to have elevated CSF gamma globulin due largely to measles antibody, which was increased in both serum and CSF. This was demonstrated to result from production of antibodies within the CNS. Electron microscopy (107) revealed inclusions similar to those found in measles virus, and finally measles virus was isolated from brains of patients with SSPE (108, 109).

There is as yet no satisfactory explanation as to how an apparently common episode of measles leads to chronic infection, disease, and death, but there is general agreement that defective strains of virus are implicated. Incomplete maturation of the virus has been described (110) in the brains of SSPE patients and in SSPE-infected tissue and organ cultures (111, 112). Furthermore, significant differences between SSPE virion structural proteins and those of normal measles virus have been described (113). The mechanism of transformation of measles virus into this aberrant infectious agent remains an enigma.

Progressive rubella panencephalitis is a similar but seemingly rarer disorder (114, 115) that appears many years after apparently uncomplicated rubella infections. This disease has been less thoroughly investigated than SSPE, but elevated rubella antibodies have been found in serum and CSF, and rubella virus has been isolated from the brain (116). Defective immune responses have not been implicated in either SSPE or progressive rubella panencephalitis.

PML, a progressive dementing disease (117–119) with multiple foci of demyelination, appears later in life than SSPE or progressive rubella panencephalitis (average age of onset is in the 50s) and occurs primarily in immunologically compromised persons. This is due most often to lymphoproliferative disease but also results from immunosuppressive drugs, sarcoid, tuberculosis, and other neoplasms. Death usually occurs within 3–6 months after onset.

vitro: an electron microscopic and immunoperoxidase study. Lab Invest 30:241–250, 1974

112. Raine CS, Feldman LA, Sheppard RD, et al: Subacute sclerosing panencephalitis virus: observations on a neuroadapted and non-neuroadapted strain in organotypic central nervous system cultures. Lab Invest 31:42–53, 1974

113. Miller CA, Fields BN: Measles and subacute sclerosing panencephalitis (SSPE) viruses: comparative characterization of purified particles (abstract). J Neuropathol Exp Neurol 35:93, 1976

114. Townsend JJ, Baringer JR, Wolinsky JS, et al: Progressive rubella panencephalitis: late onset after congenital rubella. N Engl J Med 292:990–993, 1975

115. Townsend JJ, Wolinsky JS, Baringer JR: The neuropathology of progressive rubella panencephalitis of late onset. Brain 99:81–90, 1976

116. Weil ML, Itabashi HH, Cremer NE, et al: Chronic progressive panencephalitis due to rubella virus simulating subacute sclerosing panencephalitis. N Engl J Med 292:994–998, 1975

117. Aström KE, Mancall EL, Richardson EP Jr: Progressive multi-focal leuko-encephalopathy: a hitherto unrecognized complication of chronic lymphatic leukaemia and Hodgkin's disease. Brain 81:93–111, 1958

118. Richardson EP Jr: Progressive multifocal leukoencephalopathy, in Handbook of Clinical Neurology, vol. 9. Edited by Vinken PJ, Bruyn GW. Amsterdam, North-Holland Publishing Co, 1970, pp 485–499

119. Richardson EP Jr: Our evolving understanding of progressive multifocal leukoencephalopathy. Ann NY Acad Sci 230:358–364, 1974

120. Padgett BL, Walker DL: Prevalence of antibodies in human sera against JC virus, an isolate from a case of progressive multifocal leukoencephalopathy. J Infect Dis 127:467–470, 1973

121. Shah KV, Daniel RW, Warszawski RM: High prevalence of antibodies to BK virus, an SV40-related papovavirus, in residents of Maryland. J Infect Dis 128:784–787, 1973

122. Zu Rhein GM, Chou SM: Particles resembling papova viruses in human cerebral demyelinating disease. Science 148:1477–1479, 1965

123. Padgett BL, Walker DL, Zu Rhein GM, et al: Cultivation of papova-like virus from human brain with progressive multifocal leukoencephalopathy. Lancet 1:1257–1260, 1971

124. Narayan O, Penney JB Jr, Johnson RT, et al: Etiology of progressive multifocal leukoencephalopathy: identification of papovavirus. N Engl J Med 289:1278–1282, 1973

125. Gajdusek DC, Zigas V: Degenerative disease of the central nervous system in New Guinea: the endemic occurrence of "kuru" in the native population. N Engl J Med 257:974–978, 1957

126. Hadlow WJ: Scrapie and kuru. Lancet 2:289–290, 1959

127. Klatzo I, Gajdusek DC, Zigas V: Pathology of kuru. Lab Invest 8:799–847, 1959

128. Gajdusek DC, Gibbs CJ Jr, Alpers M: Experimental transmission of a kuru-like syndrome to chimpanzees. Nature 209:794–796, 1966

129. Gibbs CJ Jr, Gajdusek DC, Asher DM, et al: Creutzfeldt-Jakob disease (spongiform encephalopathy): transmission to the chimpanzee. Science 161:388–389, 1968

130. Gajdusek DC, Gibbs CJ Jr: Slow virus infections of the nervous system and the laboratories of slow, latent, and temperate virus infections, in The Nervous System, vol 2. Edited by Tower DB. New York, Raven Press, 1975, pp 113–135

131. Roos R, Gajdusek DC, Gibbs CJ Jr: The clinical characteristics of transmissible Creutzfeldt-Jakob disease. Brain 96:1–20, 1973

132. May WW: Creutzfeldt-Jakob disease. Acta Neurol Scand 44:1–32, 1968

133. Duffy P, Wolf J, Collins G, et al: Possible person-to-person transmission of Creutzfeldt-Jakob disease. N Engl J Med 290:692–693, 1974

38. Wells CE: Diagnostic evaluation and treatment in dementia, in Dementia, 2nd ed. Edited by Wells CE, Philadelphia, FA Davis Co, 1977, pp 247–276

39. Hounsfield G, Ambrose J, Perry J, et al: Computerized transverse axial scanning. Br J Radiol 46:1016–1051, 1973

40. Paxton R, Ambrose J: The EMI scanner: a brief review of the first 650 patients. Br J Radiol 47:530–565, 1974

41. Ambrose J: Computerized X-ray scanning of the brain. J Neurosurg 40:679–695, 1974

42. Lowry J, Bahr AL, Allen JH Jr, et al: Radiological techniques in the diagnostic evaluation of dementia, in Dementia, 2nd ed. Edited by Wells CE. Philadelphia, FA Davis Co, 1977, pp 223–245

43. Wilson WP, Musella L, Short MJ: The electroencephalogram in dementia. Ibid, pp 205–221

44. Tomlinson BE, Blessed G, Roth M: Observations on the brains of non-demented old people. J Neurol Sci 7:331–356, 1968

45. Tomlinson BE: The pathology of dementia, in Dementia, 2nd ed. Edited by Wells CE. Philadelphia, FA Davis Co, 1977, pp 113–153

46. Rothschild D: Pathologic changes in senile psychoses and their psychobiologic significance. Am J Psychiatry 93:757–784, 1937

47. Rothschild D: Neuropathologic changes in arteriosclerotic psychoses and their psychiatric significance. Arch Neurol Psychiatry 48:417–436, 1942

48. Chapman LF, Wolff HG: The cerebral hemispheres and the highest integrative functions of man. Arch Neurol 1:357–424, 1959

49. Kiev A, Chapman LF, Guthrie TC, et al: The highest integrative functions and diffuse cerebral atrophy Neurology 12:385–393, 1962

50. Willanger R, Thygesen P, Nielsen R, et al: Intellectual impairment and cerebral atrophy: a psychological, neurological and radiological investigation. Dan Med Bull 15:65–93, 1968

51. Blessed G, Tomlinson BE, Roth M: The association between quantitative measures of dementia and of senile change in the cerebral grey matter of elderly subjects. Br J Psychiatry 114:797–811, 1968

52. Farmer PM, Peck A, Terry RD: Correlations among numbers of neuritic plaques, neurofibrillary tangles, and the severity of senile dementia (abstract). J Neuropathol Exp Neurol 35:367, 1976

53. Terry RD, Gonatas NK, Weiss M: Ultrastructural studies in Alzheimer's presenile dementia. Am J Pathol 44:269–297, 1964

54. Luse SA, Smith KR: The ultrastructure of senile plaques. Am J Pathol 44:553–563, 1964

55. Kidd M: Alzheimer's disease—an electron microscopic study. Brain 87:307–320, 1964

56. Krigman MR, Feldman RG, Bensch K: Alzheimer's presenile dementia: a histochemical and electron microscopic study. Lab Invest 14:381–396, 1965

57. Gonatas NK, Anderson A, Evangelista I: The contribution of altered synapses in the senile plaque: an electron microscopic study in Alzheimer's dementia. J Neuropathol Exp Neurol 26:25–39, 1967

58. Terry RD, Wisniewski H: The ultrastructure of the neurofibrillary tangle and the senile plaque, in Alzheimer's Disease and Related Conditions. Edited by Wolstenholme GEW, O'Connor M. London, J & A Churchill, 1970, pp 145–165

59. Discussion. Ibid, p 241

60. Terry RD, Peña C: Experimental production of neurofibrillary degeneration. J Neuropathol Exp Neurol 24:200–210, 1965

61. Wiśniewski H, Terry RD: An experimental approach to the morphogenesis of neurofibrillary degeneration and the argyrophilic plaque, in Alzheimer's Disease and Related Conditions. Edited by Wolstenholme GEW, O'Connor M. London, J & A Churchill, 1970, pp 223–240

62. Fraser H, Bruse ME: Argyrophilic plaques in mice inoculated with scrapie from particular sources. Lancet 1:617–618, 1973

63. Wiśniewski HM, Bruce ME, Fraser H: Infectious etiology of neuritic (senile) plaques in mice. Science 190:1108–1110, 1975

64. Terry RD: The fine structure of neurofibrillary tangles in Alzheimer's disease. J Neuropathol Exp Neurol 22:629–642, 1963

65. Kidd M: Paired helical filaments in electron microscopy in Alzheimer's disease. Nature 197:192–193, 1963

66. Iqbal K. Wiśniewski HM, Shelanski ML, et al: Protein changes in senile dementia. Brain Res 77:337–343, 1974

67. Wiśniewski HM, Terry RD: Experimental colchicine encephalopathy: I. Induction of neurofibrillary degeneration. Lab Invest 17:577–587, 1967

68. Schochet SS Jr, Lampert PW, Earle KM: Neuronal changes induced by intrathecal vincristine sulfate. J Neuropathol Exp Neurol 27:645–658, 1968

69. Wiśniewski H, Shelanski ML, Terry RD: Effects of mitotic spindle inhibitors on neurotubules and neurofilaments in anterior horn cells. J Cell Biol 38:224–229, 1968

70. Niklowitz WJ: Neurofibrillary changes after acute experimental lead poisoning. Neurology 25:927–934, 1975

71. Arab A: Plaques séniles et artériosclérose cérébrale: absence de rapports de dépendance entre les deux processus. Etude statistique. Rev Neurol 91:22–36, 1954

72. Mandybur TI: The incidence of cerebral amyloid angiopathy in Alzheimer's disease. Neurology 25:120–126, 1975

73. Malamud N: Neuropathology of organic brain syndromes associated with aging, in Aging and the Brain. Edited by Gaitz CM. New York, Plenum Press, 1972, pp 63–87

74. Olson MI, Shaw C-M: Presenile dementia and Alzheimer's disease in mongolism. Brain 92:147–156, 1969

75. Schochet SS, Lampert PW, McCormick WF: Neurofibrillary tangles in patients with Down's syndrome: a light and electron microscopic study. Acta Neuropathol 23:432–346, 1973

76. Ellis WG, McCulloch JR, Corley CL: Presenile dementia in Down's syndrome; ultrastructural iden-

tity with Alzheimer's disease. Neurology (Minneap) 24:101–106, 1974

77. Crapper DR, Krishnan SS, Quittkat S: Aluminum, neurofibrillary degeneration and Alzheimer's disease. Brain 99:67–80, 1976

78. Duckett S: Aluminum and Alzheimer's disease (ltr to ed). Arch Neurol 33:730–731, 1976

79. Perry TL, Hansen S, Kloster M: Huntington's chorea: deficiency of γ-aminobutyric acid in brain. N Engl J Med 288:337–342, 1973

80. Bird ED, Iversen LL: Huntington's chorea: postmortem measurement of glutamic acid decarboxylase, choline acetyl-transferase and dopamine in basal ganglia. Brain 97:457–472, 1974

81. Enna SJ, Bird ED, Bennett JP Jr, et al: Huntington's chorea: changes in neurotransmitter receptors in the brain. N Engl J Med 294:1305–1309, 1976

82. Terry RD: Dementia: a brief and selective review. Arch Neurol 33:1–4, 1976

83. Stahl WL, Swanson PD: Biochemical abnormalities in Huntington's chorea brains. Neurology (Minneap) 24:813–819, 1974

84. Iqbal K, Tellez-Nagel I, Grundke-Iqbal I: Protein abnormalities in Huntington's chorea. Brain Res 76:178–184, 1974

85. Hakim S, Adams RD: The special clinical problem of symptomatic hydrocephalus with normal cerebrospinal fluid pressure: observations on cerebrospinal fluid hydrodynamics. J Neurol Sci 2:307–327, 1965

86. Adams RD, Fisher CM, Hakim S, et al: Symptomatic occult hydrocephalus with "normal" cerebrospinal-fluid pressure: a treatable syndrome. N Engl J Med 273:117–126, 1965

87. Katzman R: Normal pressure hydrocephalus, in Dementia. 2nd ed. Edited by Wells CE. Philadelphia, FA Davis Co. 1977, pp 69–92

88. Benson DF: The hydrocephalic dementias, in Psychiatric Aspects of Neurologic Disease. Edited by Benson DF, Blumer D. New York, Grune & Stratton, 1975, pp 83–97

89. Crowell RM, Tew JM, Mark VH: Aggressive dementia associated with normal pressure hydrocephalus: report of two unusual cases. Neurology (Minneap) 23:461–464, 1973

90. Rice E, Gendelman S: Psychiatric aspects of normal pressure hydrocephalus. JAMA 223:409–412, 1973

91. Rosen H, Swigar ME: Depression and normal pressure hydrocephalus: a dilemma in neuropsychiatric differential diagnosis. J Nerv Ment Dis 163:35–40, 1976

92. Jacobs L, Kinkel W: Computerized axial transverse tomography in normal pressure hydrocephalus. Neurology (Minneap) 26:501–507, 1976

93. Katzman R, Hussey F: A simple constant-infusion manometric test for measurement of CSF absorption: I. Rationale and method. Neurology (Minneap) 20:534–544, 1970

94. Behrman S, Cast I, O'Gorman P: Two types of curves for transfer of RIHSA from cerebrospinal fluid to plasma in patients with normal pressure hydrocephalus. J Neurosurg 35:677–680, 1971

95. Milhorat TH, Clark RG, Hammock MK, et al: Structural, ultrastructural, and permeability changes in the ependyma and surrounding brain favoring equilibration in progressive hydrocephalus. Arch Neurol 22:397–407, 1970

96. Strecker E-P, Kelley JET, Merz T, et al: Transventricular albumin absorption in communicating hydrocephalus: semiquantitative analysis of periventricular extracellular space utilizing autoradiography. Arch Psychiatr Nervenkr 218:369–377, 1974

97. James AE Jr, Burns B, Flor WF, et al: Pathophysiology of chronic communicating hydrocephalus in dogs (Canis familiaris): Experimental studies. J Neurol Sci 24:151–178, 1975

98. James AE Jr, Strecker E-P, Novak G, et al: Correlation of serial cisternograms and cerebrospinal fluid pressure measurements in experimental communicating hydrocephalus. Neurology (Minneap) 23:1226–1233, 1973

99. Greitz T: Effect of brain distention on cerebral circulation. Lancet 1:863–865, 1969

100. Greitz TVB, Grepe AOL, Kalmér MSF, et al: Pre- and post-operative evaluation of cerebral blood flow in low-pressure hydrocephalus. J Neurosurg 31:644–651, 1969

101. Mathew NT, Hartmann A, Meyer JS: Diagnostic evaluation of normal pressure hydrocephalus. Trans Am Neurol Assoc 99:227–229, 1974

102. Shenkin HA, Greenberg J, Bouzarth WF, et al: Ventricular shunting for relief of senile symptoms. JAMA 225:1486–1489, 1973.

103. Earnest MP, Fahn S, Karp JH, et al: Normal pressure hydrocephalus and hypertensive cerebrovascular disease. Arch Neurol 31:262–266, 1974

104. Roos RP, Johnson RT: Viruses and dementia, in Dementia, 2nd ed. Edited by Wells CE. Philadelphia, FA Davis Co, 1977 pp 93–112

105. Freeman JM: The clinical spectrum and early diagnosis in Dawson's encephalitis. J Pediatr 75:590–603, 1969

106. Brody JA, Detels R: Subacute sclerosing panencephalitis: a zoonosis following aberrant measles. Lancet 2:500–501, 1970

107. Bouteille M, Fontaine C, Vedrenne C, et al: Sur un cas d'encéphalite subaiguë à inclusions. Etude anatomo-clinique et ultrastructurale. Rev Neurol 113:454–458, 1965

108. Horta-Barbosa L, Fuccillo DA, Sever JL: Subacute sclerosing panencephalitis: isolation of measles virus from a brain biopsy. Nature 221:974, 1969

109. Payne FE, Baublis JV, Itabashi HH: Isolation of measles virus from cell cultures of brain from a patient with subacute sclerosing panencephalitis. N Engl J Med 281:585–589, 1969

110. Dubois-Dalcq M, Coblentz JM, Pleet AB: Subacute sclerosing panencephalitis: unusual nuclear inclusions and lengthy clinical course. Arch Neurol 31:355–363, 1974

111. Dubois-Dalcq M, Barbosa LH, Hamilton R, et al: Comparison between productive and latent subacute sclerosing panencephalitis viral infection in

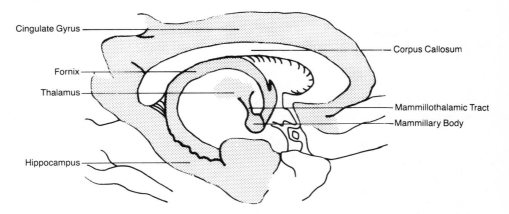

Cingulate Gyrus

Corpus Callosum

Fornix

Thalamus

Mammillothalamic Tract

Mammillary Body

Hippocampus

FIGURE 2.

trist who first identified this disorder as a specific mental illness and published a detailed description of it. This is a chronic disorder; its manifestations and prognosis differ from those of the amnesias following shock. Several of Korsakoff's patients who displayed this disorder, and most of those observed by other investigators, happened to be alcohol addicts whose disease was a direct outcome of this addiction and the associated nutritional deficiencies. Other cases have been reported to result from tumors and vascular accidents, or from degenerative or inflammatory disease, all of which affect one or another site in the brain along a functionally continuous circuit.

The relation between this circuit and the memory-process is only beginning to be understood; here, we will only point out that it comprises the cingulate cortex, the hippocampus, fornix, hypothalamus, mammillothalamic tract, and thalamus (see Figure 2). Although the analogy is quite loose, it is apparent that in the brain, as in the computer, a fault in the circuitry can disrupt the orderly retrieval of stored information.

One of the characteristic manifestations of the amnesic syndrome is "fast forgetting"—the inability to recall new information after a very short lapse of time. This has suggested that the amnesic syndrome results from a permanent impairment of the mechanisms by which information enters the memory-storage system. Other theories stress the damage in the processes of information retrieval, but neither explanation can account for all the characteristic manifestations of this disease; an inability to acquire new information; loss of temporal and situational context; lack of initiative; neglect to test for contradictions; susceptibility to interruptions; and the failure to retrieve information in an orderly manner from the memory bank.

The explanation I prefer regards the amnesic syndrome as an expression of the patient's inability to set up and carry through an action plan, either for retrieving a memory, or for acquiring new ones.

RECOVERY OF A MENTAL MAP

As an example of the amnesic syndrome and recovery from it which may occur after severe but reversible brain damage, let us take the case of a patient whom I studied through the course of his disorder and partial recovery. This young man had suffered a vascular accident in the brain. Shortly after a successful operation he displayed a number of the signs characteristic of the initial phase of the amnesic syndrome. He was entirely disoriented about the place in which he found himself, about his age, the date and year, about the persons in his surrounding. He confabulated freely, that is, he answered questions and carried on conversations without the least regard to factual truth, producing irrational and partly fictitious autobiographical material. Most of what he said was palpably impossible or improbable, contradictory and confused. Gradually these anomalies cleared up, but the memory disorder improved much more slowly. The patient remembered virtually nothing of his daily experiences, could not learn more than the odd name, and that not very reliably, and had forgotten much of what he had experienced and known before his illness.

After some months in the hospital, his very severe disturbance in memory and general orientation lessened sufficiently so that he could be discharged from the hospital and, in due course, return to work. During his spare hours, this young man used to drive a taxi in the suburb where he had lived for some four years prior to his illness. He had therefore possessed an excellent mental map of the area. When he was released from the hospital, though the skills he needed to drive a car were immediately available to him, he could not drive by himself because he was quite unable to find his way around. He had grown up in the neighboring city, however, and once he crossed the boundary into the city, he knew exactly how to get about. It was at least a year before he could dispense with someone to pilot him in the suburb where he lived, but eventually he regained his mental map of his home town.

The complex operations by which memories are rendered accessible may be permanently lost owing to irreversible brain damage, as with Korsakoff's disease. In these cases the processes governing both the acquisition of new information (learning) and the search-and-find operations of retrieving previously-stored material, remain seriously disrupted.

Alcohol addicts who develop Korsakoff's disease are typically delirious during the initial phase, grossly disoriented, and either completely apathetic or quite agitated. They are so far out of touch with their environment, so difficult to engage in an interview, that their memory disorder is scarcely apparent. Undoubtedly the memory disturbance is present and is as grave as it will be in the later, chronic stage of the disease, but it is overshadowed by the patient's total incomprehension of the situation in which he finds himself, his inability to keep his attention on any topic, and his tendency to confabulate—to jumble fragments of factual information derived from the most diverse settings and to mix them with purely imaginary matter.

While with most patients, communication is usually restricted to a fleeting moment during the first stage of the disease, the attention of some can be held for a short while. One woman, who was able to carry on a reasonably coherent interview the first day after admission, gave me her married name correctly and answered several other questions with fair accuracy. However she stated that she was unmarried and lived in her mother's house. Since her medical chart indicated that she had been married for ten years, and that her mother had been dead for quite some time, I pointed to her wedding ring, asking why she was wearing it. After a moment's bewilderment, the patient listed the names of three men in rapid succession, presenting each as her husband, and relating some plausible enough circumstances surrounding each "marriage," such as parental opposition to the man in question. Remarkably enough, the list did not include the name of her actual husband whom, however, she remembered perfectly well the next day.

A WORLD WITHOUT CONTINUITY

One could speculate about the emotional significance to the patient of the three imaginary husbands and try to discover what roles these men had played in her life. The point of immediate interest, however, is the manifold contradiction to which the patient was quite indifferent. In the later phase of the disease, as the gross disorientation subsides, examples of such utterly irrational discourse are rare. Nevertheless, one of the most salient characteristics of the amnesic patient is his propensity to make contradictory statements and to leave them unresolved. Not uncommonly a patient may talk about his grownup children and grandchildren and in the next sentence refer to himself as a 25-year-old. One man, in his sixties, widowed for many years, would always tell me that his wife had been buried only a few days before, and would describe his children as if they were in their teens until I reminded him of his real age. This he remembered accurately enough, and his logic was sufficiently sound so that he realized that his children must be adults by now.

Since many of these patients retain their capacity for reasoning and judgment, such irrational statements must be attributed to false premises they hold about the current moment in their life history. Theirs is a world without continuity. With no memories of the recent past, amnesic patients lose their anchorage in time, and in their waking hours are at apt, as we are in our dreams, to mistake the present for the past, or confuse two periods of the past with each other. This is illustrated by the wizened old woman who looked forward to going out to dances on Saturday nights once she was released from the hospital. She thought of herself as the young girl who had been helping her father run his shop, and had completely forgotten the years of her married life.

The memories of the amnesic patient are fragmented; they seem to float free of any contextual constraints. This allows them to be recombined into patterns that have little relation to actual events in the patient's life. Indeed, the manner in which these new patterns are produced may resemble the processes of artistic creation, but their content is strikingly unoriginal, and the process itself does not seem to be experienced as a creative act; there is no conscious attempt at rearrangement, no search for meaning or order. The patient who confabulates, who errs in the temporal placement of an event, is unaware of his error and makes no attempt to correct it. He does not test a specific memory for accuracy of fit as we do when

AMNESIA:
A WORLD WITHOUT CONTINUITY

GEORGE TALLAND

Everyone, at some time or other, experiences a puzzling lapse of memory. A name or a date, or the details of an experience, unaccountably vanish from our mind. "It's right on the tip of my tongue," we say, or "I know it as well as I know my own name," and we rummage around in our minds for clues, but to no avail. "Don't try to remember it", someone may say comfortingly, "it'll come back if you stop trying so hard." And sure enough, moments or hours or even days later, the forgotten information may pop back as unexpectedly as it had vanished.

If we were never conscious of having forgotten something, we might never be curious about how we remember things—about the nature of memory, its mechanisms and laws. And by the same token, studies of amnesia—a prolonged or permanent loss of memory for previous experiences—have provided us with fascinating and unique information about how memory functions.

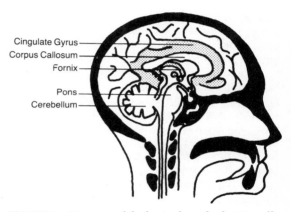

FIGURE 1. Diagrams of the brain show the functionally continuous circuit (shaded area) implicated in memory. Removal of the pons and cerebellum in the enlargement at the far right exposes the complete circuit: cingulate cortex, hippocampus, fornix, mammillary body, mammillothalamic tract, and thalamus.

EDITORS' COMMENTS:

THE AUTHOR EXAMINES THE AMNESIC PATIENT'S MEMORY DEFICIT IN QUANTITATIVE AND QUALITATIVE TERMS. HE CONCLUDES THAT THE MEMORY DEFECT IN THE AMNESTIC SYNDROME IS NOT THE SAME AS THE EVERYDAY FORGETTING OF NORMAL PEOPLE. MEMORY REQUIRES MORE THAN JUST STORAGE. APART FROM THE ASSOCIATIONAL FACTORS AND ACCESS TO STORAGE, REMEMBERING IS OFTEN PRIMARILY A SEARCHING OPERATION THAT REQUIRES FLEXIBILITY, PERSISTENCE, AND THE CAPACITY TO CHECK INFORMATION FOR ITS ACCURACY.

MODELS OF MEMORY

In attempts to conceptualize so mysterious a function as memory, people have turned to a variety of models. Perhaps the oldest is that of grooves incised in a wax tablet. In the same way that wax tablets are liable to decay, it was thought that the substance in which memories were engraved would deteriorate, causing memories to blur and fade.

Another simple model is that of a container in which an infinite collection of items—memories— are stored. Containers can leak, and if they are filled too full the contents spill out over the brim. Thus forgetting holds no mystery for those who believe that our capacity to accumulate memories is limited. It is a reasonable belief, and appears to be supported by ample evidence from observation, but it is of little value unless we can define the limits of storage capacity, and discover in what way memories are stored.

The way these memories are related to each other, how one leads to another, has for some centuries been accounted for by the laws of association; and ever since the early 1880's, when Ebbinghaus systematically investigated his own performance in tests of memorization, a steadily expanding body of experimental studies has increased our knowledge of these laws. While we can speculate only in the most tentative fashion about how information is recorded in and extracted from memory, we do know a good deal about the effects of one kind of learning on another. We know that some kinds of learning can hinder as well as help another sort, and this is important because it offers an alternative to earlier notions that forgetting is a spontaneous process.

Recently, the computer has provided us with a new and useful model for thinking about the twin processes of remembering and forgetting. In computers memories do not fade, but they can become inaccessible through some fault in the circuitry or some error in the program. Then either no information at all is forthcoming, or the wrong kind of information is printed out in place of that which is sought. While the computer model does have some features in common with human remembering, it certainly does not parallel memory processes in all important respects. The great virtue of this model is that it shifts the emphasis from the storage of memory to the processes of input and retrieval. It reminds us that unless information is properly programmed for access it will not be available on demand, and that a reliable system for storing memories is of little use if the program for reactivating them is defective. The study of various type of amnesias has shown that this is true of human memory—that is, that forgetting does not result so much from the "loss" of static memories as from the disruption of a complex on-going process.

AMNESIA

The term "amnesia" usually evokes the image of a shell-shocked soldier or, more recently, the victim of an auto accident, who has no memory of the circumstances in which he sustained his injury, and often of anything that happened over some time preceding it. Traumatic amnesia, as this type of memory loss is called, involves loss of memory of the accident itself and is usually accompanied by some degree of retrograde amnesia—the inability to recall events that occurred prior to the onset of the trauma. In such cases, the memory loss is limited and the recovery tends to be quite orderly. Step by step, more of the lost information returns, beginning with the events most remote in time, and closing in on the events that immediately preceded or involved the accident.

The memory loss in such instances is puzzling, because it usually extends to information that, quite clearly, the victim had registered up to the very moment of the accident—things he had said or done, questions he had answered. This type of amnesia suggests that information and experiences are not immediately placed on permanent record, but that the processes by which they enter into enduring memory take some time to be completed. Evidently there is a labile phase of information-intake, during which a powerful interference such as a concussion can prevent the experience from being permanently filed or consolidated in the memory system.

It is still a matter of debate how long information remains in this labile state. Very likely it varies with the individual, with the circumstance, and with the subject matter to be recorded, but its duration is on the order of seconds or minutes, and at the most, a few hours. This is also the range of the retrograde amnesia that typically follows a shock, but it does not represent the full extent of all retrograde amnesias, nor are the recovery patterns the same.

AMNESIC SYNDROME

In the retrograde amnesias following other types of brain insult—an operation, a vascular accident, or disease—the memory loss is apt to be extensive. An amnesic patient may have no recollection of having been married, although he had shared a home with his wife for several decades; he may have no memory of ever having had children, though he reared several. There is no ground for believing, as has been suggested, that this type of forgetting is motivated, that is, that such patients fail to remember because for some reason they do not want to remember; nor can their forgotten life experiences be restored to memory with hypnosis or other aids. And memories of this type, though obstinately missing for a considerable length of time, may suddenly re-emerge for no discernible reason.

The amnesic syndrome is also known as Korsakoff's disease, named for the Russian psychia-

we are in doubt—"It was just before the war started; no, it must have been a week or so afterwards, because I remember . . ." He does not test or check alternate solutions to a problem of reconstructing a memory sequence. The amnesic patient does not seem to experience the sense of doubt, the sense of imperfect closure, the need for resolution that often precedes correct recall and recognition in normal people. The amnesic patient may fail to test for "fit" because he is not aware of the contradiction, but neither does he apply the test when the contradiction is pointed out to him.

RECONSTRUCTION FROM FRAGMENTARY MEMORIES

These examples of confabulation and of errors in temporal placement not only represent an anomaly characteristic of amnesic patients, but they also point to a fundamental attribute of all remembering—its creative or constructive nature. This quality illustrates Sir Frederic Bartlett's thesis that "all remembering is a reconstructive effort after meaning." The crude and often grotesque errors in recall, characteristic of the amnesic patient, differ only in degree but not in kind from those made by normal people.

This is demonstrated by one of the studies I carried out in the course of an extensive research on amnesia. This study involved a group of some 20 patients in the chronic phase of Korsakoff's disease. Although their memory function was impaired, they had all recovered from the disorientation and other grave symptoms that are so prominent in the early stages of this illness. They were quite able to engage in an interview and follow instructions. To probe their learning and retention, I used several short narrative texts, one of which was the following news report:

> In a city in India, several thousand school children paraded in the main square to celebrate the sixty-eighth birthday of the prime minister. While reviewing the parade the prime minister released a number of doves, the symbols of peace, from the cages in which they had been kept. The white doves flew over the heads of the young marchers. One of them, however, perched atop the prime minister's head while he took the salute.

This text was read aloud to each of the patients at a measured pace, with the instruction to memorize it for reproduction; their ability to do so was compared to that of a control group of healthy people who had no memory disorder.

Even when their recall was tested immediately

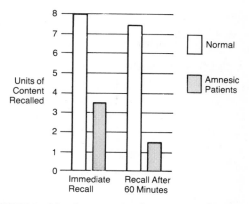

FIGURE 3. After being read a short story (see text), amnesic patients remember far fewer of 16 units of content than do normal people.

after the text had been read to them, few of the amnesic patients remembered more than four of the 16 units of content; they had forgotten almost all of them at the end of an hour; and many completely missed the gist of the story. The control group recalled twice as many items, and retained most of that information over the following hour (see Figure 3).

Quantitative measures, however, furnish only part of the evidence. When they are supplemented by an analysis of the kinds of errors in recall, we find many examples of simplification, such as the following account of the elaborately staged peace ceremony: "A group went to India to see the prime minister. They kept birds there." One patient started his report with "a man and wife celebrating his sixty-eighth birthday"; another made the principal actor a "maharajah," and a third gave the exact number of children as 5000. In the descriptions of the ceremony, there were several examples of elaboration with some gratuitous fabrication of details. These ranged from speculations about the symbolic significance of the final incident, or comments about its amusing feature, to one observation about the children watching the dove until it flew away, and another about the cheering, followed by the remark, "The prime minister thought they were cheering him; they were actually cheering the dove." An example of immediate reproduction, notable alike for its brevity and for the variety of distortions within its narrow compass was this: "Prime minister had 68 doves to celebrate his birthday. When he went to count the doves, one was missing, as it was perched on his head."

Those in the control group were quite likely to omit some of the content, but they always retained enough of it to reconstruct a coherent account, and produced nothing comparable to the distortions of the amnesic patients.

THE TELEPHONE GAME

It is possible, however, as the following study shows, to create in normal people something very much like the ambiguity and loss of direction that follow from the rapid and extensive forgetting in amnesic patients. One way to produce this effect is the method of "serial reproduction," known outside psychological laboratories as the "telephone game."

Thanks to the cooperation of my colleagues, I was able to set up seven chains composed of healthy men and women, rather above the average in intelligence. Each chain consisted of three persons; the first member of every chain was presented with the report about the Indian peace ceremony and asked to wait for a day, then pass on to the next member of the chain all that he remembered of it. The second passed on his version, after another 24 hours, to the third, who again waited for a day and then wrote down what he remembered of the story.

Under these conditions our superior normal subjects produced distortions that were remarkably similar to the immediate recall of the amnesic patients. References to the peace ceremony ranged all the way from a "large party for children" to "a party celebrated with fireworks"; references to the central figure included his designation as a

maharajah. There were gratuitously exact estimates—64 white doves; 2000 pigeons; 30,000 school children who were excused from classes to attend; there were elaborations, such as various interpretations of the significance of the episode, or comments on how amusing it must have looked. One subject produced a story that closely paralleled the fabrication of one of the amnesic patients: "In honor of this occasion he released a flock of doves, 44 in number; 43 turned up, the 44th he couldn't find, for it was perched on his head." The following gem of fabrication, however, had no match among the patients: "During the course of the celebration many more doves were released, and one of them laid an egg which hit Nehru on the head."

EXPERIMENTS IN RECOGNITION AND RECALL

Since amnesic patients retain their vocabulary unimpaired, verbal tests of their learning and memory show their deficit in the kindest light. But if they are asked to reproduce figure drawings from memory, as a test of recognition and recall, the distortions of their drawings often compound the effects of forgetting with those of faulty execution. The amnesic patient's poor observation and retention are more evident from the following experiment in recognition that demanded no skillful performance. A set of 12 cards, each bearing a different design (see Figure 4), was used with 16 patients in the chronic condition of Korsakoff's disease and with 16 control subjects matched in age; the latter were patients in psychiatric treatment for their problems of alcohol addiction, but none had any impairment of their memory function.

Each subject was shown the card bearing the

FIGURE 4. Twelve cards with different (but similar) designs are used to test the ability of amnesic patients and control subjects to remember and recognize one design (g) previously memorized.

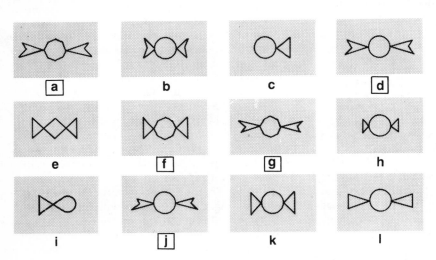

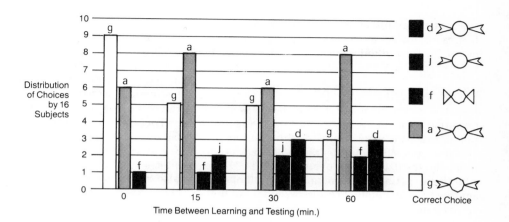

design marked "g," and was allowed to study it until he felt certain that he could remember it. Then the entire set of 12 cards was placed in front of him in the order shown and he was asked to point to the design he had seen before. The same test was repeated after 15, 30, and 60 minutes; each time the order of the cards was changed, and at no time was the subject told whether he was wrong or right. One member of the control group always chose design "a," but none of the others made a mistake in any of the four trials. On the other hand, the responses of the amnesic patients were much less consistent, and they made far fewer correct choices (*see* Figure 5).

Their mistakes were by no means random; all arose from the choice of designs that were similar, in principal outlines, to that of the model but were simpler and more symmetrical.

The amnesic patient's characteristic inability to learn new material, as well as his rapid rate of forgetting, is demonstrated by tests of memorizing lists of meaningful and nonsense syllables. Sixteen Korsakoff patients and 16 control subjects

FIGURE 5. Recall is tested by having subjects pick out the correct design from a set of 12 designs. Amnesic patients show poor recall, particularly as the time between learning and testing is increased. These patients made errors by choosing four simplified versions (a, d, f, j) of the correct design (g).

were given lists of 10 meaningful monosyllabic words (for example, hat, sun) or of 10 nonsense syllables (cuz, meb) to be learned for periods of three minutes. The subject was then instructed to recite as many of the words or syllables as he remembered, in any order he chose. Repeated tests of recall were given after different time intervals during which the subject was unoccupied. The results show the wide differences between the amnesic

FIGURE 6. Amnesic patients and normal subjects spent three minutes memorizing each of several lists of 10 words (or 10 nonsense syllables). Repeated tests of recall after different intervals of time reveal marked differences: amnesic patients learned fewer items initially and forgot much more rapidly.

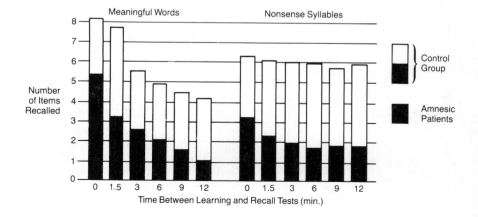

and control groups in initial acquisition, and a steep rate of forgetting in the amnesic patients during the first few minutes (*see* Figure 6).

SUSCEPTIBILITY TO INTERRUPTION

In another experiment both groups were asked to memorize a 10-word sentence; in this case, however, the subjects were occupied with a variety of tasks during the five-minute interval between the initial and the delayed test of recall.

In this experiment the immediate recall of the amnesic patient equalled or surpassed that of the control group. On the delayed tests, however, their recall never matched that of the control subjects, and the amount of material they had forgotten depended on the character of the intervening activity (*see* Figure 7). The amount forgotten was least when they were not given any task, somewhat greater when they were engaged on a manual task (working a tally counter), still greater when a learning task was interpolated, and greatest of all after a brief interview in which they were asked a few questions such as where they had gone to school as children, who their teachers were, or the address of their childhood home.

The reason why the amnesic patients remembered the test sentence least well after the interview is that the questions took their minds off the experimental task. Whereas normal people have no difficulty in reverting to an interrupted activity, amnesic patients rarely manage to pick up the thread once it is dropped. This was quite apparent from a simple experiment which required that they

FIGURE 7. The types of tasks that amnesic patients were required to perform during the five minutes between the learning of a list of 10 words and a subsequent test of recall produced various degrees of forgetting. Interviews proved to be the most disruptive activity.

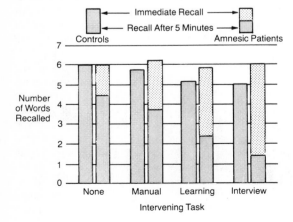

count slowly from one to 22, stop for three minutes, and then continue counting up to 37.

This experiment was run under two conditions; in one, the break was occupied by rest, in the other by drawing a picture. In both conditions all the instructions were given in advance, that is, at the end of the break the subject was told only, "now go on counting." One or two of the amnesic patients failed to stop when they reached 22; of the remainder, 10 completed their assignment without error after a rest, and two made errors of one or two places only. After three minutes of drawing, however, only four of the 16 remembered where to resume counting and where to stop.

Several other experiments demonstrated the difficulties these patients have in switching from one task to another and back again, and their disinclination to resume a task after interruption—although while engaged in an activity they persist with it, no matter how demanding it may be. This inability to depart from the track they are following is probably at the root of their failures to correct errors in the temporal placement of memories. It prevents them from exploring the contextual setting which invests each memory with its unique character.

When, on their twelfth to fifteenth visit to my laboratory, I asked the amnesic patients I was studying how many times they had been there, none of them came even close to the correct answer. Eight thought they had been there once before, and another 10 believed it was two or three times. Devoid of its contextual or associational cues, each visit is, of course, like any other, and blends with the rest into a composite memory. Experiences so incompletely registered cannot be reconstructed in retrospect, or will be reconstructed with low fidelity to the original event. The dearth of original learning and the rapid dissipation of the little that had been learned are characteristic features of the amnesic syndrome; even more characteristic than forgetting the content of an experience is forgetting its setting. This anomaly can be observed much better in clinical rather than in laboratory situations.

FORGETTING THE CONTEXT

Some amnesic patients never learn the name of their doctor, and a few may not even recognize him after innumerable encounters. More typical still are those instances in which the patient is uncertain whether he knows his doctor, or recognizes him confidently, and correctly names him, but believes that they had met in some social setting other than the hospital. Errors of this kind can persist for years, and are resistant alike to correction and to chance fluctuations in content. One woman, whom I have studied for more than 10 years, always gives my name correctly and always insists mistakenly that we had first met at her neighbor's home. Another patient, when asked how long she has been in the hospital, invariably answers that she came in yesterday for examinations and expects to be sent home later in the day. When I first confronted her with the fact that she had been in the hospital for four years, she accepted the correction but remarked that she felt as if it had been yesterday. The incident made no lasting impression on her, for each time I repeated my question during the following seven years, she has answered that she "came in yesterday."

In another example Moyra Williams and Honor Smith reported on a patient who had been through a training program prior to developing the amnesic syndrome as a result of tuberculous meningitis. Some time after his discharge from the hospital, he received a group photograph of his fellow trainees, and though he could name each of them correctly, he had no idea of where he had met them. Williams and Smith also describe another patient who always obediently rolled over on his side when the trolley with the instruments for a lumbar puncture was brought into the room; but as soon as the needle was withdrawn he would deny that he ever had anything done to his back. Jacques Barbizet reported a similar case, that of a Korsakoff patient who had been receiving shock treatments; he always seemed angry and upset at the sight of the electric shock apparatus, insisting each time that he had never seen it before.

There are several reports in the literature about amnesic patients who could play an expert game of chess or could solve quite difficult mathematical problems. Once such patients have begun a task, they can apply their well established skills to complete it. Few observations illustrate this residual capacity more impressively than Oscar Kohnstamm's report of a patient who had been buried in a shell crater during World War I and had developed an amnesic syndrome, probably as a result of carbon monoxide poisoning. Although he was a trained teacher, this man could not answer the simplest questions about geography or recent history. He was able, though, to solve problems in arithmetic, to play cards, to read music, and learn new pieces on the piano. One evening he participated in a hospital concert, accompanying one of the singers on the piano, but the next morn-

ing he had no recollection of the concert itself or his part in it.

LOSS OF SELF-REFERENCE

It is clear that the memory defect manifested in the amnesic syndrome is not the same as the everyday forgetting of normal people. It does include the unavailability of the correct response, yet quite often the patient gives the overt responses required, but is unaware of having done so, or cannot remember an earlier experience that prompted his correct response.

An experiment conducted by Edouard Claparede furnishes one more example that illustrates this characteristic disturbance. Claparede thought that the puzzling behavior of amnesic patients might be due to a loss of a sense of familiarity. To test this hypothesis, he once hid a pin between his fingers so that when he shook hands with one of his patients her hand was jabbed by the pin. A few minutes later, when he again extended his hand to her, she refused to take it. Pressed for an explanation, the woman said she was afraid she might be jabbed with a pin. She seemed entirely unaware of the fact that this was precisely what had happened to her. All she would say, to justify her apparently irrational suspicion, was that it had occurred to her that such a thing might happen, for people sometimes do hide pins between their fingers.

Perhaps the ultimate in amnesia is reached when a person correctly performs a required task, instantly forgets that he did so, and believes that the task was actually performed by the person who asked him to undertake it. This happened during the course of an interview in which I probed a patient's memory, both for some events that had taken place a few months prior to his illness, and for others that were quite recent. The first set of questions concerned an accident in which his brother had been killed; the second set concerned the forthcoming marriage of another brother. In reply to my uninformative questions —"Where?" "When?" "What is her name?" and the like—the patient gave me detailed and accurate answers relating to both events. I remarked, "You see, your memory is not so bad after all; you could remember pretty well these events in your family." The patient just stared at me with a puzzled expression, and then said, "But it was you who just told me about them." When I assured him that it was indeed he who had provided the information, he remained visibly unconvinced. Half an hour later I repeated my questions; he again answered them correctly; and again he was convinced that it was I who had just told him about those events.

REMEMBERING: AN ACTION PROGRAM

Not only was this patient able to produce the information required, but afterwards he also remembered the topic of discussion. Nevertheless, he had no recollection of his own active part in the interview. His recall was factually accurate, and it was in the proper context, but he did not register it as a performance in remembering. How can we account for the absence of the experiential quality, for his mistaking the active for the passive role— and this after almost no delay, and in regard to a subject matter of profound personal significance? It seems likely that he did not experience his performance as an active one, but perhaps more like the automatic exercise of a habitual skill. Although he produced all the information, it was I who programmed his behavior with my questions. His recall depended on external activation. He exemplified in that interview the behavior so typical of amnesic patients, that of a completely respondent organism.

For over and above their manifold and unusual memory disorders, these patients are also notable for showing little emotion and no spontaneity whatsoever. Although on rare occasions they become visibly upset or angry, they almost immediately regain their placidity and indifference. They seldom initiate an action and seem quite happy sitting about, even when surrounded by others, saying nothing, doing nothing for hours on end.

When, instead of addressing specific questions to the patient mentioned above, I asked him to talk about his brothers, leaving my questions open, he could not tell me nearly so much about them. Whereas a normal person, in attempting to retrieve a memory, sets up an action program and executes it as well as he can, checking and testing alternatives, the amnesic patient at best carries out plans imposed on him by someone else—and then only as long as the plans demand no modification or choice along the way. An interruption, a momentary distraction, is likely to loosen the amnesic patient's grasp of the action plan, and if his hold is lost, there is no prospect of its recovery. We saw examples of this in the studies described above where the action required was that of remembering a 10-word sentence.

The retrieval of a specific memory involves setting up and executing a plan. Much-practiced skills, such as those employed in dressing, eating meals, speaking or writing, and overlearned information, such as certain salient public or private events of the years past, are all as readily available to amnesic patients as they are to normal people. But information that cannot be retrieved without a plan of action is beyond the reach of amnesic patients. They may hit on it immediately, but if they do not, further efforts to find it will prove useless. Indeed, there is little evidence that they even make such efforts.

REGISTRATION OF MEMORIES

Just as an action plan is required to recover information, it is also required for registering new information so that it can be available for future reference, that is remembered. Judging from the evidence provided by studies of amnesic patients, it is not enough to perceive a message correctly, or even to respond to it overtly in the correct manner, in order to remember it at some later time. The acquisition of memories demands some further operations which can be interrupted by a violent blow, or can be permanently lost as a result of certain irreversible brain lesions. We may only speculate about these operations, but it seems reasonable to view them as some process of cross filing which defines the multiple association—that is, the context of any one event—and thus establishes its uniqueness. Multiple filing also increases the accessibility of a memory which can thus be reached from many directions, along several routes.

A systematic investigation of the amnesic syndrome leads to the discovery of a number of unexpected facts. But in this instance, fuller knowledge of a mental disease does not offer remedies. The principal value of such studies is that they increase our understanding of normal memory function. The information we can gain about human memory from animal experiments or laboratory studies with human subjects is necessarily limited. Research in abnormal memory function offers new leads, some of which can be followed up in the laboratory. For example, the finding that a faultless overt response is not sufficient proof of intact memory is one that students of normal human subjects are unlikely to discover; experimenters using animal subjects cannot even formulate the problem.

The close association between lack of spontaneity and memory defects also becomes apparent only in studies of abnormal function. Yet it is an important observation, for it stresses the crucial part played by the execution of an action program, both in the registration and in the retrieval of memories. It reminds us that, quite apart from the associational factors involved, remembering is often primarily an operation of search, requiring flexibility, persistence, the capacity to check information for its accuracy, as well as access to its storage. The student of amnesic disorders recognizes the truth in the White Queen's comment to Alice: "It is a poor sort of memory which only works backwards."

NEUROLOGIC SYNDROMES
AFFECTING EMOTIONS AND BEHAVIOR

DAVID BEAR AND GEORGE ARANA

EDITOR'S NOTE

(Weekly Psychiatry Update Series)

Two misleading assumptions make it difficult for the clinician to appreciate the close relationship between organic CNS disease and specific emotional sequelae. The first is that behavioral changes resulting from physical illness always represent an exaggeration of the patient's prior personality patterns. The second groups all emotional changes resulting from organic disorder under a single label: lability of affect. Specific emotional changes may result from specific kinds of brain involvement and, in turn, profoundly influence the clinical course of the neurological illness.

The first onset of a significant thought disorder in any patient over 40 years of age should make one suspicious of an organic etiology. Urinary incontinence is rare in psychiatric diseases and often suggests involvement of the prefrontal cortex. In alcoholic Korsakoff's psychosis, one sees apathy with impaired short-term memory, whereas in Wernicke's aphasia one commonly sees paranoia with fluent paraphasias and comprehension deficits. Other neurological disease can affect the motor expression of emotion without influencing the patient's experience of that emotion; thus, one sees the masked

EDITORS' COMMENTS:

THE AUTHORS REVIEW ORGANIC DISEASES THAT PRODUCE CHARACTERISTIC ALTERATIONS IN EMOTION AND BEHAVIOR. RECOGNITION OF SPECIFIC EMOTIONAL PROFILES IS VALUABLE BOTH IN DIFFERENTIAL DIAGNOSIS AND IN EFFECTIVE MANAGEMENT OF THE CONCOMITANT NEUROLOGICAL SYNDROMES. ORGANICALLY CAUSED EMOTIONAL CHANGES MAY FACILITATE OUR UNDERSTANDING OF THE ANATOMIC AND PHYSIOLOGICAL BASES OF PSYCHIATRIC DISORDERS.

Reprinted with permission from Weekly Psychiatry Update Series, Lesson 39:III. Princeton, NJ, Biomedia, Inc., pp. 2–7, 1980.

face of the patient with Parkinson's disease and the inappropriate laughing or crying in psuedobulbar palsy.

There are two behavioral syndromes, temporal lobe epilepsy and chronic amphetamine ingestion, in which normal or superior intellectual function may be preserved throughout. The patient with temporal lobe epilepsy often shows deepening of emotion, attributing affective significance to small details and events; sexual drives are often diminished or modified in such patients and hypergraphia may be seen. The diagnosis may often have to be established without EEG confirmation and the treatment depends upon both seizure control and personality management.

A paranoid psychosis, resembling idiopathic paranoid schizophrenia, may result from the chronic use of amphetamines in doses greater than 30 mg daily over a three-month period. Auditory and visual hallucination, euphoria, obsessive pacing, and driven rearrangement of objects in the environment are common manifestations. The acute phase usually resolves itself within three weeks after the termination of the amphetamines, but a serious depressive syndrome often follows.

Processes affecting the prefrontal cortex often produce emotional changes before cognitive ones. For example, apathy, abulia, and psychomotor retardation are characteristic of convexity lesions or disconnection of limbic input to this region; here, in contrast to an affective disorder, episodes of tearfulness and sadness are rarely persistent. By contrast, orbital frontal lesions are often associated with a loss of socially prescribed controls over behavior; the patient may seem manic but, unlike the usual manic patient, manifests gross dissocial sexual and eliminative behavior. Later, characteristic dementia usually appears. Early diagnosis of prefrontal lobe syndromes is very important since the causes are often reversible.

In this lesson the author describes specific behavioral changes associated with Huntington's disease as well as those changes seen in patients with lesions of the right hemisphere. Since lesions of the right hemisphere do not typically impair verbal memory, speech production, language comprehension, or praxis, they may easily escape early detection. Moreover, such lesions induce a curiously altered response to neurological deficits and, in this extreme form, the patient's extensive denial of a rather profound disability.

THE IMPORTANCE OF ORGANICALLY CAUSED EMOTIONAL CHANGES

Diagnosis and Clinical Course

Psychiatrists are often required to distinguish between functional and organic etiologies during the process of differential diagnosis of a behavior syndrome. Functional behavior disorders occur in patients with structurally normal nervous systems who presumably have been exposed to maladaptive emotional learning situations, perhaps early in life. In contrast, organic etiology refers to diagnostically established structural or chemical alterations of the CNS that, on the basis of current theoretical and clinical knowledge, frequently produce specific changes in emotion and behavior.

Two misleading assumptions, seemingly inconsistent but often simultaneously believed, contribute greatly to difficulties both in the diagnosis and management of organic diseases with specific emotional sequelae. The first is that emotion or behavior resulting from any physical illness represents an exaggeration of the patient's prior personality patterns. While this generalization may be true of responses to many medical diseases, it is incorrect when the disease process directly involves the emotion-mediating circuits of the brain. In these situations, characteristic changes in behavior, albeit from the baseline of prior personality, reflect the anatomy and pathophysiology of the underlying lesion.

The second troublesome assumption, embodied in current psychiatric nosology, acknowledges the existence of organically produced emotional changes but lumps all of these under the rubric of an organic brain syndrome characterized by lability of affect. In fact, this is an inaccurate description of many distinct patterns of behavior change such as those resulting from temporal lobe epilepsy or infarction of the nondominant hemisphere. In contrast, the examples in this lesson illustrate the specificity relating discrete behavioral syndromes to specific organic pathologies. In practice, the disparate emotional changes of prefrontal lobe injury, temporal lobe epilepsy, or infarction of the nodominant hemisphere can provide valuable diagnostic signs.

Following diagnosis, specific emotional changes may strongly influence the clinical course of these neurologic illnesses. Thus, patients with prefrontal lobe lesions characteristically develop a transient irritability and shallowness of emotion which leads to social rejection but rarely to dangerous behavior. Interictal changes in temporal lobe epilepsy involve deepened affect, well-tolerated by spouse and family, but with a significant risk of calculated aggression. The minimization of deficits, impairment in attention, and disrupted emotional priorities that accompany nondominant hemisphere infarction markedly impair recovery from left hemiplegia.

Models for Psychiatric Diseases

In the synopses presented below, the authors emphasize the clinical recognition of patterns of behavior and emotions associated with specific organic processes. These emotional changes, important both for diagnosis and management, are best understood as phenomena in their own right, since there is no a priori reason to believe that neurologic lesions should reproduce standard psychiatric syndromes. However, consistent changes in emotion produced by specific physical processes are of great interest as potential models for idiopathic psychiatric disease. For example, chronic amphetamine ingestion produces a psychosis similar to that of paranoid schizophrenia. This, of course, has strengthened interest in relating dopamine neurotransmission to schizophrenia. Also, the similarities between amphetamine psychosis and the schizophreniform changes of temporal lobe epilepsy may extend our understanding of localization and pathophysiology. Psychiatric symptoms in one stage of Huntington's disease strongly resemble the affective disorders; in the model neurologic disease, established genetic transmission, localized neuropathology, and specific neurotransmitter deficits enhance immediate research possibilities.

Guidelines to Organic-Function Differential Diagnosis

Since there are multiple patterns of organically produced changes in emotion, there can be no simple rule to discriminate organic from functional alternations. However, some initial observations may clarify the diagnostic territory. The onset of thought disorder in a patient over 40 years old strongly suggests an organic etiology. On the other hand, while psychomotor retardation or abulia can be mistaken for retarded depression, agitated depression with sustained weeping, rumination, or self-deprecation is usually a functional syndrome with good response to somatic psychiatric therapies. Urinary incontinence, often resulting from lesions impinging on the prefrontal cortex, is rare in psychiatric disease, unless the patient has been chronically institutionalized, heavily medicated, or given electroconvulsive treatment. Spontaneous seizures in a patient undergoing behavior changes should, of course, raise the question of an underlying neurologic disorder: convulsions can rarely be attributed to threshold effects of antipsychotic medications. While adventitious movements are often the tardive effects of antipsychotic dopamine blockers, one must consider the alternative diagnostic possibility of neurologic disease that affects both thought and movement.

Beyond such well-worn generalizations, differential diagnosis requires familiarity with the characteristic patterns of emotional change resulting from specific organic conditions. In many acute illnesses, dramatic alterations in affect coexist with disorders of cognitive mental status: agitation with defective attention in acute confusional states, apathy with impaired short-term memory in alcoholic Korsakoff's psychosis, or paranoia with fluent paraphasias and comprehension deficit in Wernicke's aphasia. These presentations are unlikely to be diagnostically overlooked, although the consequences of clinical management of, for example, paranoia in the fluent, aphasic patient are often underappreciated. Other neurologic diseases affect the motor expression of emotion without influencing the patient's experiences of affect: masked faces and hypophonia in Parkinson's disease; abrupt, inappropriate laughing or crying in pseudobulbar palsy; grimacing, barking, whistling, and cursing in Tourette's disease.

BEHAVIOR PROFILES PRODUCED BY SPECIFIC ORGANIC DISEASES

The remainder of this paper presents examples of specific changes in emotion and behavior that may occur in the setting of grossly normal cognitive status and without discrepancy between affective perception and expression. In two such behavioral syndromes, temporal lobe epilepsy and chronic amphetamine ingestion, normal or superior intellectual function may be preserved throughout; furthermore, the behavioral changes need not initially attract psychiatric or legal attention. In diseases of the prefrontal cortex or its subcortical correspondent (the caudate nucleus), dementing

changes or movement disorders may begin considerably long after personality modifications. Specific changes in emotional response with lesions in the nondominant hemisphere may overshadow subtle spatial neglect or constructional difficulty. While behavioral changes in these syndromes start from the baseline of the patient's prior personality, each may eventuate in a distinctive behavioral profile.

Temporal Lobe Epilepsy (Table 1)

Epilepsy originating from the temporal lobe has an approximate lifetime prevalence of 0.2%. This condition may produce a distinctive pattern of behavioral change which develops over months to years following the occurrence of the temporal lobe seizure focus. These behavioral changes are not episodic or contemporaneous with seizures but become enduring interictal features of personality. While occasional patients develop a schizophreniform paranoid psychosis, this represents an uncommon advanced stage of personality change seen in fewer than 5% of temporal epileptic patients.

The prevalence of the more common interictal behavior syndromes described below has not been determined and remains controversial. However, results in a recent study suggest that many patients with temporal lobe seizures, including those who do not require psychiatric treatment, may demonstrate specific behaviors to a statistically significant extent. For this reason, the interictal behavior syndrome can be an important diagnostic sign of the existence of a temporal lobe epileptic focus.

The traits summarized in Table 1 involve deepening emotions and attribution of affective significance to small details, neutral objects, and random intra- or extrapersonal events. This general mechanism may account for worsening temper, which represents a form of affective response generalized to previously neutral stimuli and situations. Anger in such patients is typically experienced in full consciousness, follows environmental provocation, and may lead to purposeful aggression. In general, the anger does not coincide with a seizure, and there is no amnesia for the aggressive acts. Alterations in sexual interest are commonly seen and range from apparent loss of sexual drive to fetishism, transvestism, and hypersexuality. A strking feature of the syndrome is hypergraphia, the tendency to compose diaries, poetry, or autobiographic texts illustrating moral or religious themes.

TABLE 1. Syndromes of Enhanced Affective Association with Intact Cognition

Process	Emotional/behavioral characteristics	Additional diagnostic features	Diagnostic/therapeutic implications
Temporal lobe epilepsy	INTERICTAL Deepened emotionality; religiosity, sense of personal destiny, hypergraphia, paranoia (may eventuate in schizophreniform paranoid psychosis) Altered sexual interests; aggressivity; circumstantiality, obsessiveness; depression; euphoric episodes	Generalized, simple, or complex partial seizures; psychomotor aura; visceral, olfactory, emotional; deja vu, jamais vu (Note: Multiple EEG records with sleep, nasopharyngeal leads, or pharmacologic activation may be necessary to demonstrate a temporal lobe focus)	Need to determine etiology: neoplasm abscess trauma; commonest is mesial temporal sclerosis resulting from febrile seizures of childhood; effective seizure control does not arrest behavioral syndrome
Chronic amphetamine ingestion	CHRONIC Deepened emotionality, paranoia ± delusions (may eventuate in schizophreniform paranoid psychosis), visual hallucinations; religiosity; decreased or altered sexual interests; relentless exploration of novel objects	Hypervigilance, insomnia; repetitive touching of hands or face; gritting, gnashing of teeth; anorexia, thirst, diaphoresis, dysuria	Caused by D-amphetamine ingestion greater than 30 mg daily; may complicate treatment of narcolepsy or obesity; repeated use of cocaine or lysergic acid may produce a similar syndrome Effects reversible with discontinuation of amphetamine, but severe depression with suicide attempts may follow

It has been proposed that an epileptic focus, by virtue of the neuranatomy of the temporal lobe, brings about additional functional connections between association cortices and limbic (emotion-mediating) structures. The behavioral syndrome may additionally reflect hemispheric asymmetries since, in recent studies, left temporal patients developed more verbally mediated intellectualized affect and right temporal subjects developed more overt emotionally.

The diagnosis of temporal lobe epilepsy is confirmed by a positive EEG. However, multiple negative EEGs do not rule out the syndrome, since temporal lobe foci often lie out of range of scalp electrodes. Recordings with sleep activation and nasopharyngeal leads may be helpful in establishing the diagnosis, but a reliable history of generalized or complex partial seizures or temporal lobe auras, in addition to the characteristic personality picture, is diagnostic.

Having established the diagnosis, the clinician should investigate etiology, since neoplasm, abscess, parasitic cyst, and encephalitis are among the causative lesions. However, the majority of patients suffer from sequelae of seizures in childhood, resulting in mesial temporal sclerosis.

Treatment of the syndrome should include both seizure control and personality management. Preventing generalized seizures is a therapeutic goal, but there is evidence that overzealous pharmacological suppression of psychomotor seizures raises the likelihood of overt psychosis. Of the available anticonvulsants, carbamazepine, which shares a tricyclic chemical structure with the antidepressants, is thought to have beneficial effects on mood and impulse control. Anterior temporal labectomy in unilateral cases may eliminate or ameliorate seizures and appears to normalize hyposexuality, but it has little effect on established paranoid delusions or overgeneralized deepened affects. Antipsychotic dopamine blockers, which may be required to control paranoid delusions or hallucinations, rarely interfere with seizure control. However, they do not appear to alter the interictal behavior pattern. In the absence of established somatic treatment for the interictal behavior changes, frank discussion with the patient, focused on excessive moralism, aggression, or circumstantiality, can be therapeutic.

Chronic Amphetamine Ingestion

A paranoid psychosis, often indistinguishable from paranoid schizophrenia, may result from chronic ingestion of amphetamine in doses greater than 30 mg daily over a three-month period. This may occur with amphetamine pharmacotherapy of narcolepsy or obesity or following the abuse of hallucinogens such as lysergic acid, cocaine, or dextroamphetamines. Prominent features, some of which are similar to the interictal behavior syndrome of temporal lobe epilepsy, include paranoid ideation, auditory and visual hallucinations, euphoria, and repetitive handling of an object or body part. Patients may pace obsessively and rearrange or order objects in their environment. Other motor behaviors seen with excessive amphetamine ingestion include twisting movements of the trunk and extremities, grimacing, and bruxism. Also present are autonomic signs of adrenergic stimulation such as tachycardia, diaphoresis, and mydriasis.

The behavioral resemblance of the hallucinogen syndrome to temporal lobe epilepsy may reflect activation of common limbic structures, since temporal lobectomy in chimpanzees or humans dramatically reduces the pharmacological responses. Animal studies have produced strong evidence that the stereotyped behavior caused by amphetamines is due to activation of dopaminergic tracts in the striatum and mesolimbic structures. Visual hallucinatory experiences with amphetamines could represent specific activation of the nondominant temporal lobe.

Psychotic hallucinatory features usually resolve within three weeks of the discontinuation of amphetamine ingestion. However, the fate of the personality syndrome has not been well-studied; there may be persistent learned emotional associations. A severe depressive syndrome often follows amphetamine withdrawal, perhaps as a result of catecholamine depletion. Suicide attempts may occur during this period.

Prefrontal Lobe Syndromes (Table 2)

Processes affecting the prefrontal (granular) cortex frequently produce emotional and behavioral changes well before cognitive dysfunction. Although different syndromes may result from impairment of the frontal convexity versus the orbital pole, many lesions will involve both regions.

Apathy, abulia, and psychomotor retardation are characteristic of convexity lesions or disconnections of limbic input to this region. The syndrome differs from retarded depression in that tearfulness and sadness, which may be momentarily elicited, are rarely persistent. All affects tend to be shallow with prefrontal impairment.

The loss of socially prescribed controls over emotional behavior produced by orbital frontal lesions is in apparent contrast to such apathy and abulia. The patient may become irreverent, inap-

TABLE 2. Syndromes of Transient, Shallow Affect with Progressive Dementia

Process	Emotional/behavioral characteristics	Additional diagnostic features	Diagnostic/therapeutic implications
Lesions of prefrontal cortex			
Convexity lesion	Motor retardation, apathy, abulia; superficial, reflexive affect; impairment in solution of multistep problem, intentional memory	Incontinence Gait disturbance Gegenhalten Deficit in alternating motor programs Grasp reflex	Normal pressure hydrocephalus Olfactory groove meningioma Multiple sclerosis Pick's disease Alzheimer's disease
Orbital lesion	Loss of learned social control over emotional behavior; irreverence, inappropriate sexuality, witzelsucht; "irritable euphoric apathy"; deterioration in dress, personal habits		

propriately facetious, vulgar, sexual, or aggressive; he may urinate or masturbate indiscriminately. Multistaged goal-directed behavior is specifically disrupted. At the same time, trivial stimuli may elicit momentarily excessive emotional reactions. This syndrome may superficially resemble mania but is differentiated by grossly dissocial (sexual and eliminative) behavior and the absence of persisting elation. Lesions that affect both the frontal convexity and the orbital pole may produce a clinical picture of reflexive, short-lived, affects. This combination of features has been described as irritable euphoric apathy.

Subsequent to changes in affect and behavior, a specific pattern of dementia usually develops. This includes slowness and poverty of speech, delay in manipulation of acquired knowledge, deficiencies in analyzing multistaged problems, and failure to remember to carry out an instruction, although the instruction itself is well remembered. Personal habits and dress become sloppy.

Frontal syndromes are associated with gait disturbances, grasp reflexes, and a characteristic form of motor resistance described as *gegenhalten*. Alternating motor patterns are impaired when the premotor cortex is specifically affected.

Early behavioral diagnosis of prefrontal lobe syndromes is of the greatest value in light of reversible causes such as olfactory groove meningiomas or normal pressure hydrocephalus. When the etiology is degenerative or otherwise irreversible, knowledge of the prefrontal changes in emotionality is essential for rational counseling of spouses and family.

Huntington's Disease (Table 3)

Huntington's disease may present with emotional changes years before the characteristic chorea or dementia manifest. In the original description of the disease, Huntington included "insanity with a tendency to suicide" as one of the three features comprising the diagnostic triad. The illness is transmitted as an autosomal dominant trait, but questionable paternity, misdiagnosis, or early death of the affected parent may obscure a familial association.

Impulse discontrol, including aggresivity, sexual promiscuity, or alcoholism, may be early behavioral manifestations. Paranoid delusions with or without visual hallucinations, frequently diagnosed as paranoid schizophrenia, follow these changes and often lead to psychiatric hospitalization. Other observers stress affective symptoms, both depressive and manic, with not infrequent suicide attempts.

Patients who present with the mood disturbance appear hopeless and guilt ridden, often with delusions of sinfulness, blameworthiness, poverty, or disease; psychomotor retardation is often associated. The depression may persist for weeks to years and often resolves spontaneously but is responsive to antidepressant medication or electroconvulsive therapy.

Table 3. Impulse Discontrol, Mood Disorder, and Progressive Frontal Dementia

Process	Emotional/behavioral characteristics	Additional diagnostic features	Diagnostic/therapeutic implications
Huntington's disease	Longitudinal progression of symptoms: Early: Aggressivity, sexual promiscuity, alcoholism, paranoid delusions Middle: Depression, euphoria ± paranoid delusions, hallucinations; suicide attempts Late: Psychomotor retardation, apathy, abulia; frontal dementia with sparing of language, praxis, perception (Table 2)	Facial tics, buccolingual dyskinesia, appendicular chorea (rigidity in Westphal variant), gaze dyskinesias; family history of autosomal dominance transmission	Motor syndrome may follow behavior change by up to 10 years Differential diagnosis includes: tardive dyskinesia, metabolic choreas, Sydenham's chorea, Wilson's disease, lupus vasculitis Antidepressant and antipsychotic medications are effective against early and middle psychiatric symptoms

TABLE 4. Indifference to Illness, Selective Inattention, and Disrupted Emotional Priorities

Process	Emotional/behavioral characteristics	Additional diagnostic features	Diagnostic/therapeutic implications
Lesion of the right hemisphere	Rare: Following right middle cerebral infarction, acute confusional state with agitation, selective inattention Rare: Explicit denial of deficit such as left hemiplegia (anosognosia) Common: Minimization of consequences of illness, unrealistic denial of lost function Impaired discrimination or expression of affective (melodic) quality in speech; deficient memory for affect-laden stories; diminished autonomic response to arousing stimuli	Spatial disorientation, construction difficulties, dressing apraxia; neglect of left hemifield	Emotional changes can be the result of any structural lesion in the right hemisphere; acute confusional state is specifically associated with right middle cerebral artery infarction, which must be differentiated from toxic, metabolic, infectious, or other vascular causes of acute confusional states Recovery from left hemiplegia and return to previous occupation may be greatly hampered by motivational changes; disrupted emotional perception and expression may be socially crippling Patient is rarely depressed and is not responsive to antidepressant medications

Depressive episodes may alternate with mania including elation, expansiveness, garrulousness, flight-of-ideas, overspending, and activity; chorea may first manifest or worsen at this time. Antipsychotic dopamine blockers are affective in treating these symptoms. Subsequently, there is a consistent progression of psychiatric symptoms into the form of dementia seen with prefrontal lobe lesions.

The caudate nucleus, site of early degeneration in Huntington's disease, is extensively connected with the prefrontal cortex. When this structure is lesioned in monkeys, resultant behavior deficits resemble those following prefrontal lesions, suggesting that a subcortical process might produce a pseudofrontal dementia. Patients with Huntington's disease do not develop an aphasia in the end stages of their dementia, as is commonly seen with the cortical degeneration of Alzheimer's, Pick's, or Creutzfeldt-Jakob disease. However, the neuropathology of Huntington's disease does include distinct degeneration of the prefrontal cortex.

Motor symptoms usually manifest in the fourth or fifth decades. As noted above, dopamine blockers, especially haloperidol, may ameliorate choreic movements, psychotic thought disorders, or manic symptoms. Tricyclic antidepressants or electroconvulsive therapy is effective against intercurrent depression. Lithium carbonate has been reported to lessen aggressivity. There is presently, however, no definitive treatment for Huntington's disease. Family and genetic counseling is, therefore, an essential part of the management.

Lesions of the Right Hemisphere (Table 4)

Since lesions of the right hemisphere typically do not impair verbal memory, speech production, language comprehension, or praxis, they may escape early detection of accurate lateralization. Rarely, an acute confusional state with agitation, disorientation, and failure of selective attention results from infarction in the distribution of the right middle cerebral artery. This syndrome may reflect acute destruction of the multisensory associational cortex analogous to polymodal language areas in the left hemisphere but subserving spatial surveillance and attentional function on the right side. This syndrome must be distinguished from more frequent toxic, metabolic, or infectious causes of acute confusional states.

More commonly, a right hemisphere lesion induces an altered response to neurologic deficits. The extreme form of this phenomenon, explicit denial, of a left hemiplegia or anosognosia, is rather rare. However, the tendency to minimize the consequences of illness—to diminish their emotional significance—is far more frequent. Patients may express blanket faith in the physician's ability to restore lost function, or they may belittle the practical significance of a left hemiparesis. Both inappropriate jocularity and expressions of hatred toward the paralyzed limbs may result, occasionally leading to requests for amputation of "a dead arm."

While such inappropriate emotional reactions to body deficits are dramatic and have been grouped as extreme forms of denial of illness, these are not the only signs of altered emotional reactions following right hemisphere injury. Patients are specifically impaired in their ability to discriminate the affective tone of verbal messages; they fail to communicate emotional cues normally through the melody and cadence of their speech. Memory for affect-laden stories, particularly those concerned with illness, is defective.

Right hemisphere lesions may produce a related deficit in arousal and emotional responses. Thus, cutaneous stimulation to either upper extremity fails to elicit normal autonomic skin reactions. These observations following right hemisphere injury and related experimental findings suggest a special role of the nondominant hemisphere in the control of affect.

The clinical consequence of these complex changes in affective response is a marked disruption of emotional priorities. Because patients minimize the significance of their deficits, they rarely sustain motivation for rehabilitation. Plans for early return to work are often unrealistic, leading to serious setbacks. Insensitivity to emotional cues and the inability to convey affective subtleties lead to crippled social relations. However, such patients rarely ruminate, become tearful, or develop vegetative signs of depression. Antidepressant medications have not proved helpful. Rather, the authors have attempted to speak to the intact left, verbally competent, hemisphere and to focus attention on the specific deficits in emotional strategy. Psychotherapy is directed toward the realities of illness, sending and receiving explicit emotional cues, and maintaining a realistic hierarchy of needs, problems, and goals.

SUGGESTED READINGS

General

Delirium, a syndrome of cerebral insufficiency. Engel GL, Romano J. Journal of Chronic Diseases 9:260–277, 1958.

Organic brain syndromes: A reformulation. Lipowski ZJ. Comprehensive Psychiatry 19:309–322, 1978.

Unsuspected Emotional and Cognitive Disturbance in Medical Patients. Knights E, Folstein M. Annals of Internal Medicine 87:723–724, 1977.

Acute organic brain syndromes: Clinical considerations. DeVaul RA. Texas Medicine 72:51–54, 1976.

The intensive care syndrome. McKegney F. Connecticut Medicine 30:633, 1966.

Psychiatric view of the intensive care unit. Kornfeld DS. British Medical Journal 1:108–110, 1969.

Delirium after cataract surgery: Review and two cases. Summers WK, Reich TC. American Journal of Psychiatry 136:386–391, 1979.

Living with the characteriologically altered brain injured patient. Lezak MD. Journal of Clinical Psychiatry 39:592–598, 1978.

Clinical differentiation of depression and dementia in the elderly. Willmuth LR. Biomedia 2:2–7, 1978.

Delirium tremens in surgical patients. Blickman L, Herbsman H. Surgery 64:882–890, 1968.

The interictal behavior syndrome of temporal lobe epilepsy. Waxman S, Geschwind N. Archives of General Psychiatry 32:1580–1586, 1975.

Biological Factors

Organic brain syndrome: differential diagnosis and investigative procedures in adults. Peterson G. Psychiatry Clinics of North America 1:21–36, 1978.

Substitute and alternative neurotransmitters in neuropsychiatric illness. Baldessarini RJ, Fischer JE. Archives of General Psychiatry 34:958–964, 1977.

The Neuropsychiatric Syndrome Associated with Hepatic Cirrhosis and an Extensive Portal Collateral Circulation. Summerskill WJH, Davidson EA, Sherlock S, Steiner RE. Quarterly Journal of Medicine 25:245–262, 1956.

Hypercapnia: Mental changes and extrapulmonary complications: An expanded concept of the "CO_2 intoxication" syndrome. Dulfano M, Ishikawa S. Annals of Internal Medicine 63:829–841, 1965.

Mental symptoms in Vitamin-B_{12} deficiency. Lancet pp. 628–629, 1965.

Electrolyte and fluid imbalance: Neuropsychiatric manifestations. Webb W Jr, Gehi, M. Psychosomatics 22:199–203, 1981.

The symptoms and behavior manifestations of Dementia. Wells CE. Contemporary Neurology Series 9:1–12, 1971.

Multi-infarct dementia: A cause of mental deterioration in the elderly. Hachinski VC, Lassen NA, Marshall J. Lancet 2:207–210, 1974.

Reversible dementia. Cummings J, Benson F, LoVerme S Jr. Journal of the American Medical Association 243:2434–2439, 1980.

"Normal-pressure" hydrocephalus. Jacobs L, Conti D, Kinkel WR, Manning EJ. Journal of the American Medical Association 235:510–512, 1976.

The Wernicke–Korsakoff syndrome. Victor M, Adams R, Collins GH. Contemporary Neurology Series 7:15–34, 1971.

Memory impairment in Korsakoff's psychosis: A correlation with brain noradrenergic activity. McEntree W, Mair R. Science 202:905–907, 1978.

Psychological Factors

Psychiatric management of operative syndromes. Hackett TP, Weisman DA. Psychosomatic Medicine 23:267–282, 1960.

Personality and psychological factors in postcardiotomy delirium. Kornfeld D, Heller S, Frank K, Moskowitz R. Archives of General Psychiatry 31:249–253, 1974.

The experience of open heart survery: IV. Assessment cf disorientation and dysphoria following cardiac surgery. Quinlan DM, Kimball CP, Osborne F. Archives of General Psychiatry 31:241–244, 1974.

GLOSSARY

Acetylcholine. A common neurotransmitter released by a nerve ending to cause excitation of an adjacent nerve ending.

Acute intermittent prophyria. An inherited metabolic disturbance, characterized by episodic attacks of abdominal pain with nausea and vomiting, at times accompanied by neurologic dysfunction such as weakness of certain muscular groups and by neurotic and psychotic behavior.

Addison's disease. A metabolic disorder, characterized by weakness, skin and mucous membrane pigmentation, hypotension, emaciation, gastrointestinal symptoms, and emotional instability, owing to insufficient production of steroids.

Affect. Emotional feedings or mood.

Agoraphobia. Fear of going out or being outside the house.

Alzheimer's disease. The most common type of dementia with diffuse cerebral cortical atrophy that particularly affects the frontal and temporal lobes.

Ambivalence. Intense contradictory feelings about similar situations or people.

Amnesia. Loss of memory; inability to recall experiences.

Amnestic confabulatory syndrome. Korsakoff's syndrome.

Amygdala. Part of the primitive brain associated with expression of rage, located in the gray matter in the lateral wall and roof of the interior horn of the lateral ventricles.

Angina pectoris. Episodic chest pain caused by an inadequate supply of blood and oxygen to the heart, generally associated with arteriosclerotic heart disease. Characteristically precipitated by effort or emotion, and relieved by nitroglycerin.

Anisocoria. Pupils of unequal size, at times a sign of neurological disorder.

Anorexia. Loss of appetite.

Anorexia nervosa. A syndrome marked by severe and prolonged refusal to eat adequately, marked weight loss, morbid fear of fatness, disturbance of body image, and amenorrhea. Found most frequently in young females.

Anticholinergic. An agent that blocks the action of acetylcholine in the transmission of impulses at certain nerve junctions.

Anxiolytic. A psychotropic agent that decreases anxiety.

Aphonia. Inability to produce normal speech sounds due to organic or psychic causes.

Association. Relationship between conscious and unconscious thoughts.

Ataxis. Incoordination of voluntary muscular action, particularly of the muscle groups used in activities, e.g., a person with an ataxic gait may appear to walk as if he were intoxicated.

Autism. Withdrawal of interest in the outside world and preoccupation with an internal fantasy life.

Basal ganglia. A group of cells in the midbrain (putamen, globus pallidus, and caudate nucleus) important in coordinating fine movements, when dysfunctional parkinsonian symptoms occur.

Behavior therapy. Therapeutic technique based on learning theory that postulates that certain maladaptive symptoms are learned patterns of behavior, which in turn can be unlearned by means of inhibition and/or extinction of the learned response.

Beta-adrenergic receptor. A specific type of neuronal receptor associated with smooth muscle and cardiac function as well as with mediation of anxiety responses.

Brain stem. Comprises the medulla, pons, and midbrain. It serves to relay afferent and efferent impulses and controls life-sustaining bodily functions and cranial nerve nuclei.

Caffeinism. A toxic condition caused by excessive ingestion of caffeine-containing substances, characterized by anxiety, tremor, and other manifestations similar to an acute anxiety attack.

Cardiac arrhythmias. Irregular heart rate.

Catatonia. Immobility with muscular rigidity and inflexibility, at times excitement.

Catecholamine. A group of amines with biological activity, including the neurotransmitters dopamine, norepinephrine, and epinephrine.

Cerebellar Purkinje cells. Layer of large cells at the junction of molecular and granular layers of the cerebellum.

Cerebellum. The inferior part of the brain lying below the cerebrum and above the pons and medulla oblongata, involved in coordination, balance, and movement.

Cerebral cortex. The external gray layer of the brain, with a high concentration of nerve cell bodies.

Cerebral edema. Swelling of the brain, especially after trauma.

Collagen diseases. A group of disorders involving inflammatory reactions of small blood vessels (vasculitis) presumably related to the interaction of an individuals' immune system with his or her own specific cellular components.

Confabulate. Filling in actual memory gaps by imagery or dimly recollected experience in response to clues from the immediate environment.

Cortisol. Steroidal hormone secreted by the adrenal cortex.

Cushing's disease. An endocrine disorder characterized by excess adrenocortical hormones and characterized by hypertension, moonlike facies, neck hump, increased body hair, thinning of certain skin layers, a tendency to develop diabetes, and emotional symptoms.

Delirium. An acute and fluctuating behavioral syndrome that often begins abruptly, even dramatically with a clouding of consciousness, a shortened attention span, and perceptual disturbances.

Delirium tremens. Also called DTs, a delirium accompanied by tremor, visual hallucinations, terror, insomnia, rapid heart rate, and sometimes fever. Typically it occurs 12 to 48 hours following cessation of heavy drinking of alcohol, and can be fatal if untreated.

Delusions. False beliefs which cannot be corrected by reason.

Dementia. Disorder caused by gradual neuronal degeneration and characterized by loss of intellectual functioning.

  Multi-infarct type. Dementia caused by multiple episodes of tiny infarctions of the brain, usually associated with hypertension or cerebral arteriolosclerosis.

Denial. An unconscious defense mechanism used to resolve emotional conflict and allay anxiety by disavowing thoughts, feelings, wishes, needs, or external reality factors that have become intolerable to the individual.

Depersonalization. Feelings of strangeness or unreality concerning body and/or personal identity, found in normal individuals as well as in those with certain types of psychopathology.

Derealization. Feelings of strangeness or unreality concerning one's environment; often accompanies depersonalization.

Diencephalon. A portion of the midbrain, including the thalamus and hypothalamus, which serves as a central integrating system for cognitive, visceral, and sensory input.

Diplopia. Double vision.

Displacement. An unconscious defense mechanism whereby an emotion is transferred, or "displaced," from its original object to a more acceptable substitute.

Dissociative disorders. A group of disorders in which there is a splitting off of components of mental activity in response to stress, producing psychogenic amnesia, multiple personalities, or fugue states.

Diurnal. Having a daily cycle. Many endocrinological functions have peak activities at certain times of the day or night.

Dopamine. A biologically active amine found in the nervous system, it is both a neurotransmitter for dopaminergic neurons and a precursor of certain other important neurotransmitters.

Double-binding. A type of interaction, noted frequently in families with a schizophrenic offspring, in which one member demands a response to a message containing mutually contradictory signals, while the other member is unable to comment on this incongruity or to escape from the situation.

Dysarthric speech. Slurred, ataxic speech, usually associated with a transient form of permanent brain or muscular dysfunction.

Dysmenorrhea. Difficult or painful menstruation.

Dysthymic disorder. A common form of affective disorder, which was formerly called chronic depressive disorder. The depressions are usually mild or moderate.

Ego. Represents perceptual, cognitive, and intellectual functions, utilizing mechanisms of adaptation and defense in negotiating between the external real world and the individual's internal perceptions and experiences.

Ego defense mechanisms. Unconscious intrapsychic processes employed to seek relief from emotional conflict and freedom from anxiety.

Ego-dystonic. Aspects of an individual's behavior, thoughts, and attitudes viewed by him/her as repugnant or inconsistent with his/her personality.

Ego-syntonic. Aspects of an individual's behavior,

thought, and attitudes viewed as compatible with his or her self-image.

Electroencephalogram (EEG). A graphic recording of minute electrical impulses arising from the activity of the outer layers of neurons in the cerebral cortex. Slowing of wave forms and asymmetry, among other abnormalities, are helpful in making neurologic diagnoses.

Encephalitis. An inflammation of the brain, at times leading to permanent neuronal damage.

Endocrinopathy. A group of disorders resulting from abnormalities in one or more of the endocrine glands, e.g., thyrotoxicosis, Cushing's disease, Addison's disease, diabetes mellitus, associated with metabolic disruption and at times mental symptoms.

Endogenous. Conditions originating predominantly within the organism, rather than external to it.

Epinephrine. A neurohormone discharged from the adrenal medulla during stress and under the direct control of the midbrain.

Exogenous. Conditions originating outside the organism, rather than intrinsic to it.

Extrapyramidal syndrome. Signs and symptoms of posture and movement disorders, such as muscular rigidity, tremor, restlessness, involuntary movements, shuffling gait, and masklike facies, secondary to inadequate supply of available dopamine in the basal ganglia, often seen as a side effect of a neuroleptic.

Formication. An abnormal sensation of insects crawling in or upon the skin, often a symptom of delirium tremens.

Fugue state. A dissociative disorder characterized by amnesia and physical flight from the individual's usual environment or field of conflict.

Glabellar reflex. A pathologic neurological reflex elicited by repeated tapping over the forehead, nasal bridge, or maxilla of a person with opened eyes. Instead of the reflex's being extinguished after the first four or five taps, blinking recurs with each tap.

Grand mal seizure. Generalized convulsion, seen in idiopathic epilepsy, delirium tremens, and other central nervous system pathologies.

Granovascular degeneration. Changes within the architecture of the neuron caused by gradually destructive processes.

Grasp reflex. A pathological reflex seen with certain types of neurological lesions, characterized by a grasping motion of the fingers or toes and induced by stimulation of the palm of the hand or the sole of the foot.

Hallucinations. Perceptions, especially auditory, not based on real stimuli from the outside world.

Hydrocephalus. Enlargement of the brain's ventricles, owing to an increase in cerebrospinal fluid pressure, following some type of block to the outflow of cerebrospinal fluid.

Hyperventilation. Abnormally rapid, deep breathing, often associated with anxiety and often accompanied by tingling of the fingertips and lips as carbon dioxide is blown off.

Hypnotic medication. A sedative agent for the induction of sleep.

Hypoglycemia. Low blood sugar, at times associated with feelings of faintness, tremor, confusion, and other neurological symptoms, which can progress to coma.

Hypomania. A syndrome of excessive elation, hyperactivity, agitation, and accelerated thinking and speaking (sometimes used interchangeably with the term "mania," and sometimes used to indicate that the condition is less intense than mania).

Id. Instinctual aspect in Freud's structural hypothesis.

Illusions. Perceptions that cause misinterpretation of actual events.

Insulinoma. A tumor arising from insulin-producing cells in the pancreas, which can produce symptoms of hypoglycemia.

Intellectualization. A defense mechanism that utilizes reasoning as a defense against confrontation with unconscious conflicts and their stressful emotions.

Intraocular pressure. The pressure within the eye, abnormally increased in glaucoma.

Jakob–Creutzfeldt disease. Progressive, gradual development of motor weakness and mental deterioration, secondary to a slow virus syndrome of low infectivity occuring months to years after initial contact.

Korsakoff's syndrome. Also referred to as the amnestic–confabulatory syndrome, characterized by confusion, loss of memory, and amnesia of events in the past. Often found in chronic alcoholics with inadequate nutrition; also following some types of traumatic brain injury.

Laparotomy. An exploratory operation of the abdominal contents, in order to establish a diagnosis.

Lesion. Small, localized area of abnormal or dysfunctional tissues.

Limbic system. A group of structures within the brain associated with feeling states, comprising the cingulate gyrus, parts of the frontal cerebral cortex, septum, hypothalamus, hippocampus, and amygdala.

Megavitamin therapy. Use of massive doses of vitamin B_1, B_3, B_6, B_{12}, folic acid, and so on, for the treatment of mental disorders. It has been seen as effective for some cases of schizophrenia, but well-controlled studies have failed to prove its efficacy, and its effectiveness is controversial.

Midbrain. Mesencephalon; that section of brain important for regulating or controlling important bodily functions.

Milieu therapy. Socioenvironmental therapy used in a hospital setting for the treatment of certain major psychiatric disorders.

Multiple personalities. A rare type of dissociative reaction in which the individual adopts two or more different personalities. These are separate and compartmentalized, with total amnesia for the one, or ones, not in awareness.

Multiple sclerosis. A disease of the nervous system of unknown etiology with episodes of muscular weakness, scanning speech, tremor, loss of bladder control, blindness, and/or emotional lability. The course of this disorder is subject to dramatic remissions and exacerbations, but it is usually gradually progressive.

Myasthenia gravis. A chronic neuromuscular disorder characterized by physical weakness and easy fatigability of voluntary skeletal muscles.

Neurofibrillary tangles. Microscopic description of brain tissue characterized by disruption of the normal relationship of axon and dendrite, producing abnormal clumping and degeneration; seen in Alzheimer's disease.

Neurohormones. Substances elaborated in the brain to assist in regulation of thought, feeling, movement, and so on.

Neuroleptic. An antipsychotic agent, or major tranquilizer, that diminishes delusions and hallucinations, decreases marked anxiety, and may help improve the thought disorder in some psychoses.

Neuronal receptors. A specialized structure on the exterior of the neuron involved in the transmission of impulses. These receptors are specific to the stimulus that excites them, so that there are dopamine receptors, acetylcholine receptors, beta-adrenergic receptors, serotonin receptors.

Neurosyphyllis. A late manifestation of syphilitic infection involving the spinal cord and/or brain.

Neurotransmitter. Substance released at the neural synapse, also called junction or cleft, when excited by a nerve impulse. The transmitter diffuses across the synaptic cleft and in turn becomes attached to the adjacent neuronal receptor, which then becomes excited and transmits the neural message.

Nondominant hemispheric lesions. A lesion in part of the brain that is not dominant for that individual (e.g., for a right-handed person, a lesion of the right side of the brain). The extent of the neurological deficit is dependent upon the location of the lesion, but nondominant lesions do not produce an inability to speak.

Nucleus. A group of brain cells controlling a specific muscular, metabolic, or circulatory function.

Organicity. Indicative of organic brain disease.

Orthostatic hypotension. Lowering of blood pressure when the individual arises suddenly, often associated with symptoms of light-headedness or even fainting.

Parkinson's disease. An often progressive neurologic disorder characterized by resting tremor, muscular rigidity, slowed or decreased spontaneous movements, masked facies, shuffling gait, slurred speech,

and difficulty swallowing associated with degeneration of neurons in the basal ganglion.

Parkinson's syndrome. Having the characteristics of Parkinson's disease, but etiologically associated with neuroleptics (antipsychotic agents) producing a relative insufficiency of dopamine in the basal ganglion.

Peristalsis. Waves of contraction of the gut, responsible for the propulsion of the stomach's contents through the remainder of the gastrointestinal tract.

Pheochromocytoma. A tumor of the adrenal medulla, associated with episodes of anxiety, tremor, and elevated blood pressure.

Pickwickian syndrome. Morbid somnolence in some people with marked obesity. It is associated with decreased ability to ventilate air into the lungs and blood gas findings of decreased oxygen and retained carbon dioxide.

Projection. The unconscious process of rejecting those qualities that are emotionally unacceptable in the self and attributing them to others.

Pseudodementia. A condition seemingly resembling dementia, with apathy, depression, and decreased motivation for using intellectual abilities, but not associated with degenerative brain changes.

Psychoanalysis. A treatment technique based on a psychologic theory of human development and behavior, originally developed by Sigmund Freud, and based on the hypothesis that unconscious mental processes exist, access to which is possible by way of free association.

Psychodynamic therapy. Psychotherapy based on psychodynamic principles.

Psychodynamics. A systematized theory of human behavior and motivation based on the assumption that there are unconscious determinants.

Psychomotor epilepsy. A type of seizure disorder characterized by repetitive, highly organized but semi-automatic behaviors occuring during a state of altered consciousness, usually associated with a temporal lobe discharge.

Psychosis. Gross inability in thinking, feeling, or remembering, resulting in poor reality testing and often inappropriate behavior associated with an organic or a functional etiology. The individual with a psychosis is usually functionally impaired.

- *Anticholinergic psychosis.* Precipitated by atropine or atropine-like substances, characterized by delirium and agitation.

- *Functional psychosis.* Affective disorder or hysterical psychosis, associated with no demonstrable organic pathology at this time (schizophrenia).

- *Reactive psychosis.* A psychosis resulting from, or precipitated by, an identifiable event.

- *Steroid psychosis.* Precipitated by an excess of endogenous or exogenous steroids, characterized by affective and/or confusional symptoms.

• *Toxic psychosis.* A delirium produced by an excess of a metabolic product, a sedative-hypnotic agent, or some other substance toxic to the central nervous system, depressing the neuron's ordinary functional capacity.

Psychotropic. Active in the brain, as with a therapeutic medication.

Pulmonary embolism. A blood clot embolic to a pulmonary artery, usually from a clot in the leg veins or abdominal veins, causing shortness of breath and at times other somatic symptoms.

Rationalization. An unconscious defense mechanism in which the individual attempts to justify, or to make something consciously tolerable, by finding explanations for those feelings, behaviors, and motives that would otherwise be intolerable.

Reaction formation. An unconscious defense mechanism wherein attitudes and behaviors are adopted that are the opposite of the individual's own conscious or unconscious impulses.

Reality testing. An important ego function, which is characterized by thought, judgment, and perception of reality.

Regression. The partial or symbolic return to some earlier level of adaptation.

Repression. An unconscious defense mechanism that banishes unacceptable ideas, affects, or impulses from consciousness, or that keeps out of consciousness that which has never been conscious.

Retroflection. A turning inward or back upon the self; for example, retroflex rage, in which one's rage is turned back upon the self.

Reuptake. A fundamental process in inactivating neurotransmitters. After a finite amount of neurotransmitter has excited an adjacent cell, it is taken back into the cell of origin. Its reuptake then has the effect of decreasing the amount of neurotransmitter available to excite adjacent neurons. Although there are other ways of inactivating neurotransmitters (metabolic degradation within some cell or outside of it), reuptake is often used to decrease the available active supply of serotonin and catecholamines.

Schisms. An interaction often noted in families with a schizophrenic child, in which two or more members of the family seem to be in continual conflict.

Senile dementia. Alzheimer's disease.

Serotonin. A central nervous system neurotransmitter, also referred to as 5-hydroxytryptamine, which has an important role in sleep and may be important is some types of affective disorders.

Short-term memory. Memory storage of experiences of the past few minutes, hours, days, or weeks. By contrast, immediate memory lasts for less than 15 seconds, and long-term memory is for events months, years, or decades in the past.

Slow virus syndrome. A progressive neurological degenerative disease that comes on months to years after the individual either has initially contacted a rare virus or else has responded in a rare fashion to a common virus. Clinically, there are a number of different types, usually involving motor weakness and often mental deterioration, e.g., Jakob–Creutzfeld disease.

Snout reflex. A pathological reflex in which sharp tapping on the upper lip results in an exaggerated automatic contraction of the lips.

Steroid. Substance secreted by the adrenal cortex (and also produced commercially) with biological properties affecting many systems; dependent on slight structural changes, sex functioning, salt retention, blood sugar level, and blood pressure can be influenced.

Subdural hemotoma. A collection of clotted blood under the skull, between the dura mater and the arachnoid covering the brain that involves one or both cerebral hemispheres; usually results from severe head trauma and causes a gradual loss of consciousness.

Superego. Conscience or moral values; used by Freud in the structural hypothesis.

Synaptic cleft. The minute space, usually one hundred to two hundred angstroms wide, found between the presynaptic plasma membrane of an axon terminal and the postsynaptic plasma membranes of a neuronal dendrite. Transmission of a neuronal impulse occurs when neurotransmitter is secreted from the presynaptic neuron, across the synaptic cleft, and couples with the plasma membrane of the postsynaptic neuron.

Systemic lupus erythematosus. One of the so-called collagen diseases (QV), characterized by fever, muscle and joint pain, anemia, skin eruptions and vascular involvement of multiple organs. The brain may be affected, causing transient, but at times dramatic, psychotic symptomatology.

Tachycardia. Heart rate over 100 beats per minute, associated with exercise, anxiety, drug effect, fever, heart disease, and so on.

Tardive dyskinesia. Permanent involuntary movements of the mouth, cheek, and tongue.

Temporal lobe epilepsy. Psychomotor epilepsy.

Therapeutic community. A treatment setting, or milieu, specifically organized and arranged to emphasize socioenvironmental and interpersonal influence and pressures in a therapeutic manner. It also encompasses the management and resocialization of long-term psychiatric patients.

Thyrotoxicosis. Hyperthyroidism; a condition caused by excess thyroxin hormone circulating in the blood, associated with tachycardia, bounding pulse, palpitations, tremor, anxiety, increased energy level, heat and tolerance, irritability, and occasionally depression or apathy.

Torticollis. An asymmetrical spasmodic contraction of the neck musculature.

Unresolved grief reaction. Continuing emotional response to an external, consciously recognized loss that has not resolved in a normal fashion with the passage of time.

Vegetative symptoms. Physical or somatic symptoms accompanying some psychiatric disorders. For example, in depression, the objective bodily effects include poor appetite, weight loss, decreased libido, poor sleep, constipation, and dry mouth.

Ventricles. The interior chambers of the cerebral cortex and brain stem.

INDEX

DSM-III QUICK CHECK FOR MAJOR PSYCHIATRIC DISORDERS

by Frederick G. Guggenheim, M.D. and Carol Nadelson, M.D.

I. SCHIZOPHRENIA DISORDERS (code on Axis I)

Require at least 6 months of illness, including prodromal and residual phases (does not include Acute Schizophrenia). Also requires psychotic features (does not include Latent, Simple or Borderline Schizophrenia). Affective syndrome, if present, develops after psychotic symptoms, or is relative brief. Onset prior to age 45.

Code in fifth digit: 1 = subchronic, 2 = chronic, 3 = subchronic with acute exacerbation, 4 = chronic with acute exacerbation, 5 = in remission, 0 = unspecified (subchronic course = less than 2 years, chronic = 2 years).

Schizophrenia

295.1x Disorganized (Hebephrenic)
295.2x Catatonic
295.3x Paranoid
295.9x Undifferentiated
295.6x Residual

II. AFFECTIVE DISORDERS (code on Axis I)

Major Affective Disorders

require discrete episodes with vegetative signs and symptoms lasting at least 2 weeks for depression or 1 week for mania.

Code in fifth digit: 2 = lacking melancholic, psychotic or endogenous features, 3 = melancholic or endogenous features, 4 = psychotic features, 6 = in remission.

296.2x Major Depression, Single Episode
296.3x Major Depression, Recurrent Episode
296.5x Bipolar I, Depression
296.4x Bipolar I, Manic
296.6x Bipolar I, Mixed

Other Specific Affective Disorders

including Chronic and Mild Partial Affective Syndromes.

301.13 Cyclothymic Disorder or Personality
300.40 Dysthymic Disorder, Depressive Neurosis or Depressive Personality (mild depression, sustained or intermittent for at least 2 years)

Atypical Affective Disorders

296.70 Atypical Bipolar Disorder, including Bipolar II (severe depression, mild hypomania)
296.82 Atypical Depression

III. PERSONALITY DISORDERS (code on Axis II)

301.00 Paranoid
301.50 Histrionic (overly dramatic, lacking genuine warmth)
301.40 Compulsive (Obsessive Compulsive Personality)
301.70 Antisocial (sociopath, begins prior to age 15)
301.83 Borderline (unstable interpersonal behavior, mood, and self image)
301.81 Narcissistic (grandiose, exhibitionistic, entitled, exploitative, unempathetic)
301.84 Passive-Aggressive (resists demands, stubborn, dawdles)
301.60 Dependent (passive; lacking confidence, subordinates own needs)
301.22 Schizotypal (oddities of thought, perception, speech and behavior)
301.20 Schizoid (defective capacity to form social relationships)
301.82 Avoidant (hypersensitive to potential rejection with social withdrawal)
301.89 Atypical, mixed, or other personality disorder (including Masochistic Personality)

IV. ANXIETY DISORDERS (code on Axis I)

Anxiety States

300.01 Panic Disorder (at least 3 attacks within a 3 week span not precipitated by life-threatening situation, exercise, or phobic stimulus)
300.02 Generalized Anxiety Disorder (persistent and generalized anxiety without panic attacks lasting continuously for more than a month)
300.30 Obsessive Compulsive Disorder (significant source of distress or interference with social or role functioning)

Phobic Disorders

300.21 Agoraphobia (marked fear of being alone or in a public place where escape might be difficult or help not available if suddenly incapacitated) with Panic Attacks
300.22 Agoraphobia without Panic Attacks
300.23 Social Phobia (fear of potentially embarrassing public situations)
300.29 Simple Phobia (heights, animals, closed spaces)

Post-traumatic Stress Disorders

(re-experiences the traumatic situation in full, or some aspect of it).

308.30 Acute
309.81 Chronic or delayed
300.00 Atypical Anxiety Disorder

V. SOMATOFORM DISORDERS   (code on Axis I)

Physical symptoms without organic basis, related to psychological factors on a temporal and/or psychodynamic basis.

300.81 Somatization Disorder (chronic polysymptomatic physical complaints, Briquet's Hysteria, Briquet's Syndrome)
300.11 Conversion Disorder
307.80 Psychogenic Pain Disorder
300.70 Hypochondriasis (preoccupation with fear of serious physical disease)
300.71 Atypical Somatoform Disorder (includes Dysmorphophobia)

VI. ORGANIC MENTAL DISORDERS   (code on Axis I)

There are nine Organic Brain Syndromes classified by etiology, when known: Dementia, Amnestic Syndrome and Delirium, in addition to Organic Delusional Syndrome, Organic Hallucinosis, Organic Affective Syndrome, Organic Personality Syndrome, Intoxication, and Withdrawal.

Organic Mental Disorders   (Axis I)
Secondary to Known Physical Disorders   (Axis III)

(do not include Alzheimer's Disease and Multi-infarct Dementia).

293.00 Delirium (clouding of consciousness, decreased attention, disorientation)
294.10 Dementia (decreased memory and cognition impairing social or occupation function)
294.00 Amnestic Syndrome (impaired short-term and long-term memory)
293.81 Organic Delusional Syndrome
293.82 Organic Hallucinosis Syndrome
293.83 Organic Affective Syndrome
310.10 Organic Personality Syndrome
924.80 Atypical or Mixed Organic Brain Syndrome

Primary Dementias   (code on Axis I, not Axis III)

290.00 Uncomplicated Senile Dementia
290.30 Senile Dementia with Delirium
290.20 Senile Dementia with Delusions
290.21 Senile Dementia with Depression (not depressive pseudodementia)

The following two primary Dementias require coding in the fifth digit: 1 = with Delirium, 2 = with Delusions, 3 = with Depression, 0 = uncomplicated

290.1x Primary Degenerative Dementia, Presenile Onset
290.4x Multi-infarct Dementia (Cerebrovascular Dementia)

Substance-induced Organic Mental Disorders   (Axis I)
Alcohol
303.00 Intoxication (simple drunkenness)
291.40 Idiosyncratic Intoxication (Pathological Intoxication)
291.80 Withdrawal
291.00 Withdrawal Delirium (Delirium Tremens, within one week of imbibing)

291.30 Hallucinosis
291.00 Amnestic Disorder (Korsakoff's Syndrome, impaired short and long-term memory)

The following Dementia requires coding in the fifth digit: 1 = mild, 2 = moderate, 3 = severe, 0 = unspecified.

291.2x Dementia associated with alcoholism (Alcoholic Dementia)

Barbiturate   (Axis I)
or similarly acting sedative or hypnotic drug

305.40 Intoxication
292.00 Withdrawal or Withdrawal Delirium
292.83 Amnestic Disorder

Other or unspecified substance   (Axis I)
(inhalants, antihypertensives, steroids, L-dopa, unlabeled pills)

305.90 Intoxication
292.00 Withdrawal
292.81 Delirium
292.82 Dementia
292.83 Amnestic Disorder
292.11 Delusional Disorder
292.12 Hallucinosis
292.84 Affective Disorder
292.89 Personality Disorder
292.90 Atypical or Mixed Organic Mental Disorder

AXIS I   CLINICAL SYNDROMES EXCEPT FOR
AXIS II   PERSONALITY DISORDER
AXIS III   PHYSICAL DISORDERS
AXIS IV   PSYCHOSOCIAL STRESSORS

1. None		
2. Minimal	Minor violation of law; small bank loan	
3. Mild	Argument with neighbors; change of work hours	
4. Moderate	New career; death of close friend, pregnancy	
5. Severe	Serious illness in self or family; major financial loss; marital separations; birth of child	
6. Extreme	Death of close relative; divorce	
7. Catastrophic	Concentration camp experience; devastating natural disaster	
0. Unspecified	No information	

AXIS V   HIGHEST LEVEL OF ADAPTIVE FUNCTIONING IN PAST YEAR

1. Superior	Unusually effective in social relations; occupational functioning; use of leisure time
2. Very Good	Better than average
3. Good	No more than slight impairment
4. Fair	Moderate impairment in either social or occupational, or some impairment in both
5. Poor	Marked impairment in social or occupational, or moderate impairment in both
6. Very Poor	Marked impairment in both social relations and occupational functioning
7. Grossly Impaired	In virtually all areas
0. Unspecified	No information